For my cousin, Pamela Greller,

who claimed at Pacific Ocean Park

when she was ten (and I was eight),

"The Sea Serpent isn't scary."

Very funny, Pam.

When large numbers of people share their joy in common
The happiness of each is greater
Because each adds fuel to the other's flame.

—ST. AUGUSTINE

CONTENTS

REMAIN SEATED

The time: the present. You are about to board the fastest roller coaster on the planet, the 149-mile-per-hour Formula Rossa, the pride of the Ferrari World Abu Dhabi theme park—where pride, like much else in this United Arab Emirates architectural showcase, comes supersized. But before being launched from inside a glistening pavilion that spans the length of seven football fields, there is the matter of adjusting your racing goggles, to keep the bugs out of your eyes.

Not a car fan? No worries, because Ferrari World is but one spoke in many amusement park wheels. According to recent figures, some one thousand fun parks span the globe, generating an annual $220 billion from visitors who total more than 475 million.

From above, Ferrari World Abu Dhabi could pass for the mother ship of a Testerossa. Inside, its high-octane rides include the world's fastest roller coaster.

The Midway Plaisance of the Chicago 1893 World's Columbian Exposition hastened the development of the American amusement park.

Formerly the prized domains of Southern California and Central Florida, amusement parks are now the expected norm in a range of far-off places from Azerbaijan to Desaru, Johor, to Darwin city, where the park's theme is crocodiles.

For those seeking pedigree, the oldest continuously running park in the world is Bakken, in Klampenborg, Denmark, which has been gladdening crowds since 1583, although an expert—that's practically any enthusiast with an annual pass and a 360fly camera—will tell you that Bakken has only had rides for the past three hundred years. That still qualifies it as the oldest.

While America won't be marking her tricentennial for more than another half century, the nation's oldest amusement park is Bristol, Connecticut's 1846 Lake Compounce, named for John Compound, a Mattatuck-Tunxis chieftain who accidentally drowned in his namesake while attempting to cross it in a large brass kettle.

In the ride arena, the world's oldest carousel, built in 1780 for Prince Wilhelm IX of Hessen-Kassel, is no longer functional, but can be seen at Wilhelmsbad Park in Hanau, Germany, birthplace of the Brothers Grimm. America's oldest, the 1876 Flying Horses, from toymaker Charles W. F. Dare, continues to make the rounds on Martha's Vineyard, one of only twenty carousels in the United States that still rewards a free ride to the grabber of the brass ring.

The longest-spinning Ferris Wheel is the 1897 Wiener Riesenrad, at the Prater in Vienna; the oldest roller coaster is the 10 mph, 1902 Leap-the-Dips, in Altoona, Pennsylvania's Lakemont Park, although the 1912 Scenic Railway in Melbourne, Australia's Luna Park also lays claim to the title, given the Leap-the-Dips' frequent and lengthy hiatuses.

The tallest? Kingda Ka, at Six Flags Great Adventure in Jackson, New Jersey, forty-five stories high, with an initial 128 mph drop of 418 feet. The longest? The 1.54-mile Steel Dragon 2000, at Nagashima Spa Land in Kuwana, Mie Prefecture, Japan.

In a realm all its own is "the world's tallest, fastest, steepest wood-steel hyper hybrid," Steel Vengeance, a 2018 addition to Cedar Point in Sandusky, Ohio, which seems to break roller coaster records more often than dishes break in a roadside diner. Its more-than-eleven-mile-long track delivers a 73 mph airtime hill with 27.2 seconds of weightlessness.

Only the biggest and best may be yet to come.

At 1.54 miles, the coaster track for Japan's Nagashima Spa Land's Steel Dragon 2000 holds the record for world's longest.

Walt Disney redefined and rejuvenated a teetering industry when he turned a deaf ear to the doubters and opened Disneyland, in 1955.

In the United Kingdom, where the 1843 Blackgang Chine on the Isle of Wight holds Britain's record for park longevity, the Al-Humaidi family's Kuwaiti European Holdings Group set a 2019 start date and 2023 opening for a £2 billion, 110-acre Hollywood theme park to occupy a former landfill in Kent.

In their own race to the gate, major international players, mostly American—the Walt Disney Company, Universal Studios, Six Flags Entertainment Corporation, and, the keeper of the keys to the world's Legolands, Merlin Entertainments—are magnifying their footholds in Asia, where an overall $24 billion investment is due to bring nearly sixty theme parks to some 220 million guests by the year 2020.

In the United Arab Emirates, Dubai ruler Sheikh Mohammed bin Rashid Al Maktoum intends to boost the city's visitor share to twenty million with the 2020 World Expo, prompting the dawn of several theme parks in the region. Not to be outdone, Russian president Vladimir Putin approved blueprints for the Magical World of Russia, described by the news agency TASS as the country's $4 billion answer to Disneyland.

Except this is getting light-years ahead of the tale.

From the beginning, amusement parks, which in their formative stage were more accurately termed amusement, or pleasure, fairs, did what they would continue to do for the ages: integrate the social classes.

What follows, for your amusement, is who mainly was responsible, and how and why they did it.

With cafés, beer halls, and promenades, the Prater flourished for
centuries before its "Venice of
Vienna" amusement sector was
added in 1895. The Giant
Wheel arrived two years later.

PART ONE

THE FUN BEGINS

ALL'S FAIR

Told his son had drowned, "King Henry fell as a man struck dead," Dante Gabriel Rosetti poeticized in his 1880 "The White Ship." The monarch's grief factored into his allowing Bartholomew Fair.

A s someone mutually blessed and blemished by fate, Henry I of England interpreted dreams as omens. Mindful of Henry's superstitious nature, his court jester, an obsequious yet opportunistic young man named Rahere, returned from a religious retreat in Italy to relay a vision he claimed had appeared to him in the throes of a malaria fever: that a winged creature with four talons plucked him out of the infirmary and carried him to the ledge of a cliff, where, in the nick of time, St. Bartholomew materialized and rescued the terrified captive from the monster's clutches.

In exchange for this act of salvation, Bartholomew instructed Rahere to return to London, where, on a "Smooth Field" outside the city wall, he was to construct a monastery and name it St. Bartholomew's.

For an apparition, Bartholomew had a remarkably shrewd head for real estate. His longed-for location, a former marsh that had been cleared for jousting, was known as Smooth Field, or Smithfield. Already home to the king's weekly trade market, it conveniently also doubled as the gallows.

As Rahere—indeed, the entire kingdom—was additionally aware, Henry was in dire need of cheering up. A dozen years before, on the night of November 25, 1120, his seventeen-year-old son, Prince William, set sail on the maiden voyage of the *White Ship* as she crossed the Channel to England. Shortly after leaving the Norman port of Barfleur, the vessel plowed bow first into rocks, killing nearly everyone aboard. This included the heir to the throne.

Rahere may have charmed the king, but historian Henry Morley dismissed the court jester as a "cheat not ignorant of Satan's wiles."

Still grieving, Henry granted Rahere his request, and further decreed—unaware this would effectively lay the foundation for the communal spectacle known as the amusement park—that there should be a fair, "celebrated," His Majesty ordered, "at the Feast of St. Bartholomew."

The first Bartholomew Fair, as Rahere's adoration of the martyred first-century AD preacher was called, was held August 24, 25, and 26, in the year 1133. Over time, the annual three-day religious festival, which also served as a cloth fair, transitioned into a two-week carnival, and then, at its peak, during the reign of Charles II, a three-week, seventeenth-century Coachella.

Rahere himself was not entirely at peace with this metamorphosis; to his dying day in 1144, he would sell the notion that miracles occurred at St. Bartholomew's, even if the bulk of his claims—a man on crutches suddenly able to walk on his own—proved questionable. Then again, one miracle did occur: the longevity of Bartholomew Fair. Presented annually, Rahere's creation ran for seven centuries, except in those years there was a plague.

Under an ever-widening expanse of colorful tents and aromatic stalls, the fair helped establish several standard practices carried out in the merriment arena: Exotic animal shows. Freak shows. Magic shows. Acrobatic shows. Theatrical spectacles. Rides. Refreshment stands. Dedicated lodgings for visitors. Prostitutes. Actually, the prostitutes were already well established; there were just more of them at fair time.

Charles Dickens described actor-producer John Richardson's Theatre, which first performed at Bartholomew Fair in 1798, the year the troupe was founded, as an "immense booth, with the large stage in front, so brightly illuminated." Note amusement rides, stage left.

The Smithfield gallows also made a substantial contribution, particularly on Bartholomew Fair's opening day in 1305. Before a standing-room-only crowd, William Wallace, the controversial Scottish patriot known as Braveheart, was brought to the fair site in shackles, strung up, hanged, and, for good measure, disemboweled.

With that, fairgoers went back to making music and merry.

Among Bartholomew Fair's infinite lures, its first animal show took to its tent in 1804, under the imprimatur of twenty-seven-year-old George Wombwell. Labeling himself a Wild Beast merchant, the former Soho shoemaker had been in show business only four years, since paying £75 on a London dock for two South American boa constrictors that had frightened off all other buyers. Within three weeks of their first exhibition, Wombwell more than made back his investment, "a circumstance which he always confessed made him partial to the serpent species," said a tribute after his death—from natural causes—at age seventy-two.

At its heartiest, Wombwell's Travelling Menagerie comprised three separate units. One year, simply to foil his chief rival, lion specialist Thomas Atkins, from having Bartholomew Fair to himself, Wombwell raced his caravan from Newcastle back to London, a 250-mile trek that fatally overtaxed his pachyderm.

When the fair opened, Atkins advertised The Only Living Elephant.

Wombwell refused to surrender. His banner read, The Only Dead Elephant.

The corpse drew the bigger crowd.

Predating animal acts by a century and a half, London's earliest documented public exhibition of what were commonly called "freaks" was held in 1665, a claim contradicted by the Oxford-educated diarist John Evelyn. He recalled that on September 15, 1657, which coincided with that season's Bartholomew Fair, "I saw the hairy woman, twenty years old, whom I had before seen when a child." Sporting a "most prolix beard" and hair growing out of her nose and ears, "she was now married," said the diarist, "and told me she had one child that was not hairy, nor were any of her parents or relations."

George Wombwell was an annual fixture at Bartholomew Fair, even if many of his attractions were not born to withstand the English climate—and didn't.

While exhibitions of human oddities were considered too graphic for women and children, who generally were barred from admittance, among their most ardent admirers was Jonathan Swift, who not only found inspiration for the Lilliputians and Brobdingnagians in his 1726 *Gulliver's Travels*, but confessed in a letter to a friend that the sight of conjoined twins from Hungary "causes a great many speculations; and raises abundance of questions in divinity, law, and physic."

Bartholomew Fair's roster of odd attractions should have quenched any such thirst, even if they only half lived up to what the handbills and placards promised:

> a Double Child without a nose, and with a mouth beneath
> the chin, and "other yet more wonderful peculiarities";
> "the Northumberland Monster,"…having the Head, Mane,
> and Feet of a Horse, with the rest like a man;
> "Girls joined together by the Crown of their Heads,"
> and therefore unable ever to "go, sit, or stand."

BEVERAGES, TOBACCO, AND FOOD, particularly roast pork—freshly butchered in the Smithfield slaughterhouse, although by 1750 the preference had switched to sausages—were "in generous supply" at Bartholomew Fair, amid "toys, gingerbread and mousetraps, puppies, purses and singing birds in a general bedlam of shouts, fiddles, drums and rattles."

Contributing loudly to the racket were puppet shows, particularly if they featured the characters Punch and Judy, whose performances were lorded over by a "violent, vulgar" male named Punch. Derived from the seventeenth-century commedia dell'arte figure Pulcinella, he was often "slapping his wife's bare buttocks, for the titillation of the adult crowd."

Amid such debauchery, the nineteenth-century radical journalist William Hone surrendered his better judgment to practitioners of legerdemain, including a fire-eater whose mouth spewed sparks "as from a blacksmith's forge," while 1825's fair found the writer captivated by something entirely new, at least to him: mechanical contraptions in a state of nearly perpetual motion.

Hone described them as "swings without number," primitive merry-go-rounds he dubbed "round abouts," and very preliminary attempts at what in 1893 would become known as Ferris Wheels or, as Hone called them, "up-and-downs," constructed "of massive wood-work, with two children in three of the boxes, and one empty box waiting for another pair."

The up-and-downs were actually a variation on what another Englishman, twenty-year-old Peter Mundy, had stumbled upon in the Middle East some two centuries before, in May 1620.

Mundy, a writer, an explorer, and a merchant trader in Asia, Russia, and continental Europe—and reputedly the first Englishman to taste tea in China—was tracking his journey through the Ottoman Balkans for his travel diary. During a midmonth stop in the city of Philippopolis, he recorded "some of their pastimes," those being (spelling and capitalizations his) "severall Sorts of Swinginge used in their Publique rejoyceings att their Feast of Biram."

From *The Travels of Peter Mundy, in Europe and Asia,* 1608–1667.

The swing, he explained, in what were essentially seminal blueprints for amusement rides, required hanging ropes from a tower, then connecting the riggings to a triangular wooden seat sturdy enough to hold a small boy, who was to be pushed by his friends "until he came to a great high." Picking up speed, the swing would boost its rider even higher, "with soe swifte a motion, equalling the flight of a Bird in the Ayre."

Mundy next witnessed an early prototype of the Ferris Wheel, which was fundamentally a revolving teeter-totter.

Compared to the swings, he said, this was "lesse dangerous and troublesome." Translated into modern English, his description likened the contraption to "a crane wheel at Custom House Key [near the Tower of London], upon which children sit on little seats dangling around its several parts…yet they always sit upright."

His final entry concerned a type of merry-go-round that he compared to "a great Cart Wheel, whose circumference has tiny seats fastened to it, on which the children sit…going around horizontal-wise."

While Mundy might have been the first to document the workings of these devices, he was by no means the first to experience them. Five years earlier, the highly regarded Roman traveler of the Renaissance, Pietro Della Valle, actually *rode* a Ferris Wheel–like invention at a Ramadan festival in Constantinople.

In correspondence, the nobleman praised the fireworks, floats, and great swings, then said of the Great Wheel: "I was delighted to find myself swept upwards and downwards at such speed. But the wheel turned round so rapidly that a Greek who was sitting near me couldn't bear it any longer, and shouted out 'Soni! Soni!'"

Translated: Enough! Enough!

≈

IN HIS 1604 PLAY *Bartholomew Fayre*, the playwright Ben Jonson lampooned the Puritans who disdained the fair, disdained him, and disdained theater (for one thing, men dressed as women). Populating his five-act play with characters whose

King Henry I (1068–1135) might have granted the charter that initiated Bartholomew Fair, but it was Henry II (1133–1189) who founded the principle on which such an assembly should uphold the law. With slight variation, the method is enforced to this day at both independent and corporate-owned theme parks, the majority of which employ their own in-house security teams.

Originally known as the Court of Pie Powder, a term dating back to the early 1200s, when pie powder dusted the feet of itinerant French merchants, the tribunal was assembled to allow an ad hoc jury of interested parties to settle issues as soon as they arose. At Bartholomew Fair, the jury was selected from among the festival's traders.

Once a case was determined, sentence was immediately rendered outside the makeshift Pie Powder courtroom—in the stocks or on the whipping post on the grounds of St. Bartholomew's.

very names were meant to elicit giggles—Win-the-Fight Littlewit, Quarlous, Zeal-of-the-Land Busy, Dame Purecraft, and Adam Over-Doo—Jonson's satire also gave voice to what was the quickly mounting criticism of the fair, complaints that would be repeated centuries later in regard to many amusement parks. As uttered by Zeal-of-the-Land Busy, "the whole Fair is the shop of Satan," and, again, by a seventeenth-century journalist: "Just as Lent is to the fishmonger, so is Bartholomew Fair to the pickpocket."

More than fifty years later, on Saturday, August 31, 1661, Secretary of the Admiralty Samuel Pepys encountered another age-old problem, as he relayed in his celebrated diary: He and a colleague went "to the tavern and after that to Bartholomew fair," and, then, at the colleague's suggestion, "to a pitiful alehouse, where we had a dirty slut or two come up that were whores." Pepys was likely on the Smithfield alleyway where the world's oldest profession was plied, the straightforwardly named Cock Lane. He claimed to have escaped before any of his friends spotted him.

"Bartholomew Fair had become an intolerable nuisance," William Hone reported, "and the lord mayor and aldermen, to abate its depravity, issued a prohibition on the 25th of June, 1700, against its lotteries and interludes."

Even greater restrictions were levied in the wake of a disturbance in 1749. Hone assigned the problem to the booth of "Mr. William Phillips, of Denbigh, fifteen years of age" and known as the "Welsh dwarf." Whatever sparked the ruckus, a silversmith, a

When Bartholomew Fair's tents went up, London's legitimate theaters shut down.

plasterer, a woman, and a child were left dead, and serious injury befell several others, including an individual whose leg required amputation the following morning.

What little remained of the fair's reputation was further compromised in 1822, said Hone, when a riot "composed of the most degraded characters of the metropolis…committed gross outrages on persons and property" throughout Smithfield. The number of culprits involved "was not less than five thousand."

The breaking point came in 1830, when the fair's negative image took a toll on its box office. Wombwell's menagerie, after several bonanza years, barely broke even. Other vendors lost money. Several shows and exhibits already had been outlawed by civic order, or else slapped with exorbitant fees to set up business. Charles Dickens further poisoned the atmosphere in 1837 with his serialized story *Oliver Twist*, which painted Smithfield as the hazardous lurking grounds of the fictitious but felonious villains Fagin and Bill Sykes.

The great cleanup began on June 19, 1840, when London's city solicitor, acknowledging the difficulties of revoking a royal charter—let alone one dating back to Henry I—moved to return Bartholomew Fair to its original strict intent of promoting trade. The resolution passed. On July 7, 1840, the Common Council accepted the solicitor's proposal and outlawed all shows, along with swings, roundabouts, and other mechanical rides.

That September, the only attractions were three paltry animal acts and a few dilapidated stalls selling toys and gingerbread. By 1842, the animals were gone.

Thirteen years after that, so was Bartholomew Fair.

ROYAL RETREAT

I.

In 1583, when Bartholomew Fair was but a tender 350 years old, across the North Sea in Denmark a 2,700-acre sylvan glade set its own stage for what for many years has carried the mantle of world's longest-operating amusement park. Dyrehavsbakken, or Deer Park's Hill, in Klampenborg about six miles north of Copenhagen, was originally established in 1583 as the exclusive hunting reserve of King Frederick III, a royal embargo that did little to dissuade nontitled trespassers from hopping the fence, often in droves.

One persistent legend surrounding Dyrehavsbakken—usually shortened to *Bakken*, meaning "hill"—involved that of a friendly spirit who met a lost little girl named Kirsten Piil at the forest's freshwater spring and safely guided her home. As the

Crowds flocked to Dyrehavsbakken after reports of a lost little girl's encounter with a spirit there in 1583.

Despite his smile, the man's party costume, circa 1915, belongs to the lovelorn clown Pierrot—or, as he's been known at Bakken since 1880, Pjerrot.

tall tale spread, so did word that the water contained mystical healing powers. Such an endorsement, however unfounded, drew mobs.

In 1756, King Frederick V opened the royal woodland to one and all, a gesture that attracted vendors of food, drink, and merchandise, along with gypsy fortune-tellers, jugglers, troubadours, and one Antonio Cetti, a thirty-five-year-old glassblower from Italy who specialized in barometers. After settling in Dyrehavsbakken around 1797, he switched to making musical instruments. With the carnival artist Pasquale Casorti and the English mime James Price, Cetti helped introduce the art of pantomime to Denmark. Their Copenhagen venue, the Hofteatret, also contained a mime creation that figures heavily into the Bakken story, a melancholy, white-faced clown known as Pierrot. Spelled *Pjerrot* in Danish, he was an Everyman character who originally debuted in February 1660 at Paris's Palais-Royal Theatre, as the hard-pressed fiancé of Charlotte in Act II of Molière's *Don Juan*.

Three years after his first Hofteatret appearance, in 1880, an actor playing Pjerrot came to Bakken and the character never left—becoming, in essence, the first-ever intellectual property in the amusement business.

Over the years, transitions at Bakken have been gradual, with neither the arrival of the steamship in the 1820s nor the introduction of the railroad in 1864 entirely considered blessings. As early as 1885, sanitation challenges caused by larger crowds necessitated the formation of a Dyrehavsbakken Tent Owners' Association, which stands to this day. In addition to banishing neon signs and commercial brands, the group dedicates itself to keeping Bakken's atmosphere discernibly low-key—except, perhaps, for a few extra-jolly days every July.

Since 1957, the park has played annual summer home to the World Santa Claus Congress, where up to 150 Kris Kringles convene to spread holiday cheer, swap stories, and, weather permitting, splash about at nearby Bellevue Beach in their most outlandish Christmas-inspired bathing garb.

In 1957, a former street performer calling himself Professor Tribini cooked up an annual World Santa Claus Congress for Bakken. Here, a whiskered Tribini swaps his winter reindeer sleigh for a summer model.

Santa's off-season spree originated with Christian Jørgen Nielsen, an effusive Copenhagen street performer who, under the legal (by decree of King Frederick IX) stage name of Professor Tribini, first appeared at Bakken in 1935, when he was twenty. In his signature top hat, British morning suit, and oversized necktie, Professor Tribini was still making his presence known in the 1950s, holding court in his own tent and presenting the Great Samson, a muscleman purported to be so strong that he could eat practically anything, including iron bars. The Professor's routine was itself ironclad.

Once an audience's patience had worn thin staring at an empty stage for twenty minutes, Professor Tribini would step into the spotlight for a somber announcement.

"Unfortunately, ladies and gentlemen," he would say, "Samson…has eaten himself."

Among its more than thirty rides, Bakken's smattering of vintage attractions include its bumper cars, miniature train, and the 1932 wooden Rutschebanen (from the Danish word for "roller coaster"), whose old-school rusticity suggests that the same spirit that guided Kirsten Piil to her miracle spring might also have overseen this coaster's design. Only don't be fooled by its grandfatherly looks. After a first-incline speed lift, the carriage jauntily rumbles along a 3,238-foot track, reaching seventy-two feet and a respectable forty-seven mph. The kick is substantial. Nonetheless, American Coaster Enthusiasts, a Texas-based group dedicated to the appreciation and preservation of roller coasters, rescinded Rutschebanen's ACE Coaster Classic status after a 2010 renovation, which, among other alterations, removed the brakeman from his position onboard.

"It is our challenge to be faithful to our history and traditions and at the same time be able to have a modern amusement park that can attract customers of all ages," said Nils-Erik Winther, the park's chief executive, who believes new entertainment is the key.

To that end, in 2018, "Efterår og Jul på Bakken" (Autumn and Christmas on the Hill) was initiated, a live celebration that keeps the park open well beyond the usual three months of summer.

And it took only 435 years.

II.

Just as Denmark's Frederick III excluded the public from his property, so did Austrian emperor Rudolf II restrict his two thousand acres of royal Viennese hunting preserve "to cavaliers and ladies." His father, Kaiser Maximilian, had claimed the land, known as the Prater (from *pratum*, Latin for "meadow"), in 1570, and Rudolf, best remembered for plunging his empire into the Thirty Years' War, was never one to share.

It was left to a successor, Emperor Josef II, on April 7, 1766, to drop the barrier dividing city from park, and embrace artists, writers, composers, coffee brewers, gingerbread bakers, a carousel, theatrical plays, and, of late, a carny-style mixed bag of mechanical attractions with such names as Dizzy Mouse, Free Fall Tower, Iceberg, and Hotel Psycho—a five-minute dark ride through a noisy battalion of ghoulish figures in various stages of electrocution.

"At the beginning" which was 1773, "there were fireworks," said Ursula Storch, curator of the Vienna Museum's Prater exhibition in 2016, marking the park's 250th anniversary. Also paid tribute were the Prater's contributions to transportation, from Czech engineer Franz von Gerstner demonstrating to technophobic Austrians, in 1823, that a train was nothing to fear, to circus-family brothers Alexander and Anatol Renner flying over the park in the first blimps, in 1909.

In 1873, to show Austria as the equal of England and France, the Prater hosted the city's one and only world's fair, the Vienna International Exhibition, devoted to industry, art, and agriculture. Twenty-six thousand exhibitors from thirty-five

On April 7, 1766, Emperor Josef II opened the Prater, Vienna's restricted royal hunting preserve, to people of all classes.

countries filled the expo's nearly two hundred pavilions, drawing some seven million fairgoers—only the fair fell short, taking place during the double whammy of a global economic crisis *and* a cholera epidemic.

On the upside, Vienna implemented a mass tourism business—albeit twenty years after Paris's and London's—and the fair cemented the Prater's status as the empire's hub for the smart set, with the *New York Times* labeling Vienna's Big Playground "the most democratic and the most aristocratic place in the world."

Deeming it a miracle that Vienna's beauty can still mask her troubled past, contemporary historian Christopher McIntosh views the Prater as one of the city's "bittersweet echoes."

British Royal Navy lieutenant and engineer Walter B. Basset built the 1897 Wiener Riesenrad. Like George Ferris before him, his wheel would be his curse.

Wurstelprater—wurstel meaning "sausage," and a little one, at that—became the nickname for the main amusement section, and the playful appellation stuck. Some pop etymologists assign the term *Wurstelprater* to the fictional Hanswurst, who starred in shows by the itinerant puppeteer Josef Anton Stranitzky (1676–1726). As the years went on, little Hanswurst's personality devolved from sly to silly, and his bearing from gnomelike to harlequin, resulting in a character so altered by time that poor little Hanswurst has all but eroded from collective Prater memory.

Equally unsung is Walter B. Basset, whose ancestors first arrived in Britain with William the Conqueror—and whose Giant Vienna Wheel opened on July 3, 1897. A dashing former cavalry officer and lieutenant in the Royal Navy under the Prince of Wales, Basset was forced to leave his commission due to ill health, driving him back to his true passion, engineering. Named, in 1891, managing director of the venerable London-based steam-engine manufacturer Maudslay, Sons, and Field, he built the sixteen-hundred-person capacity Gigantic Wheel at London's Earl's Court, to mark the 1894 Empire of India Exhibition. Blackpool's Gigantic Wheel, on that northwest England seaside town's Coronation Street, followed in 1896. Basset, who had bought design rights to George Ferris's original giant wheel after the 1893 Chicago World's Fair, confidently told one interviewer, "I'm a believer in the one-man principle, and I have carried this thing out myself."

To carry out his 212-foot Wiener Riesenrad (literally, Vienna's Giant Wheel), Basset used five hundred tons of iron and steel. "At a cost of 750,000 kronen," wrote *Life* magazine's World War II correspondent Noel F. Busch, "it was only about one fourth as high as the Eiffel Tower…but it was obviously more interesting." It was also, Busch admitted, located "over the noisy little peep shows and animal tents" of the Prater. Still, Busch maintained, "if the city changed, the Giant Wheel did not."

But then it did. With the 1938 Anschluss, the Nazis removed the Riesenrad's Jewish proprietor, Eduard Steiner, and, six years later, killed him in Auschwitz. In 1944, a fire that claimed the Prater's roller coasters, bumper cars, airships, and miniature racing cars also gutted the Wheel's engine system. The next year, air-raid bombing reduced its wooden cars to charcoal.

In the midst of postwar plans to rebuild the destroyed city, an amusement park smacked of a needless luxury; but then the cost to scrap the wheel turned out to be prohibitive. The answer turned out to be careful restoration with the materials at hand.

Due to a mechanical malfunction, Basset's Gigantic London Wheel stranded seventy passengers overnight, in 1896. Rescued the next morning, victims were treated to complimentary soup, ten shillings apiece, and their names in the newspapers.

By its fiftieth birthday in 1947, the Wiener Riesenrad was twirling again, an energized symbol of the city's strength—albeit with a noticeable concession: The number of its gondolas was forever reduced, from thirty-six to fifteen.

Its late '40s-era silhouette stands to this day, as do the larger windows and more comfortable seats installed in 2016. Recognized by cineastes as the backdrop for the Orson Welles and Joseph Cotten characters in director Carol Reed's taut 1949 adaptation of Graham Greene's novel *The Third Man*, the Riesenrad rightfully stakes its claim as a world landmark, not only for being giant cinematic eye candy, but also something uniquely Viennese.

Rotating at not quite 1.7 miles an hour, or about half the walking speed of the average person, it seems to glide habitually to the lilt of an elegant Strauss waltz.

After his success with the Wiener Riesenrad—a quarter million riders bought tickets its first two seasons alone—Walter Basset built the Grande Roue de Paris, which debuted in 1900, only to be converted fourteen years later into a wartime shelter for French families before its eventual disassembly in 1920. Closer to home, his Earl's Court and Blackpool wheels had, compared to Vienna's, relatively short runs of twelve and thirty-two years, respectively.

Basset did not fare so well himself. Wheels for amusement no longer engaged the public in numbers large enough to support his company. In 1907, at age forty-three, the engineering entrepreneur died in his ancestral castle in Watermouth, England, alone and insolvent.

Watermouth, his family castle—in truth, an 1825 country estate made to resemble a castle—met a more bearable fate. Sold off at the end of World War II by what remained of the Basset family, it went through a succession of owners until 1977, when business-man Richard Haines bought and converted it into a North Devon tourist site, one that encourages families to play in its dungeon labyrinths and adjacent amusement park.

Divided into Gnome Land, Adventure Land, and Merry Go Land, Watermouth Family Theme Park and Castle feature nine rides and other attractions.

Inexplicably, a Ferris Wheel is not among them.

VAUX POPULI

I.

Vauxhall pleasure gardens offered a more culturally refined ambience than bois-
terous Bartholomew Fair, yet still found plenty of room on its twelve acres for
hanky-panky. Starting with their adventurous Thames crossing to reach the gardens'
main entrance, Vauxhall guests were treated to "elements of masquerade, chinoiserie,
and other exotic fantasies that transported visitors to new realms of fantasy," according
to contemporary historian Jonathan Conlin. While lacking the sort of mechanical rides
"that provided New York's Coney Island with physically jarring thrills and license to
squeal," he said, places such as Vauxhall "did provide the thrill of encountering what
one might call the expected unexpected."

Modeling itself after Charing Cross's "old" gardens, Vauxhall "was a place to
gossip and stroll in," said social chronicler E. Beresford Chancellor, "a place where
acquaintances would be met, a place for assignations, and for exhibiting fine figures
and fine clothes by both sexes."

It was also the place that provided the next uptick in the development of the
amusement park.

Chief among the amusements at London's Vauxhall Gardens was
people watching—as caricaturist Thomas Rowlandson captured
in 1785. In the foreground, the style icon of her day, Georgiana,
Duchess of Devonshire (née Spencer), links arms with her sister,
Lady Duncannon. At right, the Prince of Wales whispers into the
ear of his mistress, the actress-poet Mary "Perdita" Robinson.

Vauxhall owner Jonathan Tyers—here, circa 1750, with son-in-law John Wood and daughter Elizabeth—"exhibited strains of arrogance and ambition" in seeking "to raise his own status and that of his family to gentry," said the gardens' chroniclers, David Coke and Alan Borg.

"Historically," the architecture critic Rowan Moore said of Vauxhall's 188-year run, which peaked during the Georgian era before the park closed for good in 1859, "it stood between the aristocratic gardens of the European Renaissance, and the music hall and the seaside pier of Victorian mass entertainment."

Bedecked with thousands of oil-lamp lights and extravagant pavilions, obelisks, and grottos, Vauxhall positioned itself as London's primary venue for artists and musicians to establish their professional names—a kind of *Britain's Got Talent* for its time. This promise of career opportunity allowed Vauxhall to form close ties with, among others, the composers Thomas Arne ("Rule Britannia") and George Frideric Handel ("Messiah"), whose 1738 statue by Louis-François Roubiliac could be found center court. Solidifying Vauxhall's connection with fine artists, on the recommendation of the master painter and engraver William Hogarth, Vauxhall became one of the first public spaces to display paintings and sculpture.

Its nature was not always so refined. A "much-frequented rural brothel" characterized the property for its first seventy years. (Hogarth's mordant depictions in his *A Rake's Progress* and *A Harlot's Progress* provide general impressions of what was going on.) Change arrived in the form of the South London–born entrepreneur Jonathan Tyers, who, as of 1728, had undertaken massive repair work, beginning with the site's reputation. Taking a thirty-year lease at £250 per year, Tyers, whose family traded in animal hides, bankrolled a series of property improvements before finally becoming sole owner by 1758—just as the Industrial Revolution dawned and the need for a refreshing respite from city soot became greater.

Described by one contemporary as an unrelenting pessimist who, "if he had been brought up a hatter…believed people would have been born without heads," Tyers was also praised as a "pioneer of mass entertainment." If the word *promenade* was not invented at Vauxhall, it should have been, because visitors went to great efforts to show themselves off along the gardens' main paths. The word *shrubbery*, on the other hand, *was* invented at Vauxhall, with hedges and bushes carefully situated on the landscaping grid to act as borders that shaped the grounds.

"The principal structure was the Rotunda, entered through a colonnade to the left of the Grand Walk," said Warwick William Wroth of the British Museum. "It was a circular building, seventy feet in diameter, elegantly fitted up and containing an orchestra in which the band performed on wet evenings"—or, as one 1841 journal called it, "a most august royal tent."

To level the bar, servants were kept outside the Vauxhall gate so as not to feel obliged to answer their employer's call, while inside one found an amalgam of merchants and shopkeepers, apprentices and artisans, lawyers and military men, and members of the aristocracy, all with one aim in mind—to enjoy themselves.

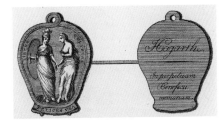

Tyer's friendship with William Hogarth yielded such distinctive flourishes to Vauxhall as Hogarth-designed tickets. Among them was a golden pass that Tyers turned around and gifted the artist.

With admission set at one shilling for most of Vauxhall's existence, and the 1750 construction of Westminster Bridge facilitating easier access, "the place was never exclusive or select, and at no other London resort could the humours of every class of the community be watched with greater interest or amusement," said Wroth, on whose word most of Vauxhall's history rests.

The artist William Hogarth, a recent arrival to South Vauxhall with his bride, Jane, befriended Jonathan Tyers and assisted in planning a grand ceremony on Wednesday, June 7, 1732, to mark Vauxhall's rebirth under the new proprietor.

What the men pulled off was a spectacular Italian-style outdoor masquerade dance called a ridotto, something that remained a Vauxhall tradition for the next thirty years. The modern amusement-park equivalent would be the holiday and special character parties, such as Halloween fright nights and Christmas light festivals, which take place outside normal operating hours and require special tickets.

At Vauxhall's premiere, for which the impresario John James Heidegger arranged the entertainment, four hundred members of haute London, including Frederick, the Prince of Wales, dressed in black-and-white, and except for a tipsy waiter and the presence of a pickpocket—later apprehended—the event was such an instant success that several more ridottos were held that same season.

Over time, Hogarth's association proved so invaluable to the Vauxhall aesthetic that Tyers commissioned the artist to design silver badges for season pass holders. The season ticket, a special bargain pass that commonly exists throughout the amusement industry to this day, was yet another Vauxhall innovation.

One frequenter watched with particular amusement was Sir John Dinely. An eccentric bachelor baronet, he made a complete spectacle of himself by placing a series of matrimonial requests in London newspapers, specifying his demand for a rich wife. He would then prepare himself to greet a surprisingly large contingent of female respondents in Vauxhall Gardens, where, according to one account, "he would parade up and down the most public parts." Sir John was all but impossible to miss. "He wore his wig fastened in a curious manner by a piece of stay-tape under his chin, and was always dressed in a cloak with long flowing folds, and a broad hat which looked as if it had started out of a picture by Van Dyke."

The madcap Sir John Dinely used Vauxhall as his private Lonely Hearts Club.

Alas, his tale did not end well. His madcap manner spiraled into insanity, and, at age eighty, "he died a bachelor, an inmate of the poor knights' quarters in Windsor Castle, in 1808."

Dinely was not the only Vauxhall standout. There was the issue of its overpriced and meagerly portioned food, particularly its ham, sliced so thin that it was joked a person could read the day's newspaper through it.

One contribution for which both Vauxhall Gardens and Bartholomew Fair could share equal glory was in the popularization of the stage spectacle, a cast-of-hundreds pageant that reenacted a scene from history, be it biblical or military, and in a later era would become the specialty of Hollywood filmmaker Cecil B. DeMille (*The Ten Commandments*) or opera director Franco Zeffirelli (Puccini's *Turandot*). In time, such

Novelist Henry Fielding wrote in his 1751 *Amelia* that Tyers's "life proves...that a truly elegant taste is generally accompanied with an excellency of heart."

productions became mainstays at American amusement parks, invariably inside specialty auditoriums with over-the-top façades. When first played at Bartholomew Fair, the stage presentation was modestly described as "a little opera called the 'Old Creation of the World newly revived, with the addition of the Glorious Battle obtained over the French and Spaniards by His Grace the Duke of Marlborough!'" At Vauxhall, the notable program was an 1827 re-creation of the relatively recent 1815 Battle of Waterloo. The cast included an army of horses and foot soldiers—one thousand of them.

As for more intimate entertainments, William Thackeray revealed in his 1848 novel *Vanity Fair* that, in seeking romance, it was de rigueur for groups of friends, including his heroine Becky Sharp, to divide into couples at Vauxhall and then reconvene and compare notes over supper. Charles Dickens, meanwhile, in one of his pseudonymous *Sketches by Boz*, made clear his preference for visiting Vauxhall at night, when darkness masked such deficiencies as the main entrance's "very roughly-painted boards and sawdust." Soon, the cracks in the plaster grew visible even at night. With them, a sense of desperation to survive crept in.

Fireworks, which climaxed with a stuntman's descent on a rope that gave the illusion of his being engulfed in flames, and hot-air balloon ascensions—in 1850, aeronaut Charles Green went aloft atop his horse—were brought in to boost attendance at the gate, which by then had long ceased to see any members of royalty.

"Vauxhall," E. Beresford Chancellor was forced to acknowledge, "was steadily deteriorating."

JONATHAN TYERS DIED IN 1767, age sixty-five, bequeathing his estate to his four children. His elder son, Jonathan Jr., ran Vauxhall until his death, in 1792, when the torch was passed to a son-in-law, Bryant Barrett, who doubled the admission to two shillings. When Bryant died in 1809, son George Barrett took over. In 1821, Vauxhall was sold for £30,000 ($3.4 million today), to T. Bish, F. Gye, and R. Hughes, operating as the London Wine Company. With permission from King George IV they began their 1822 season with a name change, to the Royal Gardens, Vauxhall. The imprimatur provided little comfort when, on July 24, 1837, in Vauxhall's darkest moment, inexperienced parachutist Robert Cocking leapt from an aerial balloon with a defective chute and plunged to his death in front of the crowd. It was history's first recorded parachute accident.

The London Wine triumvirate ran dry in 1840, when the gardens closed, only to reopen in 1841 with an Alfred Bunn listed as manager—although *mismanager* would have been more accurate. To keep the operation afloat, on September 9, Vauxhall's acreage was auctioned off, along with some accessories, which included historical paintings by Francis Hayman that went for as little as thirty shillings apiece.

While bad weather has been cited as one cause for the demise of Vauxhall, there were other factors, including upgrades in rail service to seaside resorts, residential

Vauxhall was not without its dubious distinctions: In 1837, Robert Cocking plunged to his death after leaping from a hot-air balloon, the world's first known victim of a defective parachute.

demand for land in Lambeth, and the 1854 relocation of the Crystal Palace from Hyde Park to Sydenham, which established it as a competing social attraction.

After the 1841 auction, attempts were made to resuscitate Vauxhall with the addition of gas lamps, carnivals, and masked balls—resulting in police complaints from neighbors over the site's sudden rowdiness. However, only one sound was steadily evident in those final years: a death knell.

On July 25, 1859, the evening closed with fireworks that spelled out the message "Farewell for Ever."

II.

In 1742, the same season Vauxhall Gardens debuted its Turkish Tent so visitors could dine informally, Jonathan Tyers encountered his first serious competition: Ranelagh Gardens, on the northern bank of the Thames, in Chelsea. Location alone made it preferable to Vauxhall. Half the size of Tyers's haven, this new addition to the London social scene was considered more chic than its south-of-the-river rival, partly because of its stiffer admission price of two shillings, sixpence—a factor that dissuaded the younger crowd and later proved a detriment to Ranelagh's survival, as did its stringent policy against alcohol.

Pronounced "Rawn-a-lah" or "Ran-a-ley," the park was named for the Earl of Ranelagh, whose mansion had occupied the site since 1670. Accused of misappropriating funds during his tenure as paymaster to the Forces, Ranelagh spent his later years trying to settle his accounts. That was how his estate ended up in the hands of those seeking to cash in on the success of Vauxhall; specifically, a business syndicate that included James Lacy, an owner of the Drury Lane Theatre, and Sir Thomas Robinson, a spendthrift member of Parliament.

The group secured the property in 1733, then made a public offering with their investment—a financial first for an entertainment entity. For some reason, Lacy dropped

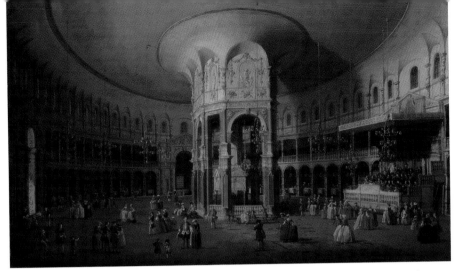

Interior of the Rotunda at Ranelagh, 1754, by Canaletto (Giovanni Antonio Canal); the prodigy Mozart performed here a decade later.

out early from the project, which threw down the creative and financial gauntlets to Robinson. With his approval, the consortium spent £16,000 on an "amazing Rotunda, which [the painter] Canaletto and [engraver Thomas] Bowles have perpetuated for all time," E. Beresford Chancellor said of the wooden structure, with its colonnade of Doric columns, 555-foot circumference, and three-thousand-person capacity.

Influenced by India's temples and the grand scale of Egypt's pyramids, William Jones of the East India Company designed the architectural marvel after Constantinople's great church of Hagia Sophia, except for giving the Rotunda's interior a thousand golden lamps, sitting rooms, gaming tables, tiered boxes, orchestra pit, and a center fireplace, to insure the facility was user-friendly in winter. Unlike Vauxhall, which was strictly a summer proposition, Ranelagh was open all year. To counter its threat to his business, Jonathan Tyres purchased the field next to Ranelagh to keep his rival from expanding.

"Every night I go constantly to Ranelagh, which has totally beat Vauxhall," the novelist Horace Walpole wrote in 1744. "Nobody goes anywhere else—everybody goes there." This included a certain eight-year-old musical prodigy. On June 29, 1764, at a benefit for the neighboring maternity hospital, the child, who had composed from the age of five, stood center stage in the Rotunda and performed his own compositions on the harpsichord and organ. His name was Wolfgang Amadeus Mozart. His family, from Salzburg, Austria, was briefly living in London's Chelsea as part of a three-year European tour.

"Now let me say something about Ranelagh and Vauxhal [*sic*]," Leopold Mozart, the boy's father, wrote in a letter to his wife, Anna. "These are 2 pleasure gardens unlike anything in the world." The patriarch was particularly taken with Ranelagh, which he found attractive, "even if not as large as Vauxhall," especially with its "amazingly large rotunda that you enter at ground level and that's lit by an incredible number of large chandeliers, lamps, and wall-lights," and the "4,500 people walking round and round

One thousand lamps lit Vauxhall. A good many of them were reserved for its Temple for Musicians.

and constantly meeting each other." What the letter didn't mention was the social custom of not bothering to remain quiet or even in one's seat during concerts—setting a precedent that recognized how an amusement venue is not the same, or as polite, as a formal concert hall.

As it was, less-than-amusing political events, such as the London riots of the 1780s and an impending war with France, were hogging the news fronts, putting a crimp in the enjoyment, even the relevance, of Ranelagh and other pleasure gardens. Although Vauxhall would tarry on for several more years, Ranelagh would not. It closed in 1803, after sixty-one years. The Rotunda was demolished two years later. Its pipe organ, whose unique position above the orchestra Leopold Mozart mentioned in his correspondence to his wife, was relocated to All Saints Church in Evesham, Worcestershire, England.

Only that, too, has vanished.

III.

One outer London amusement spot—at the foot of Ebury Bridge, over the Chelsea Waterworks reservoir—was just as unusual as its name: Jenny's Whim, "a favourite meeting-place for lovers in the happy courting seasons" that was fashionable in the daytime, "when only Londoners of the idle class were free to visit."

Like most tea gardens, the Whim was attached to a tavern, but its popularity was grounded in its distortion mirrors, which altered the shape of all those being reflected,

Jenny's Whim, a tea garden attached to a tavern at the foot of Ebury Bridge, placed funhouse-style mirrors and concealed mechanical monsters amid its hedges and pond.

and "its amusing deceptions," said an 1891 account, nearly thirty years after Jenny's Whim was removed to accommodate an expansion of Victoria Station.

The deceptions were "primitive moving mechanical monsters," said Judith A. Adams, the author of *The American Amusement Park Industry*, who likened them to contemporary "devices…in the Disney parks." Taking visitors by surprise whenever an unseen machinist cranked them up in a dark alcove or pond, the figures would be startling-looking creatures, like "large fish or mermaids," said historian Henry B. Wheatley.

How Jenny's Whim got its name remains something of a mystery. Generally it was believed that a landlady named Jenny laid out her garden in an eccentric pattern, but, in fact, there was no Jenny; the landlord was some fellow who manufactured fireworks. Wheatley ascribes the name to the unproduced 1794 play *Jenny's Whim*, by the Irish writer John O'Keefe, even though the five-act drama was about white slavery in Morocco—and 1794 was forty-four years after Jenny's Whim first opened.

Then, too, Wheatley credits Dr. Samuel Johnson for his quip upon learning that a Miss Jane Wilkinson "left a sum of money to sustain a certain number of old maids. It was so absurdly inadequate for the purpose that Johnson…being asked for a name for the institution, suggested 'Jenny's Whim.'"

IV.

Among the sixty or seventy assorted places of amusement and recreation that constituted the mid-seventeenth-century London social scene, E. Beresford Chancellor perceived that "after Vauxhall and Ranelagh, was Marylebone Gardens"—in what later would be the Marylebone district of the City of Westminster.

Thursday, May 7, 1668, diarist Samuel Pepys wrote of visiting Marylebone Gardens, "the first time I ever was there; and a pretty place it is."

What it had that the others lacked was a manor house that was formerly the hunting lodge of Henry VIII, a demonstration in 1736 by a "Flying man" who slid down a 135-foot-long rope "with a wheelbarrow before him," and the most fashionable crowd in town.

This did not guarantee decorum. The Duke of Cumberland, a frequent visitor, "often behaved here…in a scandalous manner," it was recorded, "but then he was not noted for special good behaviour anywhere."

For the majority who carried on in a civil manner, Marylebone also had gambling, operas, a bakeshop known for its plum cakes, and, for genuine razzle-dazzle, as the pioneering Victorian studies scholar Richard Daniel Altick noted, fireworks "as early as 1718," and which "became standard fare there by mid-century." William F. Mangels, the industry sage and designer—of such rides as the 1906 Tickler and, in 1914, the Whip—saved his highest praise for Marylebone's fireworks by one Morel Torré, a former pyrotechnician of Versailles.

Torré's much-repeated masterpiece, also duplicated at Ranelagh, was the "Forge of Vulcan" fireworks spectacular starring no less than the god of fire, Vulcan; the single-eyed giant, Cyclops; the goddess of love, Venus; and her cherubic son, Cupid. As the production began in a specially built pavilion, the muscular shadows of Vulcan and Cyclops were seen at their forges at the foot of Mount Etna. When Venus requests that they make arrows for Cupid, an argument ensues, which sets off Etna and Torré's handiwork—sending sparkling fire and belching smoke from its crater and faux lava down its sides, burying the cast and ending the show.

Marylebone came to a far less dazzling finish. When magicians, magic-lantern shows, and lectures failed to infuse it with new life, its keepers simply surrendered and made way for fresh land development.

The year was 1776, and, across the Atlantic, the American colonies were providing the British with something far more piercing than Cupid's arrows.

EARTHLY DELIGHTS

New York has its Vauxhall and Ranelagh; but they are poor imitations of those near London. They are, however, pleasant places of recreation for the inhabitants." Or so wrote, with blatant condescension, the British travel author R. P. Forster, in the early 1800s. If it is any consolation, Forster did concede that the "people of New York are highly distinguished amidst the surrounding states, for their urbanity, cheerfulness, and hospitality." He further found them primarily amused by "theatrical exhibitions, balls, and card parties."

On that final point, Forster was myopic. By the time its first owner, Samuel Fraunces, opened New York's Vauxhall Gardens, named for the London original, in 1767, taverns with adjoining pleasure gardens were very much in fashion in the colony—including a 1765–1769 Ranelagh rival to Vauxhall, at Thomas Street and Broadway, not to mention Governour's Garden, Cherry Garden, and Adam Vandenberg's Mead House and Garden, among others, adorning stretches of Pearl, Cherry, Fulton, Nassau, Ann, Charles, and Hudson Streets and Broadway.

Beyond New York, there were American Vauxhalls throughout the original states: Philadelphia's Vauxhall Harrowgate (1789), and Vauxhall Garden (1813); Vauxhalls in Charleston, South Carolina (1795); and Richmond, Virginia (circa 1802); as well as two in New Orleans (1850 and 1853).

That an American pleasure garden, or any leisure activity, should duplicate a tradition from Mother England was to be expected. Up until the War of 1812, when Old World culture and conventions finally started to wear away in the new country, Americans leaned heavily, if not wholly, on England for their aesthetic tastes and social pursuits.

Prior to opening his gardens, Samuel Fraunces, a native of the French West Indies, trained as an innkeeper in Philadelphia before moving to New York City sometime in the early 1750s. At the age of thirty-four, in 1757—the same year he married the former Elizabeth Dalley, with whom he would eventually have seven children—he obtained a tavern license. Within six years he had the wherewithal to purchase a forty-year-old brick building at the corner of Queen and Canal Streets (now Pearl and Broad), on the city's harbor front. Catering to the city's merchants from the Royal Exchange on neighboring Dock Street, Sam called his public house Fraunces Tavern.

Tavern owner Samuel Fraunces initiated New York's first Vauxhall Gardens in 1767, before he left to manage President George Washington's household.

Like similar establishments of the era, it specialized in rum and tobacco, but Fraunces took extra measures to distinguish his namesake, especially when it came to "cakes, tarts, jellies, whip syllabubs [a frothy cream and wine or sherry dessert], blancmange [a gelatinous version of a syllabub], sweetmeats, etc., in any quantity," according to a 1770 circular.

Still a lively enterprise today thanks to its proximity to the New York Stock Exchange and its well-stocked whiskey bar, Fraunces Tavern remains a requisite stop for tour groups because of what took place under its roof on December 4, 1783: Over a feast of turtle meat, Gen. George Washington and his Continental Army officers marked the November 25 British evacuation of the city after the War of Independence with tearful toasts and an emotional farewell—to each other, not to the British.

Framed by what would become Chambers and Warren Streets in TriBeCa, New York's Vauxhall Gardens was snugly situated on Greenwich Street near the Hudson River on the site of the former Bowling Green Garden, on land leased from nearby Trinity Church, to whose parish the Fraunces family belonged. Washington Irving, America's first man of letters and all-around bon vivant, referenced the location in one of his stories about a fictitious arbiter of social grace named Anthony Evergreen, who "often played cricket in the orchard in the rear of old Vauxhall."

Fraunces's al fresco summer "resort" specialized in "tea, coffee, cakes" available at any hour, and entertainment that included fireworks. With food and beverages extra, four shillings bought admittance to the grounds, its mansion, and displays of seashells, flowers, and ancient Roman relics. Wax likenesses of biblical and other historical figures were also exhibited—each seeming to bear an uncanny resemblance to Samuel Fraunces—and among their number were King George III and Queen Charlotte, although they quickly disappeared once the colonies' relationship with England curdled.

As it turned out, Fraunces was also removed—to Philadelphia, where he was employed as President Washington's chief household steward. (Fraunces would die in the City of Brotherly Love on October 10, 1795.) Given the heavy upkeep of the New York property, and the fact that he was now living three days away by coach, Fraunces decided it was time to unload Vauxhall Gardens.

Despite his best efforts, nine years would go by, until April 1785, before a sale could be transacted.

The delay was caused by President Washington.

Unbeknownst to Fraunces, he had arranged for Vauxhall to be rented out as federal office space.

Once Samuel Fraunces divested himself of the property, Vauxhall Gardens relocated, not once but twice. Vauxhall 2.0 opened in 1798, at the present intersection of Mulberry and Grand Streets, while Vauxhall 3.0 ended up between Broadway and the Bowery, on a rural parcel that extended all the way to what is now Astor Place.

Formerly the seed garden of a Dutch doctor named Joseph Sperry, these latter three acres became the best known of the New York Vauxhalls. John Jacob Astor, a fur trapper turned real estate mogul, had bought the land in 1804, and, the following year, a French caterer named Joseph Delacroix took out a twenty-one-year lease so he could create a miniature version of London's Vauxhall, down to its two thousand lights.

At the center of the "neat plantation," as wrote R. P. Forster, this time showing approval, stood a statue of Washington on a horse, while elsewhere were marble likenesses of Cleopatra, Cicero, Hercules, Alexander Hamilton, and other proud names. For the enjoyment of live music and theater, audience members could choose from among a number of well-placed, open-air orchestra boxes. Still, Delacroix credited his garden's success to his "elegant and appropriate" Fourth of July fireworks display, which, to give credit where credit is due, first established what was to become the time-honored tradition of shooting off bursting rockets in the air to celebrate America's independence.

This third incarnation of Manhattan's Vauxhall, which boasted, as of 1845, its own merry-go-round, was also not without its spectaculars. During the August of his very first season, Delacroix produced a live reenactment of a naval battle in the Bay of Tripoli, combining real cannon fire with fireworks, and a stage full of large-scale

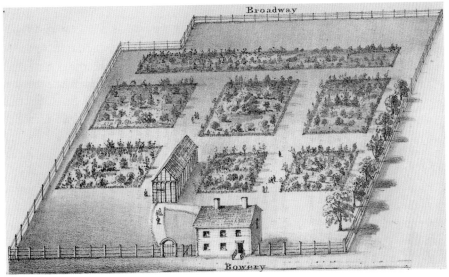

"Sperry's garden," the *New York Daily Herald* spelled out, "was the great resort of belles and beaux for the purchase of their bouquets"—that is, until 1804, when horticulturalist Joseph Sperry sold the property to John Jacob Astor for $45,000 ($7.5 million today). Astor turned it into Vauxhall Gardens.

Vauxhall Gardens' lessee Joseph Delacroix has long been credited as the first to merchandise the world's most popular frozen dessert, but as far as the Daughters of the American Revolution are concerned, the cherry on top of the sundae goes to his wife.

"The world owes a debt of gratitude to Marie Josephine Delacroix, for her peculiar genius invented *ice cream*," a DAR newsletter said in 1916. "She was a Parisian, the wife of M. Joseph Delacroix, [and] about 1784 they emigrated to the United States."

Aboard their passenger liner was Johann Jakob Astor, a prosperous German businessman who, after his arrival in New York, transformed himself into the industrialist John Jacob Astor, America's first multimillionaire—and, purely by coincidence, in 1804, the Delacroixs' Vauxhall landlord.

In Philadelphia, the couple initiated a store that rounded out its inventory of women's fashions and perfume with preserves, cookies, cakes, and ice cream.

From there, "the Frenchman and his plucky wife" moved to New York and opened Vauxhall Gardens, where, according to the scoop from the DAR, "Madame Delacroix and her beautiful daughters invented and introduced ice creams."

"The novel delicacy won instant favor," the Daughters of the American Revolution said of the product Marie Josephine Delacroix and her daughters introduced at Vauxhall, ice cream.

mechanical models of frigates and life-sized painted backdrops. For the finale, actors playing plunderers set fire to the port—while they, too, looked as if they were going up in flames, similar to the denouement of Disney's Pirates of the Caribbean attraction 162 years later.

Delacroix also sold his specialty—ice cream—at Vauxhall. The dessert, along with the inevitable balloon ascensions and circus acts, served to prolong the garden's economic health, if not its social status.

As the years progressed, the park declined markedly. When Astor refused to renew the lease, Delacroix was forced to vacate (he opened what became a successful hotel farther downtown), and the "much frequented summer resort" and "place of amusement for a much longer period than any other place…in New York," as the *Times* described Vauxhall, sat deserted until it began to be destroyed piecemeal. In 1826, John Jacob Astor permitted traffic to flow through Lafayette Place, effectively splitting the park in two. Final demolition took place in the spring of 1909, by which time Vauxhall Gardens had been closed for fifty years, not only due to the general rowdiness from the saloon that had sprung up on the property in 1838, but because of the seedy element that had seeped up from the Bowery.

It would not be the last time the deterioration of an American urban neighborhood would bring down its popular amusement area.

But it might have been the first.

HUMDINGER

I.

The saloon inside New York's Vauxhall Gardens did not spell ruin for everyone. From June to September 1841, an ambitious, thirty-year-old former farmer, grocer, newspaper editor, advertising writer, lottery manager, bootblack, and *Sears' Pictorial Illustrations of the Bible* salesman from Bethel, Connecticut, staged a variety of shows in the barroom, although, by his own admission, "I thought it would be compromising my dignity as a 'Bible man' to be known as the lessee of a theatre."

His solution was to let his brother-in-law, John Hallett, assume the venue's management while he kept his own identity concealed in the background.

It did not remain there for long.

His name was Phineas Taylor Barnum.

That same year his brother-in-law fronted for him, "I casually learned that the collection of curiosities comprising Scudder's American Museum, at the corner of Broadway and Ann Street, was for sale," Barnum recalled. He added that the collection—conveniently located at the foot of the city's Newspaper Row, where the majority of the city's numerous dailies were headquartered—"had been for several years a losing concern, and the heirs were anxious to sell it."

Barnum was in no position to buy. "My recent enterprises had not indeed been productive," he said, "and my funds were decidedly low." Still, "I desired to enjoy the blessing of a fixed home—and so I repeatedly visited that Museum as a thoughtful looker-on."

He ended up doing more than looking on.

Undaunted by his financial state, and using as collateral a fairly worthless tract of land in Connecticut left him by his grandfather, the broke but budding showman snatched up the space and, drumming up attractions that bore his personal signature, converted the repository into a kind of Barnum-land.

Here, seekers of thrills could congregate.

First established in 1791 by the Tammany Hall political organization as a members-only diversion, before later opening to the general public, the 150,000-piece American Museum was supervised by John Scudder, a naturalist and taxidermist, who eventually assumed ownership. With the curiosities in his cabinet ranging from French Revolution guillotines demonstrated on wax dummies to the bed linens

Showman and showpiece: Phineas Taylor Barnum and Charles
Sherwood Stratton, better known as Gen. Tom Thumb, circa early
1840s, around the time Barnum purchased his showplace, the
American Museum.

of Mary, Queen of Scots, and what the Museum of the City of New York termed "a
bona fide zoo," the collection proved so popular that it sometimes stayed open as late
as 9 p.m.

As tastes evolved, more visceral thrills were demanded, especially once the rival
Peale's New York Museum, at nearby 252 Broadway, had been taken over by showman
Harry Bennett, who put the kibosh on founder Rubens Peale's edifying exhibits in
favor of magicians, mentalists, and hen-eating anacondas.

Scudder's, whose collection had been appraised at $25,000, was sold to Barnum
for less than half its value, with the well-situated, five-story building housing it thrown
in as part of the bargain.

TO A PUBLICITY HOUND like Barnum, the proximity to the New York press corps was manna from heaven. In 1835, his cajolery of reporters helped make a star of Barnum's first attraction, a blind, octogenarian slave named Joice Heth, whom he imaginatively hyped as George Washington's 161-year-old former wet nurse and catapulted into a box office sensation at the Niblo's Garden downtown theater-saloon-hotel complex before sending her on tour, efficaciously launching his career as the prince of "humbug."

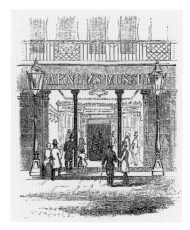

Barnum's American Museum, in Lower Manhattan, combined the formerly compartmentalized dominions of exhibitions and entertainment and presented them under a single roof.

Another geographic advantage to Barnum's American Museum, as he renamed it, was that it stood directly across the street from both City Hall and the three-hundred-room Astor House, the first luxury hotel in New York. But Barnum knew better than to limit his establishment to the elite, not when there were nickels and dimes to be made from an emerging middle class. Proving himself the showman, Barnum gussied up the former Scudder Museum's stately white marble edifice by stationing a loud live band on its outside balcony, and slapping on garish, painted placards advertising his attractions, the most prominent of which might have seemed better suited to Bartholomew Fair: a live whale, a live hippo, conjoined twins, a morbidly obese woman, and, perhaps the most notorious of them all, a baby monkey skull stitched to a fossilized fish torso and passed off as the "Fejee Mermaid."

Despite the actual fossilized look of the dead creature, billboards throughout the city—Barnum is credited with inventing the advertising medium—depicted a large illustration of a comely, humanlike, bare-breasted mermaid.

Nearly forty million customers plunked down their pennies so they could explore the wonders of Barnum's Museum.

Barnum may have been credited with the slogan "There's a sucker born every minute" (he never really said it), but he was also keenly aware that the public would settle for no less than its money's worth, and his American Museum gave it to them—if not always in quality, then in quantity. He claimed his collection contained six hundred thousand to eight hundred thousand items, and when one display fell out of public favor, he cannily renamed it and resold it as something new.

While "the intelligent public" had every right to be "disgusted" by Barnum's "innumerable sensations, [his] Museum still deserved an honorable place in the front rank of the rare and curious collections of the world," stated the *New York Times*.

Whatever his formula—which, like himself, Barnum constantly reinvented—the public simply could not get enough. Over its life span, Barnum's American Museum spun nearly forty million visitors through its turnstiles, at a time when the U.S. population was 31.4 million, and New York City's only 813,669. Despite such commercial approbation, not everyone fell under the spell of the huckster.

In addition to those who decried the exploitation of humans of any size or shape, and others still who protested the imprisoning of wild animals in unnatural habitats, there were those who simply argued that museums should be museums—that is, repositories where accomplishments of art and science should be appreciated, rather than one-stop fun houses "for stuffed birds and animals, for the exhibition of monsters, and for vulgar dramatic performances," as American educator Henry Philip Tappan, a contemporary of Barnum's, huffed after a visit to the superior British Museum in London—although it wasn't words such as his that brought down Barnum's Museum.

The force was much stronger.

New York had witnessed conflagrations before. The Great Fire of 1835, near Barnum's Museum, destroyed the twenty square blocks of the business district around Wall Street a week before Christmas, and the combined forces of fifteen hundred

In the wake of the disaster, *Harper's Weekly* extolled Barnum for having provided the public with more "amusement than could be obtained elsewhere for double the money."

local-area firefighters, with four hundred more from Philadelphia, had been required before it could be extinguished.

Ten years later, the same neighborhood was struck again. The Great Fire of 1845 began on Saturday, July 19, in a whale oil factory at 34 New Street, and spread to Broad Street, where a saltpeter warehouse exploded. "The whole area," the *New-York Daily Tribune* reported from the scene, "is one vast amphitheater of blood-red flame." Four firemen and twenty-six civilians were lost.

Few catastrophes, however, could pack the emotional wallop delivered by the fiery end to Barnum's American Museum. THE COLLECTIONS OF HALF A CENTURY ANNIHILATED, the page-one headline on the *Sun* lamented the morning after, July 14, 1865, while the *Times* anguished over the loss of "a great many relics of the Revolution, of the War of 1812, and other peculiar curiosities connected with our national and personal history," including mementos of George Washington, Thomas Jefferson, and John Adams. The timing and the rapidity of the fire also "should demand the serious attention of every one concerned in edifices for public use," the newspaper editorialized.

Only a small number of customers were inside the display halls at half past noon, when the fire was first noticed; though never confirmed, a faulty furnace was blamed, although it seems odd that it would be in use in July. No human lives were lost—a fireman named William McNamara rushed out the customers, and then evacuated the human oddities that made the Museum home—but the sacrifice of animal life was monumental, despite efforts to set the creatures free from their basement cages.

Two whales were boiled alive in their tanks. Snakes and other reptiles were never seen again. Neither were the monkeys. While there were tales of a lion roaming around City Hall, no evidence of a sighting ever came forward. The kangaroo, zebra, pigs, and dogs were all confirmed dead.

The impresario rebuilt at 539 Broadway, between Prince and Spring, but that location, too, was reduced to ash in 1868.

While the double whammies might have finished Barnum in the museum business, the showman was not finished catering to the masses.

He hitched his wagon to ringmaster James Anthony Bailey's star and ran off with the circus.

II.

While P. T. Barnum beat the drums for his manufactured wonders downtown, others, in tandem with Mother Nature, danced to a different tune uptown.

"The hills along the river were adorned with…the lordly oak, the generous chestnut, the graceful elm," said the distinguished turn-of-the-century New York historian Hopper Striker Mott, "and from the owners the territory took the name of Jones's Wood."

Mainly a place to sightsee, socialize, play sports, or even pluck little red apples from the orchard, the tract also contained a curious foreboding element: It overlooked the East River's narrow tidal strait known as Hell Gate, a passage so treacherous that it damaged or sank one out of every fifty ships that dared enter its waters.

None of this put off *New York Evening Post* editor-in-chief William Cullen Bryant, who envisioned something grand that would benefit the city's entire population—which, according to the 1840 U.S. census, had hit a staggering 312,710. Bryant's proposal was to turn the seventy acres "as they now are" over to the public as an official city park for all to enjoy—a Central Park, if you will.

"All large cities have their extensive public ground and gardens, Madrid, and Mexico their Alamedas, London its Regent's Park, Paris its Champs Elysées, and Vienna its Prater. There are none of them, we believe, which have the same natural advantages of the picturesque and beautiful which belong to this spot," Bryant wrote in his July 3, 1844, editorial, framing the location as "between Sixty-Eighth Street on the south, and Seventy-Seventh Street on the north, and extending from Third Avenue to the East River."

Bryant's words might have greased the wheels, but they were not enough to set them in motion. When the Jones family refused to relinquish their estate, State Senator James William Beekman proposed seizing it by eminent domain. "Beekman's bill passed the New York Senate," said the New-York Historical Society, but "it raised vigorous opposition among downtown businessmen."

As voiced in a letter to the *Tribune*, the merchants feared—not unreasonably, given that since the Great Fires of 1835 and 1845 there had been a massive residential and commercial migration north—that gentrifying Jones's Wood was "a scheme to enhance the value of up-town land" at the expense of their own.

In 1854, the bill's authorization was repealed, giving rise to an alternative and, as circumstances played out, a more practical suggestion.

Why not a Central Park in the middle of midtown?

Jones's Wood was not adversely affected by the debate, at least not at first. Beginning in 1855—two years before architects Frederick Law Olmsted and Calvert Vaux's glorious Central Park opened in the middle of midtown—the Jones family began renting out a portion of their property as commercial picnic grounds for private clubs, church charities, and labor unions.

"Jones's Wood eventually boasted amateur shooting galleries, bowling alleys, beer halls, and outdoor dancing stands," the Historical Society said. Additional recreation included billiards, sparring matches, theatrical presentations, puppet shows, foot races, rides on donkeys, swings, and roundabouts, earning Jones's Wood its niche as "the first large American amusement resort," according to *The Great American Amusement Park* author Gary Kyriazi, who further saluted the outpost for popularizing the term "beer garden," given its patrons' overwhelmingly favored beverage of choice.

In 1858, Valentine Mager, owner of the Jones's Wood Hotel at Seventy-First Street, promoted the destination's accessibility to the Second and Third Avenue horse-drawn trolleys. That June 26, the *Times* announced an open-air concert at the Wood at which Beethoven's Ninth Symphony would be performed "for the first time in years." The entire program consisted of fourteen hundred performers—three hundred in the orchestra, and another three hundred in the chorus. The following year, a popular, large-scale reenactment of the 1859 Battle of Magenta pitted actors playing Napoléon III's French-Sardinian troops at war against the Austrians.

Closer to home, a Civil War benefit to aid those widowed and orphaned by the Battle of Bull Run drew sixty thousand people, while a two-day May 1865 Workingmen's Union rally saw fifty thousand protestors demand that their ten-to-fourteen-hour workdays be reduced to eight.

"Before Coney Island and the Catskills," the *New Yorker* noted in 2013, when it touted a hot new bar on the site, "there was Jones's Wood, . . . a popular getaway for the island's suffocated citizens."

Jones's Wood fell to the inevitable scourge. On May 16, 1894, architect Julius Kastner's fourteen-thousand-seat Coliseum, which had stood on the property for twenty years, went down in flames, along with eleven acres of forest.

"The fire swept so furiously that engine No. 39, the 'Silver King,' had to be abandoned and was burned," according to Mott, while the *Times* told of the sixty horses set loose from the Sixty-Eighth Street stables in the hope they would run to safety. Instead, most headed directly into the burning sheds.

"No vestige of the Wood now remains," Mott eulogized in 1917, two decades after the Wood was deforested and northern Manhattan turned to concrete, "and so passes into history a region hallowed in memory for its early charm and its later identification with the amusement of former generations of pleasure-seeking New Yorkers."

III.

Venues such as Niblo's Garden, at Broadway and Prince Street, where P. T. Barnum first solidified his career, usurped the title of Garden about the same time Vauxhall and the city's other dedicated pleasure gardens had fallen out of favor with the upper and middle classes.

What replaced the traditional gardens were new sports or entertainment arenas that nonetheless identified themselves as gardens. One was the multiuse Madison Square Garden, founded, in 1874, at Madison Avenue and Twenty-Sixth Street by the bandmaster Patrick S. Gilmore and none other than P. T. Barnum. (William Vanderbilt,

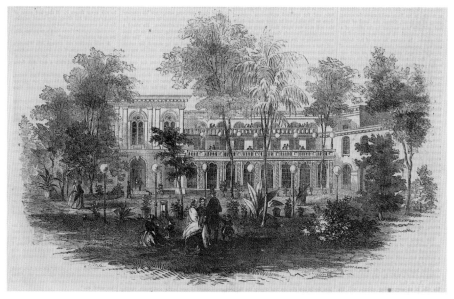

Originally "a large garden for the purposes of promenade and the partaking of refreshment," Niblo's Garden bloomed into New York City's premier amusement complex.

eldest son of railroad magnate "Commodore" Cornelius Vanderbilt, took over five years later and converted it into a sports arena.)

Another was Castle Clinton, a repurposed military fort in the Battery, which today is the central ticket office for ferries to the Statue of Liberty and Ellis Island. Remodeled and renamed Castle Gardens for thirty-one years starting in 1824, the unique, round structure was home to concerts, spectacles, even headline-worthy balloon ascensions, all with the added adventure of its patrons crossing a moat to the main entrance, as if they were stepping into a special kingdom.

Still, in terms of setting trends that became traditions, Niblo's took the blue ribbon. It was initiated in 1823 by William "Billy" Niblo, a real estate developer born in Ireland and keen on showbiz. He began on Pine Street with a coffee house specializing in locally hunted dishes, like hawks from Hoboken. His Garden was based on his correct assumption that the public would spend money on having a good time. What he offered in return was a brightly lit urban oasis modeled after London's Vauxhall that "embraces, within a space of three hundred by two hundred feet, all the conveniences of a first-class hotel, as well as a theatre, and a ball room, all of them enjoying, at present, and promising for the future, a most exceptional reputation," gushed the Boston-based *Gleason's Pictorial* in an 1852 front-page feature. With an eye toward customer safety in case of fire, the story mentioned that "the means of egress are the best of any public saloon in town."

Socially connected by sheer dint of his thriving Garden, Niblo attracted the finer classes by charging top prices, which left the less desirables to gravitate toward the Bowery. Following dictates of convention, unescorted women were refused entrance to Niblo's, for fear they might solicit. Once inside, couples were permitted to separate on the ground floor of the three-thousand-seat theater, "which has become the favorite part of the house for gentlemen, and is much frequented by ladies," said *Gleason's*.

Complementing the recurring productions of Shakespeare, fireworks, acrobats, and biblical panoramas within the enclosure, the polka was introduced in Niblo's ballroom in 1844. In 1866, Niblo's Theater debuted what is generally accepted to be the first-ever book musical, *The Black Crook*, pancaking songs with a slapdash story that was hard to follow, though its leggy chorus line was not. The show ran 474 performances.

In contrast to Barnum, Billy Niblo preferred his profile low, quietly retiring in 1861. He died in 1878, at the advanced age of eighty-nine.

Under new ownership, his Garden survived until 1895, although by that time a lively amusement resort on the Brooklyn shore was in the midst of making a lusty name for itself, by combining the best of Niblo's Garden and Barnum's Museum with its own unconventional entertainments and wanton behavior.

HORSEPLAY

I.

Say what one will of the flamboyant eighteenth-century empress of Russia, Catherine the Great—and many a false legend has been spun—one aspect of her curriculum vitae has continually rung true: Right up until her death in 1796, she was inordinately fond of having a good time.

In addition to reading—she was known to be voracious—chief among Catherine's leisure activities were cold-weather sports. One typically began with a military escort from her sprawling St. Petersburg Winter Palace to the solidly frozen Neva River. There, before an audience of admirers, Catherine would scale a multileveled stairway to the peak of a seventy-foot, man-made "ice mountain" constructed of wood, buttressed by tree stumps, and doused with water, furnishing it with an icy coat. Positioning herself luge style in a sled by sitting in the lap of the driver (known as a cavalier) and taking firm hold of his leg wherever she felt comfortable, the empress would cascade down the slippery slope at a robust angle of fifty degrees.

Among her several distinctions, Russia's Catherine the Great deserves the title of Patron Saint of Roller Coasters.

Thus was born, if not the first official incarnation of the roller coaster, then certainly a functional prototype "fit for royalty."

For at least a century before Catherine's descent, desultory "ice slides" had been popular around St. Petersburg. "In every town and village these slippery declivities are crowded with youths and maidens rushing down with the swiftness of arrows," observed Robert Sears, a seasoned traveler from New York, during his late-nineteenth-century trip to Russia, promoting a claim that the native thirst for thrills knew no class distinctions. Princes relished their indoor mahogany slides, just as peasants made do with scraps of timber in the great outdoors.

Catherine the Great Visiting the Ice Mountain, St. Petersburg, by watercolorist Benjamin Paterson, 1788

As the pastime evolved, sleds on these so-called ice or wooden mountains were kept on course by running them on tracks, which were progressively engineered to become longer, more gravity reliant (kinetic energy was key), and, once a tolerance level was evaluated, daringly hilly. "The slides built during festivals in Moscow and St. Petersburg," as described by the artist and ride enthusiast Robert Cartmell, in his *The Incredible Scream Machine: A History of the Roller Coaster,* "stretched several city blocks," with exotic adornments completing the package. "Chinese pagodas often topped the mountains, while the finest craftsmen decorated stairs and sleds."

Surviving still on the grounds of the Russian imperial palace, Oranienbaum is Italian architect Antonio Rinaldi's exquisitely baroque Katalnaya Gorka (Russian for "toboggan") pavilion, which opened in 1774—simply to complement Catherine's "flying mountain." Built of wood, it was "supported upon high brick walls [and] composed of three principal ascents, gradually diminishing its height," wrote William Coxe, an English historian, in 1784.

Upon further inspection, Coxe found that the mountain's one-person carriage—or sled, or sleigh—relied solely on gravity, and the speed it picked up going down the first hill was what propelled it to the top of the second, from which "it continue[d] to move in a similar manner until it arrive[d] at the bottom of the area, where it roll[ed] for a considerable way." The carriage then returned to the original hill by a rope, as riders were independently required to make the arduous climb by stairway to start or repeat their adventure.

Unlike the pavilion, which in 1990 was designated a UNESCO World Heritage Site, the Oranienbaum palace's wooden mountain is no more, except for a scale model on display at the estate. Having fallen into disuse by the mid-1800s, the empress's former indulgence was dismantled and its outline on the palace lawn flattened into a meadow, which was then planted over with fir trees.

Wishing to extend the joy ride beyond winter months, Catherine the Great demanded an attachment to the sleds for the elaborate wooden mountains commissioned for her properties: wheels.

Centuries later, the debate still lingers over whether these tools of convenience were a Russian or French invention.

A case can be made for both.

French winters were mild compared to Russia's, suggesting, perhaps, that the French had every reason to put rollers on their coasters.

Then again, because of the ride's country of origin, the name "Russian Mountain" fell into common use for a wheeled roller coaster—and it has tenaciously refused to go away.

"In several European languages, including French [*montagne russe*], Italian [*montagna russo*], and Spanish [*montaña rusa*]," scholar Fabrizio Tassinari, addressing matters of nomenclature, wrote in 2009, "roller coaster still translates as 'Russian mountains.'"

Curiously, he also pointed out, "The Russian term for it literally translates as 'American mountains [*Американская гора*].'"

In 1817, two years after French soldiers in the Napoléonic Wars brought home word of the thrill ride from Russia, two major mountains debuted in Paris, both featuring dual tracks, although one looked nothing like the other.

Les Montagnes Russes à Belleville laid its straight rails side by side so that riders, provided they had bought pairs of one-way tickets, could switch cars at the end of one track and then double back.

Promenades Aériennes, or "Aerial Walks," in the Jardin Beaujon, at the top of the Champs Elysées, was even fancier; it rushed riders at speeds approaching forty miles an hour down two separate curving routes to meet at the structure's base, making Promenades Aériennes the first-ever racing coaster.

The coaster's casing also contained another welcome improvement: a safety guardrail "that prevented the cars from 'jumping,' if the wheels should pass over an obstruction," said William F. Mangels. For night riding, torches were lit alongside

In 1817, the French company Les Montagnes Russes installed two attractions in Paris: Les Montagnes Russes à Belleville (shown here) and Promenades Aériennes, in the Jardin Beaujon.

A year after the debut of the Promenades Aériennes, Jardin Beaujon announced the addition of a carousel, whose "chariots of an elegant shape will provide the ladies with the pleasure of a new aerial walk."

the mountains. Another refinement, thanks to an 1826 invention by someone known only as Monsieur Lebonjer, was a return of the cars to their original position at their journey's start.

Lebonjer relied on a principle that was staring everyone in the face: He connected a cable to a pulley, and then attached the cable to the collar of a horse.

II.

Cushioned by a family fortune amassed in his native Italy, fireworks heir Claude-Fortuné Ruggieri moved to Paris, where, beginning in 1806, he placed rodents and even a sheep inside primitive rockets that he sent spiraling six hundred feet aloft. Most of the creatures parachuted safely back to earth. French authorities, however, slammed the brakes on Ruggieri's aeronautical experiments just as he stood on the brink of flight-testing an eleven-year-old boy.

Ruggieri and his family nonetheless remain lastingly associated with pyrotechnics, even when they turned their sights toward the running of several Parisian pleasure parks. For members of the dynasty, these new playgrounds were not merely a family business, but premier showcases for building their brand name.

In 1766, Pietro Ruggieri opened Jardin Ruggieri, at 20 Rue Neuve-Saint-Lazare, where the evening traditionally concluded with an impressive "fête champêtre" ("outdoor entertainment") centered on a "beautiful and brilliant promenade" with "poèms pyriques" (literally, "poetic fireworks") that could be viewed from specially built galleries or, given the perennial vagaries of the city's summer weather, rain shelters.

In 1801, the Ruggieris assumed ownership of Jardin Beaujon, first opened by Nicolas Beaujon, a former grain speculator from Bordeaux whose impressive holdings also included the Élysée Palace. Under Ruggieri guidance, the rejuvenated park began a nearly quarter-century run, gaining fame not only for its Promenades Aériennes but its chariot races, floating figure balloons that predated Macy's by a good century, and a spectacular pageant based on Homer's tale from *The Odyssey* about Calypso, the seductive daughter of Atlas, and her futile designs on Telemachus, son of Odysseus and Penelope. (Spoiler alert: He ends up with Circe.)

Slightly later, another Ruggieri family member opened Jardin Marbeuf, near the Chaillot Gate at the foot of the Champs Élysées, although its elaborate fireworks spectacular, Phaeton's Fall—after Phaeton, the son of the sun god Helios, who bungled his chance to control the sun and would have destroyed the earth had Zeus not smote him—proved so expensive that, despite selling tickets, its costs smote the park.

A year after Jardin Ruggieri opened, Morel Torré, the other Versailles virtuoso *de la pyrotechnie*, created a rival park in the Tenth Arrondissement on the Rue de Bondy (today's Rue René-Boulanger). He named it—what else?—Vauxhall Gardens. In addition to food and drink, Torré's resort provided the obligatory fireworks, along with masked balls, pantomimes, jousting tournaments, concerts, and lotteries, where one lavish giveaway was a horse and carriage. Apparently such largesse was necessary, if only to appease the neighbors, who lived in collective terror that Vauxhall's fireworks might burn down the entire neighborhood. Despite the ill will, Torré's business lasted eleven seasons, until 1778.

Throughout, Jardin Ruggieri soldiered on. After the family initiated crowd-pleasing hot-air balloon ascensions in 1784, admissions slumped three years later with the approach of the French Revolution. Torré might have managed to tackle Vauxhall's public

Claude Gillot illustrated a common sight in France: celebratory fireworks. His work is from the reign of Louis XV, benefactor to pyrotechnists Morel Torré and the Ruggieri brothers.

relations problems with his neighbors, but with so many holdings, the Ruggieris faced a greater business and social challenge: Pleasure gardens were now roundly vilified as frivolous.

The family padlocked their eponymous garden's gate on July 12, 1789, two days before the storming of the Bastille, and kept the bolt tightly fastened for a quarter of a century. When Ruggieri Gardens finally did reopen, in 1815, pronounced advances in the amusement business had taken place, and with standalone Russian mountains prospering elsewhere in the city, the Ruggieris were rightly compelled to develop a thrill ride of their own.

Called Saut du Niagara—loosely translated, "Jump over Niagara"—it was an initial step in the development of the Shoot the Chutes, which it predated by fifty years. Mangels considered it "the earliest large-scale water amusement ride," and likened its boats gliding down a ramp from a 150-foot summit to otters competing in a sliding match, while a critic for London's weekly *Literary Gazette* griped at the time the ride opened that "the descent is very inferior to that of the modest Russian Mountains."

Nevertheless, Saut du Niagara set an important architectural precedent for amusement parks.

It placed a prominent attraction in the middle of a body of water, to establish it as the main focal point of the realm.

III.

If Catherine of Russia deserves a fist bump for hastening the roller coaster's development, then so should the Aztecs be called out for their contribution to the carousel. This, according to no less an authority than Frederick P. Fried (1908–1994), whose 1964 *A Pictorial History of the Carousel*, more than half a century after its original publication, continues to remain the last word on the subject. A onetime art director at Manhattan's modish Bonwit Teller department store before he oversaw political campaigns in New York, the friendly-faced, Brooklyn-born expert called out a key element of a pre-Columbian ceremony in Mexico as a precursor of the carousel.

The concept was born, Fried explained, when the Aztecs adorned themselves in feathers representing birds of prey, then hung upside down from an eighty-foot pole. The aim was to unwind the rope from which they dangled, and, as the rope's grip loosened, go flying "outward, horizontal to the ground, spinning at great speeds." The fun was apparently so contagious that, in India, maharajahs, their elephant drivers, and household servants participated in the same sport at prayer festivals, only with less bloodshed.

What the carousel was to become started taking shape after the Crusades, when Spanish and Italian soldiers, having witnessed Arabian and Turkish horsemen play out a twelfth-century version of tag, brought the military exercise back from battle. The object of the match—called *garosello* in Italian and *carosella* in Spanish, both meaning "little war"—revolved around tossing a delicate clay ball filled with scented water before it would break and splash perfume all over their manly selves. To practice, young nobles rode crude wooden frameworks molded into the shape of horses and were pushed—in circles—by their servants.

"In primitive cultures," notes the late Russian scholar Eleazar Moiseevich Meletinskii, "the idea of repetition is specifically linked to ritual."

At the end of the fifteenth century, the exercise was introduced to France, where the court of Charles VIII christened the tournament a *carrousel* and added expressions of chivalry that culminated in spearing a beribboned ring from a wooden post. In Italian this lancing exercise was called *correre dela quintana*, and, in English, "tilting at the quintain."

Louis XIV staged carrousels for his teenaged mistress, Louise de La Vallière, who shared his bed from 1661 to 1667 and bore him four children. The court's most lavish carrousel, before fifteen thousand spectators, took place June 5, 6, and 7, 1662, to mark the birth of Louis's legitimate heir, Louis, le Grand Dauphin. King Louis wore a silver

Chivalry pageants were called *garosello* in Italian, *carosella* in Spanish, and *carrousel* in French; here, in 1656 Rome, the *garosello* in honor of Queen Christina of Sweden in the courtyard of Palazzo Barberini.

arousel music goes back to the days of young royals training for war, when servants pushed their mechanical horses into mock battle. Another servant kept pace by beating a drum, while another clashed cymbals. For dramatic effect, a flute might be added.

The carousel calliope—named for the Greek goddess Calliope, the Muse of heroic poetry—was developed sometime in the 1800s, to signal the arrival of a river showboat or traveling carnival to town.

Early versions, consisting of a steam boiler with integrated whistles and strings, were produced by the Scottish-born carousel maker Allan Herschell and his partner, James Armitage, at their Armitage-Herschell Company (1883–1899), in North Tonawanda, New York.

While the better musical organs came via slow boats from the German firms of Frati and Company, in Berlin, and Bruder, in Waldkirch (both still represented today, at Knoebels

Amusement Resort in Pennsylvania), Armitage-Herschell sped up the delivery process by hiring its own German expert. What developed was an instrument that relied on pegged cylinders programmed to read notes and play automatically—and loudly.

In 1855, when Josiah C. Stoddard, of Worcester, Massachusetts, added a physical keyboard to the steam whistles, in case a musician wished to play along, Spalding and Rogers Circus introduced the steam calliope to America, where it has been tooting ever since.

helmet plumed with ostrich feathers, "while the Queen and Princesses, seated under a gorgeous canopy cloth of gold, looked on," recalled Henrietta, Duchess of Orléans, another mistress of the monarch's.

What advanced the carrousel, because, by the end of Louis XIV's reign in 1715, these tournaments came to be passé, was a simple but ingenious development that took place around 1680, also in France.

As Fried put it, "Someone thought of suspending horses and chariots by chains from arms radiating from a center pole."

SKULDUGGERY

O ne of the most successful of the Parisian amusement resorts was the Tivoli, which opened in 1798 by two sons of the original Ruggieri family, lasted thirty years, closing in 1828," said William F. Mangels, painting a broad picture. Greater details were to be mined from Gabriel Surenne's *The New French Manual, and Traveller's Companion*, published in 1826, while the park was still up and running.

After making a comparison of Parisian pleasure gardens, Surenne, a teacher of the French language in Scotland, declared unequivocally, "Tivoli greatly excels the others [and] is quite equal to Vauxhall at London by night, and is much superior in daylight." (Surenne may have been influenced by the price of the entrance fee: one franc in the daytime, and three francs and ten sous at night—but, please, no jokes about a Scotsman's thrift.)

The travel author was not alone in his admiration. Tivoli also had a fan in Georg Carstensen, the son of the Danish consulate secretary to Algiers, Johan Carstensen. Accompanied by his wife, the former Anna Magdalene Ulrich, the elder Carstensen had been assigned to the North African post in 1810, two years before Georg's birth. Johan was next sent to Morocco as consul general in 1833, by which time Georg was twenty-one and already showing signs of the effete he was to become. An indifferent student, he switched his studies from law to philosophy. In military training, he rose to lieutenant before resigning from service.

Then, not entirely in keeping with his father's wishes, he embarked upon a lengthy sojourn to gather his impressions of southern Europe, Africa, America, England, and France, which, of all the territories he visited, exerted the strongest influence on his palate and personality.

This all would factor into Georg's building his own glorious Tivoli.

Georg Carstensen spent three years in Philadelphia, publishing an arts journal and perfecting

Born in Algeria to Danish diplomat parents and widely traveled, Georg Carstensen was susceptible to an array of international influences, particularly those from France..

the peculiarities of his personality, particularly his addictions to champagne (though never more than one glass per bottle), the latest in French waistcoats (his closet overflowed with them), and custom-made gloves (he never sported the same pair twice).

Tivoli Paris, which since 1837 has been home to the Gare Saint-Lazare rail terminal, first became a pleasure garden in 1766, under the aegis of Simon-Gabriel Boutin, the son of a wealthy financier. It was he who named it for Italy's sixteenth-century Tivoli Gardens at the Villa d'Este with its elaborate fountains, although Boutin's own mélange of English, Italian, and Dutch gardens—accessorized with water games, an orchard, and a menagerie—quickly became known as Folie Boutin (Boutin's Madness).

It just as easily could have been called Boutin's Downfall; in 1794, during the Reign of Terror, he was beheaded over his ostentatious wealth. His Folie was impounded, only to reopen in 1795.

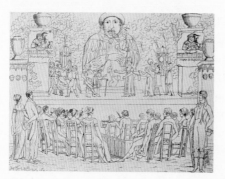

"The Giant's Dinner," at Paris Tivoli Garden

With fireworks by the Ruggieris, Tivoli played host to elaborate costumed events staged by Muscadins (men in silks and laces and with the heavy scent of musk perfume) and Incroyables (fancy women in exaggerated dress), who numbered as many as twelve thousand and carried on with their 1800s precursor of voguing until well past midnight.

"From this time," the French cultural historian Gilles-Antoine Langlois said of the garden, "all the attractions were invented. The panoramas, the puppets and the magic lantern, the rides, the Russian mountains: the ice was replaced by soap, it slipped almost as well."

Langlois also quoted doctors who prescribed a ride on the Russian mountains for their women patients, for what was believed to be the uphill journey's restorative powers to their female parts.

Apparently, another physical benefit emanated from Tivoli, singled out by Langlois as the scene of "rather salty meetings, naked dinners, served by naked servants, in an isolated pavilion in the midst of a dense park."

The cumulative result? "Sumptuous orgies."

At age twenty-seven, he settled in Copenhagen and, as a young press baron, settled scores, especially with those who belittled him—in particular, the noted playwright and critic Johan Ludvig Heiberg, who considered Carstensen a philistine who paraded around in peacock finery and the publisher's journals about fashion and opinion "the representative of stupidity." In retaliation, "Carstensen once offered me one hundred rix-dollars," said the existential theologian Søren Kierkegaard, "for an article against Heiberg."

Returning from yet another trip to Paris, Carstensen launched a series of high-profile parties he called "Vauxhall-Concerts," supplying his paying guests with a buffet, light classical music, fireworks, and stunning illuminations. His timing was propitious; in September 1841, in anticipation of Copenhagen's first railway station, gossip swirled about limited partnerships to develop a park not unlike Paris's Tivoli and London's Vauxhall—only the rumblings died down along with the negotiations, due to disputes over tax rates and the length of the lease.

Behind closed doors, another barrier was revealed.

Some Copenhagen leaders deemed it their duty to obstruct any effort to provide a common ground where the various classes of society might fraternize.

Georg Carstensen took a different tack.

Just as Rahere cannily manipulated Henry's superstitious nature to secure St. Bartholomew's, so did Carstensen seize a royal opportunity with Denmark's newly crowned King Christian VIII. Georg's foot in the door was the country's shaky political situation. Abject poverty was rampant, especially in overcrowded working-class districts such as Vesterbro and Nørrebro, where running water and a sanitation system were nonexistent. At the opposite end of the spectrum, abundant wealth was being funneled to a fortunate few able to take advantage of Copenhagen's major trading port.

King Christian VIII of Denmark faced a public-relations debacle that Georg Carstensen believed he could alleviate.

The public demanded reform, to which King Christian turned a deaf ear, sparking fears of revolution.

Emboldened by his success at Rosenborg Garden, Carstensen approached the king in the autumn of 1841 with the idea to build a site for all residents to flee the "violence and boisterousness of the town and relax in a sea of tranquility."

To back his argument, he cited "the small number of popular amusement that Copenhagen, compared to the other capital cities, offers its inhabitants and visitors"; besides the illustrious gardens of London and Paris, Tivolis flourished in Hamburg (one since the early 1800s, another starting in 1826), Berlin (since the 1820s), New York (sometime after 1840), Stockholm (albeit in 1848 and 1850, after Carstensen opened his Tivoli), and throughout Holland.

"I entertain the hope that Your Majesty will bestow upon my petition your most gracious consideration," said the cover letter. As a sign of good faith, Carstensen also formally applied for Danish citizenship, so that his income could be taxed.

Then, as if channeling the spirit of Rahere, Carstensen told King Christian, "When people amuse themselves, they do not make revolutions, Your Majesty."

Carstensen won royal approval, along with a five-year lease and 5 percent of what the park business would generate. Overseeing him to keep expenses in check would be a board of directors, chosen from among Copenhagen's business community.

Tivoli & Vauxhall, as it was named, was slated to be built on nearly fifteen available acres just outside the city wall, obliging patrons to enter through the sheltered Western Gate, or Vesterport, a fortification that required Carstensen to seek special permission from Copenhagen's military governor.

By the time Christian VIII granted Georg Carstensen his request, Western Europe, Great Britain, and Scandinavia had fallen under the spell of a philosophical school that permeated politics, literature, and art—and sensibilities in general.

"We are all Orientalists now," Victor Hugo said in the prologue to his 1829 collection of poems, *Les Orientales*, reflecting the reinvigorated Western outlook toward the East in the wake of Napoléon's 1798–1801 invasion of Egypt.

With the semimystical images—both seductive and threatening—that colonialism conjured, Greek classicism was figuratively consigned to the dust heap. Though patronizing (down to its very name), Orientalism is the reason, pure and simple, Carstensen and his architect, Harald Conrad Stilling, conceived of decorative pagodas and minarets for Copenhagen's Tivoli Gardens.

That it should resemble Aladdin's playground might also be attributed to the barefoot scamp's Danish DNA. Although Aladdin sprang from *One Thousand and One Nights*, the ancient folk tale was first given Western voice when translated in 1805 by the Copenhagen poet Adam Gottlob Oehlenschläger.

There are convincing arguments, too, that Carstensen's youth spent in Algiers and Morocco fed his personal vision, given H. C. Stilling's established reputation for rational, late-classical style.

But a new die was cast, thanks to Tivoli.

For the next century, until the art moderne movement became the definitive dreamscape design, the managed spaces of world's fairs and amusement parks would largely, if not wholly, be firmly rooted in Orientalism.

Carstensen "took from his presence in Islamic countries the idea of punctuating the park with the exoticism of new colonial empires," said architecture critic and urban planner Jean Dethier. Here is Tivoli's main entrance, circa 1900.

Private financing was secured, and prospects looked sunny, but then a surprising discovery was unearthed—one too grisly for words.

Workers in Copenhagen, preparing the future Tivoli & Vauxhall during its harried two-month construction period, stumbled upon the unexpected: human remains, compactly preserved in the excavation site. The corpses were determined to be those of soldiers, Danish, British, and Swedish, in all probability victims of the 1801 and 1807–1814 *Englandskrigene*, or English Wars, brutal extensions of the Napoléonic Wars over border trade. Some on the dig refused to continue; others saw it as their duty to honor the fallen. By and by, work did resume, and with it the city moat was reconfigured into a lake to reflect many of the aspects H. C. Stilling infused into the property to provide a sense of otherworldliness, including forcing a perspective that caused certain attractions to appear larger than they actually were.

As Tivoli & Vauxhall was being landscaped with cafés, an innovative carousel that would be drawn by live horses concealed below the carousel floor, and a Russian mountain that would incite outrage because men and women were seated side by side, Carstensen turned his attention to entertainment. He recruited composer Hans Christian Lumbye from one of Copenhagen's prestigious hotel ballrooms. Known as the Johann Strauss of Denmark, Lumbye would serve as park musical director for three decades, and proved a drawing card in his own right. Among the polkas, waltzes, fantasies, and ballet pieces he wrote during his tenure was the effervescent 1845 "Champagne Gallop," to mark the park's second anniversary and, for Carstensen, another excuse to pour his favorite drink.

Opening with the sound of a popping cork, the piece became the official tune of Tivoli Gardens—which, once the Vauxhall reference finally was dropped, became the official park name in 1915.

With Pjerrot's presence dominating Bakken only twelve and a half miles away, Carstensen hired his own actor, Niels Henrik Volkersen, to perform the silent commedia dell'arte role in Tivoli's outdoor pantomime theater. The difference between the two interpretations was that Tivoli's portrayed the figure as a comical, overgrown boy, rather than the traditional sad clown. Volkersen additionally was the first Pjerrot/Pierrot ever to speak, even if only by accident. During a performance, a dress worn on stage by an actress suddenly caught fire. Turning to the audience, Volkersen improvised that the flames were sparked by her love for him. The spectators erupted in laughter, and the line stayed in. Likewise Volkersen; he remained with the park for fifty years, until his death in 1893. He is paid tribute with his bust, as Pjerrot, on a well-trafficked Tivoli walkway.

"When he died, his funeral was enormous," said the Danish pianist and theater personality Victor Borge (1904–2000), who made his concert debut in the park at the age of fourteen. "It wound through the city streets to Tivoli, where the procession stopped, and everybody wept."

Borge, admitting that his favorite memory of Tivoli no longer existed—a restaurant that served nothing but strawberries—added that Pjerrot's statue was a park landmark, the safe place where lost children would know to wait for their worried parents.

RESTLESS SPIRITS

I.

Updates on coaster innovations did not travel the ocean the same way word of Russian mountains had swept into Paris. Waning French interest in the attraction was partly at fault, a situation that literally left Americans to their own devices. As it happened, simultaneous to Georg Carstensen's fine-tuning his chancy endeavor in Copenhagen, the completed track for what is considered the germinal roller coaster on U.S. soil was being laid amid the coal mines of eastern Pennsylvania.

It began when ironworks financiers Josiah White and Erskine Hazard partnered with Philadelphia merchant and inventor George Frederick August to develop coal mines and upgrade navigation on the Lehigh River. In 1827, they inaugurated the Mauch Chunk Railway to transport "black diamonds," as anthracite coal was called, from the quarry at the top of Sharp Mountain down to the slack water canal in the unprepossessing town of Mauch Chunk.

The nine-mile descent required half an hour and gravity, while the mule-powered return trek packed another four hours onto the schedule. To speed up return time, a parallel set of tracks and a cable were laid in 1844, bringing the train back up the slope and giving rise to the name "switchback railway."

Once Sharp Mountain's quarry was mined out and abandoned, local citizens were not content on letting the railway sit and rust. How about, it was thought, converting it into passenger mode and providing an amusing scenic tour?

They did, and it did.

Mauch Chunk—actually, *Mawsch Unk*, meaning "Bear Mountain" in the language of the Lenape—became known as the "Switzerland of America," and joy riders, from wide-eyed sightseers to bleary-eyed honeymooners, began lining up.

The Mauch Chunk Railway was not conceived as a pleasure ride, but as a means to transport coal. That changed.

The repurposed Mauch Chunk Railway was not for the faint of heart. For the price of a nickel, passengers proceeded at a tepid five to ten miles per hour toward a sweeping view of the Poconos before their transport skirted an open quarry, purported to be where Americans first discovered anthracite, followed by an "'Amazing Burning Mine,' which had been on fire since 1832," reported *American Heritage*. Shifting gears, the train hit speeds of sixty-five miles per hour in the final stretch, leaving those aboard so unnerved that "wooden seats sometimes bore the marks of fingernails."

"The car itself is worth the noting," said a 1916 issue of the *Railway Conductor*, with the recommendation that visitors attempt the ride during the change in fall foliage. "There are ten, broad, wooden benches to this, each bench intended to seat five." As for the ride, the train picked up speed while traveling upward, "and the conductor points to a handy handbrake, always ready against an accident." (In fact, only two mishaps were ever reported, neither major.)

One amusement park tradition looks to have been introduced at the Mauch Chunk station: Those with reserved seats were allowed priority boarding, but first everyone had to make a mandatory stop—at a souvenir stand.

"Descending," wrote *Railway Conductor*'s correspondent, Felix J. Koch, those seated on the end "hold on hard." At another juncture, *everyone* held on hard. Along a wild mountain brook, readers were warned, "you fairly tear over, then along…then you travel on, through endless forest, while you munch candy brought along, when

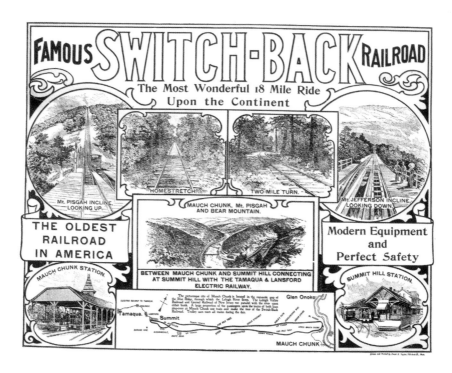

you dare." Gentlemen invariably lost their hats, while ladies strained to keep their skirts down over their knees.

The trip down the mountainside took twenty-eight minutes. "It's been a great, a wonderful experience," but "to tell the truth, you're almost glad" it ends, admitted Koch, who then confessed that he was ready to go back and ride it again.

Any fears of heights, or chances of falling out, did little to dissuade him or most others; in the mid-1870s, thirty-five thousand passengers a year rode those rails, including President Ulysses S. Grant and Thomas Alva Edison—who, when asked to convert the railway to electric power, advised leaving well enough alone. Only Niagara Falls attracted more tourists—seventy-five thousand a year—and rider demand never ceased at Mauch Chunk, until the Great Depression brought the attraction to a screeching halt.

In 1937, "America's first track roller coaster," as *The Incredible Scream Machine* author Robert Cartmell labeled the groundbreaker, was sold as scrap.

II.

To power the carousel at Paris Tivoli in 1815, a lone individual would push the platform in circles from a dark and dank subterranean pit underneath. Within another seventeen years, a hand crank was added. Pedals came next, placing the burden on the rider. Eventually, a horse or mule took control and paced the inner circle—a folksy touch that often remained even after automation kicked in.

The turning point came around 1865, with the "Steam Circus" devised by an S. G. Soames of Marsham, England. He discovered how to rotate the carriage of a carousel by attaching a flat-belt drive to a stationary steam engine. Soames ultimately found the belt drive inadequate and dropped the project altogether.

Paternity of the carousel engine, therefore, fell to Frederick Savage (1828–1897), who was born into unpromising circumstances in Norfolk, England. When he was eighteen months old, his father, William Savage, a weaver of wool, was found guilty of poaching game and sentenced to fourteen years in a Tasmanian penal colony. He never returned to his wife, Susan, and their two sons.

Starting at age ten, Frederick was successively apprenticed to a machinist, a wheelwright, and a whitesmith (in contrast to a blacksmith, who dealt with iron and steel, a whitesmith specialized in objects of metal, usually tin). Savage eventually went to work

"Father of the Carousel Engine" Frederick Savage got his start manufacturing agricultural implements for local farmers in his native Norfolk, England.

This model by an unknown American artist, circa 1890, reflects advancements made at its time. Still to come, in 1901: the mechanical crankshaft, allowing the mounts on the merry-go-round to go up and down.

for a brass smith, and assumed the business when his employer retired.

Building machinery for agricultural use, in 1868 he also developed a steam engine that could be horizontally mounted and affixed to the center of a carousel, generating a force so powerful that larger carousels for several passengers could be assembled.

"This resulted in the development of what we now think of as a traditional carousel, with carved 'galloping horses' suspended on twisted brass rods in rows of three or four abreast," according to information supplied by Savage's hometown archive. "To make the horses rise and fall, a multi-cranked driveshift was provided for each row. These carousels became known as 'Gallopers' and were painted brightly."

Although he would go on to become a popular, three-term mayor in his village, as well as a generous philanthropist—his machinery company employed four hundred employees, and by the time of his death, at age sixty-nine, he was exporting fairground rides internationally—Savage's difficult formative years left their permanent mark, albeit a creative one.

Having no formal education, leaving him only semiliterate and unable to write, he was obliged to draw instructions for clients and staff "on the cinder ash floor of his workshops using a stick."

III.

Finally, there was reason for Georg Carstensen to have so many gloves. On the opening day of Tivoli, August 15, 1843, he personally shook the hand of every one of the park's 3,615 arrivals.

"You are right to bring your offspring," Carstensen told parents as they entered. "Tivoli belongs to the future." In fact, it belonged to the investors, even though the public might have felt differently. To them, Tivoli belonged to the people, who strolled its ornamented lanes with a sense of pride bordering on possessiveness. Hans Christian Andersen claimed an affinity with Tivoli from the start: Over two days near the close of the park's first season, the thirty-eight-year-old teller of children's tales wrote his "Nattergalen" ("The Nightingale"), set in China and inspired by the architecture at Tivoli. (On the 150th anniversary of Tivoli, in 1993, Den Flyvende Kuffert [The Flying Steamer Trunk], a seven-minute, animatronic dark ride devoted to Andersen and his stories, opened in the park. Unlike Disney's, its Little Mermaid goes topless.)

In 1844, its first full season, 372,237 visitors came to Tivoli, nearly one-third of

Denmark's entire population. (Copenhagen itself had only one hundred thousand citizens.) Suddenly, the quaint little market town had flowered into a bustling urban center. Sundays at Tivoli routinely attracted ten thousand people, and overnight its access roads became cluttered with other entertainment options, though none with the polish of Carstensen's—leaving a venerable old deer park in the gravel, ridiculed for its provincial dullness compared to the glittery new entry.

By season two, in addition to already existing attractions, of which the Pantomime Theatre was a primary draw, Tivoli visitors could marvel at its new steam-powered roundabout (Denmark's first steam-powered anything), daguerreotype studio (another first in the country), early take on a switchback railroad, wax museum, in which the figures actually moved (and presented scenes from the life of Christ), and panoramas, which were vast, artistic renderings of various settings from around the globe. Another Tivoli breakthrough was a new interpretation of a restaurant. Heretofore, only men ate out; now, in a park with many meal facilities, for the first time entire families were eating out—together.

"Tivoli, will never, so to speak, be finished," Georg Carstensen announced during that second season, a sentiment that not only invited the public to keep coming back for more, but would be echoed by another storied amusement park builder, Walt Disney, when he opened Disneyland in 1955.

Tivoli's first Rutschebanen rumbled from 1843 until 1887.

"We bear the heritage of Georg Carstensen's ideas, and we remember his words that Tivoli will never be finished," Tivoli CEO Lars Liebst said on the park's 170th anniversary, in 2013. For the 175th, in 2018, Tivoli held its first-ever winter festival, in February, and a parade all through the summer.

The animator's exact words were "Disneyland will never be completed. It will continue to grow as long as there is imagination left in the world."

Carstensen held the same view, but his investors wanted to have their money returned—not poured back into a never-ending magic river of fresh ideas.

Arrogance wasn't Georg Carstensen's only flaw. Profligate spending of other people's money put a crimp in his relationship with Tivoli's board of directors, particularly after revenue from Tivoli's final night of its first season, October 11, 1843, was earmarked to

Inside Tivoli Gardens today, one finds a high-speed Demon, an anchored pirate ship for Caribbean-style casual dining, an old-fashioned fun house overrun with new-fashioned children, and environmentally correct vending machines that reimburse customers who responsibly recycle their plastic drinking cups.

The steel Demon (in Danish, Dæmonen) has been sending riders for a loop since 2004, and in 2017 added Samsung headsets that plug riders into a virtual-reality demon-and-dragon encounter through China. That's for those for whom the Immelmann loop, vertical loop, and zero-G roll are not enough. (Max Immelmann, 1890–1916, for whom the loop is named, was a World War I German aerial-fighting ace.)

The coaster comes from the Swiss engineering firm of Bollinger & Mabillard, founded in 1988 by Walter Bollinger and Claude Mabillard. To date, they are responsible for more than one hundred roller coasters worldwide, at major parks in the United States, China, Japan, and the United Kingdom.

Like some fifteen other B&M coasters, Tivoli's Demon is floorless, permitting riders to dangle their feet and risk the loss of shoes. (Coasters have been losing eyeglasses, hats, and wigs ever since their invention; floorless coasters added flying footwear and even the occasional prosthetic leg to the missing list.)

Those with more of an affinity for architecture than engineering would do well to board the 1914 Rutschebanen, with its twin mountain snowcaps. Delivering an evocative scenic-railway experience, the antique coaster requires an on-train brakeman to control its low-velocity speeds.

Among the garden's newer curiosities, Fatamorgana is a single structure with three rides: mini–bumper cars at its base, and, atop its tower, a high-speed whirling swing that shares airspace with slower, twirling Magic Carpets.

The attraction's compactness solves a practical issue; at twenty acres, park "space is limited," admits Tivoli's chief executive officer, Lars Liebst, "so we have to think outside the box."

finance Carstensen's upcoming European winter tour to gather ideas. Carstensen's "imagination and great initiative collided inadvertently with the board's petite bourgeoisie," summarized the nineteenth-century Danish theater scholar Robert Neiiendam. As a consequence, "His glory lasted only a summer and a half," concluding at the end of Tivoli's 1844 season.

Georg Carstensen had his detractors, but children's storyteller Hans Christian Andersen was not one of them.

Carstensen might also have spread himself too thin. Without negating Carstensen's creativity, or Hans Christian Andersen's appraisal of him as a genius, Neiiendam paints the Tivoli director as a tireless, perhaps tiresome, control freak intent on balancing a veritable *tagselvbord* (smorgasbord) of duties as *maître de plaisir* (master of ceremonies) at rides, concerts, and the park's ancillary ventures.

If that alone did not overtax the man, in 1845 he married for the first time. His bride, Fanny Elisabeth Webb, was twenty-one to his thirty-three, but she died barely a year after the wedding. Other than her being Carstensen's cousin, and her father English (from Cornwall) and her mother Danish, few details about their union or her cause of death are widely known.

By the autumn of 1847, Carstensen and Tivoli permanently severed all connections—and while enough time should have passed to ease any feelings of ill will, Tivoli retains what can be interpreted as a less than loving stance toward its

A bust of Carstensen pays him tribute inside Tivoli, although the founder's depature was anything but amicable.

founding father. As bluntly stated on the park's official website, "In 1848 he enlisted for the war against Prussia, and Tivoli's advisory board subsequently fired him for breach of contract."

In fact, he was called into duty during the German nationalist uprising in Schleswig-Holstein. The website also notes that when Carstensen returned to Denmark—he had to pay his own admission into Tivoli, a point not mentioned—he planned to open a new pleasure garden to rival Tivoli, Alhambra in Frederiksberg.

The Alhambra "opened in the summer of 1857," according to the Tivoli account, which then goes on to say, "Carstensen never experienced the opening; he died of pneumonia in January, at the age of 54."

In fact, he was only forty-four, and his story after leaving Tivoli proved more complicated than that.

SON OF BLUBBER

I.

Simultaneous to Georg Carstensen's moving heaven and earth to open Tivoli, 850 miles away, on an island off the southern coast of England, Alexander Dabell was facing his own quagmire. His newly established base of operations was an all-but-inaccessible cliff atop a rugged landscape onlookers have called "the Jurassic coast of the Isle of Wight" and which, given its excess of shady crevices, was known in all the right circles as an ideal hideout for smugglers.

The nineteenth-century journalist William Henry Davenport Adams found the backdrop downright "gloomy," but then Adams, who edited a newspaper on the Isle of Wight, was setting the stage for a distressing tale of a shipwreck on October 11, 1836, when the *Clarendon*, a 345-ton "gallant vessel" coming back to England from the West Indies, met her fate "on this inhospitable coast." With a crew of sixteen and a passenger load of ten, including a "husband, a wife, and their four children," the *Clarendon* "proceeded up the Channel." Gradually, on what had been placid waters, "came the wind and the tempest, and the ocean was lashed into fury by their 'pitiless smitings.'"

The *Clarendon* shattered in two, killing all aboard except three crewmembers, "while the despairing cries of men and women and children rang fearfully in the ears of the villagers who had gathered on the shore, and saw, and pitied, but could not save!"

And this is where, only seven years later, former lace salesman and hairstyling entrepreneur Alexander Dabell decided to build an amusement park.

"The name is almost enough to frighten us," George Mogridge, the prolific nineteenth-century English children's author, wrote of Blackgang Chine. "It makes one think of a dark cave, and a gang of gypsies or robbers."

In truth, Blackgang Chine embraced gypsies and robbers.

"You know the meaning of black, and therefore I have only to explain gang and chine," said Mogridge's fictitious narrator, Owen Gladdon. "Gang is, I believe, taken from the Saxon word gange, meaning a walk or way, as well as a company acting together; chine is supposed to come from cinan, a Saxon word, meaning to gape or yawn, though some say it refers to the chine or indented part of the back of an animal." Think *ravine*. "Blackgang Chine…A black, ugly-looking place, no doubt, it is, with the sea roaring at the foot of it."

The crest of a steep ravine high above Chale Bay on the Isle of Wight may seem like an unusual place for an amusement park—and it is.

Despite such logistical downsides, in 1823 the Dabell family from Nottingham settled as pioneers to the area, in the town of Newport, nine miles from Blackgang Chine. Their son Alexander was fifteen at the time and already apprenticed to his father, a lacemaker, a vocation that ultimately took the lad one hundred miles away to London, to be employed as a sales assistant. He returned to Newport at age twenty-two with the desire to run his own business, and whether due to enterprise or sheer necessity, his purview soon encompassed many businesses. These ranged from operating shops to barbering and retailing hair products.

In 1839, after a conversation with George Jones, owner of the local new hotel—which, in good weather, was said to afford a view of the southernmost point of Dorset—Dabell determined that the setting was ripe for welcoming venturesome Victorians in pursuit of a holiday out of the ordinary.

The distance from London posed little deterrent; the 1840s ushered in a boom era in British rail service, and, after all, a hundred years before, visitors to Vauxhall Gardens thought nothing of crossing the Thames from Westminster. The Isle of Wight was only four miles off the coast of Hampshire, making it close yet still far enough away for smugglers to establish a base in the late seventeenth century, when brandies, silks, and tobacco were among the favored contraband.

Not that the isle didn't have its socially prominent occupants. Queen Victoria and Prince Albert bought Osborne House on the island in 1845. Beginning in the early 1850s, Emily and Alfred Tennyson took up residence at Farringford, an estate in the south, in part because fellow poet John Keats had written nearby, from 1817 to 1819.

But what about an attraction for tourists? Inspecting the dramatic, if foreboding, landscape that would even give Agatha Christie pause, Dabell and his wife, Amelia, visualized romantic gardens, even if others only saw, as did the author of an 1824 bathing guide to England and Wales, "a vast and horrible opening."

After purchasing land, Alexander Dabell installed pathways and landscaping at the top of the cliff, and steps leading down to the beach.

Then came something largely unexpected, and unexpectedly large.

Measuring ninety feet long, thirty-five feet around, and eleven feet high, an "enormous whale was discovered, scarcely dead, and floating in Totland Bay, between Yarmouth and Allum Bay," a Southampton newspaper reported six days after the finding, on Saturday, April 9, 1842. The deputy vice admiral of the island claimed the razorback in the name of the Crown, and, as such, the deceased mammal was ordered sold at auction.

"Many sums were offered," according to the *Hampshire Advertiser & Salisbury Guardian*, quoting bids of £120 sterling (approximately U.S.$13,450 today)—£40 for the head alone. The "sums were, of course, refused," said the paper with no explanation of why. Even in its desiccated state before the auction, the whale proved an instant tourist draw. "In fact," the paper reported, "it has been like a fair there, for the last three or four days."

While the winner's bid was never revealed, his name was: Alexander Dabell. "He had the novel idea of exhibiting the skeleton of a whale," the local *Isle of Wight County Press* later explained. His investment paid off. Its blubber was sold and its bones bleached, the unfortunate whale went on display under Dabell's auspices, and "Blackgang Chine's first—and probably most bizarre—attraction was a hit with the Victorians, appealing as it did to their sense of morbid curiosity."

"Unlike the Tivoli Gardens in Denmark, Blackgang was not initially an amusement park but more of a walk down a gorge with a shop and café at the top," said Alexander's great-great grandson, Simon Dabell, who could not pinpoint exactly when Alexander

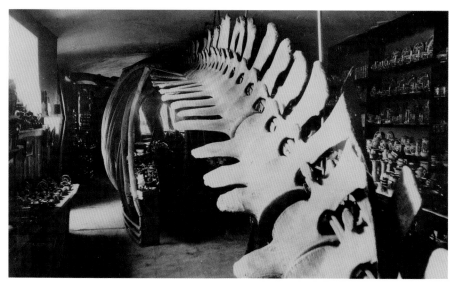

Alexander Dabell's display of a beached whale's bones is what put Blackgang Chine on the map.

first initiated what is considered Britain's longest-running amusement park, other than to say the lease on the Chine and the adjacent cliffs was signed in May 1842. "However," Simon added, "we believe that he didn't open to the public as a garden until May 1843"—which would still make it at least two and a half months older than Tivoli.

When it came to walking down the gorge, "before descending," an 1873 Isle of Wight guidebook instructed, "the visitor will walk through the bazaar, and will be expected to make a purchase." Money went to pay the groundskeeper to maintain the pathway. Also noted: "The skeleton of a whale, cast ashore some years since, is exhibited in an adjoining building for the same purpose."

From such modest enterprise grew quaintness, and from that grew whimsy, and from that grew charm, and from all that grew Blackgang Chine's reputation. Still family run, under the full name of Blackgang Chine Land of Imagination, it is a park for children, with walk-through attractions and dioramas and fiberglass figures, starting with a giant statue of a smuggler who stands at the entrance, a keg of rum hoisted onto his shoulder. The whale skeleton is still on display, though no longer in the gift shop.

In 1967, a determination was made to upgrade the park into a larger tourist attraction, so the next few years saw such additions as Smugglerland (since defunct), Buffalo Canyon (now Cowboy Town), the Mouth of Hell (more benign than it sounds), and Rumpus Mansion (a fun house with moving figures). And while there is a roller coaster—the 25 mph Cliff Hanger, which affords a spectacular view over the cliffs—the real race here is against time, as the terrain facing the sea continues its all-too-hasty erosion, the result of rain, landslides, and a coastal attrition that have totally destroyed the chine. One startling estimate places the wearing down of the cliffs at eleven and a half feet per year.

As a safety measure, rides are continually moved inland. Desolate relics of former buildings and displays are weathered and grown over, separated from the public by warning signs, gates, and fences, although in the right light (a frequent occurrence on the Isle of Wight), past glories of the park almost seem like a separate theme land unto itself: the Ghostly Blackgang.

Fortunately, the dedicated offspring of Alexander Dabell roll with the punches. The park's dinosaur area, called Restricted Area 5, makes the most of its precarious setting and the fascination children have with prehistoric giants.

In 2014, the dinosaurs were made more animated thanks to the Raspberry Pi minicomputer and IBM's Watson Internet of Things (IoT) platform. The result, said IBM's

Blackgang's Tyrannosaurus Rex, the mascot for the park's Restricted Area 5, is kid friendly.

Andy Stanford-Clark, was that rather than have a super lizard repeat the same movement all day, "we were able to introduce the element of randomness. So that sometimes it might do nothing, and then it'll suddenly roar."

That's one small step for dinosaur, one giant leap for childhood.

II.

Aggrieved by his treatment at Tivoli, Georg Carstensen set sail for the Dutch West Indies, where he served on the staff of the governor, and, in 1850, married for a second time. His bride, with whom he would have two sons, was Mary Ann Sempill, seventeen years his junior. Still very much an idea man, and still very much seeking his fortune, in 1852 Carstensen resigned his post as a captain in the West Indies Army.

That November, he relocated to New York City, where, since the start of the year, plans were percolating to hold the very first world's fair on United States soil, to show that the country had come of age internationally—at least according to a great supporter of the fair (or exposition, or exhibition—the terms were interchangeable), the persuasive editor of the *New-York Tribune*, Horace Greeley. He saw the expo's potential as "the grandest and most instructive University ever opened."

One of the two demands made by the City of New York—the first was that the admittance fee should not exceed fifty cents—was that a main structure be erected of iron and glass. Partnering with two German émigrés, the architect Charles Gildemeister and the chief engineer Christian Edward Detmold, both with excellent academic and vocational backgrounds (Detmold had supervised the laying of Fort Sumter's foundation, and was the New York fair's promoter in chief), Carstensen entered the competition to see who would build the fair's iron-and-glass exhibition hall, which would be called the Crystal Palace.

After protests by neighborhood residents shot down Madison Square as the fair site, it was decided to place the 1853 Exhibition of the Industry of All Nations on Manhattan's then-northernmost outpost, behind what was the Egyptian-style Croton Distributing Reservoir on Forty-Second Street between Fifth and Sixth Avenues, and what is now the New York Public Library and Bryant Park. Other than Carstensen, among those vying in the architectural contest were Britain's Joseph Paxton, who had designed London's Crystal Palace for the 1851 Great Exhibition of the Works of Industry of All Nations; Leopold Eidlitz, who was later responsible for the State Capitol in Albany; and James Bogardus, who proposed building a circular tower three hundred feet high, so all could see the fair's location from afar.

Carstensen got the nod over the others because of his accomplishment with Tivoli, and according to his and Gildemeister's winning design, the Crystal Palace was to be shaped like a Greek cross (the British version had been rectangular) with a Moorish crowning touch: Some sixty-two feet above the exhibition floor, and one hundred feet in diameter, its roof would be capped by the largest dome in the country, made of wood, covered in tin, and fitted with thirty-two windows.

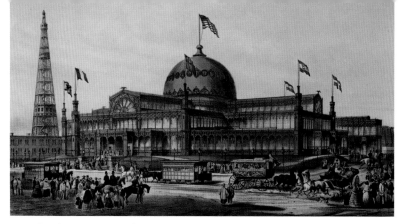

Immediately to the south of Georg Carstensen's short-lived Crystal Palace, for New York City's 1853 Exhibition of the Industry of All Nations, stood the even shorter-lived Latting Observatory, which inspired the Eiffel Tower.

"Seen at night, when it is illuminated," raved *Harper's New Monthly Magazine* once the architectural sketches became a reality, "…it is a scene more gorgeous and graceful than the imagination of Eastern story-tellers saw."

Such compliments were rare, however. "This building is very far from being ready to receive goods for exhibition, although it is more than a month after the period when its managers solemnly promised to the world that it should be open for visitors," complained *Scientific American* in June 1853. It had disparaged the notion of a fair from the very outset, coming as it was "so soon after the World's Fair in London, and by a private company whose object was gain, not honor to our country."

Rather than the first of May 1893, as had been guaranteed, the drastically over-budget $891,070 New York fair was not ready to be dedicated by President Franklin Pierce and his cabinet until July 1. Even then, the banquet following the opening ceremonies took place not in the Crystal Palace, as originally planned, but downtown, at Niblo's Garden.

Carstensen took it all as a personal affront, even if the brunt of the criticism was likely intended for the first president of the Crystal Palace Association, Theodore Sedgwick, who would later resign and be replaced by P. T Barnum.

In a blistering monograph about the Crystal Palace that shared a joint Carstensen-Gildemeister byline, the entire thirteen-page introduction railed against those who, at any point, might have wished the venture ill and "place us in a false light before the people." Every slight, negative innuendo, and outright insult ever lodged at the Crystal Palace was rehashed in the booklet and argued ad nauseam, down to its not being Carstensen and Gildemeister's fault that the stovepipes for the heating system were so unsightly.

In the end—a premature one, at that—the expo failed. A heat wave in August of the first season killed two hundred people in a single day, exacerbating what was an already dire situation. In November 1854, the exhibition closed $300,000 in the financial hole, or about $8.1 million today, making it "a corpse long before I touched it," Barnum wrote in his memoir, adding that his lesson from the experience was "the dead could not be raised." America would not hold another world's fair for twenty years.

Carstensen never received full payment for his services. The following year, he returned to Copenhagen to oversee the building of the Alhambra, only to take ill during its construction and die, physically and financially spent.

As for the Alhambra, even without Carstensen, it was decorated in his signature Moorish style, with a large theater, a bazaar, a gazebo, and lush landscaping—none of which managed to save it.

The enterprise survived only a dozen years, a victim of its auditorium's lack of heat, its grounds' lack of lighting, and, up against almighty Tivoli, its box office's lack of sizzle.

Just as Copenhagen's Alhambra turned out to be an also-ran to Tivoli, so did the 1853–1854 New York Exhibition of the Industry of All Nations pale in comparison to London's 1851 Great Exhibition of the Works of Industry of All Nations.

Gate attendance in London reached six million persons—roughly, one-third of the country's population—while in New York, 1.1 million.

What both fairs did offer were some well-received innovations, such as the public toilet—introduced in London by a Brighton plumber named George Jennings. To the great relief of 827,280 exhibition goers who used his device, Jennings installed what he called "monkey closets" in the men's restrooms of the Crystal Palace. For the price of a penny, a customer was granted a clean seat, a towel, a comb, and a shoeshine. The convenience caught on, and eventually, women were correspondingly accommodated.

In Manhattan, "New York's First Skyscraper" was raised directly next to the Crystal Palace: the 350-foot-tall, octagonal Latting Observatory, constructed mostly of wood, braced by iron, and conceived by machinist Waring Latting and designed by the architect William Naugle. From its three separate platforms, one of which housed

The Alhambra amusement complex was Cartensen's attempt to restore his reputation—and steal away Tivoli's thunder.

an ice-cream parlor, views up to sixty miles could be enjoyed. Among its admirers was Gustave Eiffel, who cited the Latting Observatory as an inspiration for his namesake 1889 tower in Paris.

Hotel and transportation expansion near the expo site was a by-product of the New York fair, as was the introduction of insignia merchandise: ashtrays, medallions, thimbles, souvenir spoons, and handkerchiefs.

For his part, fair president P. T. Barnum made his own significant contribution. Desperate to increase second-season attendance, the showman invited a handsome

Queen Victoria christened the Great Exhibition in Hyde Park, London, in 1851. Like its younger New York namesake, it, too, would succumb to a raging fire.

forty-year-old Yonkers, New York, factory engineer to demonstrate his freight hoist. The engineer called it an elevator. His name was Elisha Graves Otis, and the secret to his device, which prevented his platform from falling as it was lifted by ropes to a desired height, was a safety catch.

For all their differences, the two Crystal Palaces met similar demises. Manhattan's came crashing down on October 5, 1858, when a blaze broke out in a lumber and paper storage room. The entire framework collapsed within an hour. The Latting Observatory had predeceased its neighbor by two years, from the exact same cause of death.

London's Crystal Palace served its nation far longer—eighty-five years. After the Great Exhibition, the architectural jewel was dismantled pane by pane and moved to Sydenham in Kent, where Queen Victoria rededicated it in June 1854.

In the coming decades and into the next century, the green park around the Crystal Palace was given such embellishments as model dinosaurs and a roller coaster, both of which outlasted the grand centerpiece.

Around 7 p.m. on a windy November 30, 1936, a fire broke out in the Crystal Palace's women's cloakroom, and the flames soon spread to the central transept. Initially, it was thought the blaze might be contained, which explained why a call for emergency assistance was not placed for nearly an hour—later giving rise to rumors of arson: The Crystal Palace had been on shaky financial footing for several years, and in 1911 its owners had filed for bankruptcy.

Groan-like sounds emanating from within the structure turned out not to be trapped human victims, as feared, but the bellowing of scorched air passing through the pipes of the immense Handel organ. Incredibly, there were no human casualties.

Before everything was reduced to ash, the conflagration grew to such an intensity that its hellish embers could be seen from as far as eight counties away. Among the sullen witnesses was Winston Churchill.

Never one for a loss of words—or a loss of anything—the statesman reacted with a heavy sigh and the solemn acknowledgment, "This is the end of an age."

Coney Island bathers seldom chose to adhere to their era's rules of deportment

PART TWO

GETTING SERIOUS

THE BEACH IS DIVINE

Sometime around 1666, while on a break from Trinity College because it was closed by the Great Plague, physics prodigy Isaac Newton saw an apple fall from a tree. Not sideways, he witnessed, but perpendicular to the ground. This got Newton thinking about motion and gravity.

More than two hundred years later, during the time the Mauch Chunk Railway was pulling in visitors to Pennsylvania, LaMarcus Adna Thompson, a young manufacturer from the Midwest, traveled the six hundred miles to taste the adventure for himself.

Experiencing what could only be considered a Road to Damascus moment, not long afterward he made the daring move to sell his business and set off on an entirely different road.

Motion and gravity would grease Thompson's wheels.

One of five children, Thompson was born March 8, 1848, in the township of Jersey in Licking County, Ohio. When he was three, the family relocated to Michigan's Ransom Township in Hillsdale County, an agrarian community originally settled by former New England Puritans. Strong religious conviction would characterize Thompson throughout his life, as would ingenuity when it came to matters mechanical.

Despite the aptitude, he chose English as a major when, at eighteen, he enrolled in Michigan's Hillsdale College. The following year, 1867, financial necessity forced Thompson to drop out and seek work, landing him in Elkhart, Indiana, another Puritan sanctuary. There, he clerked in a bakery and a grocery store, rising to the position of partner. By 1877, he at last put his mechanical leaning to use, by inventing a machine that produced seamless hosiery. As founder of the Eagle

LaMarcus Adna Thompson, a stressed-out garment manufacturer from the Midwest, reinvented himself into the internationally known "Father of the Gravity Ride."

Knitting Company, Thompson had three hundred employees manufacturing stockings, scarves, and gloves and shipping them all over the United States.

Remarkably, for someone who would bring so much anxiety to others with his amusement machines, Thompson himself could not handle stress. Verging on nervous collapse from his work, he followed doctors' orders and took a leave of absence, which brought him to Mauch Chunk. Another stop was New Orleans, where an old friend was earning his bread and butter with a handmade ride on which people sat in a circle atop a seventy-foot-in-diameter wheel and were repeatedly spun at a slightly elevated angle.

Not long after, Thompson sold his interest in the Eagle Knitting Company.

"My invention relates to a gravity double track switchback railway to be used as a source or means of pleasure and amusement," Thompson, thirty-seven years old, stated in his application for U.S. Patent No. 332,762 on September 10, 1885, fourteen months after he had self-funded his Switchback Railway for a reported $1,600 (about $44,300 today). Of its novel features, the patentee outlined, "passengers may be carried from a certain starting-point at any convenient or suitable elevation in a vehicle or car over a series of descending and ascending longitudinal planes." For propulsion, the cars would rely on "gravity momentum" as they passed "over the planes to the opposite end of the course."

Other inventors may have held earlier patents—starting with John G. Taylor, of Baltimore, who received his, No. 128674 A, on July 2, 1872, for "Improvement in Inclined Railways"—but it was Thompson who first got his amusement conveyance up and undulating—or at least he encouraged the influential New York newspapers to promote his fifty-foot-tall timber structure as such. His Switchback opened on June 13, 1884.

This is why, forever after, LaMarcus A. Thompson has been called "the Father of the Gravity Ride."

"The car from the terminal point within the pavilion is elevated," Thompson's patent form detailed, and "preferably constructed of wood, but, if deemed best for the purpose, may be constructed of iron." Between eight and ten riders at a time (depending upon girth) were to climb a wooden staircase and assume seats on rolling benches facing sideways, rather than forward. Once departing the loading pavilion, the car and its passengers were then set to experience the gentle hills at a pace approaching six miles per hour, "a frightful rate of speed," judged the *New York Herald*. Crossing the full six-hundred-foot expanse of metal track on one side, riders would disembark, climb another set of stairs, and, after attendants repositioned their car, sit facing the opposite direction to slide along the second track back to the starting point.

Thompson charged five cents per person, and within three weeks found not only his investment returned but competitors nipping at his heels. Equally important, a thrill-hungry public began demanding greater gravity-ride challenges—precisely the reaction the pious Thompson had sought.

When Thompson's Switchback Railway opened on June 13, 1884, it didn't move fast. But it quickly caught on.

While never reaching the lavish, early heights achieved in Russia and France, coasting—or, at least, gliding by the seat of one's pants—on the North American continent can be traced to the Wishrams, an indigenous American tribe of about fifteen hundred people living along the Columbia River in the Pacific Northwest.

Their playground, Celilo Falls, was "where the Columbia River plunges 20 feet over a knife-edge precipice extending across the river," according to a 1941 Works Progress Administration guide to Washington State. "The falls mark the entrance to a narrow channel bordering precipitous cliffs."

Amusement inventor and historian William F. Mangels described the volcanic site as "a large inclined rock of basalt marked by two parallel grooves, worn smooth by many generations of young Wishrams, attesting their practice of the gentle art of sliding."

Coasting in America was initiated by the Wishrams, who slid down rocks at Celilo Falls, in the Pacific Northwest.

"Many of the evils of society, much of the vice and crime which we deplore come from the degrading nature of amusements," the machinist said by way of expressing his belief that "to substitute something better, something clean and wholesome, and persuade men to choose it, is worthy of all endeavor."

Thompson contended he was offering "sunshine that glows bright in the after-thought, and scatters the darkness of the tenement for the price of a nickel or a dime."

In particular, the Midwesterner was referring to the setting where he had been advised to build his first Switchback Railway, a four-mile-long, half-mile-wide coastal citadel of grime, crime, intoxication, and fornication.

Coney Island.

At the time Thompson established his Switchback Railway at the corner of Surf Avenue and Tenth Street, the Brooklyn seaside enclave was already six years into the fifteen-year reign of Tammany-tinged political poo-bah John Y. McKane, a bearded, barrel-chested character whose informal title was "the Chief," and whose formal titles the *New York Times* once listed (in an attempt to expose the myriad of duties that filled his calendar and coffers) as "Chief of Police, Commissioner of Police, Commissioner of Highways, Commissioner of Common Land, Commissioner of Excise, and commissioner of everything else in sight."

"For years McKane's methods had been questioned," the *Brooklyn Daily Eagle* reported, "but it seemed impossible to 'get anything on him.'"

Fifteen months after John McKane was born on August 10, 1841, in County Antrim, Ireland, his family immigrated to New York's Sheepshead Bay, a farming village in the town of Gravesend, which included Coney Island. Its name was derived from the seventeenth-century Dutch settlers' word for "rabbit," *konijn*, for the wild bunnies roaming the sand dunes. Long a community unto itself, Gravesend was originally colonized in 1643 by the wealthy expatriate Deborah Moody, an Anabaptist who escaped religious prosecution in England, only to be excommunicated by the Puritans of Massachusetts.

As the first woman powerbroker in the New World, Lady Moody tried to negotiate with members of the local Canarsie tribe, and she found them willing to barter for fishing rights but not ownership of their property. In the end, any debate was moot; the Mohawks annihilated the Canarsie for failing to pay a customary tribute to the Five Nations. In 1654, Gravesend settlers bought full title to the property.

Political boss John Y. McKane ruled Coney Island with an iron fist. His other fist was busy reaching into the pockets of others.

"Leasing of the common lands of Coney Island began in 1702," according to Charles Denson, author of the authoritative *Coney Island: Lost and Found*. Tobacco, corn, and cattle farming remained the principal local occupations

From antiquity onward, the ocean was to be avoided, for fear of what dark mysteries it might unleash: Leviathan, the sea monster in the Book of Job, or Kraken, his equally menacing cousin, lurking off the coast of Scandinavia and Greenland.

Novelist Jules Verne did the waters no favor, either, when he wrote, in 1870, of the *poulpes* (giant squid or octopus) attacking the submarine *Nautilus* in his *Twenty Thousand Leagues Under the Sea*.

And yet, with the onslaught of the Industrial Revolution and an awakening to the idea that physical exertion might possibly be healthy, the beach redeemed its reputation in the public's mind. Far from being a perilous pit of hell, it was a restorative paradise capable of fortifying spirit and strength.

"Cold bathing was said to spark appetite, cut the libido, keep young girls serene during puberty, make rickety children straight, give hope to barren women, and prevent men of little virility from becoming too effeminate," wrote contemporary author Alain de Botton, imparting information from Sorbonne professor Alain Corbin's *Waves of Joy and Despair: The Lure of the Seas: Seaside in the Western World, 1750-1840.*

The title told all.

until around 1800, when trespassers who had sailed over from New Jersey were discovered cutting their way through fences in search of something new.

That something new was a day at the beach.

⁓

THE TERM *RESORT* WAS first applied to Coney Island, "not only the pioneer with modern improvements for giving the crowds a good time," reporter Julian Ralph wrote for *Scribner's* in 1898, but "sui generis, enthroned, the king of all the popular resorts of America."

Coney Island might have set the stage, but making the leap from beach to amusement center was not strictly a Brooklyn phenomenon.

"On no portion of the western coast of Great Britain are the sands so level, firm, and extensive, as at Blackpool," proclaimed a travel-service guidebook to entice visitors in 1857—thirty-nine years before Blackpool's South Shore became home to the UK's first amusement park.

Granted, the 1896 sprinkling of attractions were only place settings for the satisfying buffet to come. Current managing director Amanda Thompson calls Blackpool Pleasure Beach "the world's most ride-intensive amusement park."

In 1904, business partners William George Bean and John William Outhwaite took out a £30,000 mortgage (nearly $4 million today) to develop thirty acres of shorefront rides and stalls into what they designated their Pleasure Beach.

The London-born son of a Thames riverboat pilot, Bean (1868–1929) worked in advertising in New York as a teenager, before entering amusement-machinery manufacturing in Philadelphia. Returning to England around 1895, he brought with him rights to the novelty Hotchkiss Bicycle Railway.

Outhwaite (c. 1855–1911), from West Yorkshire, also had his Philadelphia connection: His father-in-law, England-born carousel maker Edward F. Long, built mechanical rides there.

Together, Outhwaite and Bean modeled Blackpool "on a relatively stable entertainment tradition: piers, the lavish interiors, and entertainment

The coronation took place in 1823, when the newly formed Coney Island Road and Bridge Company received approval for a mile-long toll link from the town of Gravesend to Coney Island. Inaugurated that August, the road delivered horse-and-carriage traffic—so much that, in 1829, town supervisor John Terhune and his brother Abraham replaced the ramshackle wooden changing rooms with the shore's first hotel. Named the Coney Island House, its guest register bore the signatures of such illustrious personages as Washington Irving, who brought his nieces in 1848; Herman Melville, in September 1849, when he was working on *Moby Dick* (an "E. A. Poe" signed the hotel register on the same page, although the Brooklyn Public Library, which houses the historic log, insists the author of "The Raven" was lecturing in Richmond, Virginia, at the time); statesmen Henry Clay of Virginia and Daniel Webster of New England, in July 1850, the same year a second toll road materialized to handle traditions of music hall, pubs, and fish and chip shops, and customary fairground attractions," said Gary S. Cross and John K. Walton, authors of *The Playful Crowd: Pleasure Places in the Twentieth Century.*

Perennially ranked one of Britain's favorite parks—despite a 2017 kerfuffle on social media protesting the demise of a 1958 wooden Wild Mouse coaster—Blackpool Pleasure Beach's forty-two acres today offer more than forty rides, including the UK's first double-launch coaster, the £16.25 million Icon.

Deputy managing director Nick Thompson calls the 2018 addition "fast, adrenaline-fuelled, and exhilarating." Proving Amanda Thompson's claim about Blackpool's ride intensity, Icon loops through fifteen of the resort's existing attractions.

Why so many Thompsons at Blackpool? Because blood is thicker than beach water.

They are direct descendants of William Bean.

The mass-market seaside resort Blackpool Pleasure Beach, in Lancashire, England, opened in 1896, two years after construction of the Blackpool Tower—a 518-foot beacon inspired by town mayor Sir John Bickerstaffe's visit to the 1889 Paris World's Fair (and its Eiffel Tower), and financed by Victorian hoteliers and property developers.

traffic; P. T. Barnum, also in July 1850, with his singing discovery Jenny Lind, to mark her arrival in America; and that devotee of Coney, and just about all else having to do with New York, Walt Whitman, who would come to swim nude, "and declaim Homer or Shakespeare to the surf and seagulls by the hour."

A year after the Coney Island House began offering rooms, meals, and an unobstructed view of Walt Whitman, Gravesend schoolmaster John Wyckoff opened his namesake hotel directly to its south. In 1844, with the initiation of the Fort Hamilton and Coney Island Ferry Company steamship, two New Yorkers identified only as Messrs. Eddy and Hart set up flimsy shacks with only the bare bones of amenities on the far western end of the beach, called Coney Island Point. In 1845, the space was leased to ferry owner Thomas Bielby and partner Alonzo Reed for a dance hall; called the Pavilion, it is considered Coney Island's first attraction.

Only the first twenty years of fits and starts were a mere dress rehearsal.

From 1847 until the Civil War, development of the resort ran rampant, with "some improvement, some new bathing-houses run up with unplanned lumber and primitive appointments, some roughly constructed hotel or restaurant, cheap saloon, democratic eating-houses where you could bring your own luncheon or eat what was produced on the premises, lager-beer bars, and a show or two, generally of a startling character," read one disapproving account at the turn of the century—just as Coney's momentum was conscientiously kicking into high gear.

By 1875, Coney Island had taken shape, with four distinct sections catering to four distinct clienteles, each with their own transportation system. Five rail lines cut the trip from Manhattan to forty-five minutes, compared to two hours by ferry, and as long as half a day by other means.

The districts were, from west to east:

- the West End, the roughneck area. Previously known as Coney Island Point, it was renamed Norton's Point, after former political boss and pugilist Thomas "Thunderbolt" Norton. In partnership with landowner James Murray and a lot of ill-gotten Tammany Hall money, Norton assumed the property in 1874;

- West Brighton, the working-class district. Originally incorporating the Coney Island House, the zone became overshadowed by attorney Andrew R. Culver's decorative Culver Plaza, whose focal point, besides a mechanical cow that dispensed milk, was the nation's tallest structure, the three-hundred-foot-tall Iron Tower. Culver had it imported from the Philadelphia Exposition of 1876;

- Brighton Beach, formerly Duck Hill. Named for the British seaside resort, this was the most crowded, inclusive, and middle-class of the four districts. Its developer was Civil War profiteer William A. Engeman, a former carpenter who built the Brighton Beach Hotel (1878), the twelve-hundred-capacity Brighton Beach Bathing Pavilion (also 1878), and the Island's first racetrack (1879);

- and Manhattan Beach, the restricted sector. Existing as the exclusive domain of its creator, owner, and Long Island Railroad president Austin Corbin, Manhattan Beach was kept clear of minorities and anyone who did not share Corbin's beliefs.

Corbin primarily desired to keep out Jews, stating publicly, "If I could pick my Jewish guests I would never raise any objection, but this is impossible, and I am, therefore, compelled to ostracise them all."

The Brighton Beach Hotel, less restricted than Coney Island's Manhattan Beach Hotel and Oriental Hotel, catered to upper-middle-class New Yorkers.

The remark was defended by his brother, D. C. Corbin, who told the *New York Times*, "I know all you newspapers will come down upon us; but we are in the business to make money and we cannot afford to sacrifice profit to sentiment."

The reaction from the Jewish community, as well as from "all Americans who are opposed to intolerance," said the newspaper, was to "treat Mr. Corbin with silent contempt."

Contempt did not begin to describe what reformers felt toward Norton's Point, where the least of the offenses was that it never so much as adhered to the social niceties of being "in season." Its lawlessness took place year-round. "Boat trips down the bay became adventures into a perilous unknown," said Edo McCullough, whose grandfather, George C. Tilyou, became the primary mover and shaker behind Coney Island in the early twentieth century.

Practically from the time the first side-wheeler landed at its makeshift dock, the Island's far West End—an unpatrolled ten-block area known as "the Gut," from the Dutch for "gate" or, in this case, "gateway"—was home to betting parlors, opium dens, dance halls, boxing rings, and, as McCullough described them, "ladies, light of heart and loose of scruple," who considered the peepholes in the plywood dividers of the Pavilion's dressing rooms "opportunities for advertising the enticements of their ancient profession." Cubicles affording glances into the next compartment came at a premium price.

Residents of the Gut were called Gutters, and their going rate for a private nude dance was a dollar (approximately $25 today), more if physical contact was involved. A phenomenon widely known as the Coney Island Can-Can, made up of gyrating movements and gestures, was a common routine, and one that was not formally choreographed.

In saloons, sporting men renting sexual companions risked the strong likelihood of being robbed after having their drinks drugged, usually with the colorless sedative hydrate of chloral, although snuff, morphine, and laudanum also did the trick. Historians note that even though it most certainly was a red-light district, the Gut did not qualify for the label because Edison had yet to patent the lightbulb.

Over in the Bowery, despite a state law that prohibited cross-dressing, men made up as women sang in cabarets under stage names like Big Tessie and Hazel, but, as it was reported, "The la-de-la boys never caused much trouble. They did their entertaining and pretty much stayed to themselves."

"All classes of the *demi-monde*, down to the common street walker, are found here as well as rakes and others of the same class, who behave themselves so shamelessly in and out of the water," Gustav Lening, an author specializing in urban vice, warned about Coney Island in his 1873 investigation into criminality in New York.

Commissioner of Police John McKane's response was direct:

"Houses of prostitution are a necessity on Coney Island, and I don't propose to interfere with the gambling at Brighton Beach and Sheepshead Bay. After all, this ain't no Sunday school."

It was at Austin Corbin's Queen Anne–style Manhattan Beach Hotel in the 1880s, occupying its finest suite, where that living embodiment of the Gilded Age, rail tycoon and philanthropist James Buchanan "Diamond Jim" Brady, could be found on summer Sundays that somehow stretched into two-week vacations.

Scene on the Bowery, Coney Island, N.Y.

Known for an unquenchable devotion to food and horseracing, Brady generally began his day with breakfast on the Manhattan Beach Hotel veranda, where he devoured "a hefty breakfast of eggs, breads, muffins, grits, pancakes, steaks, chops, fried potatoes, and pitchers of orange juice," before a midmorning snack of "two or three dozen clams or oysters," according to contemporary food journalist John Mariani. Such conspicuous consumption generally followed the magnate's morning splash in the Atlantic, in which, as one sly biographer remarked, he was "one of the larger landmarks."

Afternoons were whiled away at the Coney Island Jockey Club, where Brady's colt, Gold Heels, managed to win as often as his owner ate. Evenings tended to be shared with longtime companion Lillian

Russell, née Helen Louise Leonard, the star of comic operas and darling of the popular press, for both her hourglass figure and the endless columns of gossip she provided. Her annulment after nine years of marriage to her bigamist husband, Edward Solomon, was the talk of New York.

In addition to the excitement of seeing the celebrated pair, the Manhattan Beach Hotel offered a radical new nocturnal amusement: swimming in the ocean after dark. The phenomenon, which at first shocked a society still skittish about allowing men and women to

Celebrity couple "Diamond Jim" Brady and his consort, the actress Lillian Russell, frequently partook of Coney Island's generous supply of sport, surf, and suppers.

Once the sea was determined to be friendly, only one mystery remained: What to wear?

"We particularly insist upon woolen as the material to be worn, as it retains the heat of the body," prescribed a nineteenth-century physician known only as Dr. Durant, who also dictated that only maroon and blue were proper fabric colors.

"Ironically, as ready-to-wear men's swimwear shed sleeves and shortened legs in the 1870s," said *World Clothing and Fashion* author Mary Ellen Snodgrass, "women's swimsuits in Europe and North America took on corsets, bathing shoes, and hose." Down Under, "Australians complemented their bathing attire with merino wool socks and oilskin caps."

The turn of the century brought the abandonment of women's bloomers and long sleeves in favor of the two-piece middy—modeled after a sailor's shirt, the blouse featured a collar cut deep, a square cut at the back, and a tapered front—while men replaced their (in some cases) nine-pound bathing costumes with streamlined yet still modest covers, as many public bathing places prohibited exposure of the chest or so much as the armpits.

Around and below men's waists, a mandatory skirt that nearly reached the knees, along with other constraints, was not lifted until the 1930s, and as late as 1937 decency laws in some states barred men from baring their chests.

Enforced by fines and jail time, Coney Island also held firm on that last restriction until as late as 1936.

swim together, was generated by loud, hissing electric and calcium arc lights aimed on the water. Thick ropes also had to be weighted into the sand for the bathers to grasp, to allay any fear of being washed out to sea.

To cash in on the craze, Electric Bathing, as it was called, was duplicated on Engeman's Brighton Beach, which also appropriated other Manhattan Beach attributes, from foot-stomping concerts by John Philip Sousa and his military band to full-scale performances by the newly founded New York City Metropolitan Opera, which brought Old World culture to the decidedly New.

Not everyone looked to Europe for inspiration. With America diving headfirst into the Mechanical Age, a former Pony Express rider and frontier scout named William F. Cody sensed an American desire for revisiting its simpler past. Anointing himself "Buffalo Bill" Cody, he assembled a Wild West spectacular that rode into William Engeman's Brighton Beach Race Track in 1883, "complete with a band of Sioux Indians, cowboys from the Doggie Camp, Oklahoma cowgirls, and Chief Bull Bear of the Cheyennes."

Only the year before, Cody, a native Iowan, had organized his first show, a modest quasi rodeo. At Brighton Beach, modesty had nothing to do with it.

The West Comes East: "Buffalo Bill" Cody's Wild West spectacular stampeded into the Brighton Beach Race Track, to cap the 1883 season.

"I have over a hundred head of stock—ten head of fine race horses, the finest six mule coach train in the world, and seventy head of good saddle horses— and the foundation laid for a fortune before long," the thirty-seven-year-old Cody wrote his sister Julia in an August 16, 1883, letter from Coney Island.

The extravaganza ran for five weeks and required extra bleachers to hold the crowds. As Cody notified his sibling, "The papers say I'm the coming Barnum."

Except Cody did Barnum one better.

He moved the spectacle outdoors.

SURF AND TURF

I.

There were karmic paybacks to John McKane's financial paybacks. "Reputable business interests began referring to central Coney Island as 'West Brighton' to avoid confusion with the corrupt activities of the West End," said Charles Denson. People also steered clear of the West End entirely in favor of West Brighton, as an 1887 New York City guidebook spelled out, with its "motley collection of hotels, large and small, concert stands, beer-gardens, variety-shows, skating-rinks, wooden toboggan-slides, shooting-galleries, bathing-houses, merry-go-rounds, inclined-railways, museums, aquariums, brass bands, pop-corn and hot sausage venders."

As further enticement, the guide compared this stretch of sand to "a great country-fair in full blast, crowded with every-day people, out for a good time."

In 1884, the best time to be had in West Brighton was aboard LaMarcus Thompson's Switchback Railway. Even if its existence was relatively brief, its impact was immense, with the line to ride the new attraction consistently many times longer than the ride itself—which caused others to take notice.

"Transportation to the island blossomed in the 1870s, when four steam-railroad lines were built to bring passengers rapidly from Downtown Brooklyn to Coney," said scholars Louis and John Parascandola.

In Thompson's very first season, a Charles Alcoke of Hamilton, Ohio, introduced his Serpentine Railway, a coaster with a continuous oval track—the first to return riders to the loading platform without their having to get out and change seats. Convenient as that was, the five-minute ride inched along just as slowly as Thompson's Switchback. No matter: The next season, a San Franciscan named Phillip Hinkle delivered to West Brighton's Iron Pier the fastest and most innovative coaster yet, the Gravity Pleasure Road, whose steam engine mechanically hoisted the car to the top of the first hill with its six passengers already inside. Its design also permitted riders to face forward, rather than sideways, making the Gravity Pleasure Road, despite its tranquil name, a thrill ride, instead of a scenic tour like its predecessors.

Hinkle, who hailed from an elevator-business background, described his coaster as something not only to be experienced, but also to be admired, given that its design allowed "an audience to observe the operation of the cars with facility and comfort." *Frank Leslie's Weekly* equated the ride to "being carried away by a cyclone."

Assigned by *Harper's New Monthly Magazine* to cover Coney Island in 1878, contributor Charles Carroll took Manhattan's Battery-to–Coney Island ferry and, reflecting the social prejudices of his time, made no attempt to mask his condescension toward the Irish, Jewish, German, and African-American passengers with whom he shared the decks.

"A showily dressed ebony couple are jammed in on the left," he wrote, "and an 'Irish lady' with a big bundle and baby compresses our right flank."

To Carroll's credit, once he landed on the Island, the restricted Manhattan Beach left him unimpressed, "because it is more aristocratic, it is less distinctive, and for the nonce we shall do better to stick to the democratic jollity of the west end and centre."

Indeed, the entire Coney Island experience made a changed man out of him.

"Delightful, isn't it?" Carroll concluded after a splash in the surf—during which, he admitted, he shared his flask with "a cheerful young Irishman, who had made my acquaintance in the water."

Daily steamships to Coney departed from uptown Manhattan's East 129th Street, and downtown's West Street and Battery Place.

Injurious as Alcoke's Serpentine Railway might have been to Thompson's livelihood, Hinkle's superior ride "drove him to near bankruptcy," according to coaster expert Robert Cartmell.

"Discouraged," said Edo McCullough, "he retreated from Coney to Atlantic City."

THE SAME YEAR THOMPSON unleashed his Switchback Railway, only two blocks away another goliath arose in the louche Bowery section of West Brighton, which was to Coney Island what Cock Lane was to Bartholomew Fair. Financial problems would plague the new structure throughout its eleven-year existence, and, not surprisingly, fire would claim it in the end. Yet much is owed the Elephantine Colossus, also known as the Elephant Hotel (1885–1896), because by its very nature, the Barnum-like structure introduced something unique to Coney Island: whimsical absurdity.

James Vincent DePaul Lafferty Jr., a Philadelphia real estate speculator from a well-to-do Irish immigrant family, first latched on to his zoomorphic notion while trying to unload isolated sand lots in South Atlantic City (since 1909 called Margate). Looking for a gimmick to enhance the potential of what was essentially the New Jersey equivalent of Florida swampland, he enlisted William H. Free, a Philly architect chiefly known for his residential work, although after his brush with Lafferty, he made a name for himself designing pavilions and bandstands for amusement parks.

Their South Atlantic City collaboration in 1881, a six-story, tin-clad, wooden restaurant in the shape of a pachyderm, cost $38,000 (just shy of $1 million today), which put

The poster for Coney's 1885 Elephantine Colossus hotel exaggerated what literally was, to the disappointment of all, a white elephant.

it at $13,000 over budget, but it quickly proved a tourist draw, and Lafferty, all of twenty-five years old, saw his future. In 1882, he patented his invention, locking up rights not only to elephant buildings, but also those "of the form of any other animal…as that of a fish, fowl, &c."

His Elephantine Colossus for Coney Island was announced to open June 1, 1884, but was not completed until a year later. It would outproportion its New Jersey cousin by nearly double, standing 175 feet high and 203 feet long. "To get to the observatory in the howdah," said Pulitzer Prize–winning historian David McCullough (no relation to Edo), "customers entered the hind leg marked Entrance and wound up a circular flight of stairs. The other rear leg—each was sixty feet around—

was the exit, and one of the front legs was a tobacco shop." The eyes contained telescopes and lit up at night.

At the invitational inspection on May 29, 1885, the Colossus's manager, C. A. Brandenburgh, treated his guests to a lavish dinner before leading them on a tour of the elephant's stomach, diaphragm, liver, and left lung, where a museum was being prepared. All thirty-one separate chambers functioned as practical amenities for hotel guests, and the pachyderm's posterior provided a view that was unmatchable—and, when described by Brandenburgh, unbelievable.

"You see that little puff of foam," the manager said with the point of a finger, "along by that pool? That is the spray above Niagara Falls." He was just warming up. "That tiny silver thread further to the west is the Mississippi River, and if I had a telescope I would show you the jetties." He claimed "a clump of trees" in the distance was Yellowstone, and a "little cluster of houses" to be Rio de Janeiro. Those with keen enough vision, he added, could spy London and Paris.

The Elephantine Colossus failed to function as well as Brandenburgh's imagination, and Lafferty was left in the lurch. He was forced to sell his animal-building patent, and in 1887, his Margate elephant's ownership was transferred to Anthony Gertzen, whose daughter-in-law, Sophia, named the attraction Lucy, a name the tusked beacon still retains, having been declared a National Historic Landmark in 1976.

Lafferty died broke a dozen years after losing Lucy, and while his failed Coney Island hotel might have been reduced to ash on September 27, 1896—perhaps not so coincidentally at the tail end of the tourist season—one legacy of his endures.

The phrase "seeing the elephant," coined at the time when the Elephantine Colossus functioned more as a brothel than a tourist attraction, took on the not-so-subtle meaning of extracurricular dallying—with a price attached.

The first woman since Lady Moody to flex real muscle in Coney Island was Lucy Devlin Vanderveer, a Newfoundland native who first came to Brooklyn as a child with her widowed mother and two sisters.

Vanderveer's impressive West Brighton real estate portfolio—initiated independently of any of the connections her husband, sewer inspector William Vanderveer, had with John McKane—began with a fruit and confectionary store, whose profits went into building twelve beachside dressing rooms, also called bathhouses, even when they were nothing more than shacks.

After a compulsory alliance with McKane, Lucy owned and operated seventy-five dressing rooms the following season and two hundred the year after. A hotel came next, then, in 1875, at West Sixth Street and Surf Avenue, the opulent, three-story, $46,000 ($1 million today) Vanderveer's Bathing Pavilion, outfitted, according to one Gravesend study, with "accommodations for 500 bathers; as well as a large Marvin safe for the reception of their valuables [thievery was widespread in Coney];... *warm* salt-water baths [swimming pools]; an excellent restaurant and bar, reception-parlors, etc."

X marks the spot where Charles I. D. Looff stands on his "Carroussel" (as the sign spells it) inside Lucy Vanderveer's pavilion, in 1875.

The restaurant's grilled clams with butter cost a penny apiece, the pavilion's livery stable kept twenty horses for visitor use, and the fifty-five hundred men's and women's bathing costumes at the rental window necessitated Vanderveer's having its own advanced washing and drying system.

In 1875, amid gossip that new racetracks were intended for Brighton Beach and Sheepshead Bay, Lucy conceived of a novelty that would increase the number of customers to her pavilion: a carousel. Designed and built by Charles I. D. Looff, a twenty-four-year-old woodworker from Schleswig-Holstein who had come to America only six years before (true or not, it was said that the Ellis Island official processing Looff's documents told the new arrival that he needed ID, so Looff took them as his initials), the carousel was mounted with mostly horses, along with a camel, zebra, giraffe, and stork. Looff had carved them at home with leftover pieces of wood from his Greenpoint, Brooklyn, furniture studio.

The frame and platform were built at the pavilion, and once finished, Looff's rotating wooden sculpture marked an important milestone.

It was Coney Island's first ride.

II.

When not dining on lobster, Diamond Jim Brady delighted in a delicacy credited to Coney, even though the sausage had been satisfying seekers of amusement since the days of Bartholomew Fair. The American twist, conceived by an immigrant, was to wrap a thirteen-inch-long—in time it would shrink to a more manageable eight inches—version of the tubular meat around a bun and call it a Coney Island.

Or a red hot.

Or a frankfurter (for the sausage's origin in the German city).

Or a wiener (for Vienna sausage, which gave rise to the weenie).

Or a hot dog—although that led to the misapprehension that actual dog meat was used, prompting a vendor at Schuetzen Park, a rival of Coney's in Union Hill, New Jersey, to compound the damage by creating a stand that gave the sick illusion of his feeding live poodles into a noisy meat grinder from which spewed a long string of linked, processed sausages.

Amid such slanders came news that the Brooklyn Board of Health had shut down a Greenpoint butcher's facility for putting horsemeat into its sausages intended for Coney Island. (Upton Sinclair's muckraking *The Jungle* was not to expose the horrors of the meatpacking industry until 1906, bringing about that same year's passage of the federal Pure Drug and Food Act.) In a public-relations move, despite the main ingredients being chuck beef and lean pork, a name change to "Coney Island chicken" was employed, briefly.

In 1867, the hot dog became synonymous with Coney Island.

With just a few embellishments, the basic facts are more or less these: The hot dog came about in 1867, when a Coney Island pushcart vendor of bread, pastries, and ice cream heeded customer suggestions to add hot sandwiches to his menu. The vendor, a German émigré named Charles Feltman, had come to America in 1856, when he was fifteen, yet still recalled the Nuremburg custom of serving sausage with a slice of bread. Turning to his wheelwright, a fellow remembered only by the name Donovan, Feltman had him attach a tin chest to the dessert wagon, to keep the milk rolls fresh, and a makeshift charcoal stove that could hold a boiling pot. Rather than ham or cheese between the bread, Feltman plunked a boiled sausage—and, in a Eureka moment that reads like something out of Hans Christian Andersen, Donovan and Feltman not only sampled the invention, but added dollops of sauerkraut and mustard. They then handed one to a sixteen-year-old boy, who, after a bite, "whooped with appreciation."

Such stories may never hold up in court, but whatever led to its creation, an empire built on a bun was launched, with no eating utensils required.

In 1871, reports the Coney Island History Project, a modern nonprofit organization that seeks to heighten awareness of the area's past, Charles Feltman rented "a small plot of land" that would expand into a full city block. By 1874, "Charles Feltman's Ocean Pavilion," wrote *Amusing the Million* author John F. Kasson, "proclaimed itself the largest building on Coney Island, with rooms for twenty thousand guests, a ballroom for three thousand dancers, and a piazza for five thousand more onlookers."

Four years later, Feltman added the one-thousand-foot Iron Pier, offering some midway attractions and twelve hundred swimmers' lockers, helping to spur, of the

German immigrant Charles Feltman went from pushing a single cart to employing twelve hundred by the turn of the century.

sixty thousand people who came to Coney Island every sunny summer Sunday, a crush of fifty thousand to West Brighton alone. In 1880, the creator of convenience food built a second Iron Pier.

"Feltman's continued to grow," the *Brooklyn Eagle* reported, while the History Project tallied "nine restaurants, a roller coaster, a carousel, a ballroom, an outdoor movie theater, a hotel, a beer garden, a bathhouse, a pavilion, a Tyrolean village, two enormous bars, and a maple garden" bearing the Feltman name. The Smithsonian counted twelve hundred Feltman's waiters by the turn of the century.

Charles Feltman died in 1910, and the business was taken over by his family. "The Great Depression and prejudice against German businesses during World War II had taken their toll," said author Charles Denson, who is also the executive director of the Coney Island History Project.

In 1954, the last section of Feltman's Ocean Pavilion closed down in the face of plans to set up a 3.1-acre amusement park called Astroland on the site. (It opened in 1962.) Feltman's hot dogs ceased production in their Brooklyn factory that same year, and in 2010, the very last remnant of the original Feltman's facility, its kitchen, was demolished. The name lay dormant until 2017, when Michael Quinn, a boyish, forty-something entrepreneur behind Coney Island Tours, having researched the company brand and its recipe, instituted a crowd-funding campaign with his younger brother Joe.

The result, after trying out pop-up stands in hip Brooklyn and Manhattan neighborhoods, was that Feltman's Red Hots—German style, with lamb casing, nitrate free, and on a toasted potato bun—returned to Coney Island, to the same 1000 Surf Avenue spot where Charles Feltman first parked his pushcart in 1871.

Quinn calls the location "the holy land of the hot dog."

Then there was the perspicacious Nathan Handwerker, a twenty-four-year-old former knish peddler from Galicia. Saving $300 from his job slicing rolls at Feltman's, he opened a nine-by-sixteen-foot hot dog stand at Schweigert Alley and Surf Avenue. There, he underpriced his former employer's dime dogs by a nickel, called his franks Nathan's Famous before they really were, and, through a myriad of other promotional schemes, such as having moonlighting actors pose as doctors and make a show out of consuming his product, launched a national institution that celebrated its centennial in 2016.

The spice recipe was his wife Ida's, but the process—"perfectly browned exteriors and much desired snap when eaten," according to food and architecture historian Bruce Kraig—was Nathan's. Over time, a side dish was added: crinkle-cut French fries.

In 1947, the same year baseball manager Branch Rickey recruited Jackie Robinson for the Brooklyn Dodgers, Handwerker hired his first African-American counterman, Derwood Jarrett. In 1968, under Nathan and Ida's son, Murray, the company went public. In 1972, Nathan's initiated a hot-dog-eating contest every Fourth of July—the first year's competition was won by a shill whom the publicists dragged over from his job on the nearby Wonder Wheel. He downed seventeen. (In 2018, eleven-time winner Joey "Jaws" Chestnut beat his own record, seventy-four.)

Nathan died in 1974, and the family sold out in 1987.

Its parent company, Virginia-based Smithfield Foods, a subsidiary of the WH Group of China since 2013, claims more than four hundred million Nathan's Famous hot dogs are consumed every year—including those sold from the still-extant twenty-four-hour service windows of 1310 Surf Avenue, Coney Island.

A sampling of steamed crustaceans representing the day's catch helped give Louis Stauch's eponymous establishment its leg up—just as Stauch's Restaurant helped popularize the tradition known as the shore dinner.

Begun in the 1880s, the meal originated with oarsmen in the waters along the upper St. Lawrence River between the United States and Canada, in a region called the Thousand Islands—which was how the dressing on the dinner salad got its name.

Born in New York's Hell's Kitchen and banging out piano in dance halls rather than attend school, Louis Stauch (1861–1929) first came to Coney as an eighteen-year-old hired to play at a wedding. Forced to sleep on the beach after the bridal party reneged on the promise of a hotel bed, he nevertheless decided the place afforded opportunity. Busing in saloons, Stauch saved $310 in two years, enough to lease his own place, only to lose the building in a storm.

He regained his footing after an arranged meeting with John McKane's brother James, who, with the tip of his shoe, outlined in the sand the boundaries inside which the aspiring young restaurateur could erect his enterprise. John McKane staked Stauch to $40,000.

The business kept growing, generally out of necessity. After a 1903 fire destroyed his West Brighton location, Stauch built a Beaux Arts palace said to be the largest restaurant-ballroom in the world.

His 1922 divorce trial from wife Mathilda was equally oversized. Married in 1896, the couple made an odd pair; he was solitary and withdrawn, while she was outgoing, to say the least. She went out with most of his employees, and even took a Manhattan apartment with one of them, Grover Muller, and called herself Mrs. Muller, as her former housekeeper testified in court.

Per the judge, Mathilda kept the apartment.

Louis kept the business.

Louis Stauch's dining establishment attracted a finer clientele than the others. Still, it was not above petty stunts.

III.

George Cornelius Tilyou was a nineteenth-century Horatio Alger hero, minus the dimwittedness of the fictional character, according to George's grandson, Edo McCullough; Alger (1832–1899) was the Harvard-educated author of countless popular fictional stories about worthy boys who rose from nothing to middle-class respectability. In the various descriptions of Tilyou—and there were many, "dreamy-eyed and abundantly mustachioed" among them—the most apt summation was that "he had sand in his shoes," a South Brooklyn expression meaning he had Coney Island salt water running through his veins. Given his decades of dedication to the area, after which his descendants assumed his protective mantle, it is safe to say that George C. Tilyou's shoes had more sand than anybody's.

Reared in Coney Island from the age of three, George Cornelius Tilyou—"dreamy-eyed and abundantly mustachioed," warbled one admirer—became the resort's single most successful entrepreneur.

He also bravely had it out for John Y. McKane.

Tilyou's forebears were Huguenots, followers of a French Calvinist Protestant movement who escaped persecution right after the 1572 St. Bartholomew's Day Massacre (yes, that St. Bartholomew), although the group's mass migration to America was not until 1685. Much less dramatic was Peter and Ellen Mahoney Tilyou's migration from New York City to Coney Island, although they did have a baby on board: three-year-old son George, born February 3, 1862.

The first year of the family's resettlement, 1865, coincided with the end of the Civil War and the first arrival of day-trippers to Coney. That year, Peter Tilyou, whose job had been to keep records for the City of New York, opened one of the first businesses in the outpost, the Surf House. Its lease cost him $35 a year, or nearly $600 today, and while he rented out "fancy flannel" bathing suits for twenty-five cents, he gave away bowls of clam chowder for free—Peter's theory being it would whet the bathers' appetite for a full meal, and, at a nickel a glass, a round or two of lager.

Reared in such an atmosphere, George early on saw economic possibilities in the beach. Spiritually, he was raised in his mother's Catholic faith. (On October 11, 1893, when he was thirty-one, George married Mary O'Donnell, and they had five children.)

George was fourteen the summer of Philadelphia's 1876 Centennial Exhibition, whose visitors spilled over into Coney and gave George a business opportunity: to sell handmade souvenirs that were nothing more than cigar boxes filled with sand, and medicine bottles with ocean water. "For my first day's labor," Tilyou later recalled, "I realized $13.45, which seemed to me a fortune, so I immediately retired." With fantasies of making his next killing in real estate, he took himself to the Philadelphia fair with the idea to buy the Crystal Palace–like Main Exhibition Building, "but after arriving on the grounds I changed my plans and bought pink lemonade and pop-corn instead."

Over the next two seasons, he set up a Coney Island shuttle service that ran from Norton's Point to Culver Plaza, with a suggested stop at his father's Surf House. Unfortunately, John McKane got wind of the business, forcing George to abandon his rented stagecoach. Next he subleased property, with his younger brother Edward, and printed a four-page dirt sheet that lasted one issue. *Tilyou's Telephone* contained local gossip written

Tilyou family enterprises first opened shop in 1865 and ran for a century, interrupted only when patriarch Peter and son George ran afoul of John McKane.

by George ("Feltman is getting his large Hotel and Dancing Pavilion in readiness [for] an early season"), as well as his stabs at poetry ("'Ocean me not,' the lover cried / 'I am your surf—to you I'm tied'"), and, in light of the resort's influx of American tycoons and British and European nobility, the first of several pithy quotes about his hometown ("If Paris is France, then Coney Island, between June and September, is the world").

With his father, Peter, he built the Island's first playhouse, Tilyou's Surf Theatre, which became the focal point of a thriving business street owned by Lucy Vanderveer, and which the Tilyous, despite having upgraded it, named the Bowery, after New York City's tawdry but widely recognized entertainment district. Hoping their theater would attract what would become known as the family trade, George took offense at the illicit activity McKane allowed on the block, and the financial kickbacks the Chief demanded. Without mentioning names, George editorialized against such corruption in *Tilyou's Telephone*.

Soon, he would have the public opportunity to point fingers. In 1887, a New York State Assembly committee, under representative Col. Alexander S. Bacon, launched an investigation into gambling, prostitution, extortion, and the awarding of land contracts in Coney Island. Throughout the hearings, McKane proclaimed his innocence and whined that maintaining law and order in Gravesend was "not an easy job." He also made prominent mention that he taught Sunday school.

In the end, Coney's political boss was indicted—but that was the extent of it. No punishment was rendered. At least, not for McKane. "Peter Tilyou was arrested again yesterday by the Coney Island police," the New York *Sun* reported June 29, 1887. As he was taken into custody, "his little thirteen-year-old daughter clung to his arm and wept as though her heart would break." The charge was breaching the peace. As the paper also noted, "He and his son George testified against John Y. McKane and others at the Bacon investigation in Brooklyn." George was arrested, too.

During Colonel Bacon's investigation, George exposed the worst of McKane's henchmen, how they fronted for the Chief, and whose whorehouses they frequented. The whistleblowing had immediate consequences. "Peter J. Tilyou, who once owned the Surf Hotel at Coney Island and was rich, opposed the methods of McKane," the *New York Times* reported. "The 'boss' took his revenge by having an avenue cut through the centre of the Surf."

With the Tilyous now pariahs, landlady Lucy Vanderveer was ordered to evict father and son from their Bowery property. It was further suggested that Peter skip town. The family fortune dried up. George covertly began assisting his mother, Ellen, in running her bathhouse, the Mikado, which was being fronted by a family friend, Theodore Kramer.

George further bided his time inventing "a primitive ride, the Aerial Racing Slide," said his grandson, "but he chafed."

IT TOOK SEVEN YEARS, but in response to a steady stream of calls for reform by press and public alike, the state legislature, seeking to unlace McKane's political grip, passed an election bill reapportioning Gravesend into six districts. Only, come voting day 1893, McKane physically stood over all six ballot boxes.

Sensing there might be trouble, the state dispatched poll monitors, led by none other than former chief investigator Col. Alexander Bacon.

"I was expecting you," McKane told his nemesis on the steps of Town Hall. "Now get out of here and be quick about it." The official and his entourage would not budge. Neither would McKane, even when Bacon flashed a Supreme Court writ in his face. "Injunctions don't go here," the fat cat bellowed.

As commissioner of police, McKane ordered the arrest of Bacon and his group before instructing a gang of drunken hirelings to rough up the interlopers.

The fallout was dramatic. In short order, a special district attorney was appointed, a grand jury convened, a trial held, and, despite his attempt at jury tampering, McKane was convicted on eleven counts that included election fraud, misuse of public funds, and contempt of court.

This time the judgment stuck. Sentenced to six years of hard labor in Sing Sing, McKane was out in four, on account of good behavior. That was 1898. A year later, he was dead.

McKane spent his final months comfortably retired at his family home in Sheepshead Bay, making only the occasional, innocuous visit to Coney before finally succumbing to the effects of Bright's disease, that period's term for kidney failure.

For Coney Island, it marked a new beginning—just as it was for George C. Tilyou.
As a businessman, he was free to resume activity.
As a newly married man, it was time to take a honeymoon.
Borrowing money from his mother, George took his bride, Mary, to the one place nearly everyone in America could not stop talking about.

WHAT GOES AROUND

For George Tilyou, growing up amid the slapdash of Coney Island, the layout of the 1893 World's Columbian Exposition in Chicago had to have been extraordinary. Everything was so precise.

"In many ways," said spatial expert Scott A. Lukas, "the World's Columbian Exposition was the world's first proto-theme park…a powerful vision of what could be in terms of an all-encompassing, enclosed amusement space."

While world's fairs of the past had traditionally honored scientific, agricultural, and technological advancements, the Chicago Fair was something different. Sure, it did all that, but with an upbeat, wholehearted American spin. Its exhibits displayed achievements already available in America—provided, like Horatio Alger, you put your shoulder to the wheel. Its location provided a harbinger for what was still available to those with fortitude—it stood on the Eastern edge of the American frontier. Its scale was grander than all previous expos—three times the size of Philadelphia's Centennial, thirty times that of London's Great Exhibition. And, unlike those other fairs, this one's attitude was not dry and pedantic—after all, George Tilyou chose it for his honeymoon.

Its pavilions, while not uniform in appearance, except for their sparkling alabaster color, were nevertheless uniformly magnificent, and so shiny clean—proud showcases for what was distinctly American: indoor American plumbing. Seeing the buildings through green-colored lenses, *The Wonderful Wizard of Oz* author L. Frank Baum found his inspiration for the Emerald City. And for the naughty child in everyone, there was the Midway Plaisance—isolated from the rarified atmosphere of the fair's two hundred main buildings, and pulsating to a honky-tonk rhythm all its own.

"Sell the cook stove if necessary and come," the Midwestern novelist Hamlin Garland implored in a letter to his father in South Dakota.

"You must see this fair."

THE SEEDS WERE FIRST planted in the late 1880s, when the United States Congress threw open a competition to find a city to host a four hundredth anniversary celebration of Christopher Columbus's 1492 discovery of America. The choices were narrowed down to Washington, DC, St. Louis, New York, and Chicago, before they were whittled down to the latter two.

The 1893 Chicago World's Columbian Exposition's Court of Honor achieved its harmonious design "through a shared vocabulary of Classical and Renaissance forms" and "the axial arrangement of the buildings"—a principle imagined for beautifying cities. It ended up being applied to amusement parks.

As the countdown closed in, Chicago banker Lyman J. Gage bettered New York's offer of $15 million, from Cornelius Vanderbilt, J. Pierpont Morgan, and William Waldorf Astor, by another $5 million, but as New York *Sun* editor Charles A. Dana assured his readership, "Don't pay any attention to the nonsensical claims of that windy city. It could not build a World's Fair even if they won it."

On February 24, 1890, the House of Representatives held its vote.

Six hours and eight ballots later, Chicago won it.

With the realization that an 1892 deadline was impractical, Congress reset May 1, 1893, for the fair's opening, and even that would be a stretch. At the time of its approval, Chicago had no architectural plans. The city had not even selected a site. There was only a committee, and its key members barely saw eye to eye, except on one central order: to erect "some novel achievement which would 'discount' the Eiffel tower—something striking and original," said the nineteenth-century economist and statistician Carl Snyder. "American pride was at stake."

Distinctive towers were considered—and rejected, including one crowned with a log cabin, and another by Gustave Eiffel himself.

"The Frenchman," Snyder noted, had already "built a tower practically one thousand feet high" in Paris, showing France to be the world's masters of iron and steel construction. A Chicago tower of twelve or fifteen hundred feet would be "merely a cheap imitation."

As debate continued, the massive fair itself was taking shape on the city's South Side, on more than six hundred acres adjacent to Lake Michigan on Jackson Park. The master plan fell to Chicago architect Daniel Hudson Burnham, as director of works for the Exposition, and the esteemed landscape architect Frederick Law Olmsted, as site designer. Both carried significant credits: Olmsted for New York's Central Park, and Burnham for Chicago's Masonic Temple Building, which he designed with his visionary partner, John W. Root. (Root did some essential groundwork for the fair but, in a loss to all concerned, developed pneumonia and died in January 1891.)

Given the substantial interest in the expo, Chicago architects and engineers organized a Saturday Afternoon Club to discuss its many facets, and it was at one club luncheon in early 1892 that Burnham chose to take the assemblage to task for the fair's lack of an identifying symbol.

"What's wrong with you scientists?" he carped. "Haven't you any sense of the unique, of the offbeat on a grandiose scale?" Burnham laid it on the line. "We must

have something, *anything*, that will make a publicity splash all over the world."

Seated in the steakhouse, a lanky, thirty-one-year-old civil engineer from Pittsburgh focused his piercing steel blue eyes on the blank scrap of paper on the table before him.

Pen in hand, he started drawing.

To say George Washington Gale Ferris Jr. was from Pittsburgh would be a misnomer. He lived in a fashionable neighborhood and kept an office there,

The Chicago Fair's Board of Architects—specifically, Daniel Burnham (above), Director of Works for the Exposition—pushed for a landmark equal in stature to the 1889 Paris Exposition's Eiffel Tower (below, in its 1888 construction phase).

but he arrived in Steel City via a circuitous route. His grandfather Sylvanus Ferris and the Presbyterian minister George W. Gale were the founders of Galesburg, the Illinois town in which George Ferris Jr. was born, on Valentine's Day 1859. Notable about Sylvanus, beyond producing accomplished progeny, was his leadership in the Underground Railroad, a cause for which, at legal and physical peril, he hid slaves in the church belfry and in his home by day, then helped them escape north by night.

Among Sylvanus and Sally's six children, all sons, Olmsted Ferris (George Jr.'s uncle) was a standout. As the story goes, besides introducing sheep to Galesburg, Olmsted introduced popcorn to Queen Victoria, taking twenty barrels of the American specialty from his farm to her in Windsor—where Her Majesty was credited with establishing the tradition of stringing popped kernels and winding the strands around a Christmas tree.

Olmsted's younger brother by seventeen years, George Washington Gale Ferris, was an agriculturalist. He married Martha Edgerton Hyde in 1840, and they had ten children, of which George Jr. was the ninth. In 1864, when the boy was five, Nevada joined the union, and the Ferrises moved by covered wagon to the new capital, Carson City, where George Sr. built a landscaping business, and George Jr. ended up at prep school more than two hundred miles away, in Oakland, California. In 1881, he received his engineering degree from Rensselaer Polytechnic Institute in Troy, New York, and was soon engaged to supervise railroad and bridge projects throughout the East and the South—and engaged to marry Margaret Ann Beatty, of Canton, Ohio. They wed in 1886 and settled in Pittsburgh, where George and James C. Hallsted, a classmate from Rensselaer Poly, established G. W. G. Ferris & Company, Inspecting Engineers. Branch offices followed in New York and Chicago, which was why George Ferris was in the second city and at that luncheon with Daniel Burnham.

"I remembered remarking," Ferris said soon afterward, "that I would build a wheel, a monster. I got some paper and began sketching it out. I fixed the size, determined the construction, the number of cars we would run, the number of people it would hold, what we would charge, the plan of stopping six times in the first revolution and loading, and then making a complete turn."

Sharing his initial drawings with fellow engineers, he was advised not to soil his reputation pursuing what could only end in disaster. "Your wheel is so flimsy it would collapse," Burnham himself told Ferris, "and even if it didn't, the public would be afraid to ride in it."

The proportions were staggering. There had been amusement wheels in the past, going back

"Physically," George Washington Gale Ferris "is a man of affairs, tall, well-proportioned, and well sent out . . . his demeanor is quiet, his tones low [and] he is rather fastidious in his dress." The writer also found the civil engineer "naïve," "boyish," and "fascinating."

to the Great Wheel ridden by Pietro Della Valle in 1615 and progressing through a number of handcrafted wheels at American county fairs as early as 1848 and 1849, but until Ferris, never was there anything on such a scale or formed from such materials.

Essentially, the engineer was proposing a perpendicular merry-go-round whose oversized circumference could support thirty-six separate railroad-car-like coaches, each twenty-four feet long, thirteen feet wide, and ten feet high, and capable of carrying anywhere from forty to sixty passengers. The double-rimmed steel wheel, resembling a gargantuan bicycle wheel, would measure 250 feet in diameter and rotate on a weighty axle supported by two parallel pyramidal-beamed towers rising 140 feet off the ground. The coaches were to be constructed of wood with openings for glass windows. Driving all that iron and steel would be two one-thousand-horsepower steam engines linked to the cogged exterior surface of the wheel's bilateral rims.

Ferris countered Burnham's rejection by responding, "You are an architect, sir, I am an engineer." He explained that his wheel had everything to do with engineering. "The spokes may seem flimsy, but they're more than strong enough."

Then, as one professional to another, despite their age difference (Burnham was fourteen years George's senior), Ferris remarked, "I feel that no man should prejudge another man's idea unless he knows what he's talking about."

Burnham consented to share Ferris's blueprints with the fair's board of directors.

PERHAPS, IF GEORGE FERRIS had consulted one of the fortune-tellers on the Midway Plaisance, he would have been told to pack up his wheel and run. Instead, Ferris persisted, even in the face of ongoing resistance.

For starters, he cut a bad deal, even if it was the only game in town. Ferris rightly saw the fair as a showcase for his idea, though he may have overestimated what long-term influence it might wield. To convince the Ways & Means Committee to give him the go-ahead, "the Man with Wheels in His Head," as he became known, spent $25,000 out of his own pocket, or nearly $680,000 today, for a feasibility study, the salaries of additional engineers, and the recruitment of investors.

After two time-consuming refusals from the board for his project, Ferris finally gained approval on December 16, 1892, barely more than five months before the fair's designated opening. (For the Paris expo, Gustave Eiffel had two years to build his tower). In addition, Ferris's rights came with the provisos that: (1) he build his wheel not on the hallowed main grounds dubbed the Court of Honor, but on the catch-all Midway, and (2) he secure all his own financing. (Eiffel had received 20 percent of his backing from the French government.)

As further impediments, that particular winter in Chicago was severe, with three-foot-deep snows, and the country itself was frozen in an equally debilitating financial depression known as the Panic of 1893.

The axle of the Ferris Wheel "sustains a burden equivalent to the great cantilever bridge at Cincinnati, and it would sustain six of these with equal ease," marveled statistician Carl Snyder.

"Make no little plans. They have no magic to stir men's blood and probably themselves will not be realized," decreed architect Daniel H. Burnham, setting into motion the sense of high-mindedness that framed plans for the World's Columbian Exhibition.

Meanwhile, at Sixty-Third and Wallace Streets, planning of a different sort was taking place.

Herman Webster Mudgett—who assumed the name H. H. Holmes, after Conan Doyle's super-sleuth—was crafting a boardinghouse for visitors to the upcoming expo. Named the World's Fair Hotel, it was where the charismatic thirty-year-old would charm, defraud, torture, and kill countless defenseless people—twenty-seven over his life's career, according to his own admission, although, by some estimates, the victim tally was closer to two hundred.

By either measure, Holmes was America's first documented serial killer.

Herman Webster Mudgett, also known as Dr. H. H. Holmes, America's first serial killer, found his numerous victims from among the fair's transitory inhabitants.

Ferris forged on. Final capitalization was $400,000 ($11 million today), with his firm contracted to keep the first $300,000 in ticket sales, after which the Ferris Company was to share 50 percent of the gross receipts with the World's Columbian Exhibition.

Construction of the more than one hundred thousand parts began in early January 1893. Steam was pumped into the snow and sand that coated the bedrock so when the concrete was poured for the thirty-two-foot-deep foundation, it would not ice over. On March 18, two days before the completion of the towers on which it would rest, the 89,320-pound axle—the largest piece of steel ever forged in the United States—arrived from the Bethlehem Iron Company in Pittsburgh.

Spring brought constant rain and Ferris's continued search for financing. New-fangled lightbulbs—there would be a total of three thousand on the wheel, visible to all of Chicago at night—were attached to the base, which was connected to two independent power generators, in case one should fail. George Westinghouse's company

As chronicled by Erik Larson in his gripping *The Devil in the White City: Murder, Magic, and Madness at the Fair That Changed America*, Burnham's story parallels that of Holmes's, except that while the architect dedicated himself to getting people to the fair, the madman did his best at doing away with them.

A New Hampshire native, Holmes was a medical student at the University of Michigan when he took to stealing cadavers for the purpose of filing false life insurance claims. By the time he reached Chicago, he cagily kept construction teams from comprehending the labyrinthine layout of his hotel by not paying them, so they would quit and be replaced by new and different crews. This left him the lone person aware of the hotel's special, soundproof chambers, where his captives—single women, mostly—succumbed to a variety of unspeakable deaths, typically by suffocation, dissection, and/or incineration.

The fair, which Holmes frequently attended, provided the perfect cover, as the police were too busy patrolling its constant activity to pay heed to the ever-growing cast of missing persons just a trolley ride away.

Holmes's anonymity ended thirteen months after the fair did. Apprehended in Boston in November 1894 for insurance fraud, the monster was exposed at last.

A trial for the murder of a Philadelphia victim began in that city on October 28, 1895, with Holmes refusing a public defender and representing himself.

On November 2, 1895, he was convicted.

On May 7, 1896, he was hanged.

Entrance to the fair cost 50 cents, the same as a ride on the Ferris Wheel.

in Pittsburgh, which owned the 1869 patent on the pneumatic airbrake for railroads, supplied the custom mechanism that would slow and stop Ferris's round colossus.

On a rain-soaked May 1, the fair opened amid great folderol, culminating in President Grover Cleveland's turning a gold key that flipped something new: an electrical switch.

"As by a touch," said the nation's leader, "the machinery that gives life to this vast Exposition is now set in motion"—everywhere, that was, except on the unfinished Ferris Wheel.

IN OCTOBER OF THE year of his lucrative Coney Island summer, Buffalo Bill Cody brought his Wild West extravaganza to the Chicago Driving Park racetrack. It was, in entertainment parlance, a smash. Two years later, back in Chicago, he introduced a five-foot-tall, twenty-three-year-old sharpshooter from Ohio, Phoebe Ann Moses. America's first female show-business personality, she became better known by her stage name (the surname she took from a Cincinnati suburb), Annie Oakley.

After shooting her first squirrel at age eight, Oakley began selling wild game to shopkeepers to support her indigent, thrice-married mother and siblings. At fifteen she beat the established marksman Frank Butler at a competition in Cincinnati, and soon the couple developed a romantic relationship. The following year they married.

Joining Cody's Wild West on tour, Oakley's only rival for attention at the Paris 1889 Exposition Universelle was *la tour Eiffel*. When Chicago started planning its expo, Cody saw the opportunity for another box office bonanza—until learning that 50 percent of every admission ticket would have to go to the fair.

Cody had a better plan.

On April 2, 1893—a month before the May 1 opening of the World's Columbian Exhibition—Buffalo Bill's Wild West and Congress of Rough Riders of the World, starring

Annie Oakley, premiered in an eighteen-thousand-seat arena built not on the fairgrounds, but right next door.

"The greatest equestrian exhibition of the century," the *Tribune* raved. "In addition to Indians, cowboys, Mexicans, Cossacks, Arabs, and Tartars are detachments from the Sixth United States Cavalry, French chasseurs, German Pottsdammer reds, and English lancers."

Besides spectacle numbers, which included a reenactment of Custer's Last Stand, the show spotlighted Oakley hitting her rapid-fire round of bull's-eyes, including shooting the cigarette out of Butler's mouth (he was by then also her manager), and Cody riding his horse while gunning down a battery of flying glass-ball targets—a feat matched with equal finesse by Oakley, whom Cody called "Missy."

Sharpshooter Annie Oakley headlined Buffalo Bill's European tour before rejoining his troupe for the Chicago Fair.

The frontiersman also took special delight in upstaging the great fair whenever possible. After its officials refused Chicago mayor Carter Harrison's request that the city's poor children receive a free day at the expo, Cody gifted fifteen thousand kids with complimentary train tickets, passes to *his* show and backstage encampment, and ice cream and candy.

His Wild West engagement also outran the fair, by one day, another publicity gimmick he turned to gold. In all, that 1893 summer in Chicago, Cody played to an

Refusing to share his box-office earnings for the privilege of staging his show on the fairgrounds, Buffalo Bill instead assembled his Wild West pageant right outside the expo.

audience of four million people and netted a profit of $1 million, more than $27 million today. But the showman was no businessman. He continued his tradition of dazzling audiences with his Western extravaganzas while also living lavishly and investing poorly. Creditors foreclosed on his troupe in July 1913, exactly thirty years after Cody took his first bow in Coney Island, and four years before his death.

On their own, Oakley and Butler went on with the show, although their true devotion was to one another. "It was a circus-folks' marriage, not a Hollywood one," said one biographer, Delancey Ferguson. "Frank and Annie were married for life."

Having no children, they gave generously to children's charities and orphanages, and in contrast to the macho braggart depicted in composer Irving Berlin's classic stage and movie musical *Annie Get Your Gun* (in fact, it was Cody who felt competitive with Annie), the real-life Butler was known to be so sentimental that he could not bear life without Oakley.

He died November 21, 1926, eighteen days after she did.

The hottest ticket at the fair was an exotic belly dancer named Little Egypt.

In the first seven and a half weeks that the fair was up and running—annoyingly, with fewer attendees than Burnham and the board had expected—its own diminutive star got the jump on the still-unfinished Ferris Wheel. Her platform was a one-thousand-seat theater amid the donkeys, camels, and dust of the "Streets of Cairo" gateway section of the Midway Plaisance, on the left side, opposite the scaffolded wheel as one approached Central Avenue.

In terms of press attention, Farida Mazar, who went by the stage name Fatima but was better known as Little Egypt, received just as much copy as Ferris, only, in her case, the vast number of myths surrounding her rivaled those of Catherine the Great. These included claims that Little Egypt performed naked for a group of men, including P. T. Barnum's grandson, at Sherry's restaurant in Manhattan (that was another Little Egypt), and Mark Twain suffered a heart attack watching her do the hoochy-cooch (never verified). Whatever the real story, Little Egypt—who, from reliable accounts, was of Syrian extraction, hailed from Arizona, and was married to a Greek restaurateur in Chicago named Spyropoulos—performed an Arabic *danse du ventre* (belly dance) to the tune of "The Streets of Cairo, or the Poor Little Country Maid," familiar on the schoolyard as "There's a Place in France Where the Ladies Wear No Pants."

Her exhibition, under a modest layer of veils but scandalously sans corset, catapulted Chicago's Midway into an international phenomenon.

Both her background music and marketing term *belly dance* sprang from the resourceful mind of Solomon Bloom, widely regarded as a savior of the fair. A first-generation American, born in Pekin, Illinois, to impoverished Orthodox Jewish parents from Poland, he was seven when his family uprooted itself to San Francisco, where his precocious gift for math got him a job keeping the books for a brush factory, despite his total lack of education. To moonlight, he acted on local stages, turning to box office work at age thirteen and, at sixteen, producing his first show. At eighteen, he entered the furniture business and earned enough to retire, a route he chose not to take.

Twenty-three years old at the time of the fair, Bloom characteristically leapt through its ranks in a few brief weeks, replacing Professor Frederic Ward Putnam, curator of the Peabody Museum of Archaeology and Ethnology at Harvard, in organizing the Midway Plaisance. "To have made this unhappy gentleman responsible for the establishment of a successful venture in the field of entertainment," Bloom later said of Professor Putnam, "was about as intelligent a decision as it would be today to make Albert Einstein manager of the Ringling Brothers and Barnum & Bailey Circus."

Bloom scrapped Putnam's pedantic plan to mold the Midway into a living museum, and used his theatrical background to see that the crowd had fun. After witnessing Paris's 1889 Exposition Universelle, with its lively and profitable Midway Plaisance, Bloom secured rights to the Algerian village and imported it in its entirety to Chicago. As its promoter, he limited Little Egypt's audience to men, convinced a local minister to condemn the belly dance, then sat back and watched the engagement sell out for the run of the fair.

Unlike the Paris exposition, where Midway offerings were integrated throughout "serious" pavilions on the Trocadéro, Les Invalides, and the other 237 acres of fairground, Chicago contained a dedicated amusement district, a world first. The dizzying array of attractions under its minarets and domes included physical-culture enthusiast Bernarr Macfadden, stripped down to his skivvies and showing off far more than Little Egypt; games of chance, where, unlike those in Coney Island, the barker patting you down to guess your weight wasn't also trying to pick your pocket; shooting galleries, which

Beholding the Chicago Fair's representations of forty-six foreign countries, every major state and territory of the United States, and the nation's latest technologies and consumer products—from Cracker Jack, Cream of Wheat, and Wrigley's Juicy Fruit gum, to zippers and Pabst Blue Ribbon beer—Frederick Douglass had a question for exhibition officials.

Douglass, a former slave who became possibly the most articulate orator of the antebellum era, wondered where were the displays to honor the accomplishments of African-Americans.

In collaboration with the journalist and civil-rights activist Ida B. Wells, Douglass published a multilingual pamphlet, *The Reason Why the Colored American Is Not in the World's Columbian Exposition*—copies of which the two distributed in the Haitian government's pavilion. In it they wrote, "The exhibit of the progress made by a race in 25 years of freedom as against 250 years of slavery, would have been the greatest tribute to the greatness and progressiveness of American institutions which could have been shown the world.

"The colored people of this great Republic…were among the earliest settlers of this continent, landing at Jamestown, Virginia in 1619 in a slave ship, before the Puritans, who landed at Plymouth in 1620." They added, "Why are they not taking part in this glorious celebration of the four-hundredth anniversary of the discovery of their country?"

Exacerbating the situation, the fair's main exhibition center, known as the Court of Honor, also bore another name, the White City—as much for the ivory-hued pavilions of plaster-of-Paris and hemp-fiber materials that hastened their construction as it was for the skin color of the site's labor pool and the patrons that fair officials sought to attract. (To its one credit, unlike amusement parks in the following century, the fair did not turn away persons of color at its admission gates.)

let you pretend to be Annie Oakley or Buffalo Bill; Carl Hagenbeck's Menagerie and World's Ethnological Museum, starring dogs, horses, and lions that were advertised to be on the attack (a hook that triggered greater attendance); a swimming facility known as a natatorium, with a bakery and lunchroom (food at the fair was pricey and poorly reviewed); a World's Congress of Beauty, boasting "40 Ladies from 40 Nations"; and various German, Dutch, Irish, Eskimo, Laplander, Turkish, Javanese, Sudanese, Nubian, Bedouin, Oceanic, and Moorish villages.

According to the *Chicago Daily Tribune*, "For Wells, the final straw came when, as a sop to blacks (but also as an attendance booster), fair officials scheduled a Colored People's Day, promising 2,000 free watermelons." Outraged, Wells called for a black boycott of the fair. Douglass, though disgusted, was not deterred.

"There is no Negro problem," the septuagenarian extemporized in a speech he gave at the fair that day, August 25, 1893. "The problem is whether the American people have loyalty enough, honor enough, patriotism enough, to live up to their own Constitution."

Two years before his death, Frederick Douglass (seated, with his grandson, the celebrated violinist Joseph Douglass) crusaded at the fair on behalf of human dignity.

Journalist and civil-rights activist Ida B. Wells (shown circa 1893) called for a black boycott of the fair.

"Compared to anything that had come before it," social historian David Nasaw said, "...the Chicago Midway was stupendous. Compared to the midways that would succeed it, it was only a beginning."

With its laissez-faire atmosphere so different from the stiff formalities performed elsewhere at the fair, Bloom created, as *American Heritage* anointed it, "the world's first amusement park."

Between the fair's opening and George Ferris's finally welcoming paying customers, only two mechanical devices on the Midway Plaisance qualified as amusement rides—two and a half, if one counted the hydrogen-filled balloon that lifted passengers one thousand feet over the fairgrounds and Lake Michigan. For the other examples, the key motivation was transportation, especially for the Hydraulic Sliding Railway, or Movable Sidewalk, a forty-five-hundred-foot, flat-ramped people mover that was meant to spare six thousand fairgoers at a time the burden of walking the full mile of Midway. Invented by a Frenchman, Charles A. Barre, and first demonstrated at the 1889 Paris expo, it broke down frequently in Chicago.

The other ride was the Ice Railway, essentially a throwback to Catherine the Great's winter pastime. Sleigh runners replaced wheels under the cars, and iced troughs served as tracks. Even in Chicago's sweltering summer, the course was kept intact by pipes filled with frozen ammonia gas and maintained by the De la Vergne Refrigeration Company of New York. The original plan was to have the Ice Railway shuttle fairgoers between the Horticulture and the Liberal Arts Buildings, but during the planning stage, the rigid Ways & Means Committee relegated it to the Midway, where it was reconfigured into an all-out roller coaster.

For the conversion, the fair turned to a specialist in the field, LaMarcus Thompson.

After his financial setback at Coney Island, the inventor rebounded handsomely, and in the six years leading up to the Chicago fair he had set up numerous switchback railways across the United States. He next "went abroad and built a score or more of such [rail]roads in England and France, which have proved a great attraction at numerous seaside resorts, watering places, and centers of public resort," reported *Scientific American*. Overseas, Thompson was responsible for three switchbacks in

LaMarcus Thompson was commissioned to build the Midway's Ice Railway.

Paris, another three in London, and many more others in the United Kingdom and on the Continent, including Boulogne and Barcelona.

"Millions of passengers have been carried on these gravity roadways," said *Scientific American*, proposing that Thompson's engineering principles be put to practical use for urban rapid transit throughout America. "We believe no serious accident has ever occurred on them," the article stated. "Probably no safer mode of conveyance was ever devised."

That is, until it wasn't. "One man was killed and five other people badly injured by an accident that occurred on the ice railway at Midway Plaisance this evening," newspapers as far away as California's Sacramento *Record-Union* reported on June 15, 1893. "The sleds on the railway were going at a high rate of speed around a curve, when one jumped the track and fell to the ground fifteen feet below."

The accident occurred during a preopening test run with fair employees, when the first and second of the three-sled train uncoupled and sent the other two sleds slamming through the guardrail. Fingers, noses, and jaws were shattered, and the one woman onboard broke both of her arms.

The fatal victim suffered internal bleeding, three broken ribs, and a face damaged beyond recognition.

EXACTLY ONE WEEK AFTER the tragedy, June 21, 1893, the Ferris Wheel opened for business. Fears over the ride's safety had been somewhat allayed on June 13—a day before the Ice Railway accident—when the site engineer, Luther V. Rice, another former classmate of Ferris's, invited the press for a ride. The reporters were greeted with a news release stating that the wheel could withstand 110 mph winds, and their stories over the following days hailed Ferris's sturdy accomplishment as "the Eighth Wonder of the World."

The Wheel's 3 p.m. opening-day ceremony was nowhere near as grand as that accorded the fair's debut, although some expo executives and other dignitaries were in attendance, along with the forty-piece Iowa State Band, which played "America." Ferris was there, with his wife, Margaret.

Thanking and attributing the success of the day to her, Ferris also assured the crowd, which included his investors, that he had "gotten the wheels" out of his head "and made them a living reality."

Amid the cheers, Margaret presented George with a gold whistle, so he could signal for the wheel to begin revolving.

The handsome couple took the first ride.

NEXT CHAPTER

I.

"**I**t lacks, to our way of thinking, character and dignity of purpose, and must awaken in the mind of the serious and thoughtful the disappointing reflection that a vast amount of money has been expended upon the production of a giant toy," grumbled the New York–based engineering journal *The Manufacturer and Builder*, although general public and professional reaction was overwhelmingly favorable. The *Journal of the Association of Engineering Societies* assessed Ferris's accomplishment as "a good promise for America in the twentieth century."

It cost fifty cents for the twenty-minute ride, the same as the general admittance

To facilitate loading and unloading, "six railed platforms of varying heights have been provided on the north side of the wheel, and six more, corresponding with these, on the south side of it," Ferris Wheel riders were instructed. "When the wheel stops, each of the six lowest cars has a platform at each of its doors. The passengers step out of the south doors, and other passengers step in at the north doors."

to the fair, or about $13.50 today. Whether or not that played a factor, once the Ferris Wheel made it past opening day and the first wave of curiosity seekers, it went begging for riders—only sixty thousand tickets were sold between June 21 and July 2, which would have filled the wheel only thirty times. Overall fair attendance was less than anticipated, too; culpability was placed on the financial Panic of 1893 and that year's poor crops, to say nothing of lingering fears as to the Ferris Wheel's genuine safety.

On Sunday, July 9, a severe thunderstorm with tornado-force winds shredded the silk shield of the Midway's hot-air balloon, which, fortunately, was grounded at the time.

At the opposite end of the pier, the Ferris Wheel survived with nary a scratch, and at the height of the weather front, its great metal mass vibrated only slightly, no more than an inch and a half—demonstrating the might, and safety, of the new landmark, an achievement quickly dispatched to the press corps.

By mid-August, the fair's box office perked up, fueled largely by growing interest in the Ferris Wheel. Burnham did some program polishing, too, at the urging of Frederick Law Olmsted, who noticed dutiful but weary facial expressions on the crowds inspecting the White City, especially when compared to the happy faces packing the Midway. Taking a cue from Sol Bloom, Burnham shook loose the stuffiness of the Court of Honor and scheduled lively concert artists, from "March King" John Philip Sousa to "King of the Ragtime Writers" Scott Joplin.

Taking their son at his word, although they may not have sold the stove, Hamlin Garland's parents made the seven-hundred-mile trek to meet him at the fair, where "rapidly did we pass from one stupendous vista to another," Hamlin recounted. The Columbian Exhibition left the elder Garlands breathless, especially the matriarch. "Her life had been spent among homely small things, and these gorgeous scenes dazzled her, overwhelmed her," said her son.

Truth to tell, it was too much to take in. "Take me home," Mrs. Garland demanded. "I can't stand any more of it."

Due to popular demand, Ferris's ride continued past the fair's October 30 expiration date, into the week of November 6, and even then security guards had to shoo trespassers away. In its entire nineteen-week existence, nearly one and a half million people rode the wheel. This resulted in gross earnings for the Ferris Wheel Company of $726,805, or nearly $20 million today, for a net profit of approximately $395,000.

George Ferris spent little time basking in the glory. While his wheel loomed large over the charred ruins of the demolished fair site, patent-right and other lawsuits showered down on him like a Lake Michigan squall. The fair organization and he battled over costs for removing his mammoth machine from Jackson Park, and Ferris sued the exposition's governing body over monies related to expenses. He did not lack for future opportunity—developers in America, England, and Europe wanted his invention, and this included George Tilyou—but Ferris rebuffed offers to focus on finding a new Chicago location for his existing wheel.

On April 29, 1894, he decided upon acreage on North Clark Street near Lincoln Park, twenty minutes from downtown, with enough space to build other attractions. By October 1896, the nearly $15,000 move was completed and the wheel was spinning again.

Only the underdeveloped Lincoln Park could not hold a candle to the world's fair. Attendance was

Among the post-fair proposals rebuffed by Ferris was to transplant the Wheel, and the Vienna Village around it, to Manhattan's Thirty-Seventh Street and Broadway.

scarce. That autumn of 1896, the same could be said of Margaret Ferris. Estranged from George for months, she returned to her parents' home in Ohio. To meet his financial obligations, primarily legal, Ferris sold his business partners his majority interest in his namesake company.

On November 17, 1896, suffering from what was alternately reported as typhoid fever, tuberculosis, renal failure, or even a possible attempt at suicide, Ferris checked himself into Pittsburgh's Mercy Hospital. Five days later, at the age of thirty-seven, the hero of the 1893 World's Columbian Exhibition was dead. A year and a half later, the undertaker was still waiting to be paid, and withholding George's ashes from the Ferris family until he was.

As for Ferris's wheel, the Lincoln Park location proved a $700,000 bust, and in 1903, the twenty-two hundred pounds of iron and steel were sold at auction to the Chicago House Wrecking Company for a pitiful $1,800.

The firm, in turn, invested $265,000 to dismantle, transport, and reassemble the wheel for the 1904 Louisiana Purchase Exposition in St. Louis, where it spent the summer giving three million people the ride of their lives.

It was a last hurrah.

Nearly two years after the fair closed, garlanded with two hundred pounds of dynamite on May 11, 1906, George Ferris's Great Wheel was blown to smithereens.

II.

George Tilyou, having failed in his bid to purchase the Chicago wheel from George Ferris, did his own bit of Barnum-ing and put up a large sign on Coney Island's Bowery, near West Eighth Street: On This Site Will Be Erected the World's Largest Ferris Wheel. Never mind that what he bought on credit from the Philadelphia Steel Company would be half the size of what had bedazzled the masses in Chicago; "We Americans," Tilyou told a reporter, "want either to be thrilled or amused, and are ready to pay well for either sensation."

Good as his word, Tilyou's sign generated enough enthusiasm for him to rent out all the surrounding concession space. Within fifty days of operation, all lit up and spinning—and, for an extra push, George's pretty, blonde sister Kathryn, bedecked in her mother's evening dress and diamond necklace, sold tickets—"the Island's first, big, glittering attraction" was showing a profit, as did his other West Brighton properties: the Aerial Racing Slide, a nascent version of the modern zip line; the Intramural Bicycle Railway, a short-distance, ground-level monorail balanced by an overhead wooden beam; and a gravity railroad called the Double Dip Chutes.

All he really needed was some kind of cohesive element to bind his varied interests together.

Coney Island began to feel its oats in the post–John McKane period.

III.

Though today his name is largely unfamiliar, and his pioneering effort in making Coney Island an amusement center overlooked, Paul Boyton was the Felix Baumgartner and Philippe Petit of his time, with equal parts David Blaine, Evel Knievel, Harry Houdini, Jacques Cousteau, and Phileas Fogg. His exploits could fill a few books—and have, including one he wrote in 1886, titled, for reasons to be explained, *Roughing It in Rubber*. While many tales of him contradict one another, especially in regard to time and place, one press description of Boyton as an aquatic adventurer rings true: On the occasion of his being presented to Queen Victoria at her marine residence on the Isle of Wight, Capt. Paul Boyton, wielding his double-bladed paddle that resembled an armored spear, looked just like a medieval crusader.

Born in either County Kildare, Ireland, or Pittsburgh—apparently he never caught his breath long enough to set the record straight, though evidence strongly points to Pittsburgh—Boyton accomplished considerable underwater exploits once he matured into adulthood. The world knew him as the "Fearless Frogman," an alias that was clearly fated to be; Boyton's birthdate, June 29, 1848, put him under the astrological sign of Cancer, a water sign. According to one relative, when swimming as a boy, he loved "to try dangerous tricks in the water, much to the dismay of his parents, who feared he would drown."

As a child, Paul Boyton would vanish from home to swim in the river, only to be found by his "angry and anxious mother, who beat a merry tattoo on a tender portion of his body with a shingle," said the daredevil's authorized biography.

"The account of his life reads like one long *Boy's Own* adventure story, encompassing as it does the American Civil War [he claimed to have joined the Union Navy at fifteen], revolution in Mexico, the Franco-Prussian War [he claimed to have fought with the French], the diamond fields of South Africa, and active service in the Peruvian Torpedo Service, quite apart from his exploits as a swimmer, a lifeguard, and a submariner," said an 1897 biographical sketch, just as Boyton was also getting his feet wet in show business, amusement parks, and ornithology.

Domestically, the adventurer was husband to "my beloved and gentle wife" (as he described her in the dedication to his autobiography), the former Margaret Connelly, and father to three sons. (Active until the end, Boyton, fatigued from a recent birding trip to South America, died of pneumonia in his Sheepshead Bay, Brooklyn, home on April 18, 1924. He was seventy-six.)

Boyton established his fame after coinventing, with Pittsburgh rubber manufacturer C. S. Merriman, the pneumatic rubber wetsuit, a "wearable kayak" that permitted him to paddle, at one hundred strokes per minute, through nearly any body of water. This he demonstrated on October 21, 1874, on the final leg of an Atlantic crossing from New York, when he leapt into the Irish Sea and survived what turned out to be a seven-hour endurance test during a treacherous storm.

"The suit weighed thirty-five pounds and had five air chambers," it was explained in *Boys' Life*, a Boy Scouts publication in the *Boy's Own* magazine mold. "These could be inflated or deflated individually, enabling the wearer to float horizontally, like a boat, or bob vertically, like a cork."

Boyton's seaworthy "life-saving dress," said the *New York Times*, "may be donned in less time than it would take to put on a pair of gloves, will sustain a person in the water for an indefinite period, and at the same time keep the wearer perfectly dry."

Hoping to mass-market his invention, Boyton spent the late 1870s onward staging aquatic shows in England, Europe, and Russia, where the Imperial Navy briefly considered suiting up its entire fleet. Returning to the States in 1881, and financially strapped due to his improvident ways, Boyton swam the Mississippi, Yellowstone, and Missouri Rivers, and toured for a time with the Barnum & Bailey Circus, which required the excavation of an artificial lake at every stop.

Independent of the circus, in August 1886, seven years before the World's Columbian Exposition, he appeared at the World's Pastime Exposition sports show at Cheltenham Beach, Illinois—"destined," according to the location's advertisements, "to become the Coney Island of Chicago."

For Boyton, it turned out to be a testing ground.

WATER WORKS

After expanding his amusement-railway empire into Europe, LaMarcus Thompson basked in the sun of Atlantic City, where, in 1887, between New York and Tennessee Avenues, he introduced the mechanical diversion that would reap him his greatest commercial success, the Scenic Railway. It may have crawled as sluggishly as his Switchback Railway, but the Thompson Scenic Railway's marketable advantage over its predecessor was that it secluded riders from the real world and transported them into a wholly imagined realm of visual wonder.

Mechanically an improvement over the Switchback, the Scenic Railway featured a return track, articulated carriages (meaning their wheels turned independently), and a steam-engine-powered cable that latched on to cars from underneath and hoisted them up the necessary inclines.

On the outside, the Scenic Railway might resemble a scaled-down Swiss Alp or other towering peak, even though its bones consisted of nothing more than a rickety wooden frame coated with chicken wire, burlap, and painted plaster. Inside, its car wheels triggered a switch to set off the lights and reveal, as the railway's name promised, "forests, landscapes, and scenes intended to horrify riders," said *Popular Science*. "The cars rarely traveled faster than ten miles an hour, and little attempt was made to thrill passengers with sharp dips."

By the late 1890s, Atlantic City was to Philadelphia what Coney Island was to New York: overcrowded, exploitative, and irresistible.

In time, Thompson managed to speed up his dark ride, and the random panoramas gradually gave way to fleeting story lines steeped in themes of biblical grandeur, often reflected on their equally grandiose façades. To create his interior tableaux, Thompson hired designers from the New York stage. He also invited, as happened with his 1884 Switchback Railway at Coney, immediate competition from rival manufacturers wishing to derail his preeminence in the field.

In 1887, the same year of Thompson's Atlantic City triumph, two designers, Stephen E. Jackman and Byron B. Floyd, introduced the figure eight track for the Toboggan Chute in Haverhill, Massachusetts—an advancement that caused coaster historian Robert Cartmell to support Jackman and Floyd's claim that they were responsible for originating the term *roller coaster*.

Even so, based on the successes of his Atlantic City attraction and subsequent formation of the Manhattan-based L. A. Thompson Scenic Railway Company, William F. Mangels designated the firm's signature product "the leading amusement ride at all major expositions and amusement parks" in the world.

By the time the first Scenic Railway was winning over crowds, Atlantic City's Boardwalk was already a seasoned seventeen years old, and, owing to storms and spurts of commercial growth, in its fifth incarnation. Like Vauxhall's promenade, the passage "became a stage," said James Lilliefors, who made a study of America's boardwalks, "a place where people could see and be seen." Furthermore, unlike the restricted resorts of New Jersey's Cape May and Stone Harbor, on the Atlantic City Boardwalk, "everyone was equal," said another assessment. "Factory owners rubbed elbows with carpenters, blue-eyed Germans mixed with olive-skinned Italians, and Irish walked next to Jews."

The melting pot did not congeal overnight. Originally called Absecon Island, from the native *absegami*, meaning "little water," the marshlands served as the summer home to the Lenape, along with mosquitos and blacksnakes. Thoughts of exploiting the healthful benefits of its coastal air and water did not take hold until the late 1840s, when Jonathan Pitney, a doctor of medicine, partnered with Richard Osborne, a civil engineer from Philadelphia, to sell Absecon as the "National Resort." Keeping with the theme, the streets were named for states and the town was rechristened Atlantic City.

On July 1, 1854, the first train carrying passengers left Camden, New Jersey, at nine thirty in the morning and arrived in Atlantic City at noon. Hotels, boardinghouses, bathhouses, and saloons quickly sprung up, less because of salt water and sea air, and more because Atlantic City, unlike Philadelphia sixty-two miles and formerly a twelve-hour stagecoach ride away, served alcohol on Sundays.

Foot traffic grew so thick that the Boardwalk was born of necessity, to address the problems of pedestrian logjams and inescapable sand. Sticking to shoes, the grit spread its damage everywhere, driving an exasperated Alexander Boardman, a conductor on the Camden & Atlantic Railroad, whose seats and floors were coated in the stuff, to take his case to the owners of similarly afflicted hotels.

The Boardwalk was born of necessity, to prevent bathers from
tracking sand into hotel lobbies.

The upshot was the May 9, 1870, approval by the city council to build a $5,000
protective path of yellow pine planks *above* the sands.

Atlantic City's first Boardwalk—for the record, the first boardwalk in the United
States—opened June 26, 1870. Two years later, an appropriately named inventor from
Bridgeport, Connecticut, Isaac Newton Forrester, came to town with his vertical
Epicycloidal Diversion, a rotary swing on a circular platform that hoisted sixty-four
passengers thirty feet above the beach before returning them to earth. (George Ferris's
much-larger wheel would employ the same principle over Lake Michigan twenty-one
years later.)

Suddenly, Atlantic City was in the amusement business. In 1880, Gustav Dentzel,
a Philadelphia cabinetmaker originally from Germany, established his own ride near
the Boardwalk, a hand-carved carousel.

What came next was something that had already been done on the Isle of Wight
as early as 1814: conversion of utilitarian boat docking wharves into a series of amusement piers attached to the Boardwalk. By 1913, Atlantic City claimed seven such
piers, the first in 1882, when entrepreneur George Howard's self-titled pier and music
pavilion began jutting out from Kentucky
Avenue. The notion caught on, and within
a few years, America's coasts had forty-two
amusement piers.

Most, too, had better luck than origina-
tor George Howard: The year he inaugurated
his pier, it got hit by a storm.

Rebuilt the year after that, it got hit by
a ship.

Predating Thompson's Scenic Railway in
Atlantic City—and George Ferris's wheel in
Chicago—Isaac N. Forrester introduced the
Epicycloidal Wheel to Atlantic City.

John Lake Young, a former carpenter turned real estate developer who had worked on Lucy the Elephant, assumed ownership of Applegate Pier on Tennessee Avenue in 1892, after its original owner, James Applegate, was run out of Philadelphia for running a brothel along with his tintype studio. Renaming it Young's Ocean Pier, John outfitted it with rides, vaudeville acts, midway games, and a nine-room Elizabethan cottage—from which he fished out the kitchen window. When the pier burned down in 1902, he created, at the foot of Arkansas Avenue, the 1,775-foot-long Young's Million Dollar Pier, Atlantic City's first genuinely successful amusement pier.

Its "world's largest" four-thousand-seat theater, the Hippodrome, at the gateway to the pier, featured such marquee names as British-American entertainer (and mistress

Of Atlantic City's amusements, a virtual reality ride, with the tantalizing name of the Haunted Swing, arrived on the Boardwalk simultaneous to Chicago's holding its 1893 fair and the reading public's lapping up a spate of such gothic-horror novels as Robert Louis Stevenson's *The Strange Case of Dr. Jekyll and Mr. Hyde*, Bram Stoker's *Dracula*, and Oscar Wilde's *The Picture of Dorian Gray*.

Devised by Amariah Lake, a member of a prominent New Jersey family, the Haunted Swing seated twenty people at a time inside its pavilion, in what resembled an open-sided Ferris Wheel car. The vehicle dangled from a steel bar near the ceiling of what otherwise looked like a cozy, Victorian parlor, complete with baby buggy, kerosene lamp, and trophy case.

Once the doors to the chamber were sealed, an attendant began pushing the swing, which rose and fell back and forth, steadily climbing higher and higher, "until…the whole swing seems to whirl over completely, [in] full circle about the bar on which it hangs," read an 1890s explanation. "It continues apparently to go round and round this way, imparting a most weird sensation to its occupant."

After a few 360-degree rotations, the ride would slow to a stop, and its wide-eyed riders would exit.

Moving the ceiling and walls around the car had done the trick, because the car remained stationary. The ride was praised as being "so complete that passengers involuntarily seize the arms of the seats without being precipitated below."

A modern variation, called Houdini's Great Escape, manufactured in 1999 by the Dutch firm Vekoma, exists at Six Flags Great Adventure and Six Flags New England. The German-based Mack Rides also makes what it calls a Mystery Swing, based on the same principle.

The entrance to John L. Young's Million Dollar Pier led the way to his Creatures of the Deep attraction and his private villa, where President William Howard Taft came to dinner in July 1911. Flanking the chief executive are Mr. and Mrs. Young.

of the Prince of Wales) Lillie Langtry, French stage actress Sarah Bernhardt, and, in the midst of seeking reelection, President Theodore Roosevelt. At the wharf's opposite end, a Creatures of the Deep attraction boasted an even greater cast: species from dog sharks to seahorses gathered by twice-daily droppings of a seventeen-hundred-foot deep-sea net. Standing by, to lecture on how humans evolved from the sea, was Young himself, decked out in boater and pantaloons.

The personal appearance was an instant walk from Young's home, given that the pier's centerpiece was his three-story, Italianate villa, whose modest address he selected himself: Number One Atlantic Ocean.

Notable about the residence, other than its over-the-top nautical theme inside and out, was that it was lit from cellar to dome by the same overqualified expert who had wired the rest of the Million Dollar Pier—Young's fishing buddy, Thomas Edison.

WHEN YOUNG, EIGHTY-FIVE, died in 1938 at his winter home in Palm Beach, Florida, management and eventually ownership of his Million Dollar Pier was taken over by George Hamid, a short, stocky, flamboyant presence who began working as

Among the more popular shops on the Boardwalk was one belonging to Enoch James, a confectioner from the Midwest. His specialty was taffy, a gummy sweet concoction of water, sugar, butter, lemon juice, vanilla, and a dash of salt, all cooked in a copper kettle, laid out to cool on a marble slab, and pulled with a hook to aerate, so it would hold its shape.

James packaged his one-inch nuggets in bright papier-mâché cartons that practically sold themselves—only, and this is a sticking point among taffy experts, it was another Atlantic City candy maker, Joseph Fralinger, who pioneered successful taffy merchandising.

Fralinger, a former Philadelphia glassblower, took over an existing candy stand on Applegate Pier in 1884, and stationed his workers in the front windows, so customers could watch the precut, two-inch square candies being wrapped and placed in one-pound oyster boxes.

While James revolutionized the taffy industry by mechanizing the pulling process, rival Fralinger introduced molasses toffee and assorted other flavors.

And so played out the Great Taffy Wars. In the 1990s, a fourth-generation Atlantic City confectioner, Frank Glaser, acquired both brands under the umbrella name James' Candy Company, and, joined by his children, has successfully kept the two labels separate.

Still, the question lingers: How did it come to be called "salt water taffy"?

Legend holds that, in 1883, the store of another Atlantic City confectioner, David Bradley, was flooded by a storm. The entire inventory waterlogged, Bradley lightheartedly asked a little girl, "Want some salt water taffy?"

Introduced to Atlantic City in the early 1880s, salt water taffy became the resort's ceremonial souvenir.

a child, performing for food in the streets of his native Brummana, Lebanon. By age nine, in 1905, he was an experienced trapeze acrobat in his Uncle Abou's traveling circus, which was seen by Buffalo Bill Cody—who imported George and his uncle to America and presented them as "Abou ben Hamid's Tumbling Arabs."

Mentoring the young boy, Cody taught George to shine his (Cody's) shoes and mix his drinks, of which Cody was perilously fond. When creditors shuttered Cody's show in 1913, seventeen-year-old George wound up in the Texas oil business, only to discover it was not his métier. Armed with a valuable list of entertainment contacts, Hamid started booking circus acts, winding up in charge of the New Jersey State Fair at a most propitious time—in the middle of Atlantic City's 1920–1960 golden age, when the town's annual visitor count was sixteen million, greater than the populations of New York City and Philadelphia combined.

For such a well-rounded game, Skee-Ball has a confoundedly checkered past.

Jonathan Dickinson Este, a Princeton graduate from Philadelphia, traditionally is credited with inventing the game, in which a player rolls wooden balls up an alley-like incline. The goal is to sink each ball into one of several holes worth different points, resulting in prize redemptions.

Este, however, did not *invent* Skee-Ball. That prize goes to the Philadelphia-born Joseph Fourestier Simpson, a fiftyish inventor and businessman who lived in Vineland, New Jersey, and was granted a patent for the game on December 8, 1908.

In 1909, Simpson formed a business alliance with William Nice Jr. and John W. Harper, with the latter two taking on the day-to-day of the Skee-Ball Alley Company. Nice died the following year, and the company closed down.

Enter the Princeton grad. "In 1913," said Thaddeus O. Cooper, coauthor of *Seeking Redemption: The Real Story of the Beautiful Game of Skee-Ball*, "Este became interested in purchasing the game after playing it for a number of years."

Installing two alleys in a Princeton pool parlor, and two game alleys across from Atlantic City's Million Dollar Pier, Este "bought the patents and rights" to manufacture and market Skee-Ball, Cooper said.

By 1931, Atlantic City had the first Skee-Ball Stadium, exclusively devoted to the game. National tournaments followed, and the fad never died, as evidenced by Cooper himself.

He became interested in the game's history while playing it on his iPhone.

The numbers racket had been flour-ishing in illegal casinos as early as 1914, when organized-crime bosses first set-tled in and ran Atlantic City as if it were their own piggy bank. From May 13 to 16, 1929, exactly three months after he likely pulled off the St. Valentine's Day Massacre, Chicago kingpin Al Capone gathered the heads of the crime families from Philadelphia, Kansas City, Detroit, New Orleans, and New York to meet in Atlantic City and iron out their differ-ences. Conferring under the guise of a celebration for mob financial-muscle man Meyer Lansky and his new bride, Anna

Prohibition-era boss Enoch "Nucky" Johnson, in straw hat, oversaw illicit operations throughout the resort. Strolling on his arm on the Boardwalk, in May 1929, is a visitor from Chicago, Al Capone. To Al's right is Meyer Lansky.

Citron, the group included Lansky cohort Charlie "Lucky" Luciano and Murder Inc. founder Albert Anastasia.

True to form, it was the charismatic Capone who stood out in the crowd. "The past few nights found him making whoopee, boom-boom or what you have in several of the resort's best-known nightclubs," the Atlantic City *Daily Press* reported during the junket, which also saw Capone rubbing "elbows with police and detectives" at a boxing match.

"The Hollywood images of a corrupt, very wet Atlantic City during Prohibition [are] pretty close to the truth," organized-crime expert Scott M. Deitche said in regard to the 2010 HBO series *Boardwalk Empire*, which was adapted from the 2002 book of the same title by New Jersey Superior Court jurist Nelson Johnson. Both were set during Prohibition, when the town was under the political thumb of Enoch "Nucky" Johnson (renamed Thompson for television, and no relation to Nelson Johnson), and vice was easily accessed in any street, hotel, or bar.

"We have whiskey, wine, women, song, and slot machines," said the real Nucky, not surprisingly sounding like John McKane. "I won't deny it and I won't apologize for it."

Convicted of tax evasion in 1941, Nucky Johnson was sent to prison for four years, then became a salesman for an oil company after his release. As opposed to his shotgun death on premium-cable television, he died peacefully, in 1968.

Three years later, in 1971, the crime bosses effectively lost their grip on Atlantic City, in the wake of a government cleanup to prepare the town for the prospect of legalized gambling.

Nineteen-seventy-one was also the year George Hamid Sr., long vociferous in his drive to rid the town of its criminal element, died of cancer at age seventy-five. For the three previous decades he had worked alongside his son, George Jr., who himself succumbed to natural causes, at ninety-four, in 2013.

Chief among the Hamids' holdings, from the 1940s into the 1970s, was Atlantic

On both page and screen, *Boardwalk Empire* placed heavy emphasis on the racial segregation that divided the resort, a dramatic reality that rang all too true.

Members of the city's large African-American labor force—by 1915, with a total population of fifty-four thousand, 21 percent of Atlantic City was black—were almost entirely relegated to menial jobs in hotel kitchens, or pushing rolling wicker sightseeing chairs along the Boardwalk, unless employed in domestic service in private households, or in minstrel shows on the piers.

They also were effectively penned into their own neighborhoods by police-enforced local and state regulations that suppressed black rights and promoted segregation.

In Atlantic City, these Jim Crow laws, named for a demeaning 1820s blackface minstrel song, "Jump Jim Crow," about a disabled slave, confined African-Americans to their own nightclubs, on Kentucky Avenue, and their own strip of shore on Missouri Avenue, known as Chicken Bone Beach.

These restrictions remained in place from about 1900 until the 1964 Civil Rights Act.

City's most famous venue, the Steel Pier, which first opened at Virginia Avenue on June 18, 1898.

By coincidence, the Steel Pier headliner that first day was the same person who had taught young George Hamid to read and write back when he was still traveling with the Buffalo Bill Cody Wild West show.

Her name was Annie Oakley.

A thirty-minute walk south from the Million Dollar Pier, the Steel Pier was built for $400,000 and advertised as half a mile in length, even if 1,650 feet was more like it. Originally a Sunday gathering place for Quakers who arrived by train from Philadelphia to partake of high-toned cultural activities, the Steel Pier hit its stride in the Roaring Twenties, when automobile salesman Frank P. Gravatt, backed by a syndicate of

The Steel Pier remained a viable national venue into the 1960s.

investors, took over the property for $2 million ($28.6 million today) and began to jazz things up. That meant more rides, more shows, more music, and more movies. Hollywood held its premieres on the Steel Pier, and Broadway its out-of-town tryouts. Television debuted there, in 1929. The next year, Alvin "Shipwreck" Kelly set a world record by sitting for 1,177 hours—forty-nine days and one hour—on a 225-foot-tall Steel Pier pole. A diving bell that lasted for generations submerged riders into water, and loudspeakers blared their echoing cries from inside.

Diving Bells submerged fifteen people at a time to depths as low as thirty feet, either in genuine waters or fish-filled specially built tanks. When the operator flipped a lever, it would release the hydraulic pressure keeping the bell underwater, and send it racing back up to the surface.

"It was fabulous," recalled Emmy-winning television producer Susan Pollock, who grew up in Atlantic City in the 1950s and ran to the Steel Pier with her brother whenever a foggy day happily precluded their going to the beach. "Our mother said we could do anything but the diving bell. She thought it was dangerous." That never stopped them.

During his tenure, Gravatt kept upping the ante. Despite Prohibition, he kept the drinks flowing, the food coming, and the entertainment spinning. Emulating Times Square and foreshadowing Las Vegas, he plastered his pavilions with electric ad signage, such as the General Motors billboard in 1926, presaging corporate sponsorship at amusement parks by decades.

It took only one admission ticket for access to the Steel Pier's food, dance, shows, and rides, and with trapeze artists, boxing kangaroos, a human cannonball, a parakeet that told fortunes (or, at least, plucked a written prediction out of a paper pile) sharing the spotlight with the biggest stars from Broadway, vaudeville, and burlesque (Bud Abbott and Lou Costello performed on the pier early in their partnership), its own baseball team, bears that bicycled, cats that played poker, and a stuffed whale, Gravatt became known as "the Salt Water Barnum," and his Steel Pier "the Playground of the World."

By the time Frank Gravatt sold the Steel Pier in 1945 for $1 million ($13.5 million today), the landmark's assets included five theaters, an ocean stadium that could accommodate five thousand, a marine ballroom for three thousand dancers, an ABC affiliate radio broadcasting studio, and scores of concession stands, exhibit halls, and lounges. The press identified the new owner as a Boston and New York theater concern headed by a New York concessionaire named Abe Ellis, when, in fact, it was George Hamid.

The Society for the Prevention of Cruelty to Animals worked overtime to halt Atlantic City's most popular attraction, the Diving Horses. But the group's inspectors could find no incident of mistreatment, no injuries, and no reason to close the show.

"It was like a thrill ride," said Arnette Webster French, who, when she was sixteen, began the first of five summers on the Steel Pier, horse-diving for W. F. "Doc" Carver, a former marksman in the Buffalo Bill Wild West show. Making $75 a week (slightly more than $1,000 today), she also met her husband, Jacob, on the pier. He piloted the boat for Rex, the Wonder Dog, who waterskied with Arnette.

Mostly, though, she dived with horses, and loved it. "Each time was different."

Her older sister, by nine years, Sonora Webster Carver—she had married "Doc" Carver's son, Albert, in 1928—also rode, and was equally enthusiastic, though she had every right not to be. Her story, told in a 1961 memoir, *A Girl and Five Brave Horses*, became a highly fictionalized 1991 movie, *Wild Hearts Can't Be Broken*, with Gabrielle Anwar as Sonora. (Sonora Webster Carver died in 2003, at age ninety-nine.)

As Arnette remembered the day in 1931 that forever changed her sister's life, the jump went wrong, "and it broke blood vessels in her eyes."

Complaining of eye pain, Sonora saw a doctor, who misdiagnosed her. "He said it will clear up, so she kept on diving."

Sonora had detachment of the retinas. Had she stopped diving even for a few days, she could have eased the pressure on her eyes, and likely would have recovered. Instead, she went permanently blind.

Nevertheless, Sonora continued to horse-dive on the Steel Pier for eleven more years.

"I relish life, and know that there is still much for me to do and to know," Sonora wrote in her memoir, decades after she had confided to her sister. "After all, I've been doing it for six or seven years. I might as well keep doing it."

Horses dived in Atlantic City from the 1920s until 1978. Current attempts to revive the act have been met with vociferous protest.

Rumors circulated that Gravatt refused to sell to someone he considered a carnival promoter, though it was Hamid, as Gravatt's Steel Pier manager in 1939, who landed what had to be the booking of the era, the Harry James Band—at least, as far as that year was concerned. There, for Easter Weekend, James introduced his new vocalist, an untested twenty-four-year-old named Frank Sinatra.

A few months later, on July 16, Hamid also brought the first African-Americans ever to headline on the Steel Pier, the Four Ink Spots.

The Hamids were not always willing to break new ground, however, as evidenced by a phone exchange George Jr. had in February 1957. On the line was a William Morris talent agent offering a new act for that year's Labor Day weekend.

"Look," Hamid told the guy after hearing out his pitch, "America will go for a Pat [Boone], a Perry [Como], a Frank. They'll never go for a guy with a crazy name like Elvis."

Today's Atlantic City is no longer the model city it once was, an all-star victim of overleveraged real estate and bottom-line casino values. The Steel Pier, fairly modern but a shadow of its former self, hangs on. Rides run from the cookie-cutter variety to helicopter charters. Still, the pier does its part to contribute to one jaw-dropping statistic: New Jersey leads the nation in number of theme parks—thirty, beating second-place Tennessee (*Tennessee!*) by one, according to a 2017 study.

Mind you, the survey was conducted by the New Jersey online casino industry.

Whatever the odds, since 1969 a sure bet has been the family-run Morey's Piers & Beachfront Waterparks, encompassing three amusement piers with one hundred rides, two waterparks, and four hotels. Seaside expert James Lilliefors calls the party-hearty Wildwood, New Jersey, spread a "perpetual carnival [with] more rides…than in any other Boardwalk resort."

Topping the list is the 1996 steel inverted Great Nor'Easter, whose 2017 update made it "so smooth, even your grandma will want to ride it," according to second-generation owner Jack Morey, who grew up in Fort Lauderdale but was born in Wildwood, for which he has a wild plan in mind.

It is to build "a really large roller coaster that will connect two piers together. It's really beautiful to look at, and it's all designed."

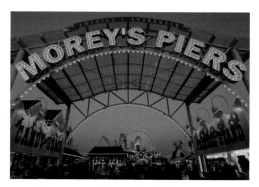

Morey's Piers, in Wildwood, New Jersey, fifty miles from Atlantic City, provide a modern take on the glory days of the older resort.

SNAKES AT A PICNIC

Mary Elitch Long, of Denver, pioneered and persevered.

Mary Elizabeth Hauck Elitch Long never became a parent with either of her two husbands, John Elitch Jr. or Thomas Long, but she did have children. Tens of thousands of them. She also had an ostrich pull her two-wheeled sulky around her sixteen-acre Denver property, a pride of lion cubs that she bottle-fed like housecats until they outgrew her house, and two pet bears named Uncle Sam and Dewey.

In Mary's trailblazing effort to tame the Wild West of the 1890s, her other charges included stray dogs and cats she boarded in her home and another bear that would waltz, although only when the music was right. "Even the snakes receive her sympathy," an observer said of Mary's animal magnetism. (Mary's rationale was "they can't help being poisonous—they were made so.") She was equally maternal about the bushes, trees, and flowers that defined her relatively tiny, but hugely celebrated, Elitch Gardens, and she claimed to know every leaf, bough, and bud by heart.

Generous to a fault, when she wasn't turning over the day's park admissions to the local fireman's brigade or the Elks Lodge or victims of the Cripple Creek flood, Mary was hosting her weekly children's day, when every Tuesday upward of five thousand racially diverse youngsters ran around her popular playground for free and "didn't do a thing but have a good time, swinging [and] traveling…at joyous speed along the circuitous route of the roller coaster," as one journalist wrote.

"I hear a great many entertaining things said by people as they pass by my cottage," said Mrs. Elitch (pronounced "EE-litch"), as she was respectfully addressed. "The other day a little boy and his father were standing out there, and the boy said: 'Papa, if you see Mrs. Elitch while we are here, I want you to show her to me.'" Why was the child so curious? "I know she's different from anybody else," he said.

Mary's individuality extended to the manner in which she conducted her business. Should a bill happen to arrive on a day there was money in the bank, she would pay it. Heaven help those creditors whose invoices arrived on the wrong day.

Some waited patiently. Others complained bitterly. But Mary determinedly went about her day-to-day duties.

If only she had paid her taxes.

One month after Mary Elizabeth Hauck's birth on May 10, 1856, in Philadelphia, the city played host to the first-ever Republican Convention. As its presidential candidate, the brand-new party nominated John C. Frémont, a former senator from the freshly minted State of California. He became rich in the 1849 Gold Rush that had propelled that far western territory toward statehood. Although Frémont ended up losing the general election to the Democratic candidate James Buchanan (at their next convention, the Republicans would nominate a lawyer from Illinois named Abraham Lincoln), the spirit of the wide-open West was fueling all quarters of the nation, including the Hauck household.

Given the size of the family, it was easy to see why. Mary was the eldest of Frederick and Augustine Hauck's six children. In 1859, when Mary was nearly three, the Haucks relocated to northern California, where Frederick raised livestock and fruit trees.

Mary was sent to the Sisters of Notre Dame convent boarding school in San Francisco, and, with her Presbyterian parents' blessing, was baptized Catholic at age thirteen.

Three years later, in 1872, without their blessing, she married John Elitch Jr.

Despite their new son-in-law's lineage—his ancestor, Colony of Rhode Island governor Stephen Hopkins, had signed the Declaration of Independence—Mary's parents saw little reason to approve of John Elitch Jr. For starters, he was six years older than their sixteen-year-old daughter and something of a dreamer. Still, their protests were outweighed, given John's muscles, dark, curly hair, and deep blue eyes.

John Elitch was born in Mobile, Alabama, eleven years before the outbreak of the Civil War, and it has been recorded that his father, John Sr., heroically served under William Rosecrans, the Union general who led the northern troops from Ohio. (This is likely an inflated account, which Mary helped promote.) John Jr. did have an Ohio connection: As a child, he was taken to the Cincinnati Zoo, where, as his wife later romanticized it, he fell in love with the idea of someday owning his own collection of animals.

Mary Hauck married John Elitch, partly, she said, because she never cared for her maiden name.

During Reconstruction, John moved to San Francisco with aspirations of becoming an actor.

When reality set in, he landed the role of restaurant manager at Manning's Oyster Grotto.

≈

EIGHT YEARS INTO THEIR marriage, during which John squandered their savings by investing in a traveling vaudeville show that flopped, the Elitches abandoned San Francisco for Durango, Colorado, recently established as the point of origin for the new Denver and Rio Grande Railroad. Trains meant a steady stream of mouths to feed, and, after first taking a job at a café, John opened his own restaurant.

"Lacking real competition, John struck it rich," according to Colorado author Rosemary Fetter. "With $4,000 profit, he returned to San Francisco and lost everything in another theatrical venture."

Once again in search of emerald pastures, the Elitches settled upon the former mining town of Denver, where John's quest for a suitable venture ended up taking five years, until the day he surprised his wife with the deed to what would be called the Elitch Palace Dining Room. *Palatial* may have been an exaggeration, but among its appointments were Mary's paintings—she had been studying art—though everyone concerned knew the real reason travelers, miners, publishers, politicians, and railroad magnates frequented the establishment: The Elitch Palace had the longest bar in Denver.

According to lore, among those who bellied up to the bar was the renowned teetotaler P. T. Barnum. By the time Elitch Gardens officially opened, the great showman was said to be such a devoted friend of the Elitches' that Mary claimed he "was nearly as excited as we were."

He must also have given her a few good lessons in humbug.

≈

IN ANOTHER SURPRISE MOVE, this time in 1888, John took the profits from the Elitch Palace and sank them into Martha and William Chilcott's sixteen-acre farm five miles northwest of town in an area called the Highlands, or, as Mary called it, "something of a wilderness." The purchase gave her the trees she always had wanted— cottonwoods and an entire apple orchard—and John a sizable vegetable patch to grow his own provisions for a restaurant. Adjacent to their property was an unexpected bonus (perhaps not that unexpected, given the Highland's sizable population of five thousand): the Denver and Berkeley Park Rapid Transit line's newly laid track, connecting the steam-driven tramway from the Highlands to central Denver. For John and Mary, here was a chance to turn their acreage into a commercial property, even if they did not know exactly quite what that should be—for Mary, a garden, surely; but, for John, a restaurant? A theater? A zoo?

Mrs. Elitch Long-Elitch Gardens, Denver, Colo.

Mary's original intention was to provide a cool, green oasis—for her animals.

Mary chose to pattern her park after hotel owner Robert B. Woodward's eponymous gardens on his San Francisco estate, where, along the tracks of his horse-trolley line at Mission and Thirteenth Streets, lush greenery, floral displays, and picnic areas shared two city blocks with a roller rink, an art museum, an aquatic merry-go-round, and a grizzly bear in his own cave. At Woodward's Gardens, women and children felt secure (the bear cave was fenced), and unlike the Elitch Palace, no intoxicating beverages were served. (Much to Mary's dismay, John sold the Elitch Palace to people who renamed it Tortoni's, thereby eliminating any possible fallback should the Elitches' new enterprise fail.)

Preparations moved apace. A steam-powered carousel came later, but by opening day, customers could count on swings, slides, seesaws, and rides in carts drawn by goats that Mary had given such names as Myrna, Maude, Leland, and Sherman. "We placed our rustic gate advantageously for the convenience of visitors arriving from 'town,'" Mary said about the front entrance, which gave visitors the impression of entering her world through a giant log cabin. Architecture inside veered toward Victorian gingerbread. A soda-fountain booth and a confectionary pavilion complemented the main restaurant, the Orchard Café.

The main selling point that first season, besides Mary's budding botanical gardens, was Elitch's distinction as America's only zoo west of Chicago—with animals, it was said, that were courtesy of P. T. Barnum. John appointed Mary guardian of the bears, lion cubs, monkeys, and ostrich, while he built their enclosures alongside the flowerbeds, bandshell gazebo, and fountains that she had placed around the wide, curved cement walkways.

"John Elitch designed the theater based on some idea he had as to what the Old Globe Theatre in London looked like," said Kevin Causey, who until 2007 served as the artistic director of an ambitious $14.2 million plan to restore the more-than-century-old structure. "He also got it very wrong."

As it was, the two-story, octagonal Theatorium, designed to John's specifications and crowned by a castle-like cupola, would not be ready to hold its first performance until the park's second season, in 1891.

Only by then, John Elitch was no longer around.

While John and Mary were still articulating plans for their property, a businessman named John Brisben Walker already had established himself on the scene.

Armed with a full résumé—Georgetown College and West Point graduate, soldier in China, iron manufacturer in West Virginia, publisher in Cincinnati and Washington, DC—along with an arsenal of ready cash, the native Pennsylvanian grabbed up five hundred lots in Colorado's Platte Valley and, sometime in the 1880s, opened the first amusement park in Denver and, more than likely, the first in the entire West.

"People were magnetically drawn to him because he was extremely handsome," the essayist and poet Helen Seeley Phillips wrote of Walker, whom she also found sincere, charming, and "the best darn alfalfa grower in America."

Walker provided his Riverfront Park with a racetrack, a world's fair–like pavilion called the Castle of Culture & Commerce, weekly fireworks, a baseball diamond, a toboggan slide,

John Brisben Walker made and lost fortunes, only to make them back again. With one, he built the first amusement park in the West, Riverfront Park.

an excursion steamer, and a five-thousand-capacity grandstand arena that housed the state's first rodeo.

Then, as was his nature—thrice married and twice widowed, Walker was the father of twelve children, which might explain his need for an amusement park—the restless entrepreneur sold his interest to the city of Denver in 1893 and moved to New York, where he bought *Cosmopolitan* magazine, built up its circulation, then, in 1905, sold it to William Randolph Hearst.

By then, Riverfront Park had been out of business for two years.

John and Mary's opening day, May 1, 1890, arrived and, with it, disaster. After their investment of time, money, and full-page newspaper ads, Elitch's Zoological Gardens—as it was first called, with a prominent photograph of John's profile dominating its logo—looked doomed to sink into the mud.

"I was filled with grief and disappointment," Mary remembered, "for rain was falling." Not just rain. A deluge. As John and Mary watched the downpour from the corner of Thirty-Eighth Avenue and Tennyson Street, they saw no sign of a single tram or buggy. Only rain.

Then, suddenly, the sound of galloping hooves broke the silence and a horseman presented himself. "Open up everything!" shouted the rider, who identified himself as Samuel C. Dorsey, of the Denver City Tramway Company. All of Denver, he said, was heading to the park.

And so it seemed, not only by train, but also by coach, carriage, bicycle, and foot. Among the faces in the crowd, according to Mary and nearly every report since, including one on the current Elitch Gardens website, was that of "Mr. Elitch's close personal friend, P. T. Barnum" and, as the guests of the impresario, the show-business headliners "Mr. and Mrs. Stratton, beloved of their public as General and Mrs. Tom Thumb." The only problem with that anecdote, no matter its source, is that by the time Elitch Gardens opened, the "most famous of the little family of liliputians [sic] introduced by P. T. Barnum to the sight-seeing world," as the New York Times described the two-foot, eleven-inch Tom Thumb, had been dead for seven years.

Regardless, it was an auspicious May Day, with much to celebrate: Elitch Gardens profitably got off the ground; between eight thousand and ten thousand customers (at a dime a head) continued to come Sundays after church, and by the end of the summer, $35,000 was sitting in the till—only not for long.

A downpour kept Denver's citizens from showing up for Elitch's 1890 opening day, but only until the clouds lifted.

John found another vaudeville troupe in which to invest: the Elitch, Schilling & Goodyear's Traveling Minstrels. John did not only bankroll the enterprise; he costarred, traveled the West, and used it to justify leaving Mary in Denver with only her animals. At least this time he was drawing a crowd. A favorable review in the February 25, 1891, *Los Angeles Herald* called the production "a decided novelty," and the singing "exceptionally fine."

From Los Angeles, the troupe moved to San Francisco's Alcazar Theater, where, two nights into the engagement, John developed a fever. Mary received a telegram, journeyed by train, and stayed at John's bedside until March 10, when, at age forty-one, he succumbed to pneumonia.

Mary was a widow at thirty-four.

"The death of my husband left me with our great venture still something of an experiment, in spite of its one successful season," said Mary, "but having been imbued with his vision…I determined to carry on." Besides, John had exhausted their money on his minstrels.

A narrow-gauge train was but one addition Mary made to her gardens in 1899. A second husband was another.

Snakes escaped their pit one day when Mary's zookeeper forgot to feed them. Finding what they wanted on the picnic grounds, "the serpents" caused "wild shrieks" among the picnickers, who "scrambled to their feet," said Mary.

On her own, Mary proved herself. Record attendance was set in 1893, and the following year, Mary bought back the investors' shares and expanded the park to twenty-eight acres, including the original sixteen purchased by John. Adding "a splendid baseball field" and "thirty healthy rattlesnakes" to her queendom, she afterward recalled a crowded picnic being interrupted by an infestation of "harmless snakes" that had escaped their pen. Once the screams subsided, "peace was restored," Mary insisted, "and the 'victims' hailed as heroes and heroines forever after."

In 1896 and 1897, respectively, Mary brought two famous names to her park: Thomas Edison, in the guise of his Vitascope projection system—making Mary the first movie exhibitor in the West—and the renowned daredevil balloonist Ivy Baldwin.

A Houston native who resettled in Denver, the former William Ivy was born in 1866, and by age eleven he was employed as an aerialist by P. T. Barnum. His stage name came about when he joined a two-man balloon act calling itself the Baldwin Brothers.

A wiry five foot three and a half and 120 pounds, Baldwin was built for flight, as he demonstrated at showtime.

Once airborne at three thousand feet, he would pretend to get caught in the balloon ropes, sending the crowd below into a panic and himself into high gear. Dangling by his toes from a bar above the passenger basket, "he would then turn loose of the bar, fall about sixty feet, pull a parachute out of a sack, and descend, hanging by his knees," one aviation journal excitedly documented.

For the Fourth of July at Elitch's, Baldwin—who would die in bed at the ripe old age of eighty-three—lit fireworks strapped to his back and then hurled himself to the ground, feet first.

Celebrated aerialist Ivy Baldwin worked for Barnum before taking flight for Mary.

She also established her theater as the nation's first home of summer stock and a springboard for future stars. Barely into his teens, an eager volunteer named Douglas Ullman got his first break when he was handed a mop and told to scrub the playhouse stage. Later, in Hollywood, he would wield something better suited to his nature—a sword—and go by the name of Douglas Fairbanks. The DeMille Brothers, William and the younger and more ambitious Cecil, acted at Elitch's in 1905. A year later, when Sarah Bernhardt's San Francisco venue was destroyed by a 7.9-magnitude earthquake, the world's most celebrated actress performed both *Camille* and *La Sorcière* in a single day under Mary's aegis.

A later Elitch coaster, the 1926–1935 Sky Rocket.

The gracious lady of the gardens also convinced the grande dame of the stage to stroke the head of one of Mary's pet lions.

Ever after, the furry feline was called Sarah.

An additional lifeline from the city was extended in 1899: Transit rails to Elitch Gardens were tripled and trolley cars went electric. In her own reenergizing effort, Mary offered shares in her business and raised $300,000 (nearly $9 million today), which she put toward an electric generator, lighting and landscaping upgrades, a penny arcade, a narrow-gauge railroad, and a Coney Island–quality staging of the Civil War naval battle between the *Monitor* and the *Merrimac*. Mary also recharged her personal life; she married one of her box office employees, the much younger (by thirteen years) Thomas Long. Following a November 1900 wedding in her Gardens residence, the two set off on a six-month honeymoon. SAT ON THE FLOOR IN A JAPANESE THEATER AND CLIMBED VESUVIUS. RODE ELEPHANTS IN INDIA, CAMELS IN EGYPT, BUT LIKES DENVER TROLLEY CARS BEST, read the headline in the *Denver Republican* that marked her return.

In the park's off-season months, the couple continued to travel, generally to see the latest plays in San Francisco or New York, with Coney Island squeezed into a 1903 itinerary. There, according to accounts, she rode a figure eight Toboggan Coaster, not once but twice.

Adjusting her hat and tightening its pin after the first attempt, she reportedly declared, before ordering a figure eight for her own park, "Let's do it again!"

RIDING THE WAVE

Having established himself as Neptune's successor, Paul Boyton was about to enter fresh waters. Watchtower Park, in Rock Island, Illinois, opened in 1882, when the former horse trader and banker Bailey Davenport linked the property, which he owned, to the Rock Island and Milan Steam and Horse Railway Company streetcar line, which he also owned. Davenport's property primarily offered musical concerts, greens for tennis and croquet, and a medicinal spring. Sometime before 1889, local inventor John P. Newburg brought a game changer to Watchtower called the Shoot the Chutes, sometimes Shooting the Chutes, and, usually, simply, the Chutes. A refinement on the old Saut du Niagara at the Jardin Ruggieri in Paris, it became the Illinois park's most popular attraction.

"Fearless Frogman" Paul Boyton purchased patent and marketing rights to a variation on Saut du Niagara, called the Shoot the Chutes.

The Shoot the Chutes took passengers in a flat-bottomed boat to the top of a bluff via a cable powered by the streetcar line. Once at the apex, a turntable reversed the boat's direction before discharging it five hundred feet down a greased double track made of oak to the Rock River below. A conductor aboard the boat (more of a gondolier, really) then returned the passengers to the loading dock, where the next set of customers would begin their turn on what William F. Mangels classified "the first American water amusement ride."

"Intrigued by the simple ride," said Jim Futrell, historian for the National Amusement Park Historical Association, "Boyton purchased the rights."

FORMED BY BOYTON AND partner John Newburg to manufacture and distribute Shoot the Chutes domestically and across the Atlantic, the Paul Boyton Company of New York sold the devices for between $8,000 ($217,000 today) and $16,000, depending on size. The first installation, at the 1893 Earl's Court Exhibition Centre, London, delivered "wild delights," as a writer for a philatelist publication said of his experience. (He had been on his way to the Juniors' Exhibition of United States postage stamps.)

Elsewhere in Britain, Chutes were established at expos and seaside pleasure piers, including Tower Grounds, New Brighton. The following year, 1894, Boyton took an even bolder plunge. On the Fourth of July, he opened Paul Boyton's Water Chute Park in Chicago, at Sixty-Third Street and Cottage Grove Avenue, not far from where

PAUL BOYTON'S
WATER CHUTE.
THE SENSATION OF
LONDON and of the
ANTWERP
EXPOSITION.
A NOVEL and....
FASCINATING
PASTIME FOR
EVERY-
BODY.

Have You Shot the Chutes ?

★
Open
TO=
DAY
and every day and even-
ing, Sunday included.
Corner 63d-st. and
Cottage Grove-av.
Admission including ride.... 25c
Additional rides, 10c.
Music by 2d Regiment Band.

Chicago, July 4, 1894: Paul Boyton opened his Water Chute Park, the first amusement park where the primary focus was on mechanical rides.

the Chicago Fair Midway had prevailed a year earlier. The intent was to rekindle the excitement of that most popular aspect of the expo, which Chute Park achieved with flying colors. It attracted more than five hundred thousand customers its first season; in its third season, it moved to a larger, seven-and-a-half-acre location, at Jackson Boulevard and Kedzie Avenue.

"The receipts during the first short season of the Chicago chute," the *Transit Journal* reported in March 1902, "were about $40,000," or $1.1 million today. "Chutes in Baltimore, Atlantic City, Atlanta, and San Francisco have all been similarly successful, some of these exceeding $2,600 in a single day." Tickets typically sold for a dime each.

Soon after the Chutes' arrival, a concern called the Aquarama Company produced the Aquarama, or Old Mill, "similar in general plan to the scenic railway," said the trade article, "except that the traveler rides by water in a boat, which floats in a shallow canal, the flow in which is provided by a water-wheel."

"The Old Mill sacrificed speed and the illusion of peril for darkness and mass privacy," reported journalists Oliver Pilat and Jo Ranson, who seemed to have as much sly fun at their typewriters as passengers had on the ride. "Three times through the Old Mill was considered equivalent to an engagement ring, and sometimes once did the trick."

Despite the separate manufacturers, some parks interwove Thompson's Scenic Railway with Aquarama's Old Mill, permitting the scenery to be shared, and the rider "taken down the Rhine and up the Nile at a cost of only 5 or 10 cents, and view, at the same time and without leaving his seat, Blarney Castle, the Pyramids, and the Parthenon," said the *Transit Journal.*

Eventually, the Philadelphia Toboggan Company attempted to combine the Railway's descents and rises in boat form, calling it the Mill Chute, a sort of grandparent

The Original and the Only Real Thing

L. A. THOMPSON SCENIC RAILWAY,

Which Combines all that is Necessary or Required for

An Enormously Profitable Investment.

Having NOVELTY, EXCITEMENT, EXHILARATION and ABSOLUTE SAFETY.

Always built upon SCIENTIFIC PRINCIPLES by Experienced Workmen under the Careful Supervision of the THOMPSON COMPANY.

L. A. THOMPSON
Scenic ⋅ Railway ⋅ Company.

308-4 BROADWAY, NEW YORK CITY.

LaMarcus Thompson's Scenic Railways elevated his stature and expanded his global reach.

of the later Log Flume, "but the motion of sailing through the route by water is considered pleasanter by some."

Attention paid the Chutes brought new recognition to Boyton, as champion of a show-stopping fun engine that, with its mechanical rides, dispensed one continuous thrill after another.

Furthermore, he located his amusement park not by the usual beach or inside a wooded picnic grove, but within an urban setting.

Foremost, he was the first to charge admission.

FRESH FROM MAKING HIS mark in the Midwest, Boyton replicated his Chutes Park in Coney Island in 1895.

Only larger.

The Frogman's foray into Gravesend began when he leased sixteen boggy acres at West Twelfth Street and Neptune Avenue, adjacent to the Elephant Hotel, a year before it burned down. He then added rides, including his signature Chutes and, later, an improved Flip-Flap Railroad (fewer broken necks), along with a new element, to underscore the proximity to the ocean.

"A park has been established at Coney Island called Sea Lion Park, where these animals are trained," said a streetcar journal, explaining, too, how the mammals had been captured by Boyton's private schooner.

New York, July 4, 1895: Paul Boyton opened his Sea Lion Park, Coney Island's first amusement park to be fenced in with a front gate.

Among the attractions at Boyton's Water Chute Park, besides Chicago's first miniature railroad, a carousel, and a giant swing, was the Loop-the-Loop coaster, first launched in 1848, in Paris's Frascati Garden, where, despite being imported from England, it was accorded the Jules Vernian title of Chemin du Centrifuge (Path of Centrifuge).

Later names were the Flip-Flap, or Topsy-Turvy.

Given its 150-miles-an-hour speed—although that sounds apocryphal—and the fact that the track and the ride's dimensions (thirteen feet in diameter, 248 feet high) were unique, its first test passenger's reaction was deemed newsworthy.

"While going down he could see everything around him," reported the *Journal du Havre*, "but within the loop he was unable to see anything."

The passenger was lucky.

"The ride had a flaw," said coaster expert Robert Cartmell. "It snapped passengers' necks."

Loop the Loop roller coasters got off to a treacherous start.

Boyton next did what no one in Coney Island had ever dared before, not even Austin Corbin: He wrapped a fence around his entire property, to keep out the undesirable element.

Respectable people would pay a dime to get in.

〜

IMPRESSED WITH BOYTON'S FENCE and signature ride, George Tilyou sought a park of his own, and a worthy rival of the Shoot the Chutes. Casting about for ideas, he "heard of a British invention—a mechanical racehorse," said his grandson, pointing to the logic of George's interest. "The most popular sport of the times was, by all odds, horseracing." Certainly that was the case at Coney, where the three local tracks drew crowds six months out of the year.

"We Britishers have been famed from time immemorial as breeders of racers," read a 1902 *Royal Magazine* account of the new Gravity Steeplechase invention by one John William Cawdery. The periodical suggested that the London-born stage designer, machinist, and inventor may "have further improved the breed. By a simple but ingenious device he has done away with the necessity for racing stable, trainer, and all other costly equipments. For—you may have guessed it already—his steeds are made of wood!"

Weighing two hundred pounds apiece, Cawdery's horses "trot, jump, and gallop, and are able to carry two to three riders at the same time," reported *Royal Magazine*'s Leonard W. Lillingston, surveying the track at Alexandra Palace, north London's answer to the Crystal Palace. The correspondent was particularly taken with the fact that Cawdery's replicas "present more than a tolerable likeness to the real animal."

Flip-Flap roller coaster designer Lina Beecher, a former Civil War captain and railroad man from Batavia, New York, began experimenting with wooden looping tracks in 1888. He improved his ride in 1904 with the introduction of an elliptical steel loop—oval, rather than circular—that reduced the G-force and its strain.

In between, manufacturer Edwin Prescott had introduced an elliptical track coaster in Coney Island in 1901, and a sister version on Young's Million Dollar Pier in Atlantic City.

Beecher, meanwhile, never ceased to create, and, in 1901, was paid tribute by *Munsey's Magazine* for his monorail system, whose cars were "lighted and heated by electricity…four feet in width…built of aluminum, and…lined with asbestos, to make it positively fire proof." This was in the days before the fire retardant was identified as a carcinogen.

As for the monorail's design, "It is little more than a projectile, pointed at the end, and is as smooth on its surface as polished steel. It contains twelve sections of four seats each, and also an observation section in the rear end, with two seats, which gives it a carrying capacity of fifty people. Entrance to these sections is from the side."

No fear of claustrophobia, either: "Each passenger has a window seat."

Improvements in safety design allowed for looping coasters in Coney Island and Atlantic City (here) by 1901, although not all the kinks were worked out.

Heavier riders were said to have had the advantage, and, in the speed department, Cawdery's ponies were no slackers. Warned a billboard at a bend in the track, before the water jump, "WHAT HO! HOLD TIGHT HERE."

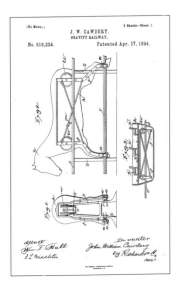

"The course is graded like the course of a switch-back railway," Lillingston wrote, "with successive hills and valleys to enable a good, but not a dangerous, speed to be kept up." The gift of gravity, he assured, "sees horse and rider safely to the end of their ride."

Not everyone was so captivated. In the midst of Cawdery's hunt for investors, the *Saturday Review of Politics, Literature, Science, and Art* raised a red flag. "For this glorified form of *petits chevaux* [little horses] the vendors are asking the modest sum of £40,000, half in cash and half in fully paid-up shares," it said. "In our opinion this price is exorbitant, and we should advise investors to think more than twice before forwarding their shillings to 23 Coleman Street."

Nevertheless, George Tilyou forwarded $41,000, the equivalent of $1.2 million today, to the Coleman Street offices, and bought the North American rights to Cawdery's Patent Steeplechase, Limited.

"To one of his indomitable nature," nineteenth-century Long Island historian Peter Ross said of thirty-five-year-old George Tilyou, "success must eventually come." And so it did, starting with his improved adaptation of the Cawdery tracked attraction. Buying up thirty-five parcels of land, Tilyou developed what he called—at least in the press releases—"655,000 square feet" (fifteen acres) in Coney Island's Bowery, at the corner of Ocean and Surf Avenues, between Sixteenth and Nineteenth Streets. The spectacle kicked off in spring 1897.

Tilyou called it Steeplechase Park.

In preparing his park's centerpiece, Tilyou spent $37,000, of which $20,000 went simply to test out what his ads promised would be "half a mile in half a minute, and fun all the time." Eight double-saddled mechanical horses were fastened atop the rolling, one-thousand-foot track that encircled the perimeter of his park, racing over a stream and past several hurdles before returning riders to an enclosed central pavilion, which housed what was christened the Blowhole Theatre.

There a barrage of indignities awaited them.

Disembarking Steeplechase riders were forced to grope their way through a dimly lit maze until they could stumble upon a brightly lit platform marked "Insanitarium." A gusting airshaft would next expose women's ankles, if not more, while their dates, forced to chase their hats in the wind, if they hadn't already forfeited them to the ride, were accosted by aggressive small men dressed as clowns, or else tall men in blackface

Imported from England, Coney's Steeplechase attracted real jockeys, who would "ride those horses in dead earnest, wagering on the outcome," said George Tilyou's nephew.

makeup. These greeters were armed with electrically charged pokers, empowering them to zap the hapless fellows in their most sensitive of places.

"The management has thoughtfully provided several hundred seats for patrons wishing to observe," the *New Yorker* noted, in 1928, of the two-decade-old, and still going strong, Steeplechase, "and the gallery, mostly but not exclusively stag, has a swell time." While the goings-on were meant to shock the early patrons to the park during the Victorian era, the Jazz Age *New Yorker* deemed the spectacle "good clean fun. Moreover, an attendant said that most of the feminine sex like the air-holes, that it was impossible to keep some women away from them."

The ceremonious main entrance to Steeplechase Park faced Surf Avenue and presented a tall, plaster arch crowned by statues of four charging horses. On the west side of the gateway was a United States Post Office, and to the east, Tilyou's Hotel. Those entering from the southern side, at the ocean, needed to brave the Barrel of Fun, a large, slowly rotating cylinder that sent couples toppling over one another as they struggled to walk through.

To add to the companionable ambience, and to protect customers' clothing—this was in the day when people dressed up to take an excursion—Tilyou rented out Pierrot-like costumes, so everyone could play the part of a clown.

"I calculated," said Tilyou, "that the American people didn't mind an occasional joke on themselves if it was a good-natured joke."

As owner of America's first grand amusement park—and, for all its naughtiness, an alcohol-free and family-friendly one, at that—George Tilyou dubbed his enterprise "the Funny Place," and for a mascot devised a maniacally smiling jester whose sardonic grin with thirty-eight teeth (in some portrayals, forty-four) made him look like *Mad* magazine's Alfred E. Neuman possessed by the Devil. People nicknamed him Tillie and Steeplechase Jack.

The "ten hours' fun for ten cents" admission not only got the working-stiff customer through the gate, but it included all rides, many of which Tilyou designed himself: "the earthquake floor, the skating floor, the falling statue, the blow hole, the electric fountain, the razzle dazzle, the pneumatic gun, the third degree regions, the electric seat, the hoodoo room, the human cage, the California bats, puzzle hall, the revolving seat, the eccentric fountain, the art room, and the maze," Peter Ross wrote in his Long Island history. He withheld any explanation of these contraptions, because, in his view, "The very names pique curiosity and the realization is in every instance more than the anticipation dreamed."

The California Bats, which cost Tilyou all of five dollars, turned out to be nothing more than a collection of broken bricks in a box that customers would discover after an elaborate treasure hunt, although the Human Cage relied on no such Barnum-like gimmicks. It let people loose in an enclosure full of monkeys.

As an example of how his ancestor let the public amuse themselves, Tilyou's grandson, Edo McCullough, cited the Razzle Dazzle, also known as the Wedding Ring or Hoop-La, "a great circle of laminated wood suspended by wires from a center pole." Seventy people could swing back and forth as "four muscular and acrobatic attendants" pushed it. When women grabbed their escorts for fear of falling off, up went their skirts; thus the name, Hoop-La!

Tilyou's Barrel of Love was a much-scaled-down adaptation of the Switchback Railway, with passengers "strapped into seats in a revolving drum that rolled gently down one incline and up another." Its (slightly bewildering) slogan was "Talk about love in a cottage! This has it beat by a mile!"

The Dew Drop was a circuitous, fifty-foot slide that ultimately dumped riders onto pillows, while the Earthquake Stairway was a collapsible platform that no

Steeplechase Park also could be entered through the Bowery, a narrow alleyway created by the Tilyous in the 1890s. Originally called Ocean Walk Avenue, its five blocks ran from Jones Walk to West Sixteenth Street.

modern insurance company would allow today. Similarly, the Human Roulette Wheel placed seated passengers on a large, circular revolving platform until the increasing speed spun them off of it as they—sometimes, their dentures first—went sailing across the floor. Tilyou came up with the idea when he saw young boys playing on the beach after they had contrived a makeshift spinning platform and put it atop the wheel of an overturned cart.

"One simply has to decide in what manner he prefers to be made uncomfortable," *Munsey's Magazine* observed, "for it is Coney Island's claim to celebrity that she is prepared to make you so in a variety of ways approaching infinity."

Noteworthy about the remark is the use of the term *Coney Island*—no longer as an umbrella term for sun and surf beach resort, as had been the case for a lifetime.

Now, *Coney Island* had a narrow, new definition.

It could only mean "amusement park."

"The Steeplechase face changed many times over the years, and sometimes there were several faces found throughout the park," said Michael P. Onorato, whose father ran Steeplechase Park from 1928 until its closure, in 1964. "The face became standardized in the late 1940s, when all former faces were removed."

In his sidesplitting 1928 *Speedy*, Harold Lloyd (as the accident-prone Harold) takes girlfriend Jane (Ann Christy) to Coney. Besides giving himself the finger in a funhouse mirror—believed to be the vulgar gesture's cinematic debut—Harold and Jane also braved the Human Roulette Wheel.

CATCHING CLOUDS

I.

Not wishing to face the same box office slump Paul Boyton suffered because the Fearless Frogman let his Sea Lion Park go stale, George Tilyou routinely added new thrills to Steeplechase Park. To Tilyou's thinking, a lavish stage spectacle might entice customers once, but a mechanical ride would bring 'em back for more. (His advice to his son, Frank, was "never hire an attraction that can eat or talk back.")

For Steeplechase, the add-ons meant natural gas–powered boats in "Venetian" canals, a miniature train to wind through the grounds, and a $40,000 LaMarcus Thompson Scenic Railway. Marking the inventor's comeback in Brooklyn, the ride proved so popular that Thompson eventually dislodged it from Tilyou and ran it independently himself, as he did with another, and even more successful, Scenic Railway, Pike's Peak. Thompson also improved his cable lift by switching its power system from smoky steam to clean electric. In fact, he became so entrenched in the Brooklyn amusement capital that he established a factory on Coney Island's Eighth Street, as did William F. Mangels.

"The reprehensible and degradin' resorts that disgraced old Coney are said to be wiped out," carped the leading character in "The Greater Coney," an O. Henry short story that took place after gentrification was set in motion. "The wipin'-out process consists of raisin' the price from 10 cents to 25 cents, and hirin' a blonde named Maudie to sell the tickets instead of Mickey, the Bowery Bite."

Steeplechase Park installed a large, saltwater swimming pool and a ballroom large enough for four bands so the music would never stop. Its owner, meanwhile, having already struck a deal with public transit to deposit streetcar passengers directly at his front archway, also added Steeplechase Pier to stream in customers arriving by boat and lead them away from rival concessionaires.

Steeplechase Park owner George Tilyou knew the public constantly craved something new, a concept his fellow park owner, Paul Boyton, failed to grasp.

Steeplechase Park's Pavilion of Fun (here, circa 1912) was built of concrete, iron, and glass, so it could withstand the destructive elements of wind, rain, and fire.

"Tilyou had a vision of a new kind of space where all the world would be on display," said modern architecture professor Michael J. Ostwald, who credits the showman for launching "the twentieth-century amusement park obsession with spatial and cultural simulation." Whether by design or convenience, Tilyou placed "a scale replica of the Eiffel Tower adjacent to a scale replica of Big Ben, thereby seeming to remove all the wasted space and time travel needed to visit the world's monuments."

Perhaps even more commercially, he placed couples in each other's laps on his runaway success, the Steeplechase. "Always the master of effect," said modern amusement park historian Paul Ruben, "Tilyou dressed his attendants as jockeys and announced the start of each ride with a bugle." Two million customers heeded the call in the first two years of the ride, and Tilyou sold facsimiles to parks elsewhere.

On the back of the Steeplechase's profits, Tilyou established other New York amusement properties and more in New Jersey, Massachusetts, Connecticut, and Missouri.

Some he named Steeplechase Park, but all of them featured the same, familiar logo with the leering, libidinous Funny Face—laughing all the way to the bank.

Across the country, others looked to cash in, too.

II.

While their glittering heydays would beam brightest in the early years of the twentieth century, amusement parks became a definitive part of the American routine beginning in the mid-1890s, rounding out people's lives with leisure hours—or, "nonproductive consumption of time," as defined by sociologist Thorstein Veblen.

Between 1910 and 1920—when such terms as *leisure time*, *vacation*, and even *paid vacation* first entered the vernacular—some two thousand amusement parks blanketed the country, grounding twentieth-century America's resolve to do things bigger and better, and solidifying President Theodore Roosevelt's conviction that "play is a fundamental need." These were permanent playgrounds, too, as opposed to itinerant carnivals and circuses, or county and state fairs, whose yearly operations, while memorable, were short-term.

Attracting sizable crowds and illuminating the landscape at a time when most American homes had yet to be wired for electricity, these gaily festooned mechanical dreamlands provided what 1920s *Baltimore Sun* columnist H. L. Mencken correctly categorized as an "escape from the horrors of reality"—with the escapes not limited to freewheeling beaches or high-density urban areas.

Near Salt Lake City, Utah, the Church of Jesus Christ of Latter-day Saints and Montana copper baron William Andrews Clark's Los Angeles & Salt Lake Railroad opened Saltair on May 30, 1893, to provide, in the words of Mormon apostle Abraham H. Cannon, "a wholesome place of recreation" under the watchful eye of church elders.

"They also intended that Saltair be a 'Coney Island of the West,' to help demonstrate that Utah was not a strange place of alien people and customs," said Utah historian John S. McCormick, admitting the incompatibility of the words *wholesome* and *Coney Island*. Nevertheless, the lakeside compound set up facilities for both swimming and dancing (women and men together), along with coasters (at one point, three), a carousel, Ferris Wheel, vaudeville shows, rodeos, midway games, boating, bicycle races, and, by the '20s, twelve hot dog stands. The focal point, an onion-domed

The Mormon Church and a Montana copper baron built Saltair in Salt Lake City, the "Coney Island of the West," only to come under fire for selling stimulants and remaining open on Sundays.

Spanish Fort, the Coney Island of New Orleans, La.

Signs at Spanish Fort, New Orleans's "Coney Island of the South," warned, "When your Desire for Mischief is too Strong to Resist, be careful that a Police Officer does not see you."

Moorish-fantasy main pavilion, with gingerbread adorning, was the work of the state's leading architect, Richard K. A. Kletting.

Despite the financial rewards, the Church found it better to focus on doctrine, and sold Saltair to a business group in 1906, which rebuilt it after a fire, in 1925. Rowdyism, so common at parks, was rarely a problem here; a receding lakefront was. After withstanding another fire in 1931, then salt damage, World War II rationing (which closed down business for the duration), and postwar apathy, Saltair ceased operation in 1958.

An arsonist torched its remains in 1970.

If Saltair was the Coney Island of the West, then Louisiana's Old Spanish Fort was the South's—"though more adult, with heavy drinking, gambling, all-night dancing, and partying," said the actor, writer, and choreographer Vernel Bagneris, a proud son of the Big Easy. "After all, this is New Orleans."

The park was developed around a 1701 French colonial citadel at Bayou St. John and Lake Pontchartrain, rebuilt by the Spanish in 1779, and decommissioned when the U.S. Government took possession as part of the Louisiana Purchase, in 1803. Insofar as a tourist trade, the fort's coincided exactly with Coney's, given that, in 1823, New Orleans developer Harvey Elkins built the Pontchartrain Hotel within fort walls.

By 1830, Elkins sold the hotel, and after a series of subsequent owners—including lawyer-politician John Slidell, who renamed it the Spanish Fort Hotel—New Orleans entrepreneur Moses Schwartz bought the property in 1877. His upgrades included a casino, restaurant, and theater, where "a very large audience," reported the June 27, 1882, *Daily Picayune*, "assembled to see Oscar Wilde." His topic was home decoration. Unfortunately, the paper complained, the venue "is so poor a hall to speak in, that a great part of the audience could hear little or nothing."

Fire took the hotel in 1897 and the remaining buildings in 1906, three years after the railroad had ceased service to the city. Picking up on the cultural trend elsewhere, in 1909 the New Orleans Railway and Light Company returned Spanish Fort to glory, as an amusement park.

To get there, patrons rode the Smoky Mary, a train named for the soot belching from her wood-burning steam engine. What emanated from the lakefront was another type of heat: early jazz players sharing their music and techniques—including, as a twelve-year-old in the uniformed brass band from the New Orleans Home for Colored Waifs, cornetist Louis Armstrong.

Prior to the Depression, Spanish Fort reigned supreme, with rides, a penny arcade, a lake bathhouse, and a picnic area. In the 1930s, the city assumed ownership and relocated the amusements a few miles east, to the end of Elysian Fields Avenue—as in the Elysian Fields working-class neighborhood that playwright Tennessee Williams used to set his *A Streetcar Named Desire*. When the park relocated, Spanish Fort was renamed Pontchartrain Beach, and the parcel developed into a full-scale amusement enterprise by Harry Batt Sr., whose sons, Harry Jr. and John, took over after his retirement in 1970.

Throughout the Jim Crow era and until the 1964 Civil Rights Act legally ended segregation, Pontchartrain Beach Park catered to whites only. In 1954, the city opened an African-American amusement park, Lincoln Beach, "along Hayne Boulevard, in the Little Woods area of New Orleans East," the *Times-Picayune* wrote, with the addendum that while "Pontchartrain Beach had the better rides, Lincoln Beach had by far the better musical acts." The roster of Fats Domino, Ray Charles, Sam Cooke, Nat King Cole, Dinah Washington, Josephine Baker, the Ink Spots, Little Richard, Ike and Tina Turner, and Guitar Slim bore out the statement.

In addition to rides and a midway—entered through the mouth of a giant clown head—Pontchartrain Beach Park provided two swimming pools, exotic animal acts, and, as of 1958, the tiki bar and restaurant Bali Ha'i, touted as New Orleans's first to serve exotic food and drink. The park also dished out the local favorite, "crayfish on newspaper," recalled the film critic Rex Reed, who'd been a student at Louisiana State University. "You'd eat the tails."

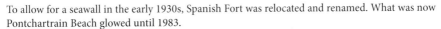

To allow for a seawall in the early 1930s, Spanish Fort was relocated and renamed. What was now Pontchartrain Beach glowed until 1983.

Of the many entertainment acts, Elvis Presley played Pontchartrain Beach, in 1955. Legend holds that he took an after-hours spin on the park's signature coaster, the sixty-eight-foot, 1939-vintage Zephyr.

While the Elvis story may be just one more unconfirmed sighting, the actor Bryan Batt (*Mad Men*), son of John Batt, did have any-hour access to the ride, and, when young, "climbed up the catwalk on the Zephyr."

When his parents found out, he was grounded.

In 1983, Pontchartrain Park met the same fate.

"Through 1908, Chicago led the nation in its number of amusement parks," said chronicler Stan Barker, starting with Paul Boyton's Water Chute Park (1894–1907) and Ferris Wheel Park (1896–1903). Boyton's Jackson Boulevard venture, though profitable, ultimately fell victim to a political chess game involving real estate and streetcar lines—a signal of similar things to come.

A ten-acre former beer garden, "Sans Souci (1899–1929) on Chicago's South Side appeared because the Chicago City Railway Company constructed it at the end of its new streetcar line to encourage trolley business," wrote *Electric Dreamland* author Lauren Rabinovitz, identifying another pattern. Named for Germany's Potsdam summer palace of Prussia's Frederick the Great, the Cottage Grove and East Sixtieth Street "Sans Souci was unlike anything Chicagoans had ever seen," said archivist Neil Gale. "The park's main entrance resembled the exterior of a German beer hall."

Named for the pavilions of the fair, White City, at Sixty-Third Street and South Parkway, "wooed thrill-seeking customers by hosting traveling carnivals," said *Jazz Age Chicago* scribe Scott A. Newman, "but curtailed the practice when the Chicago Law and Order League questioned the moral integrity of such shows."

Further proving Barker's claim of quantity, Chicago's parks also included:

- White City (1905–1934), near the old fairgrounds for which it was named, and a rendezvous spot for traveling carnivals, until the Chicago Law and Order League put the screws to it;

- Luna Park (circa 1907–1911), near the stockyards, and whose investors included former bookie James O'Leary, son of Mrs. Catherine O'Leary, who owned a legendarily pyromaniac bovine;

- Forest Park, on the West Side (1908–1923), with Art Nouveau flourishes by Frank Lloyd Wright acolyte E. E. Roberts and Frederick Ingersoll's record-breaking Chase Through the Clouds coaster—to the dismay of the Lutheran Church, it ran alongside a cemetery—as well as the only Steeplechase ride in Chicago. It also could boast more gambling and pickpocketing than any other park, until falling victim to Prohibition;

- and the largest, longest running, and still revered Riverview (1904–1967), in a glen on the North Side's Western and Belmont Avenues, where Prussian War veterans originally instituted their shooting club.

When the club dissolved, two members, Wilhelm Schmidt and George Goldman, bought the property, leading Schmidt's son, George, fresh from studying in Europe, to suggest that Sharpshooters Park be configured as a gathering spot, something along the lines of Tivoli Gardens and the Prater.

"Riverview had the world's first suspended roller coaster (1908) and first parachute ride (1936)," Stan Barker said. "Most legendary, however, was the Bobs (1924), perhaps the greatest coaster ever built."

Make that "great and popular," so much so that three simultaneously running twenty-two-passenger trains were required to handle demand. A wide, painted line stood sentry on the boarding platform, as if to stall twelve hundred riders an hour from their inevitable stampede to their favorite seats—generally in the rear, for its whiplash effect.

Commanding the park's southwest corner, beside the 1935 Flying Scooters and 1939 Boomerang, the Bobs was the work of the coaster field's holy trinity: Frederick Church, Harry Traver, and Thomas Prior, who designed it to hit 50 mph, peak at eighty-seven feet, and drop eighty-five. There were Bobs elsewhere that could twist, thunder, and turn with the same ferocity—the 1929–1971 Bobs at Belle Vue Park in Manchester, England, cost a bob, or a shilling to ride—but Chicago's "leviathan skeletal 'woody'" (as wooden roller coasters are affectionately nicknamed) was the undisputed champ. It was also reason enough to run to Riverview, but there was more: Aladdin's Castle (a fun house with a collapsing stairway, mazes, and turning barrel, from 1932), Shoot the Chutes (1907), Tilt-A-Whirl (1928), Hades (1933), Roll-O-Plane (1940), Tunnel of

Riverview was a Chicago institution. Long after its demolition, the park's 1924 Bobs roller coaster is still a source of admiration, while Riverview's 1908 Philadelphia Toboggan Carousel spreads its cheer at Six Flags Over Georgia.

Love (1951), Rotor (1952), Flying Cars (1954), Wild Mouse (1958), and, as one devotee in 2018 happily recalled about her 1953 high school junior year, "the opportunity to flirt with nineteen- and twenty-year-old sailors from the Naval Station Great Lakes."

"You could spend the entire day at Riverview, but you were never finished with Riverview," a Chicago-born baby boomer still remembered wistfully, half a century after the place to "laugh your troubles away" vanished to make way for an industrial tract and retail center.

Blame for the demise fell on juvenile delinquency and racial tensions in the neighborhood, because in its final season, 1.7 million customers packed Riverview, nearly as many as attended that year's Cubs and White Sox home games combined. Nevertheless, presented with a $6 million offer, George Schmidt pulled the plug on October 3, 1967.

"And then came winter," Chicago journalist Rick Kogan reminisced, "and then the assassinations of Dr. Martin Luther King Jr. and Bobby Kennedy, the bloody 1968 Democratic Convention here, more and more bodies coming home from Vietnam, and on and on and on, a stream of troubles that became ever more difficult to just laugh away."

Today, the only remnants of Riverview sit hundreds of miles away. In 1972, its 1908 Philadelphia Toboggan Company Model #17 carousel reopened at Six Flags Over Georgia, near Atlanta, while its 1935 John A. Miller–John Norman Bartlett Flying Turns coaster—which Riverview had purchased from Chicago's 1933–1934 Century of Progress International Exposition—was replicated in 2013, for the Knoebels Amusement Resort, in Elysburg, Pennsylvania.

With only a merry-go-round, Ferris Wheel, Whip, and Venetian Swing, Chicago's 1923 Joyland, on two acres at Wabash Avenue and Thirty-Third Street in Bronzeville, was owned and operated by, and catered to, African-Americans. Featuring "Music by the Famous Joyland Jazzers" and "the Finest Open Air Dance Hall in Chicago," the park billed itself as "a better alternative to the city cabarets."

The little jab at cabarets may have spoken volumes. Historian William Howland Kenney noted that Joyland became a favorite target of "cabaret owners and their political representatives in City Hall," perhaps a subtle way of saying mob figures and the politicians in their pockets.

Joyland closed in its second season.

III.

"Amusement parks helped to define a new concept of urban modernism—the celebration of motion and speed, the beauty of industrial technologies, and the experience of the crowd," said Lauren Rabinovitz. She also shoots down the notion of a gap as existing at the turn of the century between the "city slicker" and "the rube"— given that they were bound by the same cultural tie. As proof, the professor noted that in 1900, all but three of the fourteen cities in predominantly rural Iowa had their own amusement parks.

Arnolds Park, in the Iowa town of the same name, began when W. B. Arnold, an early homesteader, anchored a sixty-foot toboggan-style waterslide into Lake Okoboji in 1889. Since then, the expanded locale has withstood such perils as a 1965 vandal attack by seven hundred drunken college students, a 1968 tornado, a 1988 fire, and a 1999 attempt to convert the grounds to condominiums.

Following a triumphant 2017 multi-million-dollar fundraiser that would see Arnolds survive comfortably into the future, the institution's CEO Charley Whittenburg told the *Sioux City Journal*, "The park is the epicenter of our community."

What might seem surprising is that, at the turn of the century, in that densest and most inhospitable of urban areas, New York City, amusement parks were numerous and conveniently located. Five miles from Coney Island, on Jamaica Bay, the "gay, busy, teeming city" that was Bergen Beach (1896–1918) came to be when actor and vaudeville theater owner Percy G. Williams opened it with his partner, Thomas Adams, the chewing-gum mogul responsible for Chiclets.

On the Grand Colorado Canon [*sic*], its version of the L. A. Thompson Scenic Railway, "the lights fade and you find yourself in a long and narrow passageway

Arnolds Park, in Iowa, began with nothing more than a water slide, in 1889.

A standard-issue midway game variably called the African Dip, the African Dodger, the Chocolate Drop, the Soakum, the Darktown Tango, or much worse, allowed white customers to throw balls at a target board. Hitting the bull's-eye released a ledge on which sat an African-American man in a cage, sending him splashing into a tub of water.

"The exhibited 'Africans' became masters of inciting white rage by taunting young white men by complimenting their girlfriends and wives," said historian Victoria W. Wolcott, crediting the National Association for the Advancement of Colored People for closing down the affront in the late 1950s.

Riverview's African Dip was still operating in 1964, however, when *Chicago Daily News* columnist Mike Royko took to his typewriter to condemn the attraction, for "how it provided whites with malicious joy" while it stripped African-Americans of their dignity.

Readers concurred, and phoned Riverview management to express their outrage. "And within a few days,

the African Dip was no more," Royko wrote. "I had triumphed."

Not with everyone. Six African-American former Riverview employees showed up at his office, demanding he explain why they had to lose their well-paying jobs, especially when most custom ers couldn't hit the side of a barn door.

Royko explained there were "greater moral and social issues involved."

"Yeah?" one man replied. "What about the moral issue of you getting me fired?"

Royko, uncharacteristically, found himself at a loss for words.

"But I still think I was right," he wrote, "in theory."

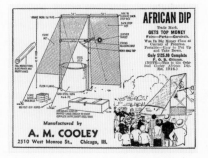

lined with pea green stalactites," the *New York Herald* reported. "It's a fairy grotto, and you should consider yourself especially blessed as an ordinary mortal for the privilege of visiting it."

Eleven miles from Coney in the other direction, under the imprimatur of George Tilyou, Rockaway Beach's Steeplechase Park (1901–1971) helped inaugurate the southern Queens beachfront as a full-fledged resort. Adjacent to Tilyou's bathhouse, the Father of the Gravity Ride established his L. A. Thompson Amusement Park (1902–1987), though in 1928 the park changed hands to become Rockaways' Playland, which it remained for the next fifty-nine years, until giving way to a high-rise apartment complex.

Playland's anchor coaster, the Atom Smasher (1938–1985), was built by Romanian émigré Aurel Vaszin, founder of the Dayton, Ohio–based National Amusement Device Company. The three-thousand-foot-long, seventy-foot-high goliath became internationally famous thirty-three years before its death, as the star of the audience-grabbing opening sequence of 1952's wide-screen phenomenon *This Is Cinerama*.

Its designer was Vernon Keenan, a civil engineer from Kentucky. Keenan built his first coaster in 1918 for Luna Park, in Schenectady, New York.

He was also the one responsible for the 1927 Cyclone at Coney Island.

In the 1880s, long before New York's Hudson Valley became a chic weekend retreat for city escapees, amusement parks popped up at such ports along the Hudson River as Bear Mountain, Indian Point, Newburgh, and as far north as Albany. In the Catskills, until a 1932 fire seized the entire property, "Monticello Amusement Park had the Pippin, reputed to be the second largest roller coaster in New York State," said John Conway, official historian for Sullivan County. "It also had one of the largest dance halls."

At Poughkeepsie's Woodcliff Pleasure Park (1927–1941), Vernon Keenan's Blue Streak coaster was situated inside an apple and peach orchard, hugging the terrain and finessing a breathtaking cliff-side turn over the Hudson. The orchard's first owner, John Winslow, was an iron magnate who helped finance the ironclad Civil War ship *Monitor*. He would have gotten quite a kick out of the Blue Streak: Its 130-foot height made it the tallest coaster in the world, a record it held until 1977 (until a so-called coaster war erupted to see which park in the country could build the biggest and best).

By then, the Blue Streak had been gone for thirty-six years, its steel rails donated to the war effort.

For a time, the 1952 movie *This Is Cinerama* turned Rockaway Beach's Playland Atom Smasher into the most famous roller coaster in the world.

Brooklyn's great resort at the shore also inspired competition in the other boroughs, with parks smaller in scale than Coney, but with an accessibility that compensated for their lack of variety. Functioning as release valves for highly pressured New Yorkers, the escapes included:

- Paradise Park (1895–1914) on the very northern tip of Manhattan, at Fort George, with food stalls, game arcade, sideshows, shooting galleries, hotel, and casino, and which would eventually sprout rides and music halls;

- Gala Amusement Park (1894–1921), built for his workers by piano manufacturer William Steinway and a partner, brewer George Ehret, on the north shore of Queens, before Prohibition bankrupted the park and the site was converted into Glenn H. Curtiss Airfield, which then became LaGuardia Airport;

- Golden City (1907–1934), near present-day Kennedy Airport, at Canarsie Beach, with a motorcycle-themed Wall of Death Ride, and, in 1911, an eighteen-year-old Mae West, shaking up the Husman Music Hall;

- Staten Island's Midland Beach (1897–circa 1929), the "Riviera of New York City," and the fifteen-acre Happyland (1906–1919), where a quarter bought admission, dancing, vaudeville, and the Scenic Railway, Dib Dab Slide, and Human Roulette Wheel;

- and, in the Bronx, Starlight Park (1918–1932), and Clason Point Amusement Park (1899–1935, and pronounced "Claw-son"), whose fresh-water pool earned the pejorative name "the Inkwell," because it drew directly from the adjacent East River.

Clason Point also weathered a freakish 1922 storm with 75 mph winds that shattered windows throughout the boroughs. The gale killed eight people aboard the Ferris Wheel, and injured fifteen when the ride hit the ground and several of its cars skidded into the river.

"Under one huge piece of steel, lying in a depression in the ground, lay a boy of 14 and his ten-year-old sister," the *Daily Star* of Oneonta, New York, reported.

For once, the outcome was happy.

"As the steel was removed," the story said, "they stood up, unhurt, and ran to the arms of their sobbing parents."

New York's Staten Island was home to Happyland and Midland Beach. From the latter in 1905, "Aunt Kate" wrote to her niece, Elsie, in Upper Montclair, New Jersey: "Just had a barrel of fun."

Building Legoland in New York's Hudson Valley was no easy snap.

In 2016, when Legoland's parent, Merlin Entertainments, first announced the $350 million theme park and resort for the town of Goshen, the company faced immediate challenges from groups calling themselves Stop Legoland and Concerned Citizens for the Hudson Valley.

Activists in nearby Haverstraw and Suffern previously had been successful in keeping Merlin—and an expected two million visitors a year—out of their towns, but an appeals court ended up denying the Goshen groups' restraining order. In March 2018, more than ninety-eight acres were cleared to begin construction in anticipation of Legoland New York's scheduled spring 2020 opening and what Merlin CEO Nick Varney vowed would be employment for thirteen hundred.

Specifically geared toward two-to-twelve-year-old children and their families, Legolands around the globe—in Scandinavia, the UK, continental Europe, Asia, the Middle East, and in Carlsbad, California, and Winter Haven, Florida—feature imaginatively themed interactive rides, pavilions, and displays that look to have been constructed entirely out of oversized, snap-together Legos (*leg godt* is Danish for "play well"). Where there are adjoining waterparks, the look is similar.

The first Legoland began in 1968 at the toy factory site in Billund, Denmark, with sculptures by the company's founder, Ole Kirk Christensen. His descendants expanded the attractions to include slides, trains, and coasters set in various "lands," and followed with a Legoland of its own, in Windsor, England, in 1996. California's opened in 1999, and the one in Gunzberg, Germany, in 2002.

Besides its Legolands, Merlin global operations include Alton Towers amusement park in Staffordshire, England; the Madame Tussauds wax museums; and what Merlin calls the Eye Brand.

Those are the supersized observation wheels one can't help but see in London, Sydney, Blackpool, and Orlando.

The first Legoland opened in the toy company's native Denmark in 1968. International expansion intensified after the parks' purchase by the Blackstone Group, whose California Legoland resort features the Sea Life Aquarium.

After the 1939–1940
New York World's Fair,
the Tilyou family brought
the Parachute Jump to
Steeplechase Park.

PART THREE

A NEW EPOCH

TO THE MOON

Having embarked in April 1901 on a six-week national tour with First Lady Ida McKinley, whose ongoing health issues included migraines, epilepsy, and phlebitis, the nation's president, William McKinley, was forced to cut the trip short on her behalf, although the couple had succeeded in venturing as far west as California—making McKinley the first president ever to set foot in the state.

When the First Couple resumed their travels in September, the leader planned to make good on his pledge to attend the Pan-American Exposition in Buffalo, New York. Originally, he was to deliver the fair's opening address on May 1.

"Expositions," McKinley said in a September 5 speech in Buffalo, where his friend, John G. Milburn, was the fair's president, "are the timekeepers of progress." Fifty thousand people turned out to hear the president that day, a testament to both his celebrity and popular respect. In keeping with the fair's theme of fostering relations with America's neighbors, McKinley visited the pavilions of Canada, Honduras, Chile, Cuba, Mexico, Santo Domingo, Puerto Rico, and Ecuador. He also took in the Midway.

The 1901 Pan-American Exposition in Buffalo, New York (with its Midway, upper left corner) aimed to outshine Chicago's 1893 World's Fair. Instead, it ended in tragedy.

The next morning, Friday, September 6, he escorted Mrs. McKinley twenty-five miles by train to see Niagara Falls, which was generating the hydroelectric power to light up the three hundred fifty acres of fairgrounds every night (and in a multitude of hues; in intentional contrast to Chicago's White City, Buffalo's fair was known as Rainbow City). The McKinleys returned to Buffalo early that afternoon for his widely promoted afternoon reception at the expo, while the First Lady retired to the couple's guest quarters in the Milburn home.

Shortly after 4 p.m., the sturdy McKinley—at age fifty-eight, he stood five foot seven and weighed two hundred pounds—began greeting the public in the fair's Temple of Music. It was there that from out of the crowd stepped "an anarchist," according to Washington, DC's newspaper of record, the *Evening Star*. The intruder was Leon Czolgosz, an unemployed factory worker of Polish descent and a resident of Detroit.

"The assassin," the *Star* reported, "had one handkerchief over one hand as if bandaged. As he moved forward he put out his hand presumably to shake the hand of the President. He shot through the handkerchief at the President two times."

Standing in line directly behind Czolgosz was James Parker, an unemployed African-American waiter who wanted to shake the hand of the president. Parker instinctively flung himself on top of the gunman as McKinley's bodyguards wrestled the assailant to the ground.

Amid piercing screams from spectators, the shooter was arrested.

Slipping into a state of shock, the twenty-fifth president of the United States entreated his protectors not to harm his attacker.

McKinley then requested, "Be careful how you tell my wife."

⁓

NEVER HAD A DISASTER of this magnitude occurred at a world's fair, and stunned exposition officers were no more equipped to handle it than McKinley's physicians were in treating him. After an optimistic initial diagnosis, the president developed gangrene and died eight days later, leaving the country without a leader for thirteen hours while a searching party scoured the Adirondacks to find McKinley's vice president, Theodore Roosevelt, who was on a hiking trip.

Leon Czolgosz's entire trial lasted but eight hours, and the jury's deliberation only half an hour. On October 29, he was executed with seventeen hundred volts of electricity—an irony, given that on the day of the assassination, the fair's infirmary had no electricity, and the staff gynecologist, Dr. Matthew Mann, the lone doctor available at the time, had to remove one of the two bullets in McKinley's stomach by the rays of the setting sun. He could not find the other. In another sorrowful example of unpreparedness, one of the expo's most popular demonstrations, the newly invented X-ray machine, was never used on the president.

In deference to the fallen leader, the fair shut down for two days.

Like McKinley, it never recovered.

The two biggest spellbinders of the Buffalo Fair Midway spun side by side: A Trip to the Moon and, looking like two Ferris Wheels attached at the hip, the Aerio-Cycle.

Midway attractions were disassembled and moved elsewhere. The LaMarcus Thompson Scenic Railway, occupying the epicenter of the fun zone, ended up in New York's Rockaway Beach. At the north end of Buffalo's Midway, two adjoining attractions attracted the attention of the mogul with sand in his shoes, George Tilyou: the Aerio-Cycle, also known as the Giant Seesaw—its name when it debuted at the 1897 Tennessee Centennial and International Exposition, in Nashville—and a combination stage spectacle and dark ride, A Trip to the Moon.

Resembling a giant, elevated bicycle stripped of its seat, the Aerio-Cycle was no match for Ferris when it came to passenger capacity—only eighteen people could fit into the total of eight cars on Aerio's two wheels—but its sheer look was a thrill in itself, and its impressive design was utilitarian. "When one wheel is down taking on and discharging passengers, the other is two-hundred and seventy feet in the air," wrote one reporter. A 240-foot beam linked the two wheels, which were spun by two separate motors, and two thousand lights outlined the elegant frame. Twenty-five cents bought a ten-minute ride.

For fifty cents—the same as admission to the exposition—one could take A Trip to the Moon, a twenty-minute immersive experience inside a forty-thousand-square-foot pavilion. Predating pioneering French filmmaker and master illusionist Georges Méliès's 1902 screen work *A Trip to the Moon*, the Buffalo attraction contained several curiously similar elements.

Those brave enough to "Get Off the Earth," as the ads phrased it, entered a space-port to board what looked like a floating spaceship. Named *Luna*, it seated thirty and was "a cross between a dirigible and an excursion steamer, with the addition of

FREDERIC THOMPSON'S

WORLD FAMOUS PRODUCTION

A TRIP TO THE MOON

ON THE AIRSHIP "LUNA".

THE GRAND NOVEL FEATURE OF THE

PAN-AMERICAN EXPOSITION

enormous red canvas wings that"—thanks to a series of pulleys—"flapped like a bird's."

A vast, shifting panorama of painted backdrops gave the illusion of flight, as blasts of air and various slide projections simulated a sense of speed while passengers spied Buffalo, Niagara, and the entire Earth growing smaller and fading into twinkling stars. After encountering a loud electrical storm, "before us, beneath us, is revealed another planet," said *Cosmopolitan*, "actually, the moon herself!"

Little people called Selenites, named for Selene, the Greek goddess of the moon, greeted and guided arrivals through lunar grottos, mazes, and the souvenir store—they also served green cheese hors d'oeuvres. After being treated to a stage extravaganza with singing and dancing extraterrestrials, guests returned to Earth by crawling through the mouth of the enormous "Avenging Spirit of the Moon."

Four hundred thousand visitors, including President McKinley, made it through the stars and back over the course of the fair, making wealthy men of its promoters, Frederic W. Thompson, a native of Irontown, Pennsylvania, and Elmer Scipio "Skip" Dundy Jr., from Omaha, Nebraska.

Granted, their subjects were dead and not able to sue for libel, but journalists Oliver Pilat and Jo Ranson showed commendable candor in observing that, individually, Fred Thompson and Skip Dundy were weak, but in tandem "they formed an unbeatable team…Thompson being a sentimental spendthrift and a dipsomaniac, and Dundy being a stuttering skirt chaser and a gambler."

Upon landing, Trip to the Moon riders were escorted by their small hosts through a maze of otherworldly experiences—and up to a merchandise sales outlet.

"Nearly a half-century before Walt Disney," said Fred Thompson biographer, Woody Register, "Thompson envisioned a Magic Kingdom: a pleasure resort operating year-round and featuring architecture and amusements organized around a single narra-tive theme."

In their business partnership, the men claimed never to quarrel, and never to keep books, only to "harmonize just because we are different." One Thompson biographer, Woody Register, acknowledging the pair's personal shortcomings, pegged Dundy as "the quietly reliable businessman in the relationship," while Thompson "made all the noise and hogged the attention…the one with imagination, the dreamer, the boy-man of the two."

Together, Thompson and Dundy assumed "the mantle of P. T. Barnum," said Pilat and Ranson, and "set styles year after year that dominated the amusement world."

What was all the more remarkable was that their association began when Dundy bamboozled Thompson.

Born on Halloween 1873, Frederic Thompson, like LaMarcus Thompson (with whom he shared no relation), was fascinated by machinery from a young age. His father, Frederic "Casey" Thompson, was an engineer, and the family traveled wherever the work would take him. In addition to a rebellious streak that did not play well in an academic setting—he quit school at fifteen—Fred showed artistic talent, which, combined with his father's tutelage in matters mechanical, landed him in his uncle's architectural firm in Nashville, tracing blueprints.

Not that any one job could pin him down. Employed as a janitor at the 1893 World's Columbian Exhibition, nineteen-year-old Fred supplemented his meager income by selling stories and drawings to a Chicago newspaper, until his father convinced him to go back to his uncle's office.

Nine years Thompson's senior, Skip Dundy—he claimed the nickname was not a derivation of his middle name Scipio, but that because of his connection to A Trip to the Moon, friends called him Skipper—was attracted to the footlights ever since childhood, when he would hear stories from a frequent visitor to the Dundy home,

Elmer "Skip" Dundy, Fred Thompson's business partner, was considered a financial genius for his role in the sale of the Union Pacific Railroad after its 1893 bankruptcy.

Buffalo Bill Cody. Dundy's father, Elmer Scipio Dundy Sr., was a prominent Omaha federal judge.

After graduation from the State University of Nebraska, Skip Jr. spent the next twenty years as a court clerk, but would solidify his reputation for financial know-how as Nebraska's Master in Chancery, when, during the Panic of 1893, he managed to sell the bankrupt Union Pacific Railroad for $90 million.

Dundy invested in a warship spectacle titled Havana and the *Maine*, for Omaha's 1898 Trans-Mississippi and International Exposition, where Fred Thompson also debuted Darkness and Dawn, an immersive experience that took customers to Hell and back. Both shows succeeded, only Thompson took his money and ran. Dundy went for a second roll of the dice.

When the fair reopened the following summer, he reopened Havana and the *Maine*, only lightning did not strike twice. Dundy lost his shirt.

Vowing to make good, Dundy marched into the Pan-American Exposition in Buffalo and, in a shifty legal maneuver, presented Darkness and Dawn under his own name, having managed to steal it out from under Thompson, who had neglected to patent it.

Rather than wrangle over it, Thompson, begrudgingly admiring Dundy for his chicanery, proposed they become partners.

"The year 1902 will figure in the local history of New York City as the year without a summer," said the 1903 *American Almanac*, which singled out June, July, and August for "practically no hot weather," a "high degree of humidity," and "rainfall on 36 days." The washout did not just dampen spirits at Paul Boyton's Sea Lion Park; it drowned them.

Matters were different across the street, at Steeplechase Park.

Once the Buffalo fair shut down, Dundy hied off for St. Louis, where there was talk of a 1904 Louisiana Purchase Exposition. Thompson headed to New York City, only to telegraph his new partner to join him there immediately. George Tilyou wanted them to open A Trip to the Moon at Steeplechase Park for the 1902 season, and in addition to a financial guarantee, he was prepared to split profits sixty-forty, with the greater share going to Thompson and Dundy.

Dundy initially was hesitant—he thought world's fairs offered greater opportunity than ragtag Coney—but the deal went through, and, with it, Tilyou's request for Thompson and Dundy's Giant Seesaw. All three entrepreneurs benefitted from the transaction.

Still, having learned from experience that novelties fade fast, at the end of his first season with the Thompson-Dundy attractions, the Steeplechase owner revised his offer. For the 1903 summer, Tilyou sought to flip the original deal, with the majority percentage going to him, into perpetuity.

The proposal did not fly.

Thompson went back to his drawing board, and Dundy contacted the financially floundering Paul Boyton to discuss the seven-year-old Sea Lion Park, specifically taking over its lease for the next twenty-five years.

⁓

LUNA PARK, THOMPSON AND Dundy's supreme effort, did not take its name from its quarter of a million lights, or from the moon, or from the spacecraft's name in the attraction that launched the men's notable alliance. It came from Luna Dundy, Skip's sister, back in Des Moines.

To find the $700,000 ($20 million today) necessary for construction of their phantasmagorical new "electric Baghdad," Dundy hit up deep-pocketed racetrack buddies with Damon Runyon–esque nicknames, like barbed-wire tycoon John Warne "Bet-a-Million" Gates and "Champagne King" George Kessler, the importer of Moët & Chandon. Whatever sums they failed to cover, Dundy sought and found on Wall Street.

Wanting their deliberately artificial realm to contrast sharply with the hard-edged Victorian reality of the outside world, the partners would leave the gags and gimmicks to George Tilyou. So, too, would they leave him the $40,000 Giant Seesaw, which the duo lost to the Steeplechase owner in a coin toss.

While he might have roiled privately over Thompson and Dundy's defection, publicly Tilyou embraced competition, as evidenced by his collaborations with LaMarcus Thompson. More attractions, insisted the Steeplechase owner, would only bring more crowds to Coney.

He even started taking credit for setting Thompson and Dundy on their own paths—by making them an offer he knew they'd refuse.

⁓

LITERALLY DOWN TO THEIR last pennies as their park's ribbon-cutting approached—when Thompson requested five dollars so he could buy a new pair of pants for the occasion, Dundy told him, "Do you know how many nails that would buy?"—the partners were suddenly minting money. Opening night, May 16, 1903, forty-five thousand people each paid their ten cents to pass through the gate. The following day, by 8 p.m., fifty thousand others did the same. That Fourth of July, attendance hit a mind-boggling 142,332. Profits their first year came to $600,000, or $16.3 million today, allowing them to reimburse Bet-a-Million, the Champagne King, and the other financial angels by that first crowded Fourth of July, truly making it Independence Day.

Park goers experiencing all that Luna had to offer would average on spending, with food and drink, $1.95 ($53 today)—the equivalent of a day's pay in the majority of blue-collar fields at the time, although factory workers out for the day were more likely to be found at the less hoity-toity Steeplechase Park.

In designing Luna Park, Fred Thompson "stuck to no style," he said, except for "the graceful, romantic curves" of the Far and Middle East.

What Luna provided free of charge was a new novelty: the picture postcard, a clever promotional tool that enabled thousands—and, by 1907, one million a week through the Gravesend post office—to spread word about the safety and suitability of Thompson and Dundy's park, where the slogan was "The Place for Your Mother, Your Wife, Your Daughter, and Your Sister."

As insurance, Luna's owners had thirty detectives patrolling the grounds against thieves and mashers.

LUNA PARK'S SINGLE HOLDOVER from Boyton's Sea Lion Park was the Shoot the Chutes, which now shared its lagoon with a glittering, two-hundred-foot Electric Tower. "Fabulous beyond conceiving, ineffably beautiful" was the opinion of visiting Soviet intellectual Maxim Gorky, who came to Luna to disparage it, only to leave singing its praises.

Contributing to the constant mix—Fred Thompson detested silences or pauses in action—were a miniature railway, similar to the one that charmed its way through the Buffalo fair; a War of the Worlds naval spectacle in miniature; the Canals of Venice, with gondoliers leading visitors through the man-made waterway; Carl Hagenbeck's Wild Animals, from the Chicago Fair; circus aerialists and clowns; marching bands; and people, lots of them, everywhere the eye could see.

"People stand in line for an hour for a ride that is 'over' in two minutes," one participant observed on a Sunday. "They ride before eating to stir up an appetite, they ride after eating to soothe the 'hot dogs,' they ride when exuberant for the fun of riding, they ride when jaded to buck themselves up." His conclusion: "The Day of Rest at Coney? There ain't none!"

Amid countless red-and-white minarets, two highlights were a Twenty Thousand Leagues Under the Sea indoor attraction and the outdoor Helter Skelter. The first took voyagers to the ocean depths aboard a modern take on the *Nautilus* submarine from Jules Verne's nearly thirty-year-old novel. Once the hatch was sealed, the sub dived into the Indian Ocean to sail into the Arctic Circle. Portholes provided views of sea monsters, reefs of vegetation and coral, and shipwrecked skeletons, and upon surfacing she'd hit an iceberg. At the North Pole, riders disembarked to witness the Aurora Borealis and a greeting by Eskimos.

Contrastingly low-tech, the Helter Skelter sat riders on burlap mats for a trip down a distorted metal slide. (Today, water-park slides offer the same surge, only wet.) "The descent itself is about fifty feet, with high sides, like a bath-tub," the author-playwright Elmer Blaney Harris wrote for *Everybody's Magazine*, "and it twists and turns" until reaching "a man standing guard at the bottom to pick up the passengers."

Yet obstacles did exist.

According to Harris: "A fat woman came to a standstill at one of the turns, and it required the combined impetus of the next four to dislodge her."

When professional colleagues scoffed at his attempt to rescue premature babies by placing them in warming chambers, Dr. Martin A. Couney (1869–1950) put his pediatric theory to work at amusement parks and world fairs.

His experiment, it has been estimated, saved sixty-five hundred lives over the course of fifty years.

The practice, utilizing an incubator, was first put to use in 1880, after French obstetrician Dr. Étienne Stéphane Tarnier observed its positive effect on chickens at the Paris Zoo, and constructed his own apparatus for human babies at L'Hôpital Paris Maternité. Primarily, the incubator solved the problem of thermoregulation, thereby reducing the alarmingly high rate of premature-infant mortality.

When Couney's hospital in Germany refused his request, he set up a small facility with his incubator at Berlin's 1896 World Exposition. His hospital did allow him to use its premature babies as guinea pigs, on the theory that they would soon die, anyway. An impressive majority did not.

Calling it Couney's Kinderbrutanstalt, or Child Hatchery, the doctor charged the public admission to see the babies from behind protective windows, with the monies going to the infants' care. (Daily cost per baby was $15, slightly more than $400 today.) Their parents were charged nothing.

After Berlin, Couney's incubators traveled with him to the Earl's Court Exhibition in London, then to the expos in Omaha, Paris, and Buffalo. It was at that last stop that he connected with Fred Thompson and Skip Dundy, who installed the Infant Incubator in Luna Park. It later moved to neighboring Dreamland, although on the early morning of that park's catastrophic 1911 fire, the babies were brought to the safety of Luna.

Couney remained at Coney Island for forty years, and also opened an incubator exhibit at Atlantic City.

His success rate was said to be 85 percent.

Dr. Martin A. Couney's Infant Incubators saved the lives of thousands of premature babies at a time when hospital staffs were ignorant of putting his principles to work.

Helter Skelter "passengers are lifted on an automatic stairway to the top of the high tower, where an attendant gives each a door-mat," said a news feature. With the mat tucked underneath, "down the slide they go, head first or heels first, as it pleases them."

"Courtesy on the part of the employee is as necessary as decency on the part of the visitor," said Fred Thompson, a pioneer in training staff to deal with crowds. "If I hear of one of my employees resenting an insult offered by a visitor, I dismiss him."

For season two, sixteen more acres were added to Luna, with the overall expenditure climbing to $1.7 million ($46 million today). Never known to budget, Thompson and Dundy "double-decked almost all of the space they occupied last year," reported the *Omaha Bee*, proud that the two Coney Island moguls had gotten their starts at Nebraska's Trans-Mississippi Exposition, "and which gives an increased capacity of over 70,000 people."

Besides a new Japanese teahouse staffed by geishas, a new, themed "land" would introduce "300 natives of India, including acrobats, snake charmers, yogi, and artisans of various crafts, [and] passing through the streets, the largest elephant herd in the world, forty camels, and 100 horses."

Luna Park's history of dealing with native peoples was nothing to write home about. Human zoos, in which nonwhites from exotic regions were placed in mock-up villages, first opened in Europe in the late nineteenth century, and were particularly success-ful at Paris's Jardin d'Acclimatation. In May 1905, Thompson and Dundy contracted physician-turned-showman Truman Hunt to exhibit at Luna Park fifty scantily clad Igor-rotes from the Philippines. Nightly in their gated compound, Hunt forced them to kill, cook, and eat a stray dog, with Hunt keeping the Igorrotes and their salaries under lock and key until legal authorities stepped in, well after Hunt had gambled away their money.

Thompson and Dundy's treatment of pachyderms was worse, considering how the owners sent elephants whooshing down the Shoot the Chutes to bring attention to their park. Luna continues to be referenced whenever the matter of animal cruelty is broached. The most egregious example served as the focus of a book, *Topsy: The Startling Story of the Crooked-Tailed Elephant, P. T. Barnum, and the American Wizard,*

Thomas Edison, by Michael Daly, published in 2013—the same year treatment of orcas at the Sea World marine-life parks came to light in the documentary feature *Blackfish*.

Topsy, a Southeast Asian elephant separated in infancy from her mother and smuggled into the United States, had been a member of the herd for the Forepaugh Circus, a rival of the Barnum and Bailey show, until founder Adam Forepaugh liquidated all assets in 1889, a year before his death from—talk about poetic justice—the Asiatic flu. Topsy, then about fifteen, ended up at Paul Boyton's Sea Lion Park. When the property switched over to Thompson and Dundy, Topsy went with it, as did inflated stories of her past misbehavior, including how she killed a drunken spectator who had sneaked into her pen and fed her a lit cigarette.

At Coney Island, her handler was William Alt, an alcoholic who mistreated her and blamed her for accidents he would cause, including, in October 1902, his stabbing her with a pitchfork and setting her loose as she was hauling the *Luna* spacecraft from Steeplechase to Luna Park. Two months later, again inebriated, Alt rode her to the Coney Island Police Station to taunt officers, who took cover from the "rogue" elephant.

Thompson and Dundy made the case for killing her—and reaping as much publicity as possible. The first thought was to hang her and charge spectators to watch, until the American Society for the Prevention of Cruelty to Animals stepped in to halt the brutal act. It was then decided to feed her carrots laced with potassium cyanide and electrocute her.

Topsy's January 4, 1903, murder—before the partially erected Electric Tower and a billboard reading OPENING MAY 2ND 1903 LUNA PARK $1,000,000 EXPOSITION, THE HEART OF CONEY ISLAND—was witnessed by slightly more than one thousand paying and nonpaying spectators and members of the press.

The Thomas Edison Company preserved the horror on film.

Luna Park's two elephants reportedly shouldered nearly ten thousand people a week.

FORTUNE'S FOLLY

I.

If imitation is the sincerest form of flattery, then William H. Reynolds (1868–1913) was the Midas of blandishment. In 1904, the former Republican state senator and suburban housing developer opened Coney Island's $3.5 million Dreamland. Its fifteen acres, while beautifully detailed, lazily piggybacked on Thompson and Dundy's effort, only more so—there were four times as many lights, making for one million, and *two* Shoot the Chutes—typifying the bigger-must-be-better corporate mind-set of the park.

At the root of the problem was that, unlike the Coney Island impresarios who preceded him, Reynolds was not a showman, though he had, in the course of a financially questionable career, run a theater company, built New York's Jamaica Racetrack, and worn the hats of a copper miner, an oil promoter, a state senator, and the chief executive of a water company and a trolley line.

The Brooklyn-born Reynolds studied law but did not graduate with a degree. Instead he followed his carpenter father, William Sr., into the building trade, where William Jr. made money for himself and the elder Reynolds by securing a 2 percent discount from creditors whenever his father paid his bills on time.

Dreamland developer William H. Reynolds amassed the bulk of his fortune in real estate. He also dabbled, somewhat nefariously, in politics.

This taught young Reynolds a dual lesson: to keep his eye on the calendar, and to make money from other people's money, including his own father's.

IT MIGHT NOT HAVE been its pretentiousness that soon curbed the public's appetite for Dreamland but its piety. A visitor might overdose on the park's morality plays, starting at the Surf Avenue front gate, with its enormous sculpted relief of a bare-breasted female angel. (Because the representation was religious, it passed muster with vigilant local clergy.) Under the angel's archway stood the entrance to the uplifting spectacle called Creation, based on the book of Genesis.

Dreamland trumpeted its arrival a year after Luna Park's debut. Critics called the newcomer cold and corporate.

One would have to venture inside the park to find its unappeasable counterpart, The End of the World.

"Both of these heavy-handed biblically themed attractions used scenes of hell and images of Satan as analogies for the then-modern terrors that might befall audience members, especially young women," said educator John S. Berman. "The End of the World frightened its viewers by depicting sinners who sank into a red pit while the angel Gabriel blew the trumpet of doom."

Respites from the fire and brimstone included a twenty-five-thousand-square-foot ballroom, which, characteristically for Dreamland, was the largest in the world. For thrills, a Coasting Thro' Switzerland scenic rail attraction whizzed past scaled-down representations of Mont Blanc and the Matterhorn, with modern cooling pipes blasting icy "mountain" air thro' its caverns—although, for a starry-eyed reporter from the *New-York Daily Tribune*, "'Fighting the Flames' is really the pièce de résistance."

Performed in a fifteen-hundred-seat alfresco auditorium, the spectacle featured the movie-set-like façade of a seven-story hotel that ignited while firemen were asleep at the engine house. Once the alarm sounded, they dressed and raced in horse-drawn trucks to rescue the occupants of the hotel, although not until the roof supporting them collapsed and "volumes of water" were tossed at the flames.

In reviewing the park on opening day, May 15, 1904, the *Trib* also sensed the wow potential of the still-uncompleted Leap Frog Railroad: "Two cars loaded with passengers approach on one track. The cars meet at the point of collision, but, instead of telescoping, one car crosses over the top of the other and continues on its trip."

Once initial interest wore off, the public stayed cool to Dreamland and remained so throughout its existence, something the *Tribune* did not predict.

In its opening-day appraisal, the paper went out on a limb and declared, "Dreamland has come to stay."

Dreamland's Fighting the Flames staged a conflagration for audiences at regularly scheduled times throughout the day.

II.

In answer to the age-old question as to what distinguishes a carousel from a merry-go-round, one need only consult the expert in the field, Frederick Fried.

After a comprehensive study that traced the ride back fifteen hundred years to a Byzantine bas-relief showing people in baskets spinning above a bear pit, the archivist concluded that a rose by any other name is still a rose.

In other words, there is no difference, although, admittedly, *carousel* has become the modern formal term, as opposed to the more carefree-sounding *merry-go-round*.

It wasn't always so. The first literary reference to the ride as a merry-go-round appeared in 1729 in a poem by George Alexander Stevens, a celebrated Covent Garden actor, who, in a lengthy sketch of Bartholomew Fair, penned the lines:

> *Here's "Whittington's cat," and "the tall dromedary,"*
> *"The chaise without horses," and "queen of Hungary."*
> *Here's the merry-go-rounds, "Come who rides, come who rides, sir,"*
> *Wine, beer, ale, and cakes, fire eating besides, sir.*

Conventional wisdom holds that as opposed to a merry-go-round, a carousel must be the exclusive sphere of horses. There is also a supposedly unwritten rule that to allow the rider to dismount on the right, using a presumably stronger right foot, a carousel (compared to a merry-go-round) must rotate counterclockwise—as is the case in the United Kingdom. Sources dispel those theories, too. Furthermore, stationary horses versus those that gallop up and down have nothing to do with separating a carousel from a merry-go-round. (In a play on words, Charles Looff once called it a "Carry Us All.")

In other words, call it what you like. That means, in Spanish, *carrusel*; in German, *karussell*; in Italian, *giostra*; in Dutch, *draaimolen*; in Polish, *karuzela*; in French, *carrousel* or *manèges de chevaux* (literally, "horse carousel"); in English (for those in the United Kingdom), a galloper or roundabout; and (in the United States), merry-go-round, whirligig, spinning or flying jennies, dip-twister, or jumping or flying horses.

Some American regions called it Kelly goats, though references to exactly why seem to have left the stable.

Meanwhile, in Chinese, it's 旋转木马轮, or *xuánzhuǎn mùmǎ lún*, and who is to argue?

The Philadelphia Toboggan Company, founded in 1904 by Henry Auchy, an amusement park manager, and Chester Albright, a veteran of his family's purse business, spelled *carousel* with a double *r*—*carrousel*—as did industry mentor William F. Mangels, while today, the meticulously restored merry-go-round at the revitalized Coney Island, with its shell by modern architectural designer David Rockwell, goes back to the original 1930s spelling.

It calls itself the B&B Carousell.

When it came to setting the gold standard during the Golden Age of the Carousel, from the early 1890s until the late 1920s, the gold ring went to Marcus Charles Illions

A Mangels-Illions merry-go-round was but one signature attraction at the "Coney Island of Michigan," Boblo Island (1898–1993), above the mouth of Michigan's Detroit River. Henry Ford bankrolled its dance hall.

(1866–1949), first at his factory in Brooklyn's Prospect Park, and then when he relocated to Coney Island—which, by the turn of the century, competed with Philadelphia as the hub of amusement-ride manufacturing.

At one time, it was tallied, as many as two dozen carousels were operating in Coney Island. Ten of them were Illions's.

Leaving his native Lithuania at the age of eight, owing to the country's policy of conscripting Jewish boys as young as nine, Illions settled in Germany, where his father, a horse trader, secured him an apprenticeship with a carver. Eventually, Illions moved to England, where, in a fortuitous series of circumstances, he connected with the carousel steam engine specialist Frederick Savage, and then Frank C. Bostock, the showman known as "the Animal King."

In 1805, Bostock's family had aligned with that of the old Bartholomew Fair impresario, George Wombwell, for the joint exhibition of exotic animals. Frank made his own name when he apprehended a lion that had gotten loose in the sewers of Birmingham.

When Bostock took his big-cat show to America in 1888, Illions followed, carving the elaborate wagons that carried the producer's precious cargo. In 1909, he paired with a blacksmith named Theodore Hunger and launched his Brooklyn carousel-horse business, principally using Arabian steeds as models, while also displaying an affinity for quarter horses and mustangs. The two oldest Illions carousels still operating are both in New York: a 1903 model in Flushing Meadows–Corona Park, in Queens, and the 1904 example in Congress Park, Saratoga Springs.

In contrast to the more staid-looking horses in the Philadelphia Style (those, for instance, by Dentzel, Daniel Muller, and Charles Leupold), or the County Fair Style (from Allan Herschell, James Armitage, and C. W. Parker), the Coney Island Style, master-crafted by Illions, was "characterized by flamboyant horses, bedecked with jewels and gold and silver leaf," according to the National Carousel Association, and "typified by proud, strong poses; long, thin heads; and round, muscular bodies,"

Inaugurating his own company in 1867, Gustav A. Dentzel, in Philadelphia, is credited with establishing the business model for a carousel industry in America—an impressive feat, given that his first carousel, installed on Smith's Island, in the Delaware River, lacked an engine.

Taking progress to the other extreme, in 1890, he created a double-decker carousel in Atlantic City, but the lengthy loading and unloading process cut into the operator's profitable ride time.

Dentzel's breakthrough came in 1881, with "a steam-powered merry-go-round, complete with band organ," which set the standard for the industry, until the arrival of gasoline- and electrical-powered engines.

Lasting through several different iterations, including a period from 1909 to 1928, when Gustav's sons took over the business following his death, the G. A. Dentzel Carousel Company survives to this day, as part of Philadelphia Toboggan Coasters.

---

as defined in *Painted Ponies: American Carousel Art*. Besides Illions's, the work of Charles Looff, as well as that of Looff acolyte Charles Carmel, the partners Solomon Stein and Harry Goldstein, and the brothers Timothy and Bartholomew Murphy also represented the Coney Island Style.

"Like a number of his fellow carvers," said Frederick Fried, Illions "also did various types of carving for synagogues." For an ark in a Brighton Beach temple, "he used

Ionic pilasters to support a pediment of moldings, crested by a pair of lions, the hands of a *kohen* [Hebrew for "priest"], the Decalogue [Ten Commandments], and a fanciful crown," said Murray Zimiles, author of *Gilded Lions and Jeweled Horses: The Synagogue to the Carousel*.

Briefly, around 1916, to repair the fire-damaged Feltman's carousel at Coney, Illions collaborated with William F. Mangels, who oversaw the metal framework and machinery, but the business union rapidly dissolved due to their strong wills.

When not carving carousel horses, M. C. Illions might be spotted in his Russian officer's uniform, cantering along Brooklyn's Ocean Parkway.

Coney Island's exquisitely refurbished B&B Carousell bears the imprints of two titans in their field: M. C. Illions and W. F. Mangels.

"We no longer cater our trade to the framemaker," Illions said in his company brochure afterward. "Our product is the product of experience and can only be had by coming to us."

Illions's once-thriving enterprise, which also involved his sons Harry, Philip, and Bernard, came to a standstill in 1929, a victim of cheaper, mass production by others and, even more crippling, the Great Depression. Illions died broke in 1949.

His work endured, however, and his horses, especially in an age of fiberglass figures, are held in reverence.

Today, a single Illions horse at auction fetches in excess of $100,000.

III.

With seventeen hundred employees to keep Luna Park running like clockwork, 1907, by all rights, should have been a banner year for Thompson and Dundy.

In many respects, it was.

Luna expansion moved apace. Twenty Thousand Leagues Under the Sea was swapped out for one of LaMarcus Thompson's most distinctive railways, Dragon's Gorge. Under a pair of giant gargoyles with glowing green eyes, coaster cars set off "on a fantastic trip from the bottom of the sea, through a waterfall, to the North Pole, Africa, the Grand Canyon, and even…over the river Styx." While the George Tilyou and the Thompson and Dundy enterprises showed profits, William Reynolds and his manager, Samuel Gumpertz, continued an ongoing struggle to awaken their somnambulant Dreamland.

Then, in a dispiriting turn of events, Skip Dundy died from a heart attack during a siege of pneumonia, after he and his mother, Mary, had gone to visit subfreezing Coney Island in late January. The death notice said that Dundy's wife was with her parents in Ohio at the time of his demise.

Married twenty years, the couple had been estranged for about nineteen and three quarters of them.

George Tilyou was dealt his own blow in 1907, when Steeplechase turned ten, although his setback was nonfatal; he was to live another seven years, and his park, run by his family, nearly another sixty.

The culprit, once again, was fire, which struck in the wee hours of Sunday, July 28, at the peak of tourist season. A lit cigar tossed into a trash container set a stairway ablaze inside the Cave of Winds attraction, which was basically a tunnel equipped with electric fans to blow away ladies' hats. In not quite thirty minutes, fire scorched thirty-five acres, nineteen of them the better part of Steeplechase. Tilyou claimed a $1 million loss (more objective estimates placed the damage at $200,000), and he may have fibbed to the *New York Times*, where news of the fire made page one, when he said, "I did not have one dollar in insurance."

Unflustered, he turned adversity into publicity. He also made it to that day's 7 a.m. Sunday Mass. Within an hour after the fire's containment, a sign went up on his smoldering property: "Mr. George C. Tilyou for 'Dear Old Steeplechase,' wishes to thank the public for their good-will and sympathy in the past and present." Soon, another sign appeared: "To inquiring friends: I have troubles today that I did not have yesterday. I had troubles yesterday that I have not today. On this site will be erected shortly a better, bigger, greater Steeplechase Park. Admission to the burning ruins: 10 cents."

The following summer, Tilyou rose from the ashes with the brand-new Pavilion of Fun.

Assembled from steel, concrete, and glass, the three-acre structure housed several of his signature attractions, resisted fire, and was immune to inclement weather, giving Steeplechase a decided advantage over Coney's more deluxe amusement parks.

It could now remain open all year.

Thirty-five acres of Steeplechase Park burned to the ground in the early hours of July 28, 1907. George Tilyou went to Sunday Mass later that morning. Customers went to his new, improved park the following summer.

JUST ADD FLAMES

I.

Fred Thompson's attractions may have defied gravity, but his career did not. After Dundy's death, Thompson's drinking intensified, leading to a precipitous decline in health. In 1907, he married the actress Mabel Taliaferro, who starred in stage shows he produced, but in 1912 he went bankrupt, listing liabilities of $664,000 ($17 million today). She divorced him.

Thompson's insolvency delivered Luna Park into the hands of creditors with little idea of what to do with the place, especially now that the public could get their kicks behind the wheels of their own automobiles. As time progressed, Luna added new rides, but minus Thompson's panache, the park simply maintained the status quo. Luna went bankrupt, and when fires swept through, first partially in 1944, and then fully in 1946, its consortium of owners chose not to rebuild. Thompson had been dead since 1919, having succumbed to a variety of ailments related to Bright's disease.

Panorama of Coney Island, N. Y.

American philosopher Elbert Hubbard defined Heaven as "The Coney Island of the Christian imagination."

On May 27, 1911, earmarked as opening day for the park's seventh season, Dreamland met its own ignominious fate, sparked by an early-morning fire set off by a spilled bucket of hot tar being used to repair, ironically enough, the Hell Gate attraction. Like the treacherous East River tidal strait off Jones's Wood for which it was named, the ride hijacked boats into the depths of a pretend Hades. The blaze burned a realistic eighteen hours.

Dreamland, farewell, 1911

Dreamland never opened again. In keeping with the park's bloated reputation, it turned out to be the biggest fire New York State had ever seen. While no human life was lost, some sixty animals perished, among them a Bostock lion whose mane caught fire as he leapt through the burning Creation arches. Frightened and bleeding, he was later shot when heard roaring inside a scenic-railway pavilion.

After the fire, Reynolds sold the lot to the city for $1.8 million. It was underutilized for years (and the city lost hope that team owner Walter O'Malley might use it to build a stadium for the Brooklyn Dodgers), and in 1957 the property became permanent home to the New York City Aquarium.

II.

Dreamland manager Samuel Gumpertz cut his teeth in showbiz by running away with the circus at age nine.

If George Tilyou had sand in his shoes, then Samuel W. Gumpertz had sawdust. Gumpertz (1868–1952) was the manager of Dreamland, and his contemporaries speculated that if he had been handed free rein from the beginning, instead of having to kowtow to Reynolds and committee approval, Dreamland might have given Steeplechase and Luna respectable runs for their money.

The Washington State native grew up in St. Louis, after his father's law practice took the family there, and when the Montgomery & Queens Circus came to town in 1877, Sam ran off with it. He was nine.

Learning under fire, he hand-walked and somersaulted in the circus, became an actor in San Francisco at twelve, and at fifteen roamed to Texas and became a cowboy in Abilene—also for three years, which seemed to be his general work cycle; he even married three times, being widowed twice.

Once Buffalo Bill's Wild West and Congress of Rough Riders of All Nations hit Abilene, Gumpertz joined, selling candy at first, before jumping into the ring as a rough rider. At twenty-five, he was back in St. Louis, running four amusement parks and seventeen theaters.

In 1904, Reynolds summoned Gumpertz to New York and hired him as Dreamland manager. Among Sam's contributions was Lilliputia, also known as Midget City. Constructed as an old German village built to half scale, with its own fire and police departments, beach, and standards of behavior, the enclave contained three hundred little people, all for the enjoyment of paying spectators.

When Reynolds's patience with Dreamland ran out and he returned to real estate, Gumpertz assumed full control, only to see the property go up in smoke. Wasting no time—within hours after the blaze, a forty-by-eighty-foot tent was pitched on Surf Avenue—he opened the Dreamland Circus Sideshow, with its Congress of the World's Greatest Living Curiosities: "wild men" from Borneo, "giraffe-necked" women from Burma, and "plate-lipped" Ubangi women, for whom Gumpertz paid the French Congo government $3,000 a week for their two-year appearance.

In all, Gumpertz escorted thirty-eight hundred unusual people through U.S. Customs—among them, Lionel the Lion-Faced Man, from Poland (who, like the hairy

In 1922, eighteen-year-old Archibald "Archie" Leach, originally from a suburb of Bristol, England, presented himself to George Tilyou Jr. for a position at Steeplechase Park. They had met at a Park Avenue supper party, where Leach, an aspiring actor, had been the arranged escort of Metropolitan Opera star Lucrezia Bori.

Tilyou had suggested Leach come see him at his Coney Island offices, "and he, true to his word, presented me with a doorman's uniform: a bright-green coat with red braid and a bright-green jockey cap," Leach recalled many decades later.

Coney was "clean, freshly painted, and well kept," said Leach, who was paid five dollars a day, except Saturdays and Sundays, when the fee doubled, owing to the hazards of the job: dealing with the constant gaggle of young brats trying to tackle Leach's legs in his role as barker, on stilts.

To keep from falling, Leach learned to grab a nearby awning, not sure "which would come away first—the awning, or me."

Leach did not stay long in the position. He had other plans.

He ditched the stilts, hammered out his Bristol accent, and, within a decade, was working in Hollywood under the name of Cary Grant.

woman at Bartholomew Fair, suffered from hypertrichosis); Violetta the Limbless Woman, from Germany; and Zip the Pinhead, a microcephalic from New Jersey (he did not have to clear customs)—though some of his scouting expeditions came up a cropper.

"On one of his trips to Egypt," it was printed, "he searched vainly for two tailors who were reported to have only one pair of legs."

GUMPERTZ'S WAX MUSEUM melted away in a 1928 fire, and the following year he left Coney Island altogether to run the Ringling Brothers and Barnum & Bailey Circus. In 1937, he joined George Hamid to supervise the Million Dollar Pier in Atlantic City.

His Dreamland Circus Sideshow parked imitators at the neighboring parks, and today a less exploitative but nevertheless direct descendant, the Coney Island Circus Sideshow, operates on Surf Avenue, at West Twelfth Street. Upon its stages have trod Zoob the Snake Boy, a contortionist ex–Brooklyn cop calling himself the Human Gumby, and the lightbulb-eating magician Todd Robbins, who's "swallowed so much glass, I could poop a chandelier."

Upstairs is the Coney Island Museum, operated by Coney Island USA, a nonprofit group founded in 1980 by Dick Zigun, who describes himself as "a tattooed author of a dozen weird American plays." The museum dedicates itself to the rebirth of the resort. An exhibit explains, "Coney Island's own history has been a bit of a roller coaster."

No sooner was Dreamland reduced to ashes than Gumpertz put up a temporary sideshow that remained permanent for decades.

State gambling laws closed the three racetracks in 1910, sending the horsey set sprinting back to their old haunts, like Saratoga. The snooty Manhattan Beach resort hotels of Austin Corbin quickly vanished. Prohibition, instituted on January 16, 1920, closed saloons and several restaurants but ushered in speakeasies, and the resort became rife with drunken sailors, who always seemed to know where the booze was.

A year later, New York City subway expansion brought large crowds to Coney's beaches, driving the resort down-market but also into huge profitability.

Once the playground of Diamond Jim Brady, Coney Island was now the Nickel Empire.

Originally called the Dip-the-Dip, the Wonder Wheel was conceived at Romanian émigré Charles Hermann's Brooklyn-based company, the appropriately named Eccentric Ferris Wheel of New York. What made this first-of-its-kind wheel eccentric was that of its twenty-four six-passenger cars, sixteen were not affixed to its rim.

Once the Eighteenth Amendment to the Constitution established the prohibition of alcoholic beverages and the nation went dry, Coney Island customers complained that the rides didn't make them as dizzy as they used to, while gyp artists complained that sober customers meant no more easy prey.

A particularly effective pre-Prohibition scam, because drunks liked to have their photo taken, routinely took place in the camera studios around Coney's Bowery.

"About the time the man had been posed in a pint-sized automobile or astride a stuffed horse," George's son, Edward F. Tilyou, told the *New-York Tribune* in 1921, "in would prance a flashy looking Jane who would insist on having her picture taken with the man."

Rarely would the inebriated subject oppose the pretty woman's suggestion that she sit in his lap and give him a nice big squeeze.

Snap, went the camera shutter. The photographer would charge nothing until delivery of the pictures, he would explain, taking down his subject's business address, so the photos could be mailed to him.

"A few days later," Tilyou disclosed, the subject would "have a visitor at his Manhattan office. It would be the Jane delivering the photographs." Instead of the agreed-upon twenty-five or fifty cents for the pictures, the price was now $250.

If the patsy balked, "a suggestion that perhaps his wife might be induced to pay more than $250 usually brought the sober and contrite husband into a different frame of mind."

Coney's ambitious nature revealed itself in 1906, when Brooklyn architect Samuel Friede proposed the largest amusement park in the world, all indoor: a $1.5-million ($42 million today), seven-hundred-foot-tall Steel Globe Tower, at the corner of Steeplechase and Surf Avenue. Investors wrote checks, a cornerstone was laid—more than once—and, ultimately, Friede's plan was exposed as a swindle.

Instead, they "swung" by rolling on flat rails between the hub and the rim, simulating the heart-racing sensation of sailing in air. Construction took place onsite at Coney Island and required two hundred tons of Bethlehem steel and two years, beginning in 1918.

In the decades since, no matter how Coney's fortunes rose or fell, the Wonder Wheel revolved, originally under the ownership of concessionaire Herman Garms and then his son, Fred—until June 7, 1983, when Fred sold it to Constantinos Dionysios "Denos" Vourderis.

A Greek immigrant who worked toward his U.S. citizenship by cooking for Germans and Italians in a New Jersey prisoner-of-war camp, Denos proposed to his girlfriend, Lula Lolas, aboard the Wonder Wheel in 1948, vowing that if she said yes, one day he would buy her the Wheel. She said yes. (Mrs. Vourderis also never rode the Wonder Wheel again because it scared her, she admitted in 2014.)

At the time of their betrothal, the only wheels Denos was operating were on a food cart, but by the 1960s he was managing a Coney Island Boardwalk eatery. When the Wonder Wheel came up for sale in the early '80s, it was Lula who informed Denos that Garms would pass him the torch. At the time, Denos was in the hospital, recovering from being stabbed at crime-ridden Coney.

Back on his feet, Denos raised $250,000 to buy the wheel, and another $250,000 to repair it. New York City landmarked the revitalized attraction in 1989.

Denos died in 1994, at the age of seventy-four, but now a third generation of Vourderises, with more than twenty rides in Coney altogether, continues his proud tradition.

Under the shadow of the Wonder Wheel is Spookarama, a genuinely scary dark ride designed by Fred Garms, and manufactured by the Pretzel Amusement Ride Company of Bridgeton, New Jersey, opened in 1955, at the height of the drive-in horror-movie craze.

Spookarama remains one of a few survivors of its kind, despite a severe battering by Superstorm Sandy in October 2012. It required a total restoration. "Everything

The landmark Wonder Wheel was called the Dip-the-Dip when its cars first swung over Coney, in 1920.

from the ghosts and goblins to the floors themselves were ripped apart," said DJ Vourderis, son of park owner Steve Vourderis.

Rest assured, the work was worth it.

Today Spookarama, along with the Wonder Wheel, the Cyclone, Feltman's, and the rooftop wine bar of Kitchen 21 (formerly Childs Restaurant and renovated after a nearly forty-year closure) are reasons enough to pay pilgrimage to what was once nothing more than Lady Deborah Moody's Utopian dream.

III.

Robert Moses, who claimed New York City parks commissioner among his many titles—twelve in all, possibly outnumbering John McKane's—viewed Coney Island, with its filth and crowds, as a place to put poor minorities, according to his biographer, Robert Caro. Targeting the amusement zone for extinction, Moses petitioned to ban sideshows outright. In 1938, he got as far as managing to muzzle the barkers.

"Although it rebounded in the '40s," said author Robert Bogdan, crediting World War II servicemen for keeping Coney afloat, "Coney Island never returned to what it had been." In the 1950s, the amusement zone was merely holding on, riding out the decade by resting on its salty goodwill of old. "Friday nights, my father would take us for fireworks and hot dogs at Nathan's," Carole Stuart, a book publisher, recalled in 2018. "I'm from Brooklyn. Coney Island was my Hamptons."

A stopgap arrived in 1962, on the old Feltman's property, in the form of Astroland, which father and son Dewey and Jerry Albert opened with Space Age–themed rides inspired by President John F. Kennedy's mission to land a man on the moon by 1970. In 2009, however, Astroland went the way of Dreamland and Luna; for an exorbitant $100 million, the city purchased Astroland's three acres plus three additional acres "to create a year-round amusement zone leased to a single operator," said Coney torchbearer Charles Denson.

Moses finally succeeded in dealing a deadly blow to Coney Island with his 1964–1965 New York World's Fair, which included its own flashy Midway, along with four attractions designed by Walt Disney. Due to a tidal wave of thoughtless urban desecration that also claimed Manhattan's Pennsylvania Station the previous year, Steeplechase Park closed for good on September 20, 1964, and in 1966, before plans were finalized to landmark the Pavilion of Fun, developer Fred Trump, the father of Donald, leveled the structure for the promise of a "Miami Beach–style" housing complex that he never built.

What remained of Steeplechase Park languished for thirty-five years, and its trademark Parachute Jump, an attraction for which the Tilyou family paid $150,000 ($2.6 million today) to bring beachside after its run at the 1939–1940 New York World's Fair, decayed into a rusty, graffiti-splattered relic.

The Jump nearly had a reprieve when writer-director Mel Brooks was shooting his 1967 theatrical spoof *The Producers*, whose original script called for filming actors Zero Mostel and Gene Wilder on the ride for the Eureka! moment when their characters agree to stage a Broadway flop. "But the ride had already closed down, and it was going to take $25,000 to get it operating again," said Alfa-Betty Olsen, who cast the movie. "There was no money for anything like that in the budget. That's how the scene ended up being shot at the fountain in Lincoln Center."

"The fiscal crisis of the 1970s took a citywide toll," the Coney Island Museum notes on a timeline. During that decade, the resort—no longer fun or safe—was at best a nostalgic memory. Woody Allen's 1977 Oscar-winning Best Picture *Annie Hall* showed its neurotic young hero, Alvy Singer, growing up in the 1940s in a house under the Thunderbolt roller coaster (the house and coaster were demolished in 2000). Director Walter Hill's 1979 *The Warriors*, about youth gangs, captured the dystopian look that the area was to project for the next quarter century.

"But this peculiar outpost has always been resilient," the Coney Island Museum accurately notes. Take the Parachute Jump. Declared a city landmark in 1989, twelve years after the City Council had ineffectually voted to dismantle it, the Jump's steel skeleton underwent a $2 million restoration that might have stripped it of its mechanical apparatuses but, since 2013, has left an iconic 250-foot reminder of Coney's glory days. Its light can even be noticed from the One World Observatory, atop the rebuilt World Trade Center complex in Lower Manhattan.

On land that was once Steeplechase Park, the Brooklyn Cyclones minor-league baseball team opened its stadium in 2001. In 2010, two new parks (even if one had an old name) opened for a new generation of Coney idlers: Luna Park and Scream Zone.

The thrills this time came from Italy's Zamperla Group, a design and manufacturing company founded in 1966. It was chosen by New York City to restore,

The '40s gave Coney a bump, while the '50s signaled a decline.

Mel Brooks nearly immortalized the Parachute Jump in his 1967 film *The Producers*, two decades before New York City landmarked the ride.

renovate, and run the revitalized resort, which also happened to get a further boost when it was used as the backdrop for Beyoncé's 2013 "XO" music video.

"Historically, Coney Island has always been on the cutting edge of the amusement industry, and iconic roller coasters like the Cyclone were a major part of that," Zamperla CEO Valerio Ferrari said in 2011. Among his firm's latest additions were New York City's first major roller coasters in more than eighty years: the sixty-six-foot-high Soaring Eagle, whose twists and turns could nauseate an astronaut, and the Steeplechase Coaster, a sixty-five-foot-high, 40 mph modern spin on the ride that made George Tilyou famous.

"With Scream Zone," said Ferrari, "we are bringing back the thrills and innovative spirit that first made Coney Island America's Playground."

Modern economic realities may have dulled the historic spirit of Coney, but the fact that an amusement zone exists at all is something of a miracle.

SHAKING THINGS UP

As the first decade of the twentieth century took shape, so did "quite the biggest thing of the kind Denver has ever had," burbled that city's *Post*, which presumably had seen big things before. With a personal investment of $175,000 toward a total cost of $250,000, Kentucky-born Denver magnate Adolph Zang, whose family brewery made him a household name, inaugurated White City on May 30, 1908. Joining him was a group calling itself the Lakeside Realty and Amusement Company, and joining them and their families on opening day were fifty thousand people—the first indication that, for once, Mary Elitch had a rival, a serious one, and only half a mile away.

Taking its name from its one hundred thousand electric lights, the new development was officially launched when Gertrude Zang, youngest of the German-Jewish brewer's five children, smashed a champagne bottle against White City's Tower of Jewels. At 150 feet, the Beaux Arts landmark was the tallest structure in all of Denver and, with sixteen thousand of its own incandescent lights, the epicenter for what park promoters called "wonders that had never been seen out West."

The design of the Chicago fair, and money from beer, combined to bring Lakeside "White City" to Denver, in 1908.

"You no doubt have seen that game on a species of billiard-table where the ball is shot up an incline and allowed to fall by gravity through an arrangement of pegs," said one shaken rider, after the fact. "This is the principle of the Tickler."

"An early ride called the Tickler was designed by its inventor to 'jostle, jolt and jounce its riders about in their seats,'" said David Forsyth, the author of a history of the park. William F. Mangels, the ride's inventor, first installed the Tickler in 1906, at Coney's Luna Park, where Frederic Thompson told him after studying its picture, "You will need barrels to take away your money." (Indeed, on a $6,000 investment, which would be $1.7 million today, Coney's Tickler in its first season grossed $42,000, or $11.7 million today, not counting what Mangels made selling the ride to other parks.) The objective was to seat up to five passengers in a round car with rubber bumpers, then set the car loose down a steep, labyrinthine course.

"Apparently it worked a little too well," Forsyth said of the Denver version. After breaking several bones, the Tickler tickled its last.

Other attractions included an indoor swimming pool, boat and train rides around the thirty-seven-acre lake, fishing, roller skating, and an exercise not always deemed acceptable in polite society: dancing.

The tower housed a casino, and Zang successfully lobbied to incorporate the town of Lakeside (pop.: 8), so he could serve alcohol at White City's German rathskeller.

AFTER WHITE CITY'S DEBUT, Elitch Gardens replaced its folksy front gate with a Greek Revival–style entrance. Gone was the log cabin; in its place was what looked like a Greek temple.

Thomas and Mary Elitch Long, meanwhile, carried out their own Olympian exploits, albeit separately—she ran the park and played the role of civic leader, donating animals to the new Denver Zoo, while he spun off a plant-nursery business from the gardens—until September 12, 1920. "T. D. Long, husband of Mary Elitch Long of Denver," the news report said, "was instantly killed in an automobile accident three miles north of Colorado Springs [when he] lost control of his machine and failed to make the turn at the bottom." He was fifty-one. Mary was sixty-four.

"Things began to slide as she got older," said Jack Gurtler, whose family ended up in control of Elitch Gardens. A sweeping fire claimed the *Monitor* and *Merrimac* pavilion (which by then had been reconfigured to be a popular reenactment of the *Titanic* disaster), and the attraction was never rebuilt. While Mary invested heavily in

In the seven-month course of the 1904 Louisiana Purchase Exposition in St. Louis, two sweets were added to the American diet: the ice-cream cone, and cotton candy—which at the fair was called Fairy Floss.

Glory for the cone goes to Ernest A. Hamwi, a Syrian concessionaire selling *zalabis*, a crisp, waffle-like wafer, and whose food stand was situated beside an ice-cream vendor who ran out of dishes and spoons—although, to be clear, Hamwi was not the one who actually *invented* the waffle cone.

Germans apparently pioneered it in the 1800s, while a Turkish entrepreneur at the Missouri fair also claimed credit, as did two brothers from Ohio and an Italian concessionaire whose cones were made of paper, which caused a litter problem.

Sugar with food coloring had been spun into creatively shaped dining-table decorations in Italy as far back as medieval times. No one thought to eat the ornaments.

That is, until cotton candy came along. It was, according to the U.S. National Library of Medicine, the product of Dr. William James Morrison, a Nashville dentist, lawyer, children's book author, and civic leader, and his partner, John C. Wharton, a Nashville confectioner.

In 1897, the two conceived and patented an electric candy machine, described as "a metal bowl containing a central spinning head filled with sugar crystals and perforated with minuscule holes." At the fair they sold their product in wooden boxes—68,655 of them, at a quarter a pop.

The process of making the candy happens so quickly—the bowl whirls at thirty four hundred revolutions per minute—"that the sugar never gets a chance to re-crystallize," explained *National Geographic*, "instead forming a disorganized, amorphous solid."

As a result, the frothy fare "is the sugar version of glass."

Cotton candy was introduced at the 1904 St. Louis World's Fair, as was another essential: the ice-cream cone. Both concoctions have remained popular for generations.

Faced with competition from Lakeside, it was crucial that Mary Elitch spruce up her gardens.

new rides, expenses were not always covered. "One thing she forgot to do was pay her bills," including "her taxes," said Gurtler, adding that it "was likely the property would be sold to satisfy that obligation."

By 1916, rumors flew that *Denver Post* publisher Frederick Gilmer Bonfils and business partner Harry Heye Tammen planned to transform Elitch's into a camp for the Sells-Floto Circus, which they also owned. The city, demonstrating a strong allegiance toward Mary, and an even stronger resentment toward Bonfils over his shifty business practices, worked quickly to thwart the effort. Mayor Robert W. Speer asked his longtime friend, John Mulvihill, to assess the state of Mary's finances.

A former executive with Carnegie Steel in Pittsburgh, before a lung condition precipitated a move West, Mulvihill was a manager at Denver Gas & Electric. He spent long weekends poring over Mary's ledgers, and found the news not good. Elitch's stack of dunning letters could have filled a library.

Speer would not be deterred. Having won on a platform of promoting Denver as "the City Beautiful"—rooted in the Chicago World's Fair's dictum that an uplifting urban environment could benefit humanity and raise the tourist market—the mayor conceived of a rescue plan. A consortium would be formed to pay down Mary's bills and clear up the taxes, while Mulvihill would be appointed manager of Elitch Gardens.

The park's founder would be provided for.

Mourning took effect with Mary's professional departure, "for no matter what happens," propounded *Denver Post* columnist Frederick White on April 16, 1916, almost twenty-six years to the day the gardens first opened, "with the personality of the Elitches gone from that lovely spot, it can never be the same to this community."

Only Mary did not go all that far. One of the many stipulations in the transference of ownership was that she live out her days rent free on the property, which was to maintain the Elitch name into perpetuity. As for her successor, Mary considered Mulvihill "a man of discernment," wrote her biographer, "for he caught the vision and

One of the conditions of Mary's relinquishing Elitch's was that she keep her home on the property.

thereafter spared neither himself nor his resources to maintain Elitch traditions." But changes did come. Among Mulvihill's first was to replace the dilapidated wooden barrier surrounding the park with a chain-link fence so passersby could see what they might enjoy inside. Mulvihill also charitably authorized that a respectably sized brick home supplant the tiny, rundown wooden cottage Mary was occupying.

But perhaps Mulvihill's most lasting contribution was to buy out the consortium and become sole proprietor of Elitch Gardens.

The same year Mary surrendered control of her park, a sixty-year-old Adolph Zang died of pneumonia. By then, he had long retreated from White City to focus on his other businesses and his hobby of breeding horses. The brewery had been sold off well before, or so the story went, in his anticipation of national Prohibition.

In 1917, a year after Zang's death, Benjamin Krasner, who operated a newsstand in Denver's Union Station, visited White City and learned the park needed someone to run its food service. Having emigrated from Russia when he was four, Krasner grew up in Binghamton, New York, which as of 1902 had a White City amusement park of its own, one that did not fill its populace with civic pride.

Like with White City in Denver, a brewer had supplied the financial backing, only unlike Denver, where rowdiness was kept in check, the drunken goings-on at the Binghamton park were "so vile, degrading, and

Lakeside owner Adolph Zang's presumption that his park could serve alcohol on Sundays landed the brewer in court.

unlawful…that a separate jail had to be erected on the property," said a local historian. (In an act of penitence, perhaps, in 1908, a cleaned-up Binghamton White City was converted into the campus of the Practical Bible Training School, now called Davis College.)

Whatever its pitfalls, in the six years of its presence, White City left a deep impression.

Especially on Ben Krasner.

Not all of John Mulvihill's alterations pleased Mary, who, lacking any say in the matter, most resented his Trocadero ballroom, which opened in 1917. Having built Elitch Gardens into an "upscale, puritan snob location [within] a no-alcohol, white, super-puritan community," according to Denver historian Phil Goodstein, Mary's technique for keeping out "roughs or rowdies," as she called them, was to use the power of positive thinking. "I do not want such people here," she said. "They know it and don't come."

In respect to matters of race, Mary may have welcomed all orphans to her Children's Days, but an adult of color was a rare sight at Elitch's. This was not necessarily out of discrimination, but simply because of their small number. Jesse T. Moore Jr., leading historian of the National Urban League, said that African-Americans "who settled in Colorado" after the Civil War "did not have to concern themselves with allaying whites' fears of their attempting to exercise political power [or of] changing the character of the West."

While couples danced on the property that bore her name, Mary toted around her well-worn copy of *The Rubaiyat of Omar Khayyam*, an affectionate reminder of husband John. She also saw that her gardens were well maintained.

Mulvihill, meanwhile, did what he had to: push Elitch's into the ride business.

≈

BY THE LATE 1930S, Denver's White City had a new name, Lakeside, and as of 1935 a new owner, concession manager Ben Krasner, after friends and family back East helped bankroll his $61,000 purchase from the Lakeside Realty and Amusement Company. The Depression had left battles scars on the park, so while Krasner lined up Big Band orchestras, demolished the 1912 Derby Racer serpentine coaster to make way for the higher and faster Cyclone, and green-lit such major additions as aviation-equipment manufacturer Lee Eyerly's Loop-O-Plane, the first item on his agenda was to devise the advertising slogan "Denver Has Gone Lakeside." Next, he hired San Diego–based architect Richard Crowther.

"Mr. Krasner wanted the park to be modern," said Crowther, who had finished adding his touches to the spires of San Francisco's 1939 Golden Gate International Exposition and, starting in the 1950s, would design futuristic Cinerama movie theaters and—as a pioneer in green development—solar-powered homes. The architect found Krasner traditional in his thinking, but "realized the park needed a new look."

New Lakeside owner Ben Krasner traded its Beaux Arts for Art Moderne, except when it came to the Tower of Jewels. The Derby Racer made way for the Cyclone.

What Crowther did was cross Buck Rogers with Ginger Rogers and Fred Astaire. Statuesque Art Deco shelters and geometrically shaped ticket booths accompanied nearly every ride, and rainbow-colored neon tubing outlined the distinctive silhouettes throughout the park. The Tower of Jewels remained untouched by order of Krasner, who judged it "too much of a landmark."

Mary Elitch died of a heart attack on July 16, 1936. She was eighty and in her declining years had trouble distinguishing between fantasy and reality. The gracious lady of the gardens was buried beside John Elitch in Denver's Fairmount Cemetery, under a single gravestone carved with his profile.

John Mulvihill predeceased her by six years. Park ownership passed on to his son-in-law, Arnold Gurtler, and by the time of Mary's death, the heir had shut down the Elitch zoo and part of the gardens, to accommodate more rides. The theater amped up its bookings—before transitioning to a screen career in Hollywood, a twenty-one-year-old Grace Kelly made what was her final stage appearance at Elitch's—and the Trocadero became a requisite stop for traveling Big Bands, as well as a high-wattage broadcast studio for *An Evening at the Troc*, a weekly live national radio show.

The slogan "Not to see Elitch's is not to see Denver" was spelled out in foliage decorating the lawn, and after half a century, there was little room for argument. With the onset of the baby boom, Arnold Gurtler's sons, Jack and Budd, who had assumed operations in 1945, grasped the trend in parks across the nation, and built a Kiddie Land with tame, junior versions of Ferris Wheels, locomotives, and motorboats. Ascertaining that the best way to deal with Saturday morning television's kidnapping their customer base was not to ignore the medium, but embrace and exploit it, astute owners like the Gurtlers added these child-friendly areas and live guest appearances by small-screen and small-fry favorites, the Three Stooges and Bozo the Clown.

To cut the ribbon on Elitch's Kiddie Land in 1954, the Gurtlers invited the hugely popular TV cowboy Hopalong Cassidy and his horse, Topper.

Both showed up for real this time, unlike the bogus sightings of Mr. and Mrs. Tom Thumb on Mary's opening day.

"Lakeside is for the working people. The carpenters, the laborers, and the firemen like my dad, and the policemen's kids," said Rhoda Krasner, who assumed control when her father died in 1965. (Ben Krasner named the park's adjoining lake for his daughter when he first bought the property, and it is still called Lake Rhoda.)

While there is no denying Lakeside is "light on the wallet and full of charm," as Denver radio personality Bree Davies put it, "some rides sit dark and dead in the midst of the other neon-lit ones." To the much-asked question of why Lakeside no longer was shining from stem to stern, as it was in its '40s prime, the Krasner family responded that it has continually refused to accept outside investment, or even outright purchase offers, that might allow a thorough update of the decidedly old-school park.

"My father's philosophy, and our philosophy, is that we want Lakeside to be affordable to everyone," said Rhoda Krasner. "The vast majority of visitors are family, with a lot of three-generation groups—Grandma, Mom and baby, and Grandma remembers being here, riding the Cyclone, when she was a child."

Mary Elitch at long last got her wish. The Trocadero dance hall was demolished in 1975, to make room for a less-passé pastime, a game arcade. More rides were added, including, in 1990, the Sidewinder from Arrow Dynamics, which not only looped (or in roller coaster parlance, "inverted"), but also sped into reverse. Still, on twenty-eight acres there was only so much room to grow.

Eyerly Aircraft Company's 1948 Rock-O-Plane still rotates at Lakeside, carrying on a tradition that began with the Loop-O-Plane and Roll-O-Plane.

Another factor was that the neighborhood was changing. Management—Budd Gurtler's son, Sandy, had taken charge in 1985—"didn't like the street kids of the northside hanging around," said historian Goodstein. "They actually put spikes along the planter beds outside the front gates so nobody could sit down on them."

One option was to shutter the original site and build anew in suburbia or, even possibly, exurbia. As was the case in 1916, however, the city of Denver rallied behind Elitch's. After voters approved a $14 million

Both the Sidewinder (foreground) and Twister II became anchor rides at the new Elitch Gardens in 1995, when the park relocated downtown.

bond issue for road improvements and flood control, the Gurtlers paid $6.1 million for sixty-five acres of formerly contaminated Central Platte River Valley land. When completed, the new Elitch's in central downtown Denver could access off-ramps from Interstate 25, making it the first amusement park to rise in an urban area of the United States in more than three decades.

The reconstituted Elitch Gardens opened on May 27, 1995, while the original site, after a number of arson fires, was turned into a $50 million housing development called Highlands Gardens Village. (In 1978, the Elitch Gardens Theatre was placed on the National Register of Historic Places and, awaiting full restoration, it at least remains standing, as does the shell that once housed the carousel.)

On the day papers were signed to relinquish John and Mary's original purchase, a maple tree on the property mysteriously upended and split in two, symbolically destroying the abandoned administration building, but sparing the theater; Mary's long-rumored ghost was credited for causing the incident.

Fifteen of the twenty rides were moved downtown, although not the 1964 Mr. Twister from veteran designer John Allen; a ten-story Twister II was built in homage. What could not be transported was that special something.

Skimpy landscaping and a paucity of homey touches made for an anemic amusement park, especially compared to its venerated predecessor, and after two disappointing seasons in the new location, the eighty-year era of John Mulvihill and the Gurtlers drew to a close. The family cashed out for $65 million in October 1996.

Since then, in a complicated network of ownership and management transfers, Elitch Gardens was bounced from one corporate parent to another. The shuffle began with Premier Parks, which sank $25 million into three new major thrill rides (including Shipwreck Falls, an update on the Shoot the Chutes) and the twenty-acre Island Kingdom family water park. Six Flags Entertainment Corporation next acquired the property, until CNL Lifestyle Properties came along. CNL retained PARC Management to handle operations (CNL dropped the Six Flags imprimatur) until 2011, when it turned management over to the Herschend Family Entertainment (Tennessee's Dollywood, Missouri's Silver Dollar City). In 2015, an investment group comprised of Kroenke Sports & Entertainment, Revesco Properties, and Second City Real Estate bought Elitch Gardens Theme & Water Park for an undisclosed sum.

The next chapter is still to be written. As the former zoological gardens looked toward its 130th anniversary in 2020, its future looked uncertain; in 2018, it was announced, city planners were examining the potential for relocating Elitch's once again, generating widespread discussion as to whether this truly was a last roundup for the frontier icon.

For the time being, it was to be business as usual, even if one strict Elitch tenet had long ago been tossed out the window: In opposition to Mary's original antialcohol edict, margarita cocktails and assorted beers are served.

At least, per Mary Elitch's wish, her husband John's surname still proudly lives on. Then again, so does that of her nemesis.

In 1997, a new theater went up within the downtown Elitch Gardens. It seats seven hundred and can also be adapted into a ballroom.

It is called the Trocadero.

Although Mary and her gardens have disappeared from the place she and John created in 1890, something is believed to remain: her ghostly spirit.

OFF THE RAILS

I.

As familiar as a hometown bank, general store, and post office—and just as integral—a trolley park often began as nothing more than a local recreational green with a dance hall and swimming pool. Once rides were added, they were also called electric parks, not only because of the crescendo of lights and the mechanical-circus fun, but because, at the time of the parks' 1890s rollout, people were switching from horse-drawn trolleys to electrical power.

That transition began in February 1888, when Frank J. Sprague, a former technical assistant to Thomas Edison, established his Richmond (Virginia) Union Railway by convincing New York financiers that electric traction was a better means to conquer the steep curbs and grades of a hilly terrain, and was certainly cheaper, than cable cars, which demanded an expensive infrastructure. All that trolley systems needed were a set of tracks and an overhead electrical wire.

By 1890, Sprague was under contract to build more than one hundred streetcar lines across America and in Italy and Germany.

Typical of city transport in the 1890s, Pittsburgh's trolleys took men to work, even though the electric-rail system extended as far as the leafy outskirts of town. To spur weekend ridership, streetcar owner Andrew Mellon leased the outlying acreage and built Kennywood.

Another popular name for the trolley park was Luna Park, a by-product of the avalanche of publicity fostered by Thompson and Dundy's New York effort since 1903. As a result, historian Mike Wallace calculated, "by 1912, Luna Parks had blossomed across the country—from Scranton to Seattle, Detroit to Denver, Chicago to Charleston, and by 1916 the roster of cities containing their own Luna Park included Berlin, Buenos Aires, Cairo, Melbourne, Mexico City, Paris, Rome, St. Petersburg, and Tokyo."

The first two Luna Parks were launched in Pittsburgh in 1905, followed shortly after by one in Cleveland. Melbourne's Luna Park, from 1912, is the oldest still operating. In Turkey, all amusement parks, no matter their name, continue to be referred to as Luna Parks, much the way Americans refer to facial tissues by the brand name Kleenex.

Remnants of the original Luna Park in Athens can be found at Ta Aidonakia, near Piraeus. There were also Lunas in Bombay, Honolulu, and the Philippines, and the list went on: Cologne, Hamburg, Leipzig, Lisbon, Madrid, Osaka—all of which, like the others, opened in the first dozen years of the twentieth century, and "represented the spread of American investments abroad at a time when American companies generally became more international in scope," said *Electric Dreamland* author Lauren Rabinovitz.

Berlin's Luna Park marked the end of the city's main shopping street, der Kurfürstendamm, where the Halensee Lake and the Grunewald (Green Forest) met. Duplicating several attractions at Coney, it included the Shoot the Chutes, the Shimmy-Treppe ("collapsing stairs"), and Scenic Railroad, not to mention its own version of Steeplechase's Blowhole Theatre. "The enjoyment here is in the mockery of human endeavor," commented Joseph Roth, the notable Weimar Republic columnist for the *Frankfurter Zeitung*, proving that George Tilyou's guiding principle knew no boundaries.

But there were limits. Except for closing down during the Great War, the park lasted from 1909 until 1933.

That was when the Nazis, brooking no truck with mockery, eradicated every last trace of Luna to make way for the 1936 Olympiastadion.

Frederick Ingersoll's constellation of Luna Parks extended to Berlin. World War I forced a temporary closure. The Nazis forced a permanent one.

Credit for Luna's global reach goes to Frederick Ingersoll, a New Jersey–born entrepreneur, slot machine manufacturer, and designer-builder of roller coasters (227 of them). Starting in 1905, he was responsible for America's first chain of amusement parks (forty-four of them, including the foreign properties), which he called Luna Parks. With architecture that smacked of the same grandeur of the (unrelated) Brooklyn park, Ingersoll's outposts were brightly lit and

Maryland's Glen Echo Park, nine miles by trolley from downtown Washington, DC, originated in 1891 as a Chautauqua for culture and the arts. In 1911, it expanded into an amusement park that would endure into the 1950s. By the next decade, skirmishes over integration decimated an already dwindling audience. Today, the restored 1921 Dentzel carousel, entrance arch, and arcade booths, now used for dance and art classes, are what remain.

colorfully electrifying. In an era when the metaphysical Chinese art of *feng shui* had yet to cross the Pacific, "the neat, orderly appearance of the midway was a hallmark of all of Fred Ingersoll's Luna Parks."

Unfortunately, Ingersoll's dreams could not keep pace with his economic resources. After declaring bankruptcy—twice in 1908 and again in 1911, when he listed liabilities of $179,668 ($4.8 million today) against assets of $75, comprised of three suits of clothes—Ingersoll was powerless against his properties closing in rapid succession. Although hampered by Prohibition, Cleveland's Luna Park held out the longest, until 1929, the year all America went bust.

Two years before, on October 24, 1927, Nebraska's *Lincoln Star* reported that Thompson, age fifty-two and suffering from ill health, was found dead inside a concession stand at Omaha's Krug Park, where he had sealed the windows and opened the gas jets. He left behind a wife and two daughters.

At his funeral, former business partner Lloyd Jeffries said in his eulogy, "Ingersoll was the tree from which the amusement limbs branched forth, as many leading park men of today came from that tree one way or another."

"The trolley parks served as an attraction at 'the end of the line,' bringing potential buyers of house lots to a new suburban development, and at the same time, building ridership on the streetcar line in the evenings and on the weekends," Maryland's Chevy Chase Historical Society explains on its website, emphasizing the two chief commercial motivations for the parks: real estate and ridership. Another reason was that the trolley companies paid the electric companies a flat monthly fee for their power supply, so they might as well have kept their trolleys rolling and fully packed.

The Chevy Chase Lake Amusement Park, where early twentieth-century ballroom dancers Vernon and Irene Castle reputedly introduced the Cakewalk, opened in 1894 on the western end of the man-made lake, near Connecticut Avenue. Its owner was the Chevy Chase Land Company, under Francis G. Newlands, a U.S. senator from Nevada and husband of a mining heiress. An avowed white supremacist, Newlands was also the promoter in chief behind the planned residential community, where covenants and strict building regulations excluded anyone but those like him from moving in.

To domesticate the rural outpost and bridge its distance from downtown Washington, DC, "Newlands and the Land Company purchased controlling shares in the Rock Creek Railway that would eventually run along newly extended Connecticut Avenue, past the recently opened National Zoo," according to the historical society. This also allowed Newlands and company to patrol exactly who rode their rails to Chevy Chase. (The streetcar line shut down in 1936, as did the amusement park the following year, but the pool, which opened in 1927, functioned until 1972, when, according to the historical society, it became "the subject of controversy over its racially exclusive admission policies.")

Revere Beach, just north of Boston, was the first public beach established in the U.S., on July 12, 1896. With its dance halls, food stands, and rides, Railroad Avenue, which smacked of Coney's Surf Avenue, even had a Traver-Church 1925 Cyclone. Standing one hundred feet above street level, it held the record as world's tallest coaster for thirty-nine years—but by 1971, when the fire-damaged Cyclone was demolished, the entire playground was no more.

Driven by land development, the Chevy Chase scenario played out similarly across the country, although metropolitan areas had their own trolley parks too, often in abundance. "Boston's Paragon Park and Revere Beach, Philadelphia's Willow Grove and nearby Atlantic City, Atlanta's Ponce de Leon Park, Cleveland's Euclid Beach, Chicago's Cheltenham Beach, Riverview, and White City, St. Louis's Forest Park Highlands, Denver's Manhattan Beach, San Francisco's The Chutes—these and others large and small became meccas for a public eagerly seeking recreation that replicated Coney Island," said *Amusing the Million* author John F. Kasson.

By 1912, New York state claimed sixty-two amusement parks; Pennsylvania, only one fewer; Ohio, not counting the "dozens of picnic groves," fifty-four; and Massachusetts, thirty-eight, said historians David and Diane Francis. "Even sparsely populated Montana could boast of four amusement parks."

"In 1907, Samuel Orcutt opened his lake outside of Tulsa to boating and swimming," said Larry O'Dell, of the Oklahoma Historical Society. Orcutt was the son of one of the first settlers to the territory, Kentucky-born rancher Col. Adolphus D. Orcutt. "By 1910, Orcutt Park, the last stop on the street car line, offered rides, a dancing pavilion, and moving pictures; the owners added a six-hundred-foot roller coaster, Tulsa's first, the next year."

The more prosperous the city or town, the more trolley parks it was likely to share, a ripple effect especially felt in Pennsylvania, particularly around Pittsburgh. At the height of the steel boom, one could choose from no fewer than nine trolley parks, including the 1899 Kennywood, which is still alive and clanging. Others mostly gave way to more lucrative development.

"The people of Philadelphia were luckier than most," said Bob Brooke, publisher of *Antiques Almanac*. "Within the area surrounding the city were four trolley parks." These were Woodside Park (1897–1955), at the intersection of Ford Road, Monument Road, and Conshohocken Avenue, and whose 1908 Dentzel Carousel, updated in 1924, was rescued (by Frederick Fried) after its closure and now occupies the City of Brotherly Love's Please Touch Museum; Point Breeze Park (1912–1923), on Penrose Ferry Bridge Road parkland that, since 1855, had been used for trotting races; and Erdenheim (1898–1912), also known as White City, which Brooke described as "a smaller park in the northern suburb of Chestnut Hill."

As the National Amusement Park Historical Association noted, "Neighborhood residents despised park—pooled their money and bought it."

The year Willow Grove opened, 1896, the one-hour, twenty-minute trolley trip from Center City Philadelphia cost fifteen cents—a nickel per zone, and there were three.

The park came about when the master builder William T. B. Roberts, whose working-class model housing was exhibited at the Chicago World's Fair, suggested it to two of his financial backers, Philadelphia magnates Peter A. B. Widener (1834–1915) and William L. Elkins (1832–1903). Partners and friends, the two met when Elkins was dealing in oil, and Widener, as city treasurer of Philadelphia, was buying up

"Staff members wore suits and dresses," the Historical Society of Pennsylvania said of Willow Grove, while "rowdy customers were promptly removed from the park." A LaMarcus Thompson Scenic Railway held court from opening day until the park's final gasp.

street-railway stocks. Besides the Philadelphia Traction Company (PTC) and its various offshoots, the men controlled major shares of U.S. Steel, American Tobacco, and, in Widener's case, Standard Oil.

What travelers would find on the 147 acres at the end of the PTC line included three picnic grounds that could accommodate twenty-five thousand people; a $100,000, fully electrified (the first in America) water-jet fountain, modeled after one at the 1893 Chicago World's Fair; and what was claimed to be the first theater anywhere in the world built exclusively for the exhibition of Thomas Edison's movies—which proved both a blessing and a curse. Faraway vistas were now brought within a viewer's reach, and amusement parks were forced by popular demand to include the new medium as part of their attractions. Its side effect was the sudden death of historic pageants and biblical spectaculars, which had already lost ground to an ever-expanding battery of new mechanical rides.

A LaMarcus Thompson Scenic Railway was up and running by the beginning of Willow Grove's first season, and would remain until the park's demise, and it would be joined by a regular series of new, improved coasters. Replacing the Shoot the Chutes in 1905, Thompson's Mountain Scenic Railway (renamed the Alps in 1935) was, for its time, the longest ride in the country.

The one-hundred-foot-high Airships also debuted in 1905, with the ships subsequently replaced over the years by miniature models of the *Spirit of St. Louis*, after the plane used in Charles Lindbergh's 1927 Atlantic crossing, then by warplanes during World War II, and finally spaceships.

Created in 1904 for British amusement parks—a glorious original continues to career at Blackpool—the Airships ride was originally called Sir Hiram Maxim's Captive Flying Machine, after its prolific inventor, whose 1884 automatic machine gun likewise bore his name.

When trolley stations, like that at Whalom Park in Fitchburg, Massachusetts, grew outdated, they were replaced by parking lots, as in Old Orchard Beach, Maine.

Born to tinker, in Sangerville, Maine, in 1840, Sir Hiram was one of the world's earliest electrical engineers, and he demonstrated an electric pressure regulator at the 1881 Paris Exposition. His other innovations included mousetraps, sprinkler systems, and hair-curling irons. (His title was bestowed by Queen Victoria in 1901, a year after he became a naturalized British citizen.)

Maxim continued to invent. When he failed to get his steam-powered airplane off the ground, he wired small, rocket-shaped passenger cars to a central armature and set them spinning, and thereby created the Airships. But when his idea to add rudders and air blades to the cars was shot down over fears that the ships might spin out of control, he dismissed his creation as nothing more than "a glorified merry-go-round."

Captive Flying Machine creator Sir Hiram Stevens Maxim with another of his inventions: the fully automatic machine gun

Inventors hemmed in by the constraints of the business world could freely express themselves at amusement parks. Take Asa Neville, of Wellsburg, West Virginia. He did just that at Coney Island, and then polished up his effort for Willow Grove.

According to a 1917 profile, Neville, born in 1852, ran the highly successful Eagle Glass & Manufacturing Company, where he "invented the clay pot that bears his name," according to a trade publication. What followed were a lock for automobiles and the Neville steering wheel, considered his masterpiece.

He also "invented and controlled several large automobile aerial races that are conducted in pleasure resorts of the country," which explained the Coney connection.

At the Brooklyn playground, in 1906, Neville took automobiles with hollowed-out motors, placed them on a coaster track, and then set them in motion with a center guide rail.

Soon, he did the same at Willow Grove.

Willow Grove's mainstays included a Mystic Moorish Maze, Shooting the Chutes on a Bicycle, 1928's 70 mph Thunderbolt roller coaster, and the electric launch on the lake, for those too lazy to row.

In 1926, society bandleader Meyer Davis took a ten-year lease on Willow Grove. Out went the formal Concerts at the Park—wireless radio and gramophone recordings had made them passé—and in came top-name bands, performing elephants, and commercial events, like the Perfect Foot Contest, sponsored by the Chiropody Society of Philadelphia.

A 1947 shopping center foretold the wave of the future, with the park's purchase by Moe, Sam, Max, and Perch Hankin, brothers in a real estate family. Their plans called for the world's largest bowling alley, a drive-in-movie theater, and an ice-skating rink.

Came the 1950s and '60s, the slogan became "Life Is a Lark at Willow Grove Park"—and it was, for most people. "I threw up there many times," recalled the Philadelphia-born writer Aimee Lee Ball. "I would ride on the roller coaster, eat cotton candy, and throw up on the ride home. Despite the ill effects, I still have happy memories of summer evenings there."

In 1971, the Hankins granted a ten-year lease to National Recreational Services, an Atlanta-based firm with parks in Florida, North Carolina, and Kentucky. National vowed to spend $1 million to refurbish, revitalize, and rebrand Willow Grove into a Western theme park called Six Gun Territory, "Where the West Comes East." Only the twain never met.

Skimping on park maintenance, by the 1975–1976 season National Recreational Services offered the Hankins $3 million to buy back the contract. NRS's years of neglect, however, carried another price. Necessary ride repairs were appraised at $1 million. With that, the Hankins decided it was time to get out of Dodge.

A fire sale was held—literally. Mysterious blazes plagued the property, including the Flying Bobs, which had replaced the Airships. After a protracted legal battle between family members, the Hankins relinquished title to a Philadelphia developer in partnership with the Cincinnati-based Federated Stores, parent of Macy's and Bloomingdale's.

In 1980, everything made in or after 1896 was demolished. Two years later, Willow Grove Park Mall, a three-story, shoppers' dreamland, opened for business.

On its third floor, flanked by an AT&T store and American Eagle Outfitters, is a merry-go-round.

When privately owned automobiles replaced public streetcars, transportation companies—which in 1911 owned 75 percent of all trolley parks in America—were reluctant to expand their real estate holdings to include enemy parking lots. Trolley parks were either shuttered or sold.

Likewise, auto companies ceded little or nothing. "In 1922," said industrial designer Hartmut Esslinger, "General Motors' longtime president Alfred P. Sloan Jr. gutted America's transportation system [using] a special unit within GM that was charged with, among other things, the task of replacing the United States' electric railways with cars, trucks, and buses. Consumers…no longer had the option of taking the streetcar."

Initially, only the wealthy could afford automobiles, and that group wanted luxury liners, not Ferris Wheels.

A tougher blow was dealt the trolley parks with Henry Ford's 1908 introduction of the Model T. Now that mass-produced automobiles were affordable, middle-class Americans in large number could hit the road to anywhere, certainly beyond the confines of their hometown trolley park.

This left the played-out playgrounds to those still riding public transportation, placing many park owners into situations they found uncomfortable.

The solution would come in offering customers sensations that could not be found on the highway.

Goodbye to the Golden Age of the Trolley Park.

Hello to the Golden Age of the Roller Coaster.

Manhattan's answer to Brooklyn's Coney Island pulsated uptown, at Fort George.

II.

Some thirty miles northwest of Coney Island, in Manhattan, atop a thousand-foot cliff overlooking the Harlem River on that island's very northern tip, a Washington Heights entertainment zone known as Fort George opened in 1895. It took full advantage of the picturesque location.

So did it also exploit its geographic location and the fiery demise of Jones's Wood, from where several of its concessionaires had been transplanted. Supported by the Third Avenue Railway System connecting Manhattan to the Bronx, Fort George also could be reached by a direct ferry.

Significant about the place, besides its Manhattan pedigree, was the number of A-list movie pioneers who got their starts there: Lillian Gish, the porcelain-doll-like star of director D. W. Griffith's epics; her younger, actress sister Dorothy; Joseph Schenck (pronounced "Skenk"), chairman of Twentieth Century-Fox; his no-nonsense, younger brother, Nicholas Schenck, president of United Artists; and their astute associate, Marcus Loew, whose New York company controlled Hollywood's Golden Age blue-ribbon studio, Metro-Goldwyn-Mayer, along with the equally enviable Loews theater chain.

The Gish sisters were born in Ohio; Lillian in 1893, and Dorothy five years later. Their father, confectioner James Leigh Gish, abandoned the family before his daughters were barely school age, although, except for church most Sundays, the girls never went to school. Their twenty-five-year-old mother, Mary Robinson McConnell Gish, a relation of Zachary Taylor, the twelfth president of the United States, supported her girls by acting, and by age three Lillian was on the stage, too. Dorothy followed in her own time, years later.

After appearing in two plays over a summer, "Mother had saved enough money to open a candy-and-popcorn stand at the Fort George amusement grounds," remembered Lillian. The Gishes lived uptown near the park, and Mary hired a helper to make taffy, leaving the girls to stand on soapboxes and hawk the output.

One day, Dorothy was nowhere to be found. Mary, beside herself, frantically scoured Fort George, only to see no sign of her younger daughter—until she came to the snake charmer's tent.

There, on a makeshift platform, surrounded by a crowd of admirers, stood fearless little Dorothy, enveloped by the star attraction.

That autumn, the Gishes were back onstage.

The Schencks' connection to Fort George proved less transient. Their family of nine—besides their parents, the boys had five siblings—originated in Rybinsk, Russia, on the Volga River, where their father sold the wood that fueled the steamers. In 1893, when Nick was eleven and Joe thirteen, the Schencks came to America. To support their mother and invalid father, the two brothers, forever inseparable, sold newspapers—school was out of the question—and, by 1899, Joe started junior-clerking at an East Harlem pharmacy. Three years later, he and Nick owned the business.

One summer morning, seeking relief from the city heat, the brothers "took a trolley ride up to Fort George," said *Liberty* magazine. "When Joe arrived he found more than a thousand other New Yorkers strolling about enjoying the breezes." Other than cooler air, all the area could offer was "a beer parlor or two, a couple of shooting galleries, and some tintype stands," barely enough to keep a large group of visitors entertained. Querying members of the crowd, Joe asked if they might return to Fort George at night, or on Sundays, if the amusement zone "offered a dance hall, a merry-go-round, and other attractions like those at Coney Island."

The overwhelming response: "'You bet!' or words to that effect."

On that assurance, before returning to the pharmacy that day, the brothers put down a $150 deposit to rent a beer concession. Not just any beer concession, either,

As tiny girls, future screen stars Dorothy and Lillian Gish helped their mother sell candy from a clapboard shack at Fort George.

The Schenck brothers' beer bar at Fort George had a whimsical shape, and an oaky aroma.

but one shaped to look like a giant old wooden barrel and called, fairly enough, the Old Barrel. In three months, the Schencks pocketed a $1,200 profit, and in 1902, $16,000 ($450,000 today)—by offering free vaudeville. "This was better than selling pills," the *New Yorker* noted.

The drugstore was sold, and the Schencks were now professional dispensers of amusement and beer. Their concession stand grew exponentially, and a Ferris Wheel, entirely of Nick's design, was added. Marcus Loew's involvement came about first as a beer customer, then as an admirer of the brothers' ambition, and finally as a consultant and business partner.

As with the Schencks, Loew's background was modest, despite his having been born, in 1870, in New York (to a Viennese waiter and a German widow with two boys). After a brief religious education, he sold newspapers in front of a saloon. At twelve, he went to work in a fur factory and slowly, and not always successfully, learned the fur trade. Right before the turn of the century, he met another peddler of pelts, the Hungarian-born Adolph Zukor, now living in Chicago, having been drawn there by the 1893 Columbian World Exhibition. Like Loew, Zukor—who would go on to found the forerunner of Paramount Pictures—was eager to find a new venture. This turned out to be penny arcades.

Little more than abandoned storefronts, the arcades offered flickering movies called Automatic Vaudeville, and the machines that showed them were called nickelodeons, because they cost a nickel to watch.

An initial investment with Zukor convinced Loew to set up his own arcades, and on November 4, 1904, his People's Vaudeville Company was born. Within eighteen months, Loew met the Schencks and, with his $10,000 starter loan, suggested they open their own amusement enclave in Fort George.

They called it Paradise Park.

"Harlem's Coney Island has one great advantage over Everybody's Coney Island, and that is it costs only a nickel to get there," reported the *Washington Post*, beneath the headline FIFTY THOUSAND PEOPLE GO SEEK AMUSEMENT ON A SUNDAY.

"Every nickel means a glass of beer or a frankfurter, and every East Sider knows the value of a nickel. That is one great reason why Fort George is popular."

In some circles, it was *too* popular. Noise complaints from neighbors kept mounting, as did the number of robberies, incidents of public drunkenness, and racial confrontations. New York City police commissioner William McAdoo vowed a cleanup but did not act fast enough. On December 10, 1911, an arsonist destroyed the Fort George Hotel and several structures around it. As community protests mounted for

Fort George's roller coaster, the Rough Rider, themed to the Spanish-American War, was not only rough but fatal.

A third-rail coaster, its power source was the same high-voltage track that ran the New York subway system. The slightest contact resulted in electrocution.

Speed was also an issue, and determined by the whim of the brakeman piloting the car. At Fort George,

Not only were the Fort George and Coney Island Rough Rider coasters rough on riders, they were fatal.

the coaster's location on the side of a particularly steep cliff added to the suspense, also to the risk of derailment.

In July 1915, Coney Island's Rough Rider capsized and killed three, leaving a twenty-eight-year-old mother and her four-year-old clinging to a precipice after their speeding car careened off the rails and plunged thirty feet when it missed a sharp left turn.

"Passengers were shot out of their seats and hurled against the double railing," the *New York Times* reported. The fence shattered from the impact.

Thomas Ward, manager of the Rough Rider, was arrested and charged with homicide.

Although the charge was later dropped, said the *Brooklyn Eagle*, Commissioner George H. Bell proposed that from then on, operators of roller coasters be licensed.

the total removal of the amusement zone, it was business as usual when Fort George reopened for the 1912 season.

It would be its last.

In the predawn hours of Monday, June 9, 1913, "flames swept through the dry wooden buildings at Paradise Park," said a report, "and in a few hours left nothing but piles of ashes and debris where the park had stood. Every building in the park was destroyed."

Five days after the calamity, Joseph Schenck issued a statement that Paradise Park would be rebuilt.

It never was.

CAUTION TO THE WIND

Graduating from picnic tables to mechanical rides and pop concerts, New Jersey's Palisades Amusement Park was a crowd magnet from 1898 to 1971.

Visible from Grant's Tomb on the Manhattan side of the Hudson River, New Jersey's Palisades Park, adjacent to the Bergen County Traction Company tracks, was purchased by the Schencks in 1910, when the only morsels the former picnic grove managed to dish up were a Ferris Wheel, diving horses, and a baby beauty pageant. The previous owners had been Cliffside, New Jersey, former mayor August Neumann and real estate developer Frank Knox, silent partners whose manager, Boston theatrical producer Alven H. Dexter, had sprinkled the grounds with games of skill and aerial acts. To the Schencks, Palisades Park was not merely an investment, but a venue to consign nickelodeon parlors.

Now called the Schenck Brothers' Palisade Park (Palisade was the name of the town), the enterprise was given a new vitality and new rides, including a simulated automobile racetrack. For Nicholas Schenck, the thirty acres held a special allure. He would devote at least half of every workweek learning the names of employees, tipping them with dimes the same way John D. Rockefeller gave them to children, enjoying the midway, and bringing his friends there by speedboat after they'd had dinner at his North Shore, Long Island, estate. He would then stay until park closing.

"His particular pet," said a *New Yorker* profile, "is the older of the two scenic railways." That would have been the Big Scenic Electric Railway, which the Palisades Amusement Park Historical Society lists as standing on the Fort Lee side of the park from 1910 until 1944. (Over time it was also called the Big Scenic, the Big Ride, the Scenic Railway, the Switchback, and, in 1916, the Big Dip Electric Coaster.) Donning overalls, Schenck supervised its construction and took personal affront when its drop was criticized as too steep. To prove otherwise, he braved the first ride, "but he nearly lost his life," said the *New Yorker*. A worker had left a stray wooden plank on the track.

Schenck came within an inch of decapitation.

Marcus Loew died in 1927, and Nick Schenck took control of the Loew's corporation. Now, with MGM stars at his fingertips, Schenck had the studio's blonde bombshell Jean Harlow pose for press photographers on the park's Scenic Railway, and former Olympic swimmer Johnny Weissmuller christen the park's pool for the 1932 season—the same year the brawny star debuted in MGM's *Tarzan the Ape Man*.

By 1935, with the movie business monopolizing their time, the Schencks sold Palisades Park for $450,000 ($8.2 million today) to Jack and Irving Rosenthal, two brothers in the Horatio Alger mold. They were Russian born, having come to America in 1902. They also had sand in their shoes.

Jack, born in 1892, was the elder, by three years, but Irving was the driving force. At age ten, he netted $1,500 selling shovels and pails at Coney Island. In his teens, with his brother, he bought a secondhand carousel at the White City trolley park in West Haven, Connecticut, and cleared $11,000. Along the way there was a boxing arena in Canarsie, Brooklyn, yet these were but warm-ups to another enterprise, the Coney Island Cyclone.

From its conception in early 1927, to its inception on June 26 of that same year, the Cyclone embodied the axiom "Speed is of the essence." Assessing other roller coasters at Coney, primarily master designer John A. Miller's 1925 Thunderbolt and

Before becoming elder statesmen of Hollywood, Nicholas (left photo, with President Franklin D. Roosevelt) and Joseph Schenck (with Marilyn Monroe) were the impresarios of Fort George and Palisades Park.

The legendary Coney Island Cyclone

LaMarcus Thompson's (with a design by Frederick Church) 1926 Tornado, the Rosenthals decided to lease a seventy-five-by-three-hundred-foot lot at 834 Surf Avenue, on the corner of West Tenth Street—ironically, the precise spot where, in 1884, Thompson launched the coaster industry.

At the time the Rosenthals decided to move forward with their Cyclone, the lot had been home to the nine-hundred-foot-long Giant Racer since 1911—the same year of the Dreamland fire, which the Racer withstood thanks to its steel frame. By the '20s, however, the Giant had outlasted its welcome, given, as *Popular Science* observed in 1927, "it is not easy to thrill people who often travel at better than sixty miles an hour in their own automobiles!"

What the Rosenthals would offer would be spiral turns and precedent-setting stature. Enlisting Kentucky-born engineer Vernon Keenan for the design, and the Henry C. Baker Company for construction (Baker's other coasters included Kennywood's 1921 Jack Rabbit, another John Miller masterwork, admired for its double dips), the Rosenthals demolished the Giant Racer and spent approximately $175,000 ($2.5 million today) for the 233,000 feet of lumber, 240 tons of steel, and 96,000 rivets to present, in the words of Robert Cartmell, "the finest coaster in the world."

Statistically, the mother of American roller coaster culture measures three thousand feet long, lasts a minute and fifty seconds, holds twenty-four passenger car lodes, and hits a top speed of 60 mph. Its biggest drop is eighty-five feet, and its descent angle is 58.1 degrees, which even after all these years still makes the Cyclone one of the steepest wooden roller coasters in the world.

National hero Charles Lindbergh, in 1929, proclaimed it a "greater thrill than flying an airplane at top speed"; six decades after the aviator's accolade, literary lion George Plimpton awarded the Cyclone ten "Lordys!"—"Lordy!" being his exclamation "at moments of extreme stress."

To ride in 1927 cost twenty-five cents ($3.60 today, although a 2018 ticket, purchased as part of a ride package, is priced around ten dollars), and with the Cyclone

Granted official New York City landmark status in 1988, the Cyclone also was named to the National Register of Historic Places in 1991. In its application to the city at the time, it was noted that "the Cyclone belongs to an increasingly rare group of wood-track coasters, there being only about eighty-five extant from the more than 1,500 that once thrilled America."

The submission went on to say:

The special qualities of wood are its natural resilience, the distinctive sound it makes, its unique aesthetic as a structural frame, and the relative ease of replacing parts. Today the Building Code of the City of New York prohibits the construction of timber-supported roller coasters; thus the Cyclone is irreplaceable.

It clearly held a place in the heart of Emilio Franco, a thirty-five-year-old coal miner from West Virginia, who in 1948 was visiting his cousin Larry in Brooklyn. For the previous five and a half years, Franco had not uttered a word, ever since keeling over in church at his Army camp in Colorado.

Described as a victim of "hysteria-phobia," he was discharged from the service for being speechless.

At Larry's prodding, the two rode the Cyclone. On the second dip, shortly after 10:15 on a Friday night in August, Franco began to scream, audibly, and did not stop until the ride came to an end.

That was when he delivered his first coherent words since that day he fell silent in church: "I feel sick."

earning back its construction costs in a matter of months, the latch was sprung for the Rosenthals to pursue other ventures.

When the Palisades Park opportunity opened up seven years into their nineteen-year lease on the Coney Island property, the Rosenthals placed the Cyclone in the experienced hands of Christian G. Feucht and George F. Kister. Feucht had built Coney's 1907 Drop the Dip, considered the seminal high-speed coaster, and the first to introduce the safety lap bar. The Kisters, meanwhile, were similar to the Tilyous, having been part of the community since the 1890s, with a family-owned hotel, restaurant, and carousel next to the entrance of Luna Park.

Hinting at what would be the remarkable longevity of the Cyclone, and why it was popular, George Kister said in 1947, on the coaster's twentieth birthday, that young boys rode it up to twenty-five times a day without ever taking a break.

"We get them Sunday after Sunday, many of the same ones, all through the summer," he said of the kids. "Then they turn up the next summer in long pants."

In New Jersey, Palisades Park had a Cyclone, too, though it was a few months younger than Coney's and could claim no relation to the Rosenthals' Brooklyn masterpiece.

"On it," the *New York Telegram* warned of the coaster on the Hudson River, "you're a fly on a racing motorcar. You're less than that, really. You're God's lowliest creature with gravitation gone back on you."

The Schencks ordered the steel-framed wooden dynamo during the same wave of construction fever that hit Ontario, Canada's Crystal Beach Amusement Park (which was only a boat ride away from Buffalo, New York, making it more of a ferry park than a trolley park), and Revere Beach, Massachusetts, just outside Boston. In fact, all three parks simultaneously bought into the Giant Cyclone Safety Coaster, made by the Traver Engineering Company of Beaver Falls, Pennsylvania. They opened their coasters within months of one another and found that what designer Harry G. Traver had sold them was so twisty and treacherous that the rides were soon pejo-

When *New Yorker* art critic Robert M. Coates interviewed the "short, pleasant-mannered" Irving Rosenthal at the Palisades' owner's "neat, compact little place," he learned that Irving "originally wanted to be a dentist, but had given up that idea because . . . 'there's more money in the amusement business.'"

ratively nicknamed "the terrible triplets"—jeopardizing both the ride's profits and the safety of its passengers. Covertly, the three tracks were also "known as a cure for unwanted pregnancies," said parks historians David and Diane Francis.

The Palisades Park Cyclone, near the cliffs framing the western side of the Hudson, had a more constrained spiral than its two brothers, given its limited space. (At Revere Beach, the model was called the Lightning, given that the park already had a coaster named the Cyclone.) Otherwise, all three Traver designs launched with the car curving out of the loading station and onto the chain lift, then plunging down a nearly ninety-foot spiral so it could ascend a second hill angled at eighty-two degrees, before taking a hairpin left turn down a fifty-two-degree drop, which was followed in rapid succession by a spiral drop, a high-speed figure eight, yet another drop, a series of hills (or "hops") under the initial incline, and then a sudden 210-degree high-speed turn under the monster's belly so riders zipped through a rattling course of bumps and turns.

Harry Guy Traver (1877–1961) has been called the Frederick Law Olmsted of roller coasters. He's also been called crazy.

In all, the eccentric Illinois-born engineer was responsible for about three thousand thrill rides that speckled the globe all the way from New Zealand to Brazil, including his challenging roller coasters, the Laff in the Dark ride-through fun house, the centrifugal-force Tumble Bug and Caterpillar flat rides, the motorized miniature Auto Ride through a trough-like racecourse, the Jazz Railway (a precursor to the Wild Mouse), and the Circle Swing, also called the Airships, for which his inspiration came while he was aboard a cattle boat recovering from diphtheria. Gazing up, he spotted a flock of seagulls circling the ship's mast.

Trained as a machinist for General Electric in Omaha, Traver went to work for a Denver trolley manufacturer before arriving in New York City and linking with a concern that made early motor-driven fire trucks. Traver founded his own company in Pennsylvania in 1903 and expanded it in 1919, when he took over the Zarro Amusement Device Company headquarters in Beaver Falls.

During World War II, Traver collaborated with the Navy and Columbia University on controlling torpedoes, and with a private New York company on launching rockets.

Married, with two daughters and four sons, Traver indulged his interest in anthropology by undertaking a history of mankind when he was seventy-three years old and starting to lose his eyesight.

He finished the manuscript the year he died, at age eighty-three, having just before that, despite his total blindness, traveled around the world—by himself.

Harry G. Traver possessed a penchant for design that would test riders' mettle.

Finally, the car returned to the station, where, at Crystal Beach, a nurse stood by with smelling salts.

The Palisades Cyclone was costly to maintain and problematic to run. Given its reputation for roughing up its riders, it was dismantled in 1934, a year after Revere Beach's Lightning careened into the same fate. Crystal Beach kept its Cyclone going until 1946, although it was completely reengineered by the Philadelphia Toboggan

Company in 1938, to balance its weight, destress its track, and prevent the structure from dismantling on its own.

The Cyclone was not the only setback. FIRE WRECKS HALF OF PALISADES PARK; 119 PERSONS HURT, read the left-column, front-page headline of the *New York Times* on August 14, 1944, although the big story that day was bannered above it: GERMANS FLEEING NORMANDY. Half of those injured in New Jersey were firemen overcome with smoke, and, among the nineteen people sent to local hospitals, six were seriously burned.

Oddly, only twenty-four hours before the Palisades fire, on Saturday, Coney Island's Luna Park had its blaze, which started in the washroom of the Dragon Gorge scenic railway. Both the Palisades Park and the Luna Park fires were estimated to have caused $500,000 damage each. Luna Park did not rebuild its lost attractions, and would close forever two years later.

Palisades rebuilt, and ran for another twenty-seven years, until 1971, when an elderly Irving Rosenthal (Jack had succumbed to the effects of Parkinson's disease, in 1967) sold the property for $12.5 million to the Texas-based Centex-Winston Corporation, for development into condominium towers.

Until its closure, Palisades Park remained profitable, which might have enhanced the local tax base but did nothing to keep locals from complaining about the traffic and crowd noise. Rides were updated—as late as 1967, the Tunnel of Love became Casper's Ghostland—as was the entertainment lineup, from the Big Bands of the Dorsey Brothers, Harry James, and Benny Goodman, to youthful pop stars like Frankie Avalon, Lesley Gore, Fabian, Diana Ross and the Supremes, and a newcomer named Billy Joel. Most were presented by WABC Top 40 deejay "Cousin" Brucie Morrow, who considered Rosenthal "Uncle Irving…a five-foot, two-inch giant."

He was also tight-fisted. When Tony Bennett sang at Palisades, Rosenthal refused to hire a backup band, forcing Bennett to lip-synch his entire concert from a record album.

Midway through his signature number, "I Left My Heart in San Francisco," the phonograph needle stuck.

For baby boomers who grew up in the Greater New York area during the '50s and '60s, Palisades Amusement Park represented a rite of passage. They tested their mettle on the Jet Star, found discount admission coupons in Superman comic books, and got turned on by the aphrodisiac aroma of the coaster's axle grease.

In the summer of '62, AM radio stations blasted the hit "Palisades Park," by Chuck Barris (creator of TV game shows, and original host of *The Gong*

Show), sung by rocker Freddy "Boom Boom" Cannon, and later covered by the Beach Boys and the Ramones.

Then there was the park's 1965 ad jingle, "Come on Over," performed by Steve Clayton, with words and music by Gladys Shelley, wife of Irving Rosenthal. The ditty sang the praises of the coaster, the free parking, and the "cool" waves in the pool—despite the fact they had not always been cool for everyone.

After World War II, African-Americans returned home from fighting overseas, only to find themselves systemically barred from entering certain public places. This included the pool as Palisades Park.

Protests mounted, the American Civil Liberties Union stepped in, and Irving Rosenthal hoped the entire unpleasantness would simply fade away. It did not.

On the morning of July 13, 1947, a twenty-year-old African-American, Melba Valle, sought admission to the Palisades pool by using a ticket purchased by a white friend. Gate attendants informed Valle she was not a member of the private pool club, and, according to news accounts, was "forcibly dragged and ejected" from the grounds.

Her removal brought about a "stand-in" demonstration by members of the Congress of Racial Equality and others, demanding that the pool be integrated.

That same summer, ten plaintiffs, including Melba Valle, sued Palisades Amusement Park and the local Chief of Police for $270,000 in damages related to the park's discriminatory policies. Rosenthal responded by arguing that if he were to admit blacks, his white customers would cease to patronize the pool. He was quoted as telling protestors, "You'll all be dead before I change." A federal judge sided with Rosenthal.

A similar lawsuit the following year was dismissed. In response, CORE stepped up protests, resulting in the arrests of twenty-two demonstrators. To discredit the antidiscrimination campaign, the FBI was asked to look into possible Communist infiltration of the group. It found none.

After three years of negative publicity, Rosenthal quietly lifted the ban in 1950, although it could be argued his motive was not out of benevolence, but by law.

The Freeman Civil Rights Act, passed by New Jersey legislators in 1949, guaranteed equal access to all public accommodations in the state, from beaches and cinemas to swimming pools and amusement parks.

SUGAR RUSH

I.

By the second decade of the twenty-first century, North America's surviving trolley parks scarcely totaled fifteen. Some calculations put the tally even lower. Generally, what kept these endurance winners grinding past their century marks was a well-oiled combination of civic pride, family ownership (or corporate takeover), managerial moxie, and never underestimating the influence of school groups when it comes to building your audience.

Of those still in the game, confectioner Milton S. Hershey's Hersheypark, in the South Central Pennsylvania foothills of the Blue Ridge Mountains, is not often classified as a trolley park—a false assumption, given that the thirty-four fern-green-and-beige streetcars of the Hershey Transit Company, which ran from 1903 to 1946 with additional service on school, church, and factory picnic days, were as vital to the health of Hersheypark as cocoa beans—or Milton Hershey himself.

Milton and Kitty Hershey: confectionary, philanthropy, and, when the time was ripe, a roller coaster

At his death in 1945, at age eighty-eight, the Derry Township farm boy who made good had also spread a lot of good. "Besides the world's biggest chocolate factory and a trust fund of $80 million," or $1.1 billion today, *American Heritage* encapsulated, "he had created the world's richest orphanage, two hotels including a huge resort, an airport, a lumber company, a department store, a drugstore, a cafeteria, a professional hockey team, a sports arena, a stadium, four golf courses, a soap division, a cold-storage plant, a slaughterhouse, a laundry and dry-cleaning business, an elaborate zoo, an amusement park, a greenhouse and nursery, a feed mill, a garden with one hundred twenty thousand plants in it, a campground, a bakery, a community center, a theatre, a dairy, a monorail, a museum, a coal business, an auto garage, a fertilizer plant, a real-estate operation, and a bank—all in Hershey."

There were also, twelve hundred miles away in Cuba, the Hershey sugar mills and a Hershey railroad to bring the processed cane to its shipping port.

Milton Snavely Hershey owed his middle name, and much else, to his mother, Veronica "Fanny" Snavely, the devout daughter of a Mennonite clergyman. His father, Henry Hershey, on the other hand, was a firm believer in get-rich-quick schemes. Henry never became so much as solvent—he failed at various jobs seventeen times; Fanny took no pleasure in keeping count. When Milton was still young, his pragmatic mother made an unorthodox move for her day: She separated from Henry. The breakup curtailed their boy's formal education but spurred him to accomplish.

Fanny Hershey kept her husband, Harry, at arm's length, and her son, Milton, under her thumb.

Apprenticed to a confectioner—through Fanny's connections—at age fourteen, and at one point staked in his own candy shop with $150 from his aunt Mattie Snavely, Milton failed in business more than once, although he picked up a technique to preserve his product so it could be sold beyond local neighborhoods to customers nationwide: Add milk.

After another of his candy shops folded, Milton returned to Pennsylvania, to the town of Lancaster, where he infused milk, first into his popular Crystal A Cream Caramels, then into his chocolates.

The milk turned to gold.

John Cadbury, in England, might have started the retail chocolate market rolling when he began selling chocolates in 1824, but his pricey product was limited to the rich. Hershey went in another direction by devising a factory method so he could deliver his product to a mass market. In 1901, he began selling his nickel Hershey Chocolate bar. That same year, he also sold his Lancaster Caramel Company in a deal that made the forty-two-year-old Hershey his first million. Adjusted for inflation, that would be $30 million today.

Hershey did take one lesson from the Englishman, however. The Cadburys had established organizations to combat poverty and human rights abuses, as well as built a model community for their factory workers in Birmingham.

In Pennsylvania, Hershey would build a Utopia of his own.

Postcards inside every wrapper of a Hershey bar presented a placid depiction of Hershey, Pennsylvania, motivating the public into wanting to see the place for themselves. Distance was no deterrent.

Even before the acres of green were planted and landscaped, standing conspicuously in view in what was to become Hershey Park (then Hersheypark, after a 1973 corporate restructuring) were Milton and his wife, the former Catherine Sweeney. The two met when she was working in an upstate New York candy store that sold Hershey caramels, and they married at Manhattan's St. Patrick's Cathedral on May 25, 1898. Milton was forty-one; Catherine, called Kitty, was fourteen years his junior. Worried how his Mennonite mother might react to his marrying a Catholic, Milton discovered his concerns were well founded. Fanny turned a frozen shoulder.

Despite the rebuke (Fanny died at eighty-four, in 1920), the Hershey marriage was solid, buoyed by Kitty's good nature and her ability to take her workaholic husband's mind off business. As inveterate travelers who just missed passage on the *Titanic*, the couple were no strangers to Coney Island, though it was coming home from Atlantic City, while Milton was tending to his factory, that Kitty caught a chill.

The year was 1915, the month was a still-frosty March, and the automobile was an open convertible.

Taking to her bed, Kitty developed pneumonia. Her final words to Milton were a request for a glass of champagne, which he promptly went to pour.

When he returned, she was no longer breathing.

An Entrance to Hershey Park, Hershey, Pa.

Milton Hershey modeled his utopian community on a British version built by fellow chocolatier John Cadbury.

Solomon Dorney's trout pond in Eastern Pennsylvania spawned an amusement park. A century later, Cedar Fair reeled it in.

II.

In 1870, years before Milton Hershey ever tasted a caramel, a carriage maker, postmaster, and general store owner named Solomon P. Dorney charged admission to his Eastern Pennsylvania farm for people to fish in his creek. Soon, Solomon's weir was "visited annually by several hundred thousand people, including sportsmen who were attracted from all sections of the country for the angling of 'speckled beauties' in season."

Dorney's Trout Ponds and Summer Resort spawned a hotel and restaurant, and, in 1884, a garden, zoo, a primitive zip line, a Venetian Swing (couples in suspended gondolas swung back and forth), and a new name: Dorney Park.

When Solomon died, in 1901, Allentown and Reading Traction Company, whose route fed the park, bought the land and added a Dentzel carousel through the efforts of attentive park manager Jacob Plarr, whose son, Robert Plarr, purchased the property in 1923. It was Robert who upgraded it to amusement park, complete with a still-extant eighty-foot-tall, 45 mph coaster of pressure-treated pine, the 1924 Thunderhawk.

Dorney Park remained a family enterprise until its 1992 sale to the Sandusky, Ohio–based Cedar Fair Entertainment Company. The purchase price was $48 million, or $85 million today.

Under the Cedar Fair corporate flag, the 210-acre Dorney Park & Wildwater Kingdom may have lost its Alfundo clown mascot—Dorney's less-foreboding version of George Tilyou's grinning face of Steeplechase—but it gained something new.

A deep-pocketed parent.

edged between Dorney Park's twenty-gondola 1989 Ferris Wheel and its 1935 gas-electric-powered miniature Zephyr train, which single-handedly helped the park ride out the Depression, is a genuine William F. Mangels Whip.

The rotating ride with its dozen small cars attached to floor cables was invented in 1914 and first unfurled at Dorney in 1920, two years after its debut at Kennywood. Today, they are the two oldest Whips still cracking. (Other parks, like New York's Rye Playland, with its 1929 version, operate later models.)

How it came to be called the Whip, its inventor explained, has to do with the fact its cars are "attached to the moving cable by flexible arms" and swing out at the curved ends of the oval course, "thus simulating the snap of a whip."

William F. Mangels promised "Action, Snap, and Thrill" in ads he placed in trade publications for the "New 8-Car 'Whip.'"

III.

After Kitty's death, Milton Hershey, having no heirs, placed his fortune into the Hershey Trust Company. (A recent appraisal placed its resources at $12.3 billion.) While the Hershey Company seeks expansion through diversification—in December 2017, it purchased the parent of SkinnyPop Popcorn, for a fat $921 million—Hersheypark seeks quite the opposite, diversification through expansion.

As the highest-attended privately owned theme park in North America (3.3 million visitors, in 2017), Hersheypark, with five themed sections, is home to seventy rides, including two 2018 additions to its Boardwalk water park. This brings the Hershey coaster count to fourteen, more than any park in Pennsylvania—a fitting legacy to Milton Hershey and a coaster tradition at his park that harks back to 1923, when, joyous over the recovery of his company after a long financial reversal, he approved a stately woody. Given the toothless name of Joy Ride, it was later suitably rechristened Wild Cat. By any name, it was created, constructed, and operated by the Philadelphia Toboggan Company. It was the work of PTC's top gun, Herbert Paul Schmeck,

CHILDREN'S PLAYGROUNDS — HERSHEY, PA.
Home of the Hershey Chocolate Co.

To entice visitors, promotional cards were inserted into Milton Hershey's chocolate bars.

who, only a year earlier, fashioned a Wildcat for Elitch Gardens. (Dorney Park's 1924 Thunderhawk was also his.)

Hershey's Wild Cat ceased growling in 1945, and was replaced the following year with the last ride Milton supervised before his death, and what is now the park's oldest roller coaster. Another Schmeck creation, it is the double out-and-back Comet. (As the description implies, the train of an out-and-back coaster travels a certain distance from the lift hill before it turns 180 degrees back to the station.)

Delivering a 50 mph, 96-foot first drop at a 43-degree angle and two 180-degree turns, and several bunny hops, the Comet may not offer the extreme thrills of Hershey's five-G-force Skyrush, but it still delivers the bone-rattling goods.

If LaMarcus Thompson is the Father of the Gravity Ride, then John A. Miller, né Augustus Johan Mueller, is the Father of the Modern High-Speed Roller Coaster.

"Anyone who has ridden a roller coaster is likely to have experienced the benefits of Miller's work and innovations," said an article on MIT's website, taking into account that even with the passage of time, "much of what Miller introduced remains standard."

A native of Homewood, Illinois, born in 1872, Miller, at nineteen, apprenticed with LaMarcus Thompson, and, after a series of successful collaborations, went on to form his own company. Contributing approximately 140 coasters to the American landscape until his death in 1941, "the Thomas Edison of the Roller Coaster" earned one hundred coaster-related patents, including one for the 1910 lift-hill safety ratchet that prevented rollback, much like the safety catch Elisha Otis attached to his elevator.

Still, it was Miller's 1919 under-friction wheel, a refinement of the earlier side-friction wheel, that truly changed the course of the ride forever.

Rather than driving trains along inner tracks via rollers fastened to their sides, he placed the wheels underneath, fastening trains to the track—thus preventing that greatest of all upsets, derailment.

The Boardwalk at Hersheypark proves that water and chocolate do mix.

With industry names of Dodgem or Auto-Skooter (or, just plain Skooter), Bumper Cars can be traced to a February 25, 1890, patent—#421877—granted James Adair, of New York, for an "Electrically Propelled Vehicle" sandwiched between a metal floor and an electrically charged ceiling.

Only, it seems, Adair was not as bumptious as his invention, lacking the motivation to set his patent in motion. (The patent grant even states, "No model.")

Picking up the electrical baton was John J. Stock, of New York, and his wealthy partner, J. J. Jones, a traveling-exposition entrepreneur in constant need of new rides. Stock formulated a bumper car capable carrying four people at most, but Jones insisted upon a lode of at least ten passengers. Called the Glideabout, the ride's test run sank under its own weight.

Stock went back to his original design, encasing his small cars on a large rectangular stage, between a metal floor and electrically charged metal mosquito netting overhead. He called it the Gadabout.

In 1912, inventor Max Stoehrer, of Massachusetts, with his son, Harold, jumped in with what they called the Dodgem car, whose similarities to Stock's design resulted in a court case. A final settlement was reached in 1923, when the Stoehrers bought out Stock and permanently unplugged his Gadabout.

Only the road ahead was anything but clear: In 1921, *Scientific American* magazine decried the Stoehrer's Dodgem cars as "highly unmanageable."

In 1928, Philadelphia-based Joseph and Robert Lusse, former manufacturers of Stock's Gadabout, perfected the standard bumper car still in use today: front-wheel steering capable of spinning ninety degrees and moving the car in both directions. They called it the Auto Skooter, and then pitted it bumper to bumper with Dodgem.

New lawsuits arose, as did new settlements.

And John Stock? He crashed. Head on.

"He died in New York City, in 1945," said William F. Mangels, "in poverty."

No one was ever immune to the temptation of a bumper car, including Elvis Presley, circa 1960.

HOLD ON TIGHT

I.

Henry Hartman Knoebel, known as Old Hen, didn't need a trolley line. He already had local families—whose husbands worked in the nearby mills or mines—stopping by his Elysburg, Pennsylvania, farm on their way home from church every Sunday so they could brush, water, and feed their horses. Henry charged them twenty-five cents. Then he got the idea to add hayrides, picnics, and refreshments.

Knoebel's grandfather, the Reverend Hartman Henry Knoebel, a German immigrant preacher, had originally bought the nearly three hundred acres, known as Peggy's Farm (and possibly named for Peggy McMaster, whose grandfather received a land patent from a son of William Penn). Reverend Knoebel paid $931, or about $21,000 today. The year was 1828.

By the time Ole Hen grew up, "the desire to farm had diminished," according to a documentary on the Knoebel family, "replaced by an entrepreneurial energy rooted in a logging operation and a uniquely personal vision inspired by the farm's prodigious shade trees and two mountain streams."

A working lumberyard continues to exist at what is today the still-family-owned Knoebels Amusement Resort.

What does not exist is an apostrophe.

Henry Hartman Knoebel's sawmill was a place for neighbors to stop on their way home from Sunday church.

Twister is Knoebels' tall and tangled tribute to Elitch's.

KNOEBELS OPENED ON JULY 4, 1926, with only a handful of games, the Crystal swimming pool, and a steam-powered Philadelphia Toboggan Company carousel. In the years since, the park has added a Whip, in 1930; its first train, the Nickel Plate Railroad, in 1940; Dodgem cars, in 1947 (the park was closed during World War II), pony rides, in 1949; a petting zoo, in 1954; and the 1960 engine Olde Smokey miniature train, which still chugs through scenic backwoods, past old park props. The park has endured a lot, too: Floods from tropical storms delivered blows in 1972, 2006, and 2011. Always, Knoebels snapped back.

Today, in addition to the Three Ponds Golf Course, the Knoebels resort's ride count tops sixty, including a terrifically satisfying Haunted Mansion, a 1973 Pretzel-like dark ride that got a 2016 facelift, to beef up the cursed abode's Bach fugue, trapped monsters, and undisciplined waterfall.

Of its two carousels, one is a 1912 kiddie merry-go-round from Coney Island stylists Solomon Stein and Harry Goldstein; the other, which the park obtained in 1941, ten days before Pearl Harbor, is a 1913, four-abreast Grand Carousel, with sixty-three horses and four chariots on a Charles Looff frame. Catching the brass ring is encouraged, as is a visit to the carousel museum, adjacent to the Tilt-A-Whirl.

In 1985, Knoebels rescued a double-out-and-back 1947 Herman Schmeck woody from the defunct Playland in San Antonio, Texas, where it was called the Rocket. Rebuilt piecemeal without benefit of any blueprints, it was renamed the Phoenix, because it rose from the dead. The park's other coaster is the 1999 Twister, a near replica honoring the Elitch Gardens original, which, despite best intentions, was too fragile to transplant from Denver.

Besides a pervasive campground atmosphere, Knoebels also has, for this day, a unique policy: It's admission free (so's the parking), a courtesy also extended to the family dog, provided Fido stays off the rides.

While some consider the Tilt-A-Whirl a pain in the neck, to the Sellner family it was nirvana.

Patriarch Herbert W. Sellner, a woodworker in Faribault, Minnesota, had already come up with his 1923 Water-Toboggan Slide when he playfully put his young son Art in a chair, placed the chair on top of the kitchen table, and then spun the table.

Art laughed; Herbert got an idea.

What came next was an "amusement apparatus wherein the riders will be moved in general through an orbit and will unexpectedly swing, snap from side to side, or rotate without in any way being able to figure what movement may next take place."

Herbert called it the Tilt-A-Whirl, and he built fourteen of them in his basement before opening the Sellner Manufacturing factory, in 1927. His first customer was the Minnesota State Fair.

Over the years, the premise remained the same, even if the power switched to electricity and the product materials changed to include lighter-weight aluminum and fiberglass.

The Sellners manufactured one thousand Tilt-A-Whirls before selling the business in 2011 to the Plainview, Texas–based Larson International, which intended to keep the Sellner name "out of respect for the long history of this company and the family."

TILT-A-WHIRL

NAME ....

STREET ....

CITY ....

Sellner Manufacturing Co.,   Faribault, Minn.

Manufacturers of Tilt-a-Whirl, Swooper, Sellner Slide and Water Wheel.

THE RIDE WITH MONEY-MAKING RECORDS. Made in two sizes: 7-Car, 28 Pass., 41 ft. diameter. Expressly for small parks, gilly and motorized shows. Weighs 10 tons. 9-Car, 36 Pass., 52 ft. diameter. For parks and wagon shows. Weighs 13 tons. Fill in and mail this coupon. It will bring complete information.

II.

Founded in 1899, and designated a National Historic Landmark in 1987, Kennywood got its name from Andrew Mellon, whose Monongahela Street Railway Company bankrolled the park. The industrialist sought to trade on the good name of Anthony Kenny, who had let the public picnic on his farm's leafy Kenny's Grove since the 1860s.

Kennywood's terrain-hugging Thunderbolt has packed a punch since 1924, when it was the Pippin.

The first signs of development at Kennywood were its dance pavilion, casino, and carousel enclosure, and in contrast to the flimsy structures at most trolley parks, these were solidly constructed. Except for the dance hall, which, before a fiery demise in 1975, had been repurposed into the walk-through Enchanted Castle, the early edifices are still in use; the former casino houses a restaurant. The oldest ride, from 1901, is the Old Mill, despite an early 1920s renovation. Since 2004, it has been given over to the Garfield's Nightmare dark ride, which, some might meow, has already used up its nine lives.

Of Kennywood's six coasters—the latest, 2010's steel Sky Rocket, power-launches from zero to fifty in fewer than three seconds—three are vintage wooden models from John Miller: the out-and-back Jack Rabbit (1920); the single-track Racer (1927), with its wooden Möbius loop and, thanks to a 1990 restoration, its original station façade; and the Pippin (1924), which, in 1968, was reconfigured and renamed Thunderbolt. The latter two delay their lift hills until the middle of the journey, because their rides start with plunges down two of nature's gullies. Thunderbolt's initial drop is fifty feet.

Beginning in 1906, when they bought out the Monongahela Railway, developer F. W. Henninger and advertising specialist Andrew McSwigan, and then their families, owned and ran Kennywood, along with their subsequent acquisitions: Idlewild & SoakZone, a former 1878 campground, in Ligonier, Pennsylvania (and, in its day, Kennywood's chief rival); the 1989 Sandcastle Waterpark, in West Homestead, Pennsylvania; the Lake Compounce Theme Park, in Bristol, Connecticut; and Story Land, in Glen, New Hampshire. Story Land dates back to 1954, when husband-and-wife founders, Bob and Ruth Morrell, brought back a large number of storybook dolls from Germany.

In the 1950s, Kennywood dealt with television by bringing the medium's name acts to the park, including *Superman* star George Reeves, and the even more popular *Lone Ranger* actor Clayton Moore. Of even greater interest to the *Pittsburgh Post-Gazette*, however, was the act that followed, Leopold "Suicide" Simon—"a

Leopold "Suicide" Simon had a dynamite act at Kennywood in the 1950s.

stocky Texan who made his money by curling himself into a coffin-sized box and setting off a stick of dynamite placed six inches from his head."

After the box was blown to pieces, "when the smoke cleared, Simon staggered unsteadily to his feet. Crowds loved it."

After more than a century as a closely held family business, Kennywood Entertainment was sold to the Madrid, Spain–based Parques Reunidos, founded in 1967 and owned (since 2011) by the London-based private equity firm Arle Capital Partners.

At first, changes to Kennywood were slow in coming—granted, in 2008, the stock market collapsed, and it took years before the amusement industry rebounded. But the park's 1936 Noah's Ark fun house, which in its years survived genuine floods, was refurbished in 2016. The original eighty-year-old teetering floorboards and the overall mechanism that rocked the boat were kept, but the attraction was restored to its popular 1969 appearance, when people entered through a whale's mouth. (What is it about amusement parks and whales?)

In a far more ambitious move reflecting contemporary public taste, Kennywood closed the Log Jammer flume ride in 2017 after a thirty-two-year run—it had replaced the 1930 pony track—to make way for Steeler Country, a themed area devoted to and named for the local National Football League team. Projected for completion in 2019, the new land represents the first time any park has linked with a professional sports franchise. Its centerpiece is the 75 mph Steel Curtain, designed to set a state record (tallest roller coaster, 220 feet), a North American record (most inversions, nine), and a world record (tallest inversion, 197 feet).

Noah's Ark fun houses first joined the amusement circuit in 1919, at Venice Pier, in California. Kennywood's was a late arrival, in 1936.

Just as Steel Country was announced in 2018, the park cut the ribbon on another brand-name addition. This, too, carried its own sense of tradition for what was, after all, a once-celebrated trolley park in a once-celebrated industrial town: Thomas the Tank Engine came to Kennywood, replacing the Olde Kennywood Railroad on its scenic Monongahela River route—and serving as the flagship (flagtrain?) attraction for an entire Thomas Town inspired by the Island of Sondo, the setting for the Reverend Wilbert Awdry and his son Christopher's The Railway Series books and the long-running television adaptation, *Thomas and Friends*.

III.

Calling them "living pieces of history that allow visitors to get a palpable sense of time and place," Arthur Levine, a contemporary travel writer who specializes in the amusement industry, says that what gives surviving trolley parks their special spark is their "decidedly un-corporate look and feel." That's because so many are independently owned and operated.

There are only fifteen trolley parks remaining—chronologically, beginning with the oldest, they are Lake Compounce, Bristol, Connecticut, 1846; Seabreeze Amusement Park, Rochester, New York, 1879; Dorney Park, Allentown, Pennsylvania, 1884; Lakemont Park, Altoona, Pennsylvania, 1894; Waldameer Park, Erie, Pennsylvania, 1896; Midway Park, Maple Springs, New York, 1898; Kennywood, West Mifflin, Pennsylvania, 1899; Bushkill Park, Easton, Pennsylvania, 1902; Canobie Lake Park, Salem, New Hampshire, 1902; Camden Park, Huntington, West Virginia, 1903; Oaks Amusement Park, Portland, Oregon, 1905; Hersheypark, Hershey, Pennsylvania, 1906; Clementon Park, Clementon, New Jersey, 1907; Lakeside Amusement Park, Denver, Colorado, 1908; and Quassy Amusement Park, Middlebury, Connecticut, 1908. Only four of them (Lake Compounce, Kennywood, Hersheypark, and Clementon) have corporate ties, while Midway is owned by New York State.

And while it is polite to say that age is only a state of mind, when it comes to their physical state, some of these parks have noticeably held up better than others.

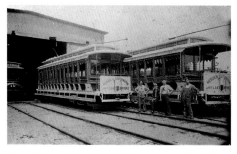

Some things change: Lake Compounce, the oldest amusement park in the United States, used to rely primarily on customers arriving by trolley.

Each has its own distinctions. Lake Compounce's rides include an 1898 Looff Carousel; the 2000 Boulder Dash, the first coaster to be built *on* a mountainside (unless one considers the perilous old Cyclone on the cliffs of Fort George); and the 1927 Wildcat, a PTC out-and-back that, for its ninetieth birthday in 2017, had its bumps unbumped and its turns made tighter.

Some things don't: Lake Compounce's sylvan setting has perennially framed the park's family experience.

In addition to its status "as the oldest amusement park in America," Lake Compounce is also where, on July 21, 1989, two model-dancer-singers from Munich known as Milli Vanilli shamed themselves live at the park's twenty-thousand-seat amphitheater.

Well into their hit "Girl You Know It's True" their prerecorded playback skipped and kept repeating the same lyric ad nauseam—revealing to the world that the lip-synching duo, Rob Pilatus and Fab Morvan, could not sing their own songs.

Seabreeze Amusement Park, in Rochester, New York, has lineage. It began when its 1925 open-air swimming pool, with its toboggan, water wheel, and water merry-go-round, failed and was made over into a bingo parlor. The outlook brightened in 1935, when George W. Long Jr. took over Seabreeze from the Rochester Transit Company. "His father was a concessionaire there before him," said Irondequoit town historian Maude I. West, referring to George Long Sr., whose family manufactured rides in Philadelphia. George Senior ran the carousel and lived in its back room "during the summer," said Rob Norris, a fifth-generation descendant of Long's. Under George Jr., the park was known as Dreamland (in 1974, it became Seabreeze), and the diligent proprietor, said West, "made many improvements, built a number of first-rate concessions, and established a well-run park, free from rowdyism."

It's alive—and landmarked. But the 1902 Leap-the-Dips, arguably the oldest roller coaster in the world, stands on shaky ground: Lakemont Park, in Altoona, Pennsylvania.

Fried dough, anyone? Make that, everyone.

Whether straight or spiral shaped, the deep-fried cruller known as the churro has been on fair and amusement park snack menus for as long as anyone can remember, even though no one seems to know where or when sugar, salt, water, butter, eggs, and flour were first mixed, fried, and dusted with cinnamon and sugar.

The name, plainly Spanish, may have to do with a U.S. government tariff classification—a "churro" was a particular kind of mountain sheep the Spanish exported to South America in 1864, and the supposition is that South American shepherds tending their flocks grew hungry, fried up strips of dough in pans over pasture fires, and through some means sent the recipe north. Squeezing it through pastry bags gave it its ridges.

The funnel cake, another fried and sugared specialty, has a slightly more transparent history, descending from German immigrants to Pennsylvania in the 1700s.

At first, the Pennsylvania Dutch—the term derived from their language, they were, in fact, Pennsylvania Deutsch—called the fried-up cake *drechter kuchen* ("the right cake"), and changed the name to "funnel cake" once bakers started pouring batter into the cooking oil through a funnel.

Seabreeze, on Lake Ontario, owed much of its development to George Long Sr. and Jr., who had family ties to Blackpool Pleasure Beach, in England.

The Norris family upholds the tradition of Seabreeze, which the National Amusement Park Historical Association recognizes as the thirteenth-oldest amusement park in the world still remaining in its original location. This places it alongside such institutions as Copenhagen's Bakken (1583), Vienna's Prater (1766), the Isle of Wight's Blackgang Chine (1842), Copenhagen's Tivoli (1843), Lake Compounce (1846), Tokyo's Hanayashiki (1853), Paris's Jardin d'Acclimatation (1860), the U.K.'s Teignmouth Grand Pier (1865) and Blackpool Central Pier (1868), Ohio's Cedar Point (1870), the U.K.'s Clacton Pier (1871), and Pennsylvania's Idlewild Park (1878).

Erie, Pennsylvania's Waldameer Park owes its magnificent view to the Great Lake from which the town took its name. If one looks quickly, its glistening blue surface can be best seen from the top of the Ravine Flyer II coaster's eighty-foot lift hill, moments before plunging 118 feet into a blackout tunnel. Crossing a bridge over a four-lane highway, the train resumes its 57 mph path into a ninety-degree banked turn. The Roller Coaster Database rates the experience as "extreme."

As for why Waldameer calls its attention-grabber the Ravine Flyer *II*, a headline in the August 8, 1938, *Erie Dispatch-Herald* tells the story: YOUTH, 19, LEAPS TO DEATH FROM RAVINE FLYER.

Stricken with fear while aboard, Clarence Sersch jumped and fell eighteen feet below, landing on the highway beneath that stretch of coaster track, according to initial news flashes. His sister later testified, however, that Clarence did not jump, but fell. The district attorney's investigation uncovered evidence of rotted planks and wheel damage, suggesting that a malfunction might have scared the teen, prompting him to stand up in the moving vehicle and causing him to tumble to his death.

Raven Flyer I, which had operated since 1921, was condemned.

And soon demolished.

Thanks to "a growing relationship with the Allan Herschell Co. in nearby North Tonawanda, a complete Herschell kiddyland of rides was installed in the 1950s," according to a factsheet supplied by the Friends of Midway Park, a state-owned playground along New York's Chautauqua Lake, originally established by the Jamestown & Lake Erie Railway. In its heyday, Midway was frequented by Jamestown's favorite daughter, a then-aspiring model and actress named Lucille Ball.

Stephen King put Canobie Lake Park on the map, even though it had been there since 1902. "I didn't want a Disney World, I didn't want a Six Flags park, and I settled on a place called Canobie Lake Park, which is in Massachusetts," the master of uneasiness told National Public Radio in 2013 while promoting his thriller *Joyland*, set in a haunted amusement park. The only problem is that Canobie Lake Park is not

The Ravine Flyer II at Erie, Pennsylvania's Waldameer Water World affords a breathtaking view of Lake Erie and the opportunity to cross a four-lane highway.

Rocky Point Amusement Park (1847–1995), on Narragansett Bay in Warwick, Rhode Island, officially became a trolley park in the summer of 1900, when Rhode Island Suburban Railway began regular electric-train service from Providence, although before that, it was the scene of a heinous murder.

On Monday, August 28, 1893, five-year-old Maggie Sheffield, whose mother had died a month after Maggie's birth, was taken to Rocky Point by her father, Frank, a forty-year-old former school principal from Pawcatuck, Connecticut.

Having suffered a freak head injury while ringing the school bell, Sheffield was prescribed medicinal opium and cocaine to ease his pain. They also played havoc with his judgment.

Father and daughter had lunch at the Shore Dining Hall before Frank escorted Maggie up a rocky cliff.

Minutes later, Sheffield wandered up to two men outside a nearby clubhouse. "I want to be turned over to an officer," he said. "I have killed my child." As the men gasped, Sheffield blurted out, "I did not know I had struck her until I saw blood."

A jury found Sheffield not guilty by reason of insanity. Among the trial witnesses was the Good Samaritan who had lifted Maggie's lifeless body from the murder scene, after her father had bashed in her head with a rock.

Sheffield died in a mental institution on March 14, 1901.

Rocky Point, Rhode Island, lays claim to the world's largest shore-dinner hall, as well as one of the most heinous cases of filicide in America.

in Massachusetts, but New Hampshire—Salem, to be exact, which was how Maine resident King may have gotten confused, given the Salem Witch Trials and all.

"We're just happy to be part of it," said Canobie Lake spokesperson Chris Nicoli of the park's link to King, who was likely inspired by the Mine of Lost Souls dark ride.

The novel, set in 1973, has the killer slitting the victim's throat and dumping her inside the Horror House. Years later, *Joyland*'s protagonist, working at the park, enters Horror House from underneath the Screaming Skull.

"And," a Horror House employee contemplates long afterward, "just suppose…a young girl's hand reached out in that darkness and took mine?"

Canobie's Nicoli supposed just that. "We are very proud of the park and that it's inspiring others' creativity," he said.

Give the author a hand.

The Stephen King novel *Joyland* may owe something to the Mine of Lost Souls at Salem, New Hampshire's Canobie Lake Park.

Camden Park originally took its name from the Camden Interstate Railway Company, which itself was named for oil tycoon and U.S. senator Johnson Newlon Camden (1828–1908), a Union sympathizer who remained a civilian during the Civil War. It is the only amusement park in West Virginia, and it draws decidedly mixed reviews on social media, where comments raise concerns about everything from alleged public smoking and cursing by the staff, to the price of the park's hand-dipped corn dog. In 2016, the Slingshot, a compact, steel-tracked spinning coaster, was brought in from Italy's SBF Visa Group, to keep company with Camden's vintage '60s Pretzel Wild Mouse, called the Hawnted House, and a 1958 woody, the Big Dipper—or IG DIPPER, as its sign reads, according to a 2017 Facebook posting.

The Oaks Amusement Park and Jantzen Beach Amusement Park, in Portland, Oregon, both vied for the title of Coney Island of the Northwest. Jantzen Beach, which was opened in 1928 by the swimwear manufacturer Carl C. Jantzen, closed in 1970. That handed the crown to Oaks, which was named for the trees along the Portland Railway, Light, and Power Company tracks. It opened May 30, 1905, two days before the ribbon was cut on the city's

Lewis and Clark Centennial Exposition, and essentially served as the fair's extended

Camden Park, in Huntington, is West Virginia's only amusement park.

midway. The Bollinger family took it over in 1909, and in 1985 donated it to the city.

In announcing a 2018 addition, Oaks Park held a naming contest for its upcoming coaster from the Bavarian rides manufacturer Gerstlauer. Five thousand submissions were received.

The winner: Adrenaline Peak.

What better name for something whose contest application promised "a 72′ vertical lift, past-vertical initial drop, 97° loop, an Immelman turn, heartline roll, 45 mph maximum speed, 1,050′ track, and a 48″ minimum height"?

CLEMENTON PARK, WHICH BEGAN a century before with trolley service from Camden, New Jersey, and its 1993 Splash World waterpark, were bought in 2007 by Adrenaline Family Entertainment—Adrenaline being a corporate name, not a family one. Family entertainment was its

A cash prize or food basket from a dance marathon at Clementon Park, or elsewhere, provided a temporary salve during the Depression.

product, or at least it became so when an Oklahoma-based private equity firm formed the company for the purpose of acquiring Clementon. Adrenaline was led by Kieran Burke and Gary Story, respectively the former chief executive officer and chief financial officer of the ten-year-old Six Flags Corporation. At Clementon, their first order of business was to update the water park, which had not been touched since the early 2000s.

Like all great inventions—the roller coaster, the ice-cream cone—the origin of the corn dog is open to debate.

On July 5, 1927, Stanley S. Jenkins, of Buffalo, New York, filed an application to patent his "combined dipping, cooking, and article-holding apparatus," which was granted on March 26, 1929. Besides "boiled ham, hard boiled eggs, cheese, sliced peaches, pineapples, bananas, and like fruit," on his list of "food impaled on a stick" was a battered wiener.

The batter included cornmeal, hence the name. The real secret to its success, however, had to do with the fact that, while hurtful to the arteries, the corn dog comforts the soul. It is deep-fried.

Despite Jenkins's patent, the Minnesota State Fair—the same forward-thinking enterprise that introduced the Tilt-A-Whirl—lays claim to debuting what it called the Pronto Pup, in 1941.

Brothers Carl and Neil Fletcher, on the other hand, insist *they* were first, at the Texas State Fair, even though most accounts give the date of their food concession as 1942.

Still, it was not until Ed Waldmire Jr. stuck a stick in it, called it a Cozy Dog, and sold it in Springfield, Illinois, on June 16, 1946, that the corn dog as it is recognized today first stuffed an American mouth.

Oaks Amusement Park has vied for the title of Portland, Oregon's "Coney Island of the Northwest" since 1905.

Three months after repairing lake damage caused by a storm that had hit twenty-three years before, Adrenaline sold Clementon Park and Splash World to the Oklahoma City–based Premier Parks for an undisclosed sum.

The following year, Adrenaline Family Entertainment folded its tent.

Quassy, on Lake Quassapaug, served as the train stop between Waterbury and Woodbury, in the aptly named Middlebury. In 1901—seven years before the arrival of the trolley line and the park—Samuel Mansfield Stone, a writer for *Forest and Stream*, referred to its setting as "the handsomest bit of natural water on the earth."

A champion of the great outdoors, Stone expressed alarm about the area's future, rather than anticipate the charm and affordability of today's Quassy Amusement Park & Waterpark.

"One feature of the lake that is likely to be destroyed by a projected line of electric cars from Waterbury," Stone warned, is "its sequestration."

Furthermore, "It is feared the trolley will introduce an objectionable element, but the wheels of progress cannot be stayed from such considerations."

The arrival of a trolley to Lake Quassapaug ignited fears that it might lead to further intrusions.

Forty thousand people turned out for
Abbot Kinney's Venice of America
opening day, July 4, 1905.

PART FOUR

BEATING A PATH

BY LAND AND SEA

uring 1910 and 1911, the big names of the amusement industry picked up their play things and brought them to Southern California: Frederick Ingersoll, to downtown Los Angeles; LaMarcus Thompson, Tom Prior, and Frederick Church, to Venice; and Charles I. D. Looff, to both Long Beach and Santa Monica. In degrees ranging from slight to extreme, new names also made their presences felt: Charles J. Sketchley, Thaddeus Lowe, Abbot Kinney, William Selig, and later, but permanently, Walter Knott and Walt Disney.

As cinema's pioneers were to discover, the key advantage to sunny California was its perennial summer. Predating the movies, amusement parks in Los Angeles and its beach cities experienced no urgencies to open and close for the season.

Every park's season ran a profitable twelve months.

Climate played something of a lesser role in the cooler north. Besides Woodward's Gardens (1866–1894), which had served as Mary Elitch's inspiration, an early roller coaster gave the City by the Bay a good ride for its money, in 1884—four months after LaMarcus Thompson opened his Switchback Railway in Coney Island.

On November 11, 1884, under the heading "A Circular Railway," San Francisco's *Evening Bulletin* told of a park at the corner of Eighth and Mission Streets that up until then had featured only outdoor sporting games. Now, however, there was "to be seen in operation something decidedly new for San Francisco. It is called the circular gravity railway."

Clearly, a precedent—and a market—had been set. Starting in the mid-1890s, San Francisco could claim three consecutive Chutes parks. Their owner was Charles Louis Ackerman (1850–1907), who purchased nonexclusive rights to the Shoot the Chutes from Paul Boyton and, from 1895 until 1901, ran the first Chutes on Haight Street between Cole and Clayton. The second, at Fulton

Attorney Charles Louis Ackerman helped legitimize vaudeville with San Francisco's Orpheum Theater. He also brought Shoot the Chutes to the city.

1023 The Chutes, Tenth Avenue and Fulton Streets, San Francisco.

Ackerman situated his three consecutive San Francisco Chutes parks (from top) on Haight, Fillmore, and Fulton Streets.

and Tenth Avenue, operated from 1902 to 1908, and the third from 1909 to 1911, in the Fillmore District.

A New Orleans native, Ackerman moved west after graduating Yale Law School. An accomplished estate lawyer, Ackerman became "president of the Equitable Gas Company before it was absorbed into the Pacific Gas and Electric Company, and was active in the Odd Fellows and B'nai B'rith," according to his papers in the San Francisco Performing Arts Library & Museum.

In addition to the Chutes, Ackerman presided over the Grand Opera House and was a founding director of vaudeville's influential Orpheum circuit theater chain. The Chutes followed the 1887 debut of San Francisco's lavish Orpheum Theater by eight years. Chief among its participatory amusements were a Scenic Railway, a carousel, a zoo, and a Camera Obscura (Latin for "dark chamber"), a sixteenth-century invention also featured at the Chicago Fair; on Haight Street, it was mounted at the top of the Chutes slide. Literally a combination of smoke and mirrors, the device used a large convex lens focused on reflective glass. "Just as the boat passengers reached the top," said city historian James R. Smith, "they entered the dark building and were mesmerized by the view reflected on the mirror." Still in the dark, boats were then sent into free-fall, ending up in the pond below.

Little Egypt made it to the Chutes in 1899, which only enhanced the park's popularity at a time when, like Egypt herself, it was already bursting at the seams. Ackerman closed the property, and, in the more spacious Richmond District, he built his next park,

Fulton Street Chutes, reputed to contain the city's first movie house and the biggest auditorium west of Chicago, the four-thousand-seat Chutes Pavilion Theater—site of the celebration for the city's survival of the April 18, 1906, earthquake and fire. (The park sustained only minor damage, and reopened within a few weeks.)

A year after the natural disaster, another unexpected threat arrived, on two blocks bordered by Fillmore, Turk, Webster, and Eddy: Coney Island Park. Charles Ackerman died a month after its November opening, but his son, Irving, then twenty-four, sprang into action. A Stanford undergrad who had gone to Harvard Law (he eventually formed his own vaudeville circuit, managed movie theaters, partnered with Marcus Loew, and helped put together Columbia Pictures), Irving shut down the Ackermans' Chutes in the Richmond District and bought Coney Island Park outright.

He then rebuilt and renamed it.

The Fillmore Street Chutes opened July 14, 1909, only to close May 29, 1911.

A faulty water heater in its barbershop caught fire, as did the rest of the park.

Adolph Sutro's land holdings incorporated a shorefront parcel in the Outer Richmond district that he devoted to public recreation.

ADOLPH HEINRICH JOSEPH SUTRO (1830–1898), a Prussian-Jewish émigré, came to America in 1850 and struck it rich with Nevada's Comstock Lode. Six years later, when San Francisco suffered its own version of the Wall Street Panic of 1873, Sutro bought real estate and became the city's largest landowner. A hero to the working class for his philanthropy, Sutro was elected mayor of San Francisco, serving from 1895 until 1897.

"I don't believe in aristocracy," said Sutro. "The aristocracy of the mind is the only aristocracy I recognize."

Recreational demand was something else he recognized. In 1887, in the Lands End area of the Outer Richmond District, the mutton-chopped mogul (the whiskers obscured a scar he got thwarting a store robbery) built an outdoor saltwater aquarium directly to the north of a resort he owned, the Cliff House.

Sutro's home, also nearby, might have been modest by magnate standards, but its gardens were lavish, with a standing invitation for anyone to come explore them, free of charge. By the early 1890s, he was willing to spring for an even bigger public enrichment, a public bathhouse—only this time, he wanted nothing modest.

The $1 million ($29 million today) steam-punk natatorium—"Imagine Madison Square Garden filled with sea water," said *Harper's Weekly*—with its "slides, trapezes, springboards and a high dive…could accommodate 10,000 people at one time, and offered 20,000 bathing suits and 40,000 towels for rent," said an account on the Golden Gate National Recreation Area website.

San Francisco's Playland, south of the Cliff House, began to take shape once Adolph Sutro built his steampunk bathhouse in 1896.

Outside, on the path called Merrie Way, Sutro installed attractions he'd purchased from the California Midwinter International Exhibition in Golden Gate Park. These included a sixteen-gondola Firth Wheel, named for its engineer, J. Kirk Firth, who cribbed his design from George Ferris's Chicago masterwork of the year before; a house of mirrors called the Mystic Maze; and the illusion that put its audience off balance, the Haunted Swing.

These paved the way for what ultimately became George K. Whitney's Playland at the Beach.

"The origins of San Francisco's first and only beachside amusement park were humble enough," said writer Robert Ehler Blaisdell, referring to the string of carnival stands to the south of the Cliff House and Sutro Baths, "near the terminus of the Park & Ocean railroad line." Around 1914, the son of carousel maker Charles I. D. Looff, Arthur Looff, put up a merry-go-round between Balboa and Fulton Streets, and around it, a Looff Hippodrome to shield the attraction from the elements. Such an encasement was essential in the Ocean Beach neighborhood, given the marine layer that leaves it in a nearly perpetual fog.

Candy and shooting gallery concessionaire John Friedle saw the big picture, and he thought it wise to purchase the property, partner with Looff, and upgrade the amusements. With

Adjacent to his baths, Sutro installed rides from the defunct California Midwinter International Exhibition, seen here.

investments of $150,000 ($2.1 million today), in 1921 they opened ten Looff-designed rides and a midway.

To satisfy the crowds at all hours, rides kept coming. By 1922, the property featured a Ferris Wheel, a Whip, an Aeroplane Swing, the Dodgem, Noah's Ark—and a change of name, one that hung around for a while: Chutes at the Beach, even though the park had no connection to the earlier Ackerman Chutes, which by then had been gone for eleven years.

By 1922, the stage was set for the park's most ambitious attraction—a gravity ride.

Arthur Looff had apprenticed with his father for sixteen years, and lent his talents to only three roller coasters: Playland's Big Dipper; the Giant

The amusement area briefly took the name Chutes at the Beach, even though it had no connection to the Ackermans' earlier efforts.

Dipper, its slightly younger sibling seventy-five miles to the south on the Santa Cruz Beach Boardwalk; and the 1906 Flying Toboggan for Crescent Park (1886–1979) in Riverside, Rhode Island, where Charles Looff settled briefly before moving to Southern California.

In creating Santa Cruz's Giant Dipper, Arthur was quoted as saying that he was seeking a "combination earthquake, balloon ascension, and aeroplane drop." It worked, and it lasted. "Fog and rain in winter make it go faster," said Aaron Sannes, who as a student operated the Dipper in the mid-1980s—not an easy task. "To bring the train in, seven brakes have to be released with just the right finesse."

The Giant Dipper, it was documented on its application to become a National Historical Landmark (granted in 1987), is the only coaster "on the West Coast that remains the centerpiece of an active amusement park." To that point, the Santa Cruz Beach Boardwalk is the oldest surviving amusement park in the State of California,

San Francisco's Big Dipper came to roost in 1922, and would hatch a younger cousin down the coast.

The Santa Cruz Beach Boardwalk's 1924 Giant Dipper has been likened to the late, great Bobs at Chicago's Riverview.

and the only privately owned major boardwalk in America. (The Canfield family has stood at the helm since 1952.)

The Boardwalk's original mastermind was Fred W. Swanton, born in Brooklyn on April 11, 1862. Fred's father, Albion, a carpenter, settled with his wife and three children in Santa Cruz in 1868. Fred graduated from business college in San Francisco in 1881 and established himself as a bookkeeper for a trading company in Fresno. He then traveled with his mother, according to an 1892 Santa Cruz County history, and while East, "obtained the State right for a telephone patent…and did a profitable business."

On Santa Cruz's Pacific Avenue, he and his father built a three-story hotel, which burned down in 1888. This led to their opening, and quickly selling, three livery stables. Fred next tried a drugstore, which he sold. In 1889 "he started in the electric light business with a three hundred light machine." Within two years, his company, Santa Cruz Electric Light and Power, was supplying the town with four thousand lights. He then campaigned for Santa Cruz to approve the building of an electric railway, which it did. This led to his laying plans for a casino and boardwalk patterned after those at Coney Island.

The casino, the onion-domed Neptune Hall, like many so-called casinos elsewhere, placed dancing above gambling (which was illegal, anyhow), and like many casinos elsewhere, burned down; in Neptune Hall's case, two years after it opened. "Undeterred," said a National Register account, "Swanton retained architect William W. Weeks, who drew plans that included a new casino, an indoor swimming pool or natatorium, a 'pleasure' pier, and a boardwalk."

Much in demand after the previous year's San Francisco earthquake, architect William W. Weeks designed the 1907 Santa Cruz Beach Boardwalk.

Launched on the Fourth of July, 1925, the Thomas Prior and Frederick Church Giant Dipper—with no involvement by Arthur Looff—for San Diego's Belmont Park, was built at what was then called Mission Beach Amusement Center. Construction of the landmark, made from Douglas fir trees, took only two months; its cost was $150,000, or $4.5 million today.

The center's driving force was San Francisco sugar magnate John Diedrich Spreckels, since 1887 a major developer of San Diego, and its wealthiest resident. A year after the Dipper opened, Spreckels died, leaving the amusement park to the city.

Through the 1940s, the ride flourished along with the park's several other attractions, until, by the '60s, the property's dilapidation became a civic embarrassment. A sliver of its former self, the Giant Dipper shut down in 1976.

A death warrant was issued—only to be stayed, thanks to a herculean "Save the Coaster Committee" public effort. The capper was the Dipper's 1978 designation as a National Historic Landmark.

It took another dozen years, however, for the ride to come back to life.

A San Diego Seaside Committee was formed as a joint venture between the new developer of Belmont Park and the Santa Cruz Boardwalk, and together they initiated a $2 million restoration.

The reopening took place August 11, 1990.

The lift hill has been rattling its chain ever since.

San Diego's 1925 Belmont Park Giant Dipper rose from the dead in 1990, thanks to public and private support.

Weeks had been much in demand, especially after the 1906 San Francisco earthquake. When the rebuilt casino opened in 1907, the recreation zone had its indoor pool, rides that included a LaMarcus Thompson Scenic Railway, and a boardwalk like Atlantic City's. President Theodore Roosevelt, who once came to Santa Cruz en route to see the redwoods, sent Swanton a telegram of congratulations.

Known to all, Swanton served as town mayor for three terms, beginning in 1927, and was credited with developing the oceanfront, which, through preservation efforts

George K. Whitney saw Playland at the Beach through the Depression, World War II, and the Television Age.

and responsible zoning restrictions, still retains the captivating charms it had in his day.

For all his dedication, however, Fred Swanton died broke, in 1940.

The wives of Arthur Looff and John Friedle reportedly did not get along. Elsie Friedle ran the Waffle House at San Francisco's Chutes at the Beach, but syrupy sweet she was not. John, again seeing the big picture, thought it best to buy out his partner. Even then, heated matters did not cool down. To keep the family at peace, in 1926 Friedle hired George Kerr Whitney to be the Chutes' general manager, after the thirty-two-year-old from Mt. Vernon, Washington, had already spent three years as a park concessionaire, with his older (by seven years) brother, Leo.

Among the Whitney wares were "quick-finish" photographs of customers poking their heads out from behind different plywood settings that were painted comically. It was an idea George came up with while in Melbourne, Australia, where he and Leo had gone to help a friend set up his nickelodeon business in the city's new Luna Park. It was Leo, the artist to George's businessman, who acquired the "Lightno" Quick Process from a contact at Eastman Kodak.

With the outbreak of World War I, Luna Park closed on government orders, so all attention could be focused on the military effort.

George first returned to Seattle, where his wife, Eva (known as Daisy), whom he had met and married in Australia, did not care for the climate. The Whitneys then moved to San Francisco. George got his foot in the door at Friedle's park by purchasing a shooting gallery, on time payments, for $3,000 ($44,000 today). Leo reactivated the quick-finish photo studio. Within a short period, George owned three shooting galleries, and, by 1928, Chutes at the Beach was renamed Playland at the Beach (sometimes with hyphens).

"It's funny how people let their hair down when they're away from home," observed George K. Whitney, whose Fun House claimed the "longest indoor slide in the world."

The Friedles left when George and Leo bought them out. As the Depression progressed, they also bought out, at bargain-basement prices, the private concessionaires, including Topsy's Roost, the fried-chicken restaurant, and Playland itself—owning it outright. Informally but widely, the park became known as Whitney's Playland. It even had its own dessert: It's-It, named for George's reaction to tasting the scoop of ice cream sandwiched between two oatmeal cookies and dipped in dark chocolate. (Presently produced in Burlingame, California, by a concern that bought the rights, the dessert's seven flavors, including green tea and pumpkin, are sold in specialty stores in the West, Manhattan, and Brooklyn.)

The Whitney buying spree continued with the Cliff House, which George purchased from the Sutro estate in 1937. In 1952, he bought the Sutro Baths building. In time, George even bought out Leo, who was ready to retire.

The park made it through the Depression by adhering to George's philosophy that "Playland is a nickel and dime business, and we'll do well as long as people have nickels and dimes in their pockets." It also made it through World War II, as a morale booster.

By 1950, Playland was referred to as "America's largest privately owned amusement park," and its owner, at the time grossing $3 million a year ($31 million today), had been crowned the "Barnum of the Golden Gate."

A musement parks, as with the rest of the entertainment industry—indeed, a good part of America—reaped a golden harvest in the years following the war.

"The first peacetime Fourth of July holiday since 1941 saw record crowds here and in Eastern Pennsylvania and Southern New Jersey," Billboard told readers in its July 20, 1946, issue. "Many reported that the holiday turn-out was the biggest in the past 10 years." An adjacent article from Atlantic City began, "The resort rode thru its first post-war July 4 holiday week in record-breaking style." And, from Coney Island: "Four-day holiday weekend, with perfect weather, exceeded every expectation."

Hollywood did particularly well; in 1946, eighty million Americans, or 57 percent of the country, went to the movies *every week*.

Those running these businesses had to move with the curves, which came quickly and unexpectedly, like on a roller coaster.

After the boom of the previous year, in 1947 homeowners became content with their new comforts, including, as of 1948, the most powerful stay-at-home magnet of all: television.

Small-screen stars Milton Berle and Sid Caesar and the situation comedy *I Love Lucy* began providing as many chuckles as could be had at amusement parks—*Lucy* alone had eleven million families watching every week, at a time when there were only fifteen million TV sets in the entire country—so the Tilyous at Coney Island's Steeplechase Park chose to fight fire with fire. Directly next door to the Pavilion of Fun, they opened a Television Hall. With benches and three TV sets (no one called them monitors then), crowds could come watch three different programs, except when important events were broadcast, like boxing matches. Then, all three sets were tuned to the same channel.

At Playland in San Francisco, George K. Whitney "was like George Tilyou," said amusement park specialist Gary Kyriazi, finding similarities in the impresarios' "keen talent for attracting customers, but not cheating them." Even so, during the 1950s, Whitney suffered some major missteps.

In a lengthy 2002 oral history with John Martini, a historian for the National Park Service, George K. Whitney Jr., born in 1922 and an active principal at Playland after World War II, said he was finally able to chide his father about something. In 1955, the elder Whitney installed a sky tram whose cable spanned the Sutro Baths basin, from the Cliff House to Point Lobos. Expensive to design, build, and maintain, the slow, one-way journey violated Whitney Sr.'s long-held rule that to be profitable, an attraction required easy entrance and exit for customers, for a quick turnaround.

"From a money standpoint," Whitney Jr. said, midway games such as "Spinning Wheels of Fortune, and so forth" were the biggest profit engines, because the games "were quasi-gambling." Tickets were two cents apiece, and the maximum betting limit was one dollar (about $9.25 today). Prizes were stuffed dolls and the like, not money, which would have classified the Midway as an illegal casino.

Still, to attract people to the games, a park needed star attractions, and in 1955, Playland made a strategic blunder by removing two of its biggest—the original Shoot the Chutes and the Big Dipper. In the case of the latter, it was a matter of high insurance premiums and maintenance costs.

In the late '60s, racial incidents broke out in the concession areas, with fistfights between rival gangs. Windows were broken, and though the violence was contained, the negative publicity delivered a blow to what was already dwindling attendance.

George Whitney Jr., who died shortly after his oral history was recorded, played down the trouble, especially in light of the full-scale riots that later played out in San Francisco neighborhoods like Hunters Point. And while he candidly admitted that his father was a cold and distant parent, George Jr. took pride in that never once did he ever hear George Sr. utter a racial or religious slur, and that their park had a long tradition of hiring people of all different backgrounds.

WHAT SET THE CLOCK ticking on Playland was George Whitney Sr.'s death in 1958.

His will essentially divided his estate, including Playland and the Cliff House and Sutro Baths properties, giving 50 percent to his widow, Eva, and 25 percent each to his son and daughter, Beatrice. George Jr. took over operations. Then, one morning in the early '60s, he read in the newspaper—as did his sister—that their mother had sold her majority interest to an outside party, a fellow named Bob Frazier. Eva Whitney's secret deal permanently divided the properties, to say nothing of the family.

Frazier announced that Playland would be turned into condos. Whitney Jr. concentrated on the Cliff House and the Sutro Baths, eventually buying out his sister. He then began five years of negotiations with the National Park Service to unload the real estate, and eventually made a deal for $6.5 million ($28.5 million today) and left San Francisco altogether, to retire in tranquil Friday Harbor, Washington.

Sutro Baths burned down mysteriously on June 26, 1966. Playland at the Beach's final day of operation was Labor Day, September 4, 1972.

"Goodbye…to part of our youth," wrote the *Chronicle*'s Herb Caen, who devoted his entire September 4 column to eulogizing the park, "and, like that youth, we expected Playland to last forever. It is an odd, sad feeling to have outlived it."

The view from the Cliff House changed considerably by 1953, but the spirit of the beach remained the same.

BEFORE ASSUMING PLAYLAND'S TOP job after his father's death, George Whitney Jr. went to Southern California, to work on a project for which the Stanford Research Institute had first approached him, in 1954.

Bringing his amusement park savvy to the table, Whitney so impressed the client that he was permanently hired to continue in an advisory position. He was Employee Number Seven.

Whitney's personal contributions to the planning were serpentine queues, to conserve space and provide customers with the illusion that the line was moving faster than it really was. He also called for separate entrances and exits on every attraction, to keep the passengers loading and unloading, and the rides in constant motion.

Whitney's ideas are still being used throughout the amusement and theme park industry, including at the original project site.

It's a place the client named after himself.

Disneyland.

BIRDS OF A FEATHER

Whether by fate or sheer coincidence, Southern California's first amusement attraction took shape on farmland bordering what would become Buena Park and Anaheim, towns where, seven decades later, Knott's Berry Farm and Disneyland would set ineradicable examples for the amusement industry. After enticing investors like Los Angeles land developer Henry Gaylord Wilshire, an English naturalist from South Africa named Dr. Charles J. Sketchley ordered a flock of ostriches from Cape Town. With dollar signs in his eyes, his plan was to pluck their plumage, a much-sought-after commodity for the fashion accessories of the time. Natural feathers sold for anywhere from $25 to $250 a pound. The birds themselves could each fetch $1,000.

After enduring the arduous passage from Africa to California via the port of Galveston, Texas, the ostriches arrived in Los Angeles on March 22, 1882—twenty-two of them, out of the two hundred that started out on the journey. The rest had perished en route. Sketchley was not deterred. Taking stock of his flock, he told a reporter, "I

Southern California's first tourist attractions to lay golden eggs were ostrich farms.

have found that not only are the ostriches quite as healthy as in Africa, but they are actually more prolific here than in their native country."

For this, he praised "the glorious climate of California, which seems to greatly increase the fertility of all animals."

It also fertilized curiosity.

Sketchley's ranch attracted so many sightseers on a daily basis that, sometime around October 1882, the rancher-cum-scientist awoke to the notion of charging visitors fifty cents each, and setting up a gift shop.

What first sparked Los Angeles's massive influx of tourists—a trend that has never abated—was the fierce competition between the Southern Pacific, which had been serving the distant agricultural outpost since 1876, and the Atchison, Topeka and Santa Fe, which chugged into town nine years later. "A hearty price war ensued," said LA historians Cory and Sarah Stargel, "with ticket prices reaching record lows in 1887."

Still prancing, to the accompaniment of a Stinson 165 Military Band Organ, the sixty-eight hand-carved horses on the merry-go-round in the Crystal Springs picnic area of Griffith Park have every reason to jump.

Originally commissioned in 1924 by John D. Spreckels for the Mission Beach Amusement Center in San Diego, the Herschell-Spillman Engineering Company's carousel moved to Griffith Park in 1937 and became the stuff of legend.

"I remember riding the merry-go-round and Daddy would be sitting there just staring at us." Diane Disney Miller, Walt Disney's oldest daughter, recalled her and sister Sharon's frequent childhood trips to Griffith Park, near her father's animation studio, on Hyperion Avenue and Griffith Park Boulevard.

Sitting on a bench watching his girls, Walt Disney began to imagine a type of amusement park where adults might also participate.

Allan Herschell founded his ride-manufacturing company in North Tonawanda, New York, in 1915.

Angelenos did not have to journey to Mauch Chunk to experience a sky train. They had their own above Altadena.

Seeking access to a greater number of customers, in 1885 Sketchley aligned with the Welsh-born Griffith J. Griffith, a former Northern California industrialist who made a fortune in mining before moving downstate. The two transported Sketchley's ostriches to Rancho Los Feliz, along the Los Angeles River, to what is now the Crystal Springs picnic area of Griffith Park—where the business lasted another four years, until financial reversals shuttered the entire operation.

All was not lost. Griffith Park came into existence, according to one theory, because as he was ridding himself of the farm in 1896, Griffith also decided to give the city his forty-two hundred acres. With this gift came the special Ostrich Farm Railway that ran up from central Los Angeles.

The flightless birds landed on their feet, too.

"By 1910," said Nathan Masters, producer-host of Los Angeles PBS station KCET's *Lost L.A.*, "Southern California boasted ten ostrich farms."

Southern California's own Mauch Chunk Railway, the Mount Lowe "Railway to the Clouds," was tucked away in the San Gabriel Mountains above Pasadena. Opening on July 4, 1893, its cable cars led to the summit of Echo Mountain (later named Mount Lowe), where a narrow-gauge mountain railway took riders on a three-and-a-half-mile tour that climaxed at a Victorian-and-Western-style resort known as the White City, for its white structures and electric lights.

New Hampshire native Thaddeus Sobieski Constantine Lowe (1831–1913), for whom the remote railway was named, was an aviation pioneer who, as a balloonist, spied on Confederate troops at the behest of President Lincoln. Arriving in Southern California in 1887, he worked in collaboration with a former Santa Fe Railway civil engineer to bring his mountain project to fruition, though it could never make back its mortgage costs, despite carrying an estimated three million people over its forty-five-year existence.

It was gone for good by 1938.

Lauded for its lushly landscaped Tampa, Florida, and Williamsburg, Virginia, theme parks, Busch Gardens actually had its origins in Pasadena, California—at what was formerly Thaddeus Lowe's estate, on Orange Grove Avenue.

St. Louis beer baron Adolphus Busch purchased the sprawling property as a winter home early in the twentieth century, prompting his pal, President William Howard Taft, to suggest Busch turn the infinity lawn into a golfing green. The brewer's wife, Lily, thought otherwise, and, enlisting Scottish botanist and landscape architect Robert Gordon Fraser, planted one hundred thousand bushes and trees along fourteen miles of walkway. The first Busch Gardens welcomed the public, free of charge, seven days a week, starting in 1906. With the addition of waterfalls, gnomes, and a souvenir seed business, the gardens drew crowds until 1937.

Lily, widowed since 1913, offered the park to the city of Pasadena, which passed. The land eventually was sold and subdivided, although sections of Lily's green glory can still be glimpsed in two classic movies.

In *Gone with the Wind*, at the barbecue at Twelve Oaks, Scarlett O'Hara is seen there, picnicking with her beaux, while, in Orson Welles's *Citizen Kane*, Busch Gardens doubles as the boundless backyard of Xanadu.

Los Angeles's first trolley park, Washington Gardens, opened in 1887, south of what is now the 10 Freeway, and east of the 110. David V. Waldron, a former U.S. marshal, owned both the park and the horse-drawn trolley that led to it. He set up a Western variety show, a small zoo, and a Battle of Gettysburg panorama he picked up from the 1884 New Orleans World Cotton Centennial. But when word got out that patrons drank and smoked at the park, its reputation was soiled.

Salvation came in the guise of the Los Angeles County Improvement Company, a business concern led by the brewer Fred Maier. In 1890, Maier installed a baseball diamond and team (the Los Angeles Angels), a monkey house, and, because Paul Boyton's signature ride was now part of the package, a new name: Chutes Park. A figure eight roller coaster followed in 1903, and Fred Ingersoll in 1910. He renamed the campus Luna Park, though Ingersoll lost his grip after only eighteen months, in September 1912.

Today, the site is mostly a macadam parking lot for an upholstery fabrics outlet.

Among his countless achievements, Abbot Kinney blanketed arid Southern California with shady eucalyptus trees imported from Australia.

Abbot Kinney was rich for life. Tobacco scions are born that way. He was also six foot two, red haired, and handsome, and born in New Jersey. Long after his death, he is recognized today in a Southern California beach town, with a hip shopping and restaurant boulevard named for him.

In the late 1880s, Kinney said, "I acquired two pieces of property at the ocean—one, a long sand spit where Ocean Park and Venice now stand, the other, the bluff back of the long wharf at Port Los Angeles."

Chutes Park, Los Angeles, Cal.

It was only a matter of time before Chutes made it to Los Angeles. The year was 1890.

Kinney lost half of the purchase in a coin toss with his ex–business partners. His remaining parcel would have convinced a lesser soul to cut his losses: an undeveloped marsh that attracted only duck hunters.

Instead, Kinney sought to develop it. What he liked about the land was that it would be easy to excavate and reshape.

"I had in mind such places as Sandy Hook, Atlantic City, and a very popular resort near Alexandria, in Egypt," he said.

His resort would end up looking like Italy.

Kinney would call it Venice of America.

SINK OR SWIM

I.

Given their planned obsolescence and elaborate façades, the temporary structures at Chicago's 1893 Columbian Exposition, for all practical purposes, gave
filmmakers their first outdoor movie sets—if only movies had already existed. (Thomas
Edison's first screening, in New York City, was on April 14, 1894, six months after
the fair closed, and the Lumière Brothers' was in Paris on March 22, 1895.) Once the
camera was out of the bag, it was obvious amusement parks made ideal locations, a
starring role they have played ever since.

Edison and producer-director-cinematographer Edwin S. Porter captured Luna
Park's lightshow for their *Coney Island at Night* in 1905, the same year the company's
Boarding School Girls followed prim and proper students as a visit to Dreamland
opened their eyes to the world.

Edison knew a good thing when he filmed it; following earlier excursions to Coney,
he secured exclusive movie rights to William Reynolds's park. His and Porter's 1903
Rube and Mandy at Coney Island, about two hayseeds romping through the resort, was
shot at Steeplechase and Luna Parks, before Dreamland entered the picture.

For land developers, moviemakers, and members of the public, the beach was
the place to shed adult inhibitions.

Charlie Chaplin secured his star when he debuted his Tramp character in slapstick-comedy producer Mack Sennett's 1914 *Kid Auto Races at Venice*, filmed in Abbot Kinney's beach town. Looming in the background of many scenes was the 1911 Race Thru the Clouds—one of fourteen rollers coasters built within a block and a half radius of one another between 1904 and 1925.

Chaplin returned again for his 1928 *The Circus*. At the film's outset, the Little Tramp hides from police by pretending to be one of the wooden figures on the pier's Noah's Ark attraction, before fleeing down the Midway and getting lost in the House of Mirrors. Given the interruptions Chaplin's global celebrity might have caused, "the location scenes," said Chaplin biographer David Robinson, "were shot in the mornings, before the regular crowds arrived."

Harold Lloyd's 1928 *Speedy*, in addition to showing his riding Coney Island Steeplechase, featured quick cuts of Luna Park's Airships, Witching Waves, Shoot the Chutes, and Bug rides. The funhouse montage, said Bruce Goldstein, director of repertory at New York's Film Forum, was actually filmed in California, on the Ocean Park Pier belonging to Kinney's fiercely competitive ex-partners. Lloyd and his film crew used their fun house's Double-Dip Slide, Revolving Drum, and Human Roulette Wheel to double for Coney.

The previous year, the same pier had been used to imply the Brooklyn playground for Clara Bow in her definitive flapper role, in *It*. Her handsome department-store boss (Antonio Moreno), wearing a suit, tie, and pocket square, takes her on the Human Roulette Wheel—they are the last to spin off—and the Revolving Drum before he wraps himself around her as they go down the slide. But when he tries for a good night kiss in the front seat of his Rolls-Royce, she slaps his face.

Producer Hal Roach's Our Gang cast also took to Ocean Park Pier, for the 1933 comedy short *Fish Hooky*. The setup had the little rascals outrun the truant officer, not knowing their teacher had secured the class a free day on the fun pier.

At the fade-out, Spanky catches the teacher and the officer about to kiss under a beach umbrella, which annoyingly interrupts his nap—he's just left designer John Miller's 1925 Hi-Boy coaster to the rest of the gang.

Abbot Kinney's former partners, who quickly became his rivals, built the Ocean Park Pier.

Scenic Railway at Ocean Park, Cal.

The title cards may have read Roscoe "Fatty" Arbuckle and Buster Keaton, but the true star of the 1917 silent comedy *Coney Island* was Coney itself, and the film can best be described as a slapstick tour of Luna Park and the Brighton Beach jail.

(Trivia note: The movie's producer was Joseph M. Schenck, even though he and brother Nick owned New Jersey's Palisades Park at the time.)

Keaton's character, lacking the dime for admission, sneaks into the park inside an empty rubbish barrel, while an uninhibited Fatty dresses in drag and hides from his wife in the women's dressing rooms of the bathhouse. Among a tireless stream of gags, Fatty picks up Buster's girlfriend, who's just gotten seasick riding a scooter over an undulating course on the Witching Waves. When Fatty takes her on the Shoot the Chutes, both do exactly what silent-screen comedians are supposed to do.

They fly out of the boat and land in the water.

Roscoe "Fatty" Arbuckle (center) and Buster Keaton flexed their comic muscle in *Coney Island*. Luna Park was the third star of the movie.

Forty thousand people stormed the beach on opening day, July 4, 1905, giving Abbot Kinney's Venice of America a promising start. There had been doubts the ambitious undertaking would open on time, if at all. Only weeks before, Kinney was forced to hire round-the-clock crews to rebuild the pier and auditorium after storms had destroyed them, and questions lingered as to whether Pacific Electric would have its new line from downtown LA up and running. It did, and the forty-minute, fourteen-mile route quickly became the company's most frequented.

To amuse the crowds, Kinney bought available attractions from the previous year's Lewis and Clark Centennial Exposition in Oregon, situating them on the southern side of what he called Venice Lagoon. Next to the pier, he docked a Ship's Hotel

The ribbon for the first roller coaster on the West Coast went to Frederick Church and Thomas Prior's 1911 Race Thru the Clouds.

that looked like an ocean liner, and for a final unconventional touch to what was, at its core, one giant theme park—arguably, the world's first, a veritable experimental prototype community of tomorrow—he wanted an equally unconventional local transport. So, he installed a miniature railroad that serviced the entire town.

The two-block business district, made up of shops under Italianate arches and colonnades, was an instant hit, as were the gondolas on seven separate canals that ran for eight miles, with islands between them.

Certain aspects of the master plan backfired—those having to do with high culture. Sarah Bernhardt in *Camille* and other class acts played to mostly empty houses in Kinney's thirty-five-hundred-seat auditorium, prompting Kinney to alter the atmosphere from La Scala to a Coney Island of the Pacific. Removing the existing attractions from the Lagoon (what is today Windward Circle), he packed his pier with as many rides as possible, having "no choice but to expand on the Atlantic City pier concept in a much bigger way," said unofficial Venice historian Jeffrey Stanton, listing a full complement of attractions that included an Aquarium, a Ferris Wheel, a Dentzel Carousel, Hades, Automobile Races, a Virginia Reel, a variation on the Old Mill called the Rapids, and the towering Johnson Captive Airplane, a contraption that looked to have been pulled together from a child's steel erector set.

On a more elevated plane, even if Kinney was not above fitting in freak shows, was Venice Pier's one-and-a-half-mile 1910 Scenic Railway, on the pier's north end, and hailed by Robert Cartmell as "Thompson's masterpiece."

Equal praise would also greet Frederick Church and Thomas Prior's dual-tracked, ninety-foot-high Race Thru the Clouds, a major achievement for 1911—James Lilliefors called it "the first roller coaster on the West Coast."

Its designer, John Miller, came west to check on its construction, while the Venice Amusement Company, as Church and Prior's partnership was newly named, set up its office bungalow beside it, snuggled up to the ride's exquisitely trellised underpinnings.

Thompson's Venice masterpiece was also a model of versatility. Remodeled in 1913, the Scenic Railway had its scenery removed in favor of greenery and steeper hills. In 1920, it was altogether replaced by the Big Dipper, which itself was replaced, in 1924, by the Giant Dipper, a figure eight twister.

Nineteen twenty also brought Prohibition, which meant new amusements of a different nature, as speakeasies and casinos with actual games of chance flourished

THE L. A. THOMPSON SCENIC RAILWAY, VENICE, CALIFORNIA.

LaMarcus Thompson's 1910 contribution to Venice's Ocean Front Walk was his most-admired Scenic Railway.

at the piers. Well into the 1940s, water taxis ferried gamblers to ships moored three miles out to sea, beyond U.S. legal boundaries.

LaMarcus Thompson did not live to see his Venice magnum opus dismantled. In declining health, he retired in 1915 to his Glen Cove, Long Island, estate, spending his days with his wife, Ada, and indulging in his hobby of astronomy at his self-designed observatory at home.

On the night of March 8, 1919, at age seventy-one, Thompson died from "acute indigestion, from which he had been a sufferer for months," said the New York *Sun*, whose respectful obituary paid him tribute as a "builder extraordinary of amusement parks in this country and England."

Venice of America ended up sinking under silt and the stench of dead fish, both of which collected in the canals. The solution was to pave them over into roads and parking lots. If that didn't kill Abbot Kinney, lung cancer did at age sixty-nine, on November 4, 1920. In May of that same year, what would be the final addition to his Venice Pier, the Big Dipper, was built, a beauteous work from designer John Miller and construction contractor Harry C. Baker. The coaster was nearly all that remained when fire devoured the pier seven months later.

Venice residents voted to annex themselves to the City of Los Angeles in 1925, and in 1929 oil was discovered in Venice. Rigs replaced ocean views and Italianate architecture. After World War II, the City of Los Angeles Parks and Recreation Department ended the lease on Venice Pier.

The Cyclone Racer survived the March 1933 Long Beach earthquake and September 1939 "El Cordonazo" tropical storm (here), but could not withstand the vicissitudes of late-1960s commercial land redevelopment.

As it was, nearly every beach town along the coast had its own roller coaster, as far down as Redondo and, even more prominent, in Long Beach, some thirty miles south of Venice.

Abbot Kinney's dream resort faded into memory.

For roller coasterists—if there isn't such a term, there should be—the Holy Grail is the Cyclone Racer at California's Long Beach Pike. Harry Traver considered it his greatest achievement, and since its demolition more than half a century ago, it has been an obsession for Larry Osterhoudt, a child of the '60s who never got to ride it. But he has doggedly spearheaded a decades-long campaign to resurrect it—and has built a 1:15 scale model of the lost landmark in his Downey, California, home.

His selling point, which convinced the City of Long Beach to launch a serious feasibility study, is that the classic racing coaster has "a high re-ride potential, compared to today's coasters that go from zero to one-hundred-twenty-five mph in three seconds, and then shoot you up over a four-hundred-foot tower—or the upside-down type coasters that ruin your day after just riding them once."

Designed by Frederick Church and his only racing coaster, the 50 mph Racer required one million feet of lumber for Traver to construct, not counting its pilings over the Pacific. At full capacity, it could handle twenty-four hundred riders an hour, and it cost $140,000, or $2.1 million today, when it opened on May 30, 1930.

Rising 110 feet above sand and sea, there was nothing gentle about the Cyclone Racer, or, for that matter, the Pike. The amusement zone, which began as a mile-long walkway (of unclear origin, *pike* was the nickname for the wooden boardwalk), catered to a rougher element than could be found on other Southern California piers, which were not exactly Sunday school picnic grounds, either. Much of their popularity largely stemmed from their providing something strictly forbidden in stuffy downtown Los Angeles: dancing on Sundays.

The Pike was the place to get down and dirty.

For the Pike, location was as much a bonus as it was a bone of contention. Its adjacent U.S. Navy Landing, pejoratively called "the Jungle," was "a warren of small, dark streets," said journalist Matt Cohn. "'Ship sailors' were notorious hell-raisers compared to their 'base sailor' brethren…and the Pike's wholesome, carnival-midway aura began to give way to something much darker and edgier."

A 1949 rebranding to Nu-Pike did nothing to upgrade its standing. In the '50s and '60s, riddled with "carnies, prostitutes, dishonorably discharged sailors, bikers, and various hustlers," said Cohn, the area, with its "Whore's Alley…had the highest crime rate in the city."

Little trace of that remains today. The Cyclone Racer was removed, ostensibly to allow for an access road when the city bought the RMS *Queen Mary*, for the luxury liner's conversion into a hotel, a business voyage that has never sailed smoothly.

The Pike itself was altogether torn down in 1979, eleven years after the Cyclone rode its last.

One of the first suspended roller coasters, Bisby's Spiral Airship greeted its first brave rider in 1902, nine years after Long Beach's Pine Avenue Pier became the first municipal wharf in the State of California.

Charles I. D. Looff actually lived with his family at the Pike, above his carousel and near his West Sixth Street factory. The Looffs were not alone. Elmer McCurdy lived at the Pike. The only difference was, McCurdy was dead.

Having served as a Laff in the Dark prop for heaven knows how many years, Elmer was accidentally found hanging inside the ride in 1976, as a Hollywood crew was prepping a location shoot for TV's *The Six Million Dollar Man*. When two handymen tried to move what they thought was a balsa-wood figure whose complexion looked like beef jerky, the arm came off, revealing bone.

Down came his pants, which led to the pronouncement, as author Mark Svengold uncovered in his 2003 *Elmer McCurdy: The Misadventures in Life and Afterlife of an American Outlaw*, "This was not 'anatomically correct.'

This was anatomical…a completely desiccated, mummified human body."

The coroner was called. Tests were conducted. Truth to tell, there was a lot of laffing.

The findings, once a bullet was dislodged from the corpse and a 1924 penny discovered inside the mouth: McCurdy had been shot by a sheriff's posse after an attempted robbery on October 7, 1911, bringing an end to a lifelong run of bad luck.

Orphaned in childhood, tubercular from working in mines, alcoholic, and comically inept at crime, McCurdy once staged an elaborate robbery, only to end up in the wrong location. Another time, he tried to blow open an iron safe, leaving the safe untouched but bringing down the entire bank building around it.

Living out this Wile E. Coyote existence, he fled to the hills, only he neglected to cover his tracks. That's when

II.

Just as Southern California had its Venice, so it had its tropics. In 1907, Francis Earnest and Joe Campbell opened the Southland's first zoological garden, the two-acre Los Angeles Alligator Farm, on the banks of a small stream in the Lincoln Heights neighborhood. Earnest had been a cook in a mining camp, and Campbell, known as "Alligator" Joe, owned the Los Angeles Ostrich Farm next to the gator enclosure, which claimed one thousand reptile inhabitants. Admission was twenty-five cents.

Inside, parents could watch their children ride on the backs of alligators (photos show the alligators' mouths wide open, without jaw harnesses), frolic in pens with tiny baby alligators (separated by fences from larger alligators, known to eat smaller the posse got him, in the Osage Hills of Oklahoma.

The local undertaker overdid it with the embalming fluid and started charging admission for people to see him. But the undertaker got his come-uppance; a flimflammer showed up five years later and claimed to be an outraged relative of the deceased. Turns out he was nothing but a traveling carnival huckster.

McCurdy's mummy hit the road, frightening people in sideshows and fun houses. It is uncertain how and when he got to Long Beach, though it was assumed he was sold to the Pike wax museum, before he ended up inside Laff in the Dark, coated in fluorescent orange paint so he could glow under a black light.

On April 22, 1977, Elmer McCurdy was finally buried, in the Boot Hill section of Summit View Cemetery, in Guthrie, Oklahoma.

A layer of concrete was poured over him, just to ensure he would never go on tour again.

Elmer McCurdy in 1911, the first time he was laid to rest

ones and, presumably, human children), and, together as a family, witness live chickens fed to the great showpieces of the farm. Among the headliners were eighty-year-old Pontchartrain Billy, who tipped the scales well north of two hundred pounds—which did not prevent his being lassoed, and made to climb a carpeted ladder and slide down a miniature Shoot the Chutes.

No cooking necessary: feeding time at the California Alligator Farm

Writing in 1910 for editor Bret Harte's *Overland Monthly*, correspondent Arthur Inkersley, while appalled, nevertheless ranked the Alligator Farm above a Texas rattlesnake ranch, and reported, "Baby alligators are sold as pets to tourists at $1.25 to $2.50 apiece."

In 1909, Earnest bought out Alligator Joe, and more cold-blooded and exotic creatures were added to the collection.

The reptile repository, which passed into the hands of Earnest's grandson, Ken Earnest, moved to Buena Park in 1953, as if to press its snout up against the parking lot fence of the main attraction across La Palma Avenue, Knott's Berry Farm.

It closed in 1984.

A STONE'S THROW FROM the original Alligator Farm, on the same 3800 block of Mission Road, was the Selig Zoo. Inaugurated in 1911 by film producer William Nicholas Selig, it was only a warm-up to the grand vision in the back of his mind: a first-of-its-kind movie-studio-zoo-and-amusement-park complex, complete with white-sand beach and artificial wave pool, like at New Jersey's Palisades Park.

At least he got the location right. The fifty-acre Eastlake Park (called Lincoln Park since 1917) put his property within the same reach as the alligator and ostrich farms, hot sulphur springs plunge, Alaskan totem pole, band shell, botanical garden, conservatory, boathouse, artificial lake, and miniature railroad; in short, the Orlando, Florida, of its day.

Selig, né William Mikolaj Zeligowsky, hailed from Chicago, which was also home to his first studio, where he shot both a 1908 and a 1910 version of *The Wizard of Oz*. It was a vehicle particularly well suited to Selig, given that in a previous career, he'd been a magician in a traveling show, much like Oz's well-meaning humbug, Professor Marvel.

Only, Selig really did pull off a marvel; in 1909, he was the first producer ever to establish a permanent studio in California. (Cecil B. DeMille's *The Squaw Man*, considered the first full-length feature to be shot in Hollywood, was not made until 1913–1914.)

Film pioneer William Selig envisioned his zoo as the first step toward an amusement empire.

Selig's was nothing but a makeshift facility downtown, "in a small building behind a Chinese laundry on Hope Street," until he set up a proper shop to the northeast, on Allesandro Street, in the Edendale section, which is called Echo Park today.

The Selig Zoo was located separately from the studio, and Selig stocked it with animals for his and other studios' jungle pictures, including the first *Tarzan*, which was shot at the zoo. When Selig sold the

Edendale facility to producer William Fox, he moved his own moviemaking to the upgraded Selig Zoo property, which by then he had outfitted with lavish trappings, nearly life-sized concrete elephants and lions at its entrance, and seven hundred animals inside, making it the largest collection of captive wild animals in the world.

He put it before the public on June 20, 1915.

Nearly ten thousand people attended the zoo's opening, and soon, groups were congregating at the tourist mecca, including schools and churches. Former president William Howard Taft spoke at a celebration of Mexicans and indigenous people. But the grand Selig Zoo Park never happened. By 1918, Selig's popular cowboy star, Tom Mix, abandoned him for greener prairies, and jungle movies fell out of favor with post–World War I audiences. The studio was sold to producer Louis B. Mayer, later to head Metro-Goldwyn-Mayer—whose logo, dating back to 1916, starred a live lion that lived at the Selig Zoo.

The facility continued under Selig until 1922, when he could no longer afford its upkeep. A 1923 auction was held, and the property rotated ownership and names in the years to come. Keeping the title Selig Zoo until 1925, it subsequently became Luna Park Zoo (1925–1931), L.A. Wild Animal Farms (1931–1932), the California Zoological Gardens (1932–1936, when it was combined with the Ostrich Farm), and Zoopark (1936–1940), although, officially, it was the California Zoological Gardens.

In February and March 1938, two horrific Pacific storms swept the Los Angeles Basin, bringing destructive floods—about 115 people drowned—and severely damaging the zoo. Many screen stars, including Richard Dix and Katharine Hepburn, rose to the animals' defense, and on April 21, 1938, appeared at a benefit on their behalf.

The animals were saved, but the decaying buildings and derelict acreage were not.

The Selig Zoo officially closed in 1940, and its inhabitants were transferred to the Los Angeles Zoo within Griffith Park, the enclave that came about as a fortuitous result of Griffith J. Griffith's liquidation of Sketchley's ostrich farm.

SALT OF THE EARTH

I.

Dudley Sherman Humphrey II was the polar opposite of Abbot Kinney. He did not come from money, although there was distinguished lineage; his grandmother, Polly Sherman Humphrey, was related to Gen. William Tecumseh Sherman. Dudley Humphrey Jr. was born on May 19, 1852, in Townsend, Ohio, where the family lived and worked on a twelve-hundred-acre farm. He was the middle child, and it was he who would transition the family into the amusement park business.

Like their father before them, Dudley's Jr.'s two brothers, Harlow and David, speculated in timber, while Dudley Jr. set off to Buchtel College in Akron, with the objective of putting his mechanical aptitude to use in civil engineering. Only, like LaMarcus Thompson, his academic career was cut short over money; in Humphrey's case, a neighbor's sawmill and barrel-making business in which his father had invested went bad.

With an outstanding debt of $15,000, the Humphreys, including Dudley Jr., his wife, Effie, their two children, and his mother, moved to the Cleveland suburb of Glenville. There, Dudley and his two brothers undertook, according to a family chronicle, "the humblest role of workers."

Fortitude prevailed, and, in good time, the Humphreys "founded on a small scale and without capital what has since become the largest concern of its kind in the United States."

Popcorn.

Dudley S. Humphrey II, with granddaughter: His financial cushion was padded with popcorn.

Euclid Beach Park, on the southern shore of Lake Erie, opened on Saturday, June 22, 1895, after five Ohio businessmen—Albert E. Thompson, John Flynn, John Irwin, Jerome B. Burrows, and the euphoniously named Hylas B. Gladwish—produced a prospectus that promised their "broad beach 75 to 100 feet wide backed by a bluff" would "make Euclid Beach to Cleveland what Coney Island is to New York." They then

Euclid Beach Park, on Lake Erie, prided itself as the Coney Island of Ohio. That was precisely what prompted Dudley Humphrey to save its soul.

finessed a deal to insert its dance pavilion, bathhouse, theater, and restaurant into the itinerary of the D&C Lines' steamers (D&C stood for "Detroit and Cleveland").

Management of the more than sixty acres fell to William R. Ryan Sr., who had a sales background in tobacco and candy. He booked Euclid Beach's entertainment, such as "Bonner, the wonderful talking and trick horse"; supervised the addition of the requisite rides, including "the mystic wonder of the century," the Crystal Maze; and saw that picnic groups regularly met on the grounds and business associations regularly met in the German Beer Garden.

The first season went so well that the Cleveland Electric Railway increased departures from downtown to every ten minutes, while the ferry service went to nine round-trips daily. The season after that, C&B Lines extended its steamship service as far as Buffalo. As if to show that Euclid Beach Park had arrived, in 1897 William Ryan booked an international star to appear: Capt. Paul Boyton.

Among the park's concessionaires were the Humphreys, who entered the popcorn market after finding street vendors' product throughout the city lacking, compared to what burst out of the family's iron kettle at home. On the street, the problem was that kernels were exposed to air, prior to seasoning. The Humphrey method, a family member revealed, was to "put our corn into the hot kettle, mix the lard and salt right with it, cover the lid, and stir it up with a big spoon. That kept all the sweetness of the corn in the popped kernel, and seasoned it at the same time."

Brother Harlow found a way for the popcorn to be stirred without having to lift the kettle lid (it involved a hole and a spoon), and "Dudley refined this idea by fitting a skillet to a Russian drum that could be turned by a hand crank," according to a Euclid Beach history. Dudley patented the product, then went about selling it—only to discover Cleveland already had too many popcorn vendors.

Their expansion coincided with the opening of Euclid Beach Park, where the family also put up a popcorn stand. Sales were hearty but, from forty-year-old Dudley's perspective, hardly worth the daily indignity. He disapproved of the drinking in

Euclid's beer garden and the immodest swimsuits on the beach.

When he complained to park owners, they collectively shrugged their shoulders.

In spite of its profits, in 1899 Dudley locked up the Humphrey popcorn stand at Euclid Beach Park and threw away the key.

Lacking a master plan and dropping a bundle, five Ohio businessmen inaugurated Euclid Beach Park on Saturday, June 22, 1895.

DUDLEY WAS IN ILLINOIS, arranging to expand his popcorn chain to Chicago, when he chanced to pick up his hometown paper. Euclid Beach manager William Ryan, he learned, was leaving the park to take the helm of a new one, Manhattan Beach, named for Austin Corbin's resort in Brooklyn and set to open one and a half miles away from Euclid Beach, on Cleveland's East 140th Street. Faced with competition they'd not even seen, and the fact they were losing $20,000 per season, Euclid's owners decided the only way out was to close their park for good.

Dudley sped home and called a family conference, where a decision was reached: The Humphreys were prepared to lease Euclid Beach Park for five years at $12,000 (nearly $360,000 today). The quintet of owners accepted the offer.

The Humphreys' new, improved Euclid Beach Park opened May 27, 1901, after they "eliminat[ed] all intoxicants, freaks, fakes, chance games, and questionable shows," said the history compiled by Ohio state senator Elroy M. Avery, "believing that the people would appreciate and patronize a resort where cleanliness in everything was the watchword."

So, too, was the admission fee eliminated, because Dudley believed enough money could be made on the individual rides and food. The policy also gave the family leeway to have its private police force expel any undesirables from the park.

Sending the message that unaccompanied women and children were safe here, the strict guidelines paid off.

Before the finish of the Humphreys' first etiquette-enforced season, the family bought 80 percent of the shares in the Euclid Beach Park Company.

Despite a necessitous thinning out of its work force, the park survived the Depression and wartime shortages fairly intact, and hit a ticket-sales record of nearly twenty million the year World War II ended, only to begin a consistent decline, except for an occasional bump in the 1950s, which was attributed to kiddie rides. Nineteen forty-six was the year an interracial group of picketers protested Euclid Beach's policy of excluding people of color. We Went to Normandy Beach Together—Why Not Euclid Beach? one sign read. Another was, Hitler and Humphrey Believe in Super Race.

On September 25, 1960, presidential candidate John F. Kennedy held one of three separate campaign rallies in Euclid Beach Park, this one accompanied by his vice presidential candidate, Lyndon B. Johnson. The Democrats did better in that era than amusement parks. Within a few years of one another, three of Euclid Beach's competitors all bid adieu: Puritas Springs Park, the Cleveland, Berea, Elyria & Oberlin Railway's trolley park that opened in 1900 and closed after a 1959 fire; "Akron's Fairyland of Pleasure," Summit Beach Park, which at its peak averaged twenty-five thousand people a day, and lasted from 1918 to 1958; and the "Park of a Thousand Trees," Vermilion's Crystal Beach Park, which blossomed every spring from 1907 until 1962, and during the 1940s Big Band era presented a young Ohio singer named Doris Day.

In 1968, Dudley Humphrey III (Senior died in 1933, and Junior in 1959) was forced to admit, "Our expenses are outrunning our income." That had been the status quo since 1963.

Euclid Beach Park was purchased in June 1968 by real estate developer Dominic Visconsi, who intended to turn it into high-rise residences.

The gates closed September 28, 1969.

Until the final day, the grounds were well kept and a dress code was in effect.

Putting the family's life savings on the line, Dudley Humphrey instituted a park policy of "One fare, free gate, no beer." It paid off.

II.

What Dudley Humphrey was to popcorn, Walter Marvin Knott was to the berry. Knott didn't look like your typical Californian. With ramrod-straight posture, sharply focused eyes, starched white shirt, and no-nonsense facial expression that rarely bore more than a slight grin, he looked like he could have sold insurance to the Iowa couple in the Grant Wood painting *American Gothic*. Yet he was Californian down to his toes, a farmer, born December 11, 1889. By then, his parents were living in San Bernardino, a former Spanish settlement incorporated in 1857, though it was little more than a remote trading post until the 1860s, when gold was discovered not so far away.

Walter's mother's side of the family had gone from Virginia to Texas, then, according to a family journal, "set out again," this time, to California, "over plains and deserts of New Mexico and Arizona." Rev. Elgin Columbus Knott, Walter's father and a Methodist minister, was born in 1859, in Bell Buckle, Tennessee, before he, too, settled in the West. In addition to preaching, Elgin owned a California orange grove. When Walter was six and his brother, Charles, was four, their father died.

Pressed for money, Walter's mother, Ginny, took in washing. Walter sold newspapers and tended neighbors' gardens, selling vegetables from his own family's yard to Santa Fe Railway workers.

Living at home with Walter, Charles, and Ginny was her mother, Rosamund Dougherty, who shared the reins on the family's wagon train across the Mojave Desert.

She also filled young Walter's ears with tales of the journey.

Walter—no one ever called him Walt—met his future wife, the former Cordelia Hornaday, when they were students at Pomona High School. Called Cordy, Cordelia was about a year younger than Walter, born January 23, 1890. They married in 1911 and had four children: Virginia, born in 1913; Russell, 1916; Rachel Elizabeth, called Toni, 1916; and Marion, 1922.

By the time of his marriage, Walter made a homesteading application to the U.S. Land Office, which required him to remain on a property for three years if he wished to take possession of it. Walter signed on, only to have a rude awakening: The land, 160 acres of it, was in the western Mojave Desert, at the foot of the Newberry Mountains, about twenty-five miles east of Barstow.

Cordelia was less than pleased. The first season, sandstorms uprooted Walter's grapevines. "About all we raised out there was a bunch of fine children," Cordelia later said.

Walter made ends meet by joining a road-construction crew on what was to become U.S. Route 66. He also did carpentering for some developers who hoped to revitalize the ghost town of Calico, which had been mined out of its silver deposits in 1896.

Through sheer stubbornness, Walter made it through the required time limit to own his desolate property.

Cordelia advised selling it.

Walter never did.

Cordelia Knott burst into tears at first glimpse of husband Walter's homestead in the California desert.

MOVING RIGHT ALONG

I.

Walter Knott recalled a cattle rancher he'd met while working on the road crew. The rancher was willing to take on a tenant farmer, to grow vegetables to feed the hands at his ranch near San Luis Obispo—340 miles from Mojave. The Knotts did not have an automobile. They got there by covered wagon.

Both the trip and Walter's vegetable crop bore fruit. Cordelia made and sold candy. But what they wanted was their own land.

On the advice of one of his cousins, in 1920 Walter bought a Model T and moved his family to Buena Park, in northwestern Orange County. The cousin, Jim Preston, had already leased acreage there close to Highway 39, the well-traveled route that well-to-do motorists from Pasadena took south to the coastal-resort towns of Newport and Huntington Beach.

Walter and Jim grew blackberries, and Cordelia made candy, preserves, relishes, sauces, and syrups. The profits from their roadside stand—the cash register was a cigar box—allowed Walter and Preston to expand their leasehold to twenty acres in 1923. They also expanded their crop to include asparagus and, because it grew fast, cherry rhubarb. The relationship between the two men, however, came to an impasse. Preston was content to produce, and leave sales and distribution to others. Walter wanted to control all three steps himself.

Walter Knott rooted his Old West in his experience near the ghost town of Calico and tales his grandmother told him.

Walter Knott's boysenberries and wife Cordelia's chicken dinners caused traffic to stop on Highway 39.

By 1927, Preston withdrew from the partnership, and with the sudden arrival of oil drilling in Buena Park, Walter was presented with a dilemma: take what money he had made and run, or keep on farming.

Farming beat running.

≈

WITH BILLS PILING UP, salvation came feathered. There were chickens all over the berry farm. Son Russell went out and caught them. Walter cleaned them. Cordelia fried them. The older girls served them—on Cordelia's wedding china—and Marion, now twelve, bussed the tables.

That was June 1934, starting with eight customers who paid sixty-five cents each ($12.11 today) for the main dish: cherry rhubarb, green salad with French dressing,

In the late '20s, through a visiting official from the U.S. Department of Agriculture, Walter met Rudolph Boysen, a superintendent of parks five miles away in Anaheim.

Crossing blackberry, red raspberry, and loganberry plants, Boysen produced a plant whose shoots yielded a larger, lusher fruit than most berry plants.

"And do you know," said a folksy Knott's brochure, "it only takes about sixty of 'em to fill a pound basket, as compared to over a hundred and fifty of blackberries."

Walter dubbed the profitable hybrid the "boysenberry."

Walter Knott put together his Ghost Town by scavenging through old Arizona mining camps.

mashed potatoes with milk gravy, boiled cabbage with bits of ham, hot biscuits with jam, and berry pie with ice cream.

Two and a half years after Cordelia had reluctantly started selling meals, the Knotts served 1,774 Thanksgiving dinners. Sundays, the waiting times were typically more than three hours. By 1938, more than *265,000* chicken dinners were served.

"That," said Walter, "was really the turning point in our economic life."

Knott's never encountered the same problem trolley parks faced when street-cars stopped running, because car traffic on Highway 39 did nothing but increase. By 1939, an average of five thousand Sunday dinners were served. On holi-days, that number doubled. What did not change was the hours-long wait for tables. To alleviate the tedium, Walter provided conversation pieces for his customers.

More low-key than anything Barnum ever would have concocted, Walter offered the homey and the hokey: a rock garden, a fern grotto, a mill wheel, old music boxes, a facsimile of George Washington's fireplace, and—perhaps giddiest of all for its smoke and noise—a small volcano powered by the Devil himself, in miniature, standing at a pumping station.

Long fascinated by the Old West, Walter had been collecting mementos, from a Wells Fargo stagecoach whose strongbox reputedly had been stolen by the bandit Black Bart, to miners' picks and shovels. It would not be until late 1940, however, that he installed a world's fair–style cyclorama on his property, to pay tribute to his grandmother's journey West and mark the beginning of his re-creating a full-scale Ghost Town, which he would call Calico.

Joining Walter on his scavenger hunts to Prescott, Arizona, and other old desert towns was Paul Swartz, an Illinois-born caricaturist and architect-manqué who came to Walter's farm in 1939 and ended up as art director. Together, they would find what they could, restore it, leaving much of the original patina, and arrange it to fit in with the rest of the standing collection in Buena Park.

By 1947, with the Western junction proving as great a visitor magnet as the Chick-en Dinner Restaurant, the family enterprise, now spread to 160 acres, was christened Knott's Berry Farm and Ghost Town.

The sign at the entrance read, "All buildings in Ghost Town are open to visitors. There is no admission charge to any of the attractions."

An illuminated sign over the main gate of Knott's Berry Farm, which today still retains enough from the old days for Walter Knott to recognize, proclaims it as America's 1st Theme Park. Some might argue.

Much depends upon where one sets the starting clock: on what was first Walter Knott's berry patch (1920), then Knott's Berry Place and tea room (1927), then Knott's Berry Place and "Covered Wagon Show" (1940), or Knott's Berry Farm and Ghost Town (1947).

Still, others hand the distinction to Holiday World, in the southwestern Indiana town of Santa Claus. In fact, it was Santa himself who gave birth to this amusement institution.

Louis J. Koch (1882–1979), an industrialist from Evanston, Indiana, nine miles away, came looking for the famous fellow who provided the town its name. All he could find was a statue of Kris Kringle and a post office, most often used for the sake of its postmark on Christmas cards.

Thinking there should be more to the happily named destination, lest children be disappointed, Koch, with his son, Bill, back from the World War II naval service, opened Santa Claus Land at 452 East Christmas Boulevard on August 3, 1946. Every aspect was linked to a Santa theme, just as Knott's attractions, once Walter set his mind to it, were connected to the Old West.

By 1986, Santa learned to embrace Halloween and the Fourth of July, and his land became Holiday World; in 2006, it added Thanksgiving.

This made the Koch and the Knott efforts *theme* parks, as opposed to amusement parks with their jumble of disassociated attractions, as presented by the likes of George Tilyou, Henry Knoebel, George Whitney, and the others.

Once Walt Disney opened Disneyland in 1955, totally discarding run-of-the-mill, off-the-shelf rides, and detailing every nook and cranny to make visitors believe they were stepping inside an animated film, the term *amusement park* faded from use—even among later chains, like Six Flags and Cedar Fair, whose properties are, by and large, amusement parks.

Perhaps the overall theme is amusement.

INDIANA ALONE COULD NOT contain Santa. Julian Reiss, a developer in Lake Placid, had raised his young daughter on tales of a baby bear that lived at the Claus summer home. Making the story real for her, on July 1, 1949, he opened a "fantasy village" called Santa's Workshop, complete with a Candy Cane Express, in upstate Wilmington, New York.

When news of this reached Glenn Holland in Southern California's semiremote San Bernardino Mountains, he got to thinking. Sketching out some preliminary ideas at

Santa's Village, in Skyforest, California, extended Christmas year-round, until its creator, Glenn Holland, overextended himself.

his kitchen table, he set into motion a commercial exploitation of perhaps the most famous figure in the public domain.

He found a business partner and acreage near Southern California's Lake Arrowhead. Santa's Village in Skyforest, California, rang its opening sleigh bell on Memorial Day, 1955, fifty days before the much-ballyhooed debut of Disneyland. A second Santa's Village opened in 1957, in Santa Cruz County's Scotts Valley, six miles north of the Santa Cruz Beach Board-walk; and a third opened near Chicago, in Dundee, Illinois, on Memorial Day, 1959.

Each afforded the opportunity to meet Mr. and Mrs. Claus, rub up against a frozen North Pole, pet reindeer, wander amid a pixieland of giant candy canes and bright pastel toadstools, and ride a twirling Christmas tree and a snowball—but, by 1965, Holland was in over his head. Inclement Midwestern winters were brutal to business, forcing him to sell all three parks.

Although new owners took over, competition from deep-pocketed theme park chains left little room for charming, Ma-and-Pa-type parks in the expanding amusement universe.

Santa Cruz's Village closed in 1979 and Skyforest's in 1998. Dundee's was nearly lost to unimaginative business concerns when, in 2010, the husband-and-wife team of Jason and Amy Sierpien opened a combination theme park and petting zoo, called Santa's Village Azoosment Park.

The Skyforest progenitor required a heartier hike back to life, but, true to the spirit of Christmas, this story has a happy ending.

Thanks to Lake Arrowhead real estate broker Bill Johnson and his wife (and compatriot mountain bike enthusiast) Michelle—Bill operated rides at the original Santa's Village when he was thirteen, and the couple quietly bought the property in 2014—on December 2, 2016, SkyPark at Santa's Village opened.

The frozen North Pole stands again, surrounded by state-of-the-art bike and hiking trails, zip line, ice rink, rock-candy mine, retail shops and eateries, bouldering, archery, fly-fishing, camping, "polar express" train ride—and visitors can still meet the great man himself.

III.

Like Knott's in California, Silver Dollar City, in Branson, Missouri, owes its theme to miners in the 1880s. Like Denver's Elitch's Gardens, it owes its success to a woman.

Close to the actual North Pole within the Arctic Circle, near Rovaniemi, Finland, is SantaPark Arctic World. It sits inside a man-made cavern.

During the Christmas season, about four hundred thousand people come to visit Santa's office, shiver in the Ice Princess's Ice Gallery, hand a letter to an elf in the post office, and decorate cookies in the Mrs. Gingerbread Bakery. The aurora borealis can also be seen, but only from outside the cave.

Opened in 1998, the park is run by Rovaniemi entrepreneurs Ilkka Länkinen and Katja Ikäheimo-Länkinen, who, in 2014, opened a second SantaPark in China.

Their motto: "We believe in the reward of a simple smile."

Mary Herschend, a housewife and mother in suburban Wilmette, Illinois, outside Chicago, and her husband, Hugo Herschend, a Danish immigrant and district manager for the Electrolux vacuum cleaning company, vacationed in the Ozarks in 1946. Liking what they saw, they repeatedly returned, and got to know the sisters Miriam and Genevieve Lynch, who ran Branson's modest tourist attraction, the five-hundred-foot-deep Marvel Cave.

First discovered by members of the Osage tribe, who called it "the Devil's Den," the natural wonder was a wet limestone cave searched in 1541 by Spanish explorers, who believed it contained the Fountain of Youth. It didn't. Nor did it contain lead, as excavators in 1869 believed. When word spread that it probably contained marble, the site became known as the Marble Cave—even if no marble was ever found, but only bat guano.

Branson, Missouri, held a buried treasure called the Marvel Cave. It led to Silver Dollar City.

When Miriam and Genevieve's father died in 1927, they took over the tourist attraction and called it the Marvel Cave. In 1950, well on in years, the sisters sold a ninety-nine-year lease to the Herschends. Hugo was delighted; Mary, far from it. It was she who was stuck running it, living in Branson with the boys in a cabin with no plumbing, while Hugo kept his day job in Illinois to keep up with expenses.

Hugo and Mary Herschend's sons built an empire, though it was Mary who triggered the process.

"When we left home, Mom would cry for the first two hours in the car," son Jack Herschend recalled. "I was fully aware of lots of nights of her crying herself to sleep."

With Mary and Hugo separated by distance, and, soon, with Jack in the Marine Corps and his brother, Pete, at the University of Missouri, the couple's marriage was in jeopardy. Mary, alone, decided to continue the business, such as it was. By 1954, Hugo was back in Branson, though only briefly. In 1955, he succumbed to a heart attack, leaving Mary, once again, alone with the cave.

This time, her sons rallied around her in force. With Pete on leave from school, Jack on early release from the Marines, and additional support from Jack's wife, Sherry, Mary sold the house in Wilmette and invested in capital improvements for the cave. Specifically, she wanted a narrow-gauge funicular to raise tourists out of it. Jack is credited with the idea to rebuild the small town that existed around the mine in the 1880s, though it was Mary who insisted upon authenticity.

The "new" old frontier town, Silver Dollar City, opened May 1, 1960, consisting of a church, a log cabin, a handful of shops, and live reenactments of the hillbilly feud between the Hatfields and the McCoys. As a publicity gimmick, all change was given in silver dollars, though a bigger public-relations boost came courtesy of the CBS sitcom *The Beverly Hillbillies*, which shot four episodes at the park that aired in October 1969.

"We scratched our heads and said, 'Okay, we must be in the amusement park business,'" Jack told *Forbes* magazine, in 2014, when his and Peter's Herschend Family Entertainment was appraised at $1 billion. Starting in the 1990s, as they focused more on their Christian-related charities, the Herschends began seeking managers outside the family. They met their soul mate in 2003, with former automobile corporate executive and Rhodes Scholar Joel Manby. After twelve years as president and CEO, Manby left Herschend in 2015 for the challenge of reversing the sliding fortunes of SeaWorld Entertainment. In 2018, he abruptly left that company.

Mary was able to witness much, but not all, of the family success.

When she died at age eighty-three, in 1983, the park was hosting 1.3 million people a season, with a staff that had mushroomed from the dozen in her day to eleven hundred.

The transformation was abetted, in large part, by the town of Branson's emergence as the country music tourist center of the world.

With three inversions, two launches, and a ten-story, ninety-degree vertical drop, Silver Dollar City's 2018 steam-punk Time Traveler stakes a claim as the world's fastest, steepest, and tallest spinning coaster.

SIX YEARS BEFORE MARY'S death, in 1976, her sons purchased the Goldrush Junction theme park in Pigeon Forge, Tennessee, which they renamed Silver Dollar City, Tennessee. Ten years later, they partnered with another strong woman: country music queen Dolly Parton, who had said, ever since first seeing the Hollywood sign in California, that she had been "aggravated about how they portray mountain people in Hollywood and in the movies, like we are all these dumb, barefoot hillbillies… personally, I think that country people are the smartest people in the world, and I've been everywhere."

Her role with the Herschends, beyond kicking up publicity, was to reimagine the old Goldrush Junction / Silver Dollar City into something on which she wanted her name. Initially, it took an estimated $40 million to, as she put it, Dolly-ize the park, into what was now called Dollywood. Every season, "Aunt" Dolly—"I think I'm kind of like a relative"—adds her exuberance to opening day, personally greeting fans and entertaining in her superstar fashion. She also stops for questions.

Dolly Parton in Dollywood, Tennessee: spreading country charm, yes; riding roller coasters, no

Asked about riding roller coasters, her eyes went wide before confessing she doesn't.

"I always make jokes, but it's the truth," she said. "I have too much to lose—like, my hair, or other parts of me that might not do well in that kind of high speed."

IV.

In the summer of 1955, Walter and Cordelia Knott, like many others, were invited to the opening of a new neighbor, Disneyland. In their case, it was at the personal behest of Walt Disney. The studio head, while in the process of imagining his own park, had been to Ghost Town more than a few times, always expressing interest in how things were done, asking Walter if he could bring his movie camera.

Walter and Cordelia were late arrivals to the opening-day festivities in Anaheim, where Disney was dedicating his park on a live national broadcast. They saw the crowds. They saw the huge expenditures of money, even though much of Disneyland still looked like a construction site. They saw what might be a challenge to their life-long investment. And they went home, certain their business would take a downturn.

It did not. It held steady, and subsequently improved. "It just proves that maybe we needed some competition," Knott said cheerily.

Perhaps more realistic was a version supplied by Harrison A. "Buzz" Price, an economist with the Stanford Research Institute hired by Walt Disney to study the feasibility of Disneyland prior to its construction. Meeting with Walter Knott, who had heard rumblings that Disney was up to something, Price sought financial data about the Farm that might be pertinent to his client's pending endeavor. He also let Knott know that Disneyland was, indeed, an approaching reality, and it would be right in the Knotts' backyard. He also assured Knott that the two parks together would form an unmatchable tourist market, "like two department stores together."

Knott would have none of it. He bristled, left Price's questions unanswered, and, rather than enthusiasm, could muster only suspicion.

"I left with none of the data I was looking for," Price admitted.

Despite Walter's pronouncement that he would keep Knott's Berry Farm as it was, his stagecoaches were joined by a "Merry-Go-Round, hurriedly installed last May by the father and son team of Ray and Wendell (Bud) Hurlbut," *Billboard* reported in 1956. By all accounts, the Hurlbuts had to convince an overly cautious Walter to allow it on his property, after his declaration that he and Cordelia wanted no "iron rides" at

Knott's Calico Mine Train marked a significant step forward for Scenic Railways—and the park itself.

GhostRider, a modern monument that pays tribute to Knott's past,
queues its riders through the old Calico Mine.

Knott's. A change of heart came sometime later. Under the terms of their contract—or,
rather, Bud's handshake deal with Walter—the Hurlbuts rented space on the Farm to
run what was their carousel, an 1896 Dentzel Menagerie model.

The homespun finally gave way to the spectacular, in 1960, when Walter contracted with Bud Hurlbut to let his imagination run wild. The result was a Carlsbad Caverns–like Scenic Railway called the Calico Mine Ride, featuring waterfalls,
mechanical-figure ore excavations, chain lift, and mock dynamite explosion. Hurlbut
financed the $1 million project himself ($8.4 million today), selling his ranch, home,
and car. In the final lap of construction, Walter forgave him the rent on the carousel.

It would take Hurlbut two years after the Mine Train opened to start seeing a profit.
In 1984, he sold his concessions to Knott's.

Before the '60s ended, he also would build Timber Mountain at Knott's, which
launched a log-flume craze at theme parks around the world.

Its first riders, on July 11, 1969, were Western screen legend John Wayne and
eighty-year-old Walter Knott.

Cordelia Knott, eighty-four, died April 12, 1974, from breast cancer. Walter, who
had suffered with Parkinson's, died December 3, 1981, at ninety-one. In the years
afterward, many suitors came calling, but when the gold dust settled at the end of
1997, the four Knott siblings had reached an agreement to sell their family-owned
Knott's Berry Farm to the publicly traded, Ohio-based Cedar Fair amusement company. The purchase price was about twice the annual revenue of the park, $245 million
($383 million today), $95 million of it in cash. "Added to that were 6.4 million limited
partnership units, valued at $23.34 per share, for a total of $150 million," reported
the *Los Angeles Times*, noting that the sale came at a time when rivals Disneyland
and Universal Studios could each afford to invest as much as $100 million in a single
new attraction.

With the addition of Snoopy and the Peanuts gang, Knott's Berry Farm and Ghost Town widened its identity.

Where once grew cherry rhubarb, asparagus, and boysenberries soon rose thrill rides, whose steel frameworks poked over the peaks of Calico Mountain. Soak City, a separate-entry water park, opened in 2000 on land that used to handle the overflow from the main Knott's parking lot.

Prior to the Cedar Fair deal, Cordelia's jams and jellies was sold to the Omaha-based Conagra Foods, in 1995. Thirteen years later, Conagra sold the brand to Ohio's J. M. Smucker Company, which expected the brand to add $40 million in sales to its annual portfolio.

In five years, the bloom was off the boysenberry.

Blaming low demand, Smuckers phased out the Knott's label in early 2013.

"Once the sale to Cedar Fair went through," said Jennifer Blazey, a former head of publicity at Knott's, "no member of the Knott family ever set foot on the property again."

That changed a dozen years later, when, in 2009, a celebration was announced to mark the seventy-fifth anniversary of the Chicken Dinner Restaurant. Word came through channels that Marion Knott was willing to loan an original china creamer and sugar bowl for display purposes.

An invitation was extended to Marion, who lived in Newport Beach, to come back and see what had transpired since her last inspection.

"We met and had lunch," Blazey recalled in 2018. (Marion died, at ninety-two, in 2014.) "We did a lot of cleanup before she came."

The sprucing-up was so thorough that the number of berries in a slice of pie was counted, simply to make sure everything was up to snuff.

Apparently, they were.

As Marion Knott left that day, her parting words were "I can just tell it's in good hands."

GRAND SLAM

An old wives' tale used to make the rounds at Disney Studios, that, late one night, Roy Disney, the older brother and business partner of Walt Disney, was walking around the lot and ended up in the animation department. Peering over the shoulder of an artist at work, Roy interrupted by offering a suggestion on how his sketch might be improved.

Looking up at this stranger, the artist asked, "And who do you think you are? God?"

"Not at all," replied Roy. "I'm God's brother."

Apocryphal or not, the anecdote expresses a certain perpetual reverence applied to Walt Disney, the twentieth-century cultural icon who gave the world Mickey Mouse and the various worlds, lands, and resorts that bear his trademarked name more than half a century after his death. Like them or not—and there are critics—they represent the diamond standard of theme parks.

Besides a peerless creativity and persistence, Diz, as his childhood friends in his native Midwest called him—first in his birthplace of Chicago, then, after age five, in the friendly town of Marceline, Missouri—was a rakishly handsome young man who maintained an eternal boyishness his entire life (1901–1966). "He is a simple person in the sense that everything about him harmonizes with everything else; his work reflects the way he lives, and vice versa," wrote the critic Gilbert Seldes in a *New Yorker* profile, when Walt was thirty and Mickey was two.

He was also, as he proved time and again, a hardheaded personality entirely immune to naysayers, and that included bankers, and even his levelheaded brother. Conversely, he was a doting father who

Not only was Walt Disney the biggest kid in the world, he also owned the world's greatest train set. (FYI: Ernest S. Marsh was president of the Santa Fe Railway.)

The Disney family moved to Marceline, Missouri, when Walt was not even four. He never got the town out of his system.

wanted to have ten children, a self-image so fixed in his mind that it devastated him when his wife, Lillian, miscarried. That was before the family grew to include daughters Diane and Sharon, born in 1933 and 1935, respectively.

Starting as a secretary at the studio—a friend had warned her not to "vamp the boss"—the former Lillian Marie Bounds (1899–1997), from Spalding, Idaho, married Walt on July 13, 1925. Both had arrived in Hollywood two years before; Walt, from Kansas City, Missouri, where he had tried, but failed, to initiate an animation studio. California seemed a natural for him. Older brother Roy (1893–1971) had gone there in 1921, to deal with respiratory issues.

Lillian came from a family of ten children, and Walt was "really taken" with his in-laws, said his daughter Diane. She also described her maternal grandparents as people who "loved to laugh, and maybe didn't appear to take life as seriously as Elias [Walt's father] did."

The trait looks to have been inherited by their daughter Lillian, who, traveling home with Walt from a trip East, convinced her husband that Mortimer was too grand a name for his cartoon mouse.

She suggested Mickey.

As with most of the emotional upheavals in his life, the loss of the child was not a topic Disney cared to discuss, nor would anyone dare broach it in his presence. Rather, he would withdraw into himself and face paralyzing bouts of self-doubt—chain-smoking and drinking scotch with a lemon peel and chipped ice were coping devices—until eventually he would allow his personal sentiments to be expressed through his screen work.

At the same time, this was also a man who, though available to his wife and children, could claim no real friends, according to PBS's *American Experience* episode "Walt Disney," directed by filmmaker Sarah Colt, which first aired in 2015.

Objective as the four-hour documentary was, hardline disciples of Disney found it cynical, even though the real eight-hundred-pound Dumbo in the room was never so much as whispered: Walt's long-debated anti-Semitism, a trait vehemently denied

Walt paid posthumous tribute to his father, Elias, with a window in his honor on Disneyland's Main Street.

by his daughter Diane. The Walt Disney Family Museum in San Francisco makes special note that Joe Rosenberg, of the Bank of America, was the one banker who approved the loan to finish *Snow White and the Seven Dwarfs,* for which Walt volubly expressed his lifelong gratitude. Further taking up Walt's defense on the issue have been some of his Jewish coworkers, including longtime Disney songwriters Richard and Robert Sherman, and "Imagineer"—Disneyspeak for "ride designer" and more—Martin Sklar, who started in publicity at Disneyland and eventually became an international ambassador for what became a multinational company.

The question cannot be put to rest—one of Walt's record twenty-six Academy Awards was for his 1943 anti-Nazi Donald Duck cartoon *Der Fuehrer's Face,* yet in 1938 he had hosted Nazi propagandist Leni Riefenstahl on her visit to Hollywood, over heated requests that he should break their appointment.

Say what one will, photos of Walt's office show that on his desk he kept a framed ten-by-twelve photographic portrait of the frequent Disney star Ed Wynn, a beloved Jewish comedian.

Disney's childhood was one of economic hardship, with the documentary suggesting that the emotionally detached father at the core of *Mary Poppins* could have been based on Walt's own father, Elias (1859-1941), described by biographer Neal Gabler, in his 2006 *Walt Disney: The Triumph of the American Imagination,* as dour, pathologically parsimonious, and wrathful. Such negativity, said Gabler, caused his artistically inclined youngest son—Walt was one of five children, four boys and a girl; Ruth, the sister, was the baby—to grow into "the antithesis of Elias Disney, almost as if he had willed himself to be so as a form of rebellion."

Flora Disney (1868–1938), Elias's wife and the children's mother, horrifically succumbed to a carbon monoxide leak in the California house that Walt and Roy built for their parents with the financial windfall from 1937's *Snow White.* She seems to represent the steady parade of dead or, at least, absentee, maternal figures that haunt the Disney animated classics—*Snow White, Pinocchio, Bambi, Dumbo, Cinderella, Alice in Wonderland, Sleeping Beauty, The Jungle Book,* and even Lady, the cocker spaniel, comes to be ignored by her human parents in *Lady and the Tramp*—but the argument is difficult to sustain. (As is, to get the topic off the table, the fatuous notion that Walt Disney was cryogenically frozen at the time of his death.) *Snow White's* release preceded Flora's passing, just as *Pinocchio* and *Bambi* were already in production at the time of the tragedy. The other stories were based on sources that already had removed the mothers from the action, although there is a possible case to be made for the examination of why Walt chose those tales in the first place.

In his choices as an employer, the picture is far less ambiguous. Disney might have been generous when it came to his boys' club of high-ranking company executives, who were granted exclusive access to the studio's penthouse steam room and gym, but the women who toiled endless hours as animation colorists were not only deprived of comfortable working surroundings but a living wage.

When, in the spring of 1941, his labor pool expressed dissatisfaction, Disney, who was drawing an annual salary of better than $100,000 (nearly $2 million today), summoned an assembly on the studio lot and berated them all. "If you're not progressing as you should," he scolded, "instead of grumbling and growling, do something about it."

They did; they went on strike, and when Walt took a swing at senior animator Art Babbitt, already fired for having joined the union, Roy suggested Walt remove himself to South America for a ten-week "vacation."

The dust settled in the fall of 1941. Roy ended the walkout by agreeing to the workers' terms.

During this same period, Elias Disney died in California.

Walt remained in South America and missed his father's funeral.

THEREAFTER DISILLUSIONED AND distrustful of the studio environment he had created, Disney returned to work in Burbank but began compiling a private dossier on those who had been "unfriendly" toward him.

"If you crossed him," a veteran Disney animator said about his onetime employer, "he was a mean S.O.B."

He also could be completely deaf when others tendered advice he refused to hear. Though warned repeatedly, Disney foresaw no problems bringing Georgia writer Joel Chandler Harris's antebellum folktales, *Song of the South*, to the screen. He deemed the combined live-action and animated project, with its sugarcoated take on race relations and its stereotypical characters, the Disney answer to *Gone with the Wind*. (The film today remains out of circulation, although it serves as the basis for the Splash Mountain log-flume attractions in the Disney parks.)

"It's as if Walt divorced himself from social context," University of Virginia art historian Carmenita Higginbotham said. "It's sort of stunning."

Then again, Walt Disney knew better than anybody the brand he had created, the artist he was, and what the world expected of him.

Such uncomplicated self-realization would allow him to create his greatest expression of himself.

Disneyland.

Walt Disney was not the only film master fixated on amusement parks.

Nine years before his *Psycho* scared the world out of taking a shower, in 1951, Alfred Hitchcock frightened movie audiences off their merry-go-round mounts with the deadly climax to his *Strangers on a Train*, based on a 1950 Patricia Highsmith mystery novel. (The scene does not exist in the book.)

"Bruno [Robert Walker], attempting to escape from Guy [Farley Granger] and the law, jumps aboard a moving merry-go-round, with Guy after him," a 1951 Warner Bros. story-department synopsis read. "The concession operator is hit in the melee of shots fired by the police at the men."

The dead ride operator falls on the control lever and, to the calliope tune of "The Band Played On," the merry-go-round spins wildly out of control. Onboard, Bruno and Guy slug it out, as riders, including children, scream and clutch their horses for dear life.

In an early screenplay by Raymond Chandler, dated August 25, 1950, that made it to final print, an "old character" who works at the park "starts crawling under the floor of the merry-go-round in a completely unconcerned manner."

Thanks to the worker's heroism, "the merry-go-round is halted, but the sudden braking causes the concession to topple over." The ride explodes, a special effect that Hitchcock shot at the studio, in miniature. Actors then stood in front of a rear-screen projection of the scene, blown up to size.

Hitchcock shot the bulk of the amusement park scenes—like the island near the Tunnel of Love, where Bruno strangles Guy's wife—on Warners' Stage 22. The merry-go-round slugfest took place on Stage 21, on December 21, 1950. The finale's exteriors were done in late November and early December, at the Roland V. Lee Ranch, in Chatsworth.

"You know," Hitch told French director François Truffaut, "that little man actually crawled under that spinning carousel. If he'd raised his head by an inch, he'd have been killed."

Recalling the situation years later, the Master of Suspense added, "I'll never do anything like that again."

Robert Walker, as Bruno Antony, zeroes in on his intended murder victim (Laura Elliot), in Alfred Hitchcock's *Strangers on a Train*— which culminates aboard an out-of-control merry-go-round.

ON WEDNESDAY NIGHT, October 27, 1954, at seven thirty in its local time zones, ABC debuted *DisneyLand*, as it was spelled in the full-page ad in *TV Guide*. "The veteran animator and producer of realistic nature films comes to TV with a weekly series," said the show's editorial listing. "Tonight he introduces both the show Dis-neyland, and the amusement park of the same name in California." The squib also related that the hour would start "with a magic-carpet journey to the Walt Disney Burbank studios, a trip around the world and then a trip to outer space."

Ratings went through the roof.

During brother Roy's whirlwind tour of Manhattan's corridors of power to sell what his brother had up his sleeve, CBS and NBC, much bigger than ABC, both passed on the program, whose deal with Disney was contingent upon the network investing in Walt's amusement park idea. For ABC, the buy-in was $15 million, in exchange for 35 percent of what was being called, in banking quarters, "Disney's Folly." Still, the figure was $2 million short of Disneyland's ultimate cost by opening day, July 17, 1955; the initial Stanford Research Institute estimate had lowballed the price at $4 million.

Since the 1930s, Disney had floated the notion of a Mickey Mouse Park, although the concept did not begin to solidify until 1950 and the release of *Cinderella*, a commercial hit but an artistic failure for Walt, who had denied it his full attention. Blame was placed on the new miniature steam locomotive he wound through his residential estate in Los Angeles's Holmby Hills neighborhood. The train was Walt's obsession—leading some Disneyologists to consider it, besides a yearning to relive his simpler Marceline past, the first significant step toward the creation of Disneyland.

"I had all my drawing things laid out at home, and I'd work on plans for the park, as a hobby, at night," Walt told *National Geographic*. The elements fell together from those daydreaming moments with his daughters at kiddie parks, about what a place representative of his creations should contain: an old-fashioned city hall and a fire station, a movie house, and a Snow White dark ride, along with a more ambitious submarine, spaceship, and steamboat, and a train protectively surrounding its circumference.

In 1952, he presented the Burbank City Council with a proposal for a $1.5 million park adjacent to his studio. It was rejected out of hand, the council fearing it would create the type of carny atmosphere plaguing the beach. Even Lillian wondered why Walt wanted to become involved in something as filthy as an amusement park.

"I talked Disneyland," he said, "but no one could see it. So I went ahead and spent my own money."

Hiring Stanford Research to scout potential locations and determine costs for what would, in fact, grant him greater leeway than the narrow strip of land in Burbank, the institute looked as far as San Fernando Valley's Chatsworth, San Gabriel Valley's

Stanford Research Institute consultant Harrison "Buzz" Price asked Walt if he had any idea of a location for his park. Replied Disney: "That's what I hired *you* for."

Pomona, Orange County's Tustin, and the county's beach town of Balboa. The last would not work at all, as Walt had definite ideas about steering clear of the shore. Besides a party crowd he did not wish to attract, and the carny atmosphere the Burbank elders feared, nature's elements would wreak havoc with the first-caliber attractions that he envisioned.

In all, forty-three sites were inspected before the possibilities were winnowed down to four in Orange County. The growing community held the promise of the Santa Ana Freeway, as well as, in Walt's words, "flat land that I could shape." The 244 acres in Anaheim he ended up with were mostly orange grove, and while trees and underbrush were cleared to make way for what would have a Neuschwanstein-like castle at its hub, the bulldozers also prepared a ten-foot earthen berm around the entire parcel.

"I don't want the public to see the real world they live in while they're in the park," Walt insisted. "I want them to feel they are in another world."

FOLLOWING WALT'S PRONOUNCEMENT THAT his park would contain no roller coasters, the Walt Disney Productions board of directors, including brother Roy, thought he was on a suicide mission and zipped their pockets shut. Roy went so far as to threaten legal action against his kid brother should any of the Disney characters appear in this self-destructive pipedream. (Roy eventually relented and partnered in the venture.)

The board's rejection spurred Walt to form a separate company, give it his initials, WED Enterprises (the *E* was for Elias), and use it exclusively to develop his park. It had no board of directors. "The artists that worked on the Disney project were usually the finest of the artists that Walt had," said George K. Whitney Jr. "He pulled them [out of his studio and] into his WED Enterprises Company."

Walt financed this independent foray by selling his Palm Springs home and borrowing $50,000 against his life insurance policy—he put the Holmby Hills estate in Lillian's name, in case, heaven forbid, the Disney board of directors was right—and it was Walt who, going against the grain of other Hollywood studio heads, decided there was money to be made from television.

Over the course of a single weekend in 1953, he worked with Hollywood graphic artist Herb Ryman, a Chicago Institute of Art graduate, whose movie credits included such MGM exemplars of detail as *David Copperfield*, *Mutiny on the Bounty*, and *The Good Earth*, for which Merry Olde England, Oceania, and China were created on that studio's backlot. Together, Ryman and Disney mapped out Disneyland—literally, on a three-by-five-foot ink-and-pencil map—drawing from Walt's ideas and trips he had taken to such places as Rye Playland in New York, Knott's Berry Farm, Coney Island (whose grittiness depressed him, never being a city boy to begin with), and Tivoli Gardens, in Copenhagen. Walt particularly appreciated Tivoli's cleanliness, to which he credited the thoughtful landscaping. Its beauty stopped people from even thinking of littering.

With a fairy-tale castle commanding the northeast corner of the 160 acres, Walt's triangle-shaped vision as rendered by Ryman had a hovering Jules Verne–style hot-air balloon and, at ground level, a train circling its perimeter. A steamboat, rocket ship, pirate frigate, and, in the Frontier Country section, a butte from Utah's Monument Valley supplied variety. Granted, there was a touch of Coney, which never made it to the finished product: Lilliputian Land.

The map accompanied Roy to New York as his sales tool.

Once ABC CEO Leonard Goldenson agreed to the financing, Ryman's map became a springboard for the actual blueprints.

Walt Disney spent the night before Disneyland's opening with his wife, Lillian, in their five-hundred-square-foot private apartment above the Main Street Firehouse. He got no sleep, dashing out several times to check on the ongoing construction progress that would continue long after the big unveil.

By morning, he was back inside the hideaway, where he stood at the window and gazed down at Town Square. What he saw were visitors filtering in.

Disneyland, at last, had people inside its gate.

As a twelve-year-old Mouseketeer from the *Mickey Mouse Club* TV show recalled of that moment (the entire Club had gathered inside the apartment with the Disneys), fifty-three-year-old Walt "had his hands behind his back, a grin from ear to ear. I could see a lump in his throat, and a tear streaming down his cheek."

Much has been made of the disastrous opening day at Disneyland, dubbed "Black Sunday." The overcapacity crowds, the gridlocked freeway, the hundred-degree weather, the faulty plumbing, the melting asphalt, the shortage of food and drink, the breakdown of rides—and, for all the world to see, the live ABC telecast with its own excess of glitches. What tends to be overlooked, if one watches the archival film—granted, it's a long slog—is the unbridled joy shown in the face of Walt Disney. The man who supposedly found it difficult to display emotion is unequivocally bursting with happiness.

Interestingly, Roy Disney and his wife, Edna, did not rush out to Disneyland on opening day. In fact, when they finally did get to Anaheim, they did not even hurry out of their Cadillac. Instead, they sat in the car and ate the cake Edna had made at home in San Fernando Valley's Toluca Lake. It was almost as if they were hesitating.

Better than anyone, Roy knew that word on the street was that Disneyland would not last beyond the summer. Still, he was pleasantly surprised to find so many cars parked outside his brother's long-gestating, pie-in-the-sky idea.

"Mr. Disney, I'm glad I found you," a young worker, approaching the car, shouted, breaking up Roy and Edna's snack time. The fellow explained that hundreds of people had been stuck in traffic for hours driving to Disneyland, and their kids couldn't wait to get to the bathrooms.

"Now they're peeing all over the lot," said the employee.

Relieved to hear there was such a large turnout, an uncharacteristically lighthearted Roy took a good look at the crowded parking lot and responded, "God bless 'em. Let 'em pee."

"It was like our own personal playground. And it had the best toys," said the dancer Marge Champion, who had grown up in Hollywood and was the Disney animators' model for Snow White, the Blue Fairy in *Pinocchio*, and the Hippo in the Tutu in *Fantasia*. She was referring to the early days of Disneyland, where she would bring her two sons with husband Gower Champion, the dancer, director, and choreographer.

The original Disneyland—just plain Disneyland, not Disneyland Park or Disneyland Resort, which were later, corporate-created tweaks as the property, crowds, and wait times expanded, and multiple-day stays were required—consisted of five lands. Main Street U.S.A., Walt's idealization of 1890s Marceline, was the corridor inside, once past the main

Despite Walt's time-honed connection to children's stories, his park was also a place adults could enjoy themselves, as one early advertisement sought to highlight.

From left: Walt dreamed it, C. V. Wood built it, and Harrison "Buzz" Price found it—Disneyland.

gate and white gingerbread-cottage ticket booths with their popcorn lights, just like the ones Walt and his sister, Ruth, used to see at Electric Park in Kansas City. Main Street was more than just a passageway; it was the beginning of the storybook adventure, setting the mood, relieving the pressure of the freeway ride to the park, and building anticipation for the excitement ahead.

Familiar commercial names leased space along Main Street's single, well-scrubbed boulevard, so that Swift sponsored the market house; Upjohn, the pharmacy; Wurlitzer, the music store; and Carnation, the ice-cream parlor. Initially Ford, General Electric, General Motors, and Coca-Cola had all said no, and not always politely. It wasn't until Swift came aboard that other companies even deigned be part of what was still perceived as a Hollywood cartoonist's kiddie park.

To grapple with the situation, Disney needed a persuasive pitchman. Fitting the bill was Cornelius Vanderbilt Wood (1920–1992), a flamboyant and cunningly convincing Oklahoma-born, Texas-reared good ol' boy who was never quite what he said he was. Neither, possibly, was his name, given that he would introduce himself, even to business associates, by saying, "Call me C.V.—that's C for Nothing, V for Nothing." Despite a doctored résumé, "Woody" was on staff at the Stanford Research Institute before Disney hired him away. If George K. Whitney was Disneyland Employee Number Seven, C.V. was Number One.

With a take-charge manner and ability to charm and strong-arm, Wood significantly contributed to getting Disneyland off the ground, under alternating titles of vice president and/or general manager and/or project supervisor (they switched, depending on how he was attempting to present himself in later deals), but his many accomplishments in Anaheim have been completely erased from Disney history.

Besides having an ego that clashed with Walt's, Wood was apparently never above accepting a kickback. This was not the Disney way—no more than it was to pose with dignitaries for Disneyland publicity photos, unless you were Walt Disney.

Walt had Roy fire Wood six months after Disneyland opened.

MAIN STREET REACHED A fork in its road at the foot of the castle, where Disneyland divided into four realms. Instinctively, the majority of "guests"—never "customers"—gravitated to the right, which took them into Tomorrowland.

In this world of the future, the "weenie"—Walt's term for a visual magnet, like the hot dog he took from the home fridge to make his pet poodle, Lady, follow him—was a seventy-six-foot rocket ship. Called the Moonliner and sponsored by Trans World Airlines, whose red and white colors the ship bore, it stood before the entrance to the Flight to the Moon. Inside the pavilion, passengers in two separate auditoriums traversed the solar system as they watched movie screens on the floor and ceiling. Technically impressive (the seats vibrated, and the auditoriums were very sci-fi cool for the '50s), but on the immersion scale, it was less proactive than Thompson and

Even though some of the splashier ideas—Donald Duck bumper boats, a Pinocchio-themed Shoot the Chutes whose boats spewed from Monstro's mouth—never got past the drawing stage, there was nothing like Disneyland, not anywhere.

Other parks modeled upon the same layout—separate themed areas branching out from a circular hub—would follow, starting with some quick imitators that immediately failed to go the distance.

In 1957 came Magic Mountain, the "Disneyland of the Rockies," in Golden, Colorado. The $3.5 million park was partially built, partially operated for three years, and then permanently closed.

In 1959 came Pleasure Island, the "Disneyland of the Northeast," near Boston. The $4 million park went bust its first season, took on an ongoing series of unfortunate subsequent owners, then closed for good in 1969.

In 1960 came Freedomland USA, the "Disneyland of the East," in the Bronx, on eighty-five acres shaped like the map of the United States. The $65

million investment—$500 million today, and, at the time, the equivalent cost of 22 movies, 195 Broadway shows, or 130 TV specials—spotlighted a miniature San Francisco that collapsed in an earthquake, an Old Chicago that spewed flames à la Dreamland's Fighting the Flames, and an Old West outfitted with taxidermied bears and wolves.

The best the *New York Times* could say of Freedomland, before it closed in 1964, was that it "was built to make the visitor seem far from the Bronx."

The one common element shared by all three parks? Leading their construction was C. V. Wood.

Of the many imitators that tried to cash in on Disneyland's success, the most blatant was Freedomland U.S.A., in the Bronx.

Trans World Airlines, owned by Howard Hughes, was one of the corporations convinced to establish a presence in Disneyland.

Dundy's A Trip to the Moon—no one at Disneyland got up to dance and share hors d'oeuvres with moon men.

Along with Imagineer John Hench, who contributed to the overall look of Disneyland, the Moonliner owed its design to space architect Werner von Braun, builder of Nazi Germany's V-2 ballistic missile program during World War II. After the war, he and his team were government approved to work in the United States, and von Braun became a key engineer in America's Apollo mission to the moon.

For youngsters, Tomorrowland's Autopia, sponsored by Richfield Oil, allowed "drivers of the future" to take their first spin behind a wheel; at least, that was the explanation for placing the attraction in Tomorrowland. Soon, bumpers had to be added to cushion collisions, and, eventually, cars had to be fixed to a track.

By 1956, a Skyway would shuttle guests from Tomorrowland to "the happiest kingdom of them all," Fantasyland, but for the first year, the sole entrance was through Sleeping Beauty's Castle. The movie *Sleeping Beauty* was still in production, so the park centerpiece, which also served as logo for Walt's ABC-TV show, was strategic prerelease publicity.

Fantasyland was conceived to look like a medieval fair, more Camelot than the Feast of St. Bartholomew, although there was a bit of that, too. Chicken of the Sea served tuna sandwiches aboard a pirate ship, and Snow White, Peter Pan, and Mr. Toad each had a single-track dark ride of his or her own. (Peter's pirate-galleon track hung overhead, provided by the Cleveland Tram Company.) Despite their thrills behind closed doors—Toad's was accurately called a "Wild Ride"—the outdoor flying Dumbo elephants and the spinning Mad Tea Party made for better photo ops. Lee Eyerly, the Loop-O-Plane manufacturer, tried selling the idea of attaching little Dumbos at the tips of the tentacles to his off-the-shelf Octopus ride, but Walt dismissed it as a cheap trick.

It was in search of the perfect Dumbo vehicle that, on the advice of Stanford Research, Walt connected with the Mountainview, California, ride manufacturer

Arrow Development. He also ended up handing them the King Arthur Carousel, his centerpiece for the Fantasyland castle's courtyard. The 1922 William Dentzel carousel, first built for Sunnyside Beach, in Toronto, certainly had enough horses to go around—Walt just didn't like the look of them. Too many galloped. He wanted them to jump. Arrow made them jump.

"I had no idea of the scope of Disneyland," Arrow cofounder Ed Morgan said about first meeting Walt, and dealing with his perfectionism. "No one had heard of a theme park at that time."

By the time Disneyland opened, Arrow—at a financial loss—had supplied the vehicles for Mr. Toad's Wild Ride, the Casey Jr. Circus Train, and the Dumbo and Snow White attractions. Landing in Walt's good graces, Arrow then got the plum assignment in 1958, when, contrary to his earlier anti-roller-coaster edict, Walt returned from Switzerland and put in an order for the greatest scenic railway ever to come down the pike—the Matterhorn.

Frontierland, at ten o'clock on the Disneyland map, was actually the most popular corner when Disneyland opened, given that the Disney-produced *Davy Crockett* TV series, which debuted in 1954, was a national phenomenon, and Westerns were the small screen's genre of choice. Except for the 105-foot *Mark Twain* stern-wheeler on the Rivers of America, and the Pepsi-Cola Golden Horseshoe Saloon, where nothing stronger than the sponsor's product was dispensed, Frontierland's Concord stagecoach, Conestoga wagon, and pack mule train were duplicates to what one could find at Knott's Berry Farm—only here they seemed to be in widescreen CinemaScope and Technicolor.

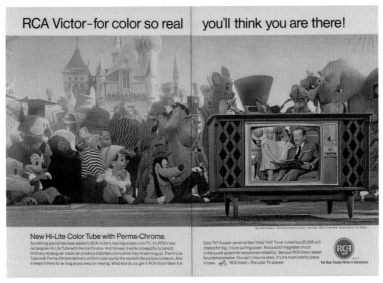

Television was responsible for making Walt Disney a household name. By the 1960s, he and his kingdom were iconic.

A private party for park sponsors was held in the Golden Horseshoe the night before Disneyland officially opened, July 16, 1955. Three days before, Walt and Lillian had celebrated their thirtieth wedding anniversary there. Dinner was preceded by a cruise on the *Mark Twain*. Because the decks were still dusty from construction, guest of honor Lillian Disney picked up a spare broom and swept them before the evening's guests arrived.

Adventureland lacked a weenie, but it did have the Rivers of the World, where floated the elaborate Explorer's Boat Ride, later called the Jungle Cruise. George K. Whitney Jr. helped quash Walt's original idea to build his own Selig's Zoo on the banks of the river, explaining the unpredictability involved, as others reminded Walt that animals tended to sleep during the day.

Walt heeded their advice—contrary to what occurred with *Song of the South*, Walt always "got it," said Whitney, complimenting Disney, too, for "being able to convey enthusiasm" like no other. The animals turned out to be robotic devices called animatronics. Once manufactured at the Disney Studios in Burbank, they were transported to Anaheim on flatbed trucks down the Santa Ana Freeway, much to the bemusement of the other drivers on the highway.

Responsibility for the ride's design fell to art director Harper Goff, whom Walt met in England in 1951, when both were in the same model-train shop. "He turned to me and said, 'I'm Walt Disney. Are you the man that wanted to buy this engine?'" Goff recalled. "Well, I almost fell over."

Walt, too, had a right to be impressed; Goff, a graduate of Los Angeles's Chouinard Art Institute—which Walt had raided in the '30s to find animators for *Snow White*—had illustrated for *Collier's*, *Esquire*, and *National Geographic* magazines in New York, set the standard for camouflage colors during the Second World War, and was a respected Warner Bros. production designer. His credits included the atmospheric *Sergeant York*, *The Charge of the Light Brigade*, and, with the simplest of touches beyond Moorish shapes, *Casablanca*.

"When you get back to America," Walt told him, "come and talk to me."

Goff did just that. Besides the steam-punk *Nautilus* submarine for Disney's screen version of *Twenty Thousand Leagues Under the Sea*, he did concept art for Main Street U.S.A. that included a haunted mansion tucked on a hill behind a church. For the Explorer's Boat Ride, he used as inspiration the 1951 film *The African Queen*, starring Humphrey Bogart, Katharine Hepburn, river rapids, and a tramp steamer. He also oversaw the ride's construction and, it is claimed, physically mapped out the boats' course by walking and marking it with a stick.

"Crocodiles, hippos, lions, and head-hunters add thrills and chills," said Disneyland's first souvenir brochure, which, the unassuming text admitted, was sent to press before all park decisions had been made.

"For that reason," it was noted, "this book may be incomplete and subject to change."

Just like Disneyland.

NEW WORLDS

I.

Word first came at a luncheon in the Waldorf-Astoria Hotel's Starlight Room, during the summer of 1963. Covering the announcement, the *New Yorker*'s Talk of the Town column delivered the news under the subhead "A Small World."

"Arriving at noon," the reporter wrote in that arch style that leads the reader to infer that every name being written up is being put down, "we found ourself in the presence of Walt Disney." Robert Moses was there, too, in his capacity as head of the upcoming 1964–1965 New York World's Fair. So were Herbert Barnet, the president of Pepsi-Cola, and D. Mitchell Cox, a public-relations representative for the soft-drink company. Speaking into a microphone, Cox's luncheon task was to enumerate "the many wonders of Mr. Disney's blueprint for an electronically powered boat trip around an animated-cartoon world of UNICEF children."

Meanwhile, at the Waldorf, actual live children, dressed in the garb of their native lands, "were busy passing out glasses of Pepsi-Cola and plastic press kits stamped with the face of Mickey Mouse."

Cox explained that when the fair opened in Flushing Meadows, Queens, the following April, Disney and Barnet would present an attraction called "It's a Small World," and it would cost more than $4 million ($33 million today).

The 1964 New York World's Fair made the case that the Disney brand could play beyond Southern California.

"Mr. Disney's writing a song for it," said Cox. "It will be *tremendous*. Another 'Heigh-Ho.'"

Cox went on to predict that people everywhere would be whistling the tune. "Everybody loves Disney," said the publicity man. "He's got friends around the world."

"Hitler didn't like me," Walt piped up, though Robert Moses broke up any ensuing friendly chat Disney had with reporters about how Der Führer had banned the sale of Mickey Mouse watches.

In any event, the cat was out of the bag.

Disney branching out beyond California? It almost didn't seem fair. Disneyland was so representative of the Golden State—and, by now, vice-versa.

The embarrassment of opening day long past—despite the negative press, crowds immediately started pouring in, 3,642,597 people in the first year, each spending an average of $2.37 ($22.05 today)—and early gaffes were hastily remedied. A Mickey Mouse Club Circus opened and closed, due to lack of interest. A Holidayland for private parties soon proved a waste of precious space, as few people wished to be isolated from the rest of Disneyland. Also during the break-in period, Tomorrowland Lagoon's Phantom Boats, mechanical hybrids between a shark and a bat-ray, constantly broke down. Walt consigned them to Davy Jones's Locker.

By the late 1950s, Disneyland was an established institution. The park not only neatly wrapped up the past on Main Street and in Frontierland, but, in 1957,

Since their 1959 unveilings, the Matterhorn has been modernized, as have the monorail and submarine (re-themed to *Finding Nemo*). Only the E ticket has faded into memory.

awarded its own seal of approval to a House of the Future, a modular plastic structure produced by Monsanto Chemical, MIT, and WED. Planted to the left of the Tomorrowland gate, it anticipated, about 75 percent correctly, what life would be like in 1986. It certainly got right the pallid colors of the plastic furniture and appliances.

In 1961, the Disneyland Alweg Monorail—the first in America—was expanded from its original sightseeing route over Tomorrowland Lagoon and past Alice's Adventures in Wonderland to beyond the berm, through the parking lot, and connecting to the Disneyland Hotel. Imagineer Bob Gurr's red-and-blue Mark I trains looked like a speeding bullet mated with a Cadillac Eldorado and, along with the Submarine Voyage and the Matterhorn Bobsleds, began operating on June 14, 1959.

The three attractions—at this stage, the term *ride* had been banished from the Disney lexicon—introduced what was called an E-ticket attraction (not to be confused with today's electronic ticket).

When the park opened, its top-shelf rides, such as the Jungle Cruise and Santa Fe & Disneyland Railroad, required a C coupon, typically purchased in a book of A, B, and C tickets that included main-gate admission (one dollar for adults, fifty cents for children) and discounted prices for the individual attractions (priced from ten to twenty-five cents). The 1959 park additions, christened by Vice President Richard M. Nixon and his family—whom Gurr inadvertently hijacked for the monorail's maiden journey before Nixon's Secret Service detail also could board—brought an expansion of the ticket books from A to E, with an E ticket priced at fifty cents. The cost of an adult "Jumbo 15" ticket book, made up of two A's, two B's, three C's, four D's, and four E's, was $4.50, a full dollar more than the "Big 10" ticket book. (A 1959 dollar is $8.55 today.)

General Dynamics sponsored the submarine, Santa Fe Railway underwrote the monorail, and the Matterhorn was now the tallest structure in Orange County. Given their sophistication and pedigrees, the E-ticket attractions raised the bar when it came to the park's standing.

They also gave Disneyland a much-needed leg up, because, forty miles away, a challenger defiantly presented itself on the shore in Santa Monica.

II.

On July 22, 1958, in a location much closer to Los Angeles Airport than Anaheim, the day's hosts, movie star Debbie Reynolds and TV host Art Linkletter, helped CBS and the Los Angeles Turf Club cut the ribbon on the two companies' joint business venture: the dressed-up old Ocean Park Pier. The newly finished version was the nautical-themed Pacific Ocean Park, or P.O.P., the brainchild of Dr. Charles Henry "Doc" Strub—he held a dentistry degree from UC Berkeley, but was better known in sports circles as the owner of baseball's San Francisco Seals. He formed the LA Turf Club in 1934, with Our Gang and Laurel and Hardy film producer Hal Roach, and it was their Santa Anita Park that introduced the photo finish.

Fleetingly perceived as a rival to Disneyland, Pacific Ocean Park slapped a maritime coating on the old Ocean Pier, but lacked effective management, financial resources, and proper maintenance. It sank in nine years.

Strub's interest in amusement parks may have harked back to his helping salvage the

The world's largest oceanarium, Marineland of the Pacific (1954–1987), in Palos Verdes Estates, held its own for several years—until competition from other Southern California theme parks and a series of disinterested corporate owners depleted it of its resources. Sea World eventually bought the facility, moved Marineland's orcas and porpoises to its San Diego flagship, and pulled the plug in Palos Verdes.

financially ailing 1939 San Francisco World's Fair, or that, during Walt's exploratory period for Disneyland investors, he approached Disney with an offer to build the park at the beach. Walt declined, but Strub followed Disneyland's progress, and took his Ocean Park proposal to CBS CEO William S. Paley, just as Roy Disney had approached ABC's Leonard Goldenson. Sadly, Strub, age seventy-three, died of a stroke on March 28, 1958, just as Pacific Ocean Park was becoming a reality.

The impressive entrance set the tone. Chief P.O.P. art director Fred Harpman had worked on Disney's Frontierland and Main Street, and as an assistant art director on Mike Todd's overblown but well-appointed *Around the World in Eighty Days*. For Strub's project, he devised a futuristic water-gushing Neptune's Kingdom courtyard, whose box office booths formed the base of soaring arches crowned by three revolving seashores. The courtyard's interior pavilion, providing a sensation of walking underwater, was sponsored by Coca-Cola, and had a live-fish tank, with sharks, rays, and a mechanical Neptune on his throne.

Design supervisors for the twenty-eight-acre P.O.P. site were William Pereira and Charles Luckman, whose architectural firm was responsible for the Beverly Hilton (1952), CBS's Television City, in Los Angeles (1953), and Marineland of the Pacific (1954), a successful oceanarium in Rancho Palos Verdes, California, and the precursor of the Sea World parks.

Existing assets—like the International Promenade, with food stands; the kick-ass Hi-Boy roller coaster, renamed the Sea Serpent; and the usual thrill rides—were all refitted with marine motifs that varied from the whimsical to the mystical, with a midway that augured SpongeBob SquarePants's Bikini Bottom. Largely, many of the attractions on the twenty-eight-acre site were but brightly coated, second-tier rip-offs of Disneyland's finest: Flight to Mars (comparable, though not really, to Disney's Flight to the Moon), Union 76 Ocean Highway (Richfield Autopia), House of Tomorrow (House of the Future, plus a Westinghouse robot from the 1939 New York World's Fair), Magic Carpet Ride (Storybook Land Canal Boats), Mystery Island Banana Train Ride (Jungle Cruise), and Ocean Skyway (advantage P.O.P.'s, because its space-age, bubble-shaped gondolas breezed over the crashing ocean, while Walt's mine buckets merely intersected with screaming bobsledders aboard the Matterhorn).

Adult admission was ninety cents, or $7.75 today, with rides extra. In terms of atmosphere and immersion, the Banana Train was by far the best P.O.P. had to offer, a combination scenic railway, tiki bar (sans rum), and South Seas oasis. Mitzi Gaynor, star of the movie musical *South Pacific*, which was in release at the time, posed there for preopening park publicity photos, alongside a beefy, bare-chested Samoan chief.

For added exotica, the Banana Train's locomotive engines were placed at the rear of each of its six trains, so the passenger cars were pushed from behind. The climax of the adventure was a goony bird popping out of its shell. En route, a headhunter stared down from the roof of a thatched hut. Arrow Development constructed the ride, and one of the train's owners—several P.O.P. attractions were leased concessions—was Walt's old nemesis, C. V. Wood.

By 1959, visitor count reached 1.2 million, and the park wittingly shut down in the winter months for a slight overhaul that brought the addition of a kiddie Fun Forest. It would be the last enhancements the park would ever see. Bleeding money on their investment despite the high attendance, CBS and the Turf Club looked for a way out. According to P.O.P. authorities Christopher Merritt and Domenic Priore, that was land developer John Moreland. An experienced dealmaker, Moreland was willing to assume the park's debt, thus sparing CBS and the Turf Club the embarrassment of a P.O.P. bankruptcy. The transfer took place in October 1959.

What Moreland could not do was come to terms with all of the park's concessionaires. His plan was to institute a Pay One Price policy (also abbreviated to P.O.P.) that would divide the $1.50 admission among himself and the others. But in making this deal, Moreland was forced to give away too much of the bank. Still, the new pricing policy worked, at least in terms of bringing in bodies.

The 1960 season saw more than two hundred thousand customers, double than that of the year before—boosted, no doubt, by Los Angeles deejay Wink Martindale's *P.O.P. Dance Party*, an LA version of TV's *American Bandstand* that started airing from the park. The lip-synching guest stars ranged from Johnny Mathis to Johnny Cash. About this same time, network producers utilized the park, arriving with crews to film episodes of *The Twilight Zone, Route 66, The Man from U.N.C.L.E., Get Smart, Mod Squad*, and the widely watched finale of *The Fugitive*.

Nineteen sixty-one saw a twenty-five-cent increase to the admission, and Martindale's introduction of a new group as the intermission act for "King of the Surf Guitar" Dick Dale & His Del-Tones: the Beach Boys. But behind the scenes, costs were not being met.

By January 1964, Moreland removed himself from the property, and the inexorable slide began.

As Walt Disney foresaw when scouting locations for his park, salt air rusted rides, and P.O.P.'s had fallen into disrepair even before a 1965 City of Santa Monica urban renewal project blocked street access to the main gate.

By then, the food in the park was no safer than the rides.

P.O.P. closed in 1967.

<h1 style="text-align:center">III.</h1>

It's a Small World—technically, the title was the all lowercase it's a small world—was one of four Disney commissions for the New York World's Fair. He was also charged with the Magic Skyway for Ford, in which riders traveled through time, past dinosaurs, in new Mustangs; the State of Illinois pavilion's Great Moments with Mr. Lincoln, in which the sixteenth president delivered a stirring address culled from several of his speeches; and, for General Electric, the Carousel of Progress, which demonstrated better living through electricity as six seated audiences simultaneously rode a giant turntable to watch a series of staged mini sitcoms—commercials for GE, really—set in 1900, 1920, 1940, and the present.

The fair work required the full creative force of the Disney Studios in Burbank, which put on hold the two major projects for Anaheim's latest "land," New Orleans Square, that Disneyland was developing in place of the old Holidayland: Pirates of the Caribbean and the Haunted Mansion.

The fair also allowed Walt to test the waters outside California, to see how Disney fare played away from home.

As international as Mickey Mouse, the It's a Small World attraction can be found within all Disney properties, except Shanghai.

Walt Disney got birds to sing—on cue—when WED Imagineering perfected Audio-Animatronics, introduced in Disneyland's Enchanted Tiki Room, in 1963.

To scoot riders through the Ford exhibit, a continuously moving conveyor-belt-like system called the Omnimover was developed by WED mechanical engineers Roger E. Broggie and Bert Brundage. It would later be used on several Disney attractions, including the Haunted Mansion's "doom buggies," Epcot's Spaceship Earth, and the Little Mermaid attractions at Disney California Adventure and at Walt Disney World's Magic Kingdom.

With water an element, Arrow sailed its canal boats for Small World with a propulsion and guidance system of its own design. The technique would eventually factor into Pirates of the Caribbean's graduating beyond its original walk-through wax museum concept, into a full-fledged adventure voyage.

What Mr. Lincoln, UNICEF's children of the world, the cast of Carousel of Progress, and Magic Skyway's sauropods, triceratops, stegosaurus, and two-story Tyrannosaurus Rex all had in common was that they were WED-patented Audio-Animatronics—moving, talking, facial-expressing robots that, among other feats, allowed Honest Abe's Duraflex face to contort fifteen different ways.

"It's just animation with sound," said Walt. The valves and controls were the products of rocket science. "This way we can get extremely subtle motions."

Audio-Animatronics were first used in a mechanical menagerie that started warbling inside Walt Disney's Enchanted Tiki Room in 1963. The seventeen-minute show, which required extra admission beyond an A to E ticket, took place inside a special thatched pavilion with its own courtyard, on prime real estate at the entrance to Adventureland.

The finely tuned Tiki Room birds inside made the animals in the Jungle Cruise look primitive, even if occasionally over the chirping, audience members could detect the sound of electronic gears shifting.

The world's fair showed that the Disney theme park brand could travel. Not only was Disneyland a money machine, but 1964 also brought Walt's critical, commercial, and Oscar-laden movie hit *Mary Poppins*. To flex his now-considerable financial and artistic muscle, he stepped up an already years-old search for a site on which to build another Disney park.

Walt's ambition for extensive new ground to conquer grew out of desire to control his surroundings, given that immediately after Disneyland opened, rampant commercial blight soiled its periphery: fast-food joints, gas stations, and motels rife with prostitution. (Contrary to suburban legend, the Orange County sheriff and Anaheim police have never had cause to deal with cases of child abduction in Disneyland.

Of all people, it was semiretired Hollywood star Joan Crawford—despite her legendary reputation for mistreating her own kids—who pushed to have Walt Disney honor the world's children.

As the widow of Pepsi-Cola's CEO Alfred Steele, the Manhattan-based former MGM and Warner Bros. star (1905–1977) sat on the Pepsi board. Crawford also knew Walt personally, said her longtime publicist, John Springer, and she was always looking for a way to maintain a link to Hollywood.

When the soft-drink company balked at the expense of hiring Disney for its fair pavilion, Crawford put down her formidable foot. Pepsi sponsored It's a Small World.

"Disney's realistic robots," said *Time* magazine, "stalk the fair. [Small World] has about 350 of them, doll-size, flanking a boat ride that children seem to like more than anything else. Scottish dolls climb steep plaid mountains, Iranian dolls fly on Persian carpets, and French dolls cancan."

During peak periods, Small World—during its harried eleven-month development, it was called Children of the World—drew up to forty thousand fairgoers a day, at ninety cents per adult (about $6.75 today), and sixty-five cents for children.

By the end of its two-year New York run, ten million people had seen it.

Like the other fair attractions by Disney, it was moved to Disneyland.

Walt may be holding the Oscar, but it was brother Roy who held the purse strings.

Security is tighter than Scrooge McDuck. However, hookers shaking down kids' fathers outside the park is another story. The 2017 movie *The Florida Project*, with Willem Dafoe, dramatized such a scenario played out at Disney World.)

One week after the New York World's Fair closed, on October 23, 1965, before an especially large gathering of press in Orlando, Florida, the state's governor, W. Haydon Burns, introduced Walt and Roy Disney. Their mission was to announce what Walt called "the biggest thing we've ever tackled."

Lincoln replaced the *Babes in Toyland* movie sets inside the Main Street Opera House; the dinos reemerged as an addendum to the Disneyland Railroad's Grand Canyon diorama; and the Carousel of Progress helped round out a new Tomorrowland until 1973, when it was transferred to Walt Disney World's Tomorrowland, in Florida. The attraction has long been acknowledged as Walt's personal favorite.

When Small World moved west, it landed directly north of the Matterhorn, expanding the outer boundary of Fantasyland, where the boat ride opened under a sparkly new edifice on May 28, 1966.

In 1971, Walt Disney World, near Orlando, Florida, debuted its own near replica, without the splashy edifice but with the same love-it-or-hate-it theme song (in nine languages) by Richard and Robert Sherman; same art direction by Walt's favorite illustrator, Mary Blair; same authentic, if Disney-fied, costumes by Alice and Marc Davis.

The children also raised their voices in subsequent Disney parks: Tokyo, in 1983; Paris, in 1992; and, once its omission triggered a barrage of criticism, Hong Kong, in 2008, bringing with it brighter lighting effects, improved sound, and an expanded display of dolls from Cambodia, the Philippines, Hong Kong, and greater China.

Good thing, too, because to date, Shanghai Disneyland, which opened in June 2016, has no It's a Small World.

The company, after a lengthy and covert exploration that conscientiously concealed the Disney identity for fear it would inflate real estate prices, had purchased forty-three thousand square acres south of Orlando. The site, strategically located near to where Interstate Highway 4 crossed with the Sunshine State Parkway, would be called Lake Buena Vista, for the Disney Studios' street in Burbank. But the day of the lively press conference, those nearly thirty thousand acres were still swampland.

From Walt's lack of prepared remarks at the gathering, it seemed like ideas were still being juggled in his head. "We have many things in mind that could make this unique and different than Disneyland," he said, off the cuff.

"Will it be a Disneyland?" the governor asked.

Walt chuckled. "Well, I've always said, there will never be another Disneyland, Governor, and I think it's going to work out that way. But it will be the equivalent of Disneyland."

He was right. And he was wrong.

Lew Wasserman admired Walt Disney. He also took a shine to corporate diversity. Given both, said Connie Bruck, a Wasserman biographer, he "started to follow Disney's amusement park lead."

Wasserman (1913–2002) was chairman and chief executive of the Music Corporation of America (MCA), and, as the *New York Times* said, "was arguably the most powerful and influential Hollywood titan in the four decades after World War II." MCA owned Universal Studios, whose backlot, soundstages, and offices sat on more than four hundred acres in North Hollywood. Though Universal, unlike Wasserman, was not the most powerful and influential Hollywood studio when it came to movies, it *was* powerful and influential when it came to television.

In 1959, MCA bought Universal, a studio that German émigré and nickelodeon distributor Carl Laemmle had started in 1909 as IMP (Independent Motion Picture Company) before renaming it Universal in 1912. In 1913, the studio ranch became known as Universal City, and tours by bus from Los Angeles were offered. In 1915, Laemmle began letting the public tour his new studio for twenty-five cents, boxed chicken lunch included. The tours would continue until 1930, when the incessant clatter of sightseers was picked up by microphones, which were now required because the talkies had arrived.

Laemmle lost the studio in 1936 during an economic downturn. For the following few decades, except for rare, quality films like the adaptations of novelist Erich Maria Remarque's *All Quiet on the Western Front* and the Jerome Kern–Oscar Hammerstein II musical *Showboat*, Universal was best known for its Dracula, Frankenstein, and Wolf Man movies, Deanna Durbin musicals, and comedies featuring Abbott and Costello and Ma and Pa Kettle. By the late 1950s, the studio's box office was kept breathing by producer Ross Hunter's vehicles for Doris Day, as she shielded her virtue from the advances of Rock Hudson.

In 1961, studio president Albert Dorskind reactivated the tours to boost the bottom line of the studio commissary. Gray Line Tours handled the logistics, until

Universal City, on opening day, March 15, 1915: Founder Carl Laemmle charged a quarter for visitors to tour his studio, boxed chicken lunch included.

Dorskind realized that handling the tours themselves could make more money. Dorskind took his idea to Wasserman, suggesting, as an added inducement, "If they come to see our studio, they're more likely to watch the shows we produce here."

According to Universal and Disney historian Sam Gennawey, Harrison "Buzz" Price, who had worked on the feasibility study for Disneyland, was called in. Recognizing the public's innate fascination with the movies, and its desire to go behind the scenes, Price assessed Universal's prime location, ample parking space, and the fact no other Hollywood studio was offering tours.

Projecting a first-year attendance of eight hundred thousand (it actually turned out to be 428,000, although numbers improved steadily from the start), Price recommended a $3 million investment, which included a $2 million visitors' center to sell souvenirs and snacks, and to serve as the depot for tour vehicles. For transport, Price examined conventional buses and a semitractor, both of which obstructed views, as well as electrical and diesel-powered trams, ultimately deciding upon the latter because of the backlot's steep, hilly terrain. To design them, Universal hired Harper Goff.

The tours began July 15, 1964. For $2.50 ($20 today), customers got a ninety-minute taste of Hollywood. Surprising to behold—while in good condition, they were so old—were the standing sets used as the Parisian façades for Lon Chaney's 1923 *The Hunchback of Notre Dame* and 1925 *The Phantom of the Opera*; the ersatz Bavarian village where Boris Karloff's Frankenstein monster did his boot-stomping in the 1930s; and, from the studio's prolonged, but at least more recent, low-budget phase, oversized props from 1957's *The Incredible Shrinking Man* and a scaly pond for *The Creature from the Black Lagoon*.

A chipper tour guide narrated a canned spiel throughout, pointing out the Bates house from *Psycho*; a display of costumes by multi-Oscar winner Edith Head; Doris Day's dressing room (at least that's what the sign outside said, as the tram bounced by); and, as if on cue, the supporting cast of TV's *McHale's Navy*, although not star Ernest Borgnine. Likewise, that old Coney Island stilt walker Cary Grant reportedly hid in his trailer until the trams passed from view.

The *McHale's* players, in their costumes, would stand outside their soundstage and wave to tourists. There was also a Keystone Kop greeter, and foam-rubber boulders that weighed nothing but looked to weigh a ton—and were available for tossing.

To youngsters and out-of-towners, this was heady stuff.

The *Psycho* house was ready for its close-up once Universal reinstated its 1915–1930 studio tours in 1964, this time aboard GlamorTrams.

ONE VISITOR TO THE Universal lot was the teenaged Steven Spielberg (born 1946), who, as he likes to tell, came into contact with the studio librarian in 1963, and then began to ingratiate himself among studio personnel.

In the next decade he would go on to direct what was up to that time the biggest hit in Universal's history, *Jaws*. The following year, 1976, an addition was made to the studio tour: a great big mechanical shark would attack a tram, during what was called the Jaws Experience.

The Spielberg-Universal relationship developed, both in terms of his making movies for the studio and having his work adapted into backlot attractions. As a result, the once-desultory studio tour, no longer a company afterthought, began to evolve into a well-planned theme park, given the restrictions imposed by the hilly terrain and the requisites of what still was a working production studio.

As the *Jurassic Park* movie franchise transitioned into *Jurassic World*, so did Universal attractions take brontosaurus-sized leaps. Among them: a Pteranodon taking flight at Universal Japan, while this Velociraptor is hungering for riders at the Universal Orlando Resort.

Years before Spielberg's involvement, the tour took a measured step in that direction. In 1967, a Western stunt show was added, and after that came a small stream of other motivators to keep people on the Universal property—and away from Disneyland and Knott's Berry Farm. Universal's offerings may not have been as slick as Disney's, but they satisfied crowds in ever-growing numbers.

At Universal Studios Hollywood, the Spielbergian attractions included, in 1990, an E.T. Adventure that put riders on simulated flying bicycles before a movie screen (it would be replaced, in 2003, by the indoor coaster Revenge of the Mummy: The Ride), and the 1996 Jurassic Park: The Ride, a river-rapids Shoot the Chute with "life-sized" dinosaurs bellowing at the boat. (The experience was completely reconceived, skull to caudal, for 2019.)

While the trams eventually discarded their pink-and-white canopies for something streamlined, they would still traverse a mechanized world of movie make-believe: the town square used for Spielberg's 1980s *Back to the Future* movies, and the crash-landed Boeing 747 prop from his 2005 *War of the Worlds*. The jumbo jet's final resting place was but one photo op on the tour, which now included 3D cinematic-effects encounters with King Kong and the main characters from the *Fast and the Furious* movies, although those had no association with Spielberg. Not that they needed to; according to one calculation, his creative consultation and licensing income from Universal between 2009 and 2017 alone was $1 billion.

The monetary figure took into account not only his attractions at Universal Studios Hollywood but at every Universal park launched since Lew Wasserman first approved the tour in 1964: Universal Studios Orlando (1990), Universal Studios Japan (2001), and Universal Studios Singapore (2011). A Beijing property is expected to open in 2020, and an indoor Universal facility is scheduled for Moscow in 2022, although that one likely depends not only upon the volatile Russian seasonal climate but also the political one.

Eighty-three hundred miles from Universal Studios, but just as Instagram-able, is Bollywood Parks Dubai, a 2017 addition to the Emirates that tips its turban to the exaggerated escapist fare of the Mumbai film industry—the only park in the world to do so.

Charming among the sixteen exotic attractions is the Lagaan: The Thrill of Victory, a vigorous motion-simulator adventure based on a 2001 Hindi sports drama. (All ride narratives are in English, though safety instructions are also delivered in Arabic.)

Lagaan can be found in the rural-village-themed Rustic Ravine, one of five zones in the not-quite-forty-acre park. Other zones are Bollywood Boulevard, Bollywood Film Studios, Royal Plaza, and Mumbai Chowk (*chowk* is Hindi for "courtyard" or, in this case, "food court and market").

"Bollywood is a lot about shows, and India is a lot about food," said park general manager Thomas Jellum, underscoring that within his gates, human experience is placed above mechanical rides.

Among these experiences is having costumed singers and dancers seemingly appear out of nowhere and break into a musical number.

For those who prefer their show-stoppers from a distance, Bollywood has the 850-seat Rajmahal Theatre, home to the elaborate stage extravaganza *Jaan-e-Jigar*, a musical melodrama about twin brothers.

"Disney has its castle, and we have the Rajmahal," Jellum said of the Taj Mahal–looking venue. "Inside is a full Broadway musical, with a cast of seventy."

That's actually about three times the size of a typical Broadway cast, but what would Bollywood be if not for its overstatement?

Hollywood on the Gulf: Bollywood Parks Dubai opened in 2017, adjacent to the larger Motiongate. Both bring a movie-theme-park experience to the Emirates.

V.

Disneyland was in full construction mode in 1965, with extensive revisions totaling $20 million. A new Tomorrowland would open in 1967, finally fulfilling its long-held goal of previewing a semirealistic future and providing it with a wow factor. In anticipation of Disneyland's original opening day, with money scarce, the initial objectives for the land were curtailed and hastily replaced with a smattering of corporate displays and unintentionally airy pavilions, one whose sales bins were stuffed with Disney merchandise—including old animation cels that sold for as little as thirty-five cents each. (Today, they fetch five and six figures.)

During the new Tomorrowland's preparatory stage, in 1965, science-fiction author Ray Bradbury, himself a boyish bundle of enthusiasm and an unabashed Disneyland fan, was having one of his semiregular studio lunches with Walt. Bradbury proposed that Walt hire him to help redo the land.

"It's no use," Walt told him. "You're a genius and I'm a genius. After two weeks, we'd kill each other."

The architecturally cohesive new Tomorrowland, with fresh attractions and an updated Skyway whose gondolas mirrored the cars on the brand-new PeopleMover, opened July 2, 1967.

(A 1998 makeover made hash of the '67 Tomorrowland, to no one's pleasure. The financial drain of the underperforming Euro Disney, later called Disneyland Paris, forced Imagineers to jettison plans for a radical redo of the entire area in favor of a cosmetic make-do. The gleaming white pavilions, including the 1977 Space Mountain roller coaster, were stained a dreadful gold and black, and the People-Mover disastrously converted into high-speed Rocket Rods that couldn't speed at all. The short-lived ride's abandoned tracks still sit, derelict, throughout Disneyland's Tomorrowland two decades later, a scar on the landscape Walt Disney never would have tolerated.)

Four months before new Tomorrowland's summer 1967 debut, on March 18, Pirates of the Caribbean opened. With 120 Audio-Animatronic pirates, two Shoot the Chute effects that sent passenger boats down waterfalls, and mysterious, dark caverns leading to a confrontation with the bandits of the seas—not to mention, a catchy "Yo Ho (A Pirate's Life for Me)" song by *Pinocchio* and *Fantasia* artist and WED Imagineer Xavier "X" Atencio—it was the most costly and ambitious attraction in amusement park history. Estimated price: $8 million, or $60 million today.

Disneyland was only twelve years old when it raised the curtain on its game-changer, Pirates of the Caribbean.

In contrast, in 2006, when Disney launched the Expedition Everest coaster in its Florida Animal Kingdom, the estimated cost was $100 million, reportedly the most expensive attraction ever. That, however, was likely surpassed by 2017's Flight of Passage in the same park, although the record breaker could well be Shanghai Disneyland's 2016 Pirates of the Caribbean: Battle for the Sunken Treasure, a remarkable advancement on the original Pirates—or any ride anywhere.

Another contender is the 2019 Millennium Falcon attraction in the Star Wars: Galaxy's Edge sections of California's Disneyland Park and Florida's Disney's Hollywood Studios.

Disney does not disclose costs.

Once a year, Disneyland's Haunted Mansion sheds its skin and assumes an autumnal overlay with characters and situations from the 1993 Tim Burton movie *The Nightmare Before Christmas.*

⚍

THE KEY TO DISNEYLAND was Walt Disney. The TV program might have worked as a multi-million-dollar promotional tool for the park, but as a warm, avuncular presence and household name, he was the best advertisement. The show wasn't even called *Disneyland* anymore; in 1961, with the debt to ABC paid off, NBC wooed Walt to its side of the fence, and, heralding itself as the first all-color network, kicked off its primetime schedule every Sunday at seven thirty with *Walt Disney's Wonderful World of Color.*

Walt Disney and Disneyland were, by then, a perdurable part of the American fabric. Whenever people suggested he run for office—the joke had already worn thin—his knee-jerk reply was "Why would I want to be president of the United States when I'm already king of Disneyland?"

Why, indeed.

As he was preparing his world's fair attractions, installing the Tiki Room, and laying the groundwork for Pirates, in 1963, a writer for *National Geographic* asked him bluntly, "What happens when there is no more Walt Disney?"

"I think about that," Walt replied, offering that he was trying to start relegating responsibilities to others.

"But I'll probably outlive them all," he added, grinning. "I plan to be around for a while."

He was given a medical prognosis in November 1966 that the malignant tumor in his lungs would probably claim him in two years. Walt Disney died the following month.

One of his final gestures was signing off on the sets and character designs for Pirates of the Caribbean.

The attraction would open three months later.

Since its 1969 debut at Disneyland, and in its subsequent versions elsewhere, the Haunted Mansion's centerpiece, the Grand Hall banquet scene, has been its major asset.

Set between the séance conducted by the tarot reader Madame Leota (whose visage appears in a crystal ball as she conjures spirits) and the musty attic (with its pop-up scary faces reminiscent of the '50s dark rides designed by cult favorite Bill Tracy), the scene contains protoplasmic dancing ghosts, dinner guests, an organist with skulls rising out of his instrument's pipes, and dueling dandies stepping out of their portraits.

To present this cast-of-tens tableau, Imagineers leaned on an 1862 stage trick, created for an adaptation of the Dickens novella *The Haunted Man and the Ghost's Bargain*. The spectral vision was known as Pepper's Ghost, an optical illusion from British scientist John Henry Pepper. According to a 1906 exposé, "A living man was seen on the stage which was otherwise empty, and presently by his side would appear, out of space, so it seemed, a shadowy figure, which moved about and spoke."

The ghost "was, in fact, a reflection transferred to a stage, with means provided for brilliantly illuminating the object to be reflected."

In the Haunted Mansion, the reflections are those of illuminated Audio-Animatronic figures.

The role that art and design play in Pepper's Ghost has to do with the stage space.

As revealed: "It is a peculiarity of images reflected from plain glass or from mirrors that they appear to be as far behind the glass as the real object in front of it."

Spoiler alert: The Haunted Mansion's protoplasmic Grand Hall banquet tableau relies on an 1860s stage trick from England.

FINISHING TOUCHES

I.

Lacking the spark of energy that characterized the company throughout the 1960s, and after the launch of the Florida project at the top of the '70s, the decade found a creative malaise settling in at Disney, fostered by an executive guessing game of what Walt might have done. Elsewhere in the amusement industry, the old trolley parks and seaside piers had either already closed down, often due to what were diplomatically referred to as neighborhood problems, or gone corporate, a trend often met with mixed results.

Despite the odds, promoters and investors still went looking for the next Disneyland. A similar ripple effect took hold in Hollywood, where the runaway success of *The Sound of Music* had sent all the studios tripping over one another for the next great big, expensive musical. The finished products sank the movie companies under the weight of their inferior—and unprofitable—imitations. Old studio regimes got the old heave-ho, and into positions of power marched corporate-minded agents and accountants referred to as "bean counters."

The Yum Yum Café at New Jersey's Great Adventure, now Six Flags Great Adventure, was a mélange of many tastes, particularly those of the park's creator, New York restaurateur Warner LeRoy.

Except for counting some boysenberries, perhaps, the groundbreakers in the amusement field—Carstensen, Barnum, Tilyou, Disney, Dudley Humphrey, Mary Elitch, George Whitney, Walter Knott, Riverview's Schmidts—were never interested in beans.

They rolled the dice on creating something different.

Warner LeRoy (1935–2001) was cut from the same cloth, with some Billy Niblo stitched in, too—had Niblo been flamboyant. An exuberant Manhattan restaurateur, LeRoy built kitschy, rococo destination-location food palaces—Maxwell's Plum, Tavern on the Green, and, later, a Russian Tea Room redone with his usual lack of restraint (a glass bear statue masquerading as a goldfish aquarium)—that were amusement parks unto themselves, as were their dishes, which included what he claimed was the world's largest ice-cream sundae. His menu, mediocre at best, always played second fiddle to the surroundings. And his taste? Warner LeRoy never met a Tiffany lamp he didn't like.

Even amidst his Wagnerian world of make-believe, Warner stood out. A large man, he was given to wearing bespoke floral-print suits. He came to his Oz-like attitude genetically; his father was the Hollywood Golden Age figure Mervyn LeRoy, who produced *The Wizard of Oz* and directed several important message films for Warner Bros. (*I Am a Fugitive from a Chain Gang*). Warner's mother was the former Doris Warner, whose father, Harry Warner, was one of the Brothers. As the son of the producer, when *Oz* finished filming, Warner got to keep Toto.

In 1974, when New York City was teetering on bankruptcy but his eight-year-old Maxwell's Plum—no, no one knew what the name meant—was raking in $5 million a year ($25 million today), LeRoy went to New Jersey. That July 1, in the Pine Barrens of rural Jackson Township, about midway between New York and Philadelphia, he opened what in its conceptual stage was called the Enchanted Forest and Safari Park. Artist renderings included a Transylvanian Banquet Hall, an Over the Rainbow land with Oz-themed dark rides, a Neptune's Kingdom, and, for shopping and eating, a Dream Street, populated, like Bakken's early days, with craftspeople and jugglers. The safari section was to be the largest drive-through animal sanctuary outside of Africa, with twelve separate themed sectors.

By the time plans were scaled down to a practical level, the entrance sign at the parking tollbooths read Great Adventure.

LeRoy thought his fifteen hundred acres would become the next Walt Disney World, with hotels, resort facilities, and campgrounds. "Projected costs quickly escalated and the plans were dramatically scaled back," said the park's unofficial historian, Harry Applegate. "Some of the oversized and over-the-top designs which he envisioned for the entire property did make their way into the park." After the first season, LeRoy dramatically scaled back his own involvement, selling off the last of his financial interest in 1993. Since 1978, the entrance sign has read Six Flags Great Adventure.

A few of its founder's touches remain to this day—one is unmistakably Warner LeRoy, the Yum Yum Café in the Fantasy Forest, housed in what looks like a giant ice-cream cake. But the real reason people go to Six Flags Great Adventure is its impressive spate of coasters. These include El Toro, one of the world's fastest woodies; Kingda Ka, the world's tallest coaster; and a rugged, ragged landscape of modern Russian Mountains themed to DC Comics heroes Batman (inverted), Superman (flying), and Green Lantern (standing).

In another bow to modern times, Yum Yum offers fare that is gluten free.

Warner LeRoy may have had a blood connection to *The Wizard of Oz*, but the eighteen-acre Land of Oz theme park, adjacent to the ski lift atop Beech Mountain in North Carolina, had a genuine Yellow Brick Road, Dorothy's farmhouse—before and after the twister—and a hot-air balloon ride.

It also had its old Hollywood studio's biggest booster, MGM star Debbie Reynolds, and her daughter, Carrie Fisher, in her pre–Princess Leia days, at the grand opening, in 1970.

Ideated by North Carolina resort developer Grover Cleveland Robbins, backed by his real estate concern, the Carolina Caribbean Corporation, and designed by Charlotte artist Jack Pentes (who also appeared on local TV as Bobo the Clown, a character he had developed as a soldier in the Korean War), Oz appeared blessed by Glinda, the Good Witch, for its few seasons, until a triple blow: the national gasoline shortage, CCC's collapse after a bad deal in St. Croix, and a deliberate post-Christmas 1975 fire.

A new owner attempted to set things right, but Oz closed for good in 1980.

Since then, its iconic remnants have remained off-limits, except, occasionally, for fan clubs and organized tours.

If only the Wicked Witch could keep away vandals.

Four hundred thousand people followed the Yellow Brick Road in the first year of North Carolina's Land of Oz theme park, but the momentum could not be sustained.

II.

Angus Gilchrist Wynne Jr. (1914–1979) was of a new breed, although, like Warner LeRoy, he was born to privilege and larger than life—in Wynne's case, like the state he hailed from. His father, Angus Sr., was a Texas land developer and president of the State Bar, which he had founded. Like his father, Angus Jr. developed property. His company, American Home Realty, was responsible for the fifty-three-acre Wynnewood Village in the Oak Cliff section of Dallas, the country's largest retail complex of its kind at the time. Having been to Disneyland with his family, and liking what he saw, Wynne approached Disney with a proposal to build an entire entertainment complex somewhere between Fort Worth and Dallas. Only by then, Walt was being courted by several others, all of whose offers he declined.

Not one to take no for an answer, Wynne set about building his own $10 million amusement kingdom in Arlington, exactly midway between the forty miles separating Fort Worth and Dallas. According to local lore, he planned to call the 150 acres Six Flags Under Texas, for the six sovereigns that ruled the land beginning in 1519—Spain, France, Mexico, the Republic of Texas, the Confederacy, and the United States—that is, until Wynne's wife, Joann, snapped, "Texas isn't under anything. "It would be called Six Flags over Texas. (In 2017, because of connotations associated with the Confederate flag, the logo's six separate banners were replaced with six Stars and Stripes, in order, said a company rep, "to focus on celebrating the things that unite us versus those that divide us.")

Randall Duell, an MGM art director and set designer, was hired to design the project, just as he later would the 1964 visitors' center at Universal Studios, Nashville's Opryland USA (1972–1997), and the thirty-three-acre MGM Grand Adventure (1993–2002) in Las Vegas. Six Flags was the first project under the banner of his own architecture firm.

For Six Flags, Duell aimed for Hollywood realism—such as making a souvenir shop look like an old hacienda by masking it with window shapes and props. One backlot technique he adapted was to use pathway curves and hills to keep distant views from spoiling the atmospheric effect of an immediate location, so that, for example, the Six Flags Missile Chaser scrambler ride could not be seen from the Indian Village. It was actually a technique H. C. Stilling had employed at Tivoli.

Laid out in similar fashion as Disneyland's hub system, with its series of spoke-like walkways and a narrow-gauge railroad around them,

In the Texas Pavilion of the 1964 New York World's Fair, Angus Wynne Jr. (right) is crowned with a ceremonial sombrero.

Duell's Six Flags edifices were built to small scale (especially second stories), with the six different themed areas each defined by its own color palette.

In all, after a year of formal planning, and another ten months for construction, by opening day, August 5, 1961, there were fourteen rides. The USA section was called Modern, and had miniature automobiles and a petting zoo, as well as the AstroLift skyway. This led to the Texas cowboy town, with its saloon, jail, and goat ride. Elsewhere, the Confederacy section had a plantation and a mule-powered Little Dixie Carousel; Mexico, an Allan Herschell La Cucaracha Wild Mouse; France, a LaSalle's River Adventure; and Spain, Los Conquistadores Mule Pack Ride. The Skull Rock skulking over its tree slide—and accessible by a Tom Sawyer–like river raft—looks remarkably like Disneyland's.

MGM art director Randall Duell designed Six Flags Over Texas. He later tackled Universal Studios' visitors center, Nashville's Opryland, and Las Vegas's MGM Grand Adventure.

Working closely with Wynne to bring Six Flags to fruition was the consulting company Marco Engineering, whose president had gone to great lengths to build a name for himself in the amusement industry: C. V. Wood.

One of his earliest contributions to Six Flags over Texas was to purchase rides from the already defunct Magic Mountain in Colorado and move them to Texas.

Otherwise, he divided his time between Arlington and the Bronx, for Freedomland.

With four hundred thousand customers required to break even its first season, attendance at Six Flags exceeded expectations: 8,374 people showed up on opening day, and 550,000 over the entire first season. Rather than rest on his laurels, Wynne accepted the offer personally extended by Vice President (and proud Texan) Lyndon B. Johnson, and state governor John Connally to head the Texas State Pavilion at the 1964–1965 New York World's Fair. After accepting, Wynne then extended the invitation to Randall Duell to design it.

Both ended up stepping into a cow pie.

In Wynne's estimation, one pavilion alone could not contain all that Texas had to offer, so seven buildings, themed very much like the six lands at Six Flags, were prepared for the three-acre site. The seventh housed a twenty-four-hundred-seat music hall, for a very unTexan *To Broadway, with Love* extravaganza, described as "an anthology packed with the moods and music of the American theater from *The Black Crook* of 1864 to recent hits."

No expense was spared, and no concept too outlandish, which explained why "an enormous Brahman bull was kept corralled inside an elegant French bedroom, as being

Now back on track, Kentucky Kingdom and Hurricane Bay, in Louisville, had an unfortunate encounter with Six Flags.

symbolic of the pampered lives that modern livestock supposedly live," said one recollection of the ill-fated Texas Pavilion. Wynne personally financed the venture and was forced into bankruptcy. Originally budgeted to cost $5 million, the project lost $100,000 a week and left Wynne with debts of $7 million, according to court filings.

The fault lay in several directions: disappointing fair attendance, which flew in the face of Robert Moses's overly optimistic projections when he was steamrolling the fair into existence; the exhausting distance from the fair entrance to the Texas compound in the Flushing Meadows hinterlands; and a widely held bias against Texas in the aftermath of President Kennedy's murder in Dallas on November 22, 1963, only five months before the fair opened.

The country was still in mourning, and in shock.

By the late 1960s, dizzying ownership and management changes left Six Flags bouncing around like one of William F. Mangels's old Ticklers—with just as jarring a descent. In 1969, Wynne sold his stake to a limited partnership called Six Flags over Texas Ltd.

In 1971, the Penn Central Railroad took over management, a tenure in which Six Flags Corp. acquired AstroWorld in Houston (1975), Warner LeRoy's Great Adventure in New Jersey (1978), and Magic Mountain in Valencia, California (1979, and no relation to C. V. Wood's Magic Mountain in Colorado). The acquisitions continued unabated; in 1984, with Marriott's Great Adventure, in Gurnee, Illinois, which the hotel chain had inaugurated, along with another Great America in Santa Clara, California, as theme park fever was spreading throughout the hospitality world. (Cedar Fair now owns California's Great America.)

Bally, which sprang to life as a pinball machine business in 1932, also chose to expand in the 1970s, getting into the casino and leisure business, and producing PacMan and other video games. In the 1980s, Bally added health clubs and Six Flags to its portfolio, though the latter only briefly, because Time Warner was looming. By 1993, the conglomerate gained control, bringing Bugs Bunny, Daffy Duck, and the other Warner Bros. Looney Tunes cartoon characters into a stable now called Six Flags Theme Parks.

The Oklahoma-based Premier Parks bought out Time Warner in 1998 for an estimated $1.86 billion ($2.86 billion today), igniting an expansion spree that splashed the Six Flags name on Premier's existing properties, which included Elitch Gardens, Lake Compounce, and, infamously, Geauga Lake, near Cleveland, a much-beloved 1887 former trolley park that Premier had bought in 1995, packed with powerhouse rides, and in 2001 merged with nearby Sea World. By 2007, Geauga Lake had been expanded out of existence.

By then, the company had Six Flags parks in Holland, Belgium, and Mexico, only to sell them in order to alleviate rising debt. Another victim was Six Flags Kentucky Kingdom, in Louisville, which Premier bought in November 1997, then, after failing to invest in new rides, ended up having to close. (The park was resuscitated in 2014 by one of its early owners, Ed Hart.)

Then came a point of no return: Wall Street's 2008 crash and burn, creating a freeze in all recreational corridors, including those of the already flagging Six Flags. The company emerged from bankruptcy in 2010, the same year Mark Shapiro, its CEO and former ESPN programming chief, was succeeded by Al Weber Jr., who had been CEO of Paramount Parks from 2002 until that chain's 2006 sale to Cedar Fair.

Weber was subsequently succeeded at Six Flags by president, chairman, and CEO James W. P. Reid-Anderson, who previously had been on the board of Siemens Healthcare and in chief executive officer positions for Dade Behring Holdings, which is a blood-testing company, and Wilson Sporting Goods.

And so it goes.

As for C. V. Wood, after the Freedomland fiasco, he joined with Robert P. McCulloch, an entrepreneurial Missouri chainsaw manufacturer known for buying London Bridge and moving it from its River Thames location to Lake Havasu City, Arizona. C.V. oversaw the transfer.

Old Woody was not quite finished. Following Universal's lead, he convinced Time Warner—the parent company of Warner Bros.—to get into the studio-tour business. This finally earned him, in his seventies, his acknowledged place in amusement park history—Down Under.

The 415-acre Warner Bros. Movie World, on Australia's Gold Coast in Queensland, opened June 3, 1991, with Clint Eastwood, Goldie Hawn, Kurt Russell, Mel Gibson, and C. V. Wood present for the ribbon cutting. Initially, the park, whose entry

Warner Bros. Movie World, on Australia's Gold Coast, was C. V. Wood's last hurrah. The Wild West Fall Adventure Ride has a ghost town inside its mountain.

area is called Main Street, was about going behind the scenes of making movies, but, over the years, movie-themed coasters and immersion rides were added to the mix.

By the time they were, C. V. Wood was gone. He died in 1992, a year after Movie World opened.

"For Woody, the lesson of Disneyland was simple: he believed that Americans were drawn to spectacle, that they wanted to live in an environment that felt as large as a Hollywood movie," said his scrupulous biographer, Todd James Pierce.

"But the work of C. V. Wood is mostly forgotten. Runners-up are rarely extolled for their vision and greatness."

III.

The choice to continue in any direction after Walt's death was left to Roy, who spoke softly but carried a big financial ledger. "Roy was never one to present himself before the public," said Michael Thomas, a partner at Lehman Brothers, the financial services firm that was vital to the capitalization of the Florida Project. "The ones responsible for pushing Florida"—which would be called Disney World until, speaking softly, Roy insisted it be Walt Disney World, in tribute to his brother—"were Donn Tatum and Card Walker."

The two sharp-minded executives helped fill the business gap at the top of Walt Disney Productions after the founder's death. Tatum held degrees from Stanford and Oxford, while Walker was a World War II Navy veteran of eight major battles in the Pacific. Their plans for Walt Disney World were slightly more ambitious than the original plans for Disneyland the decade before, but far less ambitious than Walt's plans right up until his death. He saw Central Florida as a blank canvas to build his utopia, far beyond what Milton Hershey had accomplished in his quaint rural hamlet.

Walt's vision, as he presented it to his television viewers, called for a corporate-sponsored residential, recreational, and commercial Experimental Prototype Community of Tomorrow that "can influence the future of city living for generations to come."

The theme park and resort facilities alone would be five times the size of Anaheim's Disneyland, and the overall property twice the size of Manhattan.

Air View of Orlando, Florida, "The City Beautiful"

Orlando, Florida, was taken by surprise when Walt Disney announced he was coming to town.

ON THE HORIZON

October 1, 1971, brought the successful launch of Florida's $400 million ($2.5 billion today) Walt Disney World, despite offering only a fraction of what Walt had previewed on television. The main attraction, the Magic Kingdom theme park, was California's Disneyland redone, albeit on a magnified scale—especially where the expanded Jungle Cruise, Tomorrowland Speedway, Haunted Mansion, and Mr. Lincoln were concerned (Florida's Hall of Presidents starred not one, but every chief executive). But overall, except for the placid setting, it appeared no better, no worse, no different from Anaheim.

Some attractions, if they weren't absent altogether, actually turned out to be smaller: Exhibit A being It's a Small World, couched inside Disney World's Cinderella Castle battlements, like a Disneyland dark ride. When added to Adventureland in 1973, Florida's Pirates of the Caribbean also wound up shorter than the California

At Walt Disney World, magic is not meant to happen only at the bewitching hour.

Once averse to coasters, Disney added to its collection with another mountain, Big Thunder Railroad.

original. Insofar as overnight accommodations, the Tomorrowland-themed Contemporary Resort had the wow factor of a monorail running through it; the Adventureland-themed Polynesian Resort, a lobby lava-rock waterfall; and the Frontierland-themed Fort Wilderness Resort & Campground, its own iron horse.

"May Walt Disney World bring joy and inspiration and new knowledge to all who come to this happy place," Roy Disney, age seventy-eight, said at the dedication in the Main Street Town Square, "a Magic Kingdom where the young at heart of all ages can laugh and play and learn together."

Two and a half months afterward, he was dead from a cerebral hemorrhage.

"He's my big brother," Walt said about Roy at that 1965 Florida press conference to introduce himself, Roy, and Disney World, "and he's the one, when I was a little fella, I used to go to with some of my wild ideas."

Although Roy's official title had been chairman of the Disney board and chief executive officer, his unofficial title carried greater weight: keeper of the spirit that his brother created "and that permeated their cartoons, movies, television programs, amusement parks and other enterprises," United Press International said in its obituary, which credited Roy's acumen for parlaying an original outlay of $790 in his kid brother's mouse into an empire worth several hundred millions.

The creative malaise that beset Disney in the 1970s committed the unpardonable sin of becoming a financial malaise in the 1980s. With the company ripe for hostile takeover, Roy's son, Roy E. Disney, staged a palace coup that ousted Walt's son-in-law—Diane Disney's husband, Ron Miller—and installed the triumvirate of Hollywood power players Michael Eisner, Jeffrey Katzenberg, and Frank Wells in the Disney throne room. This resulted in a controversial yet productive period for the company's movie studio and theme parks.

In their respective roles as CEO and chairman of the board of the Walt Disney Company, chairman of Walt Disney Studios, and president of the Walt Disney Company, Eisner, Katzenberg, and Wells were charged with moving that empire forward. That they did, even when Wall Street, long-term staff, and public opinion criticized their direction.

Prior to the new executives' arrival—Eisner and Katzenberg from Paramount, Wells from Warners—the Disney parks at last got their roller coasters. The Matterhorn would remain unique to Disneyland, but the concept, reimagined in space, was something Walt had kicked around with Imagineer John Hench during the 1967 Tomorrowland buildup. The catch, according to Disney histories (entire books have been devoted to nearly every E-ticket attraction), was that the technology was not yet available, at least not as Walt envisioned the finished product. A decade later, in 1975, Florida got its Space Mountain. A smaller version came to the smaller California park two years later.

By then, Imagineer Tony Baxter and ride engineer Bill Watkins, borrowing a component from Imagineer Marc Davis's idea for an unrealized Pirates of the Caribbean–like pavilion-enclosed Western Expedition, had devised a runaway train attraction. Because Disneyland space is limited, it ended up replacing Frontierland's Nature's Wonderland, where animatronic brown bears scratched their backs on trees and geysers threatened a pokey mine train through a Disney forest and painted desert.

Repurposed into Big Thunder Mountain Railroad, the steel-track coaster started running away at Disneyland in 1979. Its theming was reminiscent of Bud Hurlbut's Knott's Berry Farm Calico Mine Train and Timber Mountain Log Ride (which would, in turn, inspire Disney's Splash Mountains of the late '80s and early '90s). A Disney World version followed, in 1980; Tokyo Disneyland, in 1987; and in 1992, Euro Disney / Disneyland Paris, where the impact was compounded by the ride's intensity and location—on what is typically Tom Sawyer Island.

Also predating the Eisner regime was 1983's $1.4 billion Tokyo Disneyland, actually east of Tokyo, in the city of Urayasu, in Japan's Chiba province, where the park's owner, the travel-and-leisure-focused Oriental Land Company, is based. It pays Disney a licensing and consulting fee for what was compelled to become two parks, in order to accommodate the overflow crowds.

Unique in that it is not based on any prototype, Tokyo DisneySea opened in 2001, and, among Disney devotees, is regarded highly for shrugging off nostalgia in favor of amped-up and adult attractions, though minilands devoted to the animated features *Frozen*, *Tangled*, and *Peter Pan* are taking shape for 2022.

Another holdover from before Eisner, Epcot opened in Florida on October 1, 1982. Even at $1.2 billion ($3.1 billion today), it was a pared-down version of Walt's dream community into world's fair–like theme parks, with pavilions devoted to science and industry, along with foreign nations.

During the Eisner era, there ultimately became four Disney parks in Florida. Besides the Magic Kingdom and Epcot, there were, in 1989, Disney's Hollywood Studios, ostensibly to compete with Universal's 1990 park entry into Orlando, and, in 1998, Disney's Animal Kingdom. That zoological-themed resort was, in part, meant to thwart another potential

Epcot opened in 1982; food, art, and flower festivals followed, to give the park a warming touch.

rival, Busch Gardens Tampa, which claimed its own lavish menagerie. (Still, Busch Gardens, some eighty-five miles from the Disney property, posed far less a threat than Universal, which looms only nine miles from Cinderella's castle.)

Of the Disney parks, Epcot is roundly considered the adult favorite, a status that took time to acquire. Shortly after the park opened, technical historian Elting E. Morison said one reason he even deigned to accept the assignment to examine Epcot for *American Heritage* was because Walt Disney "tended to look upon the received tradition or the authorized version of anything as suspect."

That was said in admiration. Epcot didn't get off so easily.

While saluting its cleanliness, Morison found its narratives lacked cohesion.

He titled his treatise "What Went Wrong With Disney's World's Fair."

Once aboard, Eisner opened the Disneyland door to intellectual properties outside company archives. George Lucas and Disney Imagineers devised Star Tours, a motion-simulator—some called it a motion-sickness stimulator—attraction that opened in January 1987 and took jostled riders, along with R2-D2 and C-3PO from *Star Wars*, to the forested moon of Endor. At the same time, Lucas worked with WED—now called Walt Disney Imagineering—for Disneyland's 17-minute 3D sci-fi minimusical *Captain Eo*, starring Michael Jackson (as leader of a spaceship mission) and directed by Francis Ford Coppola. Lucas returned again for the transcendent Indiana Jones Adventure, in 1995, a gargantuan 1930s-period dark ride that involved a runaway Jeep, a crushing boulder, and several snakes.

Eisner notably green-lit major foreign park expansion, but after the $4.4 billion 1992 Euro Disney, the light quickly turned yellow—and the ink, red. The setback produced a ricochet effect throughout the company, leaving a multitude of projects on hold; some were killed outright, and the long-awaited second gate (tech talk for another park) at Disneyland, Disney California Adventure, was reduced in scope and containing the unthinkable when it debuted in 2001: anemic theming and off-the-shelf rides.

Since then, major capital investments have resulted in a nearly stem-to-stern refurbishment. Twenty twelve brought a triumphant Cars Land to California Adventure, and 2018, Pixar Pier, which rethemed the original Paradise Pier, an odd and less-than-hoped-for attempt to re-create the Santa Cruz Beach Boardwalk, the Long Beach Pike, and Santa Monica's Pacific Ocean Park in landlocked Anaheim.

Eisner and Katzenberg would famously fall out in 1994, after Wells perished in a helicopter crash and Eisner rebuffed Katzenberg's desire to fill the Wells position. Katzenberg, whose division had given the company *The Little Mermaid*, *Beauty and the Beast*, *Aladdin*, and *The Lion King*, bolted the Disney kingdom and cofounded DreamWorks SKG, a sometimes-serious rival to Disney Animation, and, eventually, a supplier of popular intellectual properties—*Shrek*, *Madagascar*, *Kung Fu Panda*, *How to Train Your Dragon*, and *Trolls*—to theme parks around the world. Motiongate, a Hollywood-studios-like park in Dubai, has an entire indoor DreamWorks Animation

uestion: How many Disney fans does it take to screw in a lightbulb?

Answer: Ten. One to screw it in, and nine to complain how much better the old lightbulb was.

In the 1980s, Disneyland and Walt Disney World replaced their old flagship stores for brand-name companies like Timex, Kodak, and Swift with one Disney merchandise store after another. Selling everything from T-shirts to silver tea sets, the Main Street Penny Arcade lost its nickelodeons to shelf upon shelf of stuffed dolls, just as the old Main Street Cinema effectively became an offshoot of the Emporium.

Throughout every park, souvenir stands popped up to surround the rider at the exits of major attractions.

Another change greeted the guest at the gate.

In his book *DisneyWar*, an examination of Michael Eisner's twenty years at the company, former *Wall Street Journal* page-one editor James B. Stewart tells of the executive's effort to woo Marriott chief financial officer Gary Wilson to join Disney, primarily to get the company into the hotel business. (The Grand Floridian Resort & Spa was but one result.)

Wilson reluctantly accepted, then "wasted no time in raising admission prices at theme parks, over the objections of some of the longtime employees," Stewart reported. In 1982, the old ticket-book formula was dropped in favor of a single admission charge, giving guests more freedom—and longer lines to the more popular rides.

Contrary to concerns, the higher price did not affect attendance in the slightest, but it did the bottom line—and significantly—for Disney.

"Indeed," wrote Stewart, the only thing that surprised Wilson "was how much guests were willing to pay."

Case in point: a three-night Adventures by Disney offer that allows purchasers to skip the lines at Disneyland and take a private tour "backstage" that includes Walt and Lillian's apartment and access to Imagineering.

Prices start at $2,129, per person.

land (its coaster, Madagascar: Mad Pursuit, like Disney's Space Mountain, is carried out almost entirely in the dark), and Universal has DreamWorks Animation attractions in all of its parks. So do Movie Park Germany and Australia's Warner Bros. Movie World.

Eisner additionally ran afoul of Apple wizard Steve Jobs, whose Pixar Animation Studios, up until then, had contributed to such efficacious Disney-Pixar collaborations as *Toy Story*, *Monsters, Inc.*, *Finding Nemo*, *The Incredibles*, and *Cars*. In 2006, for $7.4 billion, Disney bought Pixar Animation outright. By then, Robert Iger was a year into his role as Disney chairman and CEO, after Roy E. Disney won another boardroom campaign, this time to oust Michael Eisner. (Roy died in 2009.) Iger personally negotiated a Pixar peace—and the purchase—with Jobs.

Likewise, in 2008 Iger met and appeased Shanghai Communist party boss Yu Zhengsheng, ending a small but culturally significant Cold War after the Chinese government felt insulted by the 1997 Disney film *Kundun*, about the country's oppression of the Dalai Lama. The meeting opened the door to negotiations for what would culminate in the 2016 opening of the $5.5 billion Shanghai Disney Resort. (Hong Kong Disneyland opened in 2005.)

In 2009, for $4 billion, Disney acquired Marvel Entertainment, which, with certain qualifications, placed at the company's disposal such comic book superheroes as Spider-Man, Iron Man, Black Panther, the Hulk, Wolverine, Captain America, Thor, Daredevil, and Captain Marvel, and the teams of the X-Men, the Avengers, the Fantastic Four, and the Guardians of the Galaxy. While some of the characters were already under license to Disney's ramped-up rival in Florida, Universal Orlando (with such Marvel-themed attractions as the Incredible Hulk Coaster and the Amazing Adventures of Spider-Man), the Mouse House wasted little time in producing Marvel box office juggernauts and, in 2017, converting Disney California Adventure's Twilight Zone Tower of Terror into Guardians of the Galaxy—Mission: Breakout!, with an entire Marvel Land to follow.

In 2012, for $4.06 billion, Disney acquired the jewel in the intellectual property crown, Lucasfilms. Since 1977, George Lucas's intergalactic *Star Wars* movie series and spin-off programming and merchandising have turned this planet's business world on its ear, taking in an estimated $42 billion in revenues for the brand, according to a Christmas Eve 2015 article in *Fortune* titled "Star Wars Franchise Worth More Than Harry Potter and James Bond, Combined."

"I've always believed that *Star Wars* could outlive beyond me," Lucas, who donated every cent of his windfall to education, said when the deal was announced, "and I thought it was important to set up that transition in my lifetime."

By 2017, the post–George Lucas *Star Wars* movies produced by Disney, even with the slight hiccup of 2018's *Solo: A Star Wars Story*, had earned more at the box office than what the company paid for the brand in 2012. Wall Street smiled, even when considering the costs to make and market the movies. Still being factored in were profits from merchandising and, funneled even faster into the Disney coffers, revenue stemming from 2019's Star Wars: Galaxy's Edge additions to Disney World and Disneyland; these attractions

At fourteen acres, Star Wars: Galaxy's Edge, at both California's Disneyland Park and Florida's Disney's Hollywood Studios, is the largest single-themed land expansion in the history of either resort.

were expected to cause gridlock on California's Interstate 5 and Florida's Interstate 4 for years to come.

Simultaneous to the Star Wars construction, in a galaxy far, far away—Wall Street—Comcast, owner of NBCUniversal, parent of the Universal Parks, clashed with an even bigger titan, Disney. At stake was the acquisition of 21st Century Fox, whose intellectual properties included television's *The Simpsons*, James Cameron's 2009 sci-fi blockbuster *Avatar*, and the movie rights to certain Marvel Comics heroes (including the X-Men and the Fantastic Four, and their supervillains). This gets a bit complicated, because Disney already owns Marvel Studios, Universal already has a hysterically funny Simpsons ride, and—thanks to precedent-setting ride effects from Imagineering executive director Joe Rohde—in 2017 Disney's Animal Kingdom opened the tremendously innovative World of Avatar's Flight of Passage, with four-hour-plus waits to go with it.

In the end, Disney's $71.3 billion offer beat Comcast's $65 billion, with the deal solidifying just as the Themed Entertainment Association and AECOM, a development services firm, released industry visitor attendance figures for the year. "The Mouse dominated," called out the *Washington Post*, citing Disney's 150 million guests at its venues worldwide. "In North America, its parks swept the first five of 20 spots." Of those, "Almost 20.5 million parkgoers chose Walt Disney World's Magic Kingdom in Orlando as their happy place."

Which begs a couple of questions.

Is this truly how it was meant to be? After occupying a special niche in popular culture for so long, is Disney now wholly defining it?

Steve Rose, the film critic for the *Guardian*, pondered this very conundrum.

"Looking at Disney's schedule, we can practically predict the top movies for the rest of the decade: *Avengers: Infinity War*, *Avengers* sequel, Han Solo movie, *The Incredibles 2*, *Star Wars Episode IX*, *Frozen 2*, reboots of *Mary Poppins*, *Winnie the Pooh*, *Mulan*, *Aladdin*, *Dumbo*, more Marvel movies, and so on. You could call it the Infinity Slate. Where does it end?" he wrote in the spring of 2018.

"Then again," he added, "a *Star Wars*-themed hotel…pretty cool, huh?"

II.

Mekado Murphy is the senior movies editor of the *New York Times*. He also writes about theme parks for the newspaper. Asked if he could live in any amusement park in the world, which would it be, he answered without hesitation.

"Cedar Point," he said. "I love roller coasters. It has the most."

Once, all it had was a beer garden. To be fair, Cedar Point also had a dance floor and a bathhouse, and an unmatched location: sixty miles equidistant from Cleveland and Toledo, on a 364-acre sandy white tip of a seven-mile peninsula separating Sandusky Bay from Lake Erie. The resort began operations in 1870, fifty-two years after the founding of the town of Sandusky.

The Point's first developer was Louis Zistel (1830–1889), a German immigrant cabinetmaker. Settling in Sandusky in the mid-1850s, he established the bay's first fishing tug. After the Civil War, he initiated twenty-five-cents-a-passenger ferry service from town to the Point on his steamer, the *Young Reindeer*. Most of his passengers were the local German and Irish stonecutters who liked to hunt and fish. By adding swings, sandboxes, and the dance floor to the fishing spot, he also was able to attract women and children.

Throughout the 1870s, Zistel operated a boathouse saloon he called the Atlantic Garden, later adding an aquarium and a bear. After a protracted battle with throat cancer, Zistel died in 1889.

By then, Cedar Point had effectively died, too.

The action moved to other Lake Erie resorts, like Put-in-Bay and Rye Beach.

"Mr. Boeckling is one of those enterprising and wide awake business men who believes in having more than one string to his bow," said an 1893 profile of George Arthur Boeckling, still in his greenhorn days.

He was one of ten children, a lifelong bachelor, and the Indiana-born son of a German-émigré cooper. By the time he was thirty-five, Boeckling would earn Cedar Point its reputations as "the Atlantic City of the Great Lakes," "the Coney Island of the Midwest," and, in the 1920s (perhaps to indicate its role as a surreptitious antidote to Prohibition), "the Queen of the American Watering Places."

Clerking groceries instead of finishing high school, Boeckling (1862–1931) first visited Cedar Point in 1897, after a stint in wholesale lumber. One account claimed that the Michigan Central Railroad "sent Boeckling to investigate the park's potential for excursions. Boeckling saw the opportunity and seized it—for himself. He quit the railroad and organized Cedar Point Pleasure Resort Company." He later named it the George A. Boeckling Co.

When Boeckling first set foot on Sandusky's sand, there was little more than what had existed in Zistel's day, save for the additions of a wooden toboggan slide into the lake, and, from 1892, a LaMarcus Thompson Switchback Railway. The attractions were installed by an ongoing series of temporary lessees, starting with Benjamin F. Dwelle, a dealer in grain and feed, and his partner, Capt. William Slackford, a shipmaster from England.

With financial backing from the Kuebeler brewery family, Boeckling put up a midway, followed by a few rides and other amusements. By its very nature, Cedar Point was not a trolley park, because the Lake Shore Electric Railway went out of its way to steer passengers clear of Boeckling's resort, sending them instead to its own places on the shore, like Beach Park and Avon Park. To reach Cedar Point, citizens were forced to take either

George Arthur Boeckling:
Cedar Point was his baby.

The Cedar Point Midway remained a modest affair until George Boeckling returned from the 1904 St. Louis World's Fair.

a Detroit and Cleveland Steamship Navigation Company steamer or one of Sandusky's five steam railroads.

By the turn of the century, Lake Shore Electric could no longer ignore Cedar Point and opened a line that connected to a steamboat. For the Fourth of July 1901, Lake Shore Electric even promoted Cedar Point's jugglers, unicyclists, and "large vaudeville casino, ten bowling alleys, several dancing pavilions, and numerous other attractions."

That season, in which customers wishing to spend the night could take advantage of Boeckling's additions of the twenty-room Bay Shore Hotel and the fifty-five-room White House Hotel (which boasted electricity), Cedar Point attracted one million people.

The next year, Fred Ingersoll built the figure eight Racer.

"GEORGE BOECKLING," WROTE David Nasaw, "returned from the St. Louis world's fair of 1904 determined to upgrade Cedar Point into a full-fledged amusement park." This gave birth to Cedar Point's Circle of Amusement, even if Boeckling's personal taste ran to cultural amusements, rather than mechanical ones.

On June 12, 1905, he opened the six-hundred-room Hotel Breakers, the "largest and greatest hotel on the Great Lakes." Architects Wilm Knox and John H. Elliot—they met while working in the Chicago office of Burnham & Root—designed the Breakers in the style of a French country chateau, and angled the eight three-story wings off of the five-story main rotunda, so most guest rooms could have a lakefront view. One out of every six rooms had a private bathroom.

By 1908, handouts for Cedar Point described the Breakers as having "an atmosphere of refined sociability," and his park, "INNOCENT, WELL ORDERED AMUSEMENT DEVICES by the score…among them: The Scenic Railway, Circle Swing, Finest Carousel ever constructed, Figure Eight Roller Coaster, Auto Trip Around the World, Vaudeville Theater, Penny Arcade, Bowling Alleys, Trip to Rockaway, Chateau Alphonse, Miniature Railway, Box Hall, Shooting Gallery, Pony Track for Children and Saddle Horses for Ladies, Mundy's Animal Show, Egyptian Palmistry, Jap Rolling Ball, Wave-the-Wave, Roller Chairs, World in Wax."

Cedar Point's Coliseum, claiming to be the largest ballroom on the Great Lakes, split its dance floor in two, half for married couples, and half for singles seeking partners, a progressive move, considering that mixed bathing was not permitted in the lake until 1900. Then again, though fiscally conservative, Boeckling was socially liberal.

An imbiber himself, he waged lengthy battles with authorities over liquor sales on Sundays, which he ultimately lost—although he had to be arrested before he would cease selling the stuff.

"He is an architect without special training in architecture; a landscape gardener without expert experience; an amateur contractor who would take a contract to duplicate the World's Fair without having seen the original—and come very near doing it; a financier with no study of finance, and a general manager because he was simply born to manage," the *Ohio Magazine* said of the "jovial" Boeckling just short of a decade into his stewardship of Cedar Point.

Though he was slow to build a concrete highway across the peninsula so automobiles, already well established, could reach his park, Boeckling kept public interests in mind, billing his 1918 Leap Frog Railway as the nation's longest and largest, his way of boosting morale after four long years of World War I. So did he also look the other way on yacht activity in the lake during the bootlegging era.

In 1913, a star receiver from the University of Notre Dame worked as a summer lifeguard at Cedar Point and met his future wife, who was also working there. They married the following year. Her name was Bonnie Skiles, and his name was Knute Rockne.

Practicing football that summer at the Point, Rockne and his schoolmate and fellow lifeguard, Charley "Gus" Dorais, perfected the forward pass by throwing the ball in the advancing direction of the offensive team. The move proved particularly handy on November 1, 1913, when Notre Dame's team faced the heavily favored-to-win Army on a wet, cold field at West Point.

"Gus Dorais surprised Army by completing 14 of 17 passes for 243 yards and two touchdowns, with Rockne and other Notre Dame receivers catching the ball on the run," the Associated Press reported. The *New York Times* credited Notre Dame with "the most sensational football that has been seen in the East this year, baffling the cadets with a style of open play and perfectly developed forward pass, which carried the victors down the field at 30 yards a clip."

Notre Dame beat Army, 35–13, and the team's reputation was made.

Before the '20s raced fatalistically to a close, Harry Traver and Frederick Church made their contribution, too.

"Only true daredevils took on Cedar Point's Cyclone," wrote Lake Erie historians Julie Macfie Sobol and Ken Sobol. True to a Traver coaster, the 1929 model "featured tight turns and unusually steep slopes, with a seven-story lift hill to start things off."

Only from there, it all went downhill.

Cedar Point was lucky to be alive in 1950, what with Boeckling's death in 1931, the Depression, and park neglect during World War II.

Its paint chipped, its rails rusted, Traver and Church's Cyclone was demolished in 1951. At the Breakers, which in its day had seen President Taft, Annie Oakley, John Philip Sousa, and opera's Enrico Caruso inside its luxurious suites, the furnishings had faded. So had its glory.

In 1956, Toledo municipal-bond dealer George A. Roose and Cleveland investment banker Emile Legros gained controlling interest in Cedar Point, and they envisioned an upscale residential community and marina on the historic isthmus. The public outcry in opposition could be heard clear to Columbus, the state capital, where the legislature demanded Cedar Point remain a public recreation resort. Governor Frank Lausche went so far as to threaten seizing the property by eminent domain if Roose's plan went ahead.

The following year, Roose and Legros "announced that they would not only preserve the park," said Judith A. Adams, "but also develop it into a 'Disneyland of the Midwest.'"

They hired C. V. Wood.

By plane, train, boat, car, and tram, all routes led to Cedar Point.

"Roller coasters exist because we have a strong psychological need for them," claims Malcolm Burt, a contemporary researcher at Australia's Queensland University of Technology, and himself a coaster enthusiast.

Roller coasters and other thrill rides "are one way of maintaining a 'hands-on' form of release," he believes, a way "to stay in touch with our primal selves" and deliver "an adrenaline rush without being in any danger."

Not that danger shouldn't play a part: According to Dr. Seymour Epstein, a psychologist at the University of Massachusetts, "If you ask accident-prone skiers if they are scared when they are on a high-risk slope, they'll say they wouldn't bother to ski the slope if they weren't."

In fact, the professor emphasized, "It makes you feel very alive to be so scared."

Burt appears to agree, and finds roller coasters a practical means to this very end—if for no better reason than "most of us don't have the time, money, or skills to get the genuine release from doing something extreme, like climbing Mount Everest."

In April 1960, a $6 million upgrade was announced, to include expansion of the amusement zone's forty acres to one hundred, modernization of two hundred of the Breakers' one thousand rooms, and the addition of fifty cabanas on the beach.

As for the network of lagoons to the north and west of the resort area—originally formed when the marshes were dredged to clear them of mosquitos—*Billboard* reported: "After many months of intensive study by C. V. Wood Jr., of the Marco Engineering Company, Los Angeles, he recommended that the lagoons be utilized for boat rides similar to those at Disneyland."

A month after the *Billboard* article appeared, the *Sandusky Register* reported that Disneyland, Inc., and Walt Disney Enterprises requested that a Los Angeles Superior Court permanently enjoin Marco Engineering and C. V. Wood "from representing itself as having 'conceived the idea of Disneyland, or designed, engineered or constructed'" the Anaheim park.

In response, George Roose confirmed that Marco had studied Cedar Point and proposed new rides, but that "Marco did not lay out the local park nor design it." He further claimed that Marco did not "hold itself out as representing Disneyland"—which had to be the truth, because there was no Marco at the time Disneyland was being built. Wood formed the company after he was fired from Disney.

"Donn Tatum, Disneyland executive vice president, said that in filing the suit the Disney firms are not asking for monetary relief or damages," according to the *Register*. "Purpose of the action is to set the record straight that Disneyland was designed and built by the Walt Disney organization and no connection exists between it and the Wood projects."

Roose retired in 1975, the same year his partner, Legros, died, but with the plans they began effecting in the '60s, the two had set Cedar Point on the path to what it was to become.

The Roller Coaster Capital of the World.

CEDAR PARK FENDED OFF a corporate takeover in the 1970s, when MCA, Marriott, even Quaker Oats came sniffing. Instead of surrendering, in 1978 Cedar Point made its own conquest: Valleyfair, a two-year-old, twenty-five-acre park in Shakopee, Minnesota. By combining their parks' names, the management company came up with Cedar Fair.

Dorney Park was the combine's first acquisition, in 1992. Worlds of Fun, in Kansas City, Missouri, followed in 1997. Knott's Berry Farm came next, also in 1997. Other purchases, including Kings Island, in Mason, Ohio, and Kings Dominion, in Doswell, Virginia, also made the cut, as did Toronto, Ontario's Wonderland, and the attractions within the mega-shopping complex the Mall of America, in Bloomington, Minnesota.

In all, the Cedar Fair Entertainment Company owns and operates twelve amusement parks, three waterparks, and five hotels in North America—totaling 850 rides, 120 roller coasters, and 25 million visitors, annually. Cedar Point, the flagship, alone is the most visited seasonal park in America, with the yearly count at the turnstiles closing in on four million.

Thirty years after its 1987 Cedar Point debut, Iron Dragon, a suspended roller coaster, started allocating periods when it could be experienced with a virtual-reality headset. The supplement required riders—who must be at least forty-eight inches tall to begin with—to be age thirteen or older.

"Bigger Is Better" isn't strictly an American axiom.

With one hundred attractions and shows (including thirteen coasters), fourteen different lands (most themed to individual countries), and 5.5 million customers a year (Switzerland's Basel Airport is an hour's drive away), Europa Park, in the small town of Rust, Germany, is the continent's second most visited theme park, after Disneyland Paris.

When he founded Europa Park in 1975, Roland Mack had the rare luxury of being able to skip the middleman: His family makes rides—and has for well more than a century.

Today, Mack Rides GmbH & Co KG's multi-million-dollar thrill rides sell internationally. This made it all the more newsworthy when, in 2017, the major German business newspaper *Handelsblatt* reported that Roland Mack "earns more money [$337 million a year] with the amusement park than he does with his company's roller coaster business."

Having taken over the reins to the company from his father, Franz Mack (1921–2010), Roland (born 1949) was similarly prepared to hand them over to his three children, Ann-Kathrin, Thomas, and Michael.

Representing the eighth generation of Macks in the business, Thomas and Michael helm Europa Park's 2019 addition, Wasserwelt (Waterworld), because, as their father said about passing the torch, "A lifetime's experience is all very well, but that's no longer enough in these fast-moving times."

Europa Park's Atlantica SuperSplash dispatches passengers to the depths of the ocean, and then spins them backward. What really sells the experience is not so much the scenic view of Germany's Black Forest but the preride promise of "Nobody will stay dry, guaranteed!"

Thanks to its coasters, Cedar Point has been on a steadily upward trajectory since the midseventies, beginning with the 1976 Corkscrew, the world's first triple looper, and then the 1978 dual-tracked Gemini, the tallest and fastest up until then. After that, they begin to blend into memory, although not to enthusiasts who keep a credit count of every coaster ridden.

Among other Cedar Point standouts were the $8 million, 72 mph 1987 Magnum SL-200, with its two-hundred-foot drop—on a clear day, it is said, you can see Canada—and, in 2000, the world's first "giga-coaster," German designer Werner Stengel's Millennium Force. A testament to the adage "Physics can be fun," it was the first complete-circuit coaster (meaning, it completes a round trip) to hit three hundred feet, and offer an initial drop slope of eighty degrees.

It was hands up—and thumbs up—when Steel Vengeance opened at Cedar Point. Robb Alvey, of *Theme Park Review*, lauded it as "out of control," predicting, "People are going to love it." As for its noise, "They can hear this lift hill in Canada!"

In 2003, Stengel again delivered, this time with Top Thrill Dragster, the world's first four-hundred-foot complete-circuit coaster. Riders were shot up its ninety-degree hill at 120 mph in fewer than four seconds. (Stengel's Kingda Ka, at New Jersey's Six Flags Great Adventure, was installed two years later, and is fifty-six feet higher.)

In 2012, GateKeeper, so-called because it stands over the Cedar Park front gate, featured the highest inversion in the world and took honors for several of its dimensions, including those for height, speed, track length, drop height, and number of inversions.

Valravn, named for a Danish supernatural raven, sped into place in 2016 as the world's highest (223 feet), fastest (75 mph), and longest (3,415 feet) dive coaster—so called because it free-falls from a standing position and requires at least one ninety-degree-angle drop, and Valravn has two.

Twenty eighteen brought the "big and brazen" Steel Vengeance, a Rocky Mountain Construction "hyper hybrid" remake of the 1991 Mean Streak, which in its day was the tallest wooden coaster with the longest drop height in the world.

On its own, Steel Vengeance broke ten new wood-steel hybrid coaster records, and brought five new distinctions to Cedar Point: the greatest amount of steel roller coaster track at any one amusement park (57,865 feet, or eleven miles); most roller coaster track of any kind at one amusement park (60,423 feet, or 11.4 miles); most rides at one amusement park (seventy-one); most roller coasters that are higher than two hundred feet tall at one amusement park (six); and most roller coasters with a first drop of ninety degrees or more at one amusement park (five).

And now, for its next act…

QUIDDITCH, ANYONE?

Every day's a school holiday at Hogwarts, at least since Universal's Wizarding World of Harry Potter began admitting Muggles.

Just as orphaned Harry Potter found himself at Hogwarts Academy, so did the Universal Orlando Resort, forever considered an also-ran to Disney, find itself with the Wizarding World of Harry Potter. The twenty-acre themed land, which re-created the magical village of Hogsmeade down to Ollivander's Wand Shop, opened in 2010, and spawned another twenty-acre plot of Potter, Diagon Alley, in 2014. Compact versions of the Wizarding Worlds opened at Universal Studios Japan in 2014 and Universal Studios Hollywood in 2016.

Besides its hotels and waterparks, Universal Orlando has two theme parks, Islands of Adventure and Universal Studios. The $250 million Hogsmeade is located in the former and the $400 million Diagon Alley in the latter, with the Hogwarts Express connecting the two, requiring two separate admissions to the two separate parks. Their attractions require the visitor to spend at least one extra day at Universal, taking a big bite out of the Orlando pie, and putting a nice farthing or two into the pockets of the parties concerned. Wands at Ollivander's run from $25 for a toy version to $48 for a more advanced model, and that is only the beginning of the retail possibilities.

Even before Harry's arrival, Universal could be counted upon for a good time, though to appreciate its rides one needed an iron stomach. Smooth they were not. To be honest, despite several often-clever theming flourishes, and a lot of fire and smoke effects, refined they were not. Extreme, they usually were. The Incredible Hulk and the Hollywood Rip Ride Rockit coasters are extremely twisty and intense. The Simpsons Ride is extremely funny, but its motion simulators can also leave one extremely nauseous. Dudley Do-Right's Ripsaw Falls leaves one's clothing extremely wet.

Frankly, despite the first-rate experiences Universal offered, and in generous number, they lacked polish and detail when measured against their Disney counterparts, tame as they may be. Disney has since attempted to hop aboard the thrill-ride wagon—expect more as additional Marvel attractions develop—but the core audience is not the same as Universal's, or even that of other amusement parks.

Speaking on deep background, one overseas ride-company designer admitted that the prime target group for its attractions is the able-bodied between the ages of thirteen and thirty. In contrast, family-oriented Disney not only used an "Accelerometer" to gauge what impact Tower of Terror would have on the human frame, said one of its Imagineers, MIT systems-engineering graduate Kevin Parent, but the company uses a "Smellitzer—like a Howitzer, but this fires smells instead of shells—to engage every one of your senses" on its attractions.

The point is, it might have seemed that Universal was not a perfect fit for the storied J. K. Rowling. Gutsy as her narratives were, they were also detailed and descriptive.

Would Harry feel comfortable being so near Jurassic Park?

J. K. Rowling and her hero, it has been pointed out, are remarkably similar: thoughtful, private, and ready for a challenge. Both were born on July 31—Rowling, near Bristol, England, in 1965. Her name is Joanne Rowling, and she became J. K. only when her book publisher suggested boys might not read a book by a woman. (S. E. Hinton was given the same advice.) Because Rowling did not have a middle name, she took an initial from her grandmother, Kathleen.

She started writing about the boy wizard upon graduating from the University of Exeter and working for Amnesty International. Then, between teaching French and surviving with public (government) assistance in Edinburgh, she continued writing, sitting in cafés with her typewriter. Twelve publishers rejected the completed manuscript, until Bloomsbury, a small publishing house, offered a small advance, after the editor's small daughter also sat down and read Rowling's submission.

Goblins keep the ledgers and the keys to Gringotts Wizarding Bank, vault tours of which risk encounters with Voldemort and Bellatrix.

"It is impossible to live without failing at something, unless you live so cautiously that you might as well not have lived at all—in which case, you fail by default," Rowling would later say.

Nineteen ninety-seven brought out the first book in the series, *Harry Potter and the Sorcerer's Stone* (*Philosopher's Stone* in the UK). Six more books were to come over the following decade. Every one was a record-breaking best-seller, in more than two hundred countries and in eighty languages. They have sold more than five hundred million copies. Every one of the eight Warner Bros. movies based on the books topped the box office.

J. K. Rowling: The World is hers.

The Harry Potter theme park project had been on the boards for six years before the first Muggle—that's a person without magical powers—was allowed inside. Rumors persist that Rowling first huddled with Disney over a collaboration within one of its theme parks, but no one involved has ever been at liberty to confirm or deny.

"Her input has been direct and continual," said Alan Gilmore, art director for Universal's Wizarding World, a role he previously served on the movies. He also described Rowling as having "a very clear vision of her world."

When it came to bringing Harry's alternate universe into physical Universal, Rowling approved every last nail, the recipe for butterbeer, even the window display at Honeydukes Sweet Shop, whose sardine-flavored Pewking Pastilles are useful in inducing sickness when needing to skip classes at Hogwarts Academy.

Snowcapped Hogsmeade is entered through a gate at which stands a steaming Hogwarts Express engine. Beyond is the Main Village Square, with Honeydukes, Owl Post stationers, Filch's Emporium of Confiscated Goods for apparel, and the Three Broomsticks restaurant and Hogs Head pub. Towering above a wooded forest worthy of half-wizard gamekeeper Rubeus Hagrid is the town's centerpiece, the fifteen-story Hogwarts Castle. In it is housed the attraction Harry Potter and the Forbidden Journey, in which Harry and pal Ron Weasley, on Quidditch broomsticks, lead riders in special vehicles on a perilous flying chase through and around the battlements. Among the obstacles encountered en route are Aragog spiders, a Basilisk snake, Dementor phantoms, and a Hungarian Horntail dragon, whose breath should not get anywhere near a gasoline pump.

Despite its jolting turns, whose bounces reportedly were tamed for the subsequent Hollywood version, Forbidden Journey instantly became a must-ride, generating waits, when it was first unveiled, of up to seven hours.

Forbidden Journey also marked a jolting turn for Universal.

The company had, at long last, grasped hold of a family audience.

A fire-breathing dragon possessively stands guard over Gringotts Wizarding Bank.

Being, by and large, a movie business, Universal was not about to let the success of its Wizarding World go without a sequel. "We'll bring even more Harry Potter adventures to life," Universal Creative president Mark Woodbury said in January 2014, when the company announced its Diagon Alley for the Orlando resort to open that summer. Adjacent to the Muggle world, Diagon Alley is the area in London where wizards go to buy their supplies.

At Universal Studios Orlando, where the new land replaced the long-in-the-tooth Jaws ride, the entrance was a re-creation of London's King's Cross Station, where students like Harry depart for Hogsmeade on Platform 9¾. Harry Potter and the Escape from Gringotts took riders deep within the wizards' bank vaults for another motion-based projection dark ride, with some roller coaster effects for good measure. There were another complement of shops offering a wide variety of magical merchandise, but there was also greater immersion, especially in the darkened Knockturn Alley.

It was enough to make a believer out of anyone.

As a matter of fact, stepping back into the sunlight, and spying the fire-breathing Ukrainian Ironbelly dragon from *Harry Potter and the Deathly Hallows* as it hovers overhead, clawing the cupola of the Gringotts Bank, you might just swear that this was the creature that seized Rahere out of his infirmary bed and left him to hang off the edge of a cliff.

Stranger things have happened.

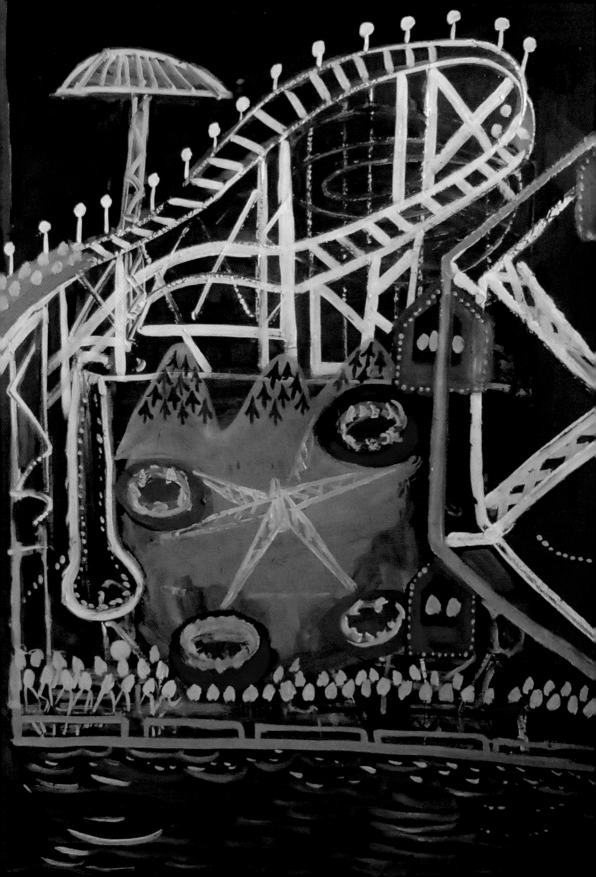

ACKNOWLEDGMENTS

My expressions of deepest gratitude begin with Mark Fletcher, of 8 Books Ltd., and Paul Stolper, owner of Paul Stolper Galleries and dinner host extraordinaire. It was Mark, at Paul's party in London, who suggested I contact the New York publisher Black Dog & Leventhal and editorial director Becky Koh—and it was Becky who responded so quickly and positively when I did.

In all these months, Becky's enthusiasm has never flagged. What a joy.

Martha Kaplan, my agent, is a pillar of wisdom, if not all seven, and she never once lost her cool, not even that time we rode the Big Apple Coaster at the New York, New York Hotel in Las Vegas. (As we climbed the lift hill, she tapped my shoulder and said, temperately, "This was a mistake.")

Diane Reid, invaluable friend of [*still counting*] years, read pages and pages, and made comments and comments. She also could be counted upon to lead the charges into Hersheypark, Knoebels, Rye Playland, and that greatest amusement park of all, New York City.

Glenn Young, lover of books and diehard fan of Chicago's late Riverview, permitted me to bounce so many ideas off of him that it's a shock he's still standing.

Michael M. Thomas, connoisseur and raconteur, greeted my announcement of this project with such gusto that it made me think the fireworks exploding around us were part of his reaction. Then I realized it was New Year's Eve.

Eve Mayer was my go-to grammar and spelling specialist, and Evelyn Renold, my frequent fixer of phrases. (Or, is that phraser of fixes?) On the picture front, as with nearly all my books, Howard Mandelbaum worked his customary wizardry, just as Keith Sherman went abracadabra with some very special illustrations.

Simone Goodman generously acted as my own personal Library of Congress, Chicago division, while the actual Library of Congress, in Washington, DC, was of such tremendous assistance that it made me think better of Congress.

In London, the British Museum's Library and Archives was Vauxhall, Ranelagh, and Jenny's Whim rolled into one. Closer to home, the glory of New York Public Library's Main Branch extended far beyond its lions, while out West, the University of Southern California's Cinematic Arts Library proved epic, and its Ned Comstock

Ludwig Bemelmans's *Coney Island*, circa late 1940s

a veritable walking encyclopedia of film. The Hitchcock cameo I owe to him, with thanks, too, to Brett Service of the Warner Bros. Archives.

Bob Stock, in Northern California, dispatched beneficial information and photographs, and Dan Gorman, in Southern California, did the same; I have known both since middle school. Katie Scott-Childress, director of the Olive Free Library in the Catskills, whom I knew for only a day, supplied the introduction to her husband, Professor Reynolds J. Scott-Childress, of the department of history at SUNY New Paltz. He shed enlightenment on Washington, DC's Marshall Hall.

Todd Moniot captained an unforgettable road trip from Bethesda, to Kennywood, to Cedar Point, to Glen Echo, with many a pit stop in between.

Jonathan Carter and Tim Ivers, dear neighbors, helped navigate the waters of Coney Island—twice—and Lake Compounce—once.

Jo Anne and Dr. Robert Simon dared Ghostrider with me at Knott's Berry Farm and California Screamin' at Disney California Adventure (on opening night)— Dr. Bob checked our pulses afterward—while Nicholas Wapshott shared the Santa Cruz Boardwalk's Giant Dipper, and, as it happened, later assigned my Walt Disney piece for *Newsweek*.

Lori Rackl, travel editor of the *Chicago Tribune*, green-lit my Shanghai and Dubai stories, and was great fun to work with. It was she who reminded me Walt Disney was born in Chicago.

Early in the construction stage of the Wizarding World of Harry Potter in Florida, Richard Corliss, of *Time* magazine, and I were handed hardhats and taken on a secret tour of the site. (Secret, because it was a no-journalist zone.) Richard adored amusement parks, although nowhere near as much as he loved his wife, Mary—and then, in 2015, something unimaginable happened: Richard died.

Dear Richard, how you are missed.

And darling Mary, how you are loved.

Harry McCracken, of *Fast Company*, graciously played host at the Walt Disney Family Museum in San Francisco, and lifelong pal Yardena Arar added to the adventure that day. (By now I hope she has seen *Pinocchio*.)

Peter Mikelbank, in Paris, sent a steady stream of relevant articles and irreverent comments, while Susanne Radzik deciphered train schedules to whisk us from the capital to Chessy, Seine-et-Marne, *très vite*.

Nina Pinsky, Susan Weaver, and Michael Weaver abetted me in a dawn raid on Hogwarts. Margaret Denk, Alex Pinsky, and Chris Hill helped soldier Six Flags Great Adventure in New Jersey; Chris unleashed an entire dictionary of expletives as we tackled the (since-defunct) Great American Scream Machine. My attorney, Diane Krausz, and our much-missed sidekick, Victor Ramos, were my companions aboard that park's El Toro, where, for once, we were speechless.

Christine La Monte (my "Belle of Crystal Beach") and Julian Siminski, both of Los Angeles, provided earfuls about their beloved Buffalo amusement park. Barbara

Cutler Emden deciphered inscrutable hotel bills and shared M&Ms (Mickey Mouse & Martinis). Marshall Efron told me Walt Disney drove a black Lincoln.

Beatrice Rich saw this all coming together, even when it wasn't.

Victoria Wilson was always there with encouragement, suggestions, and opera tickets. Sheila Nevins advised in pepping up the prologue.

Neighbor Herbert Bauernebel helped with my rusty German, son Max helped with the finer points of Thomas the Tank Engine, daughter Mia helped with the latest songs, and Estée Bauernebel helped with my spirits.

Charles B. Stovall, of the Walt Disney Company, has been a continuing source of expertise and munificence, and I also thank his colleagues Irma Smits, in France, and Jenkin Ho, in Hong Kong.

Audrey Eig, of NBCUniversal, and Meredith Danzig Bandy, at the Universal Orlando Resort, were kind in rolling out the welcome mats, as were Nick Paradise, at Kennywood, and Tony Clark, at Cedar Point. In Copenhagen Ellen Dahl personally escorted me through Tivoli.

Universal's Thierry Coup showed infinite patience while sharing lessons in design, particularly as they pertained to the Wizarding World of Harry Potter.

In Abu Dhabi, Razai Ali, Dina Bajjali, and Milica Smudja graciously assisted at their respective IMG Worlds of Adventure, Dubai Parks Resort, and Ferrari World.

While I cavorted in points north, south, east, and west, Ronny Diamond back home adoringly cared for my dog, Kingston—and all she got was this lousy T-shirt.

In New York, thanks also to Dale Burg, Carol Carey, Barbara Carroll, Fran Carpentier, Savannah Chauvet, Maria Ciaccia, Steve Cuozzo, Chip Deffaa, Yvonne Dunleavy, Frank Dunlop, Phyllis Feder, Bob Finkelstein, Tamara Glenny, the late Lesley Gore, Robert A. Harris, Robert Hofler, Robert Infarinato, Bruce Kluger, Bette and Pavel Kraus, Don Lemoine, Barbara Lowenstein, the late Sidney Mayer, Pucci Meyer McGill, Eric Myers, Carol S. Morgan, Jason Nieves, Judith Regan, Gail Clott Segal, Mary Elizabeth Simpson, Diane Stefani, Marti Stevens, Tim Teeman, Judy Twersky, Kenny Vance; in California, Susan and Frank Garfield, Daniel Greller, Sarah and Brandon Hemsath, Jeana Gamble Monroe, Babette and Steven Pinsky, Don Rath, Maryanne and Michael Sanders, Elaine and Robert Sloss, Cherie Stock, Patrick Wayne; in Florida, Nancy Beth Jackson, Charles McMurray, Sheila Stovall, Rick Sylvain; in Connecticut, Paula Conway (by way of Las Vegas, Milan, and Kenya), Patricia Funt Oxman; in Washington State, Alice B. Acheson; in Arizona (and Universal City), Duane Greeley; in England, Anna Hugo, Laura and David Rudge, Charlene Stolper; and, in Italy, Judy, Terry, Cara, and Gianni Mowschenson.

Not to mention all of the friends, acquaintances, relatives, colleagues, and perfect strangers who came along for the rides.

—S. M. S.

BIBLIOGRAPHY

BOOKS, BROCHURES, AND PAMPHLETS

Adams, Arthur, and Sarah A. Risley. *A Genealogy of the Lake Family of Great Egg Harbor, in Old Gloucester County, in New Jersey, Descended from John Lake of Gravesend, Long Island.* Hartford, CT: privately printed, 1915.

Adams, Judith A. *The American Amusement Park Industry: A History of Technology and Thrills.* Boston: Twain Publishers, 1991.

Adams, William Henry Davenport. *The History, Topography, and Antiquities of the Isle of Wight.* London: Smith, Elder, 1856.

Ady, Julia Mary Cartwright. *Madame: A Life of Henrietta, Daughter of Charles I and Duchess of Orleans.* London: Seeley, 1894.

Alberti, Samuel J. M. M., ed. *The Afterlives of Animals: A Museum Menagerie.* Charlottesville: University of Virginia Press, 2011.

Allaback, Sarah. *The First American Women Architects.* Champaign, Illinois: University of Illinois Press, 2008.

Altick, Richard D. *The Shows of London.* Cambridge, MA: Harvard University Press, 1978.

The American Almanac, Year-Book Cyclopedia, and Atlas. New York: New York American and Journal, Hearst's Chicago American, and San Francisco Examiner, 1903.

Andersen, Hemming. *Historic Scientific Instruments in Denmark.* Copenhagen: The Royal Danish Academy of Sciences and Letters, 1995.

Andersen, Kurt. *Fantasyland: How America Went Haywire: A 500-Year History.* New York: Random House, 2017.

Andersen, Lucy. *Copenhagen and Its Environs: A Guide for Travellers.* London: Walter Scott, 1888.

Anderson, Norman D. *Ferris Wheels: An Illustrated History.* Bowling Green, OH: Bowling Green State University Popular Press, 1992.

Anonymous. *Barnum's American Museum, Illustrated.* New York, 1850.

——. "Chevy Chase Lake Sector Plan," Montgomery County (MD) Planning Department, July 2012.

——. *Eighth Annual Report of the American Institute of the City of New-York.* Albany, NY: Weed, Parsons, 1850.

——. *Hotel Hershey and Cottages.* Philadelphia: Ketterlinus Lithographic Manufacturing, ca. 1960s.

——. "Matthew Schropp Henry." In *1860–1862,* Vol. 4 of *Memorial Biographies of the New England Historic Genealogical Society, 1845–1871.* Boston: The New England Historic Genealogical Society, 1885.

——. "New Publications," *North American Review,* vol. 46. Boston: Otis, Broaders, 1838.

——. *Official Catalogue and Guide Book to the Pan-American Exposition.* Buffalo, NY: Charles Ahrhart, 1901.

——. *Pennsylvania Dutch Cooking.* Gettysburg, PA: Dutchcraft, n.d. Project Gutenberg, 2008. https://www.gutenberg.org/files/26558/26558-h/26558-h.htm.

——. *Pictorial and Biographical Memoirs of Indianapolis and Marion County, Indiana.* Chicago: Goodspeed Brothers, 1893.

——. "Says Neighbor John." In *Ghost Town News.* Buena Park, CA: Knott's Berry Place, 1944.

——. *Shaw's Tourist's Picturesque Guide to the Isle of Wight.* London: The Graphotyping Co., 1873.

——. *The Story of Disneyland.* Chicago: Western Printing & Lithographing, 1955.

——. "Trolley Parks and Real Estate Development." Chevy Chase Historical Society, 2013. http://www.chevychasehistory.org/trolley-parks-and-real-estate-development.

——. *Views of the World's Fair and Midway Plaisance.* Chicago: W. B. Conkey, 1894.

Applegate, Harry, and Thomas Benton. *Six Flags Great Adventure.* Charleston, SC: Arcadia Publishing, 2009.

Ashby, LeRoy. *With Amusement for All: A History of American Popular Culture Since 1830.* Lexington, KY: University Press of Kentucky, 2012.

Ashton, Jean, Nina Nazionale, and New-York Historical Society. *When Did the Statue of Liberty Turn Green? & 101 Other Questions About New York City.* New York: Columbia University Press, 2010.

Avery, Elroy M. *A History of Cleveland and Its Environs: The Heart of New Connecticut.* Chicago: Lewis Publishing, 1918.

Baedeker, Karl. "Vienna." In *Southern Germany and Austria, Including Hungary and Transylvania: Handbook for Travellers.* 5th ed. Leipzig, Germany: Karl Baedeker, 1883.

Barnum, Phineas Taylor. *The Life of P. T. Barnum.* London: Sampson Low, Son, 1855.

Barrett, Walter. *The Old Merchants of New York.* New York: M. Doolady, 1870.

Beekman, James William. *Centenary Address Delivered Before the Society of the New York Hospital, July 24, 1871.* New York: The Society, 1871.

Bengston, John. *Silent Traces: Discovering Early Hollywood Through the Films of Charlie Chaplin.* Santa Monica, CA: Santa Monica Press, 2006.

Bergreen, Laurence. *Capone: The Man and the Era.* New York: Simon & Schuster Paperbacks, 1994.

Berman, John S. *Coney Island.* New York: Barnes & Noble Books, 2003.

Berman, Marisa L. *Historic Amusement Parks of Long Island: 118 Miles of Memories.* Charleston, SC: The History Press, 2015.

Bettencourt, David. *Rocky Point Park.* Charleston, South Carolina: Arcadia Publishing, 2015.

Bevilacqua, Fabio, and Lucio Fregonese, eds. *Nuova Voltiana: Studies on Volta and His Times.* Vol. 3. Milan: Casa Editrice Hoepli, 2001.

Black, Shirley Temple. *Child Star: An Autobiography.* New York: McGraw-Hill, 1988.

Blaisdell, Marilyn. *San Francisciana Photographs of Playland.* San Francisco: Marilyn Blaisdell, 1989.

———. *San Francisciana Photographs of Sutro Baths.* San Francisco: Marilyn Blaisdell, 1987.

Bloom, Michelle E. *Waxworks: A Cultural Obsession.* Minneapolis: University of Minnesota Press, 2003.

Bloom, Sol. *The Autobiography of Sol Bloom.* New York: G. P. Putnam's Sons, 1948.

Bogdan, Robert. *Freak Show: Presenting Human Oddities for Amusement and Profit.* Chicago: University of Chicago Press, 1990.

Bolotin, Norman, with Christine Laing. *Chicago's Grand Midway: A Walk Around the World at the Columbian Exposition.* Urbana, IL: University of Illinois Press, 2017.

Boulton, William B. *The Amusements of Old London.* London: John C. Nimmo, 1901.

"Boyton, Paul." In *A–H.* Vol. 1 of *People of the Period,* edited by A. T. Camden Pratt. London: Neville Beeman, 1897.

Boyton, Paul. *The Story of Paul Boyton.* London: George Routledge & Sons, 1892.

Brackett, Herbert I. *Brackett Genealogy.* Washington, DC: H. I. Brackett, 1907.

Braithwaite, David. *Savage of King's Lynn: Inventor of Machines & Merry-Go-Rounds.* Somerset, UK: Patrick Stephens, 1975.

Brasbridge, Joseph. *The Fruits of Experience.* 2nd ed. London: A. J. Valpy, 1824.

A Brief Historical and Descriptive Account of the Royal Gardens, Vauxhall. London: Gye and Balne, Printers, 1822.

Brigandi, Phil. *Orange County Chronicles.* Charleston, SC: The History Press, 2013.

Brock, Alan St. Hill. *Pyrotechnics: The History and Art of Firework Making.* London: Daniel O'Connor, 1922.

Brown, Brenda J. "Landscapes of Theme Park Rides: Media, Modes, Messages." In *Theme Park Landscapes: Antecedents and Variations,* edited by Terence Young and Robert Riley, 235–268. Washington, DC: Dumbarton Oaks Research Library and Collection, 2002.

Brown, Henry Collins, ed. *Valentine's Manual of the City of New York.* New Series No. 2. New York: The Old Colony Press, 1917.

Brown, Thomas. "Amusements." In *The Works of Mr. Thomas Brown.* London, 1760.

———. *The Fudge Family in Paris.* London: Longman, Hurst, Rees, Orme, and Brown, 1818.

Bruck, Connie. *When Hollywood Had a King: The Reign of Lew Wasserman, Who Leveraged Talent into Power and Influence.* New York: Random House, 2003.

Bunn, Alfred, ed. *The Vauxhall Papers.* London: John Andrews and John Mitchell, 1841.

Bunyan, Patrick. *All Around the Town: Amazing Manhattan Facts and Curiosities.* New York: Fordham University Press, 1999.

Burnes, Brian, Dan Viets, and Robert W. Butler. *Walt Disney's Missouri: The Roots of a Creative Genius.* Kansas City, MO: Kansas City Star Books 2002.

Burnham, Daniel H., Halsey C. Ives, Moses P. Handy, Roger Ballu, Angelo Del Nero, Hubert Vos, Humphrey Ward, and Ripley Hitchcock. *The Story of the Exposition, Illustrated in Its History, Architecture, and Art.* New York: D. Appleton, 1895.

Burrows, Danielle. *Clementon.* Charleston, SC: Arcadia Publishing, 2007.

Burrows, Edwin G., and Mike Wallace. *Gotham: A History of New York City to 1898.* New York: Oxford University Press, 1999.

Bush, Leo O., Edward C, Chukayne, Russell Allon Hehr, and Richard F. Hershey. *Euclid Beach Park Is Closed for the Season.* Cleveland: Dillon/Liederbach, 1977.

Bushnell, Michael G. *Historic Postcards from Old Kansas City.* Leawood, KS: Leathers Publishing, 2003.

Cairns, Stephen. "The Stone Books of Orientalism." In *Colonial Modernities: Building, Dwelling and Architecture in British India and Ceylon,* edited by Peter Scriver and Vikramaditya Prakash, 51–68. New York: Routledge, 2007.

California Coastal Commission, Madge Caughman, and Joanne S. Ginsberg, eds. *California Coastal Resource Guide.* Berkeley, CA: University of California Press, 1987.

Cannon, Daniel J. "Great Fire." In *The Encyclopedia of New York City,* edited by Kenneth T. Jackson. New Haven, CT: Yale University Press, 1995.

Carlyle, Thomas. *The Works of Thomas Carlyle (Complete).* Vol. 4. New York: P. F. Collier, 1897.

Caro, Robert A. *The Power Broker: Robert Moses and the Fall of New York.* New York: Alfred A. Knopf, 1974.

Carstensen, Georg, and Karl Gildemeister. *New York Crystal Palace: Illustrated Description of the Building.* New York: Riker, Thorne, 1854.

Cartmell, Robert. *The Incredible Scream Machine: A History of the Roller Coaster.* Bowling Green, OH: Amusement Park Books and Bowling Green State University Popular Press, 1987.

Carver, Sonora, and Elizabeth Land. *A Girl and Five Brave Horses.* Garden City, NY: Doubleday, 1961.

Cecil, Evelyn. *London Parks and Gardens.* New York: E. P. Dutton, 1907.

Chancellor, Edwin Beresford. *The Pleasure Haunts of London During Four Centuries.* London: Constable, 1925.

Charman, Isobel. *The Zoo: The Wild and Wonderful Tale of the Founding of the London Zoo, 1826–1851.* New York, Pegasus Books, 2017.

Clark, Ronald H. *The Engine Builders of Norfolk.* Yeovil, UK: Haynes, 1988.

[Cody,] Buffalo Bill [William F. Cody], and William Lightfoot Visscher. *Buffalo Bill's Own Story of His Life and Deeds.* Chicago: John R. Stanton, 1917.

Colby, Charles William, ed. *Selections from the Sources of English History: Being a Supplement to Text-books of English History B.C. 55–A.D. 1832.* New York: Longmans, Green, 1913.

Columbian Engraving and Publishing Co. *The Columbian Exposition and World's Fair Illustrated.* Chicago and Philadelphia: Columbian Engraving and Publishing, 1893.

Conlin, Jonathan. "Introduction." In *The Pleasure Garden: From Vauxhall to Coney Island,* edited by Jonathan Conlin, 1–28. Philadelphia: University of Pennsylvania Press, 2013.

Cooper, Thaddeus O., and Kevin B. Kreitman. *Seeking Redemption: The Real Story of the Beautiful Game of Skee-Ball.* San Jose, CA: Nomoreboxes, 2016.

Cowgill, Rachel. "Performance Alfresco." In *The Pleasure Garden: From Vauxhall to Coney Island ,* edited by Jonathan Conlin, 100–126. Philadelphia: University of Pennsylvania Press, 2013.

Cowles, Virginia. *The Astors.* New York: Alfred A. Knopf, 1979.

Coxe, William. *Travels into Poland, Russia, Sweden, and Denmark.* Dublin: S. Prince, R. Moncrieffe, W. Colles, T. Walker, C. Jenkin, W. Wilson, L. White, R. Burton, J. Cash and P. Byrne, 1784.

Crocker, Kathleen, and Jane Currie. *Chautauqua Lake Region*. Charleston, SC: Arcadia Publishing, 2002.

Cross, Gary S., and John K. Walton. *The Playful Crowd: Pleasure Places in the Twentieth Century*. New York: Columbia University Press, 2005.

Cudahy, Brian J. *How We Got to Coney Island: The Development of Mass Transportation in Brooklyn and Kings County*. New York: Fordham University Press, 2002.

Curtis, James. *W. C. Fields: A Biography*. New York; Alfred A. Knopf, 2003.

Daly, Michael. *Topsy: The Startling Story of the Crooked-Tailed Elephant, P. T. Barnum, and the American Wizard, Thomas Edison*. New York: Atlantic Monthly Press, 2013.

D'Antonio, Michael. *Hershey: Milton S. Hershey's Extraordinary Life of Wealth, Empire, and Utopian Dreams*. New York: Simon and Schuster, 2007.

DeGregorio, William A. *The Complete Book of U.S. Presidents*. 3rd ed. New York: Wings Books, 1991.

Deitche, Scott M. *Garden State Gangland: The Rise of the Mob in New Jersey*. London: Rowman & Littlefield, 2018.

Della Valle, Pietro. *Viaggi di Pietro Della Valle il Pellegrino*. Edited by Mario Schipano. Venice, Italy: Presso Paolo Baglioni, 1667.

Dennett, Andrea Stulman. *Weird and Wonderful: The Dime Museum in America*. New York: New York University Press, 1997.

Denson, Charles. *Coney Island and Astroland*. Charleston, SC: Arcadia Publishing, 2011.

——. *Coney Island: Lost and Found*. Berkeley, CA: Ten Speed Press, 2002.

Dewald, Christian, and Werner Michael Schwarz, eds. *Prater Kino Welt: Der Wiener Prater und die Geschichte des Kinos*. Vienna: Verlag Filmarchiv Austria, 2005.

Dickens, Charles. *Sketches by Boz: Illustrative of Every-day Life and Every-day People*. New York: The University Society, 1908.

——. "A Fancy Ball at Copenhagen," *All the Year Round*. Vol. 13. London: Chapman and Hall, 1865.

Dier, Caroline Lawrence. *The Lady of the Gardens: Mary Elitch Long*. Hollywood: Hollycrofters, 1932.

Dolkart, Andrew S. "Castle Clinton," In *The Encyclopedia of New York City*, edited by Kenneth T. Jackson, 188. New Haven, CT: Yale University Press, 1995.

Donzel, Catherine, Alexis Gregory, and Marc Walter. *Grand American Hotels*. New York: The Vendome Press, 1989.

"Dorney, Oliver Charles, C. P. A. Prominent Business Educator." In *Encyclopedia of Pennsylvania Biography*. Vol. 3, edited by John Woolf Jordan. New York: Lewis Historical Publishing, 1914.

Douglass, Frederick, and Ida B. Wells. *The Reason Why the Colored American Is Not in the World's Columbian Exposition*. Chicago: Ida B. Wells, 1893.

Dussieux, Louis. *Le Château de Versailles: Histoire et Description*. Vol. 1. Versailles, France: L. Bernard, 1881.

Easdown, Martin. *Amusement Park Rides*. Oxford, UK: Shire Library, 2012.

Editors of the *Encyclopædia Britannica*. "Hiram Maxim: American Inventor." In *Encyclopædia Britannica*, February 13, 2018. https://www.britannica.com/biography/Hiram-Maxim.

Eisenstadt, Peter R., ed. *The Encyclopedia of New York State*. Syracuse, NY: Syracuse University Press, 2005.

Elder, Abraham. *Tales and Legends of the Isle of Wight, Part the First*. London: Simpkin, Marshall, 1839.

Ely, Wally, with Bob Ott. *Dorney Park*. Charleston, SC: Arcadia Publishing, 2003.

The Encyclopedia of Canada. Vol. 3, edited by W. Stewart Wallace. Toronto: University Associates of Canada, 1948.

Erish, Andrew A. *Col. William N. Selig, the Man Who Invented Hollywood*. Austin: University of Texas Press, 2012.

Esslinger, Hartmut. *A Fine Line: How Design Strategies Are Shaping the Future of Business*. San Francisco: John Wiley & Sons, 2009.

Euclid Beach Park Now. Euclid Beach Park. Charleston, SC: Arcadia Publishing, 2012.

Evanosky, Dennis, and Eric J. Kos. *Lost San Francisco*. London: Pavilion Books, 2012.

Evelyn, John. *The Diary of John Evelyn*. Edited by William Bray. London: M. Walter Dunne, 1901.

Faulkner, Debra B. *Mary Elitch Long: First Lady of Fun*. Palmer Lake, CO: Filter Press, 2008.

Feldman, Benjamin. *East in Eden: William Niblo and His Pleasure Garden of Yore*. New York: New York Wanderer Press, 2014.

Findling, John E., ed. *Historical Dictionary of World's Fairs and Expositions, 1851–1988*. Westport, CT: Greenwood Press, 1990.

Forster, R. P. *A Collection of the Most Celebrated Voyages & Travels, from the Discovery of America to the Present Time*. Vol. 2. Newcastle upon Tyne, UK: Mackenzie and Dent, 1818.

Forsyth, David. *Denver's Lakeside Amusement Park: From the White City Beautiful to a Century of Fun*. Boulder, CO: University Press of Colorado, 2016.

Fowler, Gene. *Timber Line: A Story of Bonfils and Tammen*. Garden City, NY: Garden City Books, 1951.

Foxe, John. *The Unabridged Acts and Monuments Online or TAMO (1576 edition)*. Sheffield, England: HRI Online Publications, 2011. Available from http//www.johnfoxe.org.

Francis, David W., and Diane DeMali Francis. *Cedar Point: The Queen of American Watering Places*. Fairview Park, OH: Amusement Park Books, 1952.

——. *Cleveland Amusement Park Memories*. Cleveland: Grey, 2004.

——. *The Golden Age of Roller Coasters in Vintage Postcards*. Chicago: Arcadia Publishing, 2003.

Frank, Robin Jaffee. *Coney Island: Vision of an American Dreamland 1861–2008*. New Haven, CT: Yale University Press, 2015.

Fried, Frederick. *A Pictorial History of the Carousel*. New York: A. S. Barnes, 1964.

Friends of the Hershey Trolley and the Hershey–Derry Township Historical Society. *Hershey Transit*. Charleston, SC: Arcadia Publishing, 2013.

Funderburg, Anne Cooper. *Chocolate, Strawberry, and Vanilla: A History of American Ice Cream*. Bowling Green, OH: Bowling Green State University Popular Press, 1995.

Futrell, Jim. *Amusement Parks of New Jersey*. Mechanicsburg, PA: Stackpole Books, 2004.

——. *Amusement Parks of New York*. Mechanicsburg, PA: Stackpole Books, 2006.

——. *Amusement Parks of Pennsylvania*. Mechanicsburg, PA: Stackpole Books, 2002.

——. *Waldameer Park*. Charleston, SC: Arcadia Publishing, 2013.

Gabler, Neal. *An Empire of Their Own: How the Jews Invented Hollywood*. New York: Anchor Books, 1989.

——. *Walt Disney: The Triumph of the American Imagination*. New York: Alfred A. Knopf, 2006.

Gale, Neil. *The Midway Plaisance at the 1893 World's Columbian Exposition in Chicago*. Belleville, IL: self-published, 2017.

Galignani, A. and W. *Galignani's New Paris Guide*. 17th ed. Paris: A. and W. Galignani, 1830.

———. *Galignani's Paris Guide: Or, Stranger's Companion Through the French Metropolis*. London: G. and W. B. Whittaker, 1822.

Gargiulo, Vince. *Palisades Amusement Park: A Century of Fond Memories*. New Brunswick, NJ: Rutgers University Press, 1995.

Gee, Derek, and Ralph Lopez. *Laugh Your Troubles Away: The Complete History of Riverview Park*. Livonia, MI: Sharpshooters Productions, 2000.

Gehring, Franz Eduard. *Mozart*. London: Sampson, Low, Marston, Searle, and Rivington, 1883.

Gennawey, Sam. *The Disneyland Story: The Unofficial Guide to the Evolution of Walt Disney's Dream*. Birmingham, AL: Keen Communications, 2014.

Gindriez, Charles, and Professor James M. Hart. *International Exhibitions: Paris–Philadelphia–Vienna*. New York: A. S. Barnes, 1878.

Gish, Lillian, with Ann Pinchot. *Lillian Gish: The Movies, Mr. Griffith, and Me*. Englewood Cliff, NJ: Prentice-Hall, Inc., 1969.

Golder, Robert I. "Samuel Fraunces." In *The Encyclopedia of New York City*, edited by Kenneth T. Jackson, 438. New Haven, Connecticut: Yale University Press, 1995.

Goldman, Mark. *High Hopes: The Rise and Decline of Buffalo, New York*. Albany, NY: State University of New York Press, 1983.

Goode, Chris. *California Baseball: From the Pioneers to the Glory Years*. lulu.com, 2011.

Gottlock, Wesley, and Barbara H. Gottlock. *Lost Amusement Parks of New York City: Beyond Coney Island*. Charleston, SC: The History Press, 2013.

———. *Lost Amusement Parks of the Hudson Valley*. N.p.: CreateSpace Independent Publishing Platform, 2016.

Grant, James. *Sketches in London*. London: W. S. Orr, 1838.

Greed, Clara. *Inclusive Urban Design: Public Toilets*. Oxford, UK: Architectural Press, 2007.

Greeley, Horace. *Art and Industry as Represented in the Exhibition at the Crystal Palace, New York 1853–4*. New York: Redfield, 1853.

Green, Judith A. *Henry I: King of England and Duke of Normandy*. Cambridge, UK: Cambridge University Press, 1999.

Greenly, A. H., ed. *The Westerners: New York Posse Brand Book*. New York: The Westerners, 1954.

Grigson, Caroline. *Menagerie: The History of Exotic Animals in England*. Oxford, UK: Oxford University Press, 2016.

A Guide to All the Watering and Sea Bathing Places in England and Wales, with a Description of the Lakes; a Sketch of a Tour in Wales, and Itineraries. London, 1824.

Gurtler, Jack, and Corinne Hunt. *The Elitch Gardens Story: Memories of Jack Gurtler*. Boulder, CO: Rocky Mountain Writers Guild, 1982.

Hall, John F. *The Daily Union History of Atlantic City and County, New Jersey*. Atlantic City: Daily Union Printing, 1900.

———, and George W. Bloodgood. *The Daily Union History of Atlantic City and County, New Jersey*. Atlantic City: Daily Union Printing, 1899.

Handwerker, Lloyd, and Gil Reavill. *Famous Nathan: A Family Saga of Coney Island, the American Dream and the Search for the Perfect Hot Dog*. New York: Flatiron Books, 2016.

Handwerker, William, and Jayne A. Pearl. *Nathan's Famous: The First 100 Years*. New York: Morgan James Publishing, 2016.

Harris, James. *Santa Monica Pier: A Century on the Last Great Pleasure Pier*. Santa Monica, CA: Angel City Press, 2009.

Harris, Neil. *Humbug: The Art of P. T. Barnum*. Chicago: University of Chicago Press, 1973.

Harrison, Edward Sanford. *History of Santa Cruz County, California*. San Francisco: Pacific Press Publishing, 1892.

Harwood, Herbert H., Jr., and Robert S. Korach. *The Lake Shore Electric Railway Story*. Bloomington, IN: Indiana University Press, 2000.

Havinghust, Walter. *Annie Oakley of the Wild West*. New York: Macmillan, 1954.

Henry, Matthew Schropp. *History of the Lehigh Valley*. Easton, PA: Bixler & Corwin, 1860.

Henry, O. "The Greater Coney." In *The Complete Works of O. Henry*. Garden City, NY: Garden City Publishing, 1911.

Henry of Huntingdon. *The Chronicle of Henry of Huntingdon*. 1893. Reprint edited and translated by Thomas Forester. Felinfach, Wales: Llanerch Publishers, 1991.

Hepburn, Katharine. *The Making of the African Queen, or How I Went to Africa with Bogart, Bacall, and Huston and Almost Lost My Mind*. New York: Alfred A. Knopf, 1987.

Hepworth, T. C. "Rays of Light." In *Cassell's Popular Science*, edited by Alexander S. Galt. Vol. 2. London: Cassell, 1906.

Highfill, Philip H., Jr., Kalman A. Burnhim, and Edward A. Langhans. *Tibbett to M. West*. Vol. 15 of *A Biographical Dictionary of Actors, Actresses, Musicians, Dancers, Managers, & Other Stage Personnel in London, 1660–1800*. Carbondale and Edwardsville, IL: Southern Illinois University Press, 1993.

Hirschl, Jessie Heckman. "The Great White City," *American Heritage*, October 1960. https://www.americanheritage.com/content/great-white-city.

Hoffman, Laura J. *Coney Island*. Charleston, SC: Arcadia Publishing, 2014.

Holmes, Roger, and Paul Bailey. *Fabulous Farmer: The Story of Walter Knott and His Berry Farm*. Los Angeles: Westernlore Publishers, 1941.

Hone, William. *The Every-Day Book and Table Book: or, Everlasting Calendar of Popular Amusements, Sports, Pastimes, Ceremonies, Manners, Customs, and Events, Incident to Each of the Three Hundred and Sixty-Five Days, in Past and Present Times; Forming a Complete History of the Year, Months, and Seasons, and a Perpetual Key to the Almanac…for Daily Use and Diversion*. Vol. 1. London: T. Tegg, 1830.

Hopkins, Albert Allis, ed. *Magic: Stage Illusions and Scientific Diversions, Including Trick Photography*. New York: Munn, 1901.

Horne, Gerald. *Class Struggle in Hollywood, 1930–1950: Moguls, Mobsters, Stars, Reds, & Trade Unionists*. Austin, TX: University of Texas Press, 2011.

Hull, Betty Lynne. *Denver's Elitch Gardens: Spinning a Century of Dreams*. Boulder, CO: Johnson Printing, 2003.

Ierardi, Eric J. *Gravesend: The Home of Coney Island*. Charleston, SC: Arcadia Publishing, 2001.

Illustrated New York: The Metropolis of To-Day. New York: International Publishing, 1888.

Immerso, Michael. *Coney Island: The People's Playground*. New Brunswick, NJ: Rutgers University Press, 2002.

Iorizzo, Luciano J. *Al Capone: A Biography*. Westport, CT: Greenwood Press, 2003.

Irving, Washington. *The Works of Washington Irving*. New York: P. F. Collier, 1881.

Isherwood, Christopher. *Exhumations: Stories, Articles, and Verse*. New York: Simon and Schuster, 1966.

———. *Prater Violet*. New York: Random House, 1945.

Jacques, Charles J., Jr. *Kennywood...Roller Coaster Capital of the World*. Natrona Heights, PA: Amusement Park Journal, 1982.

James, Thomas C., M.D. "Brief Account of the Discovery of Anthracite Coal on the Lehigh," *Memoirs of the Historical Society of Pennsylvania*, edited by Edward Armstrong.Vol. 1. Philadelphia: J. B. Lippincott, 1864.

Jeffers, H. Paul. *Diamond Jim Brady: Prince of the Gilded Age*. New York: John Wiley & Sons, 2001.

Jevons, William Stanley. *Methods of Social Reform: And Other Papers*. London: Macmillan, 1883.

Jones, Robert Jameson. "Historical Society Notes and Documents: James McMaster, Jr." *Western Pennsylvania Historical Magazine* 56, no. 1 (January 1973): 99–100.

Jonson, Ben. *The Works of Ben Jonson*. Vol. 3. London: D. Midwinter, 1756.

Kahrl, William. "The Taming of American Amusement Parks." In *World's Fair*. Vols. 9–13. Corte Madera, CA: World's Fair, 1989.

Kane, Josephine. *The Architecture of Pleasure: British Amusement Parks, 1900–1939*. New York: Ashgate Publishing, 2013.

———. "Edwardian Amusement Parks." In *The Pleasure Garden: From Vauxhall to Coney Island*, edited by Jonathan Conlin, 217–246. Philadelphia: University of Pennsylvania Press, 2013.

Kasper, Shirl. *Annie Oakley*. Norman, OK: University of Oklahoma Press, 1992.

Kasson, John F. *Amusing the Million: Coney Island at the Turn of the Century*. New York: Hill & Wang, 1978.

Keels, Thomas H. *Wicked Philadelphia: Sin in the City of Brotherly Love*. Charleston, SC: The History Press, 2010.

Kestenbaum, Joy M. "Jones's Wood." In *The Encyclopedia of New York City*, edited by Kenneth T. Jackson, 626. New Haven: Yale University Press, 1995.

Khan, Azmathulla. *Risks Mitigated in World's Most Amazing Projects*. Chennai, India: Notion Press, 2017.

King, Stephen. *Joyland*. London: Titan Books, 2013.

Klein, Maury. *The Life and Legend of Jay Gould*. Baltimore: Johns Hopkins University Press, 1997.

Kraig, Bruce. "Nathan's Famous." In *Savoring Gotham: A Food Lover's Guide to New York City*, edited by Andrew F. Smith. New York: Oxford University Press, 2015.

Kraynek, Sharon L. D. *Chippewa Lake Park Chronicles*. Akron, OH: Bunnell Printing, 1994.

Kyriazi, Gary. *The Great American Amusement Parks: A Pictorial History*. Secaucus, NJ: Castle Books, 1976.

La Garde-Chambonas, Auguste Louis Charles. *Anecdotal Recollections of the Congress of Vienna*. London: Chapman & Hall, 1902.

LaGumina, Salvatore J., Frank J. Cavaioli, Salvatore Primeggia, and Joseph A. Varacalli. *The Italian American Experience: An Encyclopedia*. New York: Garland Publishing, 2000.

Lahue, Kalton C. *Motion Picture Pioneer: The Selig Polyscope Company*. South Brunswick, NJ: A. S. Barnes, 1973.

Lamb, Martha Joanna, and Mrs. Burton Harrison. *History of the City of New York: The Century of National Independence, Closing in 1880*. New York: A. S. Barnes, 1880.

"Landownership: Later Estates." In *Chelsea*, edited by Patricia E. C. Croot, 123–145. Vol. 12 of *A History of the County of Middlesex*. London: Victoria County History, 2004.

Langlois, Gilles-Antoine. *Folies, Tivolis, et Attractions*. Paris: Delegation to the Artistic Action of the City of Paris, 1991.

Larson, Erik. *The Devil in the White City: Murder, Magic, and Madness at the Fair That Changed America*. New York: Vintage Books, 2004.

Leech, Margaret. *In the Days of McKinley*. New York: Harper & Brothers, 1959.

Legato, Frank. *Atlantic City: In Living Color*. Macon, GA: Indigo Custom Publishing, 2004.

Lenček, Lena. *Making Waves: Swimsuits and the Undressing of America*. San Francisco: Chronicle Books, 1989.

Lening, Gustav. *The Dark Side of New York Life and Its Criminal Classes*. New York: Fred'k Gerhard, 1873.

Levetus, Amelia Sarah. *Imperial Vienna: An Account of Its History, Traditions, and Arts*. London: John Lane, 1905.

Levi, Vicki Gold, and Lee Eisenberg. *Atlantic City: 125 Years of Ocean Madness*. 2nd ed. Berkeley, CA: Ten Speed Press, 1979.

Lewis, Robert M. *From Traveling Show to Vaudeville: Theatrical Spectacle in America, 1830–1910*. Baltimore: John Hopkins University Press, 2003.

Liebowitz, Steve. *Steel Pier, Atlantic City: Showplace of the Nation*. West Creek, NJ: Down the Shore Publishing, 2009.

Lilliefors, James. *America's Boardwalks: From Coney Island to California*. New Brunswick, NJ: Rutgers University Press, 2006.

Litwicki, Ellen M. "The Influence of Commerce, Technology, and Race on Popular Culture in the Gilded Age." In *The Gilded Age: Essays on the Origins of Modern America*, edited by Charles W. Calhoun, 187–210. Lanham, MD: Rowman & Littlefield Publishers, 2007.

Loring, John. Introduction to *Tivoli Gardens*, by Harry Benson. New York: Abrams, 2007.

Louisiana. Supreme Court. "Roussel v. Railways Realty Co." In *Southern Reporter*. Vol. 61. St. Paul, MN: West Publishing, 1913.

Louvish, Simon. *Man on the Flying Trapeze: The Life and Times of W. C. Fields*. New York: W. W. Norton, 1999.

Lucev, Emil R., Sr. *The Rockaways*. Charleston, SC: Arcadia Publishing, 2007.

Lukas, Scott A. *Theme Park*. London: Reaktion Books, 2008.

Lust, Annette. *From Greek Mimes to Marcel Marceau and Beyond: Mimes, Actors, Pierrots, and Clowns: A Chronicle of the Many Visages of Mime in Theatre*. Lanham, MD: The Scarecrow Press, 2002.

Madden, Daniel M. *A Religious Guide to Europe*. New York: Collier Books, 1975.

Madsen, Axel. *John Jacob Astor: America's First Multimillionaire*. New York: John Wiley & Sons, 2002.

Manbeck, John B. *Brooklyn: Historically Speaking*. Charleston, SC: The History Press, 2008.

Manby, Joel. *Love Works: Seven Timeless Principles for Effective Leaders*. Grand Rapids, MI: Zondervan, 2012.

Mangels, William F. *The Outdoor Amusement Industry: From Earliest Times to the Present*. New York: Vantage Press, 1952.

Manns, William, and Peggy Shank. *Painted Ponies: American Carousel Art*. Edited by Marianne Stevens. Millwood, NY: Zon International Publishing, 1986.

Mariani, John. *America Eats Out: An Illustrated History of Restaurants, Taverns, Coffee Shops, Speakeasies, and Other Establishments That Have Fed Us for 350 Years*. New York: William Morrow, 1991.

Markham, Gervase. *The English Housewife*. Edited by Michael R. Best. Montreal: McGill-Queen's University Press, 1998.

Martin, Carol J. *Dance Marathons: Performing American Culture of the 1920s and 1930s*. Jackson, MS: University Press of Mississippi, 1994.

Matthews, William Henry. *Mazes and Labyrinths: A General Account of Their History and Developments*. New York: Longmans, Green, 1922.

Maud, Renée Gaudin de Villaine. *One Year at the Russian Court: 1904–1905*. London: John Lane, 1918.

McCormick, Nancy D., and John S. McCormick. *Saltair*. Salt Lake City: University of Utah Press, 1985.

McCown, Davis G. *Six Flags Over Texas: The First Fifty Years*. Hurst, TX: Lavaca Publications and Media, 2016.

McCullough, David W. *Brooklyn…And How It Got That Way*. New York: Dial Press, 1983.

McCullough, Edo. *Good Old Coney Island: A Sentimental Journey into the Past*. New York: Charles Scribner's Sons, 1957.

———. *World's Fair Midways: An Affectionate Account of American Amusement Areas from the Crystal Palace to the Crystal Ball*. New York: Exposition Press, 1966.

McDougal, Dennis. *The Last Mogul: Lew Wasserman, MCA, and the Hidden History of Hollywood*. New York: Crown Books, 1998.

McKenna, George. *The Puritan Origins of American Patriotism*. New Haven, CT: Yale University Press, 2007.

McLaughlin, Robert. *Pleasure Island: 1959–1969*. Charleston, SC: Arcadia Publishing, 2014.

McMechen, Edgar Carlisle. *Robert W. Speer, A City Builder*. Denver: Smith-Brooks Printing, 1919.

Merritt, Christopher, and J. Eric Lynxwiler. *Knott's Preserved: From Boysenberry to Theme Park, the History of Knott's Berry Farm*. Santa Monica, CA: Angel City Press, 2010.

Merritt, Christopher, and Dominic Priore. *Pacific Ocean Park: The Rise and Fall of Los Angeles' Space-Age Nautical Pleasure Pier*. Port Townsend, WA: Process Media, 2014.

Miller, Stephen. *Smart Blonde: The Life of Dolly Parton*. New York: Omnibus Press, 2015.

Mogridge, George. *Wanderings in the Isle of Wight*. London: The Religious Tract Society, 1846.

Moore, Norman. *The Book of the Foundation of St. Bartholomew's Church in London: The Church Belonging to the Priory of the Same in West Smithfield*. London: Oxford University Press, 1923.

Morgan, Emily Malbone. *Prior Rahere's Rose*. Hartford, CT: Belknap & Warfield, 1893.

Morley, Henry. *Memoirs of Bartholomew Fair*. London: Chapman and Hall, 1859.

Morrell, Parker. *Diamond Jim: The Life and Times of James Buchanan Brady*. New York, Simon & Schuster, 1934.

Mott, Hopper Striker. *Mott, Hopper, Striker*. New York: Historical, 1898.

———. "Jones's Wood." In *Valentine's Manual of the City of New York, 1917–1918*. New Series, No. 2, edited by Henry Collins Brown. New York: Old Colony Press, 1917.

Mozart, Wolfgang Amadeus. *Mozart: A Life in Letters*. Edited by Cliff Eisen. Translated by Stewart Spencer. London: Penguin Books, 2006.

Muelder, Owen W. *Theodore Dwight Weld and the American Anti-Slavery Society*. Jefferson, NC: MacFarland, 2011.

Munch, Richard. *Harry G. Traver: Legends of Terror*. Mentor, OH: Amusement Park Books, 1982.

Mundy, Peter. *The Travels of Peter Mundy, in Europe and Asia, 1608–1667*. Edited by Sir Richard Carnac Temple. Cambridge, UK: The Hakluyt Society, 1907.

Naroditskaya, Inna. *Bewitching Russian Opera: The Tsarina from State to Stage*. Oxford, UK: Oxford University Press, 2012.

Nasaw, David. *Going Out: The Rise and Fall of Public Amusements*. New York: Basic Books, 1993.

Nason, Henry B., ed. *Biographical Record of the Officers and Graduates of the Rensselaer Polytechnic Institute, 1824–1886*. Troy, NY: William H. Young, 1887.

National Geographic. *An Uncommon History of Common Things*. Vol. 2. Washington, DC: National Geographic Books, 2015.

Neiiendam, Robert. "Georg Carstensen." In *Danish Biographical Reading*. 3rd ed. Copenhagen: Gyldendal, 1979–1984.

Nelson, Paul. Foreword to *Waldemeer Park*, by Jim Futrell. Charleston, SC: Arcadia Publishing, 2003.

Newburger, Harriet, Anita Sands, and John Wackes. *Atlantic City: Past and Prologue, A Special Report by the Community Affairs Department*. Philadelphia: Federal Reserve Bank of Philadelphia, 2009.

Newlin, Keith. *Hamlin Garland: A Life*. Lincoln, NE: University of Nebraska Press, 2008.

The New York Times Biographical Service. Vol. 5. New York: The New York Times & Arno Press, 1974.

Nickson, John. *Our Common Good: If the State Provides Less, Who Will Provide More?* London: Biteback Publishing, 2017.

Noel, Thomas J. *Guide to Colorado Historic Places*. Boulder, CO: Westcliff Publishers, 2006.

Nollen, Scott Allen. *Abbott and Costello on the Home Front: A Critical Study of the Wartime Films*. Jefferson, NC: McFarland, 2009.

Nünlist, René. *Time in Ancient Greek Literature: Studies in Ancient Greek Narrative*, edited by Irene de Jong and René Nünlist. Boston: E. J. Brill, 2007.

O'Brien, Tim. *Dick Kinzel: Roller Coaster King of Cedar Point Amusement Park*. Nashville: Casa Flamingo Literary Arts, 2015.

O'Keefe, John. *Recollections of the Life of John O'Keefe*. Vol. 2. London: Henry Colburn, 1826.

Old York Road Historical Society. *Willow Grove Park*. Charleston, SC: Arcadia Publishing, 2005.

Ordericus Vitalis. *The Ecclesiastical History of England and Normandy*, translated by Thomas Forester. Vol. 6. London: Henry G. Bohn, 1856.

Ostwald, Michael J. "Amusement Park." In *A–F*. Vol. 1 of *Encyclopedia of Twentieth Century Architecture*, edited by R. Stephen Sennott. New York: Fitzroy Dearborn, 2004.

———. "Identity Tourism, Virtuality and the Theme Park." In *Virtual Globalization: Virtual Spaces/Tourist Spaces*, edited by David Holmes. London: Routledge, 2001.

Oxfeldt, Elisabeth. *Nordic Orientalism: Paris and Cosmopolitan Imagination 1800–1900*. Copenhagen: Museum Tusculanum Press, University of Copenhagen, 2005.

"Pan-American Exposition." In *The Pennsylvania School Journal*. Vol. 50, edited by N. C. Schaeffer. Lancaster, PA: Wickersham, 1901.

Panciroli, Guido. *The History of Many Memorable Things Lost, Which Were in Use Among the Ancients: And an Account of Many Excellent Things Found, Now in Use Among the Moderns, Both Natural and Artificial*, translated and annotated by Henricus Salmuth. Vol. 1. London: John Nicholson, 1715.

Parascandola, Louis J., and John Parascandola, eds. *A Coney Island Reader: Through Dizzy Gates of Illusion*. New York: Columbia University Press, 2015.

Pardon, George Frederick. *Porter's Guide to Blackpool*. Blackpool, UK: William Porter, 1857.

Pasko, W. W., ed. *Old New York: A Journal Relating to the History and Antiquities of New York City*. Vol. 2. New York: W. W. Pasko, 1890.

Pattison, George. "Kierkegaard and Copenhagen." In *The Oxford Handbook of Kierkegaard*, edited by John Lippitt and George Pattison. Oxford, UK: Oxford University Press, 2013.

———. *Kierkegaard, Religion, and the Nineteenth-Century Crisis of Culture*. Cambridge, UK: Cambridge University Press, 2002.

———. *Poor Paris!: Kierkegaard's Critique of the Spectacular City*. Berlin: Walter de Gruyter, 1999.

Peiss, Kathy. *Cheap Amusements: Working Women and Leisure in Turn-of-the-Century New York*. Philadelphia: Temple University Press, 1986.

Pepys, Samuel. *The Diary of Samuel Pepys*, edited by Henry B. Wheatley. Vol. 2. Boston: C. T. Brainard, 1893.

Pérez-Álvarez, Eliseo. *A Vexing Gadfly: The Late Kierkegaard on Economic Matters*. Eugene, OR: Pickwick Publications, 2009.

Perkins, Eli. "Bible Knowledge in Mauch Chunk." In *Library of Wit and Humor by Mark Twain and Others*. Chicago: J. M. Foutz, 1898.

Peter, Birgit. "Between Tradition and a Longing for the Modern: Theater in Interwar Vienna," In *Interwar Vienna: Culture Between Tradition and Modernity*, edited by Deborah Holmes and Lisa Silverman, 161–174. Rochester, NY: Camden House, 2009.

Petersen, G. Biilmann. "Tivoli." In *The Architecture of Denmark*. Oxford, UK: The Architectural Press, 1949.

Petroski, Henry. *Remaking the World: Adventures in Engineering*. New York: Alfred A. Knopf, 1997.

Pezza, Kelly Sullivan. *Murder at Rocky Point Park: Tragedy in Rhode Island's Summer Paradise*. Charleston, SC: The History Press, 2014.

Phalen, William J. *Coney Island: 150 Years of Rides, Fires, Floods, the Rich, the Poor, and Finally Robert Moses*. Jefferson, NC: MacFarland, 2016.

Pharris, Kevin. *Riding Denver's Rails: A Mile-High Streetcar History*. Charleston, SC: The History Press, 2013.

Pierce, Todd James. *Three Years in Wonderland: The Disney Brothers, C. V. Wood, and the Making of the Great American Theme Park*. Jackson, MS: University Press of Mississippi, 2016.

Pilat, Oliver, and Jo Ranson. *Sodom by the Sea: An Affectionate History of Coney Island*. Garden City, NY: Doubleday, Doran, 1941.

Pirtle, Carol. *Escape Betwixt Two Suns: A True Tale of the Underground Railroad in Illinois*. Carbondale and Edwardsville, IL: Southern Illinois University Press, 2000.

Platner, Samuel Ball, and Thomas Ashby. *A Topographical Dictionary of Ancient Rome*. London: Oxford University Press, 1929.

Prentice, Claire. *The Lost Tribe of Coney Island: Headhunters, Luna Park, and the Man Who Pulled Off the Spectacle of the Century*. New York: Amazon Publishing, 2014.

Preston, Katherine. *Scott Joplin*. Los Angeles: Melrose Square, 1989.

Pursell, Carroll. *From Playgrounds to PlayStation: The Interaction of Technology and Play*. Baltimore: John Hopkins University Press, 2015.

Rabinovitz, Lauren. *Electric Dreamland: Amusement Parks, Movies, and American Modernity*. New York: Columbia University Press, 2012.

Ralph, Julian. *Harper's Chicago and the World's Fair*. New York: Harper & Brothers, 1893.

Register, Woody. *The Kid of Coney Island: Fred Thompson and the Rise of American Amusements*. New York: Oxford University Press, 2001.

Reick, Philipp. *"Labor Is Not a Commodity!": The Movement to Shorten the Workday in Late Nineteenth-Century Berlin and New York*. Frankfurt: Campus Verlag, 2016.

Reiss, Steven A. "Madison Square Garden." In *The Encyclopedia of New York City*, edited by Kenneth T. Jackson, 712. New Haven, CT: Yale University Press, 1995.

Rhodes, Jason. *Maryland's Amusement Parks*. Charleston, SC: Arcadia Publishing, 2005.

Riefenstahl, Leni. *Leni Riefenstahl: A Memoir*. New York: St. Martin's Press, 1992.

Roberts, Steve. *Bethesda and Chevy Chase*. Charleston, SC: Arcadia Publishing, 2016.

Robinson, David. *Chaplin: His Life and Art*. London: Collins, 1985.

Robinson, Judith Helm. "Chevy Chase." In *Washington at Home: An Illustrated History of Neighborhoods in the Nation's Capital*, edited by Kathryn Schneider Smith. Washington, DC: The Historical Society of Washington, DC, 1989.

Roman, James. *Chronicles of Old Los Angeles: Exploring the Devilish History of the City of the Angels*. New York: Museyon, 2015.

Roosevelt, Theodore. *Presidential Addresses and State Papers of Theodore Roosevelt*. Vol. 6. New York: Review of Reviews, 1910.

Rorer, Sarah Tyson Heston. *Home Candy Making*. Philadelphia: Arnold, 1889.

Ross, Peter. *A History of Long Island: From Its Earliest Settlement to the Present Time*. Vol. 1. New York: Lewis Publishing, 1902.

———. *A History of Long Island: From Its Earliest Settlement to the Present Time*. Vol. 3. New York: Lewis Publishing, 1902.

Roth, Joseph. *What I Saw: Reports from Berlin 1920–1933*, translated by Michael Hoffmann. New York: W. W. Norton, 2003.

Routledge, Robert. *Discoveries and Inventions of the Nineteenth Century*. 14th ed. London: George Routledge and Sons, 1905.

Rowsome, Frank. *The Birth of Electric Traction: The Extraordinary Life and Times of Inventor Frank Julian Sprague*. Edited by John L. Sprague. North Charleston, SC: CreateSpace Independent Publishing Platform, 2013.

Rushin, Steve. *The Caddie Was a Reindeer: And Other Tales of Extreme Recreation*. New York: Grove Press, 2004.

Russell, Lynda J. *Lake Compounce*. Charleston, SC: Arcadia Publishing, 2015.

Russell, Michael S. *The Chemistry of Fireworks*. Cambridge, UK: The Royal Society of Chemistry, 2000.

Rydell, Robert W. *All the World's a Fair: Visions of Empire at America's International Expositions, 1876–1916*. Chicago: University of Chicago Press, 1984.

Sale, Richard. *Copenhagen and Denmark*. Copenhagen: New Holland Publishers, 2007.

Sally, Lynn Kathleen. *Fighting the Flames: The Spectacular Performance of Fire at Coney Island*. New York: Routledge, 2006.

Samuelson, Dale, with Wendy Yegoiants. *The American Amusement Park*. St. Paul, MN: MBI Publishing, 2001.

Sante, Luc. *Low Life*. London: Granta Books, 1998.

Savile, Rev. Bourchier W. "The Rise of the Plantagenets." In *The Gentleman's Magazine and Historical Review*. Vol. 222. London: Bradbury, Evans, January–June 1867.

Sayers, Isabelle S. *Annie Oakley and Buffalo Bill's Wild West*. New York: Dover Publications, 1981.

Schafer, Mike. *Roller Coasters*. Osceola, WI: MBI Publishing, 1998.

Schenker, Heath. "Pleasure Gardens, Theme Parks, and the Picturesque." In *Theme Park Landscapes: Antecedents and Variations*, edited by Terence Young and Robert Riley. Washington, DC: Dumbarton Oaks Research Library and Collection, 2002.

Schnitzspahn, Karen L. *Jersey Food History: Victorian Feasts to Boardwalk Treats*. Charleston, SC: American Palate, 2012.

Schorske, Carl E. *Fin-de-Siècle Vienna: Politics and Culture*. New York: Vintage Books, 1980.

Sears, Robert. *An Illustrated Description of the Russian Empire*. New York: self-published, 1885.

Seyfried, Vincent. "Seaside." In *The Encyclopedia of New York City*, edited by Kenneth T. Jackson, 1057. New Haven, CT: Yale University Press, 1995.

Shilling, Donovan A. *Rochester's Marvels and Myths*. Rochester, NY: Pancoast Publishing, 2011.

Silverman, Stephen M. *Dancing on the Ceiling: Stanley Donen and His Movies*. New York: Alfred A. Knopf, 1996.

———. *The Fox That Got Away: The Last Days of the Zanuck Dynasty at Twentieth Century-Fox*. Secaucus, NJ: Lyle Stuart, 1988.

———. *Macy's Thanksgiving Day Parade: A New York City Holiday Tradition*. New York: Rizzoli, 2016.

———. *Public Spectacles*. New York: E. P. Dutton, 1981.

Simon, Bryant. *Boardwalk of Dreams: Atlantic City and the Fate of Urban America*. New York: Oxford University Press, 2004.

Sklar, Martin. *Dream It! Do It! My Half-Century Creating Disney's Magic Kingdoms*. New York: Disney Editions, 2013.

Skrabec, Quentin R. *William McKinley, Apostle of Protectionism*. New York: Algora Publishing, 2008.

———. *The World's Richest Neighborhood: How Pittsburgh's East Enders Forged American Industry*. New York: Algora Publishing, 2010.

Slide, Anthony. *The New Historical Dictionary of the American Film Industry*. New York: Routledge, 2013.

Smiley, Jerome C. *History of Denver*. Denver: The Denver Times, 1901.

Smith, James R. *San Francisco's Lost Landmarks*. Fresno, CA: Craven Street Books, 2005.

Snedden, Robert, and David West. *A Brief Illustrated History of Space Exploration*. North Mankato, MN: Capstone Press, 2017.

Snodgrass, Mary Ellen. *World Clothing and Fashion: An Encyclopedia of History, Culture, and Social Influence*. 2 vols. New York: Routledge, 2015.

Snyder-Grenier, Ellen M. *Brooklyn! An Illustrated History*. Philadelphia: Temple University Press, 1996.

Sobol, Julie Macfie, and Ken Sobol. *Lake Erie: A Pictorial History*. Erin, ON: Boston Mills Press, 2004.

Solomon, Professor. *Coney Island*. Baltimore: Top Hat Press, 1999.

Stargel, Cory, and Sarah Stargel. *Early Los Angeles County Attractions*. Charleston, SC: Arcadia Publishing, 2008.

Starr, Kevin. *California: A History*. New York: Modern Library, 2005.

———. *Inventing the Dream: California Through the Progressive Era*. New York: Oxford University Press, 1985.

Steele, William H., ed. *Revised Record of the Constitutional Convention of the State of New York: May 8, 1894, to September 29, 1894*. Vol. 5. Albany, NY: Argus, 1900.

Stewart, James B. *DisneyWar*. New York: Simon and Schuster, 2005.

Stockdale, Patricia Ann. *The Long Beach Pike: A Collection of Memories*. Lexington, KY: AmericaUSA Publishing, 2015.

Stockwell, Austin Parsons. *A History of the Town of Gravesend, N. Y.* Brooklyn, self-published, 1884.

Stone, May N. "Astor House." In *The Encyclopedia of New York City*, edited by Kenneth T. Jackson, 63. New Haven, CT: Yale University Press, 1995.

Stone, Wilbur Fiske, ed. *History of Colorado*, Vol. 4. Chicago: S. J. Clarke, 1919.

Strachan, Edward, and Roy Bolton. *Russia & Europe in the Nineteenth Century*. London: Sphinx Fine Art, 2008.

Summers, Festus P. *Johnson Newlon Camden*. New York: G. P. Putnam's Sons, 1937.

Summit, Roland. *Flying Horses Catalog*. No. 1. Rolling Hills, CA: Flying Horses, October 1970.

Surenne, Gabriel. *The New French Manual, and Traveller's Companion*. Edinburgh: Oliver & Boyd, 1826.

Svenvold, Mark. *Elmer McCurdy: The Misadventures in Life and Afterlife of an American Outlaw*. New York: Basic Books, 2003.

Sweetser, Moses Foster, and Simeon Ford. *How to Know New York*. Boston: Rand Avery, 1887.

Swett, Richard N. *Leadership by Design: Creating an Architecture of Trust*. Atlanta: Greenway Communications, 2005.

Tassinari, Fabrizio. *Why Europe Fears Its Neighbors*. Santa Barbara, CA: ABC-CLIO, 2009.

Taylor, Robert Lewis. *W. C. Fields: His Follies and Fortunes*. Garden City, NY: Doubleday, 1949.

Teachout, Terry. *Pops: A Life of Louis Armstrong*. New York: Houghton Mifflin Harcourt, 2009.

Thackeray, William Makepeace. *Vanity Fair*. New York: P. F. Collier and Son, 1917.

Thomas, Bob. *Building a Company: Roy O. Disney and the Creation of an Entertainment Empire*. New York: Hyperion, 1998.

Thomas, Joe. *A Synopsis of the History of Upper Moreland and Willow Grove*. Willow Grove, PA: Upper Moreland Historical Association, 2000.

Thornbury, Walter. *Old and New London: A Narrative of Its History, Its People, and Its Places*. New ed., Vol. 2. London: Cassell, 1892.

Throgmorton, Todd H., and Samantha K. Throgmorton. *Roller Coasters: United States and Canada*. 4th ed. Jefferson, NC: MacFarland, 2015.

Tompkins, Eugene, and Quincy Kilby. *The History of the Boston Theatre, 1854–1901*. Boston: Houghton Mifflin, 1908.

Trager, James. *The New York Chronology: The Ultimate Compendium of Events, People, and Anecdotes from the Dutch to the Present*. New York: Harper Resource, 2003.

Truffaut, François, and Helen G. Scott. *Hitchcock*. New York: Simon and Schuster, 1983.

Trusler, Rev. Dr. John. *The Works of William Hogarth*. London: Shakspeare Press, 1831.

Tymieniecka, Anna-Teresa, ed. *Poetics of the Elements in the Human Condition: Part 2 The Airy Elements in Poetic Imagination*. Berlin: Springer, 1988.

United States. Bureau of the Census. *General Statistics of Cities: 1915*. Washington, DC: Government Printing Office, 1916.

United States. Department of Housing and Urban Development, *Brooklyn, Steeplechase Amusement Park Construction and Operation: Environmental Impact Statement*, 1989.

United States. Department of the Treasury. "Classification of Wool." In *January–December 1900*. Vol. 3 of *Treasury Decisions Under Tariff and Navigation Laws, Etc.* Washington, DC: Government Printing Office, 1901.

United States. House of Representatives. *Subversive Influences in Riots, Looting, and Burning: Hearings Before the Committee of Un-American Activities.* 90th Cong. 2061 (1967) (testimony of Edward S. Montgomery). Washington, DC: U.S. Government Printing Office, 1967.

United States. Joint Committee on Ceremonies of the World's Columbian Commission and the World's Columbian Exposition. Joint Committee on Ceremonies. *Dedicatory and Opening Ceremonies of the World's Columbian Exposition.* Chicago: Stone, Kastler, & Painter, 1893.

United States. Third Circuit Court of Appeals. "L. A. Thompson Scenic Ry. Co. v. Chestnut Hill Casino Co., Limited, et al." In *United States Circuit Courts of Appeals Reports.* Vol. 62. Rochester, NY: Lawyers' Co-Operative Publishing, 1904.

Van Hoogstraten, Nicholas. *Lost Broadway Theatres.* New York: Princeton Architectural Press, 1991.

Van Rensselaer, M. G. "The Art of Gardening—An Historical Sketch." In *Garden and Forest: A Journal of Horticulture, Landscape Art, and Forestry.* Vol. 2, edited by Charles Sprague Sargent. New York: Garden and Forest Publishing, 1889.

"Vauxhall Gardens and Kennington Lane." In *Lambeth Part 1: South Bank and Vauxhall*, edited by Howard Roberts and Walter H. Godfrey. Vol. 23 of *Survey of London.* London: London County Council, 1951.

Veblen, Thorstein. *The Theory of the Leisure Class.* New York: Macmillan, 1899. Reprint, New York: Oxford University Press, 2009.

Von Gerstner, Franz Anton Ritter. *Early American Railroads.* Edited by Frederick C. Gamst. Translated by David J. Diephouse and John C. Dexter. Stanford, CA: Stanford University Press, 1997.

Von Sneidern, Maja-Lisa. *Savage Indignation: Colonial Discourse from Milton to Swift.* Newark, DE: University of Delaware Press, 2005.

Von Sternberg, Josef. *Fun in a Chinese Laundry.* Berkeley, CA: Mercury House, 1988.

Walford, Cornelius. *Fairs, Past and Present, A Chapter in the History of Commerce.* London: Elliot Stock, 1883.

Walford, Edward. "Pimlico," *Old and New London.* Vol. 5. London: Cassell, 1878.

Wallace, Mike. *Greater Gotham: A History of New York City from 1898 to 1919.* New York: Oxford University Press, 2017.

Walton, Peter. *Blackpool Tower: A History.* Gloucester, UK: Amberley Publishing, 2016.

Waltzer, Jim, and Tom Wilk. *Tales of South Jersey: Profiles and Personalities.* New Brunswick, NJ: Rutgers University Press, 2001.

Walzer, Tina, and Stephan Templ. *Unser Wien: "Arisierung" auf österreichisch.* Berlin: Aufbau-Verlag, 2001.

Weaver, Abraham E., ed. *A Standard History of Elkhart County Indiana.* Vol. 2. Chicago and New York: The American Historical Society, 1916.

Webb, Edward A. *The Records of St. Bartholomew's Priory and of the Church and Parish of St. Bartholomew's the Great, West Smithfield.* Vol. 1. London: Oxford University Press, 1921.

Weingardt, Richard G. *Circles in the Sky: The Life and Times of George Ferris.* Reston, VA: American Society of Civil Engineers, 2009.

Weinstein, Stephen. "Gravesend." In *The Encyclopedia of New York City*, edited by Kenneth T. Jackson, 501. New Haven, CT: Yale University Press, 1995.

Wenz, Phillip I.. *Santa's Village.* Charleston, SC: Arcadia Publishing, 2007.

Werrett, Simon. *Fireworks: Pyrotechnic Arts and Sciences in European History.* Chicago: University of Chicago Press, 2010.

Wertheim, Arthur Frank. *W. C. Fields from Burlesque and Vaudeville to Broadway: Becoming a Comedian.* New York: Palgrave Macmillan, 2014.

Wertheim, Arthur Frank, and Barbara Bair, eds. *The Papers of Will Rogers: From Vaudeville to Broadway.* Vol. 3, *September 1908–August 1915.* Norman, OK: University of Oklahoma Press, 2001.

Wescott, Deborah B. "The Inspiration for Sweet Success: A Portrait of Catherine S. Hershey, Wife of Milton S. Hershey." Masters thesis, Pennsylvania State University, 1998.

West, Maude I. *Irondequoit Story.* Irondequoit, NY: The Town of Irondequoit / Franklin Press, 1957.

Wheatley, Henry B. "Jenny's Whim," *London, Past and Present.* Vol. 2. London: John Murray, 1891.

Wheatley, Henry Benjamin, and Peter Cunningham. *London, Past and Present: Its History, Associations, and Traditions.* Vol. 3. London: J. Murray, 1891.

White, H. Loring. *Ragging It: Getting Ragtime into History (and Some History into Ragtime).* New York: iUniverse, 2005.

White, William. *History, Gazetteer, and Directory of the County of Hampshire, Including the Isle of Wight.* London, Simpkin, Marshall, 1878.

Whitenack, Pamela Cassidy. *Hersheypark.* Charleston, SC: Arcadia Publishing, 2006.

Whitman, Walt. *November Boughs.* Philadelphia: David McKay, 1888.

Whitney, William Dwight, and Benjamin E. Smith, eds. *The Century Dictionary: An Encyclopedic Lexicon of the English Language.* New York: Century, 1911.

Widmer, Mary Lou. *New Orleans in the Twenties.* Gretna, LA: Pelican Publishing, 1993.

Williams, Pat, with Jim Denney. *How to Be Like Walt: Capturing the Disney Magic Every Day of Your Life.* Deerfield Beach, FL: Health Communications, 2005.

Williamson, Leland M., Richard A. Foley, Henry H. Colclazer, Louis Nanna Megargee, Jay Henry Mowbray, and William R. Antisdel, eds. *Prominent and Progressive Pennsylvanians of the Nineteenth Century.* Vol. 1. Philadelphia: Record Publishing, 1898.

Wilson, James Grant, and John Fiske, eds. *Appletons' Cyclopaedia of American Biography.* New York: D. Appleton, 1889.

Wilson, Tom. *Remembering Galesburg.* Charleston, SC: The History Press, 2009.

Wilson, Victoria. *1907–1940.* Vol. 1 of *A Life of Barbara Stanwyck, Steel True.* New York: Simon & Schuster, 2013.

Wolcott, Victoria M. *Race, Riots, and Roller Coasters: The Struggle over Segregated Recreation in America.* Philadelphia: University of Pennsylvania Press, 2012.

Woollcott, Alexander. *The Story of Irving Berlin.* New York: Da Capo Press, 1925.

Workers of the Writers' Program of the Works Projects Administration in the State of Washington. *Washington: A Guide to the Evergreen State.* Portland, OR: Binsfords & Mort, 1941.

Wroth, Warwick William, and Arthur Edgar Wroth. *The London Pleasure Gardens of the Eighteenth Century.* London: Macmillan, 1896.

Zimiles, Murray. *Gilded Lions and Jeweled Horses: The Synagogue to the Carousel: Jewish Carving Traditions.* Waltham, MA: Brandeis University Press, 2007.

Abbott, Sam. "Payland—At the Beach." *Billboard*, June 24, 1950.

———. "Rides, Attractions Build Farm Gross." *Billboard*, April 7, 1956.

Adams-Volpe, Judith. "Ferris, George Washington Gale, Jr." *American National Biography Online*. American Council of Learned Studies, January 2002. http://oxfordindex.oup.com/view/10.1093/anb/9780198606697.article.1302643.

Agrawal, Nina. "It's a Retro Southern California Christmas as Santa's Village Opens." *Los Angeles Times*, December 2, 2016.

Allyn, Scott. "Memories of Crystal Beach: Of Vermilion's Famous Park from 1907 to 1962." Lorain, (OH) *Morning Journal*, August 5, 2007.

Andrews, William. "How Niagara Has Been Harnessed." *American Monthly Review of Reviews*, June 1901.

Anonymous. "5,000 Tots Makes Children's Hospital Benefit a Real Howling Success." *Denver Post*, July 26, 1908.

———. "AC Roars Thru Record Fourth." *Billboard*, July 20, 1946.

———. "Adolph Sutro Deranged." *New York Times*, February 8, 1898.

———. "Adolphus Busch Dies in Prussia." *New York Times*, October 11, 1913.

———. Advertisement for Coasting Through Switzerland. *Street Railway Review* 14. Chicago: Kenfield Publishing, 1904.

———. "Aerial Voyages." *Temple Bar: A London Magazine for Town and Country Readers*. Vol. 114. London: Richard Bentley and Son, May–August 1898.

———. "Aged Autoist Hurled to Death Over Bridge." *Brisbee (AZ) Daily Record*, September 14, 1920.

———. "Amusement for Street Railway Parks." *Street Railway Journal*, March 1902.

———. "Amusements." *New York Times*, June 26, 1888.

———. "Angus G. Wynne Jr.; Built Theme Parks." *New York Times*, March 14, 1979.

———. "Animated History in East Bronx's Freedomland Is Revealed in Preview." *New York Times*, April 29, 1960.

———. "Bad Accident at the Fair." *New York Times*, June 15, 1893.

———. "A Baronet Who Could Not Get a Wife." *Daily Telegraph*, June 17, 1893.

———. "Big Pleasure Park Planned." *Los Angeles Times*, April 23, 1922.

———. "Blackpool's Latest Novelty." Original publication unknown, 1895. Available on Lytham & St. Anne's website, http://www.amounderness.co.uk/great_wheel_blackpool_walter_bassett_interview_1895.html.

———. "The Boynton Bicycle Electric Railway." *Scientific American*, February 17, 1894.

———. "Burning of the American Museum." *New York Times*, July 14, 1865.

———. "Captain Boynton, The Hero of the Hour." London *Daily News*, April 5, 1875.

———. "Capt. Paul Boynton, Inventor, Is Dead." *New York Times*, April 20, 1924.

———. "Cawdery's Patent Steeplechase, Limited." *Saturday Review of Politics, Literature, Science and Art*, July 25, 1896.

———. "Cedar Point Outlines $6,000,000 Project." *Billboard*, April 11, 1960.

———. "A Circular Railway." San Francisco *Evening Bulletin*, November 11, 1884.

———. "Cleveland Greets the Greatest Man-Gull of the Era." *Cleveland Leader*, September 3, 1911.

———. "Coaster Kills 3 at Coney Island." *New York Times*, July 28, 1915.

———. "Coasting Through Switzerland." *Street Railway Review*, September 20, 1904.

———. "Coney Elephant Killed." *New York Times*, January 5, 1903.

———. "Coney Island." *Life*, August 22, 1949.

———. "Coney Island Civic Leader Found Dead in Car Crash." *New York Times*, October 30, 1964.

———. "Coney Swept by $1,500,000 Fire." *New York Times*, July 29, 1907.

———. "Czolgosz Is Rapidly Breaking Down and Appears to Be a Physical and Mental Wreck—Refuses to Talk." Buffalo (NY) *Courier*, September 9, 1901.

———. "David V. Waldron," obituary. Spokane (WA) *Spokesman-Review*, November 22, 1912.

———. "Days When McKane Ruled Gravesend." *Brooklyn Daily Eagle*, January 19, 1913.

———. "Death Claims 'Fred' Maier." *Los Angeles Times*, April 12, 1909.

———. "Defective Flyer Is Blamed for Death of Youth." *Erie (PA) Dispatch-Herald*, August 19, 1938.

———. "Disastrous Conflagration." New York *Sun*, July 14, 1865.

———. "Disneyland" listing, *TV Guide* (Detroit area edition), October 23–29, 1954.

———. "Disney Sues Firm Which Did Survey for Cedar Point Park." *Sandusky Register*, May 24, 1960.

———. "Divorce for Louis Stauch." *New York Times*, August 20, 1922.

———. "Dreamland-by-the-Sea." *New-York Daily Tribune*, May 15, 1904.

———. "Editor's Easy Chair." *Harper's New Monthly Magazine*, November 1853.

———. "Elmer S. Dundy Is Dead; Won a Fortune in Shows." *New York Times*, February 6, 1907.

———. "Euclid Beach Opening Skips Dancing, Bathing." *Cleveland Press*, April 14, 1947.

———. "The Evolution of the New York Hotel." *New York Times*, December 2, 1906.

———. "The Evolution of the Roller Coaster." *Tucson (AZ) Daily Citizen*, February 8, 1914.

———. "Fairs: The World of Already." *Time*, June 5, 1964.

———. "Fairyland of Yesterday and Tomorrow." *Popular Mechanics*, December 1954.

———. "The Feeling at Coney Island." *New York Times*, July 23, 1879.

———. "Feltman's Long a Coney Institution." *Brooklyn Eagle*, May 12, 1946.

———. "Fifty Thousand People Go Seek Amusement on a Sunday." *Washington Post*, August 13, 1905.

———. "Fire Destroys Paradise Park at Fort George." *Fire and Water Engineering*, June 25, 1913.

———. "Fire Wrecks Half of Palisades Park; 119 Persons Hurt." *New York Times*, August 14, 1944.

———. "Frederic Thompson, Show Builder, Dies." *New York Times*, June 7, 1919.

———. "Fun and Industry Flourish Side-by-Side." *Grand Prairie (TX) Daily News*, April 23, 1967.

———. "The Future of Coney Island." *New York Times*, May 8, 1894.

———. "G. A. Boeckling, Cedar Point Chief, Is Dead." Unidentified Ohio newspaper clipping, Harris-Elmore Public Library, Elmore, Ohio, July 25, 1931. http://www.ohiomemory.org/cdm/ref/collection/p267401coll13/id/1669.

——. "G. A. Boeckling's Death." *Sandusky Register*, July 25, 1931.

——. "General Metropolitan News: An Alleged Exposure of Paul Boyton's Sea Serpent Story." *Chicago Tribune*, December 23, 1888, p. 12.

——. "George A. Hamid Dead at 75; Ran Steel Pier in Atlantic City." *New York Times*, June 14, 1971.

——. "The Great Fire—Full Particulars of the Buildings Burnt—Names of the Sufferers." *New York Daily Tribune*, July 21, 1845, p. 2.

——. "The Great French Show; What the Present Visitors Can See. The Eiffel Tower and Edison's Exhibit—American Pictures Very Attractive—Other Matters." *New York Times*, May 19, 1889.

——. "Hamid, George A. Jr. 94," obituary. *Press of Atlantic City*, February 25, 2013.

——. "Hanged for Many Crimes." *San Francisco Call*, May 8, 1896.

——. "He Died for Ducats." *Anaconda (MT) Standard*, November 19, 1894.

——. "Herbert P. Schmeck, Vet Ride Man, Dies in Philadelphia." *Billboard*, November 3, 1956.

——. "H. G. Traver Dead; Designer of Rides." *New York Times*, September 27, 1961.

——. "How Capt. Young Built a Villa Above the Ocean at Atlantic City—Some of Its Oddities." *New York Times*, August 7, 1910.

——. "The Inauguration of Theodore Roosevelt." *Harper's Weekly*, September 21, 1901.

——. "In the 1950s, Kennywood Was a Blast (Sometimes Literally)." *Pittsburgh Post-Gazette*, October 7, 2015.

——. "Is This a Blackgang Ghost?" *Isle of Wight County Press*, August 15, 2008.

——. "James McKane Dead." *Brooklyn Daily Eagle*, October 18, 1913.

——. "John Philip Sousa, Bandleader, Dies in Hotel at Reading." *New York Times*, March 6, 1932.

——. "John Y. M'Kane, Ex-Boss of Coney Island, Dead." Philadelphia *Times*, September 6, 1899.

——. "John Y. M'Kane Is Dead." *New York Times*, September 6, 1899.

——. "Joseph M. Schenck, 82, Is Dead; A Pioneer in the Movie Industry." *New York Times*, October 23, 1961.

——. "A Jumbo House for Coney Island." *New York Times*, February 21, 1884.

——. "Lake Side: An Art Deco Masterpiece Struggles to Survive." *American Heritage*, July–August 1992.

——. "The Late Mr. Wombwell." *Illustrated London News*, December 7, 1850.

——. "L. A. Thompson of Coney Fame Dies." New York *Sun*, March 9, 1919.

——. "The Law Guarding Bathers." *New York Times*, February 28, 1885.

——. "Losses by the Fire." *New York Times*, May 17, 1894.

——. "Lost the Balloon, Wind Wrecks the Captive Airship at Jackson Park." *Chicago Daily Tribune*, July 10, 1893, p. 1.

——. "Lucy and Her Sisters." *Marmora (NJ) Shore News Today*, July 18, 2014.

——. "Luna Park—A Modern Amusement Wonder." *Omaha Bee*, May 8, 1904.

——. "Luna Park Closed." *New York Times*, August 14, 1944.

——. "Martin A. Couney, Incubator Doctor," obituary. *New York Times*, March 2, 1950.

——. "M. C. Illions Dies." *New York Times*, August 14, 1949.

——. "McKane's Remarkable Career." *New York Times*, February 16, 1894.

——. "Motorists Don't Make Socialists, They Say." *New York Times*, March 4, 1906.

——. "Mr. Corbin and the Jews." *New York Times*, July 23, 1879.

——. "News Briefs." *Brooklyn Daily Eagle*, July 30, 1915.

——. "The New York Crystal Palace." *Scientific American*, June 4, 1853.

——. "New-York Crystal Palace: A Famous Enterprise Recalled by the Death of Its Chief Promoter." *New York Times*, July 5, 1887.

——. "New York Excursionists Riot At Woodcliff." *Poughkeepsie (NY) Eagle*, August 11, 1941.

——. "New York Swept by Record Gale." *Spectator*, June 15, 1922.

——. "Niblo's Garden." *Gleason's Pictorial*, March 6, 1852.

——. "Nicholas M. Schenck, 87, Dead; Was Head of M-G-M and Loew's." *New York Times*, March 5, 1969.

——. "N.J. Law Prohibits Racial Discrimination." *Billboard*, December 25, 1948.

——. "Obituary: Abram Baker Amusement Park Owner." *Miami Herald*, July 3, 1994.

——. "Obituary: Gen. Tom Thumb." *New York Times*, July 16, 1883.

——. "Obituary Record: Asa G. Neville." *Pottery Glass & Brass Salesman*, December 6, 1917.

——. "Old King's Lynn Fairground Master's Work to Go Digital." *Lynn (UK) News*, November 18, 2013.

——. "On an Ostrich Farm." *Shepherdstown (WV) Register*, December 14, 1888.

——. "On This Day, May 28, 1887." *New York Times*, May 28, 2001.

——. "Oscar Wilde." New Orleans *Daily Picayune*, June 27, 1882.

——. "Our Crystal Palace." *Putnam's Monthly*, August 1853.

——. "P. A. B. Widener, Capitalist, Dies." *New York Times*, November 7, 1915.

——. "Page Pendleton Robinson, Jr., Obituary." *Ocala (FL) Star-Banner*, August 30, 2011.

——. "Parisian Manners." *Literary Gazette, or Journal of Belles Lettres, Arts, Politics, & c.*, August 23, 1817.

——. "Parker Beach Dies; Gave Park Its Spirit." *Akron (OH) Beacon Journal*.

——. "Penn-Jersey Spots Feature Acts and Bands Thru Holidays." *Billboard*, July 20, 1946.

——. "Peter Tilyou Arrested." New York *Sun*, June 29, 1887.

——. "Philadelphia Items." *Contractor*, July 15, 1892.

——. "The Players." *Midland Monthly Magazine*, June 1899.

——. "POP Attracts 750,000 Under One Ticket Plan." *Billboard*, July 18, 1960.

——. "President Kennedy Breaks Ground for U.S. Pavilion." *Fair News*, December 20, 1962.

——. "President's Condition." Washington (DC) *Evening Star*, September 6, 1901.

——. "The Prison for Bosses." *New York Times*, February 27, 1894.

——. "Ravine Flyer Is Condemned in Probe of Youth's Death." *Erie (PA) Daily Times*, August 19, 1938.

——. "Representative Sol Bloom Dies of Heart Attack at 78." *New York Times*, March 8, 1949.

——. "Roller Coaster Accidents." *San Francisco Chronicle*, August 26, 1999.

——. "Roller-Coaster Ride Brings Back Speech to Army Veteran Who Lost Voice in 1943." *New York Times*, August 12, 1948.

———. "Sailors' Queer Meeting." *New York Times*, May 11, 1902.

———. "Samuel Gumpertz Dies; Ran Ringling Empire." *Billboard*, July 5, 1952.

———. "The Sea Serpent Caught." *Chicago Tribune*, December 21, 1888, p. 11.

———. "The Secret of the Success and the Fame of Elitch's Gardens." *Denver Post*, August 14, 1898.

———. "A Small World." Talk of the Town. *New Yorker*, August 31, 1963.

———. "Spanish Fort Will Be Formally Opened on Sunday Night." New Orleans *Times-Picayune*, May 23, 1911.

———. "Steel Pier Gets Three New Owners Who Are Betting on Its Future." *New York Times*, January 17, 1973.

———. "Steel Pier Is Sold." *New York Times*, May 8, 1945.

———. "Storm Hits Crowded Ferris Wheel; Six Dead, 40 Hurt." Oneonta (NY) *Daily Star*, June 12, 1922.

———. "Stranger Than Fiction." Los Angeles *Examiner*, November 21, 1894.

———. "Sutro Baths." *Harper's Weekly*, September 8, 1894.

———. "Talkers and Lecturers." *Billboard*, April 7, 1917.

———. "Thompson's Gravity System for Rapid Transit in Towns and Cities." *Scientific American*, September 8, 1888.

———. "The Times's Exposure of McKane." *New York Times*, February 16, 1894.

———. "To Overcome M'Kaneism." *New York Times*, March 5, 1894.

———. Untitled article. *Amusement Business* 82, no. 2 (date unknown, 1970).

———. "Victims Paint Lurid Picture of Tragic Coaster Train Spill." *Omaha Bee*, July 24, 1930.

———. "Vienna's Big Playground." *New York Times*, March 3, 1893.

———. "When the Mob and Al Capone Came to Atlantic City for Some Strategic Planning." *Press of Atlantic City*, January 16, 2017.

———. "W. H. Reynolds, Builder, Dead at 63." *New York Times*, October 14, 1913.

———. "William N. Selig, Pioneer in Films." *New York Times*, July 17, 1948.

———. "Will of William L. Elkins." *New York Times*, November 15, 1905.

———. "Willow Grove Sold; Owners Plan Additions." *Billboard*, December 22, 1958.

———. "Women's Realm." *New-York Daily Tribune*, August 24, 1902.

———. "The Workingmen's Union: Continuation of the Grand Festival at Jones' Wood Second Day of the Demonstration. Fifty Thousand People in the Union, and a Good Share of Them at the Frolic." *New York Times*, May 31, 1865.

———. "Youth, 19, Leaps to Death from Ravine Flyer." Erie (PA) *Dispatch-Herald*, August 8, 1938.

———. "Zoo, Circus, Spectacle All in One…" *New York Times*, July 3, 1904.

Asbury, Herbert. "That Was New York: The Great Fire of 1835." *New Yorker*, August 2, 1930.

Asimov, Eric. "Warner LeRoy, Restaurant Impresario, Is Dead at 65." *New York Times*, February 24, 2001.

Associated Press. "100 Years Ago Today: Rockne & the Forward Pass Change Notre Dame Football Forever." November 1, 2013.

———. "Attendance Falls 2% in Past Year at Tokyo Disneyland, but Families Are Still Pouring In." April 7, 1993.

———. "Fred Ingersoll Is Found Dead." *Lincoln (NE) Star*, October 24, 1927.

———. "Randall Duell." December 7, 1992.

Baca, Marie C. "Ice Cream Treat Dodges Economic Chill." *Wall Street Journal*, July 29, 2010.

———. "Inside the Disney Parks." *Life*, March 30, 2018.

Baker, J. I. "Walt Disney: From Mickey to Magic Kingdom." *Life*, April 15, 2016.

Bagley, Pat. "Living History: Original Saltair Was a Wonder of the World." *Salt Lake Tribune*, July 9, 2012.

Barboza, David, and Brooks Barnes. "How China Won the Keys to Disney's Magic Kingdom." *New York Times*, June 14, 2016.

Barrell, John. "The English Pleasures of Vauxhall." London *Times Literary Supplement*, January 27, 2012.

Barron, James. "The Carousels of Yesteryear Right Next Door." *New York Times*, September 30, 1980.

———. "Last Mob at Maxwell's Plum Bids on Glass and Menagerie." *The New York Times*, January 13, 1989.

Beck, Dana. "Oaks Amusement Park, and Its Beginnings." Portland (OR) *Bee*, December 20, 2012.

Belcher, Horace G. "Old Rocky Point." *Rhode Island History* 8, no. 2 (April 1948).

Bellandi, Deanna. "On a Big Roll: Opening of Giant Dipper Draws Crowds to Mission Beach." *Los Angeles Times*, August 12, 1990.

Belser, Ann. "Kennywood Sold to Spanish Company." *Pittsburgh Post-Gazette*, December 12, 2007.

Berger, Jennifer. "Hersheypark Secrets and Fun Facts." Long Island (NY) *Newsday*, August 22, 2017.

Berman, Jay, and Sesar Carreno. "The Short Life of a Downtown Amusement Park." *Los Angeles Downtown News*, September 4, 2006.

Bixby, Stoddard C., and Michael R. Houdart. "Focus on History: 'Nucky' Johnson and the Tuckahoe Connection." *Gazette of Upper Township*, December 22, 2014.

Blitz, Matt. "The Man in the Balloon." *Popular Mechanics*, May 9, 2017.

Block, Alex Ben. "George Lucas Will Use Disney $4 Billion to Fund Education." *Hollywood Reporter*, October 31, 2012.

Bongartz, Roy. "The Chocolate Camelot." *American Heritage*, June 1973.

Borge, Victor. "Love Letter to a Garden." *Life*, June 23, 1961.

Boswell, Charles, and Lewis Thompson. "Big Wheel from Chicago." *Coronet*, September 1958.

Bradley, Eric. "Long Beach Council Moves Forward with Cyclone Racer Roller Coaster Proposal." Long Beach (CA) *Press-Telegram*, October 1, 2013.

Briener, David M. "The Cyclone." Designation List 206 LP-1636. Landmarks Preservation Commission July 12, 1988.

———. "The Wonder Wheel." Designation List 215 LP-1798. Landmarks Preservation Commission May 23, 1989.

Brouhard, Milt. "Liberty Bell Replica Proves Crack-Proof." *Los Angeles Times*, January 4, 1966.

Brown, Abram. "The Wild Ride of the Herschends: When Amusement Parks Are the Family Business." *Forbes*, May 26, 2016.

Brown, Curt. "Minnesota History: Tilt-A-Whirl Gives Faribault, Minn., a Historic Spin." Minneapolis *Star Tribune*, April 2, 2015.

Bruck, Connie. "The Monopolist." *New Yorker*, April 21, 2003.

Brush, Edward Hale. "Pan-American Midway." *North Adams (MA) Transcript*, June 17, 1901.

Bryant, William C. "A New Public Park." *New York Evening Post*, July 3, 1844.

Buchenau, Martin-Werner, and Joachim Hofer. "A Roller Coaster Tycoon's Last Ride." *Handelsblatt*, August 19, 2017.

Busch, Noel F. "The Giant Wheel." *Life*, October 13, 1947.

Buster, Antonio. "Talk of the Day." *Gibbons Stamp Weekly*, July 3, 1909.

Caen, Herb. "We'll Never Go There Anymore." *San Francisco Chronicle*, September 4, 1972.

Calder, Rich. "Zamperla Breaks Ground on New Coney Island Coaster, Another to Follow." *New York Post*, January 31, 2011.

Carlson, Michael. "Roy Disney Obituary." *Guardian*, December 17, 2009.

Carlson, Tom. "The Woman Behind Silver Dollar City." *Springfield (MO) News-Leader*, December 9, 2014.

Carroll, Charles. "New York in Summer." *Harper's New Monthly Magazine*, October 1878.

Carryl, Guy Wetmore. "Marvelous Coney Island." *Munsey's Magazine*, September 1901.

Cavendish, Richard. "London's Last Bartholomew Fair." *History Today* 55, no. 9 (September 2005).

Chawkins, Steve. "Marion Knott Montapert, Child of Knott's Berry Farm Founders, Dies at 92." *Los Angeles Times*, November 19, 2014.

Chew, Jonathan. "Star Wars Franchise Worth More Than Harry Potter and James Bond, Combined." *Fortune*, December 24, 2015.

The Chronicler. "Among Those Present." *Ohio Magazine*, July 1906.

Clark, Neil. "What Happened the Night the Crystal Palace Burnt Down?" *Express*, November 28, 2016.

Coates, Robert M. "It's the Illusion That Counts." *New Yorker*, May 8, 1954.

Cohn, Matt. "Welcome to the Jungle: The Forgotten Tale of Long Beach's Oceanfront Slum." *Long Beach Post*, October 23, 2013.

Cons. No. 15837. "Coney Island: The World's Greatest Play Ground As It Is Today." New York State Reformatory at Elmira *Summary*, July 4, 1908.

Cook, Bob. "Will Other Amusement Parks Follow Cedar Point As It Gets Into Youth Sports Business?" *Forbes*, April 12, 2016.

Corby, Jane. "Coney His Life and Hobby, 'Cyclone' His Greatest Thrill." *Brooklyn Daily Eagle*, April 20, 1947.

Crawford, Richard. "Ostriches Were an Exotic Attraction." *San Diego Union-Tribune*, June 25, 2010.

Crissey, Elwell. "New Thrills Defy Gravity." *Popular Science*, August 1927.

Cross, Harry. "Inventing the Forward Pass." *New York Times*, November 1, 1913.

Cuozzo, Steve. "This Is the Top Dog on Coney Island—And It's Not Nathan's." *New York Post*, April 16, 2017.

Cutler, Ed. "Passage to Modernity: *Leaves of Grass* and the 1853 Crystal Palace Exhibition in New York." *Walt Whitman Quarterly Review* 16, no. 2 (Fall 1998).

Dana, Charles A. "It Shall Not Be Brought to Naught." New York *Sun*, September 17, 1889.

Daniel, Douglass K. "The Greatest Show(man) on Earth." *Boys' Life*, January 2000.

Davidson, Jim. "George Ferris, Reinventing the Wheel in Pittsburgh." *Pittsburgh Press Sunday Magazine*, July 27, 1986.

DeAngelis, Martin. "Did a Vineland Man Invent Skee-Ball?" *Press of Atlantic City*, March 1, 2016.

De Botton, Alain. "Book Review: *Waves of Joy and Despair: The Lure of the Sea: Seaside in the Western World, 1740–1840.*" London *Independent*, April 9, 1994.

De Roos, Robert. "The Magic Worlds of Walt Disney." *National Geographic*, August 1963.

De Stael, Madame. "Description of the Prater, or Public Walk, Vienna." In *The Pocket Magazine of Classic and Polite Literature*. Vol. 1. London: John Arliss, 1818.

Disneyland. Public Relations Department. "Disneyland One Year Old," press release. July 18, 1956.

Dobson, Austin. "Old Vauxhall Gardens." In *Scribner's Magazine*. Vol. 5. New York: Charles Scribner's Sons, January–June 1889.

Dorman, David. "Former Six Flags Executives Purchase Clementon Park and Splash World," press release. Clementon Park & Splash World, November 21, 2011.

Dunn, Julie, and Margaret Jackson. "Elitch's Ticket: $170 Million." *Denver Post*, August 6, 2006.

Eades, Mark. "50 Years Ago Saturday, Pirates of the Caribbean Opened at Disneyland." *Orange County (CA) Register*, March 17, 2017.

Earnest, Leslie. "As Knott's Defined O.C., 'the Farm' Has Defined Them." *Los Angeles Times*, October 22, 1997.

Ellement, John. "Anthony A. Bernie, at Age 77; Helped Run Canobie Lake Park." *Boston Globe*, August 3, 2004.

Farr, Emma-Victoria. "JK Rowling: 10 Facts About the Writer." *Telegraph*, September 27, 2012.

Ferguson, Delancey. "A Miss Who Didn't Miss." *New York Times Sunday Book Review*, September 19, 1954.

Fernandez, Bob. "Board Member at Troubled Hershey Trust Resigns." Philadelphia *Inquirer*, July 12, 2016.

Fiorillo, Victor. "I Live My Job: Jack Morey of Morey's Piers in Wildwood." *Philadelphia*, May 25, 2017.

Flint, Peter B. "Walter Knott of Knott's Berry Farm Is Dead." *New York Times*, December 5, 1981.

Foulds, Richard A. "Bro. Boyton—The Fearless Frog Man." *Northern Light*, August 2012.

Francis, David W. "Cedar Point and the Characteristics of American Summer Resorts During the Gilded Age." *Hayes Historical Journal: Cedar Point* 7, no. 2 (Winter 1988).

Frank, Walt. "Lakemont Park Trying to Sell Off Some Rides." *Altoona (PA) Mirror*, November 14, 2017.

Fricker, Dan. "Dorney Park Is Sold: $48 Million Deal Completed After Months of Talks." Allentown (PA) *Morning Call*, July 22, 1992.

Garcia, Adrian D. "Elitch Gardens 'Not Going Away Anytime Soon,' Owner Says." *Denver News*, November 4, 2017.

Garin, Nina. "Wendy Crain Is the Giant Dipper's Faithful Caregiver." *San Diego Union-Tribune*, September 2, 2014.

Ghosh, Shreesha. "Horrific Accidents on Amusement Park Rides Highlights Need for Safety." *International Business Times*, August 26, 2017.

Gibson, Christine. "The Sweetest Place on Earth." *American Heritage*, August–September 2003.

Giuffo, John. "The World's Top Christmas Destinations." *Forbes*, December 5, 2011.

Glass, Dudley. "Tivoli Is Denmark's Model Fun-Fair." *New York Times*, August 26, 1962.

Goleman, Daniel. "Why Do People Crave the Experience?" *New York Times*, August 2, 1988.

Gordon, David. "Student Film Recalls Brooklyn by the Sea." *New York Times*, May 11, 1975.

Gorky, Maksim. "Coney Island." New York *Independent*, August 8, 1907.

Granger, Bill. "'You Must See This Fair.'" *Chicago Tribune*, September 17, 1995.

Grant, Cary. "Archie Leach." *Ladies' Home Journal*, March 1963.

Green, Ed. "Ed Hart Talks About Why the New and Improved Kentucky Kingdom Will Succeed." *Louisville Business First*, April 9, 2014.

Greenhouse, Steven. "Playing Disney in the Parisian Fields." *New York Times*, February 17, 1991.

Grossman, Ron. "Flashback: When the Dancing Never Stopped." *Chicago Tribune*, January 5, 2018.

———. "History of the Ferris Wheel; 1893's Was Taller Than the Navy Pier's." *Chicago Tribune*, May 15, 2016.

Gumz, Jondi. "Rare Inside Look at Family That Keeps Boardwalk Going." Santa Cruz (CA) *Sentinel*, June 10, 2007.

Gussin, Tony. "Tributes to 'Inspirational Inventor' and Watermouth Castle Owner Richard Haines, 75." *North Devon Gazette*, June 24, 2015.

Gussow, Seth. "Going Bump in the Night." *Automobile*, November 1997.

Gutierrez, Hector. "Lakeside Speedway Ends Racing." *Rocky Mountain News*, September 2, 1988.

Gwinn, Sherman. "What He Learned at 14 Helped Him 'Come Back' at 40." *American Magazine*, April 1927.

Hagerty, James R. "Is There Life After Jim Thorpe for Jim Thorpe, Pa.?" *Wall Street Journal*, July 21, 2010.

Hall, Carla. "Zoo to Display Lion Statues from Early L.A. Menagerie." *Los Angeles Times*, May 14, 2009.

Halperin, Jennie Rose. "A Little Scandal Goes a Long Way." *Columbia Spectator*, March 27, 2013.

Hardiman, Jim. "How It Began…Walter & Cordelia Knott's Date with Destiny," Knott's Berry Farm advertising supplement. *Los Angeles Times*, July 27, 1980.

Harris, Elmer Blaney. "The Day of Rest at Coney Island." *Everybody's Magazine*, July 1908.

Harrod, Horatia. "The Phantom's New Home: Coney Island." *Telegraph*, February 17, 2010.

Hartlaub, Peter. "The Screams Still Echo from SF's Great Roller Coaster." *San Francisco Chronicle*, May 20, 2017.

———. "Woodward's Gardens Comes to Life in Book." *San Francisco Chronicle*, October 30, 2012.

Hawthorne, Julian. "Some Novelties at Buffalo Fair." *Cosmopolitan*, September 1901.

Hellman, Geoffrey T. "Calligraphic Art." *New Yorker*, February 17, 1975.

Henry, Christine. "Paris: LVMH Conserve la Gestion du Jardin d'Acclimatation." *Le Parisien*, September 26, 2016.

Hingston, Sandy. "10 Things You Might Not Know About the 1876 Centennial Exhibition," *Philadelphia*, May 10, 2016.

———. "20 More Local Native American Place Names and What They Mean." *Philadelphia*, October 22, 2015.

Hirsch, Jerry. "He's Haunted by Classic Cyclone Coaster." *Orange County (CA) Register*, December 7, 1998.

Ho, Violette, H. P. "The Ferris Wheel, the World's Columbian Exposition of 1893, and the Display of American Superiority." *Inquiries Journal*, 2016.

Holmes, Kristen E. ""Serial Killers: Could H. H. Holmes Also Be Jack the Ripper?" *Philadelphia Inquirer*, September 6, 2015.

Hong, Tan Bee. "Australia's Hollywood." *New Straits Times*, January 26, 1992.

Hynd, Alan. "The Rise and Fall of Joseph Schenck." *Liberty*, June 28, 1941.

Inkersley, Arthur. "The California Alligator Ranch." *Overland Monthly*, December 1910.

Ireland, Doug. "King Novel Based on Canobie Lake Park." North Andover (MA) *Eagle-Tribune*, June 3, 2013.

Janega, James. "The Ferris Wheel (1893)." *Chicago Tribune*, October 24, 2013.

Jenkins, Stanley S. "Combined Dipping, Cooking, and Article-Holding Apparatus," Patent No. 1,706,491. Google Patents, March 26, 1929. https://patents.google.com/patent/US1706491A/en.

Johnson, Geoffrey. "Flashback: 'Buffalo Bill' Wowed Chicago with His 'Wild West' Shows." *Chicago Tribune*, February 23, 2017.

Johnston, Richard W. "The Carrousel." *Life*, August 27, 1951.

Jones, Finn-Olaf. "On the Edge of Copenhagen, a Place to Unwind." *New York Times*, July 29, 2007.

Kandall, Jonathan. "Lew Wasserman, 89, Is Dead; Last of Hollywood's Moguls." *New York Times*, June 4, 2002.

Kauffman, Reginald D. "Why Coney? A Study of the Wonderful Playground and the Men Who Made It." *Hampton's Magazine*, August 1909.

Keller, Ilana. "NJ Ranks First in Theme Parks. Is It the Most Entertaining State in America?" *Asbury Park (NJ) Press*, October 25, 2017.

Kelly, Robert A. "Dizzy Whirl." *Popular Mechanics*, September 1960.

Kennedy, Pagan. "Who Made That Ice-Cream Cone?" *New York Times Magazine*, May 31, 2013.

Kent, Bill. "The Horse Was in Charge." *New York Times*, May 4, 1997.

———. "A Spin into the Past." *New York Times*, June 25, 1995.

Keppel, Robert D., Joseph G. Weis, Katherine M. Brown, and Kristen Welch. "The Jack the Ripper Murders: A Modus Operandi and Signature Analysis of the 1888–1891 Whitechapel Murders." *Journal of Investigative Psychology and Offender Profiling* 2, no. 1 (January 2005).

Kerby, David Ferris. "The Writer's Calendar." *Editors*, January 6, 1923.

Killen, John. "Throwback Thursday: Portland's Jantzen Beach Amusement Park Kept Things Fun for Decades." *Oregonian*, July 23, 2015.

Kirby, Irwin. "Brothers Trained Steeplechase Boss." *Billboard*, July 20, 1959.

Klasey, Jack. "Who Invented the Ferris Wheel?" *American History Illustrated*, September–October 1993, pp. 60–63.

Klaw, Spencer. "All Safe, Gentlemen, All Safe." *American Heritage*, August–September 1978.

Kleiman, Joe. "Dubai Park and Resorts: Operationally Speaking." *InPark Magazine*, August 27, 2017.

Kobler, John. "The Pride of the Eden Musee." *New Yorker*, November 20, 1943.

Koch, Felix J. "Ho! For the Oldest American Railroad." *Railway Conductor*, October 1916.

Kogan, Rick. "Remembering Riverview Park, 50 Years Later." *Chicago Tribune*, June 25, 2017.

Korb, Michael. "The Collier Family Chronicles." *Gulfshore Life*, March 2014.

Kozlov, Vladimir. "Vladimir Putin Approves $4B 'Russian Disneyland.'" *Hollywood Reporter*, June 14, 2016.

Lafferty, J. V. "Building," Patent No. 268,503. Google Patents, December 5, 1882. https://patents.google.com/patent/US268503.

Lambert, Bruce. "C. V. Wood Jr., Who Pioneered Large Theme Parks, Is Dead at 71." *New York Times*, March 16, 2002.

Lambert, Marjie. "Changing Times at Florida Theme Parks Lure You into Other Worlds." *Miami Herald*, May 19, 2017.

Larsen, Eric. "Jersey Roots: The Man Who Built Six Flags Great Adventure." *Asbury Park Press*, June 27, 2014.

Lauer-Williams, Kathy. "Former Dorney Park Head to Be Remembered Saturday." Allentown (PA) *Morning Call*, November 14, 2014.

Lavender, Dave. "Camden Park Opens for 113th Season." Huntington (WV) *Herald-Dispatch*, April 28, 2016.

Lazo, Alejandro. "For Six Flags, Debt Squeeze Looms at Latest Hurdle." *Washington Post*, March 13, 2009.

Le Mitouard, Eric. "Paris: Huit Mois de Travaux Vont Transformer le Jardin d'Acclimatation." *Le Parisien*, August 21, 2017.

Leonard, Devin. "The Inside Story of How Disney Bought Lucasfilm—and Its Plans for *Star Wars*." Bloomberg, March 7, 2013. https://www.bloomberg.com/news/articles/2013-03-07/how-disney-bought-lucasfilm-and-its-plans-for-star-wars.

Levine, Arthur. "Merry-Go-Rounds: 10 of the Oldest Carousels in the USA." *USA Today*, March 22, 2017.

Lewis, Andy. "Hand-Drawn Disney Map Sets Auction Record." *Hollywood Reporter*, June 25, 2017.

Lewis, Randy. "Ice-Skating Star Has Link to Charlie Brown." *Los Angeles Times*, January 4, 1985.

Liff, Bob. "Wonder Wheel Owner Remembered." New York *Daily News*, November 22, 1999.

Lillingston, Leonard W. "A Gravity Steeplechase." *Royal Magazine*, September 1902, pp. 486–487.

Lincoln, Natalie Sumner. "Engraved Portraits of American Patriots, Made by Saint Memin in 1796–1810." In *Daughters of the American Revolution Magazine*. Vols. 48–49. New York: The National Society of the Daughters of the American Revolution, 1916.

Lindheim, Burton. "Irving Rosenthal, 77, Is Dead; Palisades Operator 37 Years." *New York Times*, December 29, 1973.

Lindsay, David. "Terror Bound." *American Heritage*, September 1998.

Luther, Claudia. "Virginia Knott Bender, 90; Eldest Child of Founders of Knott's Berry Farm." *Los Angeles Times*, June 14, 2003.

Lyman, Rick. "Deep-Fry, and Don't Forget the Stick." *New York Times*, June 24, 2007.

Lyon, Peter. "The Master Showman of Coney Island." *American Heritage*, June 1958.

MacDonald, Brady. "Disneyland Got Off to a Nightmare Start in 1955, But 'Walt's Folly' Quickly Won Over Fans." *Los Angeles Times*, July 17, 2015.

———. "What to Expect at China's Universal Studios Beijing." *Los Angeles Times*, February 23, 2015.

———. "The World's Best Theme Park Dark Ride Just Got Better." *Los Angeles Times*, April 4, 2016.

Mahler, Jonathan. "How the Coastline Became a Place to Put the Poor." *New York Times*, December 2, 2012.

Mai-Duc, Christine. "He Dreams of Famed Roller Coaster's Return." *Los Angeles Times*, March 25, 2014.

Manbeck, John A. "Historically Speaking: Coney Island Strongman, Just Another Side Show." *Brooklyn Eagle*, January 28, 2010.

Marks, Peter. "Hooray for Dollywood." *Washington Post*, July 16, 2016.

Marroquin, Art, Mark Eades, and Sarah Tully. "Oldest Disney Daughter Dies at 79; Helped Inspire Park." *Orange County (CA) Register*, November 20, 2013.

Martin, Claire. "Nostalgia Rides on at Lakeside." *Denver Post*, July 1, 2011.

Martin, Douglas. "Wonder Wheel, Humbuggery and Freud's Fascination." *New York Times*, June 16, 1987.

Martin, Hugo. "Putin Gives Blessing to Russian Theme Park Designed by North Hollywood Firm." *Los Angeles Times*, June 14, 2016.

Marum, Anna. "Commissioner Nick Fish Found the Jantzen Beach Carousel." *Oregonian*, July 21, 2015.

———. "Jantzen Beach Carousel Location Revealed: Now It Needs a Home." *Oregonian*, September 7, 2017.

Marzulli, John. "Woman Awarded $1.5 Million over Claim She Was Seriously Injured Riding Cyclone Roller Coaster in Coney Island." New York *Daily News*, March 30, 2015.

McCabe, Kevin. "The Battle to Integrate Palisades Amusement Park." *Social Science Docket*, Summer–Fall 2011.

McClaren, Stephen. "The Phantom Venice: Hunting for Frank Gehry in L.A.'s Strangest Neighborhood." *Guardian*, September 8, 2016.

McDonough, Doug. "Larson International Acquires Tilt-A-Whirl Manufacturer." *Plainview (TX) Herald*, January 25, 2011.

McKay, Gretchen. "A New Season Means New Eats at Kennywood Park." *Pittsburgh Post-Gazette*, May 6, 2017.

McKelvey, Wallace. "From the Foundation Up: Building an Atlantic City Institution—Throughout Its History, the Steel Pier Has Continued to Change." *Press of Atlantic City*, March 11, 2012.

———. "Longtime Steel Pier Owner George Hamid Jr. Dies at 94." *Press of Atlantic City*, February 24, 2013.

McNary, Dave. "Leonardo DiCaprio, Martin Scorsese Reunite for 'Devil in the White City.'" *Variety*, August 10, 2015.

Mello, Michael. "It's Still Jam, But It's No Longer Called Knott's." *Orange County (CA) Register*, March 5, 2013.

Mello, Michael, and Mark Eades. "Knott's Berry Farm Ride Creator Bud Hurlbut Dies." *Orange County (CA) Register*, January 6, 2011.

Mendoza, Monica. "Elitch Gardens Sold to Investor Group That Includes Kroenke." *Denver Business Journal*, June 5, 2015.

Meyers, Tom. "From the Archives: The Summer of '47—Melba Valle Takes a Stand at Palisades Amusement Park." *Fort Lee(NJ) Patch*, May 10, 2013.

Miller, Bryan. "Maxwell's Plum, a Symbol of '60s, Closes Doors." *New York Times*, July 11, 1988.

Miller, Michael. "Story of Saltwater Taffy No Stretch." *Press of Atlantic City*, May 29, 2008.

Moore, H. M. "Chicago Letter." *Christian Record*, July 29, 1886.

Moore, Jesse T., Jr. "Seeking a New Life: Blacks in Post–Civil War Colorado." *Journal of Negro History* 78, no. 3 (Summer 1993).

Moore, John. "Moore: Causey Resigns as Elitch Theatre Chief." *Denver Post*, August 30, 2007.

Moore, Rowan. "*Vauxhall Gardens: A History* by David E. Coke and Alan Borg—Review." *Guardian*, July 1, 2011.

Morgan, Brian. "Frederick Savage, I Presume." *Merry-Go-Roundup*, Summer 2014.

Morison, Elting E. "What Went Wrong with Disney's World's Fair." *American Heritage*, December 1983.

Morris, David Z. "Six Flags Pulls Down Confederate Flags." *Fortune*, August 18, 2017.

Munsey, Frank A. "The Annihilation of Space." *Munsey's Magazine*, October 1900.

Murphy, Doyle. "Lula Vourderis, 82-Year-Old Matriarch of Coney Island's Deno's Wonder Wheel Family, Will Be Honored This Week." New York *Daily News*, February 13, 2014.

Muther, Christopher. "The Unintentional Horror and Camp of the House on the Rock." *Boston Globe*, October 24, 2015.

Myers, Marc. "Palisades Park: Just a Memory." *New York Times*, September 13, 1981.

Naedele, Walter F. "Gertrude Brooks Hankin, 90, Interior Decorator." Philadelphia *Inquirer*, July 24, 2012.

Nash, Lyman M. "The Incredible Floating Man." *Boys' Life*, July 1960.

"The New Switchback Steeplechase." In *Strand Magazine*. Vol. 12. London: George Newnes, 1896.

Noble, Breana. "Hillsdale Dropout Becomes 'Father of the American Roller Coaster.'" *Collegian*, Hillsdale College, October 8, 2015.

Nordland, Rod. "Santa in Finland, Where Marketing Triumphs over Geography." *New York Times*, December 20, 2017.

Obejas, Achy. "L. Frank Baum—the Man Behind 'The Wizard of Oz'—Was Really the Man Behind the Curtain." *Chicago Tribune*, October 5, 2000.

O'Brien, Ken. "A Designer's Lifetime of Ups and Downs." *Chicago Tribune*, August 18, 1996.

O'Connell, Tom. "Tradition Plus Unusual Features Secure Top Spot at Coney Island for 53-Year-Old Steeplechase." *Billboard*, June 24, 1950.

Overfelt, Maggie. "A World (Fair) of Invention." *Money*, April 1, 2003.

Palicki, Martin. "Vekoma Rides Acquired by Sansei Technologies." *InPark Magazine*, March 30, 2018.

Parasie, Nicolas. "Theme Parks Begin to Sprout in Persian Gulf Countries." *Wall Street Journal*, August 22, 2016.

Paumgarten, Nick. "Jones Wood Foundry." *New Yorker*, February 25, 2013.

Pearce, Emily. "In the Land of Imagination." *Isle of Wight County Press*, July 12, 2013.

Pedicini, Sandra. "Steven Spielberg Likely Staying with Universal Parks Past 2017, Filming Indicates." *Orlando Sentinel*, February 12, 2016.

Phillips, B. J. "Here Comes Summer: Those Roller Rides in the Sky." *Time*, July 4, 1977.

Phillips, Helen Seeley. "John Brisben Walker—Dynamic Dreamer of Denver." publication unknown, n.d.

Pierceall, Kimberly. "Castle Park Creator, Bud Hurlbut, Dies at 92." *Riverside (CA) Press-Enterprise*, January 8, 2011.

Pierpont, Claudia Roth. "Bombshells." *New Yorker*, October 19, 2015.

Pitz, Marylynne. "Luna Park's Luminary: Entrepreneur/Roller Coaster Designer Deserves His Due." *Pittsburgh Post-Gazette*, September 1, 2008.

Plimpton, George. "American Thrills." *Popular Mechanics*, May 1989.

Pollak, Michael. "Peter Stuyvesant and the Fun-House Mirrors." *New York Times*, January 29, 2016.

Pope, John. "33 Vintage Pontchartrain Beach Photos of #throwbackthursday." New Orleans *Times-Picayune*, August 21, 2014.

———. "When Smoky Mary Was Queen of the Pontchartrain Railroad." New Orleans *Times-Picayune*, July 14, 2017.

Post, Kevin. "Piers Without Peer." *Press of Atlantic City*, January 30, 2010.

Potempa, Philip. "Offbeat: TV's 'Beverly Hillbillies' Helped Put Branson on the Map." Northwest Indiana *Times*, July 25, 2011.

Previti, Emily. "Steel Pier Timeline." *Press of Atlantic City*, August 3, 2011.

Price, Mark. "NC's Failed Theme Park 'Land of Oz' Is Reopening for Just 6 Days." *Charlotte Observer*, April 3, 2018.

Price, Mark J. "Local History: Chippewa Lake Park Owner Lived Childhood Dream." *Akron (OH) Beacon Journal*, July 27, 2014.

———. "Summit Beach Park, 'Akron's Fairyland of Pleasure.'" *Akron (OH) Beacon-Journal*, July 17, 2017.

Pringle, Henry F. "Business Is Business." *New Yorker*, April 30, 1932.

PR Newswire. "John Morrell Food Group Begins Partnership with Nathan's Famous." March 20, 2014.

Radow, Craig. "The Coney Island of Canarsie." *New York Times*, July 1, 2007.

Ralph, Julian. "Coney Island." *Scribner's Magazine*, July 1896.

Rasmussen, Cecilia. "L.A. Scene/The City Then and Now." *Los Angeles Times*, October 18, 1993.

———. "Reptile Farm Gave L.A. a Wild Time." *Los Angeles Times*, August 3, 1997.

Reardon, Patrick T. "Burnham Quote: Well, It May Be." *Chicago Tribune*, June 1, 1992.

———. "The World's Columbian Exhibition at the 'White City.'" *Chicago Tribune*, 2017.

Reich, Ronni. "Fete Paradiso Turns Governor's Island into a French Carnival of the Past." Newark *Star-Ledger*, August 30, 2013.

Reil, Maxwell. "Two Authors Write Book on the Redemption of Skee-Ball." *Press of Atlantic City*, February 20, 2017.

Reuters. "Robotic Dinosaurs at U.K. Theme Park Upgraded with Cognitive Software." November 15, 2016.

Reynolds, Eileen. "The Quaker Capitalist and the Chocolate Factory." *New Yorker*, October 18, 2010.

Reynolds, Jack. "I'm the Oldest Person in the World to Ride a Rollercoaster." *Guardian*, March 9, 2018.

Riding, Alan. "The Thrills Endure as Tivoli Turns 150." *New York Times*, August 8, 1993.

Ritzer, George. "The McDonaldization of Society." *Journal of American Culture* 6, no. 1 (Spring 1983).

Roberts, Sam. "Nathan's Famous, a Hot Dog Empire Built on Hard Work and Hype." *New York Times*, July 22, 2016.

Rocco, Michael. "Those Were the Days." Lansdale (PA) *Reporter*, June 30, 2002.

Roger, Glenn. "Alternative Ideas for High Yield Investors." *Forbes*, April 20, 2018.

Rosemeyer, Mary Lou. "New Chapter in Kennywood Entertainment History Is Announced," press release. December 11, 2007.

Ross, Harold. "Down to Coney." *The New Yorker*, June 23, 1928.

Rowling, J. K. Biography. "*Harry Potter and the Cursed Child: Part One. Showbill*," April 2018.

Royko, Mike. "Tossing of Dwarfs Raises Bigger Issue." *Chicago Daily News*, July 17, 1989.

Rubin, Judith. "Peanuts/Cedar Fair Deal Shows Snoopy Is Good for the Brand, Good for the Park." *InPark Magazine*, October 24, 2017.

Rupp, Rebecca. "The Sticky-Sweet Story of Cotton Candy." *National Geographic*, July 15, 2016. https://www.nationalgeographic.com/people-and-culture/food/the-plate/2016/07/the-sticky-sweet-history-of-cotton-candy/.

Russell, Gloria. "The Mysterious Murder of Little Maggie Sheffield." Pawcatuck (CT) *Westerly Sun*, December 14. 2014.

Rutherford, Scott. "Coney's Wonder Wheel Celebrates 90th Anniversary." *Amusement Today*, November 2010.

Sachs, Andrea. "Walt Disney World's Magic Kingdom, the Louvre, Are Tops in Visitorship Survey." *Washington Post*, June 25, 2018.

Safire, William. "Why Do They Shoot Horses?" *New York Times Magazine*, January 26, 1997.

Sanghani, Radhika. "André-Jacques Garnerin: A Profile of the First Parachutist." *Telegraph*, October 22, 2013.

Schaad, Jacob, Jr. "Atlantic City, Then and Now." *Shore News Today*, February 21, 2011.

Schmidt, Chuck. "The Myths Surrounding C. V. Wood's Disney Demise Have Been Out of This World." *Staten Island (NY) Advance*, September 28, 2015.

Schneider, Kate. "First Look at the World's Steepest Coaster the Takabisha." *Australian*, July 11, 2011.

Schonberg, Harold C. "Theater: 'The Streets of New York' at SoHo Rep." *New York Times*, June 30, 1981.

Schwendener, Martha. "Sacred Skills Thrive on a Merry-Go-Round." *New York Times*, October 5, 2007.

Scott, Mike. "The Bittersweet History of Lincoln Beach in New Orleans." New Orleans *Times-Picayune*, March 3, 2017.

Searles, William H. "The Ferris Wheel." *Journal of the Association of Engineering Societies* 12, no. 12 (December 1893).

Seldes, Gilbert. "Profiles: Mickey-Mouse Maker." *New Yorker*, December 19, 1931.

Sentinel Staff Report. "Santa Cruz Seaside Co. Announces Management Changes." Santa Cruz (CA) *Sentinel*, May 12, 2015.

Shepstone, Harold J. "A Woman's Zoo." *Wide World Magazine*, October 1898.

Silverman, Stephen M. "California Screamin': Disney's New Playground Is a Thrill Ride for Daredevil Teens." *New York Post*, May 8, 2001.

———. "Dubai's Theme Parks: The Most Elaborate Sandboxes on Earth?" *Chicago Tribune*, March 6, 2017.

———. "Glowing River and All, a Sneak Peek at Disney World's New Pandora—The World of Avatar." *Chicago Tribune*, April 19, 2017.

————. "Shanghai Disneyland May Be the Best Mousetrap on Earth." *Chicago Tribune*, June 15, 2016.

Snedden, Jeffrey. "Harry Traver Took Beaver County on Thriller Roller Coaster Ride." Beaver (PA) *Times*, May 24, 2016.

Snibbe, Kurt. "San Bernardino: Lytle Creek Had Own Gold Rush." Riverside (CA) *Press-Enterprise*, July 31, 2012.

Snyder, Carl. "Engineer Ferris and His Wheel." *American Monthly Review of Reviews*, September 1893.

Sparkes, Boyden R. "What Prohibition Did to Coney Island," *New-York Tribune*, July 3, 1921.

Sparling, Polly. "Lost Amusement Parks of the Hudson Valley." *Hudson Valley Magazine*, May 20, 2014.

Spikol, Liz. "A Thousand Words." *Philadelphia Weekly*, June 30, 2004.

Stacom, Don. "Wildcat at Lake Compounce in Bristol Gets Renovation, Won't Be Ready For Opening Day." Hartford (CT) *Courant*, May 4, 2017.

Steinberg, Jim. "Skypark at Santa's Village Expansion Approved by County Supervisors." San Bernardino (CA) *Sun*, July 11, 2017.

Stephens, Kay. "Lakemont Park Closes for the Summer." Altoona (PA) *Mirror*, March 22, 2017.

Stevenson, Beatrice L. "Working Girls' Life at Coney Island." *Yearbook of the Women's Municipal League*, November 1911.

Stewart, Martha. "Texas Corn Dogs." Martha Stewart, 2018. https://www.marthastewart.com/319041/texas-corn-dogs.

Stone, Samuel Mansfield. "Fishing on Lake Quassapaug." *Forest and Stream*, June 22, 1901.

Strausbaugh, John. "When Barnum Took Manhattan." *New York Times*, November 9, 2007.

Strickland, Daryl. "Cedar Fair Completes Knott's Deal." *Los Angeles Times*, December 30, 1997.

Sudhalter, Richard M. "Benny Goodman: An Interview with the King of Swing." *American Heritage*, October–November 1981.

Sweeney, Alexis. "Atlantic City." *Baltimore Sun*, 2017.

Swiatek, Jeff. "Family Feud Rattles Holiday World." *Indianapolis Star*, May 6, 2013.

Teale, Edwin W. "A Million Kids Ride Carretta's Steeds." *American Magazine*, March 1931.

Thompson, Frederic. "Amusing the Million." *Everybody's Magazine*, September 1908.

THR Staff. "How 'I Love Lucy' Dominated Ratings from Its Start." *Hollywood Reporter*, August 15, 2011.

Thursby, Keith. "Wendell 'Bud' Hurlbut Dies at 92; Designed, Built Attractions for Knott's Berry Farm." *Los Angeles Times*, January 18, 2011.

Times Staff Writer. "Red Skelton, TV and Film's Quintessential Clown, Dies." *Los Angeles Times*, September 18, 1997.

Turque, Bill. "In Chevy Chase, a Conundrum Spouts from Fountain Named After a Racist Senator." *Washington Post*, December 26, 2014.

United Press International. "Eddie Cantor Dead, Comedy Star Was 72." October 10, 1964.

————. "Grover Robbins, 59, Resort Developer." March 6, 1970.

————. "Old Fort to Be Made into Park." March 12, 1938.

United States. Department of the Interior. National Park Service. "Santa Cruz Beach Boardwalk Roller Coaster ('The Big Dipper') and Carousel." National Register of Historic Places Inventory—Nomination Form, October 15, 1984. James H. Carleton, historian.

United States. Patent Office. "Patents Granted February 25, 1890," *Official Gazette of the United States Patent Office*. Vol. 50. Washington, D.C.: Government Printing Office, 1890.

Uno. "Coney Island, N.Y." *Billboard*, July 20, 1946.

————. "Coney Island, New York." *Billboard*, July 19, 1947.

————. "Coney Island, N.Y." *Billboard*, September 10, 1955.

Urban, Sylvanus. "The Antiquities of Bartholomew Fair." *Gentleman's Magazine and Historical Review*. Vol. 206., London: John Henry and James Parker, 1859.

Variety Staff. "Harper Goff." *Variety*, April 6, 1993.

Waltzer, Jim. "When the Pier Was Young." *Atlantic City Weekly*, July 20, 2006.

Wanko, Lauren. "History of Skee-Ball Starts in New Jersey." NJTV News, March 21, 2017. https://www.njtvonline.org/news/video/history-skee-ball-starts-new-jersey/.

Washburn, Mark. "Service Friday for Artist Jack Pentes, Who Designed Land of Oz on Beech Mountain." *Charlotte Observer*, February 12, 2015.

Wayne, Frances. "White City—Triumph of Faith." *Denver Post*, May 24, 1908.

Weiss, L. O. "Caramels Considered Only a Fad; Hershey Switches to Chocolates." Orrville (OH) *Courier Crescent*, September 7, 1967.

Wells, John D. "The Story of an Eye-Witness to the Shooting of the President." *Collier's Weekly*, September, 21, 1901.

Whalen, Jill. "Knoebels Amusement Resort Marks 90 Years of Family Fun This Summer." Pottsville (PA) *Republican Herald*, May 8, 2016.

White, Frederick. "A Recollection of Elitch's Gardens." *Denver Post*, April 16, 1916.

Williams, Ethan. "Don't Look Down! Europe's Best Rip-Roaring Rollercoasters, by Ethan the Expert, Aged Ten." *Daily Mail*, April 5, 2018.

Williams, Janette. "Pasadena's Busch Gardens, a Historic Treasure Unearthed." *Pasadena Star-News*, April 24, 2010.

Zelker, James Zeke. "Remembering Dorney Park." Allentown (PA) *Morning Call*, July 29, 1992.

Zwingle, Erla. "Catherine the Great." *National Geographic*, September 1998.

FEATURE FILMS, DOCUMENTARIES, VIDEOS, PODCASTS, AND RECORDINGS

Anonymous. *Documentary of Milton S. Hershey*. 2010; Shutter Production. YouTube, https://www.youtube.com/watch?v=GvUdc_RgVEs.

————. "History Minute—The Great Saltair." 2014; Salt Lake City Television. YouTube, https://www.youtube.com/watch?v=6QTtTQnz25I.

Arbuckle, Roscoe. *Coney Island*. Directed and written by Roscoe Arbuckle. Performed by Roscoe Arbuckle and Buster Keaton. 1917; Los Angeles: Paramount Pictures.

Bettencourt, David. *You Must Be This Tall: The Story of Rocky Point*. Directed by David Bettencourt. 2007; Providence, RI: Midway Pictures.

Burns, Ric, dir. *American Experience*. Season 3, episode 11, "Coney Island." Directed by Ric Burns, written by Richard Snow. Aired February 4, 1991, on PBS.

Campbell, Scott. *America Screams*. Directed by Scott Campbell, written by Gary Kyriazi. 1977; Los Angeles: Cyclone Productions.

Chaplin, Charles. *The Circus*. Directed and written by Charles Chaplin. 1928; Los Angeles: United Artists.

Colt, Sarah, dir. *American Experience*. Season 27, episodes 8–9, "Walt Disney—Parts 1 and 2." Aired September 14–15, 2015, on PBS.

Cutietta, Nathan, and Joanna Skye. *Welcome Back Riders*. Directed by Nathan Cutietta and Joanna Skye, written by Nathan Cutietta et al. 2007; Los Angeles: Swashbuckler Studios.

Dudley, Craig Boyton. Oral History Archive, Coney Island History Project, 2017. https://www.coneyislandhistory.org/oral-history-archive/craig-boyton-dudley.

Edison, Thomas. *The Boarding School Girls*. Produced by Thomas Edison. 1905; West Orange, NJ: Thomas A. Edison Manufacturing.

Handwerker, Lloyd. *Famous Nathan*. Directed by Lloyd Handwerker. 2014; New York: Film Movement.

Hitchcock, Alfred. *Strangers on a Train*. Directed by Alfred Hitchcock, written by Raymond Chandler and Whitfield Cook, performed by Farley Granger and Robert Walker. 1951; Los Angeles: Warner Bros.

Kane, Larry, prod. *The Bulletin with Larry Kane*. "Steel Pier Remembered," Aired circa 1995 on KYW-TV (Philadelphia). YouTube, https://www.youtube.com/watch?v=3KEypuAeIL0.

Lehrman, Henry. *Kid Auto Races at Venice*. Directed and written by Henry Lehrman, performed by Charles Chaplin, produced by Mack Sennett. 1914; Los Angeles: Keystone Film.

Leslie, Jennifer, and Catherine Park. "Dolly Parton Shares Why She Doesn't Ride the Rides at Dollywood." Aired March 16, 2018, on 11Alive (Atlanta). https://www.11alive.com/article/entertainment/dolly-parton-shares-why-she-doesnt-ride-the-rides-at-dollywood/85-529224511.

Liban, David. *Ghosts of Elitch Theatre*. Directed and written by David Liban. 2008; Denver: Tinyfist Films.

Lindner, Ashley, and Kimrey Nicholson. *Sutro Baths: A Forgotten Landmark*. Written by Ashley Lindner and Kimrey Nicholson. 2011; San Francisco State University, Broadcast & Electronic Communication Arts Department.

Osgood, Charles. *CBS Sunday Morning*. "Almanac: Milton Hershey." Hosted by Charles Osgood. Aired September 13, 2015, on CBS.

Pennsylvania College of Technology. "Brian Knoebel of Knoebels Amusement Resort." September 3, 2015. YouTube.

Porter, Edwin S. *Coney Island at Night*. Directed by Edwin S. Porter, produced by Thomas Edison. 1905; West Orange, NJ: Thomas A. Edison Manufacturing.

———. *Rube and Mandy at Coney Island*. Directed by Edwin S. Porter, produced by Thomas Edison. 1903; West Orange, NJ: Thomas A. Edison Manufacturing.

Rubin, Ann. "1959 Ferris Wheel to Be 'Retired' from Santa Cruz Beach Boardwalk." Reported by Ann Rubin. Aired March 16, 2018, on KTVU (Santa Cruz).

Sennett, Mack. *Tillie's Punctured Romance*. Directed and produced by Mack Sennett, performed by Mabel Normand, Marie Dressler, and Charles Chaplin. 1914; Los Angeles: Keystone Film.

Sherman, Gregory V., and Jeffrey C. Sherman. *The Boys: The Sherman Brothers' Story*. Directed and produced by Gregory V. Sherman and Jeffrey C. Sherman. 2009; Los Angeles: Walt Disney Studios Motion Pictures.

Sklar, Marty. "E.P.C.O.T." Written by Marty Sklar. Promotional film. Filmed October 27, 1966.

Ucicky, Gustav. *Die Pratermizzi*. Directed by Gustav Ucicky, written by Walter Reisch, performed by Anny Ondra. 1926; Vienna: Sascha-Film.

Welles, Orson. *The Lady from Shanghai*. Directed and produced by Orson Welles, written by Orson Welles and Sherwood King, performed by Orson Welles and Rita Hayworth. 1947; Los Angeles: Columbia Pictures.

Wilde, Ted, dir. *Speedy*. Directed by Ted Wilde, performed by Harold Lloyd, commentary by Bruce Goldstein. 1928; New York: The Criterion Collection, 2015. DVD and Blu-ray.

WEBSITES

Allen, Louise. "So What Was Wrong with Ranelagh?" Jane Austen's London, May 8, 2016. https://janeaustenslondon.com/2016/05/08/so-what-was-wrong-with-ranelagh/.

Anonymous. "2013 Preservation Conference." American Coaster Enthusiasts. http://www.aceonline.org/fliers/PreservationCon2013.pdf.

———. "About Lake Compounce." Lake Compounce, 2016. https://www.lakecompounce.com/plan-a-visit/lake-compounce.

———. "About Us…Our History." North Pole, Home of Santa's Workshop, 2018. http://www.northpoleny.com/about-us.

———. "Absecon & Absecon Island," Atlantic County, NJ, Government, n.d. http://www.atlantic-county.org/history/absecon-island.asp.

———. "Activities." SantaPark Arctic World, n.d. https://santaparkarcticworld.com/santa-claus-secret-forest/Activities.

———. "Adolph Sutro (1830–1876)." American Jerusalem, 2018. http://www.americanjerusalem.com/characters/adolph-sutro-1830-ae-1898/19.

———. "Almanac: Atlantic City's Steel Pier." *Sunday Morning*, CBS News, June 18, 2017. https://www.cbsnews.com/news/almanac-atlantic-citys-steel-pier/.

———. "Attendance at Amusement and Theme Parks in North America by Facility." Statista.com, 2017. https://www.statista.com/statistics/194269/attendance-at-theme-and-amusement-parks-in-north-america-since-2010/.

———. "The B&B Carousell: Restoring a Piece of Coney Island's Past." Municipal Art Society of New York, April 7, 2009. https://mas.org.

———. "Bartholomew Fair." InsideGuide to London website, 2015.

———. "Bigger and Faster: Hershey Park's Comet Roller Coaster." Hershey Community Archives, June 8, 2010. https://blog.hersheyarchives.org/2010/06/08/bigger-and-faster-hershey-parks-comet-roller-coaster/.

———. "Birthplace of Frederick Savage." Engineering Timelines, 2017. http://www.engineering-timelines.com/scripts/engineeringItem.asp?id=791.

———. "Blackgang Chine." Atlas Obscura, 2017. https://www.atlasobscura.com/places/blackgang-chine-theme-park.

———. "Blackgang Chine." Wikipedia, n.d. https://en.wikipedia.org/wiki/Blackgang_Chine.

———. "A Brief History of Watermouth Castle." Watermouth Family Theme Park and Castle, 2017. https://www.watermouthcastle.com/about/history/.

———. "Brighton Beach." Our Brooklyn, Brooklyn Collection. Brooklyn Public Library, 2005. https://www.bklynlibrary.org/ourbrooklyn/brightonbeach/.

———. "Brothers from Brooklyn…" Feltman's of Coney Island, 2016. https://feltmansofconeyisland.com.

———. "Cedar Point's Hotel Breakers Celebrates Historical Milestone." Pointbuzz.com, March 5, 2005. https://pointbuzz.com/News/Story/536.

———. "Chapter 1—Elephant to Starboard." Lucy the Elephant, 2015. http://www.lucytheelephant.org/history/chapter-1-elephant-to-starboard/.

———. "Chapter 2 Kirsten Piil Kilde." Bakken, 2016. https://www.bakken.dk/om-os/bakkens-historie/bakkens-historie-kapitel-2/ (in Danish).

———. "Charles Feltman: Inventor of the Hot Dog," Coney Island History Project, 2017. https://www.coneyislandhistory.org/hall-of-fame/charles-feltman.

———. "Christian J. Tribini (Professor)." Dansk Film Database website, 1999. https://danskefilm.dk/skuespiller.php?id=984.

———. "Cliff House." San Francisco Public Library.org, 2002–2018. https://sfpl.org/?pg=2000119601.

———. "Colorado." National Park Service, 2018. https://www.nps.gov/state/co/index.htm?program=all.

———. "Corkscrew: Knott's Berry Farm." Ultimate Rollercoaster.com, 1996–2017. https://www.ultimaterollercoaster.com/coasters/knotts-corkscrew.

———. "Doodles, Drafts, and Designs: Industrial Drawings from the Smithsonian." Smithsonian Libraries, n.d. http://www.sil.si.edu/exhibitions/doodles/.

———. "Dubai Poised for Theme Park Boom." Oxford Business Group, February 29, 2016. https://oxfordbusinessgroup.com/news/dubai-poised-theme-park-boom.

———. "The Early History of Newspaper Publishing in New York State." New York State Library, University of the State of New York, 2009. http://www.nysl.nysed.gov/nysnp/history.htm.

———. "Early Southern California Amusement Parks." Water and Power Associates, n.d. http://waterandpower.org/museum/Early_Southern_California_Amusement_Parks_Page_1.html.

———. "Early Views of Mt. Lowe Railway." Water and Power Associates, n.d. http://waterandpower.org/museum/Mt_Lowe_Railway.html.

———. "Elmer Scipio Dundy." Dundy County Nebraska Genealogy Trails, 2008. http://genealogytrails.com/neb/dundy/bios/esdundy.html.

———. "Expo 1889 Paris." Bureau International des Expositions, n.d. https://www.bie-paris.org/site/en/blog/blogger/bie.

———. "Ferris Wheel Inventor Historical Marker." ExplorePAhistory.com, 2011. http://explorepahistory.com/hmarker.php?markerId=1-A-35D.

———. "Flying Horses Carousel." Martha's Vineyard Preservation Trust, 2017. http://mvpreservation.org/properties/flying-horses-carousel/.

———. "Frank Charles Bostock (1866–1912)." National Fairground and Circus Archive, University of Sheffield, 2017. https://www.sheffield.ac.uk/nfca/projects/frankbostockbio.

———. "Frequently Asked Questions About ACE." American Coaster Enthusiasts website, 2007–2016. http://www.aceonline.org/aboutACE/.

———. "Giant Dipper Roller Coaster." Santa Cruz Beach Boardwalk, 2018. https://beachboardwalk.com/Giant-Dipper.

———. "Girl at Blackgang Chine." Myths, 2017. https://www.spookythings.iofw.co.uk/?page_id=241.

———. "Global Amusement Park Market 2018 Size, Share, Growth, Trends, Type, Applications, Analysis, and Forecast by 2025." AB Newswire, July 30, 2018. http://www.abnewswire.com/pressreleases/global-amusement-parks-market-2018-size-share-growth-trends-type-application-analysis-and-forecast-by-2025_247236.html.

———. "Grave of Elmer McCurdy." Atlas Obscura, n.d. https://www.atlasobscura.com/places/grave-elmer-mccurdy-skb.

———. "Group Honored for Saving World's Oldest Carousel." The Local (Stockholm), November 11, 2010. https://www.thelocal.de/20101111/31093.

———. "Hans Christian Lumbye (1810–1874)." The Johann Strauss Society of Great Britain, 2017. http://www.johann-strauss.org.uk/composers-a-m.php?id=182.

———. "Heard on Campus: Michael DelGrosso of DelGrosso Foods." Penn State News, Pennsylvania State University, October 23, 2015. https://news.psu.edu/story/376887/2015/10/22/heard-campus-michael-delgrosso-delgrosso-foods.

———. "Hiram Maxim: Machine Guns." Who Made America?, They Made America, PBS, 2004. http://www.pbs.org/wgbh/theymadeamerica/whomade/maxim_lo.html.

———. "History." Belmont Park, n.d. https://www.belmontpark.com/companyinfo/.

———. "History: Decades of Family Fun." Seabreeze, 2018. https://seabreeze.com/about/history/.

———. "History of Blackgang Chine." Blackgang Chine, 2008. https://blackgangchine.com/history-of-blackgang-chine/.

———. "The History of Fralinger's Salt Water Taffy." James Candy Company, 2017. https://www.jamescandy.com/our-history/fralingers/.

———. "History of Medicine: The Incubator Babies of Coney Island." Columbia University Department of Surgery, Columbia University Medical Center, August 6, 2015. http://columbiasurgery.org/news/2015/08/06/history-medicine-incubator-babies-coney-island.

———. "History of the Buffalo Bill Center of the West." Buffalo Bill Center of the West, 2017. https://centerofthewest.org/about-us/history/.

———. "The History of the Ice Cream Cone." International Dairy Foods Association, 2018. https://www.idfa.org/news-views/media-kits/ice-cream/the-history-of-the-ice-cream-cone.

———. "The History of the Vienna Prater (from 1766)." Prater, 2016. https://www.praterwien.com/en/prater/fun-in-vienna/history/.

———. "Huguenot History." The Huguenot Society of America website, n.d. http://huguenotsocietyofamerica.org/?page=Huguenot-History.

———. "Investigation of the Elitch Theater." Rocky Mountain Paranormal Research Society, July 28, 2006. https://rockymountainparanormal.com/elitch.html.

———. "John Miller." Lemelson-MIT, Massachusetts Institute of Technology, n.d. http://lemelson.mit.edu/resources/john-miller.

———. "Knoebels." WVIA Public Media, n.d. http://www.wvia.org/television/documentaries/knoebels/.

———. "Knoebels Carousel & Organ History." Knoebels, 2018. https://www.knoebels.com/history/knoebels-carousel-organ-history.

———. "Knoebels Timeline 1775–2018." Knoebels, 2018. https://www.knoebels.com/history/knoebels-timeline.

———. "Lady Deborah Moody." The National Society of Colonial Dames in the State of New York, July 2, 2015. Available at Archive Today, http://archive.is/VLcOB.

———. "Lady Deborah Moody, a Dangerous Woman, Comes to New England." New England Historical Society, January 5, 2016. http://www.newenglandhistoricalsociety.com/lady-deborah-moody-a-dangerous-woman-comes-to-new-england/.

———. "La Galerie des Glaces." Château de Versailles, n.d. http://www.chateauversailles.fr/decouvrir/domaine/chateau/galerie-glaces#le-salon-de-la-paix (in French).

———. "Lancaster Caramel Company." Hershey Community Archives, n.d. http://www.hersheyarchives.org/essay/details.aspx?EssayId=43.

———. "Lost Amusement Parks—Pennsylvania." National Amusement Park Historical Association. http://lostamusementparks.napha.org/pennsylvania-parks.html.

———. "Luna Park, Coney Island." Brooklyn Museum, n.d. https://www.brooklynmuseum.org/opencollection/objects/181511.

———. "Margaret Virginia Daugherty [sic]." Geni, November 23, 2016. https://www.geni.com/people/Margaret-Daugherty/6000000011428345050.

———. "Marvel Cave." Silver Dollar City, 2018. https://www.silverdollarcity.com/theme-park/Attractions/Rides/Marvel-Cave.

———. "Milton Hershey Biography." Biography.com, A&E Television Networks, April 27, 2017. https://www.biography.com/people/milton-hershey-9337133.

———. "Moving Sidewalk." Chicagology, 2017. https://chicagology.com/columbiaexpo/fair030/.

———. "New Hampshire Robber Baron." New England Historical Society website, 2016. http://www.newenglandhistoricalsociety.com/austin-corbin-robber-baron-new-hampshire-part-hog-part-shark/; http://www.newenglandhistoricalsociety.com/new-hampshire-robber-baron-we-do-not-like-the-jews/.

———. "No More Free Soda for All Lake Compounce Guests." NBC Connecticut, November 10, 2017. https://www.nbcconnecticut.com/news/local/No-More-Free-Soda-For-All-Lake-Compounce-Guests-456681243.html.

———. "Oldest Amusement Park in Operation." Guinness World Records website, 2016. http://www.guinnessworldrecords.com/world-records/oldest-amusement-park-in-operation.

———. "Old-Fashioned Chicken Dinner Will Drive You Absolutely Knott's." All Business Journal, September 13, 2013. http://www.allbusinessjournal.com/2013/09/13/old-fashioned-chicken-dinner-will-drive-you-absolutely-knotts/.

———. "The Origins of Jim Crow." Jim Crow Museum of Racist Memorabilia, Ferris State University, n.d. https://ferris.edu/jimcrow/origins.htm.

———. "Our History." Tivoli, 2017. https://www.tivoligardens.com/en/om/tivolis+historie.

———. "Our Parks." Parques Reunidos, 2018. https://www.parquesreunidos.com/en/global-operator/our-parks/.

———. "Park History." Elitch Gardens. https://www.elitchgardens.com/plan-a-visit/park-history/.

———. "Park History Timeline." Dorney Park & Wildwater Kingdom, Cedar Fair Entertainment, 2018. https://www.dorneypark.com/media-center.

———. "Pierre Jacques Onésyme Bergeret de Grancourt (Biographical Details)." The British Museum, 2017. http://www.britishmuseum.org/research/search_the_collection_database/term_details.aspx?bioId=25526.

———. "Quassy: One of the Last of the Old-Time Trolley Parks." ConnecticutHistory.org, Connecticut Humanities, n.d. https://connecticuthistory.org/quassy-one-of-the-last-of-the-old-time-trolley-parks/.

———. "The Real Voices Behind Milli Vanilli Share Their Side of the Lip Synching Scandal (Video)." HuffPost, February 27, 2014. https://www.huffingtonpost.com/2014/02/27/milli-vanilli_n_4860222.html.

———. "Rocky Point: A Cultural Heritage." The Rocky Point Foundation, n.d. https://rockypointfoundation.org/saga.

———. "Rutschebanen." Bakken, 2016. https://www.bakken.dk/forlystelser/alle-forlystelser/rutschebanen/. (In Danish).

———. "Samuel Fraunces." Fraunces Tavern Museum, Sons of the Revolution in the State of New York, 2002–2016. http://www.frauncestavernmuseum.org/samuel-fraunces/.

———. "Samuel Gumpertz House." Sarasota History Alive! 2007–2017. http://www.sarasotahistoryalive.com/history/postcards/samuel-gumpertz-house/.

———. "Sans Souci Amusement Park." Chicagology, 2017.

———. "Santa Monica History." Santa Monica History Museum, 2011. https://santamonicahistory.org/santa-monica-history/.

———. "Santa's Village History." Santa's Village Azoosment Park, 2018. https://santasvillagedundee.com/about-us/history/.

———. "Sir Hiram Maxim's Captive Flying Machines." Atlas Obscura, 2018. https://www.atlasobscura.com/places/sir-hiram-maxims-captive-flying-machines.

———. "'Spending a Penny': Or the First Public Flushing Toilets Open on This Day in 1852." The Victorianist, February 2, 2011. http://thevictorianist.blogspot.com/2011/02/spending-penny-or-first-public-flushing.html.

———. "Splish! Splash! At the Chutes." San Francisco Public Library, 2002–2018. https://sfpl.org/?pg=2000131701.

———. "Sutro Baths." San Francisco Public Library, 2002–2018. https://sfpl.org/?pg=2000131301.

———. "Switchback Rollercoaster." ZDT's Amusement Park, 2018.

——. "Theme Park Results Show Strong Results in 2017, and Museums Continue to Grow," AECOM, 2018. https://www.aecom.com/theme-index/.

——. "The Thrill of Rosa." Ferrari World, Ferrari World Abu Dubai, 2014.

——. "The Tilt-A-Whirl." Larson International, n.d. http://larsonintl.com/the-tilt-a-whirl/.

——. "Venice of America: Jeffrey Stanton." KCET, March 24, 2010. https://www.kcet.org/shows/departures/venice-of-america-jeffrey-stanton.

——. "Westinghouse Electric Corporation [Science and Invention] Historical Marker." ExplorePAhistory.com, 2011. http://explorepahistory.com/hmarker.php?markerId=1-A-3A0.

——. "What Are 'Crystal Palace Dinosaurs'?" Friends of Crystal Palace Dinosaurs, 2017. http://cpdinosaurs.org/what-are-crystal-palace-dinosaurs/.

——. "What Happened to the Widener Fortune?" Lynnewood Hall website, July 6, 2014. https://lynnewoodhall.wordpress.com/2014/07/06/what-happened-to-the-widener-fortune/.

——. "Who's Behind the Chinese Takeover of World's Biggest Pork Producer?" *PBS NewsHour*, September 12, 2014. https://www.pbs.org/newshour/show/whos-behind-chinese-takeover-worlds-biggest-pork-producer.

——. "Who We Are." SantaPark Arctic World, n.d. https://santaparkarcticworld.com/who-we-are.

——. "William J. Morrison (1860–1926): Co-Inventor of the Cotton Candy Machine." *Journal of the History of Dentistry* 53, no. 2 (July 2005). Abstract available at https://www.ncbi.nlm.nih.gov/pubmed/16092607.

——. "Wonders of the 1893 World's Fair." The Field Museum, Chicago History Museum, 2013. http://worldsfair.fieldmuseum.org.

——. "Woodside Park Dentzel Carousel." Please Touch Museum website, 2017. https://www.pleasetouchmuseum.org/pageblocks/explore-carousel/.

Apmann, Sarah Bean. "East 11th Street, a Slice of East Village History." Off the Grid, August 10, 2016. http://gvshp.org/blog/2016/08/10/east-11th-street-a-slice-of-east-village-history/.

Attanasio, Edmund. "Restored Yerba Buena Gardens Carousel Spins Again," Yerba Buena, July 2, 2014. http://visityerbabuena.org/stories/restored-yerba-buena-gardens-carousel-spins-again/#.W1CpiNVKjIU.

Austin, Dan. "City of Detroit III," HistoricDetroit.org, 2018. http://historicdetroit.org/building/city-of-detroit-iii/.

Baird, Sharon. "Walt's Private Apartment." JustDisney.com, n.d. http://www.justdisney.com/features/apartment.html.

Baird, Steve. "Tilt-a-Whirl Trademark, Not a Service Mark?" DuetsBlog, August 26, 2013. https://www.duetsblog.com/2013/08/articles/trademarks/tilt-a-whirl-trademark-not-service-mark/.

Barker, Stan. "Amusement Parks." *Encyclopedia of Chicago*, Chicago Historical Society website, 2006. http://www.encyclopedia.chicagohistory.org/pages/48.html.

Ben. "A Review of *East in Eden: William Niblo and His Pleasure Garden of Yore*." The New York Wanderer, November 25, 2015. http://newyorkwanderer.com/a-review-of-east-in-eden-william-niblo-and-his-pleasure-garden-of-yore/.

Bennighof, Mike. "Austrian Gasbags." Avalanche Press, March 2007. http://www.avalanchepress.com/Austrian_Gasbags.php.

Blockson, Charles L. "Black Samuel Fraunces." Temple University Libraries, 2012. https://library.temple.edu/collections/blockson/fraunces.

Braun, Matt. "Buffalo Bill Goosed the World's Fair." True West: History of the American Frontier, April 22, 2014. https://truewestmagazine.com/buffalo-bill-goosed-the-worlds-fair/.

Breznican, Anthony. "Steven Spielberg: Director's Video Tour of Universal Backlot." *Entertainment Weekly*, June 24, 2016. http://ew.com/article/2016/06/24/steven-spielberg-video-tour-universal-backlot/.

Brigandi, Paul, and Nancy Brigandi. "Coney Island's Original, Romantic Luna Park." Carousel History, June 13, 2015. http://carouselhistory.com/coney-islands-original-romantic-luna-park/.

——. "William H. Reynolds Shared His 'Dreamland' with Coney Island and the World." Carousel History, June 13, 2015. http://carouselhistory.com/coney-islands-dreamland-park-history/.

Brooke, Bob. "Trolley Parks Fade into Memory." The Antiques Almanac, 2007–2017. http://theantiquesalmanac.com/trolleyparksfadeintomemory.htm.

Bui, Ly Y. "The Rotunda of the 1873 Vienna Exhibition." A Treasury of World's Fair Art & Architecture. College Park, MD: University of Maryland Libraries Digital Collections, 2005. https://digital.lib.umd.edu/worldsfairs/essay?pid=umd:992.

Burton-Hill, Clemency. "When Christmas Carols Were Banned." BBC Culture, December 19, 2014. http://www.bbc.com/culture/story/20141219-when-christmas-carols-were-banned.

Caso, Fran. "Marcus Loew." Immigrant Entrepreneurship, September 22, 2011, last modified January 28, 2014. https://www.immigrantentrepreneurship.org/entry.php?rec=88.

Cawdery, John William. Gravity Railway U.S. Patent application, June 28, 1893, Google Patents. https://patents.google.com/patent/US518224.

Cellania, Miss. "Coney Island Freaks of Yesterday and Today." Mental Floss, February 15, 2008. http://mentalfloss.com/article/502648/if-you%E2%80%99ve-ever-seen-ghost-science-may-explain-why.

Clark, William. *Journals of the Lewis & Clark Expedition*. Center for Digital Research in the Humanities, University of Nebraska Press, October 24, 1805. https://lewisandclarkjournals.unl.edu/item/lc.jrn.1805-10-24.

Clauss, Kyle Scott. "Throwback Thursday: When Revere Beach Had Roller Coasters." *Boston*, July 23, 2015. https://www.bostonmagazine.com/news/2015/07/23/revere-beach-roller-coasters/.

Coke, David E. "Brief History." Vauxhall Gardens 1661–1859, July 2, 2016. http://www.vauxhallgardens.com/vauxhall_gardens_briefhistory_page.html.

——. "Full Chronology," Vauxhall Gardens, 1661–1859 website, July 2, 2016. http://www.vauxhallgardens.com/vauxhall_gardens_fullchronology_page.html.

Cowley, Stacy. "Disney to Buy Lucasfilm for $4 Billion." CNN Tech, October 31, 2012. https://money.cnn.com/2012/10/30/technology/disney-buys-lucasfilm/index.html.

Coyle, Millie Landis. "Milton Snavely Hershey." Hershey Derry Township Historical Society, 2016. http://hersheyhistory.org/library-archives/hershey/54-milton-snavely-hershey.

Crain, Esther. "When Subway Cars Almost Became Women-Only." Ephemeral New York, December 29, 2010. https://ephemeralnewyork.wordpress.com/2010/12/29/when-subway-cars-almost-became-women-only/.

Curtis, Ross. S. "Durango—Prehistory and History of the Durango Area." DurangoDowntown.com, 2016. https://durangodowntown.com/durango-prehistory-and-history-of-the-durango-area/.

D'Amico, Vince. "Six Gun Territory, Willow Grove Park," Historical Society of Pennsylvania, January 19, 2016. https://hsp.org/blogs/archival-adventures-in-small-repositories/life-is-a-lark-at-willow-grove-park.

Daugherty, Greg. "Seven Famous People Who Missed the Titanic." Smithsonian.com, March 1, 2012. https://www.smithsonianmag.com/history/seven-famous-people-who-missed-the-titanic-101902418/.

Daus, Susanne. "Blimps, Freak Shows and Racecars: Vienna's Prater Park Turns 250." Deutsche Welle, April 7, 2016. http://www.dw.com/en/blimps-freak-shows-and-racecars-viennas-prater-park-turns-250/a-19170709.

Davies, Bree. "Lakeside Is Awesome." Westword, August 25, 2011. http://www.westword.com/arts/lakeside-is-awesome-5780348.

———. "Ten Reasons Why Lakeside Amusement Park Rules." Westword, August 29, 2012. http://www.westword.com/arts/ten-reasons-why-lakeside-amusement-park-rules-5817844.

Del Sordo, Stephen G. "Annie Oakley." Heritage Resource Group, Dorchester County (Maryland) Public Library, n.d. http://www.dorchesterlibrary.org/library/aoakley.html.

Denaro, Adrienne. "Jantzen." The Oregon Encyclopedia, September 20, 2017. https://oregonencyclopedia.org/articles/jantzen/#.W1CzCNVKjIU.

Denney, Jim. "'Nothing Has to Die'—The Walt Disney–Ray Bradbury Friendship." The Walt Disney Family Museum, August 22, 2017. https://waltdisney.org/blog/nothing-has-to-die-walt-disney-ray-bradbury-friendship.

Desimone, Cali. "Bushkill Park Gears Up for Its Halloween Express." WFMZ, September 29, 2017. http://www.wfmz.com/news/lehigh-valley/bushkill-park-gears-up-for-its-halloween-express/628167569.

Dockrill, Peter. "The Science Behind Why We Love Terrifying Ourselves on Rollercoasters." Science Alert, January 22, 2016. https://www.sciencealert.com/the-science-behind-why-we-love-terrifying-ourselves-on-rollercoasters.

Doll, Alex. "A Brief History of America's Most Influential Pleasure Wheel." HuffPost, February 14, 2014. https://www.huffingtonpost.com/alex-doll/americas-most-influential-pleasure-wheel_b_4791101.html.

Early, Chas. "November 30, 1936: The Crystal Palace Is Destroyed by Fire." BT, May 22, 2017. http://home.bt.com/news/on-this-day/november-30-1936-the-crystal-palace-is-destroyed-by-fire-11363947170210.

Eschner, Kat. "How President William McKinley's Assassination Led to the Modern Secret Service." Smithsonian.com, September 14, 2017. https://www.smithsonianmag.com/smart-news/how-president-william-mckinleys-assassination-led-modern-secret-service-180964868/.

Fabricius, Karl. "The Amusement Park Being Swallowed by the Sea." Scribol, July 6, 2012. http://scribol.com/anthropology-and-history/urban-exploration/the-amusement-park-being-swallowed-by-the-sea/.

Farr, William. "The Watermills of Camden County." West Jersey History Project, 2002–2013. http://www.westjerseyhistory.org/books/farrwatermills/.

Feltman, Charles A. "Amusement Pneumatic Machine Gun." Patent U.S. 48460855A, August 6, 1957, Google Patents, https://patents.google.com/patent/US2801624A/en

Fetter, Rosemary. "Trail's End—John Brisben Walker Pioneered Denver's Entertainment Industry." Colorado Gambler, October 8, 2014.

———. "Trail's End–The Romantic Beginnings of the Historic Elitch Gardens Theater." Colorado Gambler, April 7, 2012.

Figalora, Sarah. "Six Flags Opens Goliath, a Record-Breaking New Roller Coaster." ABC News, June 19, 2014. https://abcnews.go.com/US/flags-opens-record-breaking-roller-coaster/story?id=24213959.

Fiore, Edna. "John Brisben Walker: A Man of Ideas." Morrison History, 2016. https://morrisonhistory.org/people/john-brisben-walker/.

Foster, Kashae. "Cliff House, Sutro Baths Display Area's Past." Our National Parks, April 27, 2009. http://www.ournationalparks.us/west/san-francisco-bay-area/cliff_house_sutro_baths_offer_look_at_bay_areas_past/.

Gale, Neil. "Paul Boyton's Water Chutes Park, Chicago, Illinois, 1894–1907." Living History of Illinois and Chicago Digital Library. http://livinghistoryofillinois.com/amusement_parks/Paul%20Boytons%20Water%20Chutes%20Park,%20Chicago,%20Illinois%201894-1907/album/.

———. "Sans Souci Amusement Park, Chicago, Illinois, 1899–1913." Living History of Illinois and Digital History of Chicago. http://livinghistoryofillinois.com/amusement_parks/Sans%20Souci%20Amusement%20Park,%20Chicago,%20Illinois%201899-1913/album/.

———. "Watchtower Amusement Park, Rock Island, Illinois, 1882–1927." Living History of Illinois and Chicago Digital Library. http://livinghistoryofillinois.com/amusement_parks/Watchtower%20Amusement%20Park,%20Rock%20Island,%20Illinois%201882-1927/album/.

Gannon, Devin. "The History of Fort George: Manhattan's Long-Lost Amusement Park in Inwood." 6sqft, July 19, 2017. https://www.6sqft.com/the-history-of-fort-george-manhattans-long-lost-amusement-park-in-inwood/.

Gardner, Richard. "Kings Dominion Carousel PTC #44—A Historic Masterpiece of Joy and Regret." The Carousel News & Trader, April 27, 2013.

Gargiulo, Vince, and Mike Chew. "A Quick Look at Palisades' Roller Coasters." Palisades Amusement Park, 1994–2017. http://www.palisadespark.com/coasters.html.

Gaunt, Ken. "Daredevil Ivy Baldwin." Airport Journals, April 1, 2003. http://airportjournals.com/daredevil-ivy-baldwin/.

Gavan, Peggy. "1896: The Alligator That Fought a Newfoundland on Coney Island." The Coney Island Blog, January 9, 2016. http://www.theconeyislandblog.com/?p=2555.

Gennawey, Sam. "How Harrison 'Buzz' Price Invented the Universal Studios Tour." blooloop, March 12, 2018. https://blooloop.com/harrison-buzz-price-universal-studios-tour/.

Gilbertat, Paul. "Katalnaya Gorka at Oranienbaum." Royal Russia News. The Romanov Dynasty & Their Legacy, Monarchy, History of Imperial & Holy Russia, October, 7, 2012. http://www.tsarnicholas.info/blog/index.blog?topic_id=1069320.

Gluck, Keith. "Harper Goff: The 'Second' Imagineer." The Walt Disney Family Museum, May 9, 2017. http://waltdisney.com/blog/harper-goff-second-imagineer.

Goss, Jared. "French Art Deco." Department of Modern and Contemporary Art, The Metropolitan Museum of Art, June 2010. https://www.metmuseum.org/toah/hd/frdc/hd_frdc.htm.

Grant, Tony. "A Visit to Vauxhall Gardens." *Jane Austen's World*, February 16, 2012. https://janeaustensworld.wordpress.com/2012/02/16/a-visit-to-vauxhall-gardens-by-tony-grant/.

Greenlees, David. "Armitage-Herschell Company, the Herschell-Spillman Company and Herschell-Spillman Engines." The Old Motor, May 30, 2013. http://theoldmotor.com/?p=82237.

Griffin, Matt. "A Chat with Frank Glaser, President/Owner, James' and Fralinger's Salt Water Taffy." Total Retail, January 1, 2007. https://www.mytotalretail.com/article/a-chat-frank-glaser-president-owner-james-fralingers-salt-water-taffy-44116/all/.

Griffiths, D. M. "Grant, James (1802–1879)," *Oxford Dictionary of National Biography* online edition, Oxford: Oxford University Press, 2004. http://www.oxforddnb.com.

Guerrasio, Jason. "The New 'Star Wars' Movies Have Already Made More Than the $4 Billion Disney Paid for the Franchise in 2012." Business Insider, December 29, 2017. http://www.businessinsider.com/star-wars-box-office-disney-4-billion-lucasfilm-purchase-2017-12.

Haidet, Ryan. "By the Numbers: Cedar Point's Valravn Roller Coaster." WKYC, January 21, 2016. https://www.wkyc.com/article/features/cedar-points-mysterious-valravn-secret-revealed/176419159

Halck, Signe, and Stine Rysgaard. "The Hill Breathes Life in Gambling Traditions, Art, and Combat." My News Desk, Bakken, May 5, 2017. https://www.bakken.dk/om-os/presserum/.

Hamilton, Ben. "Remembering Tivoli's Founder: A Showman with a Fondness for Champagne and Jazzy Waistcoats." *Copenhagen Post*, May 23, 2017. http://cphpost.dk/history/tivoli.html.

Hammerlein, Sarah. "Top Ten Places to Trace the Remains of Pasadena's Busch Gardens." KCET, January 8, 2018. https://www.kcet.org/shows/socal-wanderer/top-ten-places-to-trace-the-remains-of-pasadenas-busch-gardens.

Haugsted, Ida. "H. C. Stilling." Kunstindeks Danmark & Weilbachs Kunstnerleksikon, Castle and Cultural Agency, 1994, https://www.kulturarv.dk/kid/VisWeilbach.do?kunstnerId=10713&wsektion=alle.

Healy, Ryan. "The Strange History of NYC's Mighty Hell Gate." Gothamist, February 22, 2016. http://gothamist.com/2016/02/22/hell_gate_history_nyc.php.

Herman, Charles. "Amusement Apparatus." Patent No. 1,354,436. Google Patents, September 28, 1920. https://patents.google.com/patent/US1354436.

Hettrick, Scott. "Santa Anita's 75th Anniversary." Arcadia's Best, December 24, 2009. http://arcadiasbest.com/2009/12/santa-anitas-75th-anniversary/.

Hill, David. "Quote a Ride: Lakeside Amusement Park's Century-Old Survival." Colorado Public Radio, May 10, 2016. http://www.cpr.org/news/story/quite-ride-lakeside-amusement-parks-century-old-survival.

Hill, Jim. "Texan With Big Dreams + Big Apple = Big Trouble." Jim Hill Media, December 31, 2001. http://jimhillmedia.com/editor_in_chief1/b/jim_hill/archive/2001/12/31/texan-with-big-dreams-big-apple-big-trouble.aspx.

Hoffman, Tom. "Rides & Attractions." 1893 World's Columbian Exhibition, n.d.

Holland, Gary. "Crystal Palace: A History." BBC, July 27, 2004. http://www.bbc.co.uk/london/content/articles/2004/07/27/history_feature.shtml.

Hughes, C. J. "Harry Black: From Bootlegging Liquor to Building Skyscrapers." The Real Deal, October 1, 2017. https://therealdeal.com/issues_articles/harry-black-from-bootlegging-liquor-to-building-skyscrapers/.

Jepsen, Chris. "Bud Hurlbut (1918–2011)." Yesterland, January 8, 2011. https://ochistorical.blogspot.com/search?q=bud+hurlbut.

Johnson, Ray. "The Columbus Statue and the Cold Storage Building Fire, July 1, 1893." Chicago History Cop, May 3, 2012. http://www.chicagonow.com/chicago-history-cop/2012/05/the-columbus-statue-and-the-cold-storage-building-fire-july-10-1893-article-1-in-a-series/.

Jones, Doug. "Meet Harper Goff, The Legendary Set Designer Behind Willy Wonka's Chocolate Factory." Dangerous Minds, September 30, 2016. https://dangerousminds.net/comments/meet_harper_goff_the_legendary_set_designer_behind_willy_wonkas_chocolate_f.

Kennedy, Robert C. "On This Day: June 8, 1901." *New York Times* on the Web, June 8, 2001. https://archive.nytimes.com/www.nytimes.com/learning/general/onthisday/harp/0608.html.

Kenney, Andrew. "Much of Heritage Square Will Be History After This Weekend," Westword, October 29, 2015. http://www.westword.com/news/much-of-heritage-square-will-be-history-after-this-weekend-7285646.

Kick, Chris. "Humphrey Farm Still Popping in Huron County, and Across Ohio." Farm and Dairy, June 12, 2012. https://www.farmanddairy.com/news/humphrey-farm-still-popping-in-huron-county-and-across-ohio/38240.html.

Kirschner, Carl. "Lake Compounce: Bringing Amusements to the Star's Residents Since 1846." Connecticut History, n.d. https://connecticuthistory.org/lake-compounce-bringing-amusements-to-the-states-residents-since-1846/.

Kiss, Stephen, Sr. "On TV Westerns of the 1950s and '60s." New York Public Library, December 1, 2012. https://www.nypl.org/blog/2012/12/01/tv-westerns-1950s-and-60s.

Kjaer, Brigitte. "Tivolis far fylder rundt: Havens grundlægger var en kreativ vildbasse." Politiken, August 29, 2012. https://politiken.dk/kultur/art5453187/Tivolis-far-fylder-rundt-Havens-grundl%C3%A6gger-var-en-kreativ-vildbasse.

Koch, Richard. "How Walt Disney Funded His Dream." *HuffPost*, December 19, 2017. https://www.huffingtonpost.com/entry/how-walt-disney-funded-his-dream_us_5a38ebc1e4b0578d1beb72a1.

Kozek, Barbara. "History of Atlantic City." City of Atlantic City, n.d. https://cityofatlanticcity.org/?page_id=14.

Kudler, Adrian Glick. "The Strange and Wonderful Lost Amusement Parks of L.A." Curbed Los Angeles.com, November 12, 2015. https://la.curbed.com/maps/old-amusement-theme-parks-los-angeles-defunct-map.

Kyriazi, Gary. "Denver: A Tale of Two Parks—Part 2 (Lakeside Park)." Park World, December 12, 2012. http://www.parkworld-online.com/denver-a-tale-of-two-parks-part-2-lakeside-park/.

———. "Seabreeze—A Shining Example of Survival." Park World, February 8, 2011.

LaCross, George, and Bill Luca. "Spook-A-Rama Strikes Back." Laff in the Dark, 2017. http://www.laffinthedark.com/articles/spook3/spook3_1.htm.

Lake, Amariah. A. "Lake Theater Appliance." U.S. Patent application. May 22, 1894. Google Patents. https://patents.google.com/patent/US520236.

Lambert, Tim. "A History of English Population: The Population of England in the Middle Ages." World History Encyclopedia, 2015. http://www.localhistories.org/index.html.

Larsen, Jørgen. "Det Gamle København: Velkommen i Tivoli." *Berlingske*, April 11, 2016. https://www.b.dk/kultur/det-gamle-koebenhavn-velkommen-i-tivoli.

Levine, Arthur. "Why Are Some Amusement Parks Known As Trolley Parks?" TripSavvy, February 5, 2018. https://www.tripsavvy.com/what-is-a-trolley-park-3225649.

Long, Kat. "The Rise and Suspiciously Rapid Fall of Freedomland U.S.A." Atlas Obscura, July 8, 2015. https://www.atlasobscura.com/articles/the-rise-and-suspiciously-rapid-fall-of-freedomland-u-s-a.

Long, Tony. "June 16, 1884: A Technology with Plenty of Ups and Downs." *Wired*, June 15, 2008. https://www.wired.com/2011/06/0616gravity-roller-coaster/.

López, Tracy. "Churros: The Hidden History." *HuffPost*, last modified November 8, 2017. https://www.huffingtonpost.com/2011/08/18/churros-the-hidden-history_n_930791.html.

MacDougall, L. "Plans for a Disneyland-Style Theme Park in Kent Have Taken a Step Forward." KentLive, February 13, 2017. https://www.kentlive.news/whats-on/whats-on-news/plans-disneyland-style-theme-park-503157.

MacKinnon, Wayne. "Canobie Lake Park—An Historical Perspective." Canobie Lake History, 2018. https://clhistory.org/index.html.

Malanowski, Jamie. "The Brief History of the Ferris Wheel." Smithsonian.com, June 2015. https://www.smithsonianmag.com/history/history-ferris-wheel-180955300/.

Mangels, William F. Merry-Go-Round U.S. Patent application, June 6, 1900, Google Patents. https://patents.google.com/patent/US669842A/en.

Manning, Mike. "Man, Mountain, and Monument." MrAltadena.com, 2001.

Martini, John. "George K. Whitney, Jr. Interview, 2002." OutsideLands.org, Western Neighborhoods Project, May 18, 2010. http://www.outsidelands.org/whitney-interview1.php.

Masters, Nathan. "The Lost Canals of Venice of America." KCET, April 5, 2013. https://www.kcet.org/shows/lost-la/the-lost-canals-of-venice-of-america.

———. "Southern California's First Amusement Parks? Ostrich Farms." KCET, September 20, 2012. https://www.kcet.org/shows/lost-la/an-ornithological-curiosity-when-ostriches-ruled-socal-tourism.

———. "Who Eucalyptized Southern California?" KCET, May 16, 2012. https://www.kcet.org/shows/lost-la/who-eucalyptized-southern-california.

Maurer, Sarah. "Sloan's Lake History: Part II: Roger the Elephant Has His Revenge on Denver." 8z Real Estate, November 6, 2012. http://www.sloansdenver.com/about/history-of-the-area/.

McElfresh, Lynn E. "The Traditional Shore Dinner." *Thousand Islands Magazine*, November 13, 2013. http://www.thousandislandslife.com/BackIssues/Archive/tabid/393/articleType/ArticleView/articleId/1401/The-Traditional-Shore-Dinner.aspx.

Meares, Hadley. "Beverly Park and Ponyland: The 'Kiddieland' That Inspired Walt Disney." KCET, November 1, 2013. https://www.kcet.org/history-society/beverly-park-and-ponyland-the-kiddieland-that-inspired-walt-disney.

———. "Pasadena the Beautiful: Blossoms in Bloom at the Original Busch Gardens." KCET, October 31, 2014. https://www.kcet.org/history-society/pasadena-the-beautiful-blossoms-in-bloom-at-the-original-busch-gardens.

Meares, Joel. "Catherine the Great Put Rollers on the World's First Coaster." *Wired*, December 27, 2011. https://www.wired.com/2011/12/pl-prototyperollercoaster/.

Meehan, Patrick. "Ferris Wheel in the 1893 Chicago World's Fair." Hyde Park History Society, April 27, 2015. http://www.hydeparkhistory.org/2015/04/27/ferris-wheel-in-the-1893-chicago-worlds-fair/.

Michelson, Paul. "Chutes Park, South Los Angeles, CA." Pacific Coast Architecture Database, 2005–2015. http://pcad.lib.washington.edu/building/9825/.

———. "Sulphur Springs Hotel, South Los Angeles, CA." Pacific Coast Architecture Database, 2005–2015.

Midtown KC Poster. "Electric City Was Midtown's Coney Island." Midtown KC Post, July 7, 2014. http://midtownkcpost.com/electric-city-midtowns-coneys-island/.

Miller, Diane Disney. "Happy Birthday, Mother." The Walt Disney Family Museum website, February 15, 2011. http://www.waltdisney.com/blog/happy-birthday-mother-diane-disney-miller.

Miller, Ron. "In 1901, You Could Pay 50 Cents to Ride an Airship to the Moon." Gizmodo, May 31, 2012.

Moran, Tom. "In Kinney's Own Words." Venice of America.org, Venice Historical Society, March–April 2004. http://www.veniceofamerica.org/pdf/mar_apr_2004_newsletter.pdf.

Morgan, Adam. "Novomatic AG Opens Admiral Arena Prater in Vienna." World Casino News. https://news.worldcasinodirectory.com/novomatic-ag-opens-admiral-arena-prater-in-vienna-46588.

Morgan, Brian. "Major Carousel Builders and Carvers." National Carousel Association, 2015. http://carousels.org/Carvers_Builders.html.

Morton, Ella. "How a Real Corpse Ended Up in a Fun House Spookhouse." *Atlas Obscura* (blog), *Slate*, April 11, 2014. http://www.slate.com/blogs/atlas_obscura/2014/04/11/the_corpse_of_elmer_mccurdy_and_how_it_ended_up_in_a_long_beach_fun_park.html.

Mowbray, Peter. "Humble Beginnings: The Pleasure Beach at Blackpool." Live in Blackpool, January 2, 2011. http://www.liveinblackpool.co.uk/forum/index.php?topic=1719.0.

Mueller, Rich. "American Caramel and Its Cards: A Brief History." Sports Collectors Daily, October 28, 2009. https://www.sportscollectorsdaily.com/a-short-history-of-american-caramel-and-its-cards/.

Murdock, Gillian. "Dining for Daredevils: Amusement Park Food." Delish, August 17, 2011. https://www.delish.com/food/g1618/amusement-park-food/.

Murray, James, and Karla Murray. "The History of the Hippodrome, Once NYC's Greatest Theater." Gothamist, August 10, 2016. http://gothamist.com/2016/08/10/hippodrome_theater_history.php.

National Carousel Association. "Index of North American Carousels." 2002–2017. http://carousels.org/NCAcensus.html.

Neild, Barry. "Pandora—The World of Avatar and 10 Other Hot Theme Parks of the Future." CNN Travel, June 12, 2017. http://www.cnn.com/travel/article/pandora-world-of-avatar-future-theme-parks-2017/index.html.

Newburg, John. P. Patent No. 411255 A, U.S. Patent Office, October 23, 1886. https://patents.google.com/patent/US411255.

Nibert, Jim. Camden Park page. Facebook, July 17, 2017.

Niles, Robert. "Theme Park History: A Short History of Universal Studios Hollywood." Theme Park Insider, July 15, 2013. https://www.themeparkinsider.com/flume/201307/3564/.

Nowak, Pamela. "Before Elitch Gardens—The Early Lives of John and Mary Elitch." Pamela Nowak, December 19, 2014. http://www.pamelanowak.com/wp/?p=208.

———. "Early Denver Amusement Parks." Pamela Nowak, December 26, 2014. http://www.pamelanowak.com/wp/?p=212.

———. "Early Denver Street Car Lines." Pamela Nowak, January 2, 2015. http://www.pamelanowak.com/wp/?p=215.

O'Dell, Larry. "Amusement Parks." The Encyclopedia of Oklahoma History and Culture, Oklahoma History Society, 2009. http://www.okhistory.org/publications/enc/entry.php?entry=AM018.

Otte, Jef. "Radium and Roller Coasters: A Brief, Dirty History of Elitch Gardens." Westword, June 6, 2012. http://www.westword.com/arts/radium-and-roller-coasters-a-brief-dirty-history-of-elitch-gardens-5116922.

Parascandola, John. "America's Playground: The Development of Coney Island." The Ultimate History Project, n.d. http://www.ultimatehistoryproject.com/coney-island.html.

Petris, Mike. "A Closer Look at Thaddeus Lowe." Pasadena Museum of History, May 7, 2015. https://pasadenahistory.org/thaddeus-lowe/closer-look-lowe/.

Pierre. "Parc Monceau, Paris." French Moments, September 21, 2014. https://frenchmoments.eu/parc-monceau-paris/.

Pilgrim, David. "African Dip Carnival Game." Jim Crow Museum of Racist Memorabilia, Ferris State University, February 2007. https://ferris.edu/HTMLS/news/jimcrow/question/2007/february.htm

Platania, Joseph. "Camden Park." The West Virginia Encyclopedia, West Virginia Humanities Council, December 6, 2012. https://www.wvencyclopedia.org/articles/817.

Prentice, Claire. "How One Man Saved a Generation of Premature Babies." BBC News, May 23, 2016. https://www.bbc.com/news/magazine-36321692.

Rakoff, David. "King of the Forest." Tablet, June 12, 2006. https://www.tabletmag.com/jewish-arts-and-culture/books/861/king-of-the-forest.

Rasmussen, Nate. "Vintage Walt Disney World: A Dedication with Style at Magic Kingdom Park." Disney Parks Blog (blog), Disney, September 29, 2011. https://disneyparks.disney.go.com/blog/2011/09/vintage-walt-disney-world-a-dedication-with-style-at-magic-kingdom-park/comment-page-1/.

Reitter, Paul. "Bambi's Jewish Roots." Jewish Review of Books, Winter 2014. https://jewishreviewofbooks.com/articles/618/bambis-jewish-roots/.

Rice, Christina. "When Elephants Ruled the Intersection: The Saga of the Selig Zoo Statues." HuffPost, August 26, 2012. https://www.huffingtonpost.com/the-los-angeles-public-library/selig-zoo-statues_b_1565154.html.

Richman, Jeff. "February Birthdays." Green-Wood Cemetery, February 1, 2011. https://www.green-wood.com/2011/february-birthdays/.

Rivera, Lissa. "The Great Bygone Museum Tour." MCNY Blog: New York Stories (blog), Museum of the City of New York, December 3, 2013. https://blog.mcny.org/2013/12/03/the-great-bygone-museum-tour/.

Roller Coaster Database. "Atom Smasher." 2018. https://rcdb.com/1863.htm.

———. "Camden Park." 2018. https://rcdb.com/4607.htm.

———. "Jantzen Beach Amusement Park." 2018. https://rcdb.com/4634.htm.

———. "Luna Park." 2018. https://rcdb.com/14166.htm.

———. "Ravine Flyer II." 2018. https://rcdb.com/3917.htm.

Roncace, Kelly. "Clementon Lake Restocked with Fish After Dam is Reconstructed." NJ.com, August 9, 2011. https://www.nj.com/gloucester-county/towns/index.ssf/2011/08/clementon_lake_restocked_with.html.

———. "Clementon Park Has New Rides, Attractions and an Updated Look." NJ.com, May 17, 2011. https://www.nj.com/gloucester-county/towns/index.ssf/2011/05/clementon_park_has_new_rides_a.html.

———. "Wildwood Coaster Now 'So Smooth a Grannie Can Ride It.'" NJ.com, May 26, 2017. https://www.nj.com/entertainment/index.ssf/2017/05/wildwood_coaster_now_so_smooth_a_grannie_can_ride.html.

Rotman, Michael. "Euclid Beach Park Riot." Cleveland Historical, February 28, 2018. https://clevelandhistorical.org/items/show/562.

———. "Flight Pioneers at Euclid Beach." Cleveland Historical, April 18, 2017. https://clevelandhistorical.org/items/show/560.

Ruben, Paul. "Riding Astride." Park World, January 28, 2009. http://www.parkworld-online.com/riding-astride/.

Rubin, Judith, ed. TEA/AECOM 2015 Theme Index and Museum Index: The Global Attractions Attendance Report, Themed Entertainment Association, 2016. http://www.teaconnect.org/images/files/TEA_160_611852_160525.pdf.

Rudolph, Katie. "The Diving Elk of Denver's Chutes Park." Geneology, African American and Western History Resources, Denver Public Library, May 12, 2015. https://history.denverlibrary.org/news/diving-elk-denvers-chutes-park.

———. "The History of Lakeside Amusement Park in Photos." Geneology, African American and Western History Resources, Denver Public Library, July 13, 2015. https://history.denverlibrary.org/news/lakeside-amusement-park-celebrating-107-denver-summers.

Rydell, Robert W. "World's Columbian Exposition." Encyclopedia of Chicago, Chicago Historical Society, 2005. http://www.encyclopedia.chicagohistory.org/pages/1386.html.

Sandusky Library Archives Research Center. "Louis Zistel, an Early German Immigrant." Sandusky History, November 17, 2011. http://sanduskyhistory.blogspot.com/2011/11/louis-zistel-early-german-immigrant.html.

Sandy, Adam. "Harry G. Traver." Ultimate Rollercoaster.com, 1996–2018. https://www.ultimaterollercoaster.com/coasters/history/designer/traver.shtml.

Santoro, Lisa M. "The Upper-Class Brooklyn Resorts of the Victorian Era." Curbed New York, June 27, 2013. https://ny.curbed.com/2013/6/27/10226192/the-upper-class-brooklyn-resorts-of-the-victorian-era.

Sasha. "Bakken: The Oldest Amusement Park in the World, Revisited Today." Entertainment Designer, January 12, 2012. http://entertainmentdesigner.com/featured/bakken-the-oldest-theme-park-in-the-world-revisited-today/.

Schantz, Regena Jo. "Davenport Family." Colonel Davenport Historical Foundation, n.d. http://www.davenporthouse.org/davenport-family.php.

Schulz, Dana. "50 Years Ago, Donald Trump's Father Demolished Coney Island's Beloved Steeplechase Park." 6sqft, May 18, 2016. https://www.6sqft.com/50-years-ago-donald-trumps-father-demolished-coney-islands-beloved-steeplechase-park/.

———. "Before Nathan's There Was Feltman's: The History of the Coney Island Hot Dog." 6sqft, June 20, 2016. https://www.6sqft.com/before-nathans-there-was-feltmans-the-history-of-the-coney-island-hot-dog/.

———. "The History of Bowery Beach, the 'Coney Island of Queens.'" 6sqft, July 6, 2016. https://www.6sqft.com/the-history-of-bowery-bay-beach-the-coney-island-of-queens/.

Sieger, Edward. "Bushkill Park Carousel Building Collapses Due to Heavy Snow." LehighValleyLive, February 18, 2014. https://www.lehighvalleylive.com/breaking-news/index.ssf/2014/02/bushkill_park_carousel_buildin.html.

Silverman, Stephen M. "Disney's Small World Turns 50." People, March 21, 2014. https://people.com/celebrity/its-a-small-world-turns-50-at-disneyland-walt-disney-world/.

———. "The Godless Side of Walt Disney." Newsweek, September 11, 2015. http://www.newsweek.com/godless-side-walt-disney-371249.

———. "Harry Potter Expands His Playground at Universal Orlando." People, January 24, 2014. https://people.com/celebrity/wizarding-world-of-harry-potter-expands-in-orlando/.

———. "Harry Potter World Revealed, at Last." People, September 15, 2009. https://people.com/celebrity/harry-potters-world-revealed-at-last/.

———. "Hollywood Icon Mickey Mouse Turns 75." People, November 17, 2003. https://people.com/celebrity/hollywood-icon-mickey-mouse-turns-75/.

———. "Sneak Peek: What Fans Will Find at Universal Orlando's World of Harry Potter." People, March 25, 2010. https://people.com/celebrity/sneak-peek-what-fans-will-find-at-universal-orlandos-world-of-harry-potter/.

Silverthorn, Ann. "The Story of Waldameer's First Ravine Flyer Roller Coaster." Ann Silverthorn, May 6, 2016. http://annsilverthorn.com/index.php/4265/the-story-of-waldameers-first-ravine-flyer-roller-coaster/.

Simon, Bryant. "Atlantic City." The Encyclopedia of Greater Philadelphia, 2017. http://philadelphiaencyclopedia.org/archive/atlantic-city/.

Smith, Michael Glover. "The Secret History of Chicago Movies: Selig Polyscope." White City Cinema, April 18, 2011. https://whitecitycinema.com/2011/04/18/the-secret-history-of-chicago-movies-selig-polyscope/.

Sorenson, Douglas Kirk. "Robert Edward Bollinger." Find a Grave, August 5, 2009. https://www.findagrave.com/memorial/40308075/robert-edward-bollinger.

Squair, Ed. "The Long, Long Haunt: Artists of Walt Disney's Haunted Mansion." The Walt Disney Family Museum, October 31, 2011. https://waltdisney.org/blog/long-long-haunt-artists-walt%E2%80%99s-haunted-mansion.

Sroka-Holzmann, Pamela. "Bushkill Park's Reopening Remains a Dream of Park Owners." LehighValleyLive, December 16, 2013. https://www.lehighvalleylive.com/easton/index.ssf/2013/12/delays_in_financial_commitment.html.

Staff. "The History of Roller Coasters: The Mauch Chunk Gravity Railway." Entertainment Designer, October, 8, 2011. http://entertainmentdesigner.com/history-of-theme-parks/the-history-of-roller-coasters-the-mauch-chunk-gravity-railway/.

Stanton, Jeffrey. "Abbot Kinney Pier," Venice History Site, April 6, 1998, https://www.westland.net/venicehistory/articles/kinneypier.htm.

———. "Coney Island—First Steeplechase Park (1897–1907)." Coney Island History Site, April 1, 1998. https://www.westland.net/coneyisland/articles/steeplechase1.htm.

———. "Elitch Gardens (1890–1994)." National Amusement Park Historical Association, October 3, 2011. http://lostamusementparks.napha.org/articles/colorado/elitchgardens.html.

———. "History of Early Roller Coasters, 1870–1886." Coney Island History Site, September 6, 2013. https://www.westland.net/coneyisland/articles/EarlyRollerCoasters-1870-1886.htm.

———. "Roller Coasters & Carousels." Venice History Site, April 6, 1998. https://www.westland.net/venicehistory/articles/cc.htm.

Strassberg, Rebecca. "The OG Hot Dog Has Returned to Coney Island, 60 Years Later." Thrillist New York, May 25, 2017. https://www.thrillist.com/eat/new-york/feltmans-original-coney-island-hot-dog.

Stubbs, Naomi J. "List of Gardens." American Pleasure Gardens, March 11, 2013. https://americanpleasuregardens.com.

Sullivan, Colleen. "US Copyright: April 26th. 2006. TXu1-292-939." Captain Paul Boyton, October 7, 2009. http://www.captainboytonblogcom.blogspot.com/2009/10/book.html.

Sullivan, David A. "Coney Island History: The Story of Captain Paul Boyton and Sea Lion Park." Heart of Coney Island, 2015. http://www.heartofconeyisland.com/sea-lion-park-coney-island.html.

———. "Coney Island History: The Story of William Reynolds and Dreamland." Heart of Coney Island, 2015. http://www.heartofconeyisland.com/dreamland-coney-island.html.

Sullivan, Sady. "Coney Island Carousel Carver." Brooklyn Historical Society, November 5, 2009. https://www.brooklynhistory.org/blog/2009/11/05/coney-island-carousel-carver/.

Taylor, John G. "Improvement in Inclined Railways," Patent No. 128,674. Google Patents, July 2, 1872. https://patents.google.com/patent/US128674.

Tewes, Amanda. "The Wild West of Knott's Berry Farm Is More Fantasy Than Reality." Smithsonian.com, September 7, 2017. https://www.smithsonianmag.com/history/wild-west-knotts-berry-farm-is-more-fantasy-than-reality-180964798/.

Thompson, Charles. "Why Letting Nestlé's Candy Get Away May Be the Best Thing for Hershey." Penn Live, January 16, 2018. https://www.pennlive.com/news/2018/01/why_the_hershey_company_let_ne.html.

Thompson, Cole. "Fort George Amusement Park." My Inwood, November 14, 2013. http://myinwood.net/fort-george-amusement-park/.

Thompson, Helen. "150 Years Ago, a Fire in P. T. Barnum's Museum Boiled Two Whales Alive." Smithsonian.com, July 20, 2015. https://www.smithsonianmag.com/smart-news/pt-barnums-bizarre-museum-burned-ground-1865-180955955/.

Thompson, LaMarcus A. "Gravity Switch-Back Railway," Patent No. 332,762. Google Patents, December 22, 1885. https://patents.google.com/patent/US332762/en.

Timpano, Andrea. "Boston Landmark: Flying Horses Carousel on Martha's Vineyard." Boston, May 24, 2016. https://www.bostonmagazine.com/property/2016/05/24/flying-horses-carousel-marthas-vineyard/.

Tracy, Jordan. "The Future of Lakemont Park." WTAJ / We Are Central PA.com, November 13, 2017. https://www.wearecentralpa.com/news/the-future-of-lakemont-park/856896293.

———. "Lakemont Park to Remain Closed, Re-Open in 2019." WTAJ / We Are Central PA.com, March 6, 2018. https://www.wearecentralpa.com/news/lakemont-park-to-remain-closed-re-open-in-2019/1013540302.

Trickey, Erick. "The Origin of the Hot Dog Is a Uniquely American Story." Smithsonian.com, June 30, 2016. https://www.smithsonianmag.com/history/origins-coney-island-hot-dog-uniquely-american-story-180959659/.

Turley, Lindsay. "The Great Crystal Palace Fire of 1838." Museum of the City of New York, n.d. https://blog.mcny.org/2012/12/04/the-great-crystal-palace-fire-of-1858/.

United States. Census Bureau. "POP Culture: 1860." July 18, 2017. https://www.census.gov/history/www/through_the_decades/fast_facts/1860_fast_facts.html.

United States. Department of Commerce. National Oceanic and Atmospheric Administration. National Ocean Service. "What's the Difference Between Seals and Sea Lions?" last modified June 25, 2018. https://oceanservice.noaa.gov/facts/seal-sealion.html.

United States. Department of the Interior. National Park Service. Golden Gate National Recreation Area. "Sutro Baths History." February 28, 2015. https://www.nps.gov/goga/learn/historyculture/sutro-baths.htm.

United States. Department of the Interior. National Park Service. "Jazz Neighborhoods—New Orleans Jazz National Historic Park." April 14, 2015. https://www.nps.gov/jazz/learn/historyculture/jazz-map.htm.

United States. House of Representatives. Office of the Historian. "The House of Representatives' Selection of the Location for the 1893 World's Fair." N.d.

United States. Library of Congress. World Digital Library. "Point Breeze Park, Schottisch." June 30, 2016. https://www.wdl.org/en/item/9246/.

Vagnini, Steven. "Favorite Memories from Walt and Lillian's 30th Anniversary Party." D23 The Official Disney Fan Club, February 11, 2016. https://d23.com/favorite-memories-from-walt-and-lillians-30th-anniversary-party/.

Verlee, Megan. "Lakeside Amusement Park, A Timeless, Antique Attraction." Colorado Public Radio, August 29, 2014. http://www.cpr.org/news/story/photos-lakeside-amusement-park-timeless-antique-attraction.

Wald, Chelsea. "A Magnificent Failure: The 1873 World Exhibition in Vienna." Chelsea Wald Science Writer, October 28, 2014. http://chelseawald.com/2014/10/a-magnificent-failure-the-1873-world-exhibition-in-vienna.html.

Wall, Matthew. "Roller Coaster Technology: Bigger! Faster! Scarier!" BBC News, October 23, 2013. https://www.bbc.co.uk/news/technology-24553630.

Washington, Glynn. "The Long, Strange, 60-Year Trip of Elmer McCurdy." NPR, January 9, 2015. https://www.npr.org/2015/01/09/376097471/the-long-strange-60-year-trip-of-elmer-mccurdy.

Web staff. "A Future Move for Elitch's Possible As New Plans Develop for Downtown Denver." Fox Denver 31, KDVR, January 13, 2018. https://kdvr.com/2018/01/13/a-future-move-for-elitchs-possible-as-new-plans-develop-for-downtown-denver/.

Westerbeck, Colin L. "Frederick Douglas Chooses His Moment." Art Institute of Chicago, 1997. http://www.artic.edu/collections/books/museum-studies/preview-issue/frederick-douglass.

Young, Greg, and Tom Meyers. "The Fire at Barnum's American Museum 150 Years Ago." The Bowery Boys: New York City History, July 16, 2015. http://www.boweryboyshistory.com/2015/07/the-fire-at-barnums-american-museum-150-years-ago.html.

Zigweid, Lisa. "Whirlwind, Jantzen Beach, Portland, OR." Roller Coasters of the Pacific Northwest, 2003–2011. http://www.rollercoastersofthepacificnw.com/pages/whirlwind.html.

ENDNOTES

REMAIN SEATED

10　*an annual $220 billion*: Marjie Lambert, "Changing Times at Florida Theme Parks Lure You into Other Worlds," *Miami Herald*, May 19, 2017.

10　*total nearly 475 million*: "Theme Park Results Show Strong Results in 2017, and Museums Continue to Grow," AECOM, 2018.

11　*who accidentally drowned in…a large brass kettle*: "About Lake Compounce," Lake Compounce, 2016, https://www.lakecompounce.com/plan-a-visit/lake-compounce.

12　*Wilhelmsbad Park in Hanau, Germany*: "Group Honored for Saving World's Oldest Carousel," *Local* (Stockholm), November 11, 2010, https://www.thelocal.de/20101111/31093.

12　*the 1876 Flying Horses*: Andrea Timpano, "Boston Landmark: Flying Horses Carousel on Martha's Vineyard," *Boston*, May 24, 2016, https://www.bostonmagazine.com/property/2016/05/24/flying-horses-carousel-marthas-vineyard/.

12　*toymaker Charles W. F. Dare*: Peter R. Eisenstadt, ed., *The Encyclopedia of New York State* (Syracuse, NY: Syracuse University Press, 2005), p. 267.

12　*the grabber of the brass ring*: Arthur Levine, "Merry-Go-Rounds: 10 of the Oldest Carousels in the USA," *USA Today*, March 22, 2017.

12　*frequent and lengthy hiatuses*: Tony Long, "June 16, 1884: A Technology with Plenty of Ups and Downs," *Wired*, June 15, 2008, https://www.wired.com/2011/06/0616gravity-roller-coaster/.

13　*Britain's record for park longevity*: "History of Blackgang Chine," Blackgang Chine, 2008, https://blackgangchine.com/history-of-blackgang-chine/.

13　*a 2019 start date and 2023 opening*: Lauren MacDougall, "Plans for a Disneyland-Style Theme Park in Kent Have Taken a Step Forward," KentLive, February 13, 2017, https://www.kentlive.news/whats-on/whats-on-news/plans-disneyland-style-theme-park-503157.

13　*a former landfill in Kent*: "Hollywood Theme Park to Rival Disneyland Coming to U.K.," *North Devon Journal*, April 24, 2016.

13　*some 220 million guests by the year 2020*: Judith Rubin, ed., *TEA/AECOM 2015 Theme Index and Museum Index: The Global Attractions Attendance Report*, Themed Entertainment Association, 2016, http://www.teaconnect.org/images/files/TEA_160_611852_160525.pdf.

13　*several theme parks in the region*: Stephen M. Silverman, "Dubai's Theme Parks: The Most Elaborate Sandboxes on Earth?," *Chicago Tribune*, March 6, 2017.

13　*the Magical World of Russia*: Hugo Martin, "Putin Gives Blessing to Russian Theme Park Designed by North Hollywood Firm," *Los Angeles Times*, June 14, 2016.

13　*$4 billion answer to Disneyland*: Vladimir Kozlov, "Vladimir Putin Approves $4B 'Russian Disneyland,'" *Hollywood Reporter*, June 14, 2016.

ALL'S FAIR

17　*Henry I…interpreted dreams as omens*: Henry Morley, *Memoirs of Bartholomew Fair* (London: Chapman and Hall, 1859), p. 3.

17　*killing nearly everyone aboard*: Ordericus Vitalis, *The Ecclesiastical History of England and Normandy*, vol. 6, trans. Thomas Forester (London: Henry G. Bohn, 1856), p. 474.

17　*the heir to the throne*: Henry of Huntingdon, *The Chronicle of Henry of Huntingdon*, ed. and trans. Thomas Forester (1893; repr., Felinfach, Wales: Llanerch Publishers, 1991), p. 299.

18　*Henry granted Rahere his request*: Edward A. Webb, *The Records of St. Bartholomew's Priory and of the Church and Parish of St. Bartholomew's the Great, West Smithfield*, vol. 1 (London: Oxford University Press, 1921), pp. 42–58.

18　*"at the Feast of St. Bartholomew"*: Sylvanus Urban, "The Antiquities of Bartholomew Fair," *Gentleman's Magazine and Historical Review*, vol. 206 (London: John Henry and James Parker, 1859), p. 126.

18　*a three-week, seventeenth-century Coachella*: Edwin Beresford Chancellor, *The Pleasure Haunts of London During Four Centuries* (London: Constable, 1925), p. 321.

18　*the bulk of his claims…proved questionable*: Morley, *Memoirs of Bartholomew Fair*, pp. 8–9.

18　*there was a plague*: Tim Lambert, "A History of English Population: The Population of England in the Middle Ages," World History Encyclopedia, 2015, http://www.localhistories.org/index.html.

18 *carried out in the merriment arena*: Cornelius Walford, *Fairs, Past and Present, A Chapter in the History of Commerce* (London: Elliot Stock, 1883), pp. 171–173.

19 *took to its tent in 1804*: Samuel J. M. M. Alberti, ed., *The Afterlives of Animals: A Museum Menagerie* (Charlottesville: University of Virginia Press, 2011), p. 39.

19 *his death…at age seventy-two*: "The Late Mr. Wombwell," *Illustrated London News*, December 7, 1850, p. 440.

19 *public exhibition…was held in 1665*: Richard D. Altick, *The Shows of London* (Cambridge, MA: Harvard University Press, 1978), p. 37.

19 *"nor were any of her parents, or relations"*: John Evelyn, *The Diary of John Evelyn*, ed. William Bray (London: M. Walter Dunne, 1901), p. 318.

20 *"divinity, law, and physic"*: Maja-Lisa von Sneidern, *Savage Indignation: Colonial Discourse from Milton to Swift.* (Newark, DE: University of Delaware Press, 2005), p. 142.

20 *what the handbills and placards promised*: Altick, *The Shows of London*, p. 36.

20 *"shouts, fiddles, drums, and rattles"*: Richard Cavendish, "London's Last Bartholomew Fair," *History Today* 55, no. 9 (September 2005).

20 *: "the titillation of the adult crowd"*: "Bartholomew Fair," InsideGuide to London website, 2015.

20 *"waiting for another pair"*: William Hone, *The Every-Day Book and Table Book: or, Everlasting Calendar of Popular Amusements, Sports, Pastimes, Ceremonies, Manners, Customs, and Events, Incident to Each of the Three Hundred and Sixty-Five Days, in Past and Present Times; Forming a Complete History of the Year, Months, and Seasons, and a Perpetual Key to the Almanac…for Daily Use and Diversion*, vol. 1 (London: T. Tegg, 1830), pp. 623–625.

21 *"going around horizontal-wise"*: Peter Mundy, *The Travels of Peter Mundy, in Europe and Asia, 1608–1667*, ed. Sir Richard Carnac Temple (Cambridge, UK: The Hakluyt Society, 1907), pp. 57–59.

21 *"shouted out 'Soni! Soni!'"*: Pietro Della Valle, *Viaggi di Pietro Della Valle il Pellegrino*, ed. Mario Schipano (Venice, Italy: Presso Paolo Baglioni, 1667), p. 102.

22 *from among the festival's traders*: Morley, *Memoirs of Bartholomew Fair*, p. 77.

22 *on the grounds of St. Bartholomew's*: Henry Benjamin Wheatley and Peter Cunningham, *London, Past and Present: Its History, Associations, and Traditions*, vol. 3 (London: J. Murray, 1891), p. 111.

22 *"the whole Fair is the shop of Satan"*: Ben Jonson, *The Works of Ben Jonson*, vol. 3 (London: D. Midwinter, 1756), p. 330.

22 *"so is Bartholomew Fair to the pickpocket"*: "Bartholomew Fair," *New Monthly Magazine*, vol. 115 (London: Chapman and Hall, 1859), pp. 186–187.

22 *"that were whores"*: Samuel Pepys, *The Diary of Samuel Pepys*, vol. 2, ed. Henry B. Wheatley (Boston: C. T. Brainard, 1893), p. 86.

22 *the "Welsh dwarf"*: Hone, *The Every-Day Book and Table Book*, p. 594.

23 *several bonanza years*: Chancellor, *The Pleasure Haunts of London*, p. 329.

ROYAL RETREAT

24 *world's longest-operating amusement park*: "Oldest Amusement Park in Operation," Guinness World Records, 2016, http://www.guinnessworldrecords.com/world-records/oldest-amusement-park-in-operation.

24 *often in droves*: Finn-Olaf Jones, "On the Edge of Copenhagen, a Place to Unwind," *New York Times*, July 29, 2007, p. TR10.

24 *a lost little girl named Kirsten Piil*: "Kirsten Piil Kilde," Bakken, 2016, https://www.bakken.dk/om-os/bakkens-historie/bakkens-historie-kapitel-2/ (in Danish).

24 *safely guided her home*: Daniel M. Madden, *A Religious Guide to Europe* (New York: Collier Books, 1975), p. 394.

25 *the water contained mystical healing powers*: Lucy Andersen, *Copenhagen and Its Environs: A Guide for Travellers.* (London: Walter Scott, 1888), p. 146.

25 *who specialized in barometers*: Hemming Andersen, *Historic Scientific Instruments in Denmark* (Copenhagen: The Royal Danish Academy of Sciences and Letters, 1995), p. 13.

25 *making musical instruments*: Fabio Bevilacqua and Lucio Fregonese, eds., *Nuova Voltiana: Studies on Volta and His Times*, vol. 3 (Milan: Casa Editrice Hoepli, 2001), p. 21.

25 *Christmas-inspired bathing garb*: "Santas from All over the World Meet to Talk Shop," Reuters, July 21, 2016.

26 *when he was twenty*: "Christian J. Tribini (Professor)," Dansk Film Database, 1999, https://danskefilm.dk/skuespiller.php?id=984.

26 *a respectable forty-seven miles per hour*: "Rutschebanen," Bakken, 2016, https://www.bakken.dk/forlystelser/alle-forlystelser/rutschebanen/ (in Danish).

26 *the appreciation and preservation of roller coasters*: "Frequently Asked Questions About ACE," American Coaster Enthusiasts, 2007–2016, http://www.aceonline.org/aboutACE/.

26 *embrace artists, writers, composers*: Franz Eduard Gehring, *Mozart.* (London: Sampson, Low, Marston, Searle, and Rivington, 1883), p. 128.

26 *coffee brewers, gingerbread bakers*: "The History of the Vienna Prater (from 1766)," Prater, 2016, https://www.praterwien.com/en/prater/fun-in-vienna/history/.

26 *a carousel, theatrical plays*: Amelia Sarah Levetus, *Imperial Vienna: An Account of Its History, Traditions, and Arts* (London: John Lane, 1905), p. 372.

27 *the park's 250th anniversary*: Susanne Daus, "Blimps, Freak Shows and Racecars: Vienna's Prater Park Turns 250," Deutsche Welle, April 7, 2016, http://www.dw.com/en/blimps-freak-shows-and-racecars-viennas-prater-park-turns-250/a-19170709.

27 *Alexander and Anatol Renner*: Mike Bennighof, "Austrian Gasbags," Avalanche Press, March 2007, http://www.avalanchepress.com/Austrian_Gasbags.php.

27 *industry, art, and agriculture*: Charles Gindriez and Professor James M. Hart, *International Exhibitions: Paris–Philadelphia–Vienna* (New York: A. S. Barnes, 1878).

27 *seven million fairgoers*: Ly Y. Bui, "The Rotunda of the 1873 Vienna Exhibition," A Treasury of World's Fair Art & Architecture (College Park, MD: University of Maryland Libraries Digital Collections, 2005), https://digital.lib.umd.edu/worldsfairs/essay?pid=umd:992.

27 *a cholera epidemic*: Chelsea Wald, "A Magnificent Failure: The 1873 World Exhibition in Vienna," Chelsea Wald Science Writer, October 28, 2014, http://chelseawald.com/2014/10/a-magnificent-failure-the-1873-world-exhibition-in-vienna.html.

27 *the smart set*: Karl Baedeker, "Vienna," in *Southern Germany and Austria, Including Hungary and Transylvania: Handbook for Travellers*, 5th ed. (Leipzig, Germany: Karl Baedeker, 1883), p. 225.

27 *"the most aristocratic place in the world"*: "Vienna's Big Playground," *New York Times*, March 3, 1893, p. 2.

28 *William the Conqueror*: "A Brief History of Watermouth Castle," Watermouth Family Theme Park and Castle, 2017, https://www.watermouthcastle.com/about/history/.

28 *under the Prince of Wales*: Norman D. Anderson, *Ferris Wheels: An Illustrated History* (Bowling Green, OH: Bowling Green State University Popular Press, 1992), p. 97.

28 *"I have carried this thing out myself"*: "Blackpool's Latest Novelty," original publication unknown, 1895. Available on Lytham & St. Anne's website, http://www.amounderness.co.uk/great_wheel_blackpool_walter_bassett_interview_1895.html.

28 *"the Giant Wheel did not"*: Noel F. Busch, "The Giant Wheel," *Life*, October 13, 1947, pp. 6–15.

28 *killed him in Auschwitz*: Tina Walzer and Stephan Templ, *Unser Wien: "Arisierung" auf österreichisch* (Berlin: Aufbau-Verlag, 2001).

29 *more comfortable seats installed in 2016*: Daus, "Blimps, Freak Shows and Racecars."

30 *its first two seasons alone*: Busch, "The Giant Wheel."

30 *alone and insolvent*: "8 Decembris 1896," in *Journals of the House of Lords*, vol. 128 (Great Britain: Parliament, House of Lords), p. 436.

30 *adjacent amusement park*: Tony Gussin, "Tributes to 'Inspirational Inventor' and Watermouth Castle Owner Richard Haines, 75," *North Devon Gazette*, June 24, 2015.

VAUX POPULI

31 *new realms of fantasy*: "Introduction," in *The Pleasure Garden: From Vauxhall to Coney Island*, ed. Jonathan Conlin (Philadelphia: University of Pennsylvania Press, 2013), p. 1.

31 *"the expected unexpected"*: Ibid., p. 9.

31 *"fine clothes by both sexes"*: Chancellor, *The Pleasure Haunts of London*, p. 197.

32 *"Victorian mass entertainment"*: Rowan Moore, "*Vauxhall Gardens: A History* by David E. Coke and Alan Borg—Review," *Guardian*, July 1, 2011.

32 *establish their professional names*: Rachel Cowgill, "Performance Alfresco," in Conlin, *The Pleasure Garden*, pp. 106–110.

32 *"much-frequented rural brothel"*: Alfred Bunn, ed., *The Vauxhall Papers* (London: John Andrews and John Mitchell, 1841), p. 113.

32 *"people would have been born without heads"*: Joseph Brasbridge, *The Fruits of Experience*, 2nd ed. (London: A. J. Valpy, 1824), p. 149.

32 *"a most august royal tent"*: Bunn, *The Vauxhall Papers*, p. 84.

33 *to enjoy themselves*: William B. Boulton, *The Amusements of Old London*, vol. 1 (London: John C. Nimmo, 1901), p. 263.

33 *for the next thirty years*: Chancellor, *The Pleasure Haunts of London*, p. 221.

33 *Heidegger arranged the entertainment*: David E. Coke, "Brief History," Vauxhall Gardens 1661–1859, July 2, 2016, http://www.vauxhallgardens.com/vauxhall_gardens_briefhistory_page.html.

33 *a pickpocket—later apprehended*: Warwick William Wroth and Arthur Edgar Wroth. *The London Pleasure Gardens of the Eighteenth Century* (London: Macmillan, 1896), p. 310.

33 *that same season*: Chancellor, *The Pleasure Haunts of London*, p. 206.

33 *yet another Vauxhall innovation*: Scott A. Lukas, *Theme Park* (London: Reaktion Books, 2008), p. 24.

34 *"a picture by Van Dyke"*: "A Baronet Who Could Not Get a Wife," *Daily Telegraph*, June 17, 1893, p. 2.

35 *"the Duke of Marlborough!"*: Rev. Dr. John Trusler, *The Works of William Hogarth* (London: Shakspeare Press, 1831), p. 246.

35 *compare notes over supper*: William Makepeace Thackeray, *Vanity Fair* (New York: P. F. Collier and Son, 1917), chapter 6.

35 *"very roughly-painted boards and sawdust"*: Charles Dickens, *Sketches by Boz: Illustrative of Every-day Life and Every-day People* (New York: The University Society, 1908), chapter 14.

35 *went aloft atop his horse*: A Brief Historical and Descriptive Account of the Royal Gardens, Vauxhall. (London: Gye and Balne, 1822), p. 27.

35 *"steadily deteriorating"*: Chancellor, *The Pleasure Haunts of London*, p. 225.

35 *the London Wine Company*: "Vauxhall Gardens and Kennington Lane," in *Survey of London*, ed. Howard Roberts and Walter H. Godfrey, vol. 23, *South Bank and Vauxhall: The Parish of St. Mary Lambeth, Part I* (London: London County Council, 1951).

35 *first recorded parachute accident*: "Aerial Voyages," in *Temple Bar: A London Magazine for Town and Country Readers*, vol. 114 (London: Richard Bentley and Son, May–August 1898), p. 122.

35 *as thirty shillings apiece*: Chancellor, *The Pleasure Haunts of London*, p. 225.

36 *a competing social attraction*: Moore, "Vauxhall Gardens: A History."

36 *the site's sudden rowdiness*: Chancellor, *The Pleasure Haunts of London*, p. 226.

36 *occupied the site since 1670*: Evelyn Cecil, *London Parks and Gardens* (New York: E. P. Dutton, 1907), p. 315.

36 *trying to settle his accounts*: "Landownership: Later Estates," in *A History of the County of Middlesex*, vol. 12, Chelsea, ed. Patricia E. C. Croot (London: Victoria County History, 2004), pp. 123–145.

36 *an entertainment entity*: Judith A. Adams, *The American Amusement Park Industry: A History of Technology and Thrills* (Boston: Twain Publishers, 1991), p. 6.

37 *three-thousand-person capacity*: Chancellor, *The Pleasure Haunts of London*, p. 229.

37 *Egypt's pyramids*: Stephen Cairns, "The Stone Books of Orientalism," in *Colonial Modernities: Building, Dwelling and Architecture in British India and Ceylon*, ed. Peter Scriver and Vikramaditya Prakash (New York: Routledge, 2007), pp. 60–61.

37 *to keep his rival from expanding*: Louise Allen, "So What Was Wrong with Ranelagh?" Jane Austen's London, May 8, 2016, https://janeaustenslondon.com/2016/05/08/so-what-was-wrong-with-ranelagh/.

37 *"everybody goes there"*: Cecil, *London Parks and Gardens*, p. 315.

38 *"constantly meeting each other"*: Wolfgang Amadeus Mozart, *Mozart: A Life in Letters*, ed. Cliff Eisen, trans. Stewart Spencer (London: Penguin Books, 2006), pp. 40–41.

38 *Only that, too, has vanished*: Allen, "So What Was Wrong with Ranelagh?"

38 *the happy courting seasons*: Walter Thornbury, *Old and New London: A Narrative of Its History, Its People, and Its Places*, new ed., vol. 2 (London: Cassell, 1892), p. 46.

38 *"were free to visit"*: William F. Mangels, *The Outdoor Amusement Industry: From Earliest Times to the Present* (New York: Vantage Press, 1952), p. 9.

39 *"in the Disney parks"*: Adams, *The American Amusement Park Industry*, p. 7.

39 *"large fish or mermaids"*: Henry B. Wheatley, "Jenny's Whim," *London, Past and Present*, vol. 2 (London: John Murray, 1891), p. 306.

39 *who manufactured fireworks*: Edward Walford, "Pimlico," in Thornbury, *Old and New London*, vol. 5 (London: Cassell, 1878), pp. 39–49.

39 *white slavery in Morocco*: John O'Keefe, *Recollections of the Life of John O'Keefe*, vol. 2 (London: Henry Colburn, 1826), p. 337.

39 *"suggested 'Jenny's Whim'"*: Wheatley, "Jenny's Whim," *London, Past and Present*, vol. 2, p. 306.

40 *"with a wheelbarrow before him"*: Mangels, *The Outdoor Amusement Industry*, p. 8.

40 *the most fashionable crowd in town*: Chancellor, *The Pleasure Haunts of London*, p. 348.

40 *"special good behaviour anywhere"*: Ibid., p. 351.

40 *"by mid-century"*: Altick, *The Shows of London*, p. 36.

40 *former pyrotechnician of Versailles*: Louis Dussieux, *Le Château de Versailles: Histoire et Description*, vol. 1 (Versailles, France: L. Bernard, 1881), p. 494.

EARTHLY DELIGHTS

41 *"for the inhabitants"*: R. P. Forster, *A Collection of the Most Celebrated Voyages & Travels, from the Discovery of America to the Present Time*, vol. 2 (Newcastle upon Tyne, UK: Mackenzie and Dent, 1818), pp. 199–200.

41 *"and card parties"*: Ibid., p. 181.

41 *Hudson Streets and Broadway*: W. W. Pasko, ed., *Old New York: A Journal Relating to the History and Antiquities of New York City*, vol. 2 (New York: W. W. Pasko, 1890), p. 12.

41 *the French West Indies*: Charles L. Blockson, "Black Samuel Fraunces," Temple University Libraries, 2012, https://library.temple.edu/collections/blockson/fraunces.

41 *the city's harbor front*: Robert I. Golder, "Samuel Fraunces," in *The Encyclopedia of New York City*, ed. Kenneth T. Jackson (New Haven: Yale University Press, 1995), p. 438.

41 *Fraunces Tavern*: "The Evolution of the New York Hotel," *New York Times*, December 2, 1906, p. 3.

42 *not to the British*: "History in Biography," *New York Times*, September 22, 1931, p. 26.

42 *"rear of old Vauxhall"*: Washington Irving. *The Works of Washington Irving.* (New York: P. F. Collier, 1881), p. 20.

42 *Wax likenesses*: Walter Barrett, *The Old Merchants of New York* (New York: M. Doolady, 1870), p. 176.

42 *chief household steward*: "Samuel Fraunces," Fraunces Tavern Museum, Sons of the Revolution in the State of New York, 2002–2016, http://www.frauncestavernmuseum.org/samuel-fraunces/.

42 *federal office space*: Ibid.

43 *America's independence*: Naomi Stubbs, "Pleasure Gardens of America," in Conlin, *The Pleasure Garden*, p. 133.

43 *its own merry-go-round*: Frederick Fried, *A Pictorial History of the Carousel* (New York: A. S. Barnes, 1964), p. 51.

44 *162 years later*: Heath Schenker, "Pleasure Gardens, Theme Parks, and the Picturesque," in Terence Young and Robert Riley, eds., *Theme Park Landscapes: Antecedents and Variations* (Washington, DC: Dumbarton Oaks Research Library and Collection, 2002), p. 77.

44 *cookies, cakes, and ice cream*: Anne Cooper Funderburg, *Chocolate, Strawberry, and Vanilla: A History of American Ice Cream* (Bowling Green, OH: Bowling Green State University Popular Press, 1995), p. 12.

45 *to be destroyed piecemeal*: "Historic Site to Be Sold," *New York Times*, April 11, 1909, p. 13.

46   *ruin for everyone*: Luc Sante, *Low Life* (London: Granta Books, 1998), p. 97.

46   *in the barroom*: Douglass K. Daniel, "The Greatest Show(man) on Earth," *Boys' Life*, January 2000, p. 13.

46   *in the background*: Phineas Taylor Barnum, *The Life of P. T. Barnum.* (London: Sampson Low, Son, 1855), p. 214.

46   *"anxious to sell it"*: Ibid., pp. 215–216.

46   *by his grandfather*: Ibid., pp. 218–219.

47   *"a bona fide zoo"*: Lissa Rivera, "The Great Bygone Museum Tour," *MCNY Blog: New York Stories* (blog), Museum of the City of New York, December 3, 2013, https://blog.mcny.org/2013/12/03/the-great-bygone-museum-tour/.

47   *part of the bargain*: Andrea Stulman Dennett, *Weird and Wonderful: The Dime Museum in America.* (New York: New York University Press, 1997), pp. 24-25.

48   *theater-saloon-hotel complex*: Neil Harris, *Humbug: The Art of P. T. Barnum* (Chicago: University of Chicago Press, 1973), p. 21.

48   *first luxury hotel in New York*: May N. Stone, "Astor House," in Jackson, *The Encyclopedia of New York City*, p. 63.

49   *and New York City's only 813,669*: "POP Culture: 1860," United States Census Bureau, July 18, 2017, https://www.census.gov/history/www/through_the_decades/fast_facts/1860_fast_facts.html.

50   *before it could be extinguished*: Herbert Asbury, "That Was New York: The Great Fire of 1835," *New Yorker*, August 2, 1930, pp. 32–37.

50   *"blood-red flame"*: "The Great Fire—Full Particulars of the Buildings Burnt—Names of the Sufferers," *New York Daily Tribune*, July 21, 1845, p. 2.

50   *made the Museum home*: "Disastrous Conflagration," New York *Sun*, July 14, 1865, p. 1.

51   *in their tanks*: Helen Thompson, "150 Years Ago, a Fire in P. T. Barnum's Museum Boiled Two Whales Alive," Smithsonian.com, July 20, 2015, https://www.smithsonianmag.com/smart-news/pt-barnums-bizarre-museum-burned-ground-1865-180955955/.

51   *were all confirmed dead*: Greg Young and Tom Meyers, "The Fire at Barnum's American Museum 150 Years Ago," The Bowery Boys: New York City History, July 16, 2015, http://www.boweryboyshistory.com/2015/07/the-fire-at-barnums-american-museum-150-years-ago.html.

51   *Hopper Striker Mott*: Hopper Striker Mott, *Mott, Hopper, Striker* (New York: Historical, 1898), p. 3.

51   *"Jones's Wood"*: Hopper Striker Mott, "Jones's Wood," in *Valentine's Manual of the City of New York, 1917–1918*, new series no. 2, ed. Henry Collins Brown (New York: Old Colony Press, 1917), p. 140.

51   *from the orchard*: "Losses by the Fire," *New York Times*, May 17, 1894.

51   *dared enter its waters*: Ryan Healy, "The Strange History of NYC's Mighty Hell Gate," Gothamist, February 22, 2016, http://gothamist.com/2016/02/22/hell_gate_history_nyc.php.

51   *a Central Park, if you will*: William C. Bryant, "A New Public Park," *New York Evening Post*, July 3, 1844.

51   *downtown businessmen*: Jean Ashton, Nina Nazionale, and New-York Historical Society, *When Did the Statue of Liberty Turn Green? & 101 Other Questions About New York City* (New York: Columbia University Press, 2010), p. 141.

52   *the expense of their own*: Edwin G. Burrows and Mike Wallace, *Gotham: A History of New York City to 1898* (New York: Oxford University Press, 1999), p. 791.

52   *and labor unions*: Joy M. Kestenbaum, "Jones's Wood," in Jackson, *The Encyclopedia of New York City*.

52   *the Historical Society said*: Ashton, *When Did the Statue of Liberty Turn Green?*, p. 142.

52   *favored beverage of choice*: Gary Kyriazi, *The Great American Amusement Parks: A Pictorial History* (Secaucus, NJ: Castle Books, 1976), p. 16.

52   *horse-drawn trolleys*: Mott, "Jones's Wood," in *Valentine's Manual of the City of New York*, p. 147.

52   *in the chorus*: "Amusements," *New York Times*, June 26, 1888, pg. 4.

52   *war with the Austrians*: Mangels, *The Outdoor Amusement Industry*, p. 18.

52   *sixty thousand people*: Ashton, *When Did the Statue of Liberty Turn Green?* p. 142.

52   *Workingmen's Union rally*: "The Workingmen's Union: Continuation of the Grand Festival at Jones' Wood Second Day of the Demonstration. Fifty Thousand People in the Union, and a Good Share of Them at the Frolic," *New York Times*, May 31, 1865.

52   *reduced to eight*: Burrows and Wallace, *Gotham*, p. 987.

53   *architect Julius Kastner's*: Sarah Bean Apmann, "East 11th Street, a Slice of East Village History," Off the Grid, August 10, 2016, http://gvshp.org/blog/2016/08/10/east-11th-street-a-slice-of-east-village-history/.

53   *according to Mott*: Mott, "Jones's Wood," in *Valentine's Manual of the City of New York*, p. 156.

53   *the burning sheds*: "Losses by the Fire."

53   *"pleasure-seeking New Yorkers"*: Mott, "Jones's Wood," in *Valentine's Manual of the City of New York*, p. 159.

53   *upper and middle classes*: Burrows and Wallace, *Gotham*, p. 585.

54   *a sports arena*: Steven A. Reiss, "Madison Square Garden," in Jackson, *The Encyclopedia of New York City*, p. 712.

54   *balloon ascensions*: Andrew S. Dolkart, "Castle Clinton," in Jackson, *The Encyclopedia of New York City*, p. 188.

54   *"any public saloon in town"*: "Niblo's Garden," *Gleason's Pictorial*, March 6, 1852, p. 1.

54   *within the enclosure*: Ben Feldman, "A Review of *East in Eden: William Niblo and His Pleasure Garden of Yore*," The New York Wanderer, November 25, 2015, http://newyorkwanderer.com/a-review-of-east-in-eden-william-niblo-and-his-pleasure-garden-of-yore/.

55   *having a good time*: Erla Zwingle, "Catherine the Great," *National Geographic*, September 1998, p. 95.

55   *"fit for royalty"*: Edward Strachan and Roy Bolton, *Russia & Europe in the Nineteenth Century* (London: Sphinx Fine Art, 2008), p. 80.

55   *desultory "ice slides"*: Joel Meares, "Catherine the Great Put Rollers on the World's First Coaster," *Wired*, December 27, 2011, https://www.wired.com/2011/12/pl-prototyperollercoaster/.

55   *late-nineteenth-century trip to Russia*: Robert Sears, *An Illustrated Description of the Russian Empire* (New York: self-published, 1885), pp. 548, 549.

56   *"stairs and sleds"*: Robert Cartmell, *The Incredible Scream Machine: A History of the Roller Coaster* (Bowling Green, OH: Amusement Park Books, and Bowling Green State University Popular Press, 1987), p. 20.

56   *an English historian, in 1784*: William Coxe, *Travels into Poland, Russia, Sweden, and Denmark* (Dublin: S. Prince, R. Moncrieffe, W. Colles, T. Walker, C. Jenkin, W. Wilson, L. White, R. Burton, J. Cash, and P. Byrne, 1784).

56   *repeat their adventure*: Ibid.

57   *"American mountains [Американская гора]"*: Fabrizio Tassinari, *Why Europe Fears Its Neighbors* (Santa Barbara, CA: ABC-CLIO, 2009), p. 130.

57   *first-ever racing coaster*: Cartmell, *The Incredible Scream Machine*, p. 25.

57   *William F. Mangels*: Mangels, *The Outdoor Amusement Industry*, pp. 84–85.

58   *Monsieur Lebonjer*: David Lindsay, "Terror Bound," *American Heritage*, September 1998.

58   *collar of a horse*: A. and W. Galignani, *Galignani's New Paris Guide*, 17th ed. (Paris: A. and W. Galignani, 1830), p. 566.

58   *an eleven-year-old boy*: Robert Snedden and David West, *A Brief Illustrated History of Space Exploration* (North Mankato, MN: Capstone Press, 2017), p. 4.

59   *the Élysée Palace*: "Pierre Jacques Onésyme Bergeret de Grancourt (Biographical Details)," The British Museum, 2017, http://www.britishmuseum.org/research/search_the_collection_database/term_details.aspx?bioId=25526.

59   *eleven seasons, until 1778*: Philip H. Highfill Jr., Kalman A. Burnhim, and Edward A. Langhans, *A Biographical Dictionary of Actors, Actresses, Musicians, Dancers, Managers, & Other Stage Personnel in London, 1660–1800*, vol. 15, *Tibbett to M. West* (Carbondale and Edwardsville, IL: Southern Illinois University Press, 1993), pp. 31–33.

60   *"the modest Russian Mountains"*: Anonymous, "Parisian Manners," *The Literary Gazette, or Journal of Belles Lettres, Arts, Politics, & c.* (London), August 23, 1817, p. 125.

60   *political campaigns in New York*: Barbara Williams, "Remembering Fred Fried, the Historic Carousel's Best Friend," *Carousel News & Trader*, December 2007, p. 14.

60   *Brooklyn-born expert*: Geoffrey T. Hellman, "Calligraphic Art," *New Yorker*, February 17, 1975, pp. 27–28.

60   *only with less bloodshed*: Fried, *A Pictorial History of the Carousel*, pp. 13, 18.

62   *another mistress of the monarch's*: Julia Mary Cartwright Ady, *Madame: A Life of Henrietta, Daughter of Charles I and Duchess of Orleans* (London: Seeley, 1894), p. 118.

62   *"radiating from a center pole"*: Fried, *A Pictorial History of the Carousel*, p. 19.

62   *North Tonawanda, New York*: David Greenlees, "Armitage-Herschell Company, the Herschell-Spillman Company and Herschell-Spillman Engines," The Old Motor, May 30, 2013, http://theoldmotor.com/?p=82237.

63   *painting a broad picture*: Mangels, *The Outdoor Amusement Industry*, p. 12.

63   *three years in Philadelphia*: Robert Neiiendam, "Georg Carstensen," in *Danish Biographical Reading*, 3rd ed. (Copenhagen: Gyldendal 1979–1984).

63   *publishing an arts journal*: Anonymous, "New Publications," in *North American Review*, vol. 46 (Boston: Otis, Broaders, 1838), p. 567.

64   *peculiarities of his personality*: John Loring, introduction to *Tivoli Gardens*, by Harry Benson (New York: Abrams, 2007), p. 9.

64   *overflowed with them*: Ben Hamilton, "Remembering Tivoli's Founder: A Showman with a Fondness for Champagne and Jazzy Waistcoats," *Copenhagen Post*, May 23, 2017, http://cphpost.dk/history/tivoli.html.

64   *sported the same pair twice*: Jørgen Larsen, "Det Gamle København: Velkommen i Tivoli," *Berlingske*, April 11, 2016, https://www.b.dk/kultur/det-gamle-koebenhavn-velkommen-i-tivoli.

64   *"it slipped almost as well"*: Gilles-Antoine Langlois, *Folies, Tivolis, et Attractions* (Paris: Delegation to the Artistic Action of the City of Paris, 1991).

64   *"Sumptuous orgies"*: Ibid.

65   *in peacock finery*: Neiiendam, "Georg Carstensen."

65   *"the representative of stupidity"*: George Pattison, "Kierkegaard and Copenhagen," in *The Oxford Handbook of Kierkegaard*, ed. John Lippitt and George Pattison (Oxford, UK: Oxford University Press, 2013), p. 60.

65   *"an article against Heiberg"*: Eliseo Pérez-Álvarez, *A Vexing Gadfly: The Late Kierkegaard on Economic Matters* (Eugene, OR: Pickwick Publications, 2009), p. 117.

65   *"Vauxhall-Concerts"*: Elisabeth Oxfeldt, *Nordic Orientalism: Paris and Cosmopolitan Imagination 1800–1900* (Copenhagen: Museum Tusculanum Press, University of Copenhagen, 2005), p. 68.

65   *and stunning illuminations*: Neiiendam, "Georg Carstensen."

65   *the length of the lease*: Af Jørgen Larsen, "Det Gamle København."

65   *major trading port*: Ben Hamilton, "Remembering Tivoli's Founder."

65   *fears of revolution*: Alan Riding, "The Thrills Endure as Tivoli Turns 150," *New York Times*, August 8, 1993.

65   *Rosenborg Garden*: Robert Neiiendam, "Georg Carstensen."

65   *"a sea of tranquility"*: Hamilton, "Remembering Tivoli's Founder."

66   *the cover letter*: Oxfeldt, *Nordic Orientalism*, pp. 68–69.

66   *park business would generate*: Ibid.

66   *Copenhagen's business community*: Larsen, "Det Gamle København."

66   *as it was named*: Loring, introduction to *Tivoli Gardens*, p. 9.

66   *rational, late-classical style*: Ida Haugsted, "H. C. Stilling," Kunstindeks Danmark & Weilbachs Kunstnerleksikon, Castle and Cultural Agency, 1994, https://www.kulturarv.dk/kid/VisWeilbach.do?kunstnerId=10713&wsektion=alle.

67   *two-month construction period*: Oxfeldt, *Nordic Orientalism*, pp. 68–69.

67   *the excavation site*: Hamilton, "Remembering Tivoli's Founder."

67   *a sense of otherworldliness*: Dudley Glass, "Tivoli Is Denmark's Model Fun-Fair," *New York Times*, August 26, 1962, p. 19.

67   *larger than they actually were*: Lukas, *Theme Park*, p. 23.

67   *seated side by side*: Brigitte Kjaer, "Tivolis far fylder rundt: Havens grundlægger var en kreativ vildbasse," Politiken, August 29, 2012, https://politiken.dk/kultur/art5453187/Tivolis-far-fylder-rundt-Havens-grundl%C3%A6gger-var-en-kreativ-vildbasse.

67   *1845 "Champagne Gallop"*: "Hans Christian Lumbye (1810–1874)," The Johann Strauss Society of Great Britain, 2017, http://www.johann-strauss.org.uk/composers-a-m.php?id=182.

68   *the line stayed in*: Annette Lust, *From the Greek Mimes to Marcel Marceau and Beyond: Mimes, Actors, Pierrots, and Clowns: A Chronicle of the Many Visages of Mime in the Theatre* (Lanham, MD: Scarecrow Press, 2002), p. 60.

68   *his death in 1893*: Loring, introduction to *Tivoli Gardens*, p. 11.

68   *their worried parents*: Victor Borge, "Love Letter to a Garden," *Life*, June 23, 1961, pp. 87–88.

RESTLESS SPIRITS

69   *the unprepossessing town of Mauch Chunk*: Thomas C. James, MD "Brief Account of the Discovery of Anthracite Coal on the Lehigh," in *Memoirs of the Historical Society of Pennsylvania*, vol. 1, ed. Edward Armstrong (Philadelphia: J. B. Lippincott, 1864), p. 331.

69   *began lining up*: Mangels, *The Outdoor Amusement Industry*, pp. 86–87.

70   *"the marks of fingernails"*: Lindsay, "Terror Bound."

70   *change in fall foliage*: Felix J. Koch, "Ho! For the Oldest American Railroad," *Railway Conductor*, October 1916, pp. 680–685.

71   *sold as scrap*: "The History of Roller Coasters: The Mauch Chunk Gravity Railway," Entertainment Designer, October, 8, 2011, http://entertainmentdesigner.com/history-of-theme-parks/the-history-of-roller-coasters-the-mauch-chunk-gravity-railway/.

71   *a stationary steam engine*: Fried, *A Pictorial History of the Carousel*, p. 31.

71   *objects of metal, usually tin*: Brian Morgan, "Frederick Savage, I Presume," *Merry-Go-Roundup*, Summer 2014.

72   *could be assembled*: David Braithwaite, *Savage of King's Lynn: Inventor of Machines & Merry-Go-Rounds* (Somerset, UK: Patrick Stephens, 1975).

72   *"were painted brightly"*: "Birthplace of Frederick Savage," Engineering Timelines, 2017, http://www.engineering-timelines.com/scripts/engineeringItem.asp?id=791.

72   *fairground rides internationally*: "Old King's Lynn Fairground Master's Work to Go Digital," *Lynn (UK) News*, November 18, 2013.

72   *"using a stick"*: Ronald H. Clark, *The Steam Engine Builders of Norfolk* (Sparkford Nr. Yeovil, Somerset, UK: Faulis Haynes, 1988).

72   *"Tivoli belongs to the future"*: Loring, introduction to *Tivoli Gardens*, p. 11.

73   *the life of Christ*: George Pattison, *Poor Paris!: Kierkegaard's Critique of the Spectacular City* (Berlin: Walter de Gruyter, 1999), p. 23.

74   *river of fresh ideas*: Kjaer, "Tivolis far fylder rundt."

75   *to gather ideas*: Loring, introduction to *Tivoli Gardens*, p. 10.

75   *"a summer and a half"*: Neiiendam, "Georg Carstensen."

75   *a year after the wedding*: Ibid.

75   *Carstensen's cousin*: G. Biilmann Petersen, "Tivoli," in *The Architecture of Denmark* (Oxford, UK: The Architectural Press, 1949).

75   *his own admission into Tivoli*: Hamilton, "Remembering Tivoli's Founder."

75   *"the age of 54"*: "Our History," Tivoli, 2017, https://www.tivoligardens.com/en/om/tivolis+historie.

SON OF BLUBBER

76   *"the Isle of Wight"*: "Blackgang Chine," Atlas Obscura, 2017, https://www.atlasobscura.com/places/blackgang-chine-theme-park.

76   *"but could not save!"*: William Henry Davenport Adams, *The History, Topography, and Antiquities of the Isle of Wight* (London: Smith, Elder, 1856), p. 209.

76   *"roaring at the foot of it"*: George Mogridge, *Wanderings in the Isle of Wight* (London: The Religious Tract Society, 1846), pp. 118–119.

77   *to operating shops retailing hair products*: "History of Blackgang Chine," Blackgang Chine Land of Imagination, 2017, https://blackgangchine.com/history-of-blackgang-chine/.

77   *southernmost point of Dorset*: William White, *History, Gazetteer, and Directory of the County of Hampshire, Including the Isle of Wight* (London: Simpkin, Marshall, 1878), p. 189.

77   *"a vast and horrible opening"*: Editor of the *Picture of London, A Guide to All the Watering and Sea Bathing Places in England and Wales, with a Description of the Lakes; a Sketch of a Tour in Wales; and Itineraries* (London: Longman, Hurst, Rees, Orme, & Brown, 1824), p. 147.

78   *"sense of morbid curiosity"*: Emily Pearce, "In the Land of Imagination," *Isle of Wight County Press*, July 12, 2013.

79   *"until May 1843"*: Simon Dabell, quoted in "Blackgang Chine," Wikipedia, n.d., https://en.wikipedia.org/wiki/Blackgang_Chine.

79   *"for the same purpose"*: *Shaw's Tourist's Picturesque Guide to the Isle of Wight* (London: The Graphotyping Co., 1873), p. 76.

79   *eleven and a half feet per year*: Karl Fabricius, "The Amusement Park Being Swallowed by the Sea," Scribol, July 6, 2012, http://scribol.com/anthropology-and-history/urban-exploration/the-amusement-park-being-swallowed-by-the-sea/.

80   *"then it'll suddenly roar"*: Reuters, "Robotic Dinosaurs at U.K. Theme Park Upgraded with Cognitive Software," November 15, 2016.

80   *married for a second time*: Richard N. Swett, *Leadership by Design: Creating an Architecture of Trust* (Atlanta: Greenway Communications, 2005), p. 27.

80   *New York City*: Neiiendam, "Georg Carstensen."

80   *"most instructive University ever opened"*: Horace Greeley, *Art and Industry as Represented in the Exhibition at the Crystal Palace, New York 1853–4* (New York: Redfield, 1853), p. iv.

80   *should not exceed fifty cents*: "New-York Crystal Palace: A Famous Enterprise Recalled by the Death of Its Chief Promoter," *New York Times*, July 5, 1887.

80   *James Bogardus*: "Our Crystal Palace," *Putnam's Monthly*, August 1853, p. 123.

80   *the fair's location from afar*: John E. Findling, ed., *Historical Dictionary of World's Fairs and Expositions, 1851–1988* (Westport, CT: Greenwood Press, 1990).

80   *thirty-two windows*: Swett, *Leadership by Design*, pp. 27–28.

81   *"Eastern story-tellers saw"*: "Editor's Easy Chair," *Harper's New Monthly Magazine*, November 1853, p. 844.

81   *"honor to our country"*: "The New York Crystal Palace," *Scientific American*, June 4, 1853, p. 301.

81   *were as unsightly*: George Carstensen and Karl Gildemeister, *New York Crystal Palace: Illustrated Description of the Building* (New York: Riker, Thorne, 1854), pp. 9–22.

81   *a single day*: David Ferris Kerby, "The Writer's Calendar," *Editors*, January 6, 1923, p. v.

82   *"the dead could not be raised"*: Barnum, *The Life of P. T. Barnum*, p. 387.

82   *physically and financially spent*: Swett, *Leadership by Design*, p. 29.

82   *the Crystal Palace*: Clara Greed, *Inclusive Urban Design: Public Toilets* (Oxford, UK: Architectural Press, 2003), p. 42.

82   *and a shoeshine*: "'Spending a Penny': Or the First Public Flushing Toilets Open on This Day in 1852," The Victorianist, February 2, 2011, http://thevictorianist.blogspot.com/2011/02/spending-penny-or-first-public-flushing.html.

82   *Waring Latting*: *Eighth Annual Report of the American Institute of the City of New-York* (Albany, NY: Weed, Parsons, 1850), p. 57.

83   *namesake 1889 tower in Paris*: Azmathulla Khan, *Risks Mitigated in World's Most Amazing Projects* (Chennai, India: Notion Press, 2017).

83   *souvenir spoons, and handkerchiefs*: Lindsay Turley, "The Great Crystal Palace Fire of 1838," *MCNY Blog: New York Stories* (blog), Museum of the City of New York, December 4, 2012, https://blog.mcny.org/2012/12/04/the-great-crystal-palace-fire-of-1858/.

83   *a safety catch*: Spencer Klaw, "All Safe, Gentlemen, All Safe," *American Heritage*, August–September 1978.

83   *in June 1854*: Gary Holland, "Crystal Palace: A History," BBC, July 27, 2004, http://www.bbc.co.uk/london/content/articles/2004/07/27/history_feature.shtml.

83   *the immense Handel organ*: Chas Early, "November 30, 1936: The Crystal Palace Is Destroyed by Fire," BT, May 22, 2017, http://home.bt.com/news/on-this-day/november-30-1936-the-crystal-palace-is-destroyed-by-fire-11363947170210.

83   *"This is the end of an age"*: Neil Clark, "What Happened the Night the Crystal Palace Burnt Down?," *Express*, November 28, 2016.

THE BEACH IS DIVINE

87   *motion and gravity*: Amanda Gefter, "Newton's Apple: The Real Story," *New Scientist*, January 18, 2010, https://www.newscientist.com/article/2170052-newtons-apple-the-real-story/.

87   *taste the adventure for himself*: Martin Easdown, *Amusement Park Rides* (Oxford, UK: Shire Library, 2012), p. 10.

87   *former New England Puritans*: George McKenna, *The Puritan Origins of American Patriotism* (New Haven, CT: Yale University Press, 2007), p. 87.

87   *The following year, 1867*: Breana Noble, "Hillsdale Dropout Becomes 'Father of the American Roller Coaster,'" *Collegian*, Hillsdale College, October 8, 2015.

87   *another Puritan sanctuary*: Abraham E. Weaver, ed., *A Standard History of Elkhart County Indiana*, vol. 2 (Chicago and New York: The American Historical Society, 1916), p. 523.

87   *the position of partner*: "L. A. Thompson of Coney Fame Dies," New York *Sun*, March 9, 1919, p. 13.

88   *the United States*: Neil Gale, *The Midway Plaisance at the 1893 World's Columbia Exposition in Chicago* (Belleville, IL: self-pub., 2017), p. 21.

88   *nervous collapse from his work*: Cartmell, *The Incredible Scream Machine*, p. 40.

88   *a slightly elevated angle*: Jeffrey Stanton, "History of Early Roller Coasters, 1870–1886," Coney Island History Site, September 6, 2013, https://www.westland.net/coneyisland/articles/EarlyRollerCoasters-1870-1886.htm.

88   *"opposite end of the course"*: LaMarcus A. Thompson, "Gravity Switch-Back Railway," Patent No. 332,762, Google Patents, December 22, 1885, https://patents.google.com/patent/US332762/en.

88   *"Improvement in Inclined Railways"*: John G. Taylor, "Improvement in Inclined Railways," Patent No. 128,674, Google Patents, July 2, 1872, https://patents.google.com/patent/US128674.

88   *"the Father of the Gravity Ride"*: "Coney Island," *Life*, August 22, 1949, p. 53.

89   *"precipitous cliffs"*: Workers of the Writers' Program of the Works Projects Administration in the State of Washington, *Washington: A Guide to the Evergreen State* (Portland, OR: Binsfords & Mort, 1941), p. 397.

89   *"the gentle art of sliding"*: Mangels, *The Outdoor Amusement Industry*, p. 81.

90   *"a nickel or a dime"*: William Kahrl, "The Taming of American Amusement Parks," in *World's Fair*, vols. 9–13 (Corte Madera, CA: World's Fair, 1989), p. 21.

90   *"everything else in sight"*: "McKane's Remarkable Career," *New York Times*, February 16, 1894.

90   *"get anything on him"*: "Days When McKane Ruled Gravesend," *Brooklyn Daily Eagle*, January 19, 1913, p. 13.

90   *which included Coney Island*: Stephen Weinstein, "Gravesend," in Jackson, *The Encyclopedia of New York City* (New Haven, Connecticut: Yale University Press, 1995), p. 501.

90   *the sand dunes*: United States Department of Housing and Urban Development, *Brooklyn, Steeplechase Amusement Park Construction and Operation: Environmental Impact Statement* (1989).

90   *a community unto itself*: Edo McCullough, *Good Old Coney Island: A Sentimental Journey into the Past* (New York: Charles Scribner's Sons, 1957), p. viii.

90   *wealthy expatriate Deborah Moody*: Oliver Pilat and Jo Ranson, *Sodom by the Sea: An Affectionate History of Coney Island* (Garden City, New York: Doubleday, Doran, 1941), p. 11.

90   *the Puritans of Massachusetts*: "Lady Deborah Moody," The National Society of Colonial Dames in the State of New York, July 2, 2015; available at Archive Today, http://archive.is/VLcOB.

90   *the New World*: "Lady Deborah Moody, a Dangerous Woman, Comes to New England," New England Historical Society, January 5, 2016, http://www.newenglandhistoricalsociety.com/lady-deborah-moody-a-dangerous-woman-comes-to-new-england/.

90   *ownership of their property*: Ibid.

90   *the Five Nations*: Pilat and Ranson, *Sodom by the Sea*, p. 12.

90   *to the property*: Eric J. Ierardi, *Gravesend: The Home of Coney Island* (Charleston, SC: Arcadia Publishing, 2001), p. 30.

90   *Coney Island: Lost and Found*: Charles Denson, *Coney Island: Lost and Found* (Berkeley, CA: Ten Speed Press, 2002), p. 2.

90   *and cattle farming*: James Lilliefors, *America's Boardwalks: From Coney Island to California* (New Brunswick, NJ: Rutgers University Press, 2006), p. 27.

91   *Western World, 1750-1840*: Alain de Botton, "Book Review / Waves of Joy and Despair: The Lure of the Sea: Seaside in the Western World, 1740–1840)," (London) *Independent*, April 9, 1994.

91   *The term resort*: Catherine Donzel, Alexis Gregory, and Marc Walter, *Grand American Hotels* (New York: The Vendome Press, 1989), p. 20.

91   *"popular resorts of America"*: Julian Ralph, "Coney Island," *Scribner's Magazine*, July 1896, p. 16.

92   *a travel-service guidebook*: George Frederick Pardon, *Porter's Guide to Blackpool* (Blackpool, UK: William Porter, 1857), p. 33.

92   *their Pleasure Beach*: Josephine Kane, "Edwardian Amusement Parks," in Conlin, *The Pleasure Garden*, p. 221.

92   *manufacturing in Philadelphia*: Peter Mowbray, "Humble Beginnings: The Pleasure Beach at Blackpool," Live in Blackpool, January 2, 2011, http://www.liveinblackpool.co.uk/forum/index.php?topic=1719.0.

92   *Hotchkiss Bicycle Railway*: Easdown, *Amusement Park Rides*, p. 28.

92   *his Philadelphia connection*: Josephine Kane, *The Architecture of Pleasure: British Amusement Parks, 1900–1939* (New York: Ashgate Publishing, 2013), pp. 29–30.

92   *mechanical rides there*: Gary Kyriazi, "Seabreeze—A Shining Example of Survival," Park World, February 8, 2011, http://www.parkworld-online.com/seabreeze-a-shining-example-of-survival/.

92   *horse-and-carriage traffic*: Denson, *Coney Island: Lost and Found*, p. 6.

92   *his brother Abraham*: Austin Parsons Stockwell, *A History of the Town of Gravesend, N. Y.* (Brooklyn, self-pub., 1884), p. 37.

92   *Coney Island House*: Pilat and Ranson, *Sodom by the Sea*, p. 15.

93   *"seagulls by the hour"*: McCullough, *Good Old Coney Island*, p 23.

93   *directly to its south*: Michael Immerso, *Coney Island: The People's Playground* (New Brunswick, NJ: Rutgers University Press, 2002), p. 13.

93   *Ferry Company steamship*: Robin Jaffee Frank, *Coney Island: Vision of an American Dreamland, 1861–2008* (New Haven, CT: Yale University Press, 2015), p. 12.

93   *Coney Island Point*: Stockwell, *A History of the Town of Gravesend*, p. 39.

93   *the space was leased*: Denson, *Coney Island: Lost and Found*, p. 7.

93   *Coney Island's first attraction*: Ellen M. Snyder-Grenier, *Brooklyn! An Illustrated History* (Philadelphia: Temple University Press, 1996), p. 171.

93   *Twentieth Century*: Gary S. Cross and John K. Walton, *The Playful Crowd: Pleasure Places in the Twentieth Century* (New York: Columbia University Press, 2005), p. 55.

94   *kicking into high gear*: Peter Ross, *A History of Long Island: From Its Earliest Settlement to the Present Time*, vol. 1 (New York: Lewis Publishing, 1902), pp. 373–374.

94 *own transportation system*: Ross, *A History of Long Island*, p. 374.

94 *by other means*: John S. Berman, *Coney Island* (New York: Barnes & Noble Books, 2003), p. 15.

94 *a former carpenter*: Burrows and Wallace, *Gotham*, p. 1135.

94 *first racetrack (1879)*: Lisa M. Santoro, "The Upper-Class Brooklyn Resorts of the Victorian Era," Curbed New York, June 27, 2013, https://ny.curbed.com/2013/6/27/10226192/the-upper-class-brooklyn-resorts-of-the-victorian-era.

95 *"sacrifice profit to sentiment"*: "The Feeling at Coney Island," *New York Times*, July 23, 1879, p. 1.

95 *"with silent contempt"*: "Mr. Corbin and the Jews," *New York Times*, July 23, 1879, p. 1.

95 *being "in season"*: *Illustrated New York: The Metropolis of To-Day: 1888* (New York: International Publishing, 1888), p. 97.

95 *known as "the Gut"*: Burrows and Wallace, *Gotham*, p. 1134.

95 *"their ancient profession"*: McCullough, *Good Old Coney Island*, p. 31.

96 *also did the trick*: Pilat and Ranson, *Sodom by the Sea*, p. 99.

96 *"stayed to themselves"*: Ibid., pp. 110–111.

96 *criminality in New York*: Gustav Lening, *The Dark Side of New York Life and Its Criminal Classes* (New York: Fred'k Gerhard, 1873), pp. 400–401.

96 *"no Sunday school"*: *American Experience*, season 3, episode 11, "Coney Island," directed by Ric Burns, written by Richard Snow, aired February 4, 1991, on PBS.

96 *on summer Sundays*: H. Paul Jeffers, *Diamond Jim Brady: Prince of the Gilded Age* (New York: John Wiley & Sons 2001), p. 120.

96 *Manhattan Beach Hotel veranda*: Ierardi, *Gravesend*, p. 57.

96 *John Mariani*: John Mariani, *America Eats Out: An Illustrated History of Restaurants, Taverns, Coffee Shops, Speakeasies, and Other Establishments That Have Fed Us for 350 Years.* (New York: William Morrow, 1991).

96 *"one of the larger landmarks"*: Parker Morrell, *Diamond Jim: The Life and Times of James Buchanan Brady* (New York: Simon & Schuster, 1934).

96 *as his owner ate*: McCullough, *Good Old Coney Island*, p. 128.

97 *proper fabric colors*: McCullough, *Good Old Coney Island*, pp. 8–9.

97 *"and oilskin caps"*: Mary Ellen Snodgrass, *World Clothing and Fashion: An Encyclopedia of History, Culture, and Social Influence*, vols. 1–2 (New York: Routledge, 2015), p. 565.

97 *baring their chests*: Lena Lenček, *Making Waves: Swimsuits and the Undressing of America* (San Francisco: Chronicle Books, 1989).

97 *and jail time*: Frank, Robin Jaffee. *Coney Island: Vision of an American Dreamland, 1861–2008*, p. 106.

97 *as late as 1936*: Brian J. Cudahy, *How We Got to Coney Island: The Development of Mass Transportation in Brooklyn and Kings County* (New York: Fordham University Press, 2002), p. 20.

98 *aimed on the water*: William J. Phalen, *Coney Island: 150 Years of Rides, Fires, Floods, the Rich, the Poor, and Finally Robert Moses* (Jefferson, NC: MacFarland, 2016), p. 39.

98 *"of the Cheyennes"*: "Brighton Beach," Our Brooklyn, Brooklyn Collection, Brooklyn Public Library, 2005, https://www.bklynlibrary.org/ourbrooklyn/brightonbeach/.

98 *a native Iowan*: Buffalo Bill [William F. Cody] and William Lightfoot Visscher, *Buffalo Bill's Own Story of His Life and Deeds* (Chicago: John R. Stanton, 1917), p. 23.

98 *"I'm the coming Barnum"*: Isabelle S. Sayers, *Annie Oakley and Buffalo Bill's Wild West* (New York: Dover Publications, 1981), p. 15.

SURF AND TURF

99 *"for a good time"*: Moses Foster Sweetser and Simeon Ford, *How to Know New York* (Boston: Rand Avery, 1887), p. 117.

100 *get out and change seats*: Mangels, *The Outdoor Amusement Industry*, p. 89.

100 *like its predecessors*: David W. Francis and Diane DeMali Francis, *The Golden Age of Roller Coasters in Vintage Postcards* (Chicago: Arcadia Publishing, 2003), p. 8.

100 *"with facility and comfort"*: L. A. Thompson Scenic Ry. Co. v. Chestnut Hill Casino Co., Limited, et al., 62 C.C.A. 455 (3rd Circ. 1904).

100 *"in the water"*: Charles Carroll, "New York in Summer," *Harper's New Monthly Magazine*, October 1878, pp. 694–699.

101 *"to near bankruptcy"*: Cartmell, *The Incredible Scream Machine*, p. 47.

101 *"from Coney to Atlantic City"*: McCullough, *Good Old Coney Island*, p. 308.

101 *Florida swampland*: "Chapter 1—Elephant to Starboard," Lucy the Elephant, 2015, http://www.lucytheelephant.org/history/chapter-1-elephant-to-starboard/.

101 *for amusement parks*: Sandra L. Tatman, "Free, William H. (fl. 1881–1904)," Philadelphia Architects and Buildings, 2017, https://www.philadelphiabuildings.org/pab/app/ar_display.cfm/25831.

101 *"a fish, fowl, &c."*: J. V. Lafferty, "Building," Patent No. 268,503, Google Patents, December 5, 1882, https://patents.google.com/patent/US268503.

101 *open June 1, 1884*: "A Jumbo House for Coney Island," *New York Times*, February 21, 1884.

102 *"a tobacco shop"*: David W. McCullough, *Brooklyn...And How It Got That Way* (New York: Dial Press, 1983), p. 149.

102 *London and Paris*: "Coney Island's Big Elephant," *New York Times*, May 30, 1885.

102 *National Historic Landmark in 1976*: "Lucy and Her Sisters," (Marmora, NJ) *Shore News Today*, July 18, 2014.

102 *initiated independently*: Stockwell, *A History of the Town of Gravesend*, p. 44.

102 *had with John McKane*: McCullough, *Good Old Coney Island*, p. 50.

102 *compulsory alliance with McKane*: Pilat and Ranson, *Sodom by the Sea*, p. 30.

102 *"reception-parlors, etc."*: Stockwell, *A History of the Town of Gravesend*, p. 46.

103 *a penny apiece*: Laura J. Hoffman, *Coney Island* (Charleston, SC: Arcadia Publishing, 2014), p. 67.

103 *a carousel*: John B. Manbeck, *Brooklyn: Historically Speaking* (Charleston, SC: The History Press, 2008).

103 *as his initials*: Patricia Ann Stockdale, *The Long Beach Pike: A Collection of Memories* (Lexington, KY: AmericaUSA Publishing, 2015), p. 7.

103 *Coney Island's first ride*: Fried, *A Pictorial History of the Carousel*, p. 62.

104 *linked, processed sausages*: McCullough, *Good Old Coney Island*, p. 239.

104 *to his menu*: Stockwell, *A History of the Town of Gravesend*, p. 44.

104 *when he was fifteen*: Dana Schulz, "Before Nathan's There Was Feltman's: The History of the Coney Island Hot Dog," 6sqft, June 20, 2016, https://www.6sqft.com/before-nathans-there-was-feltmans-the-history-of-the-coney-island-hot-dog/.

104 *a slice of bread*: Pilat and Ranson, *Sodom by the Sea*, p. 239.

104 *sauerkraut and mustard*: McCullough, *Good Old Coney Island*, pp. 235–236.

104 *"whooped with appreciation"*: Pilat and Ranson, *Sodom by the Sea*, p. 239.

105 *West Brighton alone*: John F. Kasson, *Amusing the Million: Coney Island at the Turn of the Century* (New York: Hill & Wang, 1978), p. 33.

105 *a second Iron Pier*: Immerso, *Coney Island: The People's Playground*, p. 125.

105 *the* Brooklyn Eagle *reported*: "Feltman's Long a Coney Institution," *Brooklyn Eagle*, May 12, 1946, p. 13.

105 *the Feltman name*: "Charles Feltman: Inventor of the Hot Dog," Coney Island History Project, 2017, https://www.coneyislandhistory.org/hall-of-fame/charles-feltman.

105 *turn of the century*: Erick Trickey, "The Origin of the Coney Island Hot Dog Is a Uniquely American Story," Smithsonian.com, June 30, 2016, https://www.smithsonianmag.com/history/origins-coney-island-hot-dog-uniquely-american-story-180959659/.

106 *Coney Island History Project*: Charles Denson, *Coney Island and Astroland* (Charleston, SC: Arcadia Publishing, 2011), p. 7.

106 *brand and its recipe*: "Brothers from Brooklyn…," Feltman's of Coney Island, 2016, https://feltmansofconeyisland.com.

106 *a toasted potato bun*: Steve Cuozzo, "This Is the Top Dog on Coney Island—And It's Not Nathan's," *New York Post*, April 16, 2017.

106 *"the holy land of the hot dog"*: Rebecca Strassberg, "The OG Hot Dog Has Returned to Coney Island, 60 Years Later," Thrillist New York, May 25, 2017, https://www.thrillist.com/eat/new-york/feltmans-original-coney-island-hot-dog.

106 *knish peddler from Galicia*: *Famous Nathan*, directed by Lloyd Handwerker (New York: Film Movement, 2014).

106 *architecture historian Bruce Kraig*: Bruce Kraig, "Nathan's Famous," in *Savoring Gotham: A Food Lover's Companion to New York City*, ed. Andrew F. Smith (New York: Oxford University Press, 2015), p. 405.

106 *Derwood Jarrett*: Lloyd Handwerker and Gil Reavill, *Famous Nathan: A Family Saga of Coney Island, the American Dream, and the Search for the Perfect Hot Dog* (New York: Flatiron Books, 2016), p. 218.

106 *He downed seventeen*: Sam Roberts, "Nathan's Famous, a Hot Dog Empire Built on Hard Work and Hype," *New York Times*, July 22, 2016.

106 *Virginia-based Smithfield Foods*: PR Newswire, "John Morrell Food Group Begins Partnership with Nathan's Famous," March 20, 2014.

106 *since 2013*: "Who's Behind the Chinese Takeover of World's Biggest Pork Producer?," *PBS NewsHour*, September 12, 2014, https://www.pbs.org/newshour/show/whos-behind-chinese-takeover-worlds-biggest-pork-producer.

107 *the Thousand Islands*: Lynn E. McElfresh, "The Traditional Shore Dinner," *Thousand Islands Magazine*, November 13, 2013, http://www.thousandislandslife.com/BackIssues/Archive/tabid/393/articleType/ArticleView/articleId/1401/The-Traditional-Shore-Dinner.aspx.

107 *erect his enterprise*: McCullough, *Good Old Coney Island*, p. 320.

107 *staked Stauch to $40,000*: "Louis Stauch Dead; Pioneer at Coney," *New York Times*, April 5, 1929.

107 *a Beaux Arts palace*: Denson, *Coney Island: Lost and Found*, p. 31.

107 *largest restaurant-ballroom in the world*: Hoffman, *Coney Island*, p. 92.

107 *testified in court*: "Divorce for Louis Stauch," *New York Times*, August 20, 1922, p. 10.

108 *"abundantly mustachioed"*: Horatia Harrod, "The Phantom's New Home: Coney Island," *Telegraph*, February 17, 2010.

108 *forebears were Huguenots*: Pilat and Ranson, *Sodom by the Sea*, p. 131.

108 *not until 1685*: "Huguenot History," The Huguenot Society of America, n.d., http://huguenotsocietyofamerica.org/?page=Huguenot-History.

108 *born February 3, 1862*: Jeff Richman, "February Birthdays," Green-Wood Cemetery, February 1, 2011, https://www.green-wood.com/2011/february-birthdays/.

108 *for the City of New York*: Peter Lyon, "The Master Showman of Coney Island," *American Heritage*, June 1958.

108 *clam chowder for free*: Pilat and Ranson, *Sodom by the Sea*, p. 131.

108 *they had five children*: Luciano J. Iorizzo, *Al Capone: A Biography* (Westport, CT: Greenwood Press, 2003), pp. 24–25.

108 *Main Exhibition Building*: Sandy Hingston, "10 Things You Might Not Know About the 1876 Centennial Exhibition," *Philadelphia*, May 10, 2016/.

109 *"lemonade and pop-corn instead"*: McCullough, *Good Old Coney Island*, p. 288.

109 *younger brother Edward*: Ibid., p. 289.

109 *lasted one issue*: Denson, *Coney Island: Lost and Found*, p. 32.

109 *"is the world"*: Pilat and Ranson, *Sodom by the Sea*, pp. 131–132.

109 *In 1887*: "On This Day, May 28, 1887," *New York Times*, May 28, 2001.

109 *Alexander S. Bacon*: William H. Steele, ed., *Revised Record of the Constitutional Convention of the State of New York: May 8, 1894, to September 29, 1894*, vol. 5 (Albany, NY: Argus, 1900), p. 500.

109 *land contracts in Coney Island*: Berman, *Coney Island*, 17.

109   *"not an easy job"*: Professor Solomon, *Coney Island* (Baltimore: Top Hat Press, 1999), p. 28.

109   *George was arrested, too*: "Peter Tilyou Arrested," *New York Sun*, June 29, 1887, p. 1.

110   *whose whorehouses they frequented*: Lyon, "The Master Showman of Coney Island."

110   *"the centre of the Surf"*: "To Overcome M'Kaneism," *New York Times*, March 5, 1894, p. 9.

110   *"but he chafed"*: McCullough, *Good Old Coney Island*, pp. 294–295.

110   *"be quick about it"*: Pilat and Ranson, *Sodom by the Sea*, p. 47.

110   *rough up the interlopers*: "The Times's Exposure of McKane," *New York Times*, February 16, 1894, p. 2.

110   *The fallout was dramatic*: "The Prison for Bosses," *New York Times*, February 27, 1894, p. 4.

110   *contempt of court*: Snow and Burns, *Coney Island*.

110   *Sheepshead Bay*: "Days When McKane Ruled Gravesend."

110   *Bright's disease*: "James McKane Dead," *Brooklyn Daily Eagle*, October 18, 1913, p. 2.

110   *could not stop talking about*: McCullough, *Good Old Coney Island*, p. 295.

WHAT GOES AROUND

111   *"enclosed amusement space"*: Lukas, *Theme Park*, p. 30.

111   *for the Emerald City*: Achy Obejas, "L. Frank Baum—the Man Behind 'The Wizard of Oz'—Was Really the Man Behind the Curtain," *Chicago Tribune*, October 5, 2000.

111   *"You must see this fair"*: Keith Newlin, *Hamlin Garland: A Life* (Lincoln, NE: University of Nebraska Press, 2008), p. 175.

111   *New York, and Chicago*: Daniel H. Burnham et al., *The Story of the Exposition, Illustrated in Its History, Architecture, and Art* (New York: D. Appleton, 1895).

111   *to the latter two*: Jessie Heckman Hirschl, "The Great White City," *American Heritage*, October 1960.

112   *another $5 million*: Robert W. Rydell, "World's Columbian Exposition," Encyclopedia of Chicago, Chicago Historical Society, 2005, http://www.encyclopedia.chicagohistory.org/pages/1386.html.

112   *"even if they won it"*: Charles A. Dana, "It Shall Not Be Brought to Naught," *New York Sun*, September 17, 1889, p. 1.

112   *Chicago won it*: Hirschl, "The Great White City."

112   *for the fair's opening*: Rydell, "World's Columbian Exposition."

112   *"American pride was at stake"*: Carl Snyder, "Engineer Ferris and His Wheel," *American Monthly Review of Reviews*, September 1893, p. 269.

112   *were considered—and rejected*: "Doodles, Drafts, and Designs: Industrial Drawings from the Smithsonian," Smithsonian Libraries, n.d., http://www.sil.si.edu/exhibitions/doodles/.

113   *discuss its many facets*: Erik Larson, *The Devil in the White City: Murder, Magic, and Madness at the Fair That Changed America* (New York: Vintage Books, 2004), p. 155.

113   *"all over the world"*: Charles Boswell and Lewis Thompson, "Big Wheel from Chicago," *Coronet*, September 1958, p. 126.

114   *the Underground Railroad*: Owen W. Muelder, *Theodore Dwight Weld and the American Anti-Slavery Society* (Jefferson, NC: McFarland2011), p. 140.

114   *Sylvanus and Sally's six children*: Richard G. Weingardt, *Circles in the Sky: The Life and Times of George Ferris* (Reston, VA: American Society of Civil Engineers, 2009).

114   *introducing sheep to Galesburg*: Carol Pirtle, *Escape Betwixt Two Suns: A True Tale of the Underground Railroad in Illinois* (Carbondale and Edwardsville, IL: Southern Illinois University Press, 2000), p. 40.

114   *around a Christmas tree*: Tom Wilson, *Remembering Galesburg* (Charleston, SC: The History Press, 2009).

114   *a landscaping business*: Anderson, *Ferris Wheels*, p. 47.

114   *settled in Pittsburgh*: Judith Adams-Volpe, "Ferris, George Washington Gale, Jr.," *American National Biography Online*, American Council of Learned Studies, January 2002, http://oxfordindex.oup.com/view/10.1093/anb/9780198606697.article.1302643.

114   *a classmate from Rensselaer Poly*: Henry B. Nason, ed., *Biographical Record of the Officers and Graduates of the Rensselaer Polytechnic Institute, 1824–1886.* (Troy, NY: William H. Young, 1887), p. 526.

114   *"making a complete turn"*: Snyder, "Engineer Ferris and His Wheel," p. 270.

115   *as early as 1848 and 1849*: Jamie Malanowski, "The Brief History of the Ferris Wheel," Smithsonian.com, June 2015, https://www.smithsonianmag.com/history/history-ferris-wheel-180955300/.

115   *"what he's talking about"*: Boswell and Thompson, "Big Wheel from Chicago," pp. 126–127.

115   *the recruitment of investors*: Malanowski, "The Brief History of the Ferris Wheel."

115   *to build his tower*: Alex Doll, "A Brief History of America's Most Influential Pleasure Wheel," *HuffPost*, February 14, 2014, https://www.huffingtonpost.com/alex-doll/americas-most-influential-pleasure-wheel_b_4791101.html.

115   *from the French government*: Violette, H. P. Ho, "The Ferris Wheel, the World's Columbian Exposition of 1893, and the Display of American Superiority," *Inquiries Journal*, 2016, p. 21.

116   *"will not be realized"*: Patrick T. Reardon, "Burnham Quote: Well, It May Be," *Chicago Tribune*, June 1, 1992.

117   *dissection, and/or incineration*: Larson, *The Devil in the White City*, p. 34.

117   *for insurance fraud*: "He Died for Ducats," *Anaconda (MT) Standard*, November 19, 1894, p. 1.

117   *and representing himself*: "Stranger Than Fiction," *Los Angeles Examiner*, November 21, 1894, p. 1.

117   *he was hanged*: "Hanged for Many Crimes," *San Francisco Call*, May 8, 1896, p.1.

117   *World's Columbian Exhibition*: Patrick Meehan, "Ferris Wheel in the 1893 Chicago World's Fair," Hyde Park History Society, April 27, 2015, http://www.hydeparkhistory.org/2015/04/27/ferris-wheel-in-the-1893-chicago-worlds-fair/.

117   *in early January 1893*: Anderson, *Ferris Wheels*, p. 58.

117   *it would not ice over*: Ho, "The Ferris Wheel."

117   *Bethlehem Iron Company in Pittsburgh*: Boswell and Thompson. "Big Wheel from Chicago," pp. 127–128.

117   *continued search for financing*: Adams, *The American Amusement Park Industry*, pp. 31–32.

118   *Ferris's round colossus*: "Westinghouse Electric Corporation [Science and Invention] Historical Marker," ExplorePA-history.com, 2011, http://explorepahistory.com/hmarker.php?markerId=1-A-3A0.

118   *"now set in motion"*: Hirschl, "The Great White City."

118   *unfinished Ferris Wheel*: Larson, *The Devil in the White City*, pp. 236–237.

118   *Annie Oakley*: Walter Havighurst, *Annie Oakley of the Wild West* (New York: Macmillan, 1954).

118   *first squirrel at age eight*: Shirl Kasper, *Annie Oakley* (Norman, OK: University of Oklahoma Press, 1992), p. 4.

118   *following year they married*: Stephen G. Del Sordo, "Annie Oakley," Heritage Resource Group, Dorchester County (Maryland) Public Library, n.d., http://www.dorchesterlibrary.org/library/aoakley.html.

118   *was la tour Eiffel*: "The Great French Show; What the Present Visitors Can See. The Eiffel Tower and Edison's Exhibit—American Pictures Very Attractive—Other Matters," *New York Times*, May 19, 1889, p. 1.

118   *to go to the fair*: Matt Braun, "Buffalo Bill Goosed the World's Fair," *True West*, April 22, 2014, https://truewestmagazine.com/buffalo-bill-goosed-the-worlds-fair/.

119   *"and English lancers"*: Geoffrey Johnson, "Flashback: 'Buffalo Bill' Wowed Chicago with His 'Wild West' Shows," *Chicago Tribune*, February 23, 2017.

119   *whom Cody called "Missy"*: Victoria Wilson, *A Life of Barbara Stanwyck, Steel True*, vol. 1, *1907–1940* (New York: Simon & Schuster, 2013), p. 441.

119   *ice cream and candy*: Braun, "Buffalo Bill Goosed the World's Fair."

120   *in July 1913*: Johnson, "Flashback: 'Buffalo Bill' Wowed Chicago."

120   *four years before his death*: "History of the Buffalo Bill Center of the West," Buffalo Bill Center of the West, 2017, https://centerofthewest.org/about-us/history/.

120   *"were married for life"*: Delancey Ferguson, "A Miss Who Didn't Miss," *New York Times Sunday Book Review*, September 19, 1954, p. 6.

121   *he chose not to take*: "Representative Sol Bloom Dies of Heart Attack at 78," *New York Times*, March 8, 1949, p. 1.

121   *"Barnum & Bailey Circus"*: Sol Bloom, *The Autobiography of Sol Bloom* (New York: G. P. Putnam's Sons, 1948), p. 119.

122   *a dedicated amusement district*: David Nasaw, *Going Out: The Rise and Fall of Public Amusements* (New York: Basic Books, 1993), pp. 66–67.

122   *the antebellum era*: Colin L. Westerbeck, "Frederick Douglass Chooses His Moment," Art Institute of Chicago, 1997, http://www.artic.edu/collections/books/museum-studies/preview-issue/frederick-douglass.

122   *"the discovery of their country?"*: Frederick Douglass and Ida B. Wells, *The Reason Why the Colored American Is Not in the World's Columbian Exposition*. Chicago: Ida B. Wells, 1893.

123   *pricey and poorly reviewed*: Tom Hoffman, "Rides & Attractions," 1893 World's Columbian Exhibition, n.d.

123   *"2,000 free watermelons"*: Patrick T. Reardon, "The World's Columbian Exhibition at the 'White City,'" *Chicago Tribune*, 2017.

123   *black boycott of the fair*: Rydell, "World's Columbian Exposition."

123   *"to their own Constitution"*: Westerbeck, "Frederick Douglass Chooses His Moment," Art Institute of Chicago website.

124   *only a beginning*: Nasaw, *Going Out*, p. 68.

124   *"the world's first amusement park"*: Hirschl, "The Great White City."

124   *the full mile of Midway*: "Moving Sidewalk," Chicagology, 2017, https://chicagology.com/columbiaexpo/fair030/.

124   *broke down frequently in Chicago*: Gale, *The Midway Plaisance*, p. 20.

124   *frozen ammonia gas*: Ibid., p. 21.

124   *Refrigeration Company of New York*: Norman Bolotin with Christine Laing, *Chicago's Grand Midway: A Walk Around the World at the Columbian Exposition* (Urbana, IL: University of Illinois Press, 2017).

125   *"was ever devised"*: "Thompson's Gravity System for Rapid Transit in Towns and Cities," *Scientific American*, September 8, 1888, p. 149.

125   *damaged beyond recognition*: "Bad Accident at the Fair," *New York Times*, June 15, 1893, p. 1.

125   *with his wife, Margaret*: United States, World's Columbian Commission and the World's Columbian Exposition, Joint Committee on Ceremonies, *Dedicatory and Opening Ceremonies of the World's Columbian Exposition* (Chicago: Stone, Kastler & Painter, 1893), p. 191.

125   *"a living reality"*: Meehan, "Ferris Wheel in the 1893 Chicago World's Fair."

125   *took the first ride*: Boswell and Thompson, "Big Wheel from Chicago," p. 129.

NEXT CHAPTER

126   *"in the twentieth century"*: William H. Searles, "The Ferris Wheel," *Journal of the Association of Engineering Societies* 12, no. 12 (December 1893), p. 623.

126   *between June 21 and July 2*: Anderson, *Ferris Wheels*, p. 71.

126   *grounded at the time*: "Lost the Balloon, Wind Wrecks the Captive Airship at Jackson Park," *Chicago Daily Tribune*, July 10, 1893, p. 1.

126   *an inch and a half*: Anderson, *Ferris Wheels*, p. 66.

127   *packing the Midway*: Dale Samuelson with Wendy Yegoiants, *The American Amusement Park* (St. Paul, MN: MBI Publishing, 2001), p. 14.

127   *Scott Joplin*: Katherine Preston, *Scott Joplin* (Los Angeles: Melrose Square, 1989), pp. 60–61.

127   *"any more of it"*: Bill Granger, "'You Must See This Fair,'" *Chicago Tribune*, September 17, 1995.

127 *rode the wheel*: Jack Klasey, "Who Invented the Ferris Wheel?," *American History Illustrated*, September–October 1993, pp. 60–63.

127 *approximately $395,000*: Meehan, "Ferris Wheel in the 1893 Chicago World's Fair."

127 *monies related to expenses*: Malanowski, "The Brief History of the Ferris Wheel."

127 *Europe wanted his invention*: Hirschl, "The Great White City."

127 *this included George Tilyou*: Berman, *Coney Island*, p. 31.

127 *build other attractions*: "Ferris Wheel Inventor Historical Marker," ExplorePAhistory.com, 2011, http://explorepa history.com/hmarker.php?markerId=1-A-35D.

127 *the wheel was spinning again*: Anderson, *Ferris Wheels*, p. 75.

128 *her parents' home in Ohio*: Adams-Volpe, "Ferris, George Washington Gale, Jr."

128 *typhoid fever*: Anderson, *Ferris Wheels*, p. 75.

128 *tuberculosis*: Meehan, "Ferris Wheel in the 1893 Chicago World's Fair."

128 *renal failure*: Malanowski, "The Brief History of the Ferris Wheel."

128 *possible attempt at suicide*: Jim Davidson, "George Ferris, Reinventing the Wheel in Pittsburgh," *Pittsburgh Press Sunday Magazine*, July 27, 1986, pp. 8–9.

128 *until he was*: "Ferris Wheel Inventor Historical Marker."

128 *for a pitiful $1,800*: Meehan, "Ferris Wheel in the 1893 Chicago World's Fair."

128 *the ride of their lives*: "Ferris Wheel Inventor Historical Marker."

128 *blown to smithereens*: Reardon, "The World's Columbian Exhibition at the 'White City.'"

128 *"World's Largest Ferris Wheel"*: Jeffrey Stanton, "Coney Island—First Steeplechase Park (1897–1907)," Coney Island History Site, April 1, 1998, https://www.westland.net/coneyisland/articles/steeplechase1.htm.

128 *"for either sensation"*: Hirschl, "The Great White City."

128 *sold tickets*: McCullough, *Good Old Coney Island*, p. 51.

128 *showing a profit*: Ibid., p. 295.

128 *an overhead wooden beam*: "The Boynton Bicycle Electric Railway," *Scientific American*, February 17, 1894, p. 1.

129 *a medieval crusader*: "Captain Boyton, The Hero of the Hour," London *Daily News*, April 5, 1875.

129 *"he would drown"*: Colleen Sullivan, "US Copyright: April 26th. 2006. TXu1-292-939," Captain Paul Boyton, October 7, 2009, http://wwwcaptainboytonblogcom.blogspot.com/2009/10/book.html.

130 *an 1897 biographical sketch*: "Captain Paul Boyton," The Library of Nineteenth-Century Photography, http://www.19thcenturyphotos.com/Captain-Paul-Boyton-125033.htm. See also "Boyton, Paul," in *People of the Period*, vol. 1, *A–H*, ed. A. T. Camden Pratt (London: Neville Beeman, 1897).

130 *dedication to his autobiography*: Paul Boyton, *The Story of Paul Boyton* (London: George Routledge & Sons, 1892).

130 *He was seventy-six*: "Capt. Paul Boyton, Inventor, Is Dead," *New York Times*, April 20, 1924.

130 *strokes per minute*: McCullough, *Good Old Coney Island*, p. 296.

130 *"vertically, like a cork"*: Lyman M. Nash, "The Incredible Floating Man," *Boys' Life*, July 1960, p. 18.

130 *"the Coney Island of Chicago"*: H. M. Moore, "Chicago Letter," (Boston) *Christian Record*, Volume LXV, Number 30, July 29, 1886, p. 6.

WATER WORKS

132 *"with sharp dips"*: Elwell Crissey, "New Thrills Defy Gravity," *Popular Science*, August 1927, p. 38.

132 *his interior tableaux*: Francis and Francis, *The Golden Age of Roller Coasters*, p. 14.

132 *the term* roller coaster: Cartmell, *The Incredible Scream Machine*, pp. 72–73.

132 *in the world*: Mangels, *The Outdoor Amusement Industry*, pp. 90–91.

132 *"could see and be seen"*: Lilliefors, *America's Boardwalks*, p. 8.

132 *"Irish walked next to Jews"*: Bryant Simon, *Boardwalk of Dreams: Atlantic City and the Fate of Urban America* (New York: Oxford University Press, 2004), p. 36.

132 *meaning "little water"*: Sandy Hingston, "20 More Local Native American Place Names and What They Mean," *Philadelphia*, October 22, 2015.

132 *Atlantic City at noon*: Frank Legato, *Atlantic City: In Living Color*, photographs by Jennifer Shermer Pack and David Verdini (Macon, GA: Indigo Custom Publishing, 2004), p. 10.

132 *served alcohol on Sundays*: Lilliefors, *America's Boardwalks*, p. 5.

133 *similarly afflicted hotels*: Barbara Kozek, "History of Atlantic City," City of Atlantic City, https://cityofatlanticcity.org/?page_id=14.

133 above *the sands*: Lilliefors, *America's Boardwalks*, p. 6.

133 *from Bridgeport, Connecticut*: Herbert I. Brackett, *Brackett Genealogy* (Washington, DC: H. I. Brackett, 1907).

133 *Epicycloidal Diversion*: Bill Kent, "A Spin into the Past," *New York Times*, June 25, 1995.

133 *returning them to earth*: Anderson, *Ferris Wheels*, pp. 25–26.

133 *a hand-carved carousel*: Kent, "A Spin into the Past."

133 *as early as 1814*: Peter Walton, *Blackpool Tower: A History* (Gloucestershire, UK: Amberley Publishing, 2016).

133 *forty-two amusement piers*: Kevin Post, "Piers Without Peer," *Press of Atlantic City*, January 30, 2010.

134 *hit by a ship*: Legato, *Atlantic City: In Living Color*, p. 16.

134 *with his tintype studio*: Liz Spikol, "A Thousand Words," *Philadelphia Weekly*, June 30, 2004.

134 *genuinely successful amusement pier*: Lilliefors, *America's Boardwalks*, p. 9.

134 *Devised by Amariah Lake*: Arthur Adams and Sarah A. Risley, *A Genealogy of the Lake Family of Great Egg Harbor, in Old Gloucester County, in New Jersey, Descended from John Lake of Gravesend, Long Island* (Hartford, CT: privately printed, 1915).

134   *riders would exit*: Albert Allis Hopkins, ed., *Magic: Stage Illusions and Scientific Diversions, Including Trick Photography* (New York: Munn, 1901), p. 94.

134   *the car remained stationary*: Amariah Lake, "A. Lake. Theater Appliance," Patent No. 520,236, Google Patents, May 22, 1894, https://patents.google.com/patent/US520236.

135   *President Theodore Roosevelt*: Jim Waltzer, "When the Pier Was Young," *Atlantic City Weekly*, July 20, 2006.

135   *boater and pantaloons*: Ibid.

135   *Thomas Edison*: "How Capt. Young Built a Villa Above the Ocean at Atlantic City—Some of Its Oddities," *New York Times*, August 7, 1910.

136   *His specialty was taffy*: Karen L. Schnitzspahn, *Jersey Food History: Victorian Feasts to Boardwalk Treats* (Charleston, SC: American Palate, 2012).

136   *a dash of salt*: Sarah Tyson Heston Rorer, *Home Candy Making* (Philadelphia: Arnold, 1889), p. 53.

136   *practically sold themselves*: Schnitzspahn, *Jersey Food History*.

136   *one-pound oyster boxes*: "The History of Fralinger's Salt Water Taffy," James Candy Company, 2017, https://www.jamescandy.com/our-history/fralingers/.

136   *the two labels separate*: Matt Griffin, "A Chat with Frank Glaser, President/Owner, James' and Fralinger's Salt Water Taffy," Total Retail, January 1, 2007, https://www.mytotalretail.com/article/a-chat-frank-glaser-president-owner-james-fralingers-salt-water-taffy-44116/all/.

136   *"salt water taffy?"*: Michael Miller, "Origin of 'Saltwater Taffy' No Stretch," *Press of Atlantic City*, May 29, 2008.

137   *"Abou ben Hamid's Tumbling Arabs"*: "George A. Hamid Dead at 75; Ran Steel Pier in Atlantic City," *New York Times*, June 14, 1971, p. 40.

137   *started booking circus acts*: Simon, *Boardwalk of Dreams*, p. 133.

137   *sixteen million*: Harriet Newburger, Anita Sands, and John Waches, *Atlantic City: Past as Prologue: A Special Report by the Community Affairs Department.* (Philadelphia: Federal Reserve Bank of Philadelphia, n.d.), p. 4. Available at https://www.philadelphiafed.org/-/media/community-development/publications/special-reports/AC-report_April-29-2009.pdf.

137   *and Philadelphia combined*: Bryant Simon, "Atlantic City," The Encyclopedia of Greater Philadelphia, 2017, http://philadelphiaencyclopedia.org/archive/atlantic-city/.

137   *Vineland, New Jersey*: Martin, DeAngelis, "Did a Vineland Man Invent Skee-Ball?," *Press of Atlantic City*, March 1, 2016.

137   *December 8, 1908*: Thaddeus O. Cooper and Kevin B. Kreitman, *Seeking Redemption: The Real Story of the Beautiful Game of Skee-Ball* (San Jose, CA: Nomoreboxes, 2016), p. 44.

137   *Skee-Ball Alley Company*: Maxwell Reil, "Two Authors Write Book on the Redemption of Skee-Ball," *Press of Atlantic City*, February 20, 2017.

137   *Cooper said*: Lauren Wanko, "History of Skee-Ball Starts in New Jersey," NJTV News, March 21, 2017, https://www.njtvonline.org/news/video/history-skee-ball-starts-new-jersey/.

137   *on his iPhone*: Cooper and Kreitman, *Seeking Redemption*, p. ix.

138   *iron out their differences*: Iorizzo, *Al Capone: A Biography*, p. 52.

138   *stood out in the crowd*: "When the Mob and Al Capone Came to Atlantic City for Some Strategic Planning," *Press of Atlantic City*, January 16, 2017.

138   *a boxing match*: Ibid.

138   *"close to the truth"*: Scott M. Deitche, *Garden State Gangland: The Rise of the Mob in New Jersey* (London: Rowman & Littlefield, 2018), p. 14.

138   *"won't apologize for it"*: Nelson Johnson, *Boardwalk Empire: The Birth, High Times, and Corruption of Atlantic City* (Medford, NJ: Plexus Publishing, 2002), p. 83.

138   *after his release*: Stoddard C. Bixby and Michael R. Houdart, "Focus on History: 'Nucky' Johnson and the Tuckahoe Connection," *Gazette of Upper Township*, December 22, 2014.

138   *alongside his son*: Wallace McKelvey, "Longtime Steel Pier Owner George Hamid Jr. Dies at 94," *Press of Atlantic City*, February 24, 2013.

138   *ninety-four, in 2013*: "Hamid, George A. Jr., 94," obituary, *Press of Atlantic City*, February 25, 2013.

139   *fifty-four thousand*: United States, Bureau of the Census, *General Statistics of Cities: 1915* (Washington, DC: Government Printing Office, 1916), p. 10.

139   *Atlantic City was black*: Newburger et al., *Atlantic City: Past as Prologue*, p. v.

139   *a disabled slave*: David Pilgrim, "The Origins of Jim Crow," Jim Crow Museum of Racist Memorabilia, Ferris State University, n.d., https://ferris.edu/jimcrow/origins.htm.

139   *1964 Civil Rights Act*: Vicki Gold Levi and Lee Eisenberg, *Atlantic City: 125 Years of Ocean Madness*, 2nd ed. (Berkeley, CA: Ten Speed Press, 1979).

139   *the Steel Pier*: John F. Hall, *The Daily Union History of Atlantic City and County, New Jersey* (Atlantic City: Daily Union Printing, 1900), p. 482.

139   *Annie Oakley*: "Almanac: Atlantic City's Steel Pier," *Sunday Morning*, CBS News, June 18, 2017, https://www.cbsnews.com/news/almanac-atlantic-citys-steel-pier/.

139   *more like it*: John F. Hall and George W. Bloodgood, *The Daily Union History of Atlantic City and County, New Jersey* (Atlantic City: Daily Union Printing Company, 1899), p. 74.

139   *the Roaring Twenties*: "Steel Pier Remembered."

140   *to jazz things up*: Wallace McKelvey, "From the Foundation Up: Building an Atlantic City Institution—Throughout Its History, the Steel Pier Has Continued to Change," *Press of Atlantic City*, March 11, 2012.

140   *That never stopped them*: Susan Pollock, interview with the author, January 1, 2018.

140   *early in their partnership*: Scott Allen Nollen, *Abbott and Costello on the Home Front: A Critical Study of the Wartime Films* (Jefferson, NC: McFarland, 2009), p. 8.

140   *named Abe Ellis*: "Steel Pier Is Sold," *New York Times*, May 8, 1945, p. 16.

141   *Wild West show*: Bill Kent, "The Horse Was in Charge," *New York Times*, May 4, 1997.

141   *"Each time was different"*: "Steel Pier Remembered," produced by Larry Kane, *The Bulletin with Larry Kane*, KYW-TV (circa 1995); available on YouTube, https://www.youtube.com/watch?v=3KEypuAeIL0.

141   *"to do and to know"*: Sonora Carver and Elizabeth Land, *A Girl and Five Brave Horses* (Garden City, NY: Doubleday 1961), p. 208.

141   *"keep doing it"*: "Steel Pier Remembered."

142   *a carnival promoter*: Simon, *Boardwalk of Dreams*, pp. 133–134.

142   *the Four Ink Spots*: Steve Liebowitz, *Steel Pier, Atlantic City: Showplace of the Nation* (West Creek, NJ: Down the Shore Publishing, 2009), p. 80.

142   *according to a 2017 study*: Ilana Keller, "NJ Ranks First in Theme Parks. Is It the Most Entertaining State in America?," *Asbury Park (NJ) Press*, October 25, 2017.

142   *"any other Boardwalk resort"*: Lilliefors, *America's Boardwalks*, p. 102.

142   *"will want to ride it"*: Kelly Roncace, "Wildwood Coaster Now 'So Smooth a Grannie Can Ride It,'" NJ.com, May 26, 2017, https://www.nj.com/entertainment/index.ssf/2017/05/wildwood_coaster_now_so_smooth_a_grannie_can_ride.html.

142   *"and it's all designed"*: Victor Fiorillo, "I Love My Job: Jack Morey of Morey's Piers in Wildwood," *Philadelphia*, May 25, 2017.

SNAKES AT A PICNIC

143   *Uncle Sam and Dewey*: Harold J. Shepstone, "A Woman's Zoo," *Wide World Magazine*, October 1898, p. 16.

143   *"of the roller coaster"*: "5,Tots Makes Children's Hospital Benefit a Real Howling Success," *Denver Post*, July 26, 1908, p. 6.

143   *"from anybody else," he said*: "The Secret of the Success and the Fame of Elitch's Gardens," *Denver Post,* August 14, 1898, p. 15.

144   *six children*: Caroline Lawrence Dier, *The Lady of the Gardens: Mary Elitch Long* (Hollywood: Hollycrofters, 1932), p. 9.

144   *and deep blue eyes*: Pamela Nowak, "Before Elitch Gardens—The Early Lives of John and Mary Elitch," Pamela Nowak, December 19, 2014, http://www.pamelanowak.com/wp/?p=208.

144   *under William Rosecrans*: Dier, *The Lady of the Gardens*, p. 18.

145   *vaudeville show that flopped*: Jack Gurtler and Corinne Hunt, *The Elitch Gardens Story: Memories of Jack Gurtler* (Boulder CO: Rocky Mountain Writers Guild, 1982), p. 3.

145   *Denver and Rio Grande Railroad*: Ross. S. Curtis, "Durango—Prehistory and History of the Durango Area," DurangoDowntown.com, 2016, https://durangodowntown.com/durango-prehistory-and-history-of-the-durango-area/.

145   *another theatrical venture*: Rosemary Fetter, "Trail's End—The Romantic Beginnings of the Historic Elitch Gardens Theater," Colorado Gambler, April 7, 2012.

145   *mining town of Denver*: Debra B. Faulkner, *Mary Elitch Long: First Lady of Fun* (Palmer Lake, CO: Filter Press, 2008), p. 4.

145   *the longest bar in Denver*: Hull, *Denver's Elitch Gardens*, pp. 7–8.

145   *"excited as we were"*: Dier, *The Lady of the Gardens*, p. 21.

145   *population of five thousand*: Pamela Nowak, "Early Denver Amusement Parks," Pamela Nowak, December 26, 2014, http://www.pamelanowak.com/wp/?p=212.

145   *to central Denver*: Kevin Pharris, *Riding Denver's Rails: A Mile-High Streetcar History* (Charleston, SC: The History Press, 2013).

146   *his San Francisco estate*: Gurtler and Hunt, *The Elitch Gardens Story*, p. 3.

146   *in his own cave*: Peter Hartlaub, "Woodward's Gardens Comes to Life in Book," *San Francisco Chronicle*, October 30, 2012.

146   *renamed it Tortoni's*: Hull, *Denver's Elitch Gardens*, p. 12.

146   *Myrna, Maude, Leland, and Sherman*: Faulkner, *Mary Elitch Long*, p. 19.

146   *"visitors arriving from 'town'"*: Dier, *The Lady of the Gardens*, p. 20.

146   *courtesy of P. T. Barnum*: Gurtler and Hunt, *The Elitch Gardens Story*, p. 5.

146   *monkeys, and ostrich*: Nowak, "Before Elitch Gardens."

146   *wide, curved cement walkways*: Hull, *Denver's Elitch Gardens*, p. 11.

147   *more-than-century-old structure*: John Moore, "Moore: Causey Resigns as Elitch Theatre Chief," *Denver Post*, August 30, 2007.

147   *"got it very wrong"*: *Ghosts of Elitch Theatre*, written and directed by David Liban (Denver: Tinyfist Films, 2008).

147   *octagonal Theatorium*: John Stanton, "Elitch Gardens (1890–1994)," National Amusement Park Historical Association, October 3, 2011.

147   *to John's specifications*: Thomas J. Noel, *Guide to Colorado Historic Places* (Boulder, CO: Westcliff Publishers, 2006), p. 146.

147   *Cincinnati and Washington, DC*: "John Brisben Walker," obituary, *Charleston Gazette*, July 8, 1931.

147   *first amusement park in Denver*: Rosemary Fetter, "Trail's End—John Brisben Walker Pioneered Denver's Entertainment Industry," Colorado Gambler, October 8, 2014.

147   *"alfalfa grower in America"*: Helen Seeley Phillips, "John Brisben Walker—Dynamic Dreamer of Denver," publication unknown, n.d.

147   *father of twelve children*: Edna Fiore, "John Brisben Walker: A Man of Ideas," Morrison History, 2016, https://morrisonhistory.org/people/john-brisben-walker/.

148   *"General and Mrs. Tom Thumb"*: Dier, *The Lady of the Gardens*, p. 25.

148   *Tom Thumb*: "Obituary: Gen. Tom Thumb," *New York Times*, July 16, 1883, p. 8.

148   *sitting in the till*: Fetter, "Trail's End—The Romantic Beginnings of the Historic Elitch Gardens Theater."

149   *"exceptionally fine"*: "The Merry Minstrels," *Los Angeles Herald*, February 25, 1891, p. 5.

149   *"I determined to carry on"*: Dier, *The Lady of the Gardens*, p. 29.

150   *purchased by John*: Stanton, "Elitch Gardens."

150   *"forever after"*: Dier, *The Lady of the Gardens*, pp. 53–54.

150   *"hanging by his knees"*: Ken Gaunt, "Daredevil Ivy Baldwin," Airport Journals, April 1, 2003, http://airportjournals.com/daredevil-ivy-baldwin/.

151   the Monitor *and the* Merrimac: David Forsyth, *Denver's Lakeside Amusement Park: From the White City Beautiful to a Century of Fun* (Boulder, CO: University Press of Colorado, 2016), p. 15.

151   *"Let's do it again!"*: Faulkner, *Mary Elitch Long*, p. 31.

RIDING THE WAVE

152   *banker Bailey Davenport*: Regena Jo Schantz, "Davenport Family," Colonel Davenport Historical Foundation, n.d., http://www.davenporthouse.org/davenport-family.php.

152   *Sometime before 1889*: Mangels, *The Outdoor Amusement Industry*, p. 120.

152   *to the loading dock*: Neil Gale, "Watchtower Amusement Park, Rock Island, Illinois 1882–1927," Living History of Illinois and Chicago Digital Library, 2014–2017, http://livinghistoryofillinois.com/amusement_parks/Watchtower%20Amusement%20Park,%20Rock%20Island,%20Illinois%201882-1927/album/.

152   *"Boyton purchased the rights"*: Jim Futrell, *Amusement Parks of New York* (Mechanicsburg, PA: Stackpole Books, 2006), p. 4.

153   *depending on size*: "Amusement for Street Railway Parks," *Street Railway Journal*, March 1902, p. 225.

153   *United States postage stamps*: Antonio Buster, "Talk of the Day," *Gibbons Stamp Weekly*, July 3, 1909, p. 8.

153   *Tower Grounds, New Brighton*: Easdown, *Amusement Park Rides*, p. 24.

153   *Kedzie Avenue*: Jim Futrell, *Amusement Parks of Pennsylvania* (Mechanicsburg, PA: Stackpole Books, 2002), p. 4.

153   *"in a single day"*: "Amusement for Street Railway Parks," p. 225.

153   *"once did the trick"*: Pilat and Ranson, *Sodom by the Sea*, p. 214.

153   *the Mill Chute*: Mangels, *The Outdoor Amusement Industry*, p. 121.

154   *"considered pleasanter by some"*: "Amusement for Street Railway Parks," p. 227.

154   *Boyton's private schooner*: "Amusement for Street Railway Parks," p. 225.

155   *and a giant swing*: Neil Gale, "Paul Boyton's Water Chutes Park, Chicago, Illinois, 1894–1907," Living History of Illinois and Chicago Digital Library, http://livinghistoryofillinois.com/amusement_parks/Paul%20Boytons%20Water%20Chutes%20Park,%20Chicago,%20Illinois%201894-1907/album/.

155   *"unable to see anything"*: Mangels, *The Outdoor Amusement Industry*, pp. 99-100.

155   *"It snapped passengers' necks"*: Cartmell, *The Incredible Scream Machine*, p. 86.

155   *"by all odds, horseracing"*: McCullough, *Good Old Coney Island*, p. 300.

156   *G-force and its strain*: Francis and Francis, *The Golden Age of Roller Coasters*, p. 27.

156   *"has a window seat"*: Frank A. Munsey, "The Annihilation of Space," *Munsey's Magazine*, October 1900, pp. 37–38.

157   *"the end of their ride"*: Leonard W. Lillington, "A Gravity Steeplechase," *Royal Magazine*, September 1902, pp. 486–487.

157   *hunt for investors*: "The New Switchback Steeplechase," in *Strand Magazine*, vol. 12 (London: George Newnes, 1896), p. 479.

157   *"to 23 Coleman Street"*: "Cawdery's Patent Steeplechase, Limited," *Saturday Review of Politics, Literature, Science and Art*, July 25, 1896, p. 88.

157   *$1.2 million today*: Paul Ruben, "Riding Astride," Park World, January 28, 2009, http://www.parkworld-online.com/riding-astride/.

157   *"success must eventually come"*: Peter Ross, *A History of Long Island: From Its Earliest Settlement to the Present Time*, vol. 3 (New York: Lewis Publishing, 1902), p. 51.

157   *thirty-five parcels of land*: Denson, *Coney Island: Lost and Found*, p. 32.

157   *Sixteenth and Nineteenth Streets*: McCullough, *Good Old Coney Island*, p. 300.

157   *of which $20,000*: Ross, *A History of Long Island*, vol. 3, p. 41.

157   *marked "Insanitarium"*: Adams, *The American Amusement Park Industry*, p. 45.

158   *"away from them"*: Harold Ross, "Down to Coney," *New Yorker*, June 23, 1928, p. 10.

158   *to the east, Tilyou's Hotel*: Denson, *Coney Island: Lost and Found*, pp. 32–33.

158   *"a good-natured joke"*: Reginald Wright Kauffman, "Why Is Coney? A Study of a Wonderful Playground and the Men That Made It," *Hampton's Magazine*, August 1909, p. 224.

159   *"the anticipation dreamed"*: Ross, *A History of Long Island*, vol. 3, p. 41.

159   *an elaborate treasure hunt*: Berman, *Coney Island*, p. 32.

160   *would allow today*: McCullough, *Good Old Coney Island*, pp. 309–310.

160   *an overturned cart*: Mangels, *The Outdoor Amusement Industry*, p. 40.

160   *"approaching infinity"*: Guy Wetmore Carryl, "Marvelous Coney Island," *Munsey's Magazine*, September 1901, p. 810.

161   *"can eat or talk back"*: Irwin Kirby, "Brothers Trained Steeplechase Boss," *Billboard*, July 20, 1959, p. 44.

161   *through the grounds*: John Parascandola, "America's Playground: The Development of Coney Island," The Ultimate History Project, n.d., http://www.ultimatehistoryproject.com/coney-island.html.

161   *Scenic Railway, Pike's Peak*: McCullough, *Good Old Coney Island*, p. 309.

161   *smoky steam to clean electric*: Francis and Francis, *The Golden Age of Roller Coasters*, p. 40.

161   *"Mickey, the Bowery Bite"*: O. Henry, "The Greater Coney," in *The Complete Works of O. Henry* (Garden City, NY: Garden City Publishing, 1911), p. 709.

161   *music would never stop*: Berman, *Coney Island*, p. 32.

162   *"with spatial and cultural simulation"*: Michael J. Ostwald, "Amusement Park," in *Encyclopedia of Twentieth Century Architecture*, vol. 1, *A–F*, ed. R. Stephen Sennott (New York: Fitzroy Dearborn, 2004), p. 52.

162   *"with a bugle"*: Ruben, "Riding Astride."

162   *first two years of the ride*: James Trager, *The New York Chronology: The Ultimate Compendium of Events, People, and Anecdotes from the Dutch to the Present* (New York: Harper Resource, 2003), p. 254.

162   *"nonproductive consumption of time"*: Thorstein Veblen, *The Theory of the Leisure Class* (1899; repr., New York: Oxford University Press, 2009), p. 31.

163   *entered the vernacular*: David Nasaw, *Going Out*, p. 63.

163   *blanketed the country*: *Welcome Back Riders*, written by Nathan Cutietta et al., and directed by Nathan Cutietta and Joanna Skye (Swashbuckler Studios, 2007).

163   *"play is a fundamental need"*: Theodore Roosevelt, *Presidential Addresses and State Papers*, vol. 6 (New York: Review of Reviews, 1910), p. 1163.

163   *"the horrors of reality"*: Jason Rhodes, *Maryland's Amusement Parks* (Charleston, SC: Arcadia Publishing, 2005), p. 8.

163   *wholesome* and Coney Island: Nancy D. McCormick and John S. McCormick, *Saltair* (Salt Lake City: University of Utah Press, 1985).

163   *twelve hot dog stands*: Pat Bagley, "Living History: Original Saltair Was a Wonder of the World," *Salt Lake Tribune*, July 9, 2012.

164   *its remains in 1970*: "History Minute—The Great Saltair," Salt Lake City Television, YouTube, 2014, https://www.youtube.com/watch?v=6QTtTQnz25I.

164   *"this is New Orleans"*: Vernel Bagneris, interview with the author, December 29, 2016.

164   *Louisiana Purchase, in 1803*: United Press, "Old Fort to Be Made into Park," March 12, 1938.

164   *within fort walls*: Roussel et al. v. Railways Realty Co., 61 So. 409 (1913).

164   *"little or nothing"*: "Oscar Wilde," New Orleans *Daily Picayune*, June 27, 1882, p. 3.

165   *as an amusement park*: Mary Lou Widmer, *New Orleans in the Twenties* (Gretna, LA: Pelican Publishing, 1993), p. 66.

165   *wood-burning steam engine*: John Pope, "When Smoky Mary Was Queen of the Pontchartrain Railroad," New Orleans *Times-Picayune*, July 14, 2017.

165   *their music and techniques*: "Jazz Neighborhoods—New Orleans Jazz National Historic Park," National Park Service, U.S. Department of the Interior, April 14, 2015, https://www.nps.gov/jazz/learn/historyculture/jazz-map.htm.

165   *cornetist Louis Armstrong*: Terry Teachout, *Pops: A Life of Louis Armstrong* (New York: Houghton Mifflin Harcourt, 2009), p. 37.

165   *renamed Pontchartrain Beach*: Widmer, *New Orleans in the Twenties*, p. 67.

165   *and Guitar Slim*: Mike Scott, "The Bittersweet History of Lincoln Beach in New Orleans," New Orleans *Times-Picayune*, March 3, 2017.

165   *"You'd eat the tails"*: Rex Reed, interview with the author, February 2, 2018.

166   *1939-vintage Zephyr*: Cartmell, *The Incredible Scream Machine*, p. 150.

166   *"the catwalk on the Zephyr"*: John Pope, "33 Vintage Pontchartrain Beach Photos of #throwbackthursday," New Orleans *Times-Picayune*, August 21, 2014.

166   *Ferris Wheel Park (1896–1903)*: Stan Barker, "Amusement Parks," *Encyclopedia of Chicago*, Chicago Historical Society website, 2006, http://www.encyclopedia.chicagohistory.org/pages/48.html.

166   *similar things to come*: Gale, "Paul Boyton's Water Chutes Park."

166   *"encourage trolley business"*: Lauren Rabinovitz, *Electric Dreamland: Amusement Parks, Movies, and American Modernity* (New York: Columbia University Press, 2012), p. 26.

166   *"a German beer hall"*: Neil Gale, "Sans Souci Amusement Park, Chicago, Illinois, 1899–1913," Living History of Illinois and Chicago Digital History, November 12, 2017, http://livinghistoryofillinois.com/amusement_parks/Sans%20Souci%20Amusement%20Park,%20Chicago,%20Illinois%201899-1913/album/.

167   *and the Prater*: Derek Gee and Ralph Lopez, *Laugh Your Troubles Away: The Complete History of Riverview Park* (Livonia, MI: Sharpshooters Productions, 2000), pp. 3–7.

167   *"greatest coaster ever built"*: Barker, "Amusement Parks."

167   *"leviathan skeletal 'woody'"*: Adams, *The American Amusement Park Industry*, pp. 71–72.

168   *"Naval Station Great Lakes"*: Helga Trolli, interview with the author, February 3, 2018.

168   *"never finished with Riverview"*: Glenn Young, interview with the author, December 21, 2017.

168   *home games combined*: John Owens, "The Remnants of Riverview," *Chicago Tribune*, June 22, 2011.

168   *"to just laugh away"*: Rick Kogan, "Remembering Riverview Park, 50 Years Later," *Chicago Tribune*, June 25, 2017.

169   *"representatives in City Hall"*: William Howland Kenney, *Chicago Jazz: A Cultural History, 1904–1930* (New York: Oxford University Press, 1994), p. 28.

169   *said Lauren Rabinovitz*: Rabinovitz, *Electric Dreamland*, p. 26.

169   *their own amusement parks*: Ibid., pp. 16–17.

169   *Lake Okoboji*: Brett Hayworth, "Okoboji Amusement Park Celebrates 125 Years," *Sioux City (IA) Journal*, March 22, 2015.

169 *"epicenter of our community"*: Russ Oechslin, "New Roof Garden Ballroom Part of $112M Renovation Project at Arnolds Park," *Sioux City (IA) Journal*, May 10 2017.

169 *responsible for Chiclets*: "Famous Staten Islanders," New York Public Library, 2009.

170 *a tub of water*: David Pilgrim, "African Dip Carnival Game," Jim Crow Museum of Racist Memorabilia, Ferris State University, February 2007, https://ferris.edu/HTMLS/news/jimcrow/question/2007/february.htm.

170 *in the late 1950s*: Victoria M. Wolcott, *Race, Riots, and Roller Coasters: The Struggle over Segregated Recreation in America* (Philadelphia: University of Pennsylvania Press, 2012), p. 219.

170 *"in theory"*: Mike Royko, "Tossing of Dwarfs Raises Bigger Issue," *Chicago Daily News*, July 17, 1989.

170 *"the privilege of visiting it"*: "Gay Bergen Beach," *New York Herald*, August 9, 1896, p. 6.

170 *Amusement Park (1902–1987)*: Emil R. Lucev Sr., *The Rockaways* (Charleston, SC: Arcadia Publishing, 2007), p. 65.

171 *next fifty-nine years*: Marisa L. Berman, *Historic Amusement Parks of Long Island: 118 Miles of Memories* (Charleston, SC: The History Press, 2015), p. 52.

171 *National Amusement Device Company*: "Atom Smasher," Roller Coaster Database, 2018, https://rcdb.com/1863.htm.

171 *as far north as Albany*: Polly Sparling, "Lost Amusement Parks of the Hudson Valley," *Hudson Valley Magazine*, May 20, 2014.

171 *"the largest dance halls"*: John Conway, text message to the author, November 22, 2017.

172 *LaGuardia Airport*: Dana Schulz, "The History of Bowery Beach, the 'Coney Island of Queens,'" 6sqft, July 6, 2016, https://www.6sqft.com/the-history-of-bowery-bay-beach-the-coney-island-of-queens/.

172 *Husman Music Hall*: Craig Radow, "The Coney Island of Canarsie," *New York Times*, July 1, 2007, p. 144.

172 *and injured fifteen*: Wesley Gottlock and Barbara H. Gottlock, *Lost Amusement Parks of New York City: Beyond Coney Island* (Charleston, SC: The History Press, 2013), p. 111.

172 *skidded into the river*: "New York Swept by Record Gale," *Spectator*, June 15, 1922, p. 3.

172 *"their sobbing parents"*: "Storm Hits Crowded Ferris Wheel; Six Dead, 40 Hurt," Oneonta (NY) *Daily Star*, June 12, 1922.

173 *spring 2020 opening*: Richard J. Bayne, "Legoland Completes Tree Clearing Phase Before Deadline," Albany (NY) *Times Herald-Record*, March 27, 2018.

173 *employment for thirteen hundred*: Glenn Blaine, "Legoland to Open New York Theme Park in 2020," New York *Daily News*, October 25, 2017.

TO THE MOON

178 *Rainbow City*: William Andrews, "How Niagara Has Been Harnessed," *American Monthly Review of Reviews*, June 1901.

178 *two hundred pounds*: William A. DeGregorio, *The Complete Book of U.S. Presidents*, 3rd ed. (New York: Wings Books, 1991), p. 355.

178 *a resident of Detroit*: "Czolgosz Is Rapidly Breaking Down and Appears to Be a Physical and Mental Wreck—Refuses to Talk." Buffalo (NY) *Courier*, September 9, 1901, p. 3.

178 *"the President two times"*: "President's Condition," Washington (DC) *Evening Star*, September 6, 1901.

178 *behind Czolgosz*: John D. Wells, "The Story of an Eye-Witness to the Shooting of the President," *Collier's Weekly*, September, 21, 1901.

178 *the hand of the president*: Quentin R. Skrabec, *William McKinley, Apostle of Protectionism* (New York: Algora Publishing, 2008), p. 177.

178 *the shooter was arrested*: Kat Eschner, "How President William McKinley's Assassination Led to the Modern Secret Service," Smithsonian.com, September 14, 2017, https://www.smithsonianmag.com/smart-news/how-president-william-mckinleys-assassination-led-modern-secret-service-180964868/.

178 *"tell my wife"*: Margaret Leech, *In the Days of McKinley* (New York: Harper & Brothers, 1959).

178 *on a hiking trip*: "The Inauguration of Theodore Roosevelt," *Harper's Weekly*, September 21, 1901, p. 957.

178 *the setting sun*: Mark Goldman, *High Hopes: The Rise and Decline of Buffalo, New York* (Albany, NY: State University of New York Press, 1983).

178 *on the president*: Robert C. Kennedy, "On This Day: June 8, 1901," New York Times on the Web, June 8, 2001, https://archive.nytimes.com/www.nytimes.com/learning/general/onthisday/harp/0608.html.

178 *it never recovered*: Michael Daly, *Topsy: The Startling Story of the Crooked-Tailed Elephant, P. T. Barnum, and the American Wizard, Thomas Edison* (New York: Atlantic Monthly Press, 2013), p. 294.

179 *Rockaway Beach*: Vincent Seyfried, "Seaside," in Jackson, *The Encyclopedia of New York City*, p. 1057.

179 *in Nashville*: Anderson, *Ferris Wheels*, p. 117.

179 *Aerio's two wheels*: Ibid., p. 120.

179 *wrote one reporter*: "Pan-American Exposition," *Pennsylvania School Journal*, July 1901, p. 13.

180 *"Flapped like a bird's"*: Ron Miller, "In 1901, You Could Pay 50 Cents to Ride an Airship to the Moon," Gizmodo.com, May 31, 2012.

180 *"the moon herself!"*: Julian Hawthorne, "Some Novelties at Buffalo Fair," *Cosmopolitan*, September 1901, p. 490.

180 *the souvenir store*: *Official Catalogue and Guide Book to the Pan-American Exposition* (Buffalo, NY: Charles Ahrhart, 1901), p. 44.

180 *"Avenging Spirit of the Moon"*: Woody Register, *The Kid of Coney Island: Fred Thompson and the Rise of American Amusements* (New York: Oxford University Press, 2001), p. 71.

181 *"we are different"*: Pilat and Ranson, *Sodom by the Sea*, p. 147.

181 *"the boy-man of the two"*: Register, *The Kid of Coney Island*, p. 87.

181 *"the amusement world"*: Pilat and Ranson, *Sodom by the Sea*, pp. 141–142.

181 *quit school at fifteen*: Register, *The Kid of Coney Island*, p. 87.

181 *in matters mechanical*: "Frederic Thompson, Show Builder, Dies," *New York Times*, June 7, 1919, p. 13.

181 *to his uncle's office*: Register, *The Kid of Coney Island*, p. 28.

182 *Buffalo Bill Cody*: Pilat and Ranson, *Sodom by the Sea*, p. 142.

182 *a court clerk*: "Elmer S. Dundy Is Dead; Won a Fortune in Shows," *New York Times*, February 6, 1907, p. 9.

182 *for $90 million*: Pilat and Ranson, *Sodom by the Sea*, p. 143.

182 *they become partners*: Ibid.

182 *"rainfall on 36 days"*: *The American Almanac, Year-Book Cyclopedia, and Atlas* (New York: New York American and Journal, Hearst's Chicago American, and San Francisco Examiner, 1903), p. 59.

182 *join him there immediately*: "Elmer S. Dundy Is Dead."

183 *the next twenty-five years*: Pilat and Ranson, *Sodom by the Sea*, p. 145.

183 *back in Des Moines*: McCullough, *Good Old Coney Island*, p. 305.

183 *"electric Baghdad"*: Frederic Thompson, "Amusing the Million," *Everybody's Magazine*, September 1908, pp. 378–387.

183 *found on Wall Street*: Pilat and Ranson, *Sodom by the Sea*, p. 146.

183 *with LaMarcus Thompson*: McCullough, *Good Old Coney Island*, p. 303.

183 *more crowds to Coney*: Lyon, "The Master Showman of Coney Island," *American Heritage*.

183 *"that would buy?"*: Thompson, "Amusing the Million."

183 *came to $600,000*: Denson, *Coney Island: Lost and Found*, p. 36.

183 *making it Independence Day*: Lynn Kathleen Sally, *Fighting the Flames: The Spectacular Performance of Fire at Coney Island* (New York: Routledge, 2006), pp. 112–113.

183 *at the time*: Cross and Walton, *The Playful Crowd*, p. 264.

183 *hoity-toity Steeplechase Park*: Mike Wallace, *Greater Gotham: A History of New York City from 1898 to 1919* (New York: Oxford University Press, 2017), p. 437.

185 *the Gravesend post office*: Ibid., p. 436.

185 *singing its praises*: Maxim Gorky, "Coney Island," New York *Independent*, August 8, 1907.

185 *naval spectacle in miniature*: Cross and Walton, *The Playful Crowd*, p. 41.

185 *from the Chicago Fair*: Mangels, *The Outdoor Amusement Industry*, p. 44.

185 *a greeting by Eskimos*: Paul Brigandi and Nancy Brigandi, "William H. Reynolds Shared His 'Dreamland' with Coney Island and the World," Carousel History, June 13, 2015, http://carouselhistory.com/coney-islands-dreamland-park-history/.

185 *"to dislodge her"*: Elmer Blaney Harris, "The Day of Rest at Coney Island," *Everybody's Magazine*, July 1908, p. 34.

186 *more than $400 today*: "History of Medicine: The Incubator Babies of Coney Island," Columbia University Department of Surgery, Columbia University Medical Center, August 6, 2015, http://columbiasurgery.org/news/2015/08/06/history-medicine-incubator-babies-coney-island.

186 *the safety of Luna*: "Martin A. Couney, 'Incubator Doctor,'" obituary, *New York Times*, March 2, 1950, p. 27.

187 *"I dismiss him"*: Thompson, "Amusing the Million."

187 *"and 100 horses"*: "Luna Park—A Modern Amusement Wonder," *Omaha Bee*, May 8, 1904.

187 *from the Philippines*: Claire Prentice, *The Lost Tribe of Coney Island: Headhunters, Luna Park, and the Man Who Pulled Off the Spectacle of the Century* (New York: Amazon Publishing, 2014), p. 27.

188 *the Asiatic flu*: Daly, *Topsy*, p. 231.

FORTUNE'S FOLLY

189 *suburban housing developer*: Wallace, *Greater Gotham*, p. 435.

189 *Shoot the Chutes*: Cross and Walton, *The Playful Crowd*, p. 42.

189 *his bills on time*: "W. H. Reynolds, Builder, Dead at 63," *New York Times*, October 14, 1913, p. 23.

190 *John S. Berman*: Berman, *Coney Island*, p. 36.

190 *and the Matterhorn*: Paul Brigandi and Nancy Brigandi, "Coney Island's Original, Romantic Luna Park," CarouselHistory.com, June 13, 2015, http://carouselhistory.com/coney-islands-original-romantic-luna-park/.

190 *thro' its caverns*: "Coasting Through Switzerland, *Street Railway Review*, September 20, 1904, p. 646.

190 *"Dreamland has come to stay"*: "Dreamland-by-the-Sea," *New-York Daily Tribune*, May 15, 1904, p. 10.

191 *Byzantine bas-relief*: Fried, *A Pictorial History of the Carousel*, p. 19.

191 *above a bear pit*: Richard W. Johnston, "The Carrousel," *Life*, August 27, 1951, p. 108.

191 *fire eating besides, sir*: As quoted in Hone, *The Every-Day Book and Table Book*, p. 625.

192 *Ten of them were Illions's*: Roland Summit, *Flying Horses Catalog*, no. 1 (Rolling Hills, CA: Flying Horses, October 1970), p. 4.

192 *as young as nine*: Sady Sullivan, "Coney Island Carousel Carver," Brooklyn Historical Society, November 5, 2009, https://www.brooklynhistory.org/blog/2009/11/05/coney-island-carousel-carver/.

192 *a horse trader*: Martha Schwendener, "Sacred Skills Thrive on a Merry-Go-Round," *New York Times*, October 5, 2007, p. E42.

192 *George Wombwell*: Mangels, *The Outdoor Amusement Industry*, p. 171.

192 *exhibition of exotic animals*: "Frank Charles Bostock (1866–1912)," National Fairground and Circus Archive, University of Sheffield, 2017, https://www.sheffield.ac.uk/nfca/projects/frankbostockbio.

192 *Illions followed*: Eisenstadt, *Encyclopedia of New York State*, p. 267.

192   *quarter horses and mustangs*: "M. C. Illions Dies," *New York Times*, August 14, 1949, p. 68.

192   *National Carousel Association*: Brian Morgan, "Major Carousel Builders and Carvers," National Carousel Association, 2015, http://carousels.org/Carvers_Builders.html.

193   *lacked an engine*: Johnston, "The Carrousel." p. 108.

193   *profitable ride time*: Fried, *A Pictorial History of the Carousel*, p. 58.

193   *"complete with band organ"*: Johnston, "The Carrousel," p. 108.

193   *Painted Ponies: American Carousel Art*: William Manns and Peggy Shank, *Painted Ponies: American Carousel Art*, ed. Marianne Stevens (Millwood, NY: Zon International Publishing, 1986), p. 127.

193   *"carving for synagogues"*: Fried, *A Pictorial History of the Carousel*, pp. 126–128.

193   *The Synagogue to the Carousel*: Murray Zimiles, *Gilded Lions and Jeweled Horses: The Synagogue to the Carousel: Jewish Carving Traditions* (Waltham, MA: Brandeis University Press, 2007), p. 34.

193   *William F. Mangels*: "M. C. Illions Dies."

194   *"by coming to us"*: Summit, *Flying Horses Catalog*, p. 4.

194   *"over the river Styx"*: "Luna Park, Coney Island," Brooklyn Museum, n.d., https://www.brooklynmuseum.org/opencollection/objects/181511.

194   *in late January*: "Elmer Scipio Dundy," Dundy County Nebraska Genealogy Trails, 2008, http://genealogytrails.com/neb/dundy/bios/esdundy.html.

194   *three quarters of them*: "Elmer S. Dundy Is Dead."

195   *blow away ladies' hats*: Cons. No. 15837, "Coney Island: The World's Greatest Play Ground As It Is Today," New York State Reformatory at Elmira *Summary*, July 4, 1908), p. 8.

195   *better part of Steeplechase*: "Coney Swept by $1,500 Fire," *New York Times*, July 29, 1907, p. 3.

195   *"one dollar in insurance"*: Ibid., p. 1.

JUST ADD FLAMES

196   *She divorced him*: "Frederic Thompson, Show Builder, Dies," *New York Times*, p. 13.

197   *the burning Creation arches*: Kyriazi, *The Great American Parks*, p. 70.

197   *the Brooklyn Dodgers*: Uno, "Coney Island, N.Y.," *Billboard*, September 10, 1955, p. 55.

198   *jumping into the ring*: "Samuel Gumpertz Dies; Ran Ringling Empire," *Billboard*, July 5, 1952, p. 56.

198   *a rough rider*: "Samuel Gumpertz House," Sarasota History Alive!, 2007–2017, http://www.sarasotahistoryalive.com/history/postcards/samuel-gumpertz-house/.

198   *and seventeen theaters*: "The Players," *Midland Monthly Magazine*, June 1899, p. 504.

198   *as Dreamland manager*: Phalen, *Coney Island*, p. 66.

198   *name of Cary Grant*: Cary Grant, "Archie Leach," *Ladies' Home Journal*, March 1963.

199   *to clear customs*: Kyriazi, *The Great American Amusement Parks*, pp. 72–74.

199   *"one pair of legs"*: "Samuel Gumpertz Dies."

199   *"poop a chandelier"*: Todd Robbins, interview with the author, August 20, 2003.

200   *old haunts, like Saratoga*: Santoro, "The Upper-Class Brooklyn Resorts."

200   *where the booze was*: Boyden R. Sparkes, "What Prohibition Did to Coney Island," *New-York Tribune*, July 3, 1921, p. 4. Illustrated by Edmund Duffy.

200   *Brooklyn-based company*: Charles Hermann, "Amusement Apparatus," Patent No. 1,354,436, Google Patents, September 28, 1920, https://patents.google.com/patent/US1354436.

200   *"different frame of mind"*: Sparkes, "What Prohibition Did to Coney Island."

201   *prisoner-of-war camp*: Bob Liff, "Wonder Wheel Owner Remembered," New York *Daily News*, November 22, 1999.

201   *She said yes*: Douglas Martin, "Wonder Wheel, Humbuggery and Freud's Fascination," *New York Times*, June 16, 1987.

201   *she admitted in 2014*: Doyle Murphy, "Lula Vourderis, 82-Year-Old Matriarch of Coney Island's Deno's Wonder Wheel Family, Will Be Honored This Week," New York *Daily News*, February 13, 2014.

201   *crime-ridden Coney*: Scott Rutherford, "Coney's Wonder Wheel Celebrates 90th Anniversary," *Amusement Today*, November 2010, p. 4.

201   *to repair it*: Martin, "Wonder Wheel, Humbuggery and Freud's Fascination."

201   *revitalized attraction in 1989*: David M. Briener, "The Wonder Wheel," Designation List 215 LP-1798, Landmarks Preservation Commission, May 23, 1989. Additional research by Janet Adams; edited by Nancy Goeschel.

202   *said DJ Vourderis*: George LaCross and Bill Luca, "Spook-A-Rama Strikes Back," Laff in the Dark, 2017, http://www.laffinthedark.com/articles/spook3/spook3_1.htm.

202   *filth and crowds*: Robert A. Caro, *The Power Broker: Robert Moses and the Fall of New York* (New York: Alfred A. Knopf, 1974), p. 152.

202   *biographer, Robert Caro*: Jonathan Mahler, "How the Coastline Became a Place to Put the Poor," *New York Times*, December 2, 2012, p. A29.

202   *muzzle the barkers*: John A. Manbeck, "Historically Speaking: Coney Island Strongman, Just Another Side Show," *Brooklyn Eagle*, January 28, 2010.

202   *"what it had been"*: Robert Bogdan, *Freak Show: Presenting Human Oddities for Amusement and Profit* (Chicago: University of Chicago Press, 1990), p. 58.

202   *"Coney Island was my Hamptons"*: Carole Stuart, interview with the author, January 10, 2018.

202   *Coney torchbearer Charles Denson*: Denson, *Coney Island and Astroland*, p. 9.

202   *leveled the structure*: Martin, "Wonder Wheel, Humbuggery and Freud's Fascination."

202   *that he never built*: Dana Schulz, "50 Years Ago, Donald Trump's Father Demolished Coney Island's Beloved Steeplechase Park," 6sqft., May 18, 2016, https://www.6sqft.com/50-years-ago-donald-trumps-father-demolished-coney-islands-beloved-steeplechase-park/.

203   *"fountain in Lincoln Center"*: Alfa-Betty Olsen, interview with the author, May 20, 2016.

204   *"Coney Island America's Playground"*: Rich Calder, "Zamperla Breaks Ground on New Coney Island Coaster, Another to Follow," *New York Post*, January 31, 2011.

SHAKING THINGS UP

205   *seen big things before*: Frances Wayne, "White City—Triumph of Faith," *Denver Post*, May 24, 1908, p. 49.

205   *Lakeside Realty and Amusement Company*: Katie Rudolph, "The History of Lakeside Amusement Park in Photos," Geneology, African American and Western History Resources, Denver Public Library, July 13, 2015, https://history.denverlibrary.org/news/lakeside-amusement-park-celebrating-107-denver-summers.

205   *"seen out West"*: "Lake Side: An Art Deco Masterpiece Struggles to Survive," *American Heritage*, July–August 1992.

206   *tickled its last*: David Hill, "Quite a Ride: Lakeside Amusement Park's Century-Old Survival," Colorado Public Radio, May 10, 2016, http://www.cpr.org/news/story/quite-ride-lakeside-amusement-parks-century-old-survival.

206   *Lakeside (pop.: 8)*: Rudolph, "The History of Lakeside Amusement Park in Photos."

206   *"turn at the bottom"*: "Aged Autoist Hurled to Death Over Bridge," *Brisbee (AZ) Daily Record*, September 14, 1920.

207   *the waffle cone*: "The History of the Ice Cream Cone," International Dairy Foods Association, 2018, https://www.idfa.org/news-views/media-kits/ice-cream/the-history-of-the-ice-cream-cone.

207   *a litter problem*: Pagan Kennedy, "Who Made That Ice-Cream Cone?," *New York Times Magazine*, May 31, 2013.

207   *electric candy machine*: Arden G. Christen and Joan A. Christen, "William J. Morrison (1860–1926): Co-Inventor of the Cotton Candy Machine," *Journal of the History of Dentistry* 53, no. 2 (July 2005); abstract available at https://www.ncbi.nlm.nih.gov/pubmed/16092607.

207   *"sugar version of glass"*: Rebecca Rupp, "The Sticky-Sweet Story of Cotton Candy, *National Geographic*, July 15, 2016, https://www.nationalgeographic.com/people-and-culture/food/the-plate/2016/07/the-sticky-sweet-history-of-cotton-candy/.

208   *"satisfy that obligation"*: Gurtler and Hunt, *The Elitch Gardens Story*, p. 10.

208   *which they also owned*: Gene Fowler, *Timber Line: A Story of Bonfils and Tammen* (Garden City, NY: Garden City Books, 1951.)

208   *Denver Gas & Electric*: Dier, *The Lady of the Gardens*, p. 132.

208   *raise the tourist market*: Edgar Carlisle McMechen, *Robert W. Speer, A City Builder* (Denver: Smith-Brooks Printing, 1919).

208   *"to this community"*: Frederick White, "A Recollection of Elitch's Gardens," *Denver Post*, April 16, 1916, p. 40.

209   *"maintain Elitch traditions"*: Dier, *The Lady of the Gardens*, p. 131.

209   *might enjoy inside*: Gurtler and Hunt, *The Elitch Gardens Story*, p. 13.

209   *Mary was occupying*: Ibid., p. 15.

209   *hobby of breeding horses*: Wilbur Fiske Stone, ed., *History of Colorado*, vol. 4 (Chicago: S. J. Clarke, 1919), p. 106.

209   *run its food service*: Megan Verlee, "Photos: Lakeside Amusement Park, A Timeless, Antique Attraction," Colorado Public Radio, August 29, 2014, http://www.cpr.org/news/story/photos-lakeside-amusement-park-timeless-antique-attraction.

210   *"super-puritan community"*: Jef Otte, "Radium and Roller Coasters: A Brief, Dirty History of Elitch Gardens," Westword, June 6, 2012, http://www.westword.com/arts/radium-and-roller-coasters-a-brief-dirty-history-of-elitch-gardens-5116922.

210   *"and don't come"*: "The Secret of the Success and the Fame of Elitch's Gardens."

210   *"character of the West"*: Jesse T. Moore Jr., "Seeking a New Life: Blacks in Post–Civil War Colorado," *Journal of Negro History* 78, no. 3 (Summer 1993).

210   *Amusement Company*: "Lake Side," *American Heritage*.

210   *"Denver Has Gone Lakeside"*: Forsyth, *Denver's Lakeside Amusement Park*, p. 106.

210   *"needed a new look"*: "Lake Side."

211   *between fantasy and reality*: Gurtler and Hunt, *The Elitch Gardens Story*, p. 15.

211   *stage appearance at Elitch's*: Hull, *Denver's Elitch Gardens*, p. 99.

212   *his horse, Topper*: Gurtler and Hunt, *The Elitch Gardens Story*, p. 25.

212   *"and the policemen's kids"*: Verlee, "Lakeside Amusement Park."

212   *"and full of charm"*: Bree Davies, "Ten Reasons Why Lakeside Amusement Park Rules," Westword, August 29, 2012, http://www.westword.com/arts/ten-reasons-why-lakeside-amusement-park-rules-5817844.

212   *"the other neon-lit ones"*: Bree Davies, "Lakeside Is Awesome," Westword, August 25, 2011, http://www.westword.com/arts/lakeside-is-awesome-5780348.

212   *"she was a child"*: Claire Martin, "Nostalgia Rides On at Lakeside," *Denver Post*, July 1, 2011.

212   *"sit down on them"*: Otte, "Radium and Roller Coasters."

213   *National Register of Historic Places*: "Colorado," National Park Service, 2018, https://www.nps.gov/state/co/index.htm?program=all.

213   *causing the incident*: Hull, *Denver's Elitch Gardens*, pp. 129–130.

213   *in October 1996*: Julie Dunn and Margaret Jackson, "Elitch's Ticket: $170 Million," *Denver Post*, August 6, 2006.

214   *an undisclosed sum*: Monica Mendoza, "Elitch Gardens Sold to Investor Group That Includes Kroenke," *Denver Business Journal*, June 5, 2015.

214   *Elitch's once again*: "A Future Move for Elitch's Possible As New Plans Develop for Downtown Denver," Fox Denver 31, January 13, 2018, https://kdvr.com/2018/01/13/a-future-move-for-elitchs-possible-as-new-plans-develop-for-downtown-denver/.

214   *business as usual*: Adrian D. Garcia, "Elitch Gardens 'Not Going Away Anytime Soon,' Owner Says," *Denver News*, November 4, 2017.

OFF THE RAILS

215   *in Italy and Germany*: Frank Rowsome, *The Birth of Electric Traction: The Extraordinary Life and Times of Inventor Frank Julian Sprague*, ed. John L. Sprague (North Charleston, SC: CreateSpace Independent Publishing Platform, 2013), pp. 87–89.

216   *"St. Petersburg, and Tokyo"*: Wallace, *Greater Gotham*, p. 438.

216   *and the Philippines*: Cartmell, *The Incredible Scream Machine*, p. 95.

216   *author Lauren Rabinovitz*: Rabinovitz, *Electric Dreamland*, p. 63.

216   *"for the Frankfurter Zeitung"*: Joseph Roth, *What I Saw: Reports from Berlin 1920–1933*, trans. Michael Hoffmann (New York: W. W. Norton, 2003), p. 159.

217   *"Fred Ingersoll's Luna Parks"*: David Francis and Diane Francis, *Cleveland Amusement Park Memories* (Cleveland: Gray 2004), p. 36.

217   *three suits of clothes*: Marylynne Pitz, "Luna Park's Luminary: Entrepreneur/Roller Coaster Designer Deserves His Due," *Pittsburgh Post-Gazette*, September 1, 2008.

217   *the longest, until 1929*: Futrell, *Amusement Parks of Pennsylvania*, pp. 27–28.

217   *opened the gas jets*: Associated Press, "Fred Ingersoll Is Found Dead," *Lincoln (NE) Star*, October 24, 1927, p. 12.

217   *business partner Lloyd Jeffries*: "Talkers and Lecturers," *Billboard*, April 7, 1917, p. 38.

217   *"one way or another"*: Cartmell, *The Incredible Scream Machine*, p. 94.

217   *explains on its website*: "Trolley Parks and Real Estate Development," Chevy Chase Historical Society, 2013, http://www.chevychasehistory.org/trolley-parks-and-real-estate-development.

218   *introduced the Cakewalk*: Steve Roberts, *Bethesda and Chevy Chase* (Charleston, SC: Arcadia Publishing, 2016), p. 69.

218   *An avowed white supremacist*: Bill Turque, "In Chevy Chase, a Conundrum Spouts from Fountain Named After a Racist Senator," *Washington Post*, December 26, 2014.

218   *from moving in*: Judith Helm Robinson, "Chevy Chase," in *Washington at Home: An Illustrated History of Neighborhoods in the Nation's Capital*, ed. Kathryn Schneider Smith (Washington, DC: The Historical Society of Washington, DC, 1989).

218   *which opened in 1927*: "Chevy Chase Lake Sector Plan," Montgomery County (MD) Planning Department, July 2012.

219   *author John F. Kasson*: Kasson, *Amusing the Million*, p. 7.

219   *"four amusement parks"*: Francis and Francis, *Cleveland Amusement Park Memories*, pp. 5–6.

219   *"the next year"*: Larry O'Dell, "Amusement Parks," The Encyclopedia of Oklahoma History and Culture, Oklahoma History Society, 2009, http://www.okhistory.org/publications/enc/entry.php?entry=AM018.

219   *more lucrative development*: Futrell, *Amusement Parks of Pennsylvania*, p. 26.

219   *"four trolley parks"*: Bob Brooke, "Trolley Parks Fade into Memory," The Antiques Almanac, 2007–2017, http://theantiquesalmanac.com/trolleyparksfadeintomemory.htm.

219   *Please Touch Museum*: "Woodside Park Dentzel Carousel," Please Touch Museum, 2017, https://www.pleasetouchmuseum.org/pageblocks/explore-carousel/.

219   *used for trotting races*: "Point Breeze Park, Schottisch," World Digital Library, U.S. Library of Congress, June 30, 2016, https://www.wdl.org/en/item/9246/.

219   *"and bought it"*: "Lost Amusement Parks—Pennsylvania," National Amusement Park Historical Association, http://lostamusementparks.napha.org/pennsylvania-parks.html.

219   *and there were three*: Old York Road Historical Society, *Willow Grove Park* (Charleston, SC: Arcadia Publishing, 2005), p. 12.

220   *Chicago World's Fair*: Columbian Engraving and Publishing Co., *The Columbian Exposition and World's Fair Illustrated* (Chicago and Philadelphia: Columbian Engraving and Publishing, 1893), p. 343.

220   *street-railway stocks*: "What Happened to the Widener Fortune?," Lynnewood Hall, July 6, 2014, https://lynnewoodhall.wordpress.com/2014/07/06/what-happened-to-the-widener-fortune/.

220   *new mechanical rides*: Rabinovitz, *Electric Dreamland*, p. 59.

220   *debuted in 1905*: Old York Road Historical Society, *Willow Grove Park*, p. 60.

221   *hair-curling irons*: Editors of *Encyclopædia Britannica*, "Hiram Maxim: American Inventor," in *Encyclopædia Britannica*, February 13, 2018, https://www.britannica.com/biography/Hiram-Maxim.

221   *a naturalized British citizen*: "Hiram Maxim: Machine Guns," Who Made America?, They Made America, PBS, 2004, http://www.pbs.org/wgbh/theymadeamerica/whomade/maxim_lo.html.

221   *"a glorified merry-go-round"*: "Sir Hiram Maxim's Captive Flying Machines," Atlas Obscura, 2018, https://www.atlasobscura.com/places/sir-hiram-maxim-s-captive-flying-machines.

222   *the same at Willow Grove*: "Obituary Record: Asa G. Neville," *Pottery Glass & Brass Salesman*, December 6, 1917, p. 45.

222   *Chiropody Society of Philadelphia*: Joe Thomas, *A Synopsis of the History of Upper Moreland and Willow Grove* (Willow Grove, PA: Upper Moreland Historical Association, 2000), pp. 34–36.

222   *a real estate family*: Walter F. Naedele, "Gertrude Brooks Hankin, 90, Interior Decorator," Philadelphia *Inquirer*, July 24, 2012.

222 *an ice-skating rink*: "Willow Grove Sold; Owners Plan Additions," *Billboard*, December 22, 1958, p. 45.

222 *"summer evenings there"*: Aimee Lee Ball, interview with the author, December 27, 2017.

222 *North Carolina, and Kentucky*: "Page Pendleton Robinson, Jr., Obituary," *Ocala (FL) Star-Banner*, August 30, 2011.

223 *"Where the West Comes East"*: Old York Road Historical Society, *Willow Grove Park*, p. 116.

223 *buy back the contract*: Old York Road Historical Society presentation to Upper Moreland Free Public Library, Willow Grove, Pennsylvania, May 2011.

223 *trolley parks in America*: Rabinovitz, *Electric Dreamland*, p. 9.

223 *"taking the streetcar"*: Hartmut Esslinger, *A Fine Line: How Design Strategies Are Shaping the Future of Business* (San Francisco: John Wiley & Sons, 2009), p. 108.

224 *the picturesque location*: Cole Thompson, "Fort George Amusement Park," My Inwood, November 14, 2013, http://myinwood.net/fort-george-amusement-park/.

224 *Loews theater chain*: Stephen M. Silverman, *The Fox That Got Away: The Last Days of the Zanuck Dynasty at Twentieth Century-Fox* (Secaucus, NJ: Lyle Stuart, 1988), p. 59.

225 *were back onstage*: Lillian Gish with Ann Pinchot, *Lillian Gish: The Movies, Mr. Griffith, and Me* (Englewood Cliff, NJ: Prentice-Hall, 1969), pp. 23–24.

225 *fueled the steamers*: "Joseph M. Schenck, 82, Is Dead; A Pioneer in the Movie Industry," *New York Times*, October 23, 1961, p. 1.

225 *came to America*: "Nicholas M. Schenck, 87, Dead; Was Head of M-G-M and Loew's," *New York Times*, March 5, 1969, p. 47.

225 *owned the business*: Neal Gabler, *An Empire of Their Own: How the Jews Invented Hollywood* (New York: Anchor Books, 1989), p. 113.

225 *"words to that effect"*: Alan Hynd, "The Rise and Fall of Joseph Schenck," *Liberty*, June 28, 1941.

226 *the* New Yorker *noted*: Henry F. Pringle, "Business Is Business," *New Yorker*, April 30, 1932, pp. 23–25.

226 *learned the fur trade*: Fran Caso, "Marcus Loew," Immigrant Entrepreneurship, September 22, 2011, last modified January 28, 2014, https://www.immigrantentrepreneurship.org/entry.php?rec=88.

226 *"Fort George is popular"*: "Fifty Thousand People Go Seek Amusement on a Sunday," *Washington Post*, August 13, 1905, p. 24.

227 *charged with homicide*: "Coaster Kills 3 at Coney Island," *New York Times*, July 28, 1915.

227 *roller coasters be licensed*: "News Briefs," *Brooklyn Daily Eagle*, July 30, 1915, p. 12.

227 *"in the park was destroyed"*: "Fire Destroys Paradise Park at Fort George," *Fire and Water Engineering*, June 25, 1913, p. 447.

227 *would be rebuilt*: Gottlock and Gottlock, *Lost Amusement Parks of New York City*, p. 29.

CAUTION TO THE WIND

228 *Traction Company tracks*: Vince Gargiulo, *Palisades Amusement Park: A Century of Fond Memories* (New Brunswick, NJ: Rutgers University Press, 1995), p. 3

228 *Alven H. Dexter*: Eugene Tompkins and Quincy Kilby, *The History of the Boston Theatre, 1854–1901* (Boston: Houghton Mifflin, 1908), p. 366.

228 *skill and aerial acts*: Gargiulo, *Palisades Amusement Park*, p. 8.

229 *Big Dip Electric Coaster*: Vince Gargiulo and Mike Chew, "A Quick Look at Palisades' Roller Coasters," Palisades Amusement Park, 1994–2017, http://www.palisadespark.com/coasters.html.

229 *an inch of decapitation*: "Pringle, Business Is Business," p. 25.

229 Tarzan the Ape Man: Gargiulo, *Palisades Amusement Park*, p. 44.

229 *in Canarsie, Brooklyn*: Burton Lindheim, "Irving Rosenthal, 77, Is Dead; Palisades Operator 37 Years," *New York Times*, December 29, 1973, p. 28.

230 *"their own automobiles!"*: Crissey, "New Thrills Defy Gravity," p. 38.

230 *precedent-setting stature*: Cartmell, *The Incredible Scream Machine*, p. 142.

230 *and 96,000 rivets*: Crissey, "New Thrillers Defy Gravity," p. 39.

230 *"an airplane at top speed"*: B. J. Phillips, "Here Comes Summer: Those Roller Rides in the Sky," *Time*, July 4, 1977.

230 *"of extreme stress"*: George Plimpton, "American Thrills," *Popular Mechanics*, May 1989, p. 41.

231 *the Cyclone is irreplaceable*: David M. Briener, "The Cyclone," Designation List 206 LP-1636, Landmarks Preservation Commission, July 12, 1988, p. 5. Additional research by Janet Adams; edited by Nancy Goeschel.

231 *"I feel sick"*: "Roller-Coaster Ride Brings Back Speech to Army Veteran Who Lost Voice in 1943," *New York Times*, August 12, 1948, p. 14.

231 *and George F. Kister*: Jane Corby, "Coney His Life and Hobby, 'Cyclone' His Greatest Thrill," *Brooklyn Daily Eagle*, April 20, 1947, p. 23.

231 *the safety lap bar*: Cartmell, *The Incredible Scream Machine*, p. 91.

231 *entrance of Luna Park*: "Coney Island Civic Leader Found Dead in Car Crash," *New York Times*, October 30, 1964, p. 26.

232 *"in long pants"*: Corby, "Coney His Life and Hobby," *Brooklyn Daily Eagle*, p. 23.

232 *"gone back on you"*: Lindsay, "Terror Bound."

232 *and Diane Francis*: Francis and Francis, *The Golden Age of Roller Coasters*, p. 95.

232 *western side of the Hudson*: Gargiulo and Chew, "A Quick Look at Palisades' Roller Coasters."

232 *bumps and turns*: Richard Munch, *Harry G. Traver: Legends of Terror* (Mentor, OH: Amusement Park Books, 1982), pp. 99–100.

233 *of roller coasters*: Kyle Scott Clauss, "Throwback Thursday: When Revere Beach Had Roller Coasters," *Boston*, July 23, 2015, https://www.bostonmagazine.com/news/2015/07/23/revere-beach-roller-coasters/.

233 *been called crazy*: Jeffrey Snedden, "Harry Traver Took Beaver County on Thriller Roller Coaster Ride," Beaver (PA) *Times*, May 24, 2016.

233 *the ship's mast*: Adam Sandy, "Harry G. Traver," Ultimate Rollercoaster.com, 1996–2018, https://www.ultimateroller coaster.com/coasters/history/designer/traver.shtml.

233 *the world—by himself*: "H. G. Traver Dead; Designer of Rides," *New York Times*, September 27, 1961, p. 42.

233 *with smelling salts*: Samuelson and Yegoiants, *The American Amusement Park*, p. 109.

233 *into the same fate*: Gargiulo, *Palisades Amusement Park*, p. 40.

234 *dismantling on its own*: Sandy, "Harry G. Traver."

234 *six were seriously burned*: "Fire Wrecks Half of Palisades Park; 119 Persons Hurt," *New York Times*, August 14, 1944, pp. 1, 17.

234 *$500,000 damage each*: "Luna Park Closed," *New York Times*, August 14, 1944, p. 17.

234 *"a five-foot, two-inch giant"*: Gargiulo, *Palisades Amusement Park*, p. ix.

234 *the phonograph needle stuck*: Tom Meyers, "From the Archives: Palisades Park Music Man Cousin Brucie," *River Dell (NJ) Patch*, June 2, 2013.

235 *patronize the pool*: Kevin McCabe, "The Battle to Integrate Palisades Amusement Park," *Social Science Docket*, Summer–Fall 2011, p. 49.

235 *"dead before I change"*: Wolcott, *Race, Riots, and Roller Coasters*, p. 60.

235 *sided with Rosenthal*: "N.J. Law Prohibits Racial Discrimination," *Billboard*, December 25, 1948, p. 54.

235 *lifted the ban in 1950*: Tom Meyers, "From the Archives: The Summer of '47—Melba Valle Takes a Stand at Palisades Amusement Park," *Fort Lee (NJ) Patch*, May 10, 2013.

SUGAR RUSH

236 *factory picnic days*: Friends of the Hershey Trolley and the Hershey–Derry Township Historical Society, *Hershey Transit* (Charleston, SC: Arcadia Publishing, 2013), p. 7.

237 *"all in Hershey"*: Roy Bongartz, "The Chocolate Camelot," *American Heritage*, June 1973.

237 *a Mennonite clergyman*: Millie Landis Coyle, "Milton Snavely Hershey," Hershey Derry Township Historical Society, 2016, http://hersheyhistory.org/library-archives/hershey/54-milton-snavely-hershey.

237 *She separated from Henry*: "Milton Hershey Biography," Biography.com, A&E Television Networks, April 27, 2017, https://www.biography.com/people/milton-hershey-9337133.

237 *Lancaster Caramel Company*: Rich Mueller, "American Caramel and Its Cards: A Brief History," Sports Collectors Daily, October 28, 2009, https://www.sportscollectorsdaily.com/a-short-history-of-american-caramel-and-its-cards/.

237 *his first million*: "Lancaster Caramel Company," Hershey Community Archives, n.d., http://www.hersheyarchives.org/essay/details.aspx?EssayId=43.

237 *factory workers in Birmingham*: Eileen Reynolds, "The Quaker Capitalist and the Chocolate Factory," *New Yorker*, October 18, 2010.

237 *a Utopia of his own*: Christine Gibson, "The Sweetest Place on Earth," *American Heritage*, August–September 2003.

238 *to Coney Island*: Pamela Cassidy Whitenack, *Hersheypark* (Charleston, SC: Arcadia Publishing, 2006), p. 11.

238 *no longer breathing*: Deborah B. Wescott, "The Inspiration for Sweet Success: A Portrait of Catherine S. Hershey, Wife of Milton S. Hershey" (masters thesis, Pennsylvania State University, 1998).

239 *"'speckled beauties' in season"*: "Dorney, Oliver Charles, C. P. A. Prominent Business Educator," in *Encyclopedia of Pennsylvania Biography*, vol. 3, ed. John Woolf Jordan (New York: Lewis Historical Publishing, 1914), p. 975.

239 *Dorney Park*: Wally Ely with Bob Ott, *Dorney Park* (Charleston, SC: Arcadia Publishing, 2003), p. 10.

239 *fed the park*: "Dorney, Oliver Charles, C. P. A. Prominent Business Educator."

239 *the 1924 Thunderhawk*: "Park History Timeline," Dorney Park & Wildwater Kingdom, Cedar Fair Entertainment, 2018, https://www.dorneypark.com/media-center.

240 *"snap of a whip"*: Mangels, *The Outdoor Amusement Industry*, pp. 133–134.

240 *at $12.3 billion*: Bob Fernandez, "Board Member at Troubled Hershey Trust Resigns," Philadelphia *Inquirer*, July 12, 2016.

240 *visitors, in 2017*: "Attendance at Amusement and Theme Parks in North America by Facility," Statista, 2017, https://www.statista.com/statistics/194269/attendance-at-theme-and-amusement-parks-in-north-america-since-2010/.

241 *"remains standard"*: "John Miller," Lemelson-MIT, Massachusetts Institute of Technology, n.d., http://lemelson.mit.edu/resources/john-miller.

241 *all upsets, derailment*: Lindsay, "Terror Bound."

242 *"No model"*: "Patents Granted February 25, 1890," in United States Patent Office, *Official Gazette of the United States Patent Office*, Volume 50. (Washington, D.C.: Government Printing Office, 1890), p. 995.

242 *the Gadabout*: Mangels, *The Outdoor Amusement Industry*, pp. 137–139.

242 *"highly unmanageable"*: Seth Gussow, "Going Bump in the Night," *Automobile*, November 1997.

242 *in both directions*: Easdown, *Amusement Park Rides*, p. 46.

242 *"in poverty"*: Mangels, *The Outdoor Amusement Industry*, p. 139.

243   *a son of William Penn*: Robert Jameson Jones, "Historical Society Notes and Documents: James McMaster, Jr.," *Western Pennsylvania Historical Magazine* 56, no. 1 (January 1973): 99–100.

243   *about $21,000 today*: "Knoebels Timeline 1775–2018," Knoebels, 2018, https://www.knoebels.com/history/knoebels-timeline.

243   *"two mountain streams"*: "Knoebels," WVIA Public Media, n.d., http://www.wvia.org/television/documentaries/knoebels/.

244   *Charles Looff frame*: "Knoebels Carousel & Organ History," Knoebels, 2018, https://www.knoebels.com/history/knoebels-carousel-organ-history.

245   *Herbert got an idea*: Curt Brown, "Minnesota History: Tilt-A-Whirl Gives Faribault, Minn., a Historic Spin," Minneapolis *Star Tribune*, April 2, 2015.

245   *"may next take place"*: Steve Baird, "Tilt-a-Whirl Trademark, Not a Service Mark?," DuetsBlog, August 26, 2013, https://www.duetsblog.com/2013/08/articles/trademarks/tilt-a-whirl-trademark-not-service-mark/.

245   *"and the family"*: Doug McDonough, "Larson International Acquires Tilt-A-Whirl Manufacturer," *Plainview (TX) Herald*, January 25, 2011.

246   *solidly constructed*: Charles J. Jacques Jr., *Kennywood...Roller Coaster Capital of the World* (Natrona Heights, PA: Amusement Park Journal, 1982), pp. 1–4.

246   *and renamed Thunderbolt*: Jacques, *Kennywood*, p. 40.

247   *"Crowds loved it"*: "In the 1950s, Kennywood Was a Blast (Sometimes Literally)," *Pittsburgh Post-Gazette*, October 7, 2015.

248   *"time and place"*: Arthur Levine, email to the author, April 2, 2018.

248   *owned and operated*: Arthur Levine, "Why Are Some Amusement Parks Known As Trolley Parks?," TripSavvy, February 5, 2018, https://www.tripsavvy.com/what-is-a-trolley-park-3225649.

249   *sing their own songs*: "The Real Voices Behind Milli Vanilli Share Their Side of the Lip Synching Scandal (Video)," *HuffPost*, February 27, 2014, https://www.huffingtonpost.com/2014/02/27/milli-vanilli_n_4860222.html.

249   *rides in Philadelphia*: Maude I. West, *Irondequoit Story* (Irondequoit, NY: The Town of Irondequoit / Franklin Press, 1957).

249   *descendant of Long's*: Kyriazi, "Seabreeze—A Shining Example of Survival."

249   *free from rowdyism*: West, *Irondequoit Story.*

250   *South America in 1864*: "Classification of Wool," in United States, Department of the Treasury, *Treasury Decisions Under Tariff and Navigation Laws, Etc.*, vol. 3, *January-December 1900* (Washington, D.C., Government Printing Office, 1901), pp. 1043–1044.

250   *gave it its ridges*: Tracy López, "Churros: The Hidden History," *HuffPost*, last modified November 8, 2017, https://www.huffingtonpost.com/2011/08/18/churros-the-hidden-history_n_930791.html.

250   *through a funnel*: *Pennsylvania Dutch Cooking* (Project Gutenberg, 2008), https://www.gutenberg.org/files/26558/26558-h/26558-h.htm.

251   *experience as "extreme"*: "Ravine Flyer II," Roller Coaster Database, 2018, https://rcdb.com/3917.htm.

251   *initial news flashes*: "Youth, 19, Leaps to Death from Ravine Flyer," *Erie (PA) Dispatch-Herald*, August 8, 1938.

251   *tumble to his death*: "Defective Flyer Is Blamed for Death of Youth." *Erie (PA) Dispatch-Herald*, August 19, 1938.

251   *was condemned*: "Ravine Flyer Is Condemned in Probe of Youth's Death." *Erie (PA) Daily Times*, August 19, 1938.

251   *named Lucille Ball*: Kathleen Crocker and Jane Currie, *Chautauqua Lake Region* (Charleston, SC: Arcadia Publishing, 2002), p. 81.

252   *service from Providence*: David Bettencourt, *Rocky Point Park* (Charleston, SC: Arcadia Publishing, 2015), p. 92.

252   *from Pawcatuck, Connecticut*: Gloria Russell, "The Mysterious Murder of Little Maggie Sheffield," Pawcatuck (CT) *Westerly Sun*, December 14. 2014.

252   *with his judgment*: Kelly Sullivan Pezza, *Murder at Rocky Point Park: Tragedy in Rhode Island's Summer Paradise* (Charleston, SC: The History Press, 2014), p. 13.

252   *"until I saw blood"*: Russell, "The Mysterious Murder of Little Maggie Sheffield."

252   *March 14, 1901*: Pezza, *Murder at Rocky Point Park*, p. 71.

252   *link to king*: Doug Ireland, "King Novel Based on Canobie Lake Park," North Andover (MA) *Eagle-Tribune*, June 3, 2013.

252   *"and took mine?"*: Stephen King, *Joyland* (London: Titan Books, 2013.)

253   *SBF Visa Group*: "Camden Park," Roller Coaster Database, https://rcdb.com/4607.htm.

253   *a 2017 Facebook posting*: Jim Nibert, Camden Park page, Facebook, July 17, 2017.

253   *fair's extended midway*: Dana Beck, "Oaks Amusement Park, and Its Beginnings," Portland (OR) *Bee*, December 20, 2012.

254   *Adrenaline Family Entertainment*: Kelly Roncace, "Clementon Park Has New Rides, Attractions and an Updated Look," NJ.com, May 17, 2011, https://www.nj.com/gloucester-county/towns/index.ssf/2011/05/clementon_park_has_new_rides_a.html.

254   *Six Flags Corporation*: David Dorman, "Former Six Flags Executives Purchase Clementon Park and Splash World," press release, Clementon Park & Splash World, November 21, 2011.

254   *since the early 2000s*: Roncace, "Clementon Park Has New Rides."

254   *a battered wiener*: Stanley S. Jenkins, "Combined Dipping, Cooking, and Article-Holding Apparatus," Patent No. 1,706,491, Google Patents, March 26, 1929, https://patents.google.com/patent/US1706491A/en.

254   *an American mouth*: Rick Lyman, "Deep-Fry, and Don't Forget the Stick," *New York Times*, June 24, 2007.

255   *"from such considerations"*: Samuel Mansfield Stone, "Fishing on Lake Quassapaug," *Forest and Stream*, June 22, 1901, pp. 448–449.

259   *"circular gravity railway"*: "A Circular Railway," San Francisco *Evening Bulletin*, November 11, 1884.

259   *in the mid-1890s*: "Splish! Splash! At the Chutes," San Francisco Public Library, 2002–2018, https://sfpl.org/?pg=2000131701.

260   *in the Fillmore District*: Robert Ehler Blaisdell, *San Francisciana: Photographs of Ocean Beach and Playland* (San Francisco: Marilyn Blaisdell, 1989), p. i.

260   *Orpheum circuit theater chain*: Arthur Frank Wertheim and Barbara Blair, eds., *The Papers of Will Rogers*, vol. 3, *From Vaudeville to Broadway, September 1908–August 1915* (Norman, OK: University of Oklahoma Press, 2001), p. 53.

260   *"reflected on the mirror"*: James R. Smith, *San Francisco's Lost Landmarks* (Fresno, CA: Craven Street Books, 2005), p. 38.

261   *earthquake and fire*: Smith, *San Francisco's Lost Landmarks*, p. 41.

261   *Coney Island Park*: Dennis Evanosky and Eric J. Kos, *Lost San Francisco* (London: Pavilion Books, 2012).

261   *the rest of the park*: Smith, *San Francisco's Lost Landmarks*, p. 44.

261   *Nevada's Comstock Lode*: Kevin Starr, *California: A History* (New York: Modern Library, 2005), p. 123.

261   *for his philanthropy*: "Adolph Sutro (1830–1876)," American Jerusalem, 2018, http://www.americanjerusalem.com/characters/adolph-sutro-1830-ae-1898/19.

261   *from 1895 until 1897*: "Adolph Sutro Deranged," *New York Times*, February 8, 1898, p. 3.

261   *Outer Richmond District*: Marilyn Blaisdell, *San Francisciana Photographs of Sutro Baths* (San Francisco: Marilyn Blaisdell, 1987), p. i.

261   *the Cliff House*: "Sutro Baths History," Golden Gate National Recreation Area, National Park Service, U.S. Department of the Interior, February 28, 2015, https://www.nps.gov/goga/learn/historyculture/sutro-baths.htm.

261   *said Harper's Weekly*: "Sutro Baths," *Harper's Weekly*, September 8, 1894, p. 855.

261   *Recreation Area website*: "Sutro Baths History."

262   *J. Kirk Firth*: Anderson, *Ferris Wheels*, p. 87.

262   *the Haunted Swing*: Blaisdell, *San Francisciana Photographs of Sutro Baths*, p. i.

262   *"Park & Ocean railroad line"*: Marilyn Blaisdell, *San Francisciana Photographs of Playland* (San Francisco: Marilyn Blaisdell, 1989), p. i.

262   *Arthur Looff*: Cartmell, *The Incredible Scream Machine*, p. 150.

263   *Noah's Ark*: Blaisdell, *San Francisciana Photographs of Playland*, p. i.

263   *to Southern California*: Fried, *A Pictorial History of the Carousel*, p. 63.

263   *and aeroplane drop*: "Giant Dipper Roller Coaster," Santa Cruz Beach Boardwalk, 2018, https://beachboardwalk.com/Giant-Dipper.

263   *"just the right finesse"*: Aaron Sannes, interview with the author, August 9, 2017.

264   *major boardwalk in America*: Lilliefors, *America's Boardwalks*, p. 189.

264   *"did a profitable business"*: Edward Sanford Harrison, *History of Santa Cruz County, California* (San Francisco: Pacific Press Publishing, 1892), pp. 318–319.

265   *telegram of congratulations*: Lilliefors, *America's Boardwalks*, pp. 193–194.

265   *from Douglas fir trees*: Nina Garin, "Wendy Crain Is the Giant Dipper's Faithful Caregiver," *San Diego Union-Tribune*, September 2, 2014.

265   *to the city*: "History," Belmont Park, n.d., https://www.belmontpark.com/companyinfo/.

265   *August 11, 1990*: Deanna Bellandi, "On a Big Roll: Opening of Giant Dipper Draws Crowds to Mission Beach," *Los Angeles Times*, August 12, 1990.

266   *older (by seven years) brother, Leo*: Sam Abbott, "George Whitney's Showmanship Turns Playland into Payland," *Billboard*, June 24, 1950, p. 74

266   *new Luna Park*: John Martini, "George K. Whitney, Jr. Interview, 2002," OutsideLands.org, Western Neighborhoods Project, May 18, 2010, http://www.outsidelands.org/whitney-interview1.php.

267   *Manhattan, and Brooklyn*: Marie C. Baca, "Ice Cream Treat Dodges Economic Chill," *Wall Street Journal*, July 29, 2010.

267   *"in their pockets"*: Martini, "George K. Whitney, Jr. Interview, 2002."

267   *as a morale booster*: Abbott, "Payland—At the Beach," p. 74.

267   *$31 million today*: Ibid., p. 52.

267   *"the past 10 years"*: "Penn-Jersey Spots Feature Acts and Bands Thru Holidays," *Billboard*, July 20, 1946, p. 83.

267   *"record-breaking style"*: "AC Roars Thru Record Fourth," *Billboard*, July 20, 1946, p. 83.

267   *"every expectation"*: Uno, "Coney Island, N.Y.," *Billboard*, July 20, 1946, p. 82.

268   *in the entire country*: THR Staff, "How 'I Love Lucy' Dominated Ratings from Its Start," *Hollywood Reporter*, August 15, 2011.

268   *the same channel*: Tom O'Connell, "Tradition Plus Unusual Features Secure Top Spot at Coney Island for 53-Year-Old Steeplechase," *Billboard*, June 24, 1950, p. 73.

268   *"but not cheating them"*: Kyriazi, *The Great American Amusement Parks*, p. 139.

268   *was one dollar*: Martini, "George K. Whitney, Jr. Interview, 2002."

268   *Windows were broken*: *Subversive Influences in Riots, Looting, and Burning: Hearings Before the Committee of Un-American Activities*, 90th Cong. 2061 (1967) (testimony of Edward S. Montgomery).

269   *"to have outlived it"*: Herb Caen, "We'll Never Go There Anymore," *San Francisco Chronicle*, September 4, 1972.

269   *in constant motion*: Martini, "George K. Whitney, Jr. Interview, 2002."

BIRDS OF A FEATHER

270 *each fetch $1,000*: Richard Crawford, "Ostriches Were an Exotic Attraction," *San Diego Union-Tribune*, June 25, 2010.

271 *"of all animals"*: "On an Ostrich Farm, *Shepherdstown (WV) Register*, December 14, 1888.

271 *a gift shop*: Nathan Masters, "Southern California's First Amusement Parks? Ostrich Farms," KCET, September 20, 2012, https://www.kcet.org/shows/lost-la/an-ornithological-curiosity-when-ostriches-ruled-socal-tourism.

271 *might also participate*: Art Marroquin, Mark Eades, and Sarah Tully, "Oldest Disney Daughter Dies at 79; Helped Inspire Park," *Orange County (CA) Register*, November 20, 2013.

272 *"ten ostrich farms"*: Ibid.

272 *behest of President Lincoln*: Michael Patris, "A Closer Look at Thaddeus Lowe," Pasadena Museum of History, May 7, 2015, https://pasadenahistory.org/thaddeus-lowe/closer-look-lowe/.

272 *its forty-five-year existence*: "Early Views of Mt. Lowe Railway," Water and Power Associates, n.d., http://waterand power.com/museum/Mt_Lowe_Railway.html.

273 *a golfing green*: Hadley Meares, "Pasadena the Beautiful: Blossoms in Bloom at the Original Busch Gardens," KCET, October 31, 2014, https://www.kcet.org/history-society/pasadena-the-beautiful-blossoms-in-bloom-at-the-original-busch-gardens.

273 *starting in 1906*: Sandi Hemmerlein, "Top Ten Places to Trace the Remains of Pasadena's Busch Gardens," KCET, January 8, 2018, https://www.kcet.org/shows/socal-wanderer/top-ten-places-to-trace-the-remains-of-pasadenas-busch-gardens.

273 *widowed since 1913*: "Adolphus Busch Dies in Prussia," *New York Times*, October 11, 1913.

273 *Los Angeles County Improvement Company*: Paul Michelson, "Chutes Park Theatre, South Los Angeles, Los Angeles, CA," Pacific Coast Architecture Database, 2005–2015, http://pcad.lib.washington.edu/building/21445/.

273 *the brewer Fred Maier*: "Death Claims 'Fred' Maier," *Los Angeles Times*, April 12, 1909.

273 *Chutes Park*: Jay Berman and Sesar Carreno, "The Short Life of a Downtown Amusement Park," *Los Angeles Downtown News*, September 4, 2006.

273 *followed in 1903*: "Luna Park," Roller Coaster Database, 2018, https://rcdb.com/14166.htm.

273 *"Port Los Angeles"*: Tom Moran, "In Kinney's Own Words," Venice of America.org, Venice Historical Society, March–April 2004, http://www.veniceofamerica.org/pdf/mar_apr_2004_newsletter.pdf.

274 *excavate and reshape*: Lilliefors, *America's Boardwalks*, p. 176.

SINK OR SWIM

275 *William Reynolds's park*: Sally, *Fighting the Flames*, p. 112.

276 *Race Thru the Clouds*: John Bengston, *Silent Traces: Discovering Early Hollywood Through the Films of Charlie Chaplin* (Santa Monica, CA: Santa Monica Press, 2006), p. 19.

276 *between 1904 and 1925*: Jeffrey Stanton, "Roller Coasters & Carousels," Venice History Site, April 6, 1998, https://www.westland.net/venicehistory/articles/cc.htm.

276 *"regular crowds arrived"*: David Robinson, *Chaplin: His Life and Art* (London: Collins, 1985), p. 369.

276 *New York's Film Forum*: Bruce Goldstein, commentary, in *Speedy*, directed by Harold Lloyd, disc 1 (1928; New York: The Criterion Collection, 2015), DVD.

276 *Ocean Park Pier*: Christopher Merritt and Dominic Priore, *Pacific Ocean Park: The Rise and Fall of Los Angeles' Space-Age Nautical Pleasure Pier* (Port Townsend, WA: Process Media, 2014), pp. 16–17.

277 *a promising start*: "Venice of America: Jeffrey Stanton," KCET, March 24, 2010, https://www.kcet.org/shows/departures/venice-of-america-jeffrey-stanton.

277 *Venice Lagoon*: Adrian Glick Kudler, "The Strange and Wonderful Lost Amusement Parks of L.A.," Curbed Los Angeles.com, November 12, 2015, https://la.curbed.com/maps/old-amusement-theme-parks-los-angeles-defunct-map.

278 *eight miles*: Nathan Masters, "The Lost Canals of Venice of America," KCET, April 5, 2013, https://www.kcet.org/shows/lost-la/the-lost-canals-of-venice-of-america.

278 *islands between them*: Bengston, *Silent Traces*, p. 17.

278 *Johnson Captive Airplane*: Jeffrey Stanton, "Abbot Kinney Pier," Venice History Site, April 6, 1998, https://www.westland.net/venicehistory/articles/kinneypier.htm.

278 *"Thompson's masterpiece"*: Cartmell, *The Incredible Scream Machine*, p. 51.

278 *"on the West Coast"*: Lilliefors, *America's Boardwalks*, p. 177.

278 *a figure eight twister*: "Giant Dipper Roller Coaster," Calisphere, University of California, n.d., https://calisphere.org/item/b71a907483870a4fbf4fcd9269802c2c/.

279 *U.S. legal boundaries*: Cecilia Rasmussen, "L.A. Scene The City Then and Now," *Los Angeles Times*, October 18, 1993.

279 *seven months later*: Kudler, "The Strange and Wonderful Lost Amusement Parks of L.A."

280 *Larry Osterhoudt*: Jerry Hirsch, "He's Haunted by Classic Cyclone Coaster," *Orange County (CA) Register*, December 7, 1998.

280 *Downey, California, home*: Christine Mai-Duc, "He Dreams of Famed Roller Coaster's Return," *Los Angeles Times*, March 25, 2014.

280 *feasibility study*: Eric Bradley, "Long Beach Council Moves Forward with Cyclone Racer Roller Coaster Proposal," *Long Beach (CA) Press-Telegram*, October 1, 2013.

280   *"riding them once"*: Larry Osterhoudt, text message to the author, March 15, 2018.

281   *rebranding to Nu-Pike*: Samuelson and Yegoiants, *The American Amusement Park*, p. 123.

281   *"in the city"*: Matt Cohn, "Welcome to the Jungle: The Forgotten Tale of Long Beach's Oceanfront Slum," *Long Beach Post*, October 23, 2013.

282   *"mummified human body"*: Mark Svenvold, *Elmer McCurdy: The Misadventures in Life and Afterlife of an American Outlaw* (New York: Basic Books, 2003), p. 6.

282   *bank building around it*: Glynn Washington, "The Long, Strange, 60-Year Trip of Elmer McCurdy," NPR, January 9, 2015, https://www.npr.org/2015/01/09/376097471/the-long-strange-60-year-trip-of-elmer-mccurdy.

283   *traveling carnival huckster*: Ella Morton, "How a Real Corpse Ended Up in a Fun House Spookhouse," *Atlas Obscura* (blog), *Slate*, April 11, 2014, http://www.slate.com/blogs/atlas_obscura/2014/04/11/the_corpse_of_elmer_mccurdy_and_how_it_ended_up_in_a_long_beach_fun_park.html.

283   *in Guthrie, Oklahoma*: "Grave of Elmer McCurdy," Atlas Obscura, n.d., https://www.atlasobscura.com/places/grave-elmer-mccurdy-skb.

282   *twenty-five cents*: Cecilia Rasmussen, "Reptile Farm Gave L.A. a Wild Time," *Los Angeles Times*, August 3, 1997.

283   *presumably, human children*: Cory Stargel and Sarah Stargel, *Early Los Angeles County Attractions* (Charleston, SC: Arcadia Publishing, 2008), pp. 39–40.

283   *showpieces of the farm*: Kudler, "The Strange and Wonderful Lost Amusement Parks of L.A."

284   *"$1.25 to $2.50 apiece"*: Arthur Inkersley, "The California Alligator Ranch," *Overland Monthly*, December 1910, pp. 533–538.

284   *his first studio*: Kalton C. Lahue, *Motion Picture Pioneer: The Selig Polyscope Company* (South Brunswick, NJ: A. S. Barnes, 1973).

284   *permanent studio in California*: Michael Glover Smith, "The Secret History of Chicago Movies: Selig Polyscope," White City Cinema, April 18, 2011, https://whitecitycinema.com/2011/04/18/the-secret-history-of-chicago-movies-selig-polyscope/.

284   *"on Hope Street"*: "William N. Selig, Pioneer in Films," *New York Times*, July 17, 1948, p. 15.

284   *the Edendale section*: Anthony Slide, *The New Historical Dictionary of the American Film Industry* (New York: Routledge, 2013), p. 183.

285   *Louis B. Mayer*: Christina Rice, "When Elephants Ruled the Intersection: The Saga of the Selig Zoo Statues," *HuffPost*, August 26, 2012, https://www.huffingtonpost.com/the-los-angeles-public-library/selig-zoo-statues_b_1565154.html.

285   *California Zoological Gardens*: "Early Southern California Amusement Parks," Water and Power Associates, n.d., http://waterandpower.org/museum/Early_Southern_California_Amusement_Parks_Page_1.html.

SALT OF THE EARTH

286   *twelve-hundred-acre farm*: Elroy M. Avery, *A History of Cleveland and Its Environs: The Heart of New Connecticut* (Chicago: Lewis Publishing, 1918), p. 331.

286   *went bad*: Leo O. Bush et al., *Euclid Beach Park Is Closed for the Season* (Cleveland: Dillon/Liederbach, 1977), p. 17.

286   *suburb of Glenville*: Ibid., p. 18.

286   *"in the United States"*: Avery, *A History of Cleveland and Its Environs*, p. 332.

287   *D&C Lines' steamers*: Bush et al., *Euclid Beach Park Is Closed for the Season*, pp. 2–4.

287   *"Detroit and Cleveland"*: Dan Austin, "City of Detroit III," HistoricDetroit.org, 2018, http://historicdetroit.org/building/city-of-detroit-iii/.

287   *more than sixty acres*: Euclid Beach Park Now, *Euclid Beach Park.* (Charleston, SC: Arcadia Publishing, 2012), p. 7.

287   *"at the same time"*: Sherman Gwinn, "What He Learned at 14 Helped Him 'Come Back' at 40," *American Magazine*, April 1927, p. 61.

287   *too many popcorn vendors*: Bush et al., *Euclid Beach Park Is Closed for the Season*, pp. 18–19.

288   *accepted the offer*: Ibid., p. 25.

288   *"was the watchword"*: Avery, *A History of Cleveland and Its Environs*, p. 332.

288   *from the park*: Bush et al., *Euclid Beach Park Is Closed for the Season*, p. 27.

289   *in Super Race*: Michael Rotman, "Euclid Beach Park Riot," Cleveland Historical, last modified February 28, 2018, https://clevelandhistorical.org/items/show/562.

289   *Lyndon B. Johnson*: Bush et al., *Euclid Beach Park Is Closed for the Season*, p. 207.

289   *from 1918 to 1958*: Mark J. Price, "Summit Beach Park, 'Akron's Fairyland of Pleasure,'" *Akron (OH) Beacon-Journal*, July 17, 2017.

289   *singer named Doris Day*: Scott Allyn, "Memories of Crystal Beach: Of Vermilion's Famous Park from 1907 to 1962," Lorain (OH) *Morning Journal*, August 5, 2007.

289   *status quo since 1963*: Francis and Francis, *Cleveland Amusement Park Memories*, p 32.

290   *not so far away*: Kurt Snibbe, "San Bernardino: Lytle Creek Had Own Gold Rush," Riverside (CA) *Press-Enterprise*, July 31, 2012.

291   *settled in the West*: Chris Jepsen, email to the author, March 26, 2018.

291   *took in washing*: Jim Hardiman, "How It Began…Walter & Cordelia Knott's Date with Destiny," Knott's Berry Farm advertising supplement, *Los Angeles Times*, July 27, 1980, p. 6.

291   *Cordelia later said*: "Says Neighbor John," *Ghost Town News* (Buena Park, CA: Knott's Berry Place), p. 4.

291   *silver deposits in 1896*: Phil Brigandi, *Orange County Chronicles* (Charleston, SC: The History Press, 2013).

292   *twenty acres in 1923*: Peter B. Flint, "Walter Knott of Knott's Berry Farm Is Dead," *New York Times*, December 5, 1981.

293   *"of blackberries"*: "Says Neighbor John," *Ghost Town News*, p. 8.

294   *berry pie with ice cream*: "Old-Fashioned Chicken Dinner Will Drive You Absolutely Knott's," All Business Journal, September 13, 2013, http://www.allbusinessjournal.com/2013/09/13/old-fashioned-chicken-dinner-will-drive-you-absolutely-knotts/.

294   *"our economic life"*: Christopher Merritt and J. Eric Lynxwiler, *Knott's Preserved: From Boysenberry to Theme Park, the History of Knott's Berry Farm* (Santa Monica, CA: Angel City Press, 2010), pp. 22–25.

294   *other old desert towns*: Ghost Town News, pp. 28–29.

294   *"any of the attractions"*: "Says Neighbor John," Ibid., p. 17.

295   *on Christmas cards*: John Giuffo, "The World's Top Christmas Destinations," *Forbes*, December 5, 2011.

295   *on August 3, 1946*: Jeff Swiatek, "Family Feud Rattles Holiday World," *Indianapolis Star*, May 6, 2013.

295   *Wilmington, New York*: "About Us…Our History," North Pole Home of Santa's Workshop, 2018, http://www.northpoleny.com/about-us.

295   *he got to thinking*: Phillip L. Wenz, *Santa's Village* (Charleston, SC: Arcadia Publishing, 2007), p. 11.

296   *Memorial Day, 1959*: "Santa's Village History," Santa's Village Azoosment Park, 2018, https://santasvillagedundee.com/about-us/history/.

296   *the property in 2014*: Nina Agrawal, "It's a Retro Southern California Christmas as Santa's Village Opens," *Los Angeles Times*, December 2, 2016.

296   *Santa's Village opened*: Jim Steinberg, "Skypark at Santa's Village Expansion Approved by County Supervisors," San Bernardino (CA) *Sun*, July 11, 2017.

297   *"a simple smile"*: "Who We Are," SantaPark Arctic World, n.d., https://santaparkarcticworld.com/who-we-are.

297   *Mrs. Gingerbread Bakery*: "Activities," SantaPark Arctic World, n.d., https://santaparkarcticworld.com/santa-claus-secret-forest/Activities.

297   *outside the cave*: Rod Nordland, "Santa in Finland, Where Marketing Triumphs over Geography," *New York Times*, December 20, 2017.

297   *Marvel Cave*: Tom Carlson, "The Woman Behind Silver Dollar City," *Springfield (MO) News-Leader*, December 9, 2014.

297   *bat guano*: "Marvel Cave," Silver Dollar City, 2018, https://www.silverdollarcity.com/theme-park/Attractions/Rides/Marvel-Cave.

297   *to the Herschends*: Abram Brown, "The Wild Ride of the Herschends: When Amusement Parks Are the Family Business," *Forbes*, May 26, 2016.

297   *keep up with expenses*: Carlson, "The Woman Behind Silver Dollar City."

298   *in October 1969*: Philip Potempa, "Offbeat: TV's 'Beverly Hillbillies' Helped Put Branson on the Map," Northwest Indiana *Times*, July 25, 2011.

298   *appraised at $1 billion*: Brown, "The Wild Ride of the Herschends."

298   *eighty-three, in 1983*: United Press International, "Silver Dollar City Founder Dead," March 16, 1983.

299   *"I've been everywhere"*: Stephen Miller, *Smart Blonde: The Life of Dolly Parton* (New York: Omnibus Press, 2015), p. 225.

299   *"like a relative"*: Peter Marks, "Hooray for Dollywood," *Washington Post*, July 16, 2016.

299   *"of high speed"*: Jennifer Leslie and Catherine Park, "Dolly Parton Shares Why She Doesn't Ride the Rides at Dollywood," 11Alive.com, March 16, 2018, https://www.11alive.com/article/entertainment/dolly-parton-shares-why-she-doesnt-ride-the-rides-at-dollywood/85-529224511.

300   *Knott said cheerily*: Merritt and Lynxwiler, *Knott's Preserved*, p. 97.

300   *Price admitted*: Todd James Pierce, *Three Years in Wonderland: The Disney Brothers, C. V. Wood, and the Making of the Great American Theme Park* (Jackson, MS: University Press of Mississippi, 2016), p. 81.

301   *Dentzel Menagerie model*: Keith Thursby, "Wendell 'Bud' Hurlbut Dies at 92; Designed, Built Attractions for Knott's Berry Farm," *Los Angeles Times*, January 18, 2011.

301   *seeing a profit*: Merritt and Lynxwiler, *Knott's Preserved*, pp. 101–103.

301   *concessions to Knott's*: Kimberly Pierceall, "Castle Park Creator, Bud Hurlbut, Dies at 92," *Riverside (CA) Press-Enterprise*, January 8, 2011.

301   *single new attraction*: Daryl Strickland, "Cedar Fair Completes Knott's Deal," *Los Angeles Times*, December 30, 1997.

302   *in early 2013*: Michael Mello, "It's Still Jam, But It's No Longer Called Knott's," *Orange County (CA) Register*, March 5, 2013.

302   *"before she came"*: Jennifer Blazey, interview with the author, March 16, 2018.

GRAND SLAM

303   *"I'm God's brother"*: Stephen M. Silverman, "The Godless Side of Walt Disney," *Newsweek*, September 11, 2015, http://www.newsweek.com/godless-side-walt-disney-371249.

303   *a New Yorker profile*: Gilbert Seldes, "Profiles: Mickey-Mouse Maker," *New Yorker*, December 19, 1931, p. 23.

304   *"Elias [Walt's father] did"*: Diane Disney Miller, "Happy Birthday, Mother," The Walt Disney Family Museum, February 15, 2011, http://www.waltdisney.com/blog/happy-birthday-mother-diane-disney-miller.

304 *his cartoon mouse*: Stephen M. Silverman, "Hollywood Icon Mickey Mouse Turns 75," *People*, November 17, 2003, https://people.com/celebrity/hollywood-icon-mickey-mouse-turns-75/.

305 *Richard and Robert Sherman*: *The Boys: The Sherman Brothers' Story*, produced and directed by Gregory V. Sherman and Jeffrey C. Sherman (2009; Burbank, CA: Walt Disney Studios Home Entertainment, 2010), DVD.

305 *a multinational company*: Martin Sklar, *Dream It! Do It! My Half-Century Creating Disney's Magic Kingdoms* (New York: Disney Editions, 2013), p. 45.

305 *break their appointment*: Leni Riefenstahl, *Leni Riefenstahl: A Memoir* (New York: St. Martin's Press, 1992), pp. 239–240.

305 *"a form of rebellion"*: Neal Gabler, *Walt Disney: The Triumph of the American Imagination* (New York: Alfred A. Knopf, 2006), pp. 22–23.

306 *"do something about it"*: J. I. Baker, "Walt Disney: From Mickey to Magic Kingdom," *Life*, April 15, 2016, p. 50.

306 *"unfriendly" toward him*: Gerald Horne, *Class Struggle in Hollywood, 1930–1950: Moguls, Mobsters, Stars, Reds, & Trade Unionists* (Austin, TX: University of Texas Press, 2001), p. 175.

306 *"a mean S.O.B."*: *American Experience*, season 27, episodes 8–9, "Walt Disney—Parts 1 and 2," directed by Sarah Colt, written by Sarah Colt, Mark Zwonitzer, and Tom Jennings, aired September 14–15, 2015, on PBS.

306 *"sort of stunning"*: Ibid.

307 *in Chatsworth*: *Strangers on a Train* production notes, Warner Bros. Archives, USC School of Cinematic Arts.

307 *"anything like that again"*: François Truffaut and Helen G. Scott, *Hitchcock* (New York: Simon and Schuster, 1983), p. 198.

308 *"trip to outer space"*: "Disneyland" listing, *TV Guide* (Detroit area edition), October 23–29, 1954, pp. A46–A47.

308 *Walt told National Geographic*: Robert De Roos, "The Magic Worlds of Walt Disney," *National Geographic*, August 1963, p. 191.

308 *plaguing the beach*: Brady MacDonald, "Disneyland Got Off to a Nightmare Start in 1955, But 'Walt's Folly' Quickly Won Over Fans," *Los Angeles Times*, July 17, 2015.

308 *"my own money"*: De Roos, "The Magic Worlds of Walt Disney," p. 191.

308 *beach town of Balboa*: MacDonald, "Disneyland Got Off to a Nightmare Start in 1955."

309 *"in another world"*: De Roos, "The Magic Worlds of Walt Disney," p. 192.

310 *"WED Enterprises Company"*: Martini, "George K. Whitney, Jr. Interview," 2002.

310 *Lilliputian Land*: "Fairyland of Yesterday and Tomorrow," *Popular Mechanics*, December 1954, pp. 118–119.

310 *"streaming down his cheek"*: Sharon Baird, "Walt's Private Apartment," JustDisney.com, n.d., http://www.justdisney.com/features/apartment.html.

311 *"Let 'em pee"*: Bob Thomas, *Building a Company: Roy O. Disney and the Creation of an Entertainment Empire* (New York: Hyperion, 1998), p. 195.

311 *the dancer Marge Champion*: Marge Champion, conversation with the author, August 3, 2010.

312 *Swift came aboard*: Pierce, *Three Years in Wonderland*, p. 145.

312 *"V for Nothing"*: Michael Thomas, conversation with author, April 12, 2018.

312 *after Disneyland opened*: Chuck Schmidt, "The Myths Surrounding C. V. Wood's Disney Demise Have Been Out of This World," *Staten Island (NY) Advance*, September 28, 2015.

313 *permanently closed*: Andrew Kenney, "Much of Heritage Square Will Be History After This Weekend," Westword, October 29, 2015, http://www.westword.com/news/much-of-heritage-square-will-be-history-after-this-weekend-7285646.

313 *for good in 1969*: Robert McLaughlin, *Pleasure Island: 1959–1969* (Charleston, SC: Arcadia Publishing, 2014), pp. 7–8.

313 *or 130 TV specials*: Kat Long. "The Rise and Suspiciously Rapid Fall of Freedomland U.S.A.," Atlas Obscura, July 8, 2015. https://www.atlasobscura.com/articles/the-rise-and-suspiciously-rapid-fall-of-freedomland-u-s-a.

313 *"from the Bronx"*: "Animated History in East Bronx's Freedomland Is Revealed in Preview," *New York Times*, April 29, 1960, p. 64.

314 *Cleveland Tram Company*: Pierce, *Three Years in Wonderland*, p. 87.

314 *as a cheap trick*: Ibid., p. 88.

315 *"at that time"*: Ibid., p. 89.

316 *the evening's guests arrived*: Steven Vagnini, "Favorite Memories from Walt and Lillian's 30th Anniversary Party," D23: The Official Disney Fan Club, February 11, 2016, https://d23.com/favorite-memories-from-walt-and-lillians-30th-anniversary-party/.

316 *Moorish shapes, Casablanca*: Variety Staff, "Harper Goff," *Variety*, April 6, 1993.

316 *"talk to me"*: Doug Jones, "Meet Harper Goff, The Legendary Set Designer Behind Willy Wonka's Chocolate Factory," Dangerous Minds, September 30, 2016. https://dangerousminds.net/comments/meet_harper_goff_the_legendary_set_designer_behind_willy_wonkas_chocolate_f.

316 *behind a church*: Ed Squair, "The Long, Long Haunt: Artists of Walt's Haunted Mansion," The Walt Disney Family Museum, October 31, 2011, https://waltdisney.org/blog/long-long-haunt-artists-walt%E2%80%99s-haunted-mansion.

316 *The African Queen*: Keith Gluck, "Harper Goff: The 'Second' Imagineer," The Walt Disney Family Museum, May 9, 2017, http://waltdisney.com/blog/harper-goff-second-imagineer.

316 *a tramp steamer*: Katharine Hepburn, *The Making of "The African Queen," or How I Went to Africa with Bogart, Bacall, and Huston and Almost Lost My Mind* (New York: Alfred A. Knopf, 1987), pp. 7–78.

316 *"subject to change"*: *The Story of Disneyland* (Chicago: Western Printing & Lithographing, 1955), p. 19.

NEW WORLDS

318   *Mickey Mouse watches*: "A Small World," Talk of the Town, *New Yorker*, August 31, 1963, pp. 20–21.

318   *average of $2.37*: "Disneyland One Year Old," press release, Disneyland, July 18, 1956.

319   *introduced the photo finish*: Scott Hettrick, "Santa Anita's 75th Anniversary," Arcadia's Best, December 24, 2009, http://arcadiasbest.com/2009/12/santa-anitas-75th-anniversary/.

320   *becoming a reality*: Chris Goode, *California Baseball: From the Pioneers to the Glory Years* (lulu.com, 2011), p. 357.

320   *Frontierland and Main Street*: Pierce, *Three Years in Wonderland*, p. 234.

321   *C. V. Wood*: Merritt and Priore, *Pacific Ocean Park*, p. 131.

321   *the Beach Boys*: Ibid., p. 171.

322   *and the present*: Stephen M. Silverman, "Disney's Small World Turns 50," *People*, March 21, 2014, https://people.com/celebrity/its-a-small-world-turns-50-at-disneyland-walt-disney-world/.

323   *fifteen different ways*: De Roos, "The Magic Worlds of Walt Disney," p. 207.

323   *"extremely subtle motions"*: Ibid., p. 202.

324   *a link to Hollywood*: John Springer, conversation with the author, 1999.

324   *"French dolls cancan"*: "Fairs: The World of Already," *Time*, June 5, 1964.

325   *no It's a Small World*: Stephen M. Silverman, "Shanghai Disneyland May Be the Best Mousetrap on Earth," *Chicago Tribune*, June 15, 2016.

325   *"the equivalent of Disneyland"*: Newsreel of press conference, October 23, 1965.

326   *"after World War II"*: Jonathan Kandall, "Lew Wasserman, 89, Is Dead; Last of Hollywood's Moguls," *New York Times*, June 4, 2002.

327   *"we produce here"*: Dennis McDougal, *The Last Mogul: Lew Wasserman, MCA, and the Hidden History of Hollywood* (New York: Crown Books, 1998), p. 321.

327   *steep, hilly terrain*: Sam Gennawey, "How Harrison 'Buzz' Price Invented the Universal Studios Tour," blooloop, March 12, 2018, https://blooloop.com/harrison-buzz-price-universal-studios-tour/.

327   *For $2.50*: Robert Niles, "Theme Park History: A Short History of Universal Studios Hollywood," Theme Park Insider, July 15, 2013, https://www.themeparkinsider.com/flume/201307/3564/.

328   *among studio personnel*: Anthony Breznican, "Steven Spielberg: Director's Video Tour of Universal Backlot," *Entertainment Weekly*, June 24, 2016, http://ew.com/article/2016/06/24/steven-spielberg-video-tour-universal-backlot/.

328   *was $1 billion*: Sandra Pedicini, "Steven Spielberg Likely Staying with Universal Parks Past 2017, Filming Indicates," *Orlando Sentinel*, February 12, 2016.

329   *open in 2020*: Brady MacDonald, "What to Expect at China's Universal Studios Beijing," *Los Angeles Times*, February 23, 2015.

329   *the political one*: Barry Neild, "Pandora—The World of Avatar and 10 Other Hot Theme Parks of the Future," CNN Travel, June 12, 2017, http://www.cnn.com/travel/article/pandora-world-of-avatar-future-theme-parks-2017/index.html.

329   *"cast of seventy"*: Thomas Jellum, interview with the author, February 1, 2017.

330   *"we'd kill each other"*: Jim Denney, "'Nothing Has to Die'—The Walt Disney–Ray Bradbury Friendship," The Walt Disney Family Museum, August 22, 2017, https://waltdisney.org/blog/nothing-has-to-die-walt-disney-ray-bradbury-friendship.

331   *any ride anywhere*: Silverman, "Shanghai Disneyland May Be the Best Mousetrap on Earth."

331   *"for a while"*: De Roos, "The Magic Worlds of Walt Disney," p. 207.

331   *Pirates of the Caribbean*: Mark Eades, "50 Years Ago Saturday, Pirates of the Caribbean Opened at Disneyland," *Orange County (CA) Register*, March 17, 2017.

332   *"in front of it"*: T. C. Hepworth, "Rays of Light," in *Cassell's Popular Science*, vol. 2, ed. Alexander S. Galt (London: Cassell, 1906), p. 351.

FINISHING TOUCHES

333   *as "bean counters"*: Silverman, *The Fox That Got Away*, p. 163.

334   *he didn't like*: Stephen M. Silverman, *Public Spectacles* (New York: E. P. Dutton, 1981), pp. 3–4.

334   *got to keep Toto*: Eric Asimov, "Warner LeRoy, Restaurant Impresario, Is Dead at 65," *New York Times*, February 24, 2001.

334   *$5 million a year*: Bryan Miller, "Maxwell's Plum, a Symbol of '60s, Closes Doors," *New York Times*, July 11, 1988, p. B1.

334   *separate themed sectors*: Harry Applegate and Thomas Benton, *Six Flags Great Adventure* (Charleston, SC: Arcadia Publishing, 2009), pp. 11–12.

334   *"into the park"*: Eric Larsen, "Jersey Roots: The Man Who Built Six Flags Great Adventure," *Asbury Park Press*, June 27, 2014.

334   *financial interest in 1993*: Ibid.

335   *Grover Cleveland Robbins*: United Press International, "Grover Robbins, 59, Resort Developer," March 6, 1970.

335   *in the Korean War*: Mark Washburn, "Service Friday for Artist Jack Pentes, Who Designed Land of Oz on Beech Mountain," *Charlotte Observer*, February 12, 2015.

335   *keep away vandals*: Mark Price, "NC's Failed Theme Park 'Land of Oz' Is Reopening for Just 6 Days," *Charlotte Observer*, April 3, 2018.

336   *"those that divide us"*: David Z. Morris, "Six Flags Pulls Down Confederate Flags," *Fortune*, August 18, 2017.

336   *and set designer*: Stephen M. Silverman, *Dancing on the Ceiling: Stanley Donen and His Movies* (New York: Alfred A. Knopf, 1996), p. 156.

336   *own architecture firm*: Associated Press, "Randall Duell," December 7, 1992.

337   *its own color palette*: Davis G. McCown, *Six Flags Over Texas: The First Fifty Years* (Hurst, TX: Lavaca Publications and Media, 2016), pp. 17–18.

338   *ill-fated Texas Pavilion*: Jim Hill, "Texan With Big Dreams + Big Apple = Big Trouble," Jim Hill Media, December 31, 2001, http://jimhillmedia.com/editor_in_chief1/b/jim_hill/archive/2001/12/31/texan-with-big-dreams-big-apple-big-trouble.aspx.

338   *according to court filings*: "Angus G. Wynne Jr.; Built Theme Parks," *New York Times*, March 14, 1979, p. 17.

339   *invest in new rides*: Ed Green, "Ed Hart Talks About Why the New and Improved Kentucky Kingdom Will Succeed," *Louisville Business First*, April 9, 2014.

339   *C.V. oversaw the transfer*: Bruce Lambert, "C. V. Wood Jr., Who Pioneered Large Theme Parks, Is Dead at 71," *New York Times*, March 16, 2002, p. B8.

340   *of making movies*: Tan Bee Hong, "Australia's Hollywood," *New Straits Times*, January 26, 1992, p. 4.

340   *"vision and greatness"*: Pierce, *Three Years in Wonderland*, p. 5.

340   *"Donn Tatum and Card Walker"*: Michael Thomas, interview with the author, April 12, 2018.

340   *"for generations to come"*: "EPCOT," written by Marty Sklar, promotional film, filmed October 27, 1966.

ON THE HORIZON

342   *"and learn together"*: Nate Rasmussen, "Vintage Walt Disney World: A Dedication with Style at Magic Kingdom Park," *Disney Parks Blog* (blog), Disney, September 29, 2011, https://disneyparks.disney.go.com/blog/2011/09/vintage-walt-disney-world-a-dedication-with-style-at-magic-kingdom-park/comment-page-1/.

343   *Tokyo Disneyland*: Associated Press, "Attendance Falls 2% in Past Year at Tokyo Disneyland, but Families Are Still Pouring In," April 7, 1993.

344   *"Disney's World's Fair"*: Elting E. Morison, "What Went Wrong with Disney's World's Fair," *American Heritage*, December 1983.

344   *Euro Disney*: Steven Greenhouse, "Playing Disney in the Parisian Fields," *New York Times*, February 17, 1991.

344   *off-the-shelf rides*: Stephen M. Silverman, "California Screamin': Disney's New Playground Is a Thrill Ride for Daredevil Teens," *New York Post*, May 8, 2001.

345   *"willing to pay"*: James B. Stewart, *DisneyWar* (New York: Simon and Schuster, 2005), p. 66.

345   *entirely in the dark*: Silverman, "Dubai's Theme Parks," *Chicago Tribune*.

346   *Roy died in 2009*: Michael Carlson, "Roy Disney Obituary," *Guardian*, December 17, 2009.

346   *and the purchase—with Jobs*: Devin Leonard, "How Disney Bought Lucasfilm—and Its Plans for *Star Wars*," Bloomberg, March 7, 2013, https://www.bloomberg.com/news/articles/2013-03-07/how-disney-bought-lucasfilm-and-its-plans-for-star-wars.

346   *the Dalai Lama*: David Barboza, and Brooks Barnes, "How China Won the Keys to Disney's Magic Kingdom," *New York Times*, June 14, 2016.

346   *Shanghai Disney Resort*: Silverman, "Shanghai Disneyland May Be the Best Mousetrap on Earth."

346   *"James Bond, Combined"*: Jonathan Chew, "Star Wars Franchise Worth More Than Harry Potter and James Bond, Combined," *Fortune*, December 24, 2015.

346   *windfall to education*: Alex Ben Block, "George Lucas Will Use Disney $4 Billion to Fund Education," *Hollywood Reporter*, October 31, 2012.

346   *"in my lifetime"*: Stacy Cowley, "Disney to Buy Lucasfilm for $4 Billion," CNN Tech, October 31, 2012, https://money.cnn.com/2012/10/30/technology/disney-buys-lucasfilm/index.html.

346   *the brand in 2012*: Jason Guerrasio, "The New 'Star Wars' Movies Have Already Made More Than the $4 Billion Disney Paid for the Franchise in 2012," Business Insider, December 29, 2017, http://www.businessinsider.com/star-wars-box-office-disney-4-billion-lucasfilm-purchase-2017-12.

347   *to go with it*: Stephen M. Silverman, "Glowing River and All, a Sneak Peek at Disney World's New Pandora—The World of Avatar," *Chicago Tribune*, April 19, 2017.

347   *"as their happy place"*: Andrea Sachs, "Walt Disney World's Magic Kingdom, the Louvre, Are Tops in Visitorship Survey," *Washington Post*, June 25, 2018.

347   *"It has the most"*: Mekado Murphy, interview with the author, March 31, 2018.

348   *and a bear*: Sandusky Library Archives Research Center, "Louis Zistel, an Early German Immigrant," Sandusky History, November 17, 2011, http://sanduskyhistory.blogspot.com/2011/11/louis-zistel-early-german-immigrant.html.

348   *and Rye Beach*: David W. Francis and Diane DeMali Francis, *Cedar Point: The Queen of American Watering Places* (Fairview Park, OH: Amusement Park Books, 1995), p. 24.

348   *George Arthur Boeckling*: *Pictorial and Biographical Memoirs of Indianapolis and Marion County, Indiana* (Chicago: Goodspeed Brothers, 1893), p. 181.

348   *German-émigré cooper*: "G. A. Boeckling, Cedar Point Chief, Is Dead," unidentified Ohio newspaper clipping, Harris-Elmore Public Library, Elmore, Ohio, July 25, 1931, http://www.ohiomemory.org/cdm/ref/collection/p267401coll13/id/1669.

348   *"George A. Boeckling Co"*: Untitled article, *Amusement Business* 82, no. 2 (date unknown, 1970).

348   *shipmaster from England*: Francis and Francis. *Cedar Point*, p. 24.

349   *five steam railroads*: Herbert H. Harwood Jr. and Robert S. Korach, *The Lake Shore Electric Railway Story* (Bloomington, IN: Indiana University Press, 2000), pp. 13–14.

349   *"numerous other attractions"*: Ibid., p. 14.

349   *figure eight Racer*: Francis and Francis. *Cedar Point*, p. 41.

349   *"full-fledged amusement park"*: Nasaw, *Going Out*, p. 85.

350   *singles seeking partners*: Ibid., p. 90.

350   *selling the stuff*: David W. Francis, "Cedar Point and the Characteristics of American Summer Resorts During the Gilded Age," *Hayes Historical Journal: Cedar Point* 7, no. 2 (Winter 1988).

350   *the Associated Press reported*: Associated Press, "100 Years Ago Today: Rockne & the Forward Pass Change Notre Dame Football Forever," November 1, 2013.

350   *stewardship of Cedar Point*: The Chronicler, "Among Those Present," *Ohio Magazine*, July 1906, p. 80.

350   *could reach his park*: Adams, *The American Amusement Park Industry*, p. 79.

350   *"30 yards a clip"*: Harry Cross, "Inventing the Forward Pass," *New York Times*, November 1, 1913.

351   *"to start things off"*: Julie Macfie Sobol and Ken Sobol, *Lake Erie: A Pictorial History* (Erin, ON: Boston Mills Press, 2004), p. 189.

351   *"'Disneyland of the Midwest'"*: Adams, *The American Amusement Park Industry*, p. 82.

352   *"in any danger"*: Daniel Goleman, "Why Do People Crave the Experience?," *New York Times*, August 2, 1988.

352   *"climbing Mount Everest"*: Peter Dockrill, "The Science Behind Why We Love Terrifying Ourselves on Rollercoasters," Science Alert, January 22, 2016, https://www.sciencealert.com/the-science-behind-why-we-love-terrifying-ourselves-on-rollercoasters.

352   *"to those at Disneyland"*: "Cedar Point Outlines $6,000,000 Project," *Billboard*, April 11, 1960, p. 87.

353   *"the Wood projects"*: "Disney Sues Firm Which Did Survey for Cedar Point Park," *Sandusky Register*, May 24, 1960, p. 5.

353   *25 million visitors annually*: Glenn Roger, "Alternative Ideas for High Yield Investors," *Forbes*, April 20, 2018.

354   *"fast-moving times"*: Martin-Werner Buchenau and Joachim Hofer, "A Roller Coaster Tycoon's Last Ride," *Handelsblatt*, August 19, 2017.

QUIDDITCH, ANYONE?

357   *thirteen and thirty*: Ride-company designer, interview with the author, February 1, 2017.

357   *on its attractions*: Kevin Parent, interview with the author, April 13, 2018.

358   *five hundred million copies*: J. K. Rowling, biography, *Harry Potter and the Cursed Child: Part One*, in *Showbill*, April 2018.

358   *"of her world"*: Stephen M. Silverman, "Harry Potter World Revealed, at Last," *People*, September 15, 2009, https://people.com/celebrity/harry-potters-world-revealed-at-last/.

358   *near a gasoline pump*: Stephen M. Silverman, "Sneak Peek: What Fans Will Find at Universal Orlando's World of Harry Potter," *People*, March 25, 2010, https://people.com/celebrity/sneak-peek-what-fans-will-find-at-universal-orlandos-world-of-harry-potter/.

358   *subsequent Hollywood version*: Brady MacDonald, "The World's Best Theme Park Dark Ride Just Got Better," *Los Angeles Times*, April 4, 2016.

359   *open that summer*: Stephen M. Silverman, "Harry Potter Expands His Playground at Universal Orlando," *People*, January 24, 2014, https://people.com/celebrity/wizarding-world-of-harry-potter-expands-in-orlando/.

ILLUSTRATION CREDITS

Courtesy of HeliclineFineArt.com, Oliver Smith, designer, Coney Island backdrop, *On the Town*, (1945): endpapers

Courtesy of Digital Commonwealth, Boston Public Library, Tichnor Brothers Postcard Collection: 6–7, 232 (top, middle, bottom)

Courtesy of Ferrari World Abu Dhabi: 10

Courtesy of Alpsdake/CC-BY-SA 4.0: 12

Courtesy of Walt Disney Pictures: 13

Courtesy of Bakken/PR/CC-BY 3.0: 25 (bottom)

Courtesy of George Pachantouris/Getty Images: 27 (bottom)

Courtesy of Metropolitan Museum of Art, Elisha Whittelsey Collection, Elisha Whittelsey Fund, 1959: 31

Courtesy of Yale Center for British Art, Paul Mellon Collection, Francis Hayman, artist: 32

Courtesy of *Scribner's Magazine*: 33, 34 (bottom)

Courtesy of National Portrait Gallery, Smithsonian Institution; gift of Mr. and Mrs. Paul Mellon: 44

Courtesy of *Gleason's Pictorial*: 48 (top), 49

Courtesy of Metropolitan Museum of Art, Harris Brisbane Dick Fund, 1934: 59

Courtesy of Museo di Roma a Palazo Braschi, Filippo Gagliardi e Filippo Lauri, artists: 61 (bottom)

Courtesy of Library of Congress: 62, 67, 109, 120, 123 (left and right), 124, 131, 133 (top), 135 (all), 156, 163, 180 (bottom), 181, 190 (bottom), 206, 207, 214, 217, 224, 261, 287

Courtesy of Smithsonian American Art Museum, gift of Mrs. Edith Gregor Halpert: 72

Courtesy of Bob Cullinan: 73 (bottom)

Courtesy of American Historical Society, New York: 87

Courtesy of Portland State University and the Oregon Historical Society: 89 (bottom)

Courtesy of Boston Public Library, H. D. Nichols, artist: 112

Courtesy of Buffalo Bill Museum and Grave: 119 (bottom)

Courtesy of National Park Service: 133 (bottom)

Courtesy of Brinks38200: 138

Courtesy of New Jersey Education Association: 142

Courtesy of Grinnell College Libraries Special Collections: 169

Courtesy of Legoland: 173

Courtesy of Jonathan Carter: 194 (left and right), 204 (bottom)

Courtesy of Deno's Wonder Wheel: 202

Courtesy of lakesideamusementpark.com: 211

Courtesy of Carol M. Highsmith's America Project, Carol M. Highsmith Archive, Library of Congress, Prints and Photographs Division: 212, 253 (bottom)

Courtesy of Elitch Gardens: 213

Courtesy of Bundesarchiv, Bild 102-00075/CC-BY-SA 3.0: 216

Courtesy of iowagirlonthego.com: 230

Courtesy of Hershey Entertainment & Resorts Company: 241 (bottom)

Courtesy of Knoebel Lumber: 243

Courtesy of knoebels.com: 244

Courtesy of Lake Compounce Family Theme Park: 249 (top)

Courtesy of Seabreeze Amusement Park: 250

Courtesy of Waldameer: 251

Courtesy of National Photo Company Collection, Library of Congress: 254

Courtesy of Chester Copperpot/CC-BY-SA 3.0: 255 (top)

Courtesy of Jewish Museum of the American West: 259

Courtesy of Matthew Evans Resource Room, San Francisco State University: 262 (bottom)

Courtesy of Visitor 7/CC-BY-SA 3.0: 265

Courtesy of San Francisco History Center, San Francisco Public Library: 269

Courtesy of Herschell Carrousel Factory Museum: 271

Courtesy of Photofest: 277

Courtesy of San Diego State University, Library Digital Collections: 280 (top)

Courtesy of Herschend Family Entertainment: 299 (top)

Courtesy of Knott's Berry Farm: 301, 302

Courtesy of Disney Enterprises, Inc./Photofest: 303, 305

Courtesy of Warner Bros./Photofest: 307

Courtesy of Paul Hiffmeyer, photographer/Disney Parks: 318, 322, 330

Courtesy of Walt Disney Pictures/Photofest: 323

Courtesy of Universal Studios Hollywood: 327

Courtesy of Universal Orlando Resort: 328

Courtesy of Disneyland Resort: 331

Courtesy of Land of Oz: 335

Courtesy of Chensiyuan/CC-BY-SA 4.0: 339

Courtesy of Kent Phillips, photographer/Disney Parks: 341

Courtesy of Garth Vaughn, photographer/ Disney Parks: 342

Courtesy of Matt Stroshane, photographer/Disney Parks: 343

Courtesy of Disney Parks: 346

Courtesy of Nick Nolte/CC-BY-SA 2.5: 353

Courtesy of Europa Park: 354

Courtesy of Cedar Point: 355

Courtesy of Courtesy of HeliclineFineArt.com: 360

INDEX

ILLUSTRATIONS ARE INDICATED IN BOLD